RESEARCH HANDBOOK ON THE ECONOMICS OF EUROPEAN UNION LAW

RESEARCH HANDBOOKS IN LAW AND ECONOMICS

Series Editors: Richard A. Posner, *Judge, United States Court of Appeals for the Seventh Circuit and Senior Lecturer, University of Chicago Law School, USA* and Francesco Parisi, *Oppenheimer Wolff and Donnelly Professor of Law, University of Minnesota, USA and Professor of Economics, University of Bologna, Italy*

Edited by highly distinguished scholars, the landmark reference works in this series offer advanced treatments of specific topics that reflect the state-of-the-art of research in law and economics, while also expanding the law and economics debate. Each volume's accessible yet sophisticated contributions from top international researchers make it an indispensable resource for students and scholars alike.

Titles in this series include:

Research Handbook on Public Choice and Public Law
Edited by Daniel A. Farber and Anne Joseph O'Connell

Research Handbook on the Economics of Property Law
Edited by Kenneth Ayotte and Henry E. Smith

Research Handbook on the Economics of Family Law
Edited by Lloyd R. Cohen and Joshua D. Wright

Research Handbook on the Economics of Antitrust Law
Edited by Einer Elhauge

Research Handbook on the Economics of Corporate Law
Edited by Brett McDonnell and Claire A. Hill

Research Handbook on the Economics of European Union Law
Edited by Thomas Eger and Hans-Bernd Schäfer

Research Handbook on the Economics of European Union Law

Edited by

Thomas Eger

University of Hamburg, Germany

Hans-Bernd Schäfer

University of Hamburg, Germany

RESEARCH HANDBOOKS IN LAW AND ECONOMICS

Edward Elgar

Cheltenham, UK • Northampton, MA, USA

Published by
Edward Elgar Publishing Limited
The Lypiatts
15 Lansdown Road
Cheltenham
Glos GL50 2JA
UK

Edward Elgar Publishing, Inc.
William Pratt House
9 Dewey Court
Northampton
Massachusetts 01060
USA

A catalogue record for this book
is available from the British Library

Library of Congress Control Number: 2012930569

MIX
Paper from
responsible sources
FSC® C018575

ISBN 978 1 84980 100 3 (cased)

Typeset by Servis Filmsetting Ltd, Stockport, Cheshire
Printed and bound by MPG Books Group, UK

Contents

Contributors

Herbert Brücker, Professor of Economics at the University of Bamberg; Institute for Employment Research, Nürnberg, Germany.

Fabrizio Cafaggi, Professor of Comparative Law at the European University Institute in Florence, Italy.

Emanuela Carbonara, Assistant Professor of Economics, Department of Economics, University of Bologna, Italy.

Thomas Eger, Professor of Law and Economics, Faculty of Law, University of Hamburg, Germany.

Michael G. Faure, Faculty of Law, Maastricht University, and Erasmus University Rotterdam, the Netherlands.

Jan Fidrmuc, Department of Economics and Finance and Centre for Economic Development and Institutions (CEDI), Brunel University, Uxbridge, UK; and CES-Ifo Munich.

Nuno Garoupa, Professor of Law and the H. Ross and Helen Workman Research Scholar, University of Illinois College of Law, USA.

Fernando Gomez, Professor of Law and Economics, School of Law, Universitat Pompeu Fabra, Barcelona, Spain.

Manfred J. Holler, Senior Research Fellow, Public Choice Research Centre at Turku, Finland and Professor Emeritus of Economics, Institute of Socioeconomics, University of Hamburg, Germany.

Patrick C. Leyens, Junior Professor of Civil Law and Economic Analysis of Law, Faculty of Law, University of Hamburg, Germany.

Barbara Luppi, Assistant Professor of Economics, University of Modena and Reggio Emilia, Italy.

Antonio Nicita, Professor of Economic Policy, Department of Economics and Statistics, University of Siena and Professor of Economic Analysis of Law, Department of Law, LUISS Guido Carli, Rome, Italy.

Roberto Pardolesi, Professor of Comparative Law, LUISS Guido Carli, Rome, Italy.

Francesco Parisi, Oppenheimer Wolff and Donnelly Professor of Law, University of Minnesota, USA and Professor of Economics, University of Bologna, Italy.

Jacques Pelkmans, Jan Tinbergen Chair in European Economic Integration and Director of the Economic Studies Department, College of Europe, Bruges and Senior Fellow, CEPS (Centre for European Policy Studies), Brussels, Belgium.

Hans-Bernd Schäfer, Affiliate Professor, Bucerius Law School and Professor Emeritus of Economics, Institute for Law and Economics, University of Hamburg, Germany.

Helmut Siekmann, Professor of Money, Currency and Central Bank Law, Johann Wolfgang Goethe-Universität, Frankfurt am Main, Germany.

George Tsebelis, Anatol Rapoport Collegiate Professor of Political Science, University of Michigan, USA.

Stefan Voigt, Professor of Law and Economics, Faculty of Law, University of Hamburg, Germany.

Hans-Jürgen Wagener, Professor Emeritus of Economics, European University Viadrina, Frankfurt (Oder), Germany.

Introduction

Thomas Eger and Hans-Bernd Schäfer

This book provides the reader with an economic analysis of the most important elements of EU law and the mechanisms of decisions within the EU. All the authors are well-known scholars of this discipline and have written their chapters especially for this volume. The authors presented a first draft of their chapters at a manuscript conference in Hamburg and improved their drafts on the basis of invited and prepared comments and the general discussion.

The process of European integration is, on the one hand, a "truly unique endeavor. Nowhere else in the world has a group of countries come to be so integrated by peaceful means" (Baldwin and Wyplosz 2004, XXI). On the other hand, the actual architecture of the European Union has evolved as a compromise between conflicting philosophies of integration. First of all, there has been a conflict between intergovernmentalists, who look at European integration as an increased coordination and cooperation between sovereign governments, and federalists, who imagine the United States of Europe as a true political federation, characterized by powerful supranational institutions. However, there is another, much more important, conflict in the views on European integration: "the dirigiste economic management style of France and the free market, laissez faire style of the United Kingdom" (Alesina and Giavazzi 2006, 125).

The history of European integration after World War II comprises a multitude of facets and can be described in a nutshell as follows (Eichengreen 2007; Nello 2009, Chapters 1 and 2). Originally, European integration was triggered by the political motivation to avoid war between European countries in the future. After the failure of the European Defence Community and the European Political Community in 1954 the founding members decided to relaunch European integration on an *economic* basis. Having started already in 1952 with the European Coal and Steel Community (ECSC) as a community of six Member States (Belgium, France, Italy, Luxembourg, the Netherlands and West Germany), aimed at coordinating and controlling some economic activities in the coal and steel sector (at the time the key industry for both the military sector and the economy as a whole), the community extended its scope in 1958 in the Treaties of Rome – the Treaty establishing the European Economic Community (EEC Treaty), which was the most important one for the daily life of the European citizens, and the Treaty establishing the European Atomic Energy Community (EAEC Treaty) – by making all economic activities subject to integration. Several revisions and consolidations of the Treaties affected the allocation of competences between the community level and the Member States as well as the rules of the collective decision making processes at the community level. In 1967 the Merger Treaty fused the institutions of the three Communities.

After long controversial discussions the former EFTA countries Denmark, Ireland and the UK joined the Community in 1973. The European Parliament decided in 1975 by a resolution to replace the term "European Economic Community" by "European

Community." After the end of dictatorship, Greece (1981), Spain and Portugal (both in 1986) became Member States.

The Single European Act from 1986 enacted the first major revisions of the Treaty in order to complete the internal market by the end of 1992. The Treaty of Maastricht (1993) formally confirmed the term "European Community" and included *inter alia* a time schedule for establishing a monetary union and a legal framework for the organization and operation of a European Central Bank. It added to the "supranational pillar," consisting of the three Communities, two "intergovernmental pillars" ("Common Foreign and Security Policy" and "Justice and Home Affairs"), and established the "European Union" as a kind of common roof for the three pillars.

After the fall of the iron curtain, the formerly neutral countries Austria, Finland and Sweden decided to join the Union in 1995. Five years later, as a consequence of the German reunification, the territory of Eastern Germany was integrated into Germany and the European Union. Already in 1993, the heads of Member States' governments had met in Copenhagen and invited the Central and Eastern European countries to join the Union, provided they meet the so-called Copenhagen Criteria, consisting of some political criteria (democracy and rule of law), economic criteria (a functioning and competitive market economy) and the ability to take on the *acquis communautaire*, i.e. the body of EU legislation, jurisdiction, practices, principles and objectives binding for the Member States.

Since the then existing institutions were designed to enable and support collective decision making in a small community, consisting of six members, the expectation of enlarging the European Union by a large number of Central and Eastern European countries triggered several attempts to adapt the architecture of the institutions to a much larger and more heterogeneous Union. The Treaty of Amsterdam (1999) introduced some minor changes, shifted some issues such as visa, asylum and immigration policies from the third (intergovernmental) pillar to the first (supranational) pillar and renamed the former as "Police and Justice Co-operation on Criminal Matters." These measures aimed at the development of the European Union as an "Area of Freedom, Security and Justice." However, already at the moment they signed the Treaty of Amsterdam it was clear to all Member States that the objective, to prepare the EU for Eastern enlargement, had not been achieved. The Treaty of Nice, which followed in 2003, was also not very successful in this respect. The next attempt of further integration, the Constitutional Treaty drafted by a Constitutional Convention, was rejected in 2005 by a French and a Dutch referendum.

However, even without major institutional reforms, ten new Member States joined the EU in 2004 (Cyprus, the Czech Republic, Estonia, Hungary, Latvia, Lithuania, Malta, Poland, Slovakia and Slovenia), and two more followed in 2007 (Bulgaria and Romania). Four years later, after controversial discussions within and between the Member States, the Lisbon Treaty entered into force, which consists of the Treaty on European Union (TEU), the Treaty on the Functioning of the European Union (TFEU) and the Charter of Fundamental Rights of the European Union. Some institutional reforms aim at facilitating collective decision making at the EU level, the "pillar structure" has been abolished and the European Union replaces the European Community as a legal personality. Today (2011), the EU consists of 27 Member States with a population of about 500 million people and produces a GDP of more than 12 trillion euros, which implies that the EU is the largest integrated economic area in the world.

From a law and economics point of view, at least three stories of European integration have to be told. The first one is the single market story. This story is about the development of European integration from fragmented national markets to a single (internal) European market, based on the four fundamental freedoms: the free movement of goods, services, persons and capital. The first step towards achieving this objective was the establishment of a customs union, i.e. a free trade area plus common external tariffs, which was completed already in July 1968. Only in 1985, however, when Jacques Delors became president of the European Commission, were many remaining non-tariff barriers identified and a legislative program was enacted in order to complete the internal market by the end of 1992. Further steps to open national markets already had been triggered in 1979 by the famous *Cassis de Dijon* judgment of the European Court of Justice, which stated that in general all goods lawfully manufactured and marketed in one Member State should also be accepted in the other Member States. This means that the prohibition of discrimination on grounds of nationality has been extended to the prohibition of (even non-discriminatory) barriers to trade. Instead of forcing the Member States to apply the same standards to domestic and foreign products, each Member State had to mutually recognize the product standards applied in other Member States. Only if some "mandatory requirement in the general interest" of the importing country would be violated, this country would not necessarily infringe EU law by refusing the import of the goods concerned. Later on, the tendency to extend the prohibition of discrimination to the prohibition of barriers to free movement and to apply the principle of mutual recognition has been extended, more or less, to the other fundamental freedoms as well. Consequently, the price of opening national markets has been accompanied by some loss of national sovereignty. From this "market-oriented" point of view, the power of the supranational EU authorities has been used to open the fragmented national markets by keeping protectionism of the Member States down.

The second story is about centralization of policy instruments in Brussels to the detriment of Member States' sovereignty. Basically, national sovereignty may be undermined by two forces: by market forces (mutual recognition, see first story) or by the supranational authorities in Brussels. According to the principle of conferral, a supranational authority "can act only within the limits of the competences conferred upon it by the Treaties" (Article 5(2) TEU). On the one hand, more competences have been conferred on the supranational authorities in the course of time by the revisions of the Treaties. On the other hand, there has been a tendency towards "competence creep" to the benefit of the EU, due to the fact that there are some open provisions concerning the allocation of competences between the EU and its Member States. The principle of subsidiarity, designed to slow down this centralization process in areas with shared competences, has not been completely successful so far. According to the theory of fiscal federalism (Oates 1972, 1999), centralization of competences can only be justified if there are economies of scale and regional spill-overs and if the preferences of the decentralized regional units (the Member States) are not too heterogeneous. When applying this idea to the actual allocation of competences between the EU and Member States it turns out that in some areas, such as agricultural policy and parts of environmental policy, we face too much centralization, whereas in other areas, such as defence policy and international relations, the role of the Member States is still too strong. We should add that the controversial discussions on how to allocate competences between supranational institutions and Member States refer not only to public law issues, such as quality, safety and environmental standards but also to the question of how rules of private law should come into being (Faure and van der Walt 2010; Wagner 2009). The range of opinions reaches from "no need for harmonizing private law" to the request by the European Parliament to create a unified European civil code. However, when talking about the allocation of competences, one should not forget about the implications for political decision making and the related information and incentive problems. This brings us to the third story.

The third story is about democracy in a multi-level system. Apart from the question at which level the collective decision making should be done it has to be decided how to organize the representation of the Member States at the EU level. The actual solution reached by the EU is a compromise between two conflicting principles: "One man one vote," which would give the smallest countries a weight close to zero, or "one country one vote," which would be less appealing for the bigger countries. The main institutions at the Community level have been the European Commission, the Council of Ministers, the European Council, the European Parliament, and the European Court of Justice. In the course of the last 50 years there has been a tendency to give the supranational component in collective decision making at the EU level a larger weight, by reducing unanimity voting to the benefit of qualified majority voting and by increasing the importance of the directly elected European Parliament with respect to the Council of Ministers. Today, regular law-making at the EU level requires an initiative by the European Commission and majority votes by both the Council of Ministers and the European Parliament (co-decision procedure).

When putting the three stories together, we face the phenomenon which has been recently described by Rodrik (2011) as the "globalization paradox." According to this paradox, which holds not only for the globalized world as a whole but also for regionally integrated parts of the world, such as the European Union, it is not possible to achieve at the same time complete economic integration (a single market), national sovereignty and political democracy. With sovereign nation states and complete economic integration, characterized by the free movement of goods, services, persons and capital, the national parliaments and governments are not free any more to follow their policies based on political majorities within the countries, but have to make their policies dependent on the markets. The price is a loss of political democracy. With economic integration and centralization of the policies at the federal level political democracy may be re-established. However, the price is a loss of national sovereignty, to the benefit of the supranational authorities. If one wants to keep national sovereignty and political democracy as well, one has to accept some loss of economic integration, i.e. some fragmentation of the markets due to obstacles to the free movement of goods, services, persons and capital.

European Union law crucially affects the everyday life of the people living in the 27 Member States, and also of those parties outside the European Union who engage in transactions with EU citizens. As Pelkmans (2001, 36) put it: "The EEC is a regulatory machinery, not a spending tree." On the one hand, the EU budget is comparatively small: whereas the EU budget amounts to around 1 percent of the European Union's GDP, the corresponding share in the Member States varies between one-third and more than 50 percent. On the other hand, the European Union produces every year thousands of legislative acts that address every facet of people's life. The following legislative instruments are available (Article 288 TFEU). A *Regulation* is directly binding in all Member States. A *Directive* has to be transposed into national law before entering into force. It leaves discretion to Member States with regard to some of its content and with regard to its systematic place in the body of the national law. It can for instance be transformed as a separate law or imputed into an existing law such as the civil code. A *Decision* is only binding on those to whom it is addressed. Moreover, there are two types of "soft law" with no binding force: *Recommendations* and *Opinions*. Whereas the number of binding legislative acts (regulations, directives and decisions) issued in the period 1971–75 amounts to about 2,600, the number increased in the period 1996–2000 to around 11,400 – a 500 percent increase (Alesina and Giavazzi 2006, 121–3). According to recent data by EUR-Lex the corresponding number of legislative acts issued in the period 2006–10 amounts to more than 12,400.

The European Court of Justice (ECJ) specified in a series of landmark decisions in the 1960s and 1970s the legal relationship between the Community and the Member States. In 1963 the ECJ ruled that provisions of the Treaty could have *direct effect*; i.e. provisions of binding EC law which are clear, precise and unconditional enough to be considered justiciable can be revoked and relied on by individuals before national courts (*Van Gend & Loos*, case 26/62). In *Costa v ENEL* (case 6/64) the ECJ established the *supremacy* of EC law with respect to the national law of the Member States: "The transfer, by Member States, from their national orders in favour of the Community order of the rights and obligations arising from the Treaty, carries with it a clear limitation of their sovereign right upon which a subsequent unilateral law, incompatible with the aims of the Community, cannot prevail." Moreover, in 1984 the ECJ required national courts to interpret domestic law, as far as possible, *in the light of and in conformity with Community law* (*Colson and Kamann v Land Nordrhein-Westfalen*, case 14/83). Finally, the ECJ established in a series of decisions, starting with *Francovich* in 1991 (case 6 & 9/90), the principle of *state liability* for breach of Community law.

In all areas of Community (European Union) law, the ECJ has extensively relied on one specific procedure, the so-called *preliminary ruling procedure* (Article 267 TFEU), to develop the substantive law. Since the national courts of the Member States have to ensure that EU law is properly applied in each state there is a risk that the interpretation of EU law might differ between the Member States. The preliminary ruling procedure has been introduced to prevent such a divergence. If a national court is in doubt about the interpretation or validity of some EU law, it may – and sometimes must – interrupt the proceeding and ask the Court of Justice for advice. This advice is called a preliminary ruling and has become, since the middle of the 1990s, the most important way to trigger rulings by the Court of Justice, more important than all *direct actions*, such as, in particular, actions by the Commission against Member States that have failed to fulfill their obligations under European Union law and actions by individuals or organizations to challenge the validity of EU legislation that affects them.

This research handbook analyzes important parts of European Union law from an economic point of view. The focus is on how the development of European Union Law copes with the tension between market integration, national sovereignty and political democracy.

The first part of the book deals with "constitutional issues." There has been an ongoing controversial discussion for many years on "democratic deficits," "lack of transparency" and "over-centralization" and "over-bureaucratization" of political decision making in Brussels. It is discussed, for example, whether the European Union strengthens the positions of national governments vis-à-vis national parliaments, whether the European Commission dominates the European Parliament, or whether the European Court of Justice has gained importance to the detriment of the European legislator and to the detriment of the Member States as the "masters of the treaty." Stefan Voigt compares the constitutional framework of the European Union with nation state constitutions. George Tsebelis analyzes some crucial features of decision making at the European Union level. Manfred Holler also copes with collective decision making in a multi-level system, but with the focus on the allocation of responsibility. Hans-Bernd Schäfer asks the question whether Member States' liability for the infringement of EU law can deter national legislators from violating European law. Finally, Emanuela Carbonara, Barbara Luppi and Francesco Parisi assess the principle of subsidiarity from an economic point of view.

The second part of the book is related to a central policy issue of many years, the establishment of a single (internal) market, which is closely related to the four fundamental freedoms. Whereas Jacques Pelkmans elaborates on the important principle of mutual recognition with respect to goods and services, Herbert Brücker and Thomas Eger discuss the development of the free movement of persons in the last 50 years and its economic implications. Also important for the establishment of an integrated market are corporation law and corporate governance, which are discussed in Part 3 by Patrick Leyens. It is still far from clear whether it is required, helpful, needless or detrimental to harmonize private law in Europe. This issue is discussed in Part 4 by Michael Faure (tort law) and Fernando Gomez (contract law). In Part 5, Fabrizio Cafaggi and Antonio Nicita address the highly controversial question whether a specific legislation in favor of consumers should supplement the standard remedies in contract law, property law, tort law and antitrust law, and – if the answer is yes – whether the European Union or the Member States should be responsible for consumer protection.

An important question refers to law enforcement in a multi-level governance system, such as the European Union. The two contributions in Part 6 deal with this problem. Nuno Garoupa takes a skeptical view on the harmonization of the enforcement of European Union law. Roberto Pardolesi discusses the recent initiative by the European Commission to strengthen the importance of private enforcement of European antitrust law.

At latest after the Eastern enlargements of 2004 and 2007 the question arose how to cope with an increasing club of heterogeneous countries with different economic structures, different quality of institutions and different cultures and languages (Part 7). Hans-Jürgen Wagener discusses the economic and political implications of the recent and possible future enlargements. Jan Fidrmuc addresses the specific economic problems resulting from the fact that within the European Union today 23 official languages exist.

Finally, the most urgent problems today result from the serious sovereign debt crises in Greece and some other Member States of the Eurozone. In Part 8, Helmut Siekmann provides a detailed analysis of the architecture of the monetary institutions and the monetary policy and their implications for the sovereign debt crisis, with reference to the support mechanisms that have been established or discussed.

REFERENCES

Alesina, A. and F. Giavazzi (2006), *The Future of Europe: Reform or Decline*, Cambridge, MA: The MIT Press.

Baldwin, R. and Ch. Wyplosz (2004), *The Economics of European Integration*, Maidenhead, UK: McGraw-Hill.

Eichengreen, B. (2007), *The European Economy Since 1945: Coordinated Capitalism and Beyond*, Princeton, NJ: Princeton University Press.

Faure, M. and A. van der Walt (eds) (2010), *Globalization and Private Law*, Cheltenham, UK: Edward Elgar Publishing.

Nello, S.S. (2009), *The European Union: Economics, Policies and History*, Maidenhead, UK: McGraw-Hill.

Oates, W.E. (1972), *Fiscal Federalism*, New York: Harcourt, Brace and Jovanovic.

Oates, W.E. (1999), "An Essay on Fiscal Federalism," *Journal of Economic Literature*, 37, 1120–49.

Pelkmans, J. (2001), *European Integration: Methods and Economic Analysis*, second edition, Harlow, UK: Prentice Hall.

Rodrik, D. (2011), *The Globalization Paradox: Democracy and the Future of the World Economy*, New York: W.W. Norton.

Wagner, G. (ed.) (2009), *The Common Frame of Reference: A View from Law & Economics*, Munich: Sellier.

PART 1

THE CONSTITUTIONAL FRAMEWORK OF THE EU

1 A constitution like any other? Comparing the European constitution with nation state constitutions

*Stefan Voigt**

1 INTRODUCTION

The Treaty of Lisbon went into force in December 2009. From an economic point of view, this treaty is equivalent with the constitutional framework of the European Union. Its institutional traits are, hence, analyzed in this chapter.

The Treaty of Lisbon is the way EU governments have coped with the failure of the attempt to install a fully fledged constitution, due to the negative referendum results in both France and the Netherlands. The Treaty of Lisbon was subject to referendums in only one member state, namely Ireland. Ironically, it possibly owes its ratification to the global financial crisis that occurred in 2008 and 2009: after having turned down the Lisbon treaty once, the Irish opted in its favor as soon as they realized that their own country was in deep trouble and that the support of the EU might be crucial for getting it out of the crisis.

The financial crisis is further evidence for the precarious nature of constitutions. Before some members of the Eurozone got into serious trouble, there was unanimous consent that the Treaty of Lisbon contained a very clear and unambiguous no bail-out clause. After a protective shield worth €750 billion was created in May 2010, we all know better.

This chapter provides an evaluation of both the genesis and the content of the Treaty of Lisbon. The normative benchmarks on which the evaluations are based are taken mainly from both constitutional political economy and fiscal federalism. The chapter spells out some of the key features of the EU's constitutional framework. The likely effects of these features will be speculated upon.

The rest of this chapter is organized as follows. Section 2 briefly summarizes the main elements of constitutional political economy. Some normative considerations regarding the genesis as well as the content of constitutions are spelled out in Section 3. Section 4 presents some key features of the Treaty and deals with their likely effects in isolation, while Section 5 makes the attempt to look at the broader picture. It tries to evaluate the kind of separation of powers established with the Treaty of Lisbon and christens it "diagonal separation of powers." The most important question that the constitution of the EU needs to come to terms with appears to be the balance between Brussels and the

* The author thanks Anne van Aaken for interesting discussions on the topic as well as David Börn, Matthias Dauner, Felix Horbach, Jerg Gutmann, Katharina Stepping, Agnes Strauß, George Tsebelis and the other participants of the author conference leading to this volume.

member states. Section 6 thus inquires whether the current measures are likely to create a sustainable balance. Section 7 concludes.

2 CONSTITUTIONAL POLITICAL ECONOMY – A BRIEF SURVEY OF OUR FRAME OF REFERENCE

One of the founders of constitutional political economy, James Buchanan, defines constitutions in their most basic sense as "a set of rules which constrain the activities of persons and agents in the pursuits of their own ends and objectives" (Buchanan 1977, 292). Defined as such, quite a few rule systems can be analyzed as constitutions: a firm's partnership agreement as well as the statute of a church. According to Buchanan's definition, a sovereign nation state is no precondition for having a constitution. The definition implies that the European Union has had a constitution for a long time.

Approaching constitutions from a functional point of view, the following functions could be named:

1. Constitutions serve to *create authority* by defining the organs that are to provide public goods, and by specifying the *modi* according to which representatives of these organs are appointed and the specific competences of these organs including their interplay. In federal polities, constitutions also have the function to determine the competence of the various levels of government. With regard to the European Union, this means that the allocation of competences between Union and member state competences should be clear-cut.
2. Constitutions also create protected private spheres which are exempt from public decision-making. Formulated differently: they *restrict the authority* of the governing.
3. States claim to command the monopoly of the legitimate use of force. Both the procedure by which constitutions are generated and their content can help to establish a state's legitimacy. Constitutions thus serve to *make the actions of the governing legitimate*.
4. Constitutions are a specific subset of institutions. Institutions have the function of enabling individuals to form expectations that have a good chance of turning out to be correct. This refers to possible actions of both private actors and representatives of the state. Predictability is a necessary condition for forming a long time horizon, for being willing to specialize, for making long-term investment, etc. Predictability is thus a crucial precondition for economic growth. Constitutions serve to *increase predictability*.

Two broad avenues in the economic analysis of constitutions can be distinguished: (1) the normative branch is interested in legitimizing the state and the actions of its representatives; (2) the positive branch is interested in explaining (a) the emergence and modification of constitutional rules and (b) the outcomes that are the consequence of (alternative) constitutional rules (for a similar demarcation of the topic, see Mueller (1996); Voigt (2011) is an up-to-date survey of the field). In this chapter, no attempt is made to endogenize the constitutional framework of the European Union (but see Vaubel (2002) for such an attempt).

Normative constitutional economics could deal with a variety of questions, e.g. (1) how should societies proceed in order to bring about constitutional rules that fulfill some criterion like being "just" or "efficient"? (2) what contents should the constitutional rules have? (3) which issues should be dealt with in the constitution and which should be left to sub-constitutional choice? (4) what characteristics should constitutional rules have? and many more. Buchanan answers none of these questions directly but hopes to offer a conceptual frame that would make them answerable. The frame is based on social contract theory as developed most prominently by Hobbes. According to Buchanan (1987, 249), the purpose of this contractarian approach is justificatory in the sense that "it offers a basis for normative evaluation. Could the observed rules that constrain the activity of ordinary politics have emerged from agreement in constitutional contract? To the extent that this question can be affirmatively answered, we have established a legitimating linkage between the individual and the state."

3 NORMATIVE CONSIDERATIONS

In this section, three normative aspects are dealt with: the procedure used to generate the Treaty of Lisbon, some criteria for evaluating its content and a measure for evaluating the success of constitutions.

3.1 Criteria for Evaluating a Constitution's Creation

In their approach, Buchanan and Tullock (1962) take a rational individual who is interested in her own utility as the starting point. Applied to a European constitution, this individual would have to decide (1) which goods should be provided by collective action and which ones by private action, (2) whether the publicly provided goods should be provided on the European level or the nation state level,[1] and (3) what the respective majorities used in order to decide upon the provision of public goods should be. Buchanan and Tullock (1962) gave the following basic answers: (1) goods should be provided by collective action only if private action is more expensive (57f.); (2) where possible, collective action should be organized in small rather than in large units (114f.); (3) the decision-rule should lead to the minimization of interdependence costs, which are defined as the sum total of external costs ("costs that the individual expects to endure as a result of the actions of others over which he has no direct control") and decision-making costs ("costs which the individual expects to incur as a result of his own participation in an organized activity") (45f.).

The European Union was founded by six countries in 1957. Today, it has 27 members – and it is likely to grow further. The broadening of EU membership has led to an increase in the heterogeneity of the preferences of the citizens who are part of the Union. Suppose preferences were completely homogeneous in some – supposedly – small polity:

---

1 Or, possibly, on a level beyond the European one.

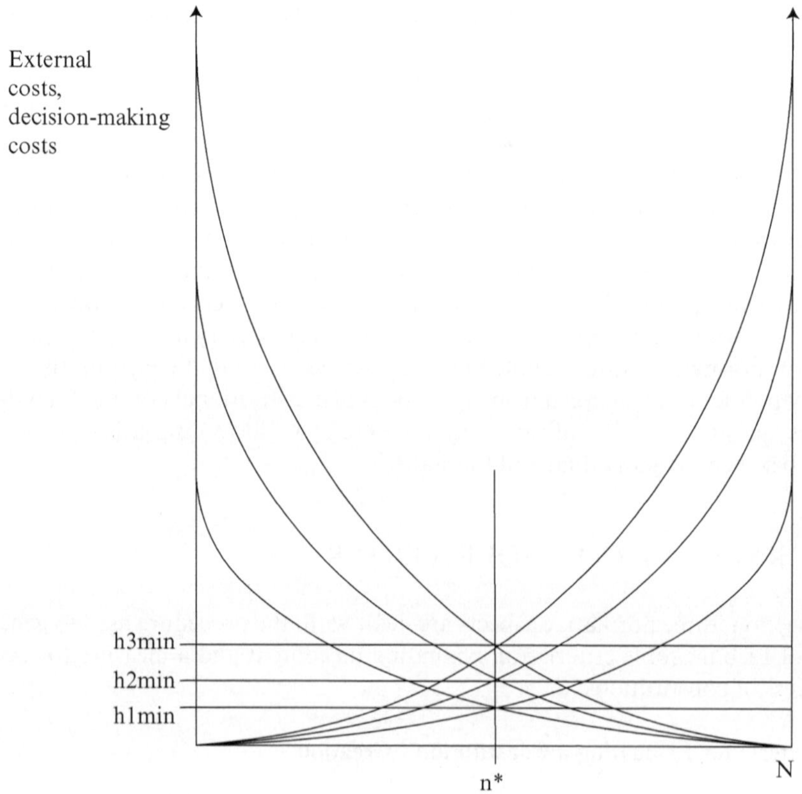

Figure 1.1 Increasing heterogeneity always means increasing interdependence (external plus decision-making) costs

this would mean that the external cost that any individual would have to bear because it is in the minority should be minuscule.[2] The same holds for decision-making costs: if all are of the same opinion, getting to a collective decision should not be difficult and thus rather cheap. Such a community could easily reach unanimity but decisions made by a single individual could be just as good as long as all individuals have identical preferences. The more heterogeneous the preferences become, the larger the expected external costs. This can be seen in Figure 1.1, in which two levels of heterogeneity lead to two different external cost functions. A similar argument can be made for decision-making costs: the more heterogeneous the preferences with regard to public goods, the steeper the slope of the curve. This means that the sum of both curves – the interdependence costs – increases with the degree of heterogeneity. Public goods should be provided on the level of government on which they can be provided at least costs. The larger the Union, the greater are

[2] More precisely: if preferences were completely identical among all members of a polity, external costs would be zero.

the costs of provision on the European level. This means that the chances that the provision of public goods on the level of the nation state are less costly increase with the size of the Union. The larger the Union, the fewer the public goods which should be optimally provided by the Union itself.

Let us now turn to the decision-making rules used to determine the quality and quantity of the public goods to be provided at the Union level. In the abstract, this should be that majority rule where interdependence costs are at a minimum. *Ex ante*, it is unclear whether higher degrees of heterogeneity lead to more or less inclusive majorities, which means that the minimum of the interdependence costs can move to the right as well as to the left.

It is, however, unlikely that the optimal level of provision for a large bundle of public goods is either the nation state or the European Union. The optimal level in many cases might be beyond the nation state but only comprise a number of other states that is clearly below the level of all 27 members. This possibility can be taken into consideration by providing for the possibility of *géométrie variable*,[3] i.e. the possibility that different goods can be provided by a different number of states cooperating on specific issues.

To sum up. The interdependence cost calculus has been used to derive some insights concerning the optimal level on which public goods should be provided as well as optimal decision-making rules concerning decisions about these goods. Given that policy areas and decision-making rules are chosen such that interdependence costs are minimized, unanimous consent in favor of such a constitution should be attainable, if only conceptually. This calculus would take care of the first two functions of constitutions, namely to create authority and to restrict it at the same time. We now turn to the third function, namely to secure legitimacy.

If real people are to accredit an organization with legitimacy, purely conceptual consent is unlikely to be sufficient. Transparency during the constitutional negotiations and the participation of representatives of civil society are possible means to create legitimacy for a constitution that shifts competence away from the nation state to Brussels. The Convention following the Declaration of Laeken did make some attempts in that direction. The Treaty of Lisbon was, however, created in the traditional Union style.

Among many citizens, the European Union is not particularly popular. Referendums instigate public discussion and increase the general knowledge concerning the functioning of the relevant institutions (Benz and Stutzer 2004). Referendums on the European constitution could, thus, have increased the familiarity of many citizens with the basic rules and could also have improved the legitimacy of the document. It is a pity that the Treaty of Lisbon was generated and ratified excluding the citizens for which it was purportedly drafted.

---

[3] One can often read similar ideas under the heading of "multiple speeds," implying that some are faster in integrating than others. We explicitly do not use this metaphor here because some societies might be better off never integrating the provision of certain public goods. The possibility of a variable geometry is explicitly mentioned in Art. 20 TEU. Examples of more integrationist endeavors are "Schengen" and the European Economic and Monetary Systems.

3.2 Criteria for Evaluating a Constitution's Content

Economics in general, and fiscal federalism in particular, has produced a number of criteria for the allocation of competence onto various government levels. The possibility to realize economies of scale (and possibly also of scope) and the presence of spillover effects are features in favor of "unionizing" policy areas. The heterogeneity of preferences but also the availability of local information are features in favor of providing public goods on levels below the European Union. Based on these criteria, Alesina and Wacziarg (1999) as well as Alesina et al. (2005a) argue that the Union might suffer from a centralization bias. They argue that social as well as agricultural policies should be allocated to the level of the member states. On the other hand, defence and foreign policies as well as environmental issues should be dealt with more at the European level.

Alesina et al. (2005b) draw on survey data to inquire into citizen preferences concerning the level on which a number of public goods should be provided. Out of nine policy domains delineated by the authors (international trade; common market; money and finance; education, research, and culture; environment; business relations (sectoral and non-sectoral); international relations; citizen and social protection), citizens would prefer that education, research, and culture as well as agriculture be dealt with on the national level, whereas money and finance, environment and international relations should be dealt with at the Union level. Broadly speaking, *vox populi* is largely in line with economic theory but constitutional reality is not.

3.3 Criteria for Evaluating a Constitution's Success

Many constitutions promise paradise on earth whereas constitutional reality is frequently rather nasty and brutish. Some constitutions successfully constrain the governing whereas others do not. Elster (1991) proposes three criteria for evaluating whether a constitution is "successful," namely that it matters, that it works, and that it lasts. Whether it is considered to be working depends on subjective evaluation and Elster does not address this issue further. For a constitution to matter, he points to three conditions: (1) it must contain precise and enforceable action implications, which (2) have to be actually enforced, and (3) whose enforcement must causally be linked to the existence of the constitution (Elster 1991, 15).

To increase the likelihood of constitutional provisions being factually implemented, a number of tools have been created. One of them, checks and balances, implies that the different organs of government are to check each other. But checks and balances will be unsuccessful if the governing form a cartel. In such cases, informal institutions become crucial: will a sizable number of individuals and/or groups manage to overcome the dilemma of collective action (Olson 1965) to protest against the infringement of constitutional rights? is there a press criticizing the infringement? and so on. It has often been pointed out that Europe lacks a *demos* (e.g. by Grimm 2002). Relying on informal norms in Europe might, hence, be premature.

Prima facie, the longevity of a constitution as such does not enjoy normative status. Returning to the basic function of all institutions – namely to make the future more predictable – the lasting of a constitution can have important positive effects. Elkins et al. (2009, 139ff.) deal with the endurance of constitutions and find that (1) constitutions written under inclusive conditions (e.g. public ratification), (2) constitutions that are easier to amend and (3) constitutions with more scope and detail all have a longer expected lifespan. Their empirical results are based on nation state constitutions. Assuming that the results can also be applied to supranational constitutions, aspects (1) and (2) seem problematic whereas the third one is definitely not.

Aspect (1) appears problematic because the European constitution was created largely excluding the public. Aspect (2) appears problematic because the EU constitution is probably more difficult to amend than any nation state constitution that has ever existed. After all, every member state needs to consent according to the domestically established ratification procedures. The third aspect appears less problematic because the EU constitution contains considerable detail. If the length of a constitution in words is used as a proxy for detail, the EU constitution is definitely one of the most detailed constitutions ever written (a word count of the consolidated version of the Treaty gives 124,203 words; the US constitution consists of less than 5000 words).[4]

To sum up Section 3: we have seen that the allocation of competences in the European constitution is hard to justify drawing on economic theory; we have further seen that some doubts concerning the possible success of this constitution seem well grounded. We now move on to describe a number of key features of the constitution and their likely effects.

4 THE KEY FEATURES OF THE EUROPEAN CONSTITUTION – AND THEIR LIKELY CONSEQUENCES

Research into the economic effects of nation state constitutions has made important progress over the last years (Persson and Tabellini (2003) is a seminal contribution, Voigt (2011) offers a broad survey). Before making predictions regarding the likely effects of the EU constitution, a caveat seems in order: the EU is not a nation state and many complex interactions between the supranational and the national level do not play any role in the analysis of the effects of nation state constitutions.

With regard to nation state constitutions, electoral systems (including the electoral rule but also the size of the voting districts and the proportion of individually elected candidates) have been shown to have far-reaching effects (Persson and Tabellini 2003; Blume et al. 2009). It is, however, unclear how to transfer these insights onto the European level: the function of the European Parliament might be different from that of national parliaments. What is more, the parliamentarians are still elected on the basis of national election laws (though there are common principles; Art. 223 TFEU).

In the remainder of this section, the constitutional traits most commonly mentioned in the context of nation state constitutions are briefly discussed.

---

4 Voigt (2009) is an attempt to identify determinants of the extreme differences in constitutional length.

4.1 Creating Legislation: the Decision-making Rules

Section 3 developed some criteria for determining (1) the level on which public goods should be provided and (2) the decision-making rules that ought to be applied when deciding about their exact provision. Under the Treaty of Lisbon, a standard procedure for generating legislation was created. Under it, both the Council (representing the member states) and the European Parliament (EP; representing the citizens) need to consent to a proposal initiated by the Commission. Fifty-five percent of the Council votes suffice given that they originate from at least 15 member states and those member states represent at least 65 percent of the entire population.[5] The awkward construction that the Commission – the equivalent of the executive on the nation state level – keeps its monopoly as an agenda-setter for the legislature remains unchanged.

The Treaty of Lisbon has reduced the number of policy areas for which unanimity is required. To be more precise: it has increased the number of policy areas to which the newly created ordinary legislative procedure (formerly called qualified majority voting) is applied from 137 to 181. European legislation has thus become easier, implying that more laws and further centralization can be expected. It could, however, be argued that legislation has become more difficult in some policy areas as not only the consent of the Council but also that of the Parliament is needed. But the refraining effect of the EP seems to be more of a hypothetical possibility than a real option: it is reasonable to assume that the median voter of the EP is more integrationist than the pivotal player of the Council. In all likelihood, the extended competence of the EP will therefore not prove to be a counterweight against the higher number of laws passed by the Council due to the change from unanimity to the ordinary legislative procedure.

4.2 The Form of Government: Presidential or Parliamentary?

The form of government and its economic effects have been one of the central topics in research in positive constitutional economics. Persson et al. (1997) argue that the presidential form of government implies more separation of powers than the parliamentary one, because in the latter the prime minister depends for survival on securing a parliamentary majority on a daily basis. Presidents would be more independent from parliament and could, hence, be a real check on parliament. Later on, Persson and Tabellini (2003) showed that compared with parliamentary systems, presidential systems would tend to have lower taxes, to spend less and to accrue lesser deficits. Additionally, they would achieve better governance scores (e.g. less rent seeking and less corruption). Critics of this conceptualization (e.g. Robinson and Torvik 2008 or Hayo and Voigt 2010) point out that this model of presidential systems was largely based on the US example. In other settings, reality would be less rosy. Empirically, governance scores of presidential systems are shown to be worse than parliamentary ones (e.g. with regard to corruption) and general output measures, such as total factor productivity, are better under parliamentary systems. In this debate, the only criterion for distinguishing parliamentary from

[5] Before the Treaty of Lisbon, qualified majority voting meant that some 70 percent of the Council votes were necessary.

presidential systems is whether the survival of the head of government depends on the consent of parliament (this has been criticized by Keefer 2004).

Before asking to what degree these findings are relevant to the form of government chosen in the European Union, we need to ascertain what form of government has been chosen according to the Treaty of Lisbon. The Treaty established the president of the European Council (Art. 15 TEU), who is elected by the European Council with qualified majority for a term of two and a half years. He is eligible for re-election once. Now, the task of the European Council is to give the Union impulses necessary for its development, to determine the general political goals and priorities but not to function as a legislator (ibid.). Nor does it function as the executive. In that sense, the newly created position has little to do with a presidential system as discussed above.

The Commission is more similar to nation state governments. Its head is also called president (Art. 17 TEU). He is elected by the European Parliament after having been proposed by the European Council. The Commission as a group is accountable to the European Parliament. The Parliament can vote it down via a vote of no confidence. According to the criterion used in positive constitutional economics, the form of government realized in the European Union is, thus, more parliamentary than presidential.

Research with regard to nation state constitutions has found that presidential systems incur less deficits than parliamentary ones. Other fiscal variables such as revenue, expenditure and the structure of the budget are also correlated with the form of government. When analyzing the EU constitution, these criteria make little sense: as of now, the EU does not have the competence to charge taxes of its own; its budget is balanced by definition. Referring to the quality of governance, research on nation state constitutions has looked at both rent seeking and corruption perceptions. A pretty straightforward conjecture is that resources spent on rent seeking are a function of the prospective rents to be reaped. Corruption is conjectured to be high where large sums are being distributed. In the European Union, almost three-quarters of the entire budget is still spent on the common agricultural policy and on structural policy. The common agricultural policy cannot be justified on economic grounds. Following economic arguments would not only make the Union more efficient but would also make it less prone to corruption.

4.3 The Number of Chambers: Uni-, Bi- or Tricameral?

The economic effects of bicameralism have long been neglected. Buchanan and Tullock (1962) demonstrated that the effects of a second chamber could theoretically also be reached by establishing supra-majority decision-rules in a single legislative chamber. All federations have, by definition, at least two chambers, namely the one representing the nation and the one representing the constituent units. Sometimes, presidential federations, such as the United States, are characterized as having a third house, namely the president.

The legislative process according to the Treaty of Lisbon has been briefly described in Section 4.1 above. One innovation of the Treaty has, however, not been mentioned there. The nation state parliaments have been established as an additional veto player by the Treaty (Art. 12 TEU). It is they who have the possibility to monitor that the organs of the European level are not reneging on the principle of subsidiarity (itself enshrined in Art. 5 TEU). The Treaty arranges for two ways to do so: a third of all parliaments can, within eight weeks after receiving draft legislation from the Union, send a comment in which the reasons for the incompatibility of said legislation with the subsidiarity principle is spelled out. The other way is to go directly to the European Court of Justice (ECJ).

Both ways are unlikely to have substantial effects. For the use of the first tool, national parliaments would have to find mechanisms to overcome the problem of collective action. Agreeing on a comment within just eight weeks seems rather unlikely. Use of the second tool is likely to make little impact for a different reason: here, the ECJ is the final arbiter about compliance with the subsidiarity principle. In the past, the ECJ has probably been the most important driver toward ever more integration. Making integration-friendly judges the arbiters on subsidiarity seems to be a mistaken idea.

4.4 The Possibility of Initiatives: Power to the People?

It has been argued that direct democratic institutions help to align policies better with citizen preferences. The existence of direct democratic institutions as such could already have an important effect: given that politicians do not like to be corrected by their voters, they have incentives to take voter preferences explicitly into account when producing new legislation. Empirical results obtained from a cross-country study (Blume et al. 2009) show, first, that effects are larger when direct democratic institutions are actually used – and are not merely a possibility; and, second, that institutional detail greatly matters: whereas referendums are correlated with less expenditure, initiatives are correlated with more.

The Treaty of Lisbon introduced the possibility of a citizens' initiative (Art. 11 TEU). At least one million citizens must support the initiative. According to a regulation proposed jointly by the Parliament and the Commission (COM (2010) 119), the supporters must be citizens of at least nine member states. The supporters "may take the initiative of inviting the European Commission . . . to submit any appropriate proposal on matters where citizens consider that a legal act of the Union is required for the purpose of implementing the Treaties" (ibid., number 4).

It is difficult to predict the effects of the citizens' initiative. Compared with many nation states, the number of signatures needed is rather small. So kicking it off does not seem an insurmountable hurdle. Yet, in substance, this form of direct democratic participation falls far short of many nation state institutions: citizens never have the final word on any issue, i.e. there is no referendum. It is also unclear whether they can even be regarded as agenda-setters. Citizens do not have the right to make concrete proposals, but may only "invite" the Commission to become active. The invitations are furthermore confined to issues within the Treaties. In other words, Constitutional change, or primary legislation, cannot be kicked off by using this provision. Direct democracy is frequently defined as the competence of citizens to make final decisions on substantive issues (e.g. IRI 2005, 228). By that definition, the Treaty of Lisbon does not contain any direct democratic elements. As of today, it seems very likely that the Commission will use the citizens' initiative as an instrument supporting ever more activities on the European level.

4.5 The Charter of Fundamental Rights: Protecting Citizens – or Increasing the Influence of Brussels?

There seems to be a trend that modern constitutions include ever more individual rights (Law and Versteeg 2011). Economists have often been rather critical concerning the likely effects of long enumerated lists: Hayek (e.g. 1976), pointed out that every positive right granted implies by necessity the allocation of some duty to others to implement that right. He was very much in favor of negative rights, protecting the individual from abuse by the state, but was very critical of positive rights because they would lead to a thinning out of property rights of those who have to pay for such rights. Sen (1999) develops an entirely different conjecture: according to him, formally spelled-out rights that have a rather aspirational status at their inception might develop as focal points and become constitutional reality later on.

The constitutional framework of the European Union contains an extended list of individual rights. The Charter of Fundamental Rights had already been agreed upon in 2000 but did not enjoy any formal status. This has changed with the Treaty of Lisbon. The Charter now enjoys the same legal status as the Treaties (Art. 6, TEU).[6]

In principle, a catalogue of rights that protect citizens against intrusions of European organs into their private sphere makes eminent sense. Genuine law-making power on the European level should be accompanied by genuine and directly applicable negative rights of the citizens who are subject to such legislation.

The Charter does, however, contain not only a number of negative rights but also a number of problematic articles:

- Formally, the provisions are to bind the organs of the Union only when they implement Union law; at the same time, Union law is to take primacy over the laws of the member states; it is thus unclear in which cases the rights laid down in the Charter do not enjoy primacy over the basic rights as found in the constitutions of the member states. A decision of the ECJ in order to clarify is most likely – and it seems further likely that it will decide in favor of a broad application of the European Charter.
- Materially, the Charter contains a number of positive rights, e.g. the right to work (Art. 15, Charter) and the right to a free placement service (Art. 29, Charter). Again, the European Court of Justice can be expected to use the Charter as an additional instrument to increase the influence of the European organs.

Even if many "rights" spelled out in the Charter cannot be enforced directly, the European Court of Justice is likely to take them into account in its jurisdiction, as they allow the Court to push centralization even further.

---

[6] Except in Poland and the UK (see Protocol No. 30). This is another example of a variable geometry.

4.6 Leaving the Union: A Credible Threat?

The discussion regarding a constitutionally safeguarded right to secede has not produced consensus. Sunstein (1991) conjectures that such a right would encourage strategic behavior by certain subgroups whose resources are indispensable for the further existence of the state but who do not depend themselves on its further existence. He also fears that such a right would produce large destabilizing effects which may disrupt expectations whose existence is indispensable both to economic prosperity and democratic self-determination (ibid., 651). Others have argued the exact opposite. The government of a federal union could be restrained effectively by a right to secede established for the members of the union: should the utility of being a member become negative, the respective member could credibly threaten its withdrawal. A right to secede would thus be an instrument to constrain government activities on the federal level (e.g. Buchanan 1990). Chen and Ordeshook (1994) point out that if secession is the dominant strategy, then a unit will secede no matter whether it has that right or not. A formal right to secede will only make sense if there are at least two alternative equilibria and the formal right to secede can help society to coordinate on one of them. They venture that these conditions could hold in cases where a subgroup disposes of credible commitments and if the decision of a subgroup to exit from a state or to remain within it depends on prior agreement. To sum up: our positive knowledge concerning the effects of a constitutional right to secede remains rather scarce; I am not aware of any systematic empirical results.

The Treaty of Lisbon establishes the formal right to exit from the Union (Art. 50, TEU). This can be interpreted as an ultimate veto right. A government alluding to the possibility of using it can constrain a majority of other states from systematic neglect of the interests of the member contemplating its use. Its effects should, however, not be overestimated: the threat of leaving will only remain credible if it is not used too often.

4.7 Changing the Constitution: So Difficult to Entail the Danger of Non-compliance?

A very important decision-rule in every constitution is the rule that specifies how it can be amended. Constitution makers face a tradeoff: on the one hand, a high threshold makes constitutional change more expensive and, hence, less likely. This can be considered beneficial because institutional stability increases predictability. Yet, it also entails the danger that constitutional provisions will be amended implicitly, i.e. through a modified interpretation of a formally unchanged document, or simply be ignored if it is too difficult to ever change the constitution.

Although the Treaty of Lisbon introduced some simplified revision procedures (Art. 48, 6 and 7 TEU), the European constitution is very likely to be the most difficult one to change.[7] The competence of constitutional change remains with the member states; i.e. the European organs do not have the so-called "competence competence" at their disposal. All member states need to ratify the change according to the relevant national procedures. The simplified procedures are unlikely to significantly reduce that threshold.

---

[7] Very costly explicit change is likely to foster less costly implicit change. The notion of explicit as opposed to implicit constitutional change is further developed in Voigt (1999, Chapter 7).

The extraordinary difficulty to change the European constitution explicitly has endowed the European Court of Justice with considerable leeway in amending it implicitly. The decisions *Van Gend en Loos* and *Costa vs. Enel* are the two best-known cases in which the ECJ swiftly enlarged the relevance of European law. Both decisions date back to the first half of the 1960s, when the Union only had six members. With the current 27 members, explicitly amending the constitution has become a lot more difficult in the meantime. Accordingly, the leeway of the Court has tremendously increased (Voigt 2003 is a more detailed analysis).

It was argued in Section 3.1 that the explicit introduction of a *géométrie variable* would make sense as the optimal level of provision could lie somewhere between the entire EU and the nation state. In Art. 20, the Treaty of Lisbon provides for such an opportunity as "a last resort."

To sum up: the institutional innovations brought about by the Treaty of Lisbon have been described briefly. Looked at in isolation, they are likely to bring about the following effects: (i) The increased number of policy areas to which the newly created ordinary legislation procedure will be applied is likely to lead to more legislation. (ii) The creation of a president of the European Council will not make the Union presidential. (iii) The subsidiarity principle in combination with the monitoring competence of the national parliaments is unlikely to create an important brake to ever more centralization. (iv) Since citizens' initiatives do not have any formally binding effects, they are unlikely to have any such effects factually. (v) The Charter of Fundamental Rights gives the ECJ yet another tool to enhance its influence which it is expected to use. (vi) The possibility of exiting from the Union is unlikely to change much, as the Union could not have prevented any member state from exiting even before. (vii) The tremendous hurdles to explicitly change the constitution in combination with the large number of member states further re-enforce the influence of the ECJ.

5 A NEW SEPARATION OF POWERS?

A democratic deficit of the European Union has often been deplored. The Declaration of Laeken, which marked the beginning of the ill-fated attempt to create a constitution for the European Union that also carries that name, explicitly mentioned that democracy – as well as transparency and efficiency – should be improved. For economists, democracy is a collective decision-making procedure but often not a value per se. This is especially true for Buchanan and Tullock (1962) who devise criteria for areas in which collective decision-making is worse than private decision-making.

The second half of the 20th century has witnessed the rise of many independent agencies on the nation state level. It is argued that a number of policy areas that share a number of traits can better be handled by technocrats who are not subject to the re-election constraint characteristic of democracies (Maskin and Tirole 2004). The most important single reason seems to be the problem of time inconsistency in which short-term and long-term incentives to act diverge. Politicians who have the competence over monetary policy have an incentive to promise a stable money supply. Shortly before the elections, however, they have an incentive to increase monetary supply to push economic growth which will increase their popularity and thus increase their chances of being re-elected.

Higher inflation, the cost of such a policy, will – if timed correctly – only appear well after the election date. As a consequence, the competence over monetary supply has been taken away from politicians and allocated to independent central bankers not subject to the re-election constraint. Such "non-majoritarian" institutions (Majone, e.g. 2001) have been created with regard to a few other policy areas such as competition policy, environmental policy and so forth.

Independent agencies have usually been legitimized by answering the question whether time inconsistency poses a serious problem in the respective policy area. But the cumulative effects of such agencies are seldom discussed: will they undermine democracy? will they make efficiency-enhancing logrolling less likely? In other words: the normative foundations are underdeveloped.

It seems intuitively clear that there must be some upper bound to the number of policy areas that can be exempt from majoritarian decision-making. It also seems clear that care must be taken that representatives of non-majoritarian institutions are not able to extend their own competences to the detriment of majoritarian institutions. Therefore, some mechanisms are needed to keep representatives of non-majoritarian institutions accountable. By definition, democratic elections are not an option. It seems fair to assume that accountability mechanisms – both democratic and other – are more highly developed on the nation state level than on the European level.

This leads to the following conjecture. For many politicians, it is extremely attractive to circumvent the stricter accountability standards valid at home by getting the desired measures passed on the European level. Take a minister with a specific portfolio, e.g. environment. At home, he might not be able to secure a majority in favor of his projects because other ministers might have competing goals. But as a member of "his" European Council, he meets with 26 other ministers all sharing the same portfolio – and supposedly attaching more weight to it than to other policy areas. In such cases, getting legislation initiated can thus be relatively less difficult on the European level – and is therefore very likely to occur.

This leads directly to a second conjecture. Assume that some of the policies just described are incapable of getting government support on the nation state level because they are unpopular. The frequent use of the European level for such policies would thus imply that many policy decisions of the European Union should be unpopular. This phenomenon has often been described as the European Union having the function of a scapegoat which would ensure that rational, but unpopular, policies could be implemented simply because democratic accountability on the European level was low.

In economics, principal agent reasoning is used to identify accountability deficits and monitoring problems. It seems intuitive that the longer the principal agent chains are, the more difficult it becomes to monitor the relevant agent. Conceptually, all European citizens are the principals. There are at least two relevant principal agent chains: one via the Council and the other one via the European Parliament. The first chain is quite long: citizens elect parliamentarians, who elect the government (at least in parliamentary systems), which sends a representative to the (European) Council; the European Council nominates members to the Commission. This leads us to the second chain: the Commission is accountable to the European Parliament; its members are elected by the citizens.

It is not very daring to conjecture that the agents' capacity to deviate from the preferences of the principal increases in the length of the principal agent chains. In addition, some of the chain links are not individuals but groups. This implies that they are prone to the problem of collective action (Olson 1965): even if every member of the group preferred that they become active in controlling their agents, they might be unable to do so because they find themselves in a prisoners' dilemma situation. It has been argued that representatives of international organizations often enjoy broad leeway due to this problem (Vaubel 2006).

Ackerman (2000) proposed to talk of a "new" separation of powers. What he had in mind was a separation of powers that would substantially deviate from the US model that still seems to be the epitome of the separation of powers for many. In political science, "multi-level systems" and "multi-level governance" have been analyzed for a number of years. We propose to christen the currently realized accountability structure of the European union as a "diagonal separation of powers".

It has often been mentioned that mandatory referendums that need to be held before the European constitution can be changed (on the nation state level) can increase the bargaining leeway of the government of the respective state. Ireland is the example. The referendum also helps to shorten the principal agent chain considerably: a majority of citizens give the government the binding mandate to bring a change about (or not). Recently, another national actor is said to have influenced the results of a European Council meeting: the German Federal Constitutional Court. If constitutional review on the nation state level is sufficiently strong, the threat of getting a decision of the European Council declared unconstitutional can make the European Council decide differently than had the Court been less strong or entirely absent. Here, the nation state judiciary checks upon the behavior of one (non-judicial) European organ. This is why we propose to talk of a "diagonal separation of powers".

6 MAINTAINING THE FEDERAL BALANCE?

Riker (1975, 101) defines federalism as "a political organization in which the activities of government are divided between regional governments and a central government in such a way that each kind of government has some activities on which it makes final decisions." In other words, federations consist of constituent governments (with regard to the European Union, the nation states) and one central government ("Brussels") and both levels of government are endowed with final decision-making power in some areas. Art. 3 TFEU defines five areas over which the Union has exclusive competence (customs union, competition rules, monetary policy for euro members, conservation of marine biological resources, and common commercial policy). Interestingly, the final decision-making powers of the constituent governments are formulated less precisely. Art. 5 TEU introduces the principle of conferral according to which the Union only becomes active in those areas conferred to it by decisions of the nation state governments. A formal precondition for the (constitutional) stability of this allocation of decision-making competence is that it cannot be changed by either of the power centers unilaterally, which is the case.

Maintaining a sustained balance between the constituent governments and the central one is a perennial problem of all federal entities. Scharpf (1991) has called the promise of federations to contain the power of the central government their "living lie." He is, in other words, concerned with the tendency of federal entities to centralize.

But the exact opposite, where constituent units shirk on the central unit, is also relevant. Bednar (2009, 9) has recently identified three relevant types of opportunism: (1) the center could encroach on the authority of the constituent states, (2) the states might shirk on their responsibilities toward the Union and (3) states may shift burdens among themselves.

To be sustainable, the constitution of a federation needs to be self-enforceable. Weingast (1995) has identified three conditions under which he deems this to be the case: (1) subnational governments retain primary responsibility over the economy, (2) a common market is assured through the central government and (3) the states face a hard budget constraint with no potential for bailout by the center.

The Union has been strong on the second condition. Conditions (1) and (3) could, however, become problems sooner rather than later. Let us begin with the obvious: Art. 125 TFEU contains the so-called "no bail-out clause," which spells out that neither the Union nor other member states are liable for the commitments of any nation state government. Before the crisis, there seemed to be unanimous consent that protective shields and the like would be outright unconstitutional. By now, it is obvious that the states do not face a hard budget constraint. The Union is, hence, likely to face problems similar to those of Argentina, Brazil or Germany.

As a consequence of the crisis, some politicians have demanded a joint economic policy. In the long run, this could put the primary responsibility over the economy on the Union level, which would, hence, be a transgression of condition (1).

Next to the structural safeguards established by the constitution, a number of additional safeguards for sustaining a federation are discussed. Bednar (2009) names three: (1) political (referring to the party system), (2) judicial and (3) popular. Let us have a quick look at each of them in turn.

One of the foremost students of federalism, William Riker, frequently emphasized the importance of political parties for sustaining the federal balance. If the same parties are active both on the constituent and the central level, then they can serve as one important device to secure unity and prevent the system from falling apart. As of now, the unifying role of parties regarding the Union seems limited, to say the least. No parties that are active on the Union level have emerged, hence parties are unlikely to stabilize the European federation.

An independent judiciary can create focal points in the interpretation of the relevant constitutional articles. Courts, however, command neither the sword nor the purse. They will only be able to create focal points if their decisions are perceived as carrying a high degree of visibility as well as legitimacy. The solution offered by the courts will only turn out to be the equilibria of the respective games if a sufficiently large number of relevant actors accepts these proposals. It is doubtful whether the ECJ can be relied upon to uphold the federal balance in the European Union. It has a history as one of the most consistent centralizers. Given that an issue relating to the right balance between constituent and central units emerges, it is doubtful whether its decision will enjoy the degree of legitimacy needed.

This leaves us with the third potential safeguard mentioned by Bednar, namely popular control. There are ample reasons to be rather skeptical concerning the possibility of direct popular control as many of the most important EU positions are not subject to direct democratic control. There might be a certain role for popular control via elections on the nation state level, namely, when parties gain that are rather critical with regard to "Brussels."

Currently, the allocation of competences between the member states and "Brussels" can be compared to a one-way street: due to the logic of the *acquis communautaire*, competences once allocated to Brussels are almost impossible to re-allocate back to the nation state level. But it was shown above that due to the increasing heterogeneity that is a logical consequence of every enlargement, the re-allocation of competences could be very rational. This is why mechanisms that slow down the rush through the one-way street – which might eventually turn out to be a dead end street – are needed. One could, for example, discuss the possibility of "sunset competence": a competence is allocated to European Union level for a given number of years after which it automatically extinguishes if it is not prolonged unanimously by the Council. This would definitely increase the rationality of the European political architecture. It might also help to ensure the survival of the European Union in the long run.

7 CONCLUSION AND OUTLOOK

This chapter compares key features of the EU constitution with nation state constitutions. Many criteria regularly used to classify nation state constitutions, such as form of government or electoral systems, are of little use due to the special nature of the EU constitution. But one of the criteria, namely the way in which policy responsibilities are allocated between a higher and a lower level of government ("federalism"), is conjectured to be crucial for the future of the European Union. Recent insights on the sustainability of federations are applicable to the EU. It is argued that some of the policy measures implemented as a consequence of the debt crisis in some member states and, even more so, some of the currently discussed measures, such as a joint economic policy, seriously endanger the federal balance.

REFERENCES

Ackerman, Bruce (2000), "The New Separation of Powers," *Harvard Law Review*, 113 (3): 633ff.

Alesina, A. and R. Wacziarg (1999), "Is Europe Going Too Far?," *Carnegie-Rochester Conference Series on Public Policy*, 51 (1): 1–42.

Alesina, A., I. Angeloni and F. Etro (2005a), "International Unions," *American Economic Review* 95 (3): 602–15.

Alesina, A., I. Angeloni and L. Schuknecht (2005b), "What does the European Union do?," *Public Choice* 123 (3–4): 275–319.

Bednar, J. (2009), *The Robust Federation – Principles of Design*, Cambridge: Cambridge University Press.

Benz, M. and A. Stutzer (2004), "Are Voters Better Informed When They Have a Larger Say in Politics? – Evidence for the European Union and Switzerland," *Public Choice* 119: 31–59.

Blume, L., J. Müller and S. Voigt (2009), "The Economic Effects of Direct Democracy – A First Global Assessment," *Public Choice* 140: 431–61.

Buchanan, James M. (1977), *Freedom in Constitutional Contract – Perspectives of a Political Economist*, College Station/London: Texas A&M University Press.

Buchanan, J. (1987), "The Constitution of Economic Policy," *American Economic Review*, 77: 243–50.

Buchanan, J. (1990), "Europe's Constitutional Opportunity," in *Europe's Constitutional Future*, IEA Readings, London.

Buchanan, J. and G. Tullock (1962), *The Calculus of Consent – Logical Foundations of Constitutional Democracy*, Ann Arbor: University of Michigan Press.

Chen. Y. and P. Ordeshook (1994), "Constitutional Secession Clauses," *Constitutional Political Economy* 5 (1): 45–60.
Elkins, Z., T. Ginsburg and J. Melton (2009), *The Endurance of National Constitutions*, Cambridge: Cambridge University Press.
Elster, J. (1991), *Arguing and Bargaining in Two Constituent Assemblies*, The Storrs Lectures.
Grimm, D. (2002), "Constitutionalism Beyond the Nation State," in S. Voigt and H.J. Wagener (eds), *Constitutions, Markets and Law – Recent Experiences in Transition Economies*, Cheltenham: Edward Elgar.
Hayek, F. (1976), *Law, Legislation and Liberty*, Vol. 2, *The Mirage of Social Justice*, Chicago: University of Chicago Press.
Hayo, B. and S. Voigt (2010), "Determinants of Constitutional Change: Why Do Countries Change Their Form of Government?," *Journal of Comparative Economics* 38 (3): 283–305.
Initiative and Referendum Institute Europe (IRI) (2005), *Guidebook to Direct Democracy*, Amsterdam.
Keefer, Phil (2004), "What Does Political Economy Tell Us About Economic Development – And Vice Versa?," *Annual Review of Political Science* 7: 247–72.
Law, David and Mila Versteeg (2011), "The Evolution and Ideology of Global Constitutionalism," *California Law Review*, 99 (5): 1163–257.
Majone, G. (2001), "Nonmajoritarian Institutions and the Limits of Democratic Governance: A Political Transaction-Cost Approach," *Journal of Institutional and Theoretical Economics*, 157 (1): 57–78.
Maskin, E. and J. Tirole (2004), "The Politician and the Judge: Accountability in Government," *American Economic Review* 94 (4): 1034–54.
Mueller, D. (1996), *Constitutional Democracy*, Oxford: Oxford University Press.
Olson, M. (1965), *The Logic of Collective Action*, Cambridge, MA: Harvard University Press.
Persson, T. and G. Tabellini (2003), *The Economic Effects of Constitutions*, Cambridge, MA: MIT Press.
Persson, Torsten, Gerard Roland and Guido Tabellini (1997), "Separation of Powers and Political Accountability," *Quarterly Journal of Economics* 112: 310–27.
Riker, W. (1975), "Federalism," in F.I. Greenstein and N. Polsby (eds), *The Handbook of Political Science*, Volume V: *Government Institutions and Processes*, Reading, MA: Addison Wesley.
Robinson, James Alan and Ragnar Torvik (2008), "Endogenous Presidentialism," NBER Working Paper 14603.
Scharpf, F. (1991), "Kann es in Europa eine stabile föderale Balance geben?," in R. Wildenmann (ed.), *Staatswerdung Europas: Optionen für eine Europäische Union*, Baden-Baden, 415–28.
Sen, A. (1999), *Development as Freedom*, Oxford: OUP.
Sunstein, C. (1991), "Constitutionalism and Secession," *University of Chicago Law Review* 58 (2): 633–70.
Vaubel, R. (2002), "Die Politische Ökonomie des Europäischen Verfassungskonvents," *Wirtschaftsdienst*, Oktober: 636–40.
Vaubel, R. (2006), "Principal–Agent Problems in International Organizations," *The Review of International Organizations*, 1(2): 125–38.
Voigt, S. (1999), *Explaining Constitutional Change*, Cheltenham.: Edward Elgar.
Voigt, S. (2003), "Iudex Calculat – the ECJ's Quest for Power," *Jahrbuch für Neue Politische Ökonomie*.
Voigt, S. (2009), "Explaining Constitutional Garrulity," *International Review of Law and Economics*, 29 (4): 290–303.
Voigt, S. (2011), "Positive Constitutional Economics II – A Survey of Recent Developments," *Public Choice* 146 (1–2): 205–56.
Weingast, B. (1995). "The Economic Role of Political Institutions: Market-Preserving Federalism and Economic Development," *Journal of Law, Economics & Organization* 11 (1): 1–31.

2 The rules of decisionmaking in EU institutions

*George Tsebelis**

For much of the first decade of the twenty-first century (2001–09) the EU has tried to reform its institutions. These efforts began in the mid-1980s and continued through the early 2000s, resulting in a new agreement every three to four years with little ultimate success (Tsebelis and Yataganas 2002). Further, the initial institutions adopted in the Single European Act (SEA 1986) were essentially replicating the decisionmaking rules in the Council adopted in the Rome Treaty (1957) and adding an important role for the European Parliament (Tsebelis 1994; Tsebelis and Kreppel 1999). So, the *de jure* decisionmaking rules in the Council have remained essentially stable (although not applied until the SEA) and changed for the first time under the institutional reform process initiated after the Nice Treaty (2000). Table 2.1 demonstrates this stability of the required qualified majority in the Council (over 70 percent from 1958 until the Convention).

The reform process that led to the first real change in European institutions started with the Laeken declaration (2001) and took almost ten years to be completed. So, in the EU case, stasis was followed by painstakingly slow change. The reason for the slow rate of change was that while the target was set and known (set by the significant institutional change produced by the European Convention), it was not acceptable by all the political actors whose assent was required to instigate change. These actors engaged in a strategic exercise during which they each tried to achieve an outcome slightly different from the shared goal, but still quite close to it. In other words, they were engaging in a "tatonnement" process, to reach the closest possible solution to the existing default solution. So, what occurred was a trial and error process that led to an outcome quite close to their

Table 2.1 Council qualified majority requirements over time

Year	Total number of MS	Total votes	QM: votes	QM: percentage
1958	6	17	12	70.59
1973	9	58	42	72.41
1981	10	63	45	71.43
1986	12	76	54	71.05
1995	15	87	62	71.26
2000	25	232	321	72.27
Convention				60
Lisbon				65

Source: Opinion of the Commission entitled "Adapting the institutions to make a success of enlargement" delivered on 26 January 2000, COM (2000) 34.

* I would like to thank Cassandra Grafström for very efficient help.

shared goal. These activities occurred many times, but I will focus on two main clusters of them: one in the Constitutional Convention, and one in the preparation of the Lisbon Treaty.

In this chapter I will argue that this tatonnement process had two components: first, elimination of obstacles that would derail the whole enterprise, and second, fine-tuning to reach the outcome as close as possible to the goal. Actually, it is remarkable that the goal during the fine-tuning phase consistently remained the agreement reached in the previous round, so that the final outcome was as close as possible to the initial draft despite the fact that very few of the principal actors had remained the same. Actually, only Denmark (A.F. Rasmussen, three terms), Belgium (Verhofstadt, three terms) and Luxembourg (Juncker, three terms) had the same prime minister throughout this eight-year period. All other countries changed several chief executives. And although for some of them this change may not have had political significance (the UK moved from Blair to Brown within the Labour Party, France moved from Chirac to Sarkozy), for most the changes in leadership signified significant changes in policies (Germany from Schröder to Merkel, Greece from Simitis to Karamanlis, Spain from Aznar to Zapatero, Italy from Berlusconi to Prodi, etc.).

It was apparent that institutional reform was necessary as soon as the Nice Treaty was signed. Tony Blair provided a pessimistic appraisal of the Treaty: "As far as Europe is concerned we cannot do business like this in the future" (BBC News, 11 December 2000). Yet, the process of reform was to fail several times (e.g. "the erratic [Italian] Presidency of Silvio Berlusconi was one reason why the Brussels summit failed" (*The Economist*, 18 December 2003); referendums in France and the Netherlands) and declared dead several times by the press (e.g. "the Constitution is dead" (*The Economist*, 2 June 2005) or "Irish Voters sign Death Warrant for Lisbon Treaty" (*Times Online*, 14 June 2008)) or "in equilibrium" by academics, which is the same ("the failure of Constitutional reform is, paradoxically, evidence of the success and stability of the existing European constitutional settlement" (Moravcsik 2006: 219)). And yet, ultimately, major reforms to the workings of the European Union were achieved.

The chapter is organized into three parts. The first explains some of the differences between the old and the new institutions and their significance; the second describes some of the tatonnement that occurred in the Constitutional Convention; the third describes the tatonnement by national governments surrounding the Lisbon Treaty.

1 THE EU INSTITUTIONS OLD AND NEW

This section compares the policy and political outcomes that followed from the institutional structures generated by the European Convention, the Lisbon Treaty, and the Nice Treaty. The institutions produced under these different arrangements empowered different actors in the creation of policies within the Union. The comparison is based on the theory of veto players (Tsebelis 2002) and is aimed at demonstrating the potential differences in policy outcomes for the EU had future policies been made in each of these institutional settings. In other words, what is the most productive institutional design for the EU? I answer this by examining the expected effects of different institutional arrangements.

I analyze the outcomes of the decisionmaking processes generated by these various procedures and discuss the policy, political, and structural implications of the different arrangements. The argument is that the procedures proposed in the Convention text resolved a series of problems facing the European Union, and the rejection of these proposals could have had unfortunate consequences if the Lisbon Treaty had not been ratified.

The supermajority required by the Nice rules made the passage of new legislation much more difficult than under either the Convention's proposal or the slightly amended Treaty of Lisbon. The second-order consequences were that the Council's inability to act would allow the bureaucracy and judiciary to act with a freer hand than they would have been able to under the alternative institutional arrangements. As I will discuss below, the inability of the member states to reach agreement meant that those actors charged with implementing (bureaucrats) and interpreting (judges) the law would have had a larger range of positions that they could take that would be difficult for the Council to overturn. The movement of the locus of policy determination away from (indirectly) elected EU politicians to (wholly unelected) judges and bureaucrats is problematic for those who argue that the European Union suffers from a democratic deficit.

More specifically, the argument is that the European Union is characterized by a plethora of veto players, which makes decisionmaking very difficult. The Nice arrangements – which hinder decisionmaking in the Council because of their stringent qualified majority requirements – had increased the powers of the judiciary and the bureaucracies (de Witte 2001; Tsebelis and Yataganas 2002; Yataganas 2001a). Valéry Giscard d'Estaing, President of the Convention, was able to reverse all of these features with one stroke of his pen: supported by a Convention unique for its synthesis (Closa 2004; Magnette 2001), he eliminated the triple qualified majority decisionmaking rule in the Council. As a result, he made political decisions easier to adopt, reduced the relative power of any individual member state, increased the role of the European Parliament, and resultantly decreased the importance of the bureaucracy and the judiciary. In the Lisbon Treaty a compromise (located close to the Convention proposal, as Table 2.1 demonstrates) was adopted. This compromise results in a clearer delineation of who is responsible for decisions and leads to more of the Union's important decisions being made by politically accountable individuals. Referendum results notwithstanding, this constitutional document constituted a focal point for projects of EU integration. Despite press analyses which focused upon the EU's failure to integrate, national politicians realized that what was rejected in 2005 was worth resurrecting and adopting in the form of the Treaty of Lisbon – no other alternative was workable within the current configuration of the EU.

1.1 Judges and Bureaucrats

Before examining the specific institutional changes proposed by the Convention and the Brussels IGC, it is relevant to discuss broader problems faced by the European Union and their relationships to European institutions more generally. In particular, this subsection explores a hotly discussed set of problems that is thought to plague the European Union: the power of the EU's bureaucracy and judiciary. The strength of these groups' independent decisionmaking powers is related to the sets of institutions that shape decisionmaking in the EU and was amplified by the use of the Nice rules.

Regardless of their intentions (public-spirited or otherwise), increasing the latitude with which judges and bureaucrats act is problematic to those interested in maintaining or enhancing democratic accountability within the European Union. The bureaucracy and the judiciary are involved with legislatures in a sequential game. They interpret the law and then the legislature can decide to overrule their statutory interpretation or not (Tsebelis 2002). As more and more legislators' agreement becomes necessary to overrule the statutory interpretation of the bureaucracy or the court, these actors' interpretations become increasingly likely to determine how policy is implemented. While they may choose to implement policies in a fashion quite similar to that envisioned by the legislature, this is not guaranteed. Indeed, as I show below, as the number and ideological diversity of actors who need to agree to change the interpretation of the bureaucracy/judiciary increases, these non-elected actors have greater leeway in choosing how to interpret and implement public policy.

If the courts are rendering *constitutional* interpretations, then the high thresholds that need to be breached to change the constitution make it nearly impossible for the legislature to overrule the courts' interpretations. In a recent analysis Santoni and Zucchini found that the Italian Constitutional Court became more proactive the greater the ideological distance between the government parties and the Communists in the period 1956–92 (because the government with the cooperation of the Communists formed a sufficiently large majority during this period to modify the Italian Constitution) (Santoni and Zucchini 2004). No matter what the interests and/or preferences of the bureaucracy and the courts, the real question is should the political decisions of the Union be made by the citizens' elected representatives or should these decisions be left to unelected agents?

The question may seem provocative and the answer obvious: elected representatives. I do not share this belief without condition. There are decisions that are better left to judges than to elected representatives: for example, issues of human rights are better left to courts. Similarly, there are decisions that are better left to independent agencies (like an ombudsman or perhaps an independent central bank) than to governments (Yataganas 2001b). However, these arguments cannot be made for the majority of political decisions, and reducing the capacity of a political body to generally make decisions increases the likelihood that these decisions will be made by unelected (and non-politically-accountable) agents. This is an important point: reducing the capacities of elected representatives of the EU does not necessarily increase the power of national governments. In issues of EU jurisdiction (decided by the treaties) the power to define and implement policy reverts to unelected representatives when elected representatives are deadlocked, not to national politicians who have given up those rights to the European Union. I doubt that this is the goal of national governments or citizens when they vote "no" in referendums.

While the problems identified in this subsection already exist within the European Union, how are they related to the form of the institutions that make up the EU and the proposed changes in the European Constitution? As I have tried to lay out above, the increased power of the bureaucracy and judiciary is directly related to the number of actors whose consent is needed to overrule their interpretations of the law. How do the institutional rules that the European Union operates under affect these problems and what framework can be used to think about all of these issues? This is explored in the next subsection through the lens of veto players.

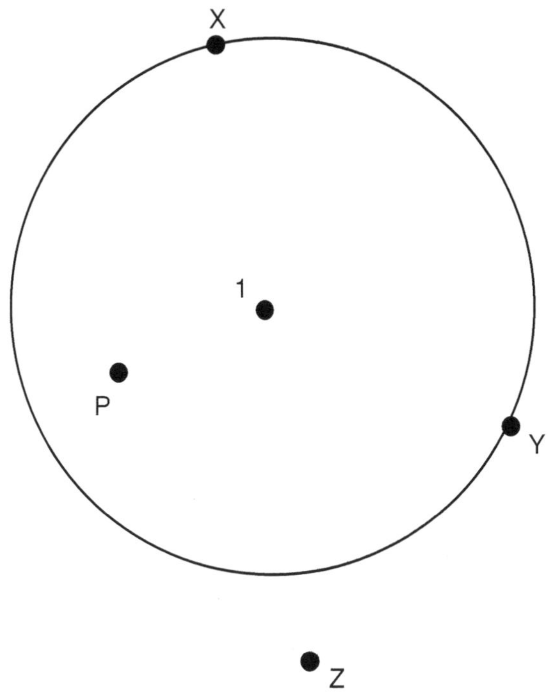

Figure 2.1 Circular indifference curve of a veto player

1.2 Veto Players and their Policy and Institutional Implications

Veto players are individual or collective decisionmakers whose agreement is necessary to change the legislative status quo. We can represent such players in a two-dimensional policy space by their ideal points. Each player will prefer points closer to him over points further away, or will have circular indifference curves. Indeed, in Figure 2.1 veto player 1 among the points P, X, Y, and Z prefers P rather than the rest (located inside the circle going through X), then X or Y (indifferent between these two), and has Z as his last preference.

From the definition of veto player follows that the higher the number of veto players, the more difficult it is to change the status quo. Tsebelis calls the "difficulty of changing the status quo" *policy stability*. He demonstrates that the higher the number of veto players, and the larger the ideological distances among them, the higher is policy stability.

Here I will use some ideas from Tsebelis (2002) that help us understand European Union institutions. First, I present the two concepts that Tsebelis uses in order to operationalize policy stability (the core and the winset of the status quo). Second, I explain the effect of increasing the required qualified majorities for a decision. Third, I show that increasing the qualified majority requirement in one chamber of a bicameral legislature shifts the policy outcome towards this chamber: in the EU case, increasing the qualified majority requirements in the Council increases its power and adds to the "democratic deficit." Finally, I discuss the structural implications of increasing the number of (legislative) veto players: in particular, I will describe how more legislative veto players increase the importance and independence of the judiciary and the bureaucracy.

1.2.1 The core and the winset of the status quo of veto players as measures of policy stability

In the discussion that follows I will introduce two concepts that will help us understand EU institutions. The first is the *winset of the status quo* (W(SQ)), the set of outcomes that can defeat the status quo. Think of the status quo as current policy. The winset of the status quo is the set of policies that can replace the existing one. The second concept is the *core*, the set of points with empty winset–the points that cannot be defeated by any other point if we apply the decisionmaking rule. I usually refer to the core along with the decision-making rule that produces it. For example, the "unanimity core" refers to the set of points that cannot be defeated if the decision is unanimous. An alternative name for "unanimity core" that is frequently used in law and economics is "Pareto set."

In Figure 2.2, I present a system with three veto players A, B and C and two different positions of the status quo: SQ1 and SQ2. As noted, all decisions must be made by unanimity, since A, B, and C are veto players. In order to identify the winset of SQ1 (W(SQ1)) one draws the indifference curves of A, B, and C that pass through SQ1, and identifies their intersection. I have hatched this intersection in Figure 2.2. A similar operation indicates that W(SQ2) = ∅, or that SQ2 belongs to the unanimity core of the three veto players system. It is easy to verify that W(SQ2) = ∅ as long as SQ2 is located inside the triangle ABC.[1] Thus the unanimity core is the entire triangle ABC as shaded in Figure 2.2.

I use both the smallness of the winset of SQ and the size of the unanimity core as indicators of policy stability. Here I will study two different cases, one focusing on the winset of the status quo, and the other on the core, so that the reader becomes familiar with the subsequent reasoning.

(i) Winset of status quo is non-empty Figure 2.3 replicates Figure 2.2 and adds one more veto player: D. It is easy to see by comparison of the two figures that the winset of SQ1 shrinks with the addition of D as a veto player. Indeed, D vetoes some of the points that were acceptable by veto players A, B, and C. This is the generic case. Under special spatial conditions the addition of a veto player may not affect the outcome. For economy of space I do not present another figure here, but the reader can imagine the following: if D is located on the BSQ line between B and SQ so that the circle around D is included inside the circle around B, the addition of D as a veto player would not influence the size of the winset of SQ1. I could continue the process of adding veto players, and watch the winset of the status quo shrinking or remaining the same ("not expanding") with every new veto player. It is possible that as the process of adding veto players unfolds, at some point the winset of the status quo becomes empty such that there is no longer a point that can defeat the status quo. This would have been the case if D were located in an area so that SQ1 were surrounded by veto players. We will deal with this case in the next few

---

1 If, however, SQ2 is located outside the triangle ABC, then it can be defeated by its projection on the closest side, so its winset is not empty.

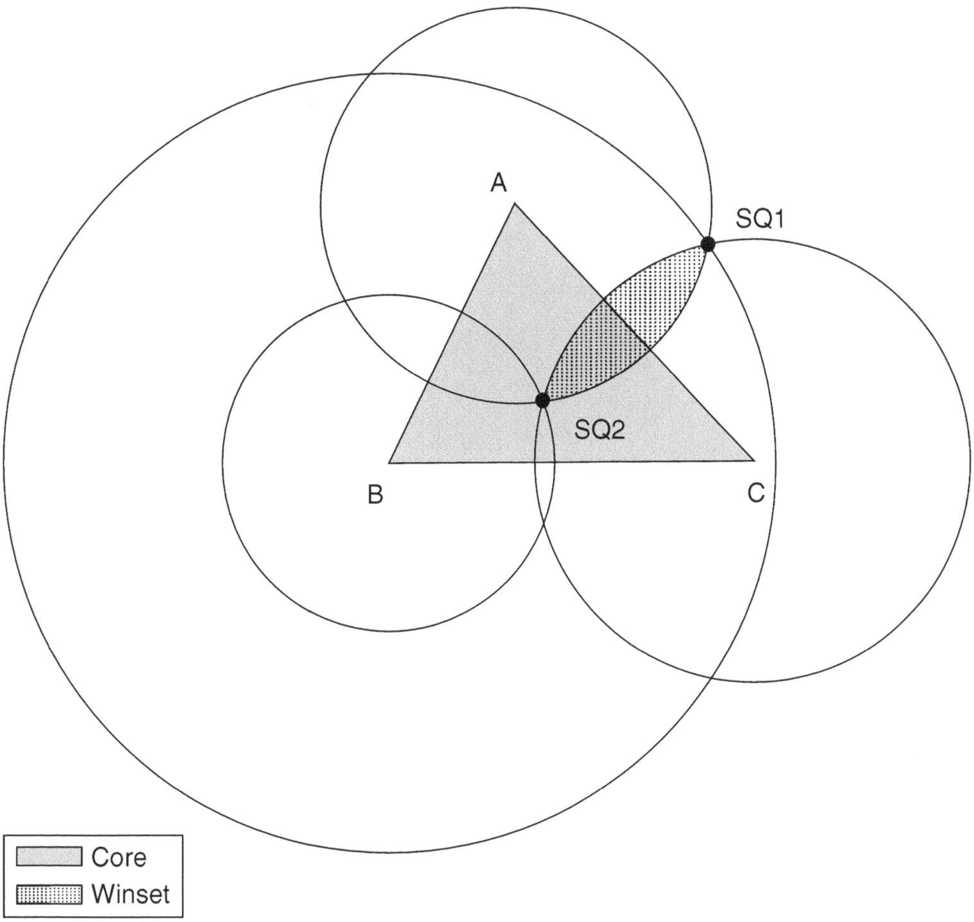

Figure 2.2 Winset and core of a system with three veto players

paragraphs. Here let me summarize the result of the analysis so far. *If the winset of the status quo exists, its size decreases or remains the same with the addition of new veto players.*

(ii) Winset of status quo is empty Let us now focus on SQ2 in Figure 2.3. It presents the case where the winset of the status quo with three veto players is empty. Given that W(SQ2) = ∅, the size of W(SQ) is not going to change no matter how many veto players one adds. However, the addition of D as one more veto player has another interesting result: it expands the unanimity core. The reader can verify that the unanimity core now is the whole area ABCD. Again, it is not necessary that an additional veto player expands the unanimity core. It is possible that it leaves the size of the unanimity core the same, as would have been the case if D were located inside the triangle ABC. We will deal with this case in the next section. For the time being, the conclusion of this paragraph is as follows. *The size of the unanimity core increases or remains the same with the addition of new veto players.*

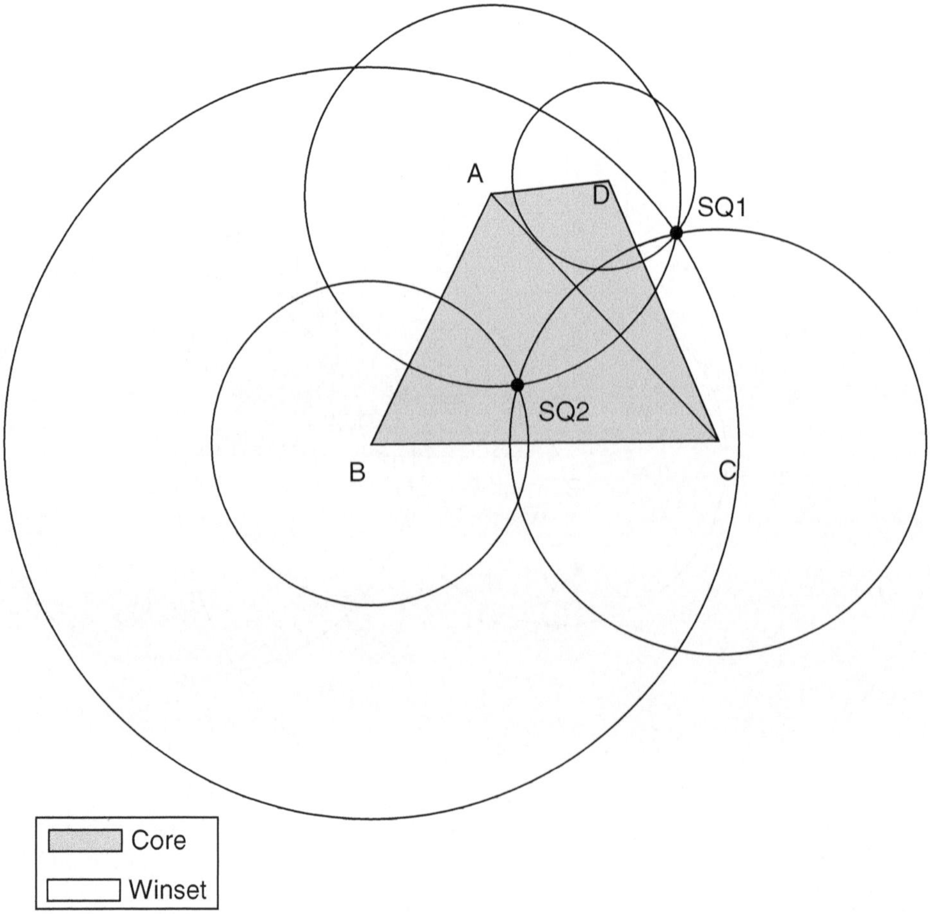

Figure 2.3 Winset and core of a system with four veto players

From the previous analysis follows that the larger the size of the core, and the smaller the size of winset of the status quo, the higher policy stability is. The argument is best represented in Figure 2.4.

1.2.2 Changing the qualified majority requirements

Let us now consider a "collective veto player" that decides by qualified majority rule in a manner much like the Council of Ministers of the EU. In Figure 2.5, I present a seven-member Council that decides by a qualified majority of 5/7. This is approximately the same majority required by the weighted voting of the Council (around 70 percent) prior to the 2004 expansion, so I will be able to use the same figure to discuss the European Union in the next part of this section.

We can divide this collective veto player several times in the following way: we can select any five points (say 1–5) and then consider the pentagon composed of these five points (the unanimity core of these five players). Any point included in this pentagon

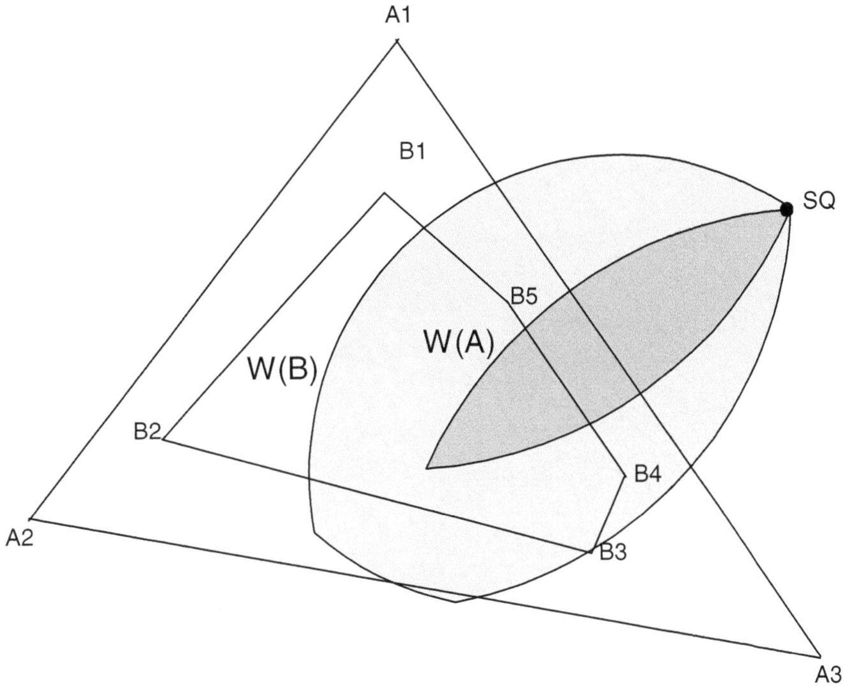

Figure 2.4 *Veto players A1–A3 produce more policy stability than B1–B5 (no matter where the status quo is)*

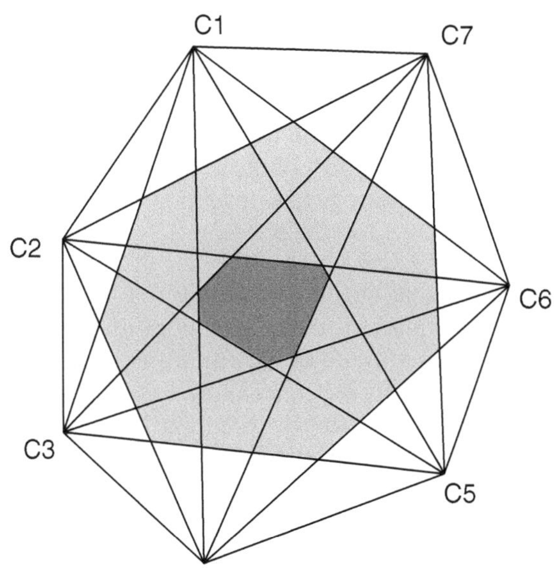

Figure 2.5 *Core of Council with 5/7 and 6/7 majorities*

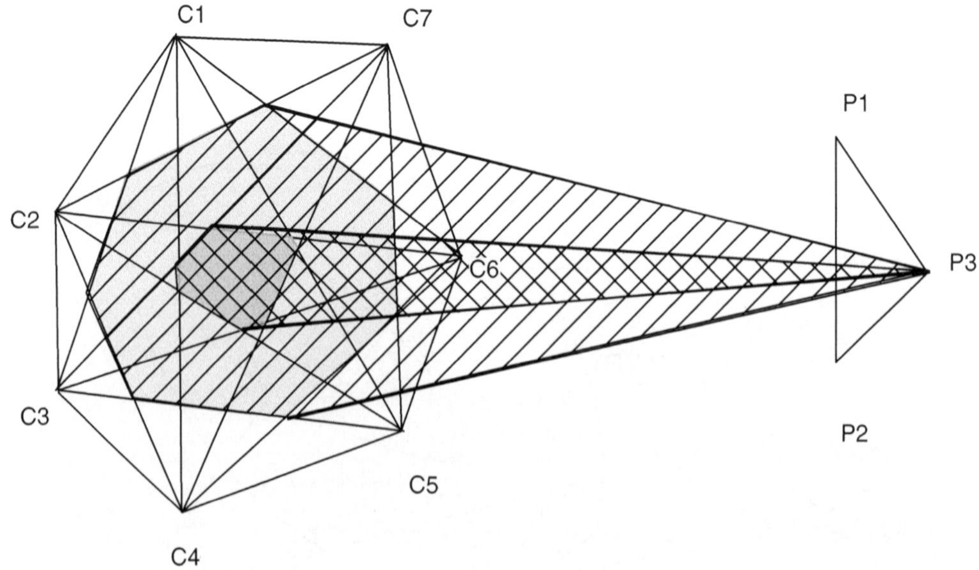

Figure 2.6 Core EU with Council (5/7 and 6/7) and EP majority

cannot be defeated by a unanimous agreement of the five selected players. If now we select all possible such combinations of five players the area composed of the intersection of their unanimity cores cannot be defeated by any 5/7 qualified majority. This intersection is the heavily shaded area in Figure 2.5. This area is the 5/7 core of the collective veto player. This exercise can be repeated with 6 out of the seven members to find the 6/7 core of the Council. The 6/7 core is represented by the addition of the lightly shaded area to the 5/7 core in Figure 2.5. One can see that the core expands when the required majority for a decision increases. This is the basic property that I will use in this chapter. I argue that the Treaty of Nice (particularly combined with the expansion of 2004) produced institutions with an exceptionally large core, making political decisionmaking practically impossible. The agreements proposed at the European Convention in 2003, and those subsequently adopted in the Lisbon Treaty, rectified the problem.

1.2.3 Bicameralism and changing qualified majorities

What happens if decisions are made by the congruent position of two distinct chambers, as is the case in the European Union? In particular, what are the effects of changing the threshold of qualified majority decisionmaking in one chamber while keeping the decisionmaking rules in the other chamber unchanged? Two different effects of such a change have been identified (Tsebelis 2002). First, the overall policy stability of the system increases. Second, power shifts in favor of the chamber whose threshold *increases.* Let us examine each one of these effects separately.

What happens to the overall policy stability of the system? Figure 2.6 replicates the Council we presented in Figure 2.5, and adds a three-member Parliament. The core of the system includes the core of the Council. The reader can verify that as the core of the Council increases from a 5/7 to a 6/7 qualified majority threshold, the overall core,

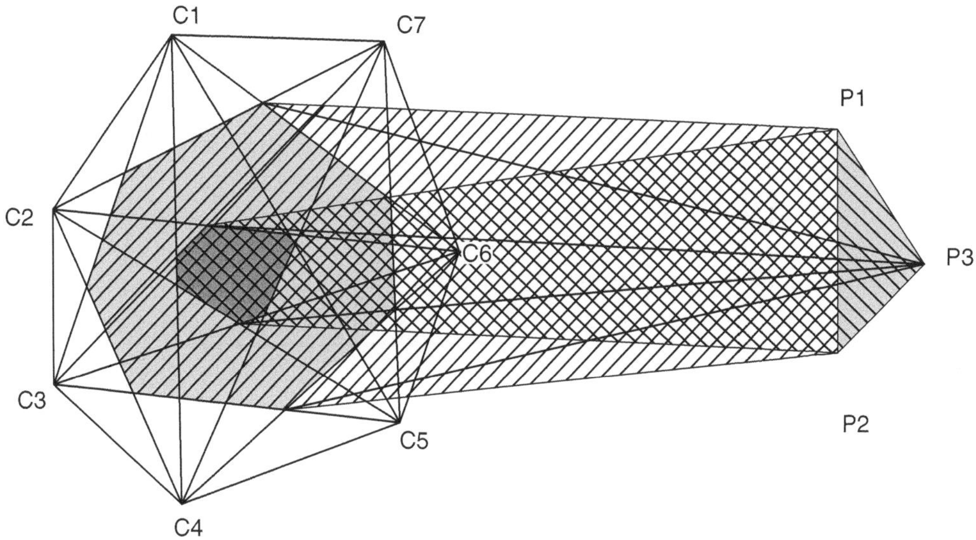

Figure 2.7 Core EU with Council (5/7 and 6/7) and EP unanimity

as indicated by the double-hatched area to include the single hatched area, increases as well. Increasing the required majority in the Council from a 5/7 to a 6/7 qualified majority has two consequences. The first is distributive: it makes agreement in the Council more important, and restricts the outcomes of a compromise to those closer to the preferences of the Council. Second, it increases the overall policy stability of the system, and makes changes to the status quo more difficult.

Figure 2.7 makes the same point about the European Parliament. If a constitutional convention decided to increase the required majority threshold of the Parliament, the result would be an increase in the size of the Union's core. Figure 2.7 presents a three-member Parliament that decides by unanimity (all three of its members) instead of majority (two of them). The reader can verify that the core increases significantly.

More interesting, and perhaps counterintuitive, are the political (or redistributive) consequences of changing the qualified majority threshold in one of the chambers. As Tsebelis and Money (1997) demonstrate, this shifts the policy outcomes *towards* the chamber where decisionmaking becomes more difficult. Figure 2.8 shows the winset of the status quo of a bicameral legislature composed of two three-member chambers. In the first case congruent majorities in both chambers make decisions; in the second, unanimity in the Council is required (along with a majority in the Parliament). The lightly shaded area indicates the winset of the status quo by congruent majorities, while the heavily shaded area indicates the winset of the status quo when unanimity is required in the Council. The reader can verify the outcome shifts in favor of the Council in the second case. The reason is that an additional member (whose preferences were ignored in the case of congruent majorities) is now taken into account. This member has the most "stringent" preferences because his location was so close to the status quo that the other members preferred to ignore him when negotiating a new policy under simple majority rules. Now that his agreement is required he restricts the winset of the status quo,

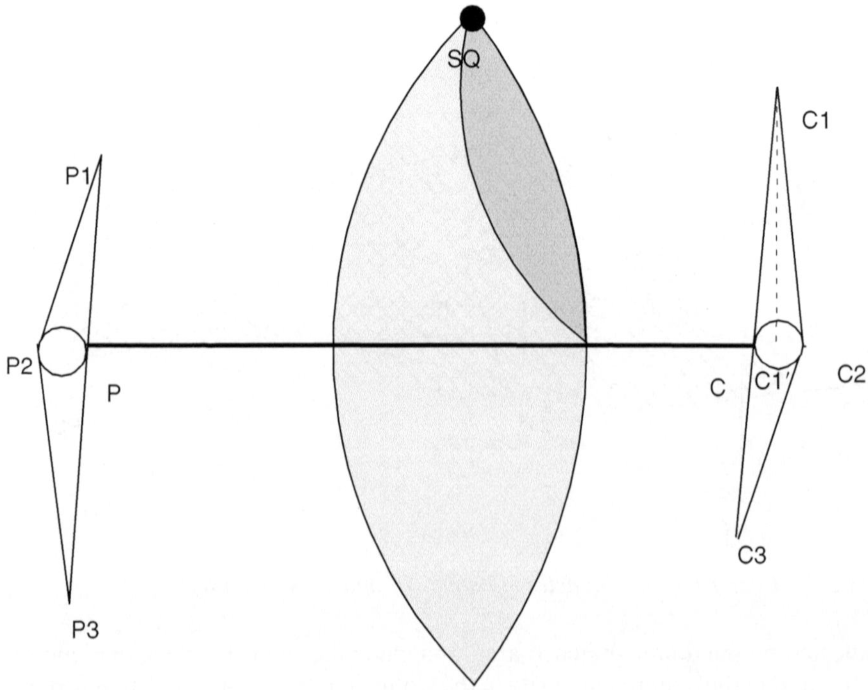

Figure 2.8 Winset by concurrent majorities, and by unanimity in the Council

moving it toward his preferred outcome and towards the location of the Council. Thus, we can see that the reversion to the Nice rules, by increasing the number of veto players in the Council, reduces the influence of the European Parliament in determining policy outcomes and increases the relative weight of national executives as represented in the Council of Ministers. This increases (or generates, depending on the initial point of view) the Union's democratic deficit.

Returning to the question of bureaucratic and judiciary strength, it can be shown that the same institutions that serve to weaken the European Parliament also empower these unelected institutions in the EU. Let us assume that there are three legislative veto players. Figure 2.9 demonstrates such a case, where the triangle 1–2–3 is defined as their core, the set of points that they cannot agree to change. Consequently, if the first mover (the bureaucracy or judiciary) selects one of the points in the core there will be no legislative overrule. Figure 2.9 presents three different possibilities. In the first two cases, the first movers' ideal points J and K are outside of the legislative core and they select the closest core point to them (J′ and K′ respectively). Despite the fact that these two choices are significantly different from each other, the veto players are incapable of changing either of them. In the third case, the first mover is located inside the legislative core but changes her mind and moves from point L1 to point L2. Since the first mover is inside the core, she can always select her own ideal point.

This simple example shows that the Nice Treaty rules, by increasing the number of veto players and likely increasing the size of the core, increase the latitude of the courts and bureaucracy to interpret and implement policy as they wish. There is one additional

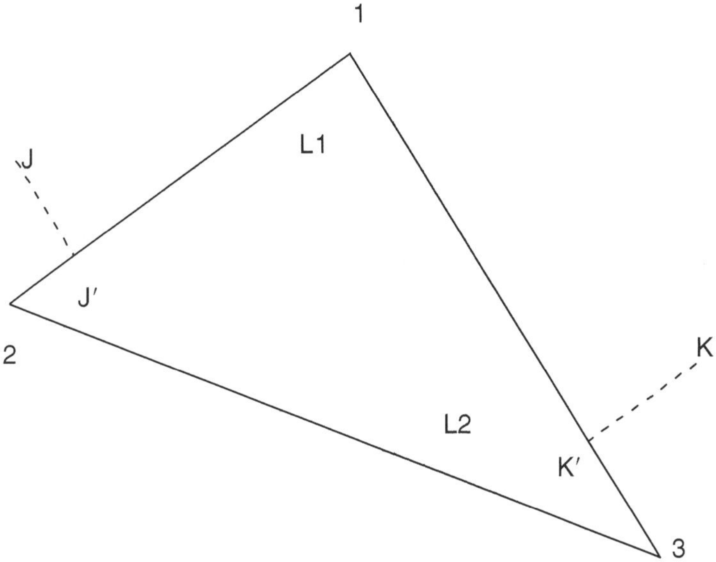

Note: First mover outside core (J or K) selects closest point inside core (J′ or K′); first mover inside core (L1 or L2) selects own ideal point.

Figure 2.9 Selection of a policy within the core by first mover (bureaucracy or judiciary)

point concerning the simple account raised in the literature. Given that the courts or bureaucracy in the game presented above will be able to select a policy close or identical to their own ideal point, what will the legislative branch do to prevent this event from materializing? There is an extensive literature arguing that legislation will be written more restrictively when there are many veto players (Huber and Shipan 2002; McCubbins et al. 1987, 243; 1989, 430; Moe 1990, 213; Moe and Caldwell 1994, 171). This is a valid point, and if the legislature can come to an agreement, then they will restrict both bureaucrats and judges. Consequently, multiple veto players will lead to more lengthy, specific, and bureaucratic legislation when legislation can be agreed upon. The changes proposed by the Convention and in the Lisbon Treaty make it easier to come to such agreements, restricting the independent power of judges and bureaucrats. In the next subsection I discuss the evidence, both theoretical and empirical, supporting the arguments presented here about the substantive impact of these institutional changes on decisionmaking in the EU.

1.2.4 Qualified majority in the Council: to what extent does it impede decisionmaking?

In the previous subsection I argued that, in principle, increasing the qualified majority threshold makes reaching decisions more difficult. The argument is simple and straightforward, but the actual differences between the sets of procedures introduced at Nice in 2001 and at the Convention in 2003 (and later put into effect through the ratification of the Treaty of Lisbon) may have been effectively inconsequential. Here I will use results from Tsebelis (2005) as well as König and Bräuninger (2004) to argue quite the opposite: the differences between the proposals put forth at Nice and the Convention are significant and consequential. The failure to adopt these new proposals would have had deleterious effects.

Tsebelis and Yataganas (2002, 283) have analyzed the dynamics of bargaining at Nice and argued that it was the first time that the Council's three voting criteria (qualified majority of weighted votes, majority of states, and qualified majority of populations (62 percent)) did not coincide and that different countries were attached to different principles. The Nice Treaty required a triple majority to pass anything by QMV: 72 percent of the weighted votes must be cast in favor of the proposal, comprising a majority of member states and 62 percent of the EU's population.[2] As a result, the conferees in Nice adopted the detrimental strategy of including all three criteria for valid decision-making. In other words, the countries bargaining at Nice were involved in a collective prisoners' dilemma in which it was individually rational to insist on their own preferred criterion but that collectively resulted in a suboptimal collective outcome. As a result, they became collectively worse off by their inability to strike a compromise (see also Galloway 2001).

Tsebelis (2006) used the number of winning coalitions in the Council to represent the different decisionmaking rules. The short-term effects of Nice were minor. Indeed, under the 62/87 qualified majority rule, which was in effect before the Treaty of Nice, the number of winning coalitions with the single qualified majority criterion was 2549/32768 (7.77 percent). This number would have been slightly restricted by the triple majority to 2513/32768 (7.67 percent).

The effects of the triple majority become even less significant in a European Union of 15 members with the weighting system adopted by the Nice Treaty itself. Now with the simple qualified majority criterion (169/237) the number of winning coalitions became 2707/32768 (8.26 percent), while with the triple majority it was reduced to 2692/32768 (8.21 percent).

With the expansion to 25 members, the difference between the simple qualified majority criterion (255/345) and the triple majority criterion remains insignificant (the number of winning coalitions goes down from 1,204,448 to 1,203,736). What is significant is that these numbers identify only 3.58 percent of all possible winning majorities in the Council following expansion.

It is to the great credit of the Convention and its leader Valéry Giscard d'Estaing that they correctly identified the source of the high policy stability generated by the Nice Treaty: two of the decisionmaking requirements (majority of countries and qualified majority (60 percent) of the population) significantly decrease the restrictions on the decisionmaking process. The key restriction comes from the qualified majority requirement of weighted votes. As a result, the Convention leadership introduced the much more permissive double criterion. The frequency of valid decisions increases by a factor of 6: from 3.58 to 22.5 percent. So, the frequency of valid decisions went from 8 percent in a Union of 15 (before or after Nice) to 3.58 percent in a Union of 25 (after Nice) to 22.5 percent under the Convention proposal, and back down to 10 percent under the Brussels IGC (the text rejected by the referendums).

However, Tsebelis' (2006) numbers can be challenged on the grounds that they do not

[2] Votes were weighted, roughly, by population size under the Nice criteria.

incorporate the preferences of the actors. As becomes clear in Figure 2.4 it is not always the case that more veto players lead to more policy stability; the distance of these players matters too. Tsebelis' (2006) results are based on the assumption that all potential coalitions are equally probable. This is not necessarily the case: it is more likely that countries located close to one another in the policy space will make coalitions more frequently. In addition, if countries enter into competition as to which one will be included in winning coalitions, then the "competitive" price for entering a coalition will be the same per unit of support (each vote, or the representation of each million voters, depending on the decisionmaking rule in the Council).

An alternative way of calculating the size of the core of EU institutions is provided in König and Bräuninger (2004). They consider the positions of the different countries in a two-dimensional policy space. The first dimension is a general left–right dimension using the per capita income of the different countries as a proxy of this underlying preference. The second is policy positions on agricultural issues, approximated by the size of agriculture as a share of the country's GDP.

Using both these indicators, they calculate the core of the Council, presenting a comparison before and after the expansion as well as a comparison between Nice and the Convention text. In both cases, the core expands significantly with more countries, as well as with the Nice Treaty rules. This method also has its own drawbacks. The proxy variables may be considered objectionable. However, because the new countries have not participated very much in voting either in the Council or in the European Parliament, one cannot use their voting records to approximate their policy positions, so this is perhaps the best proxy available to establish their policy positions.

Despite the differences in assumptions about coalition formation in the EU constituent bodies, all of these different methods come to very similar conclusions: the core of the EU expands because of the rules introduced in Nice and the expansion to 27 countries. But is there any empirical evidence to support them? I have to point out that it is very early for empirical tests, and that the evidence is going to be sparse, but there are considerable indications in support of these contentions. Here I will use only some data presented by the Commission (for additional evidence see Tsebelis (2008)).

In a report entitled "Better Lawmaking 2005," the Commission finds that the number of legislative proposals significantly declined during the first year of the application of the Nice rules following enlargement. According to the report, "[g]enerally, the number of legislative proposals fell in 2005 by 17.5 percent compared to 2004 and by 10.5 percent compared to the 2003–04 average. That decrease applies for all types of proposal: regulations (–21), directives (–24), decisions (–46) and recommendations (–2). The biggest relative drop is in the number of directives, which fell by 47 percent compared to 2004."

1.2.5 Policy implications

In the previous subsections I demonstrated that imposing constraints on the decisionmaking of the Council (or the Parliament) leads to further difficulties in Union decisionmaking, since increasing the core of the Council increases (or at best leaves unchanged) the size of the core of the Union as a whole. I explained that the restrictions imposed by the Nice Treaty are very significant, and that the proposals made at the Convention to drop one of the qualification requirements for Council agreement increases by a factor of 6 the number of decisive coalitions possible in the Council (according to Tsebelis 2006) or decreases significantly the size of the policy core (according to König and Bräuninger 2004). In both cases, changes of the status quo are made much easier under the Convention proposal, or the Lisbon compromise, than under the status quo (Nice Treaty). These are quantitatively significant differences, but why should one care whether the Union is able to make political decisions or not? Could we perhaps say that a Union that is unable to decide politically is a better institution than a politically active Union? After all, decisions will be made at the national level and maybe the people of Europe will have more control over the decisions affecting them. The debate over the proper extent of Union competencies is one that has become increasingly urgent. The tradeoff between greater efficiency through coordination at the European level and the specific needs and demands of individual countries, along with concerns about national sovereignty, is fuzzy.

While there is no general "philosophy" about which issues should or should not be in what jurisdiction (why is it better for countries to have fiscal but not monetary discretion, as determined by the Maastricht treaty?), the Union's ability to make political decisions is directly linked to which decisions will be made, de facto, by the political institutions of the Union and which will be made by other institutions (national or supranational). I focus here on the national ones.

Is it better for a political system to have more or less policy stability? There is no general answer, unless a political system occupies some kind of extreme position (e.g. if unanimity is required for decisionmaking in a parliament like the Polish *Sejm* prior to 1791, or decisions on human rights are made by simple majority in which case a majority can decide to oppress the human rights of a minority) (Tsebelis 2002). Obviously the European Union does not fall into an extreme category like either of these. However, whether it should choose a set of institutions that allow for greater policy flexibility (stability) depends on what type of environment we expect to encounter in the future. Will the EU be facing an economic and political environment with lots of shocks (and, therefore, high variance of external conditions)? The developments of terrorism, potential trade conflict with the United States, globalization and the opening of new markets are all external shocks that may be too big for individual European countries to effectively respond, and may therefore require a coordinated adjustment. In this case, decisions by the European Union will become more necessary, not less. If this is an accurate prospect for Europe, then restricting the Council's decisionmaking capabilities undermines the Union today more than it did in the past. This is as much the crux of the federalist debate today as it was when the Union began in the 1960s: is coordination among the individual countries necessary in order to create an entity able to negotiate with superpowers like the US and the Soviet Union (in the past) or China (in the future) and influence decisions worldwide? Or will individual countries have to negotiate on their own (with a high probability of becoming "pricetakers")?

As a result of this analysis and a reasonable expectation that common shocks will become bigger in the future, I argue that the steps taken in Nice in a Union of 27 countries are negative, and the ratification of the Lisbon Treaty has been a positive development for citizens of the European Union. After the negative referendums in France and the Netherlands, the Nice rules risked becoming permanent. The insistence of countries on their own rights and a continued lack of focus on collective consequences would inevitably lead to an inability of the Union to address new issues. Ultimately, this would leave each country to make its own decisions, but with only its own forces, facing situations where its own weight may not be enough to confront difficult conditions. Thus, the institutional changes agreed to under the Lisbon Treaty are important because they will allow member states greater opportunities to coordinate when this is needed in the future. In the next two sections I describe the most important parts of the process that produced the Convention document first, and the Lisbon Treaty second.

2 TATONNEMENT IN THE EUROPEAN CONVENTION

This section describes how one of the procedural impossibilities of reforming European institutions was removed.[3] The President of the Convention was able to produce results through the astute use of several significant agenda control tools that he developed. He limited the number of amendments from Convention delegates by restricting the amount of time that the Convention would spend on the whole process, by eliminating amendments, and juxtaposing them; he prohibited voting, and produced results "by consensus," with him defining the meaning of the term. Here I will focus on two major uses of procedures as political weapons: the first negative, the second positive.

Negative tatonnement (elimination of discussion of Nice) On 15 May 2003, President Giscard summarized the amendments on institutions, and referred to some of them, of a significant number, which demanded maintenance of the status quo. He went on to wonder "whether such a status quo approach was compatible with the mandate which the Convention had received at Laeken" (European Convention 2003). Giscard reiterated the mandate given to the Convention by the Laeken European Council:

> First question: how can we increase the democratic legitimacy and the transparency of the three current institutions? Second question: how can we reinforce the authority and efficiency of the European Commission – which proves well that we cannot be satisfied with the current situation? And third question: can we keep the six month rotation of the Council? Your amendments must respond to these questions of Laeken and it is a matter of fact that the group of amendments which insists on retention of the current system obviously does not respond to the Laeken questions. (ibid.)

The importance of this statement should not be understated. The implicit rule in all IGCs was a comparison of the proposed solution with the status quo. This was the reason that all expansions were moving around the previous decisionmaking rule. Given the required unanimity the only possible modifications were essentially incremental. Looking back at Table 2.1 we can verify that moving from 12 countries to 15 in 1995 led to a change in the required majorities from 54/76 (a percentage of 71.05) to 62/87 (a percentage of 71.26).

---

[3] For a more extended discussion of the agenda-setting procedures that Giscard followed in the convention see Tsebelis and Proksch (2007).

Giscard applies the "successive agenda" (Rasch 2000: 9) where alternatives are introduced one after the other, and whichever achieves a majority (in the Convention case "consensus") is adopted. Giscard is buttressed here by the fact that successive agenda procedures prevail in most European countries (including the EU Parliament), but it is the elimination of the status quo from the comparison set that enables him (and the Convention) to produce a clear alternative deviating significantly from the status quo.

There is another, methodological reason that we should pay attention to Giscard's statement. While he refers to the mandate from Laeken, at this point it is not clear what the new set of rules will be (or for that matter, whether there will be a new set of rules). The mandate was asking for more efficient institutions, but could not specify the exact form these institutions should take. In other words, while we have some general rules of endogenous institutional design (Laeken), the specific form can only be achieved by the interactions between the individual actors involved in the Convention. Had Giscard not taken this position, or had he been defeated on the issue by his opponents in the convention, or had the representatives not approved the final document, we would have been back to square one, despite the "need" for such a document expressed in Laeken.

Positive tatonnement (iterated agenda setting) Giscard introduced iterated agenda setting as a standard procedure of the Convention. In a one-shot game the agenda-setter makes a proposal that is amended, accepted, or rejected by the floor. This approach assumes that there are procedures in place that determine which amendments eventually prevail (e.g. amendments with the largest support coalition). In the European Convention, a one-shot agenda-setting game could have resulted in either failure (no amendments get accepted) or in the modification of the proposed amendments and the acceptance of constitutional provisions by shifting majorities. Through iteration, however, the Presidency guaranteed a systematic influence on outcomes. The procedure Giscard applied in the Convention was that he and the Praesidium would propose amendments, and if alternative amendments were available they would synthesize them and produce new amendments until consensus was reached. But the major feature of the system is that the floor of the Convention cannot introduce amendments directly, but has to go always through the Praesidium.

This is one instance where political elites invented an institution that promoted tatonnement as much as possible: that is, reached their preferred outcome or, if this was impossible, a different point that was as close as possible to it.

President Giscard d'Estaing (G) had a central position inside the Praesidium, which was centrally located inside the Convention (Tsebelis 2006). Here I will show how it is possible for such a centrally located figure to achieve outcomes very close to his ideal point. Figure 2.10 shows the effects of iterated agenda setting. There are four members in the Convention (A, B, C, and D) and, for simplicity, I assume that decisions require the support of a majority (3/5). If the President (centrally located at G) proposes his own position G, it can be amended by proposal G′. Through iteration this amended proposal can be amended back to G″ and still enjoy majority support. While the proposal G′ is far away from the preferences of Giscard, the alternative proposal G″ brings the final outcome close to the President's preferences.

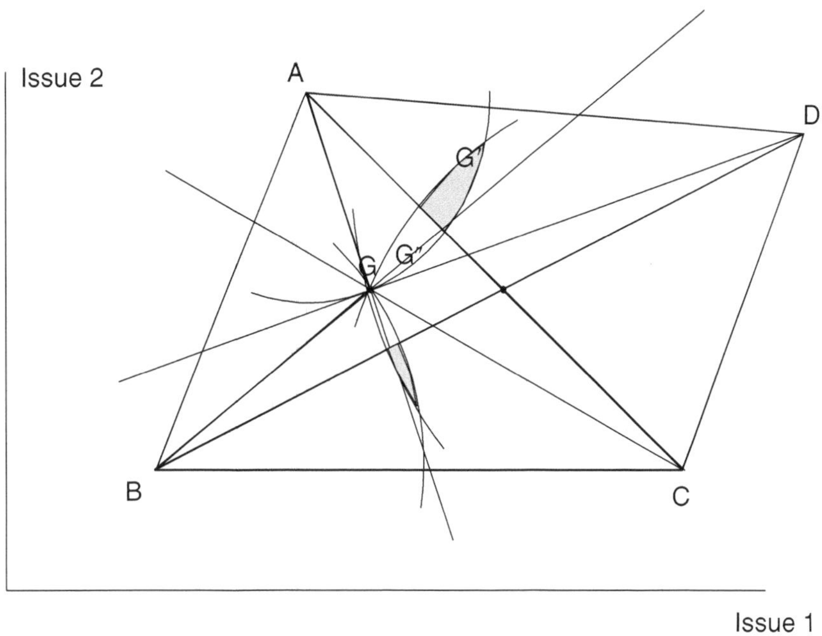

Figure 2.10 Effect of iterated agenda setting

3 TATONNEMENT FROM THE "NO" REFERENDUMS TO BRUSSELS AND LISBON: ACHIEVING THE IMPOSSIBLE

This section discusses the last obstacle to the reform of the EU institutions: bypassing the announced and failed referendums for the final adoption of the new institutions of the EU.[4] Following the "no" votes in France and the Netherlands, avoiding another set of referendums became a necessity for national politicians interested in a more flexible EU. Even then, the referendum in Ireland (the only unavoidable one) had to be repeated (just like The Godfather, the EU made Ireland an offer it could not refuse) and a constitutional decision in the Czech Republic nearly derailed the process before today's plain sailing to EU reform (to be fully materialized in the year 2013). New obstacles emerged from intergovernmental bargaining under the Merkel EU Presidency that were difficult to subdue until the Lisbon agreement was reached. I will deal here with two issues: the problems arising from national referendums (and the "no" votes in France and the Netherlands; negative measures enabling subsequent tatonnement) and the way that the subsequent

---

4 This section is based on the JCMS Lecture I gave in the EUSA Conference in Montreal on 17 May 2007, under the title: "Thinking about the recent past and the future of the EU" (Tsebelis 2008). The lecture was given before the Brussels conference, when the prevailing belief was that of an impasse of the reform process and I was predicting the advancement of EU reform as the only possible solution. I would like to thank Sven Oliver Proksch and Lisa Blaydes for their help.

dispute surrounding agreement at the Brussels IGC under the Merkel presidency was resolved (positive tatonnement).

3.1 The Referendums and the Impasse They Generated

I will not deal with the referendum process and why it was adopted by some countries. For what follows here we need to know only one thing, a piece of common knowledge gained from the whole history of the EU: referendums are highly uncertain events. Even in countries with strong parliamentary majorities in favor of the EU, referendums are events that can produce positive or negative results with a probability of almost 50 percent (as can be inferred by the numerous referendum results that have 4 or 5 as the first digit of their percentage). The reason for this disconnect between the parliaments and voters on the EU, I argue, is because legislators consider changes to the European Union texts relative to the status quo while voters consider only the text, ignoring the status quo policy outcome.

Given the large number of blocking coalitions possible under the Nice institutions, politicians desiring an effective European Union were in favor of moving institutions toward those laid out in the Convention text. However, the voters in these countries are not engaged in the same complex comparisons as their parliamentary representatives between the status quo and the new option presented to them when deciding to vote up or down in an EU referendum. The evidence shows that EU voters did not consider the status quo reversion point when making their vote choices. They, by and large, considered issues largely unrelated to the treaty text up for a vote. Of those objections that were related to the actual document, voters largely failed to account for the fact that the rejection of the Constitution implied that the Nice institutions would continue to dictate the movements of policy (which, as discussed above, would worsen the issues that voters were concerned with relative to the Constitutional Treaty) and not something that they prefer more than the Constitution.

Knowing this truism of the unpredictability of referendum outcomes, and confirming it with the two "no" referendums in France and the Netherlands, European governments were determined to avoid the referendum process at all costs. There was one country where this strategy was a legal impossibility: Ireland, which has a constitutional requirement for a referendum on issues of European integration. Despite the ratification failure, the constitutional document was the EU's only negotiated and agreed-upon solution to its problem of increasing policy immobility. While the document itself has been subjected to many criticisms from diverse political perspectives, it is the only document approved by the governments of all EU countries. Finding agreement between 25 countries is an impressive feat and abandoning that agreement would have been quite costly.

In order to bypass voters, the governments sacrificed two of the unifying symbols of the EU (the "Ode to Joy" as EU anthem and the 12-star flag) and removed the "constitutional" tag from the document, but these were small prices to pay to improve the performance of European institutions. So, this is another brilliant example of the removal of obstacles in order to apply the tatonnement process. European leaders removed the serious institutional constraints that were making the adoption of the institutions impossible (referendums) by providing only "symbolic" sacrifices in the process. Proceeding in the old way led to the abandonment of the term "constitution" as well. However, the practice has always been that intergovernmental treaty agreements have served as the working European constitution. So the text was left largely unchanged with the "constitution" tag eliminated. This small concession avoided ratification by referendum (with the exception of Ireland).

The Convention (and IGC) decision to decrease policy stability in the European Union was an important one because under the Nice rules the European Union would have been unable to function. Regardless of the legal form of the new compromise and the method selected for its ratification, the substance of the new EU treaty had to be derived from the existing document. In other words, the compromise agreed upon in Brussels had to be the focal point of any EU constitution. The IGCs in Brussels and Lisbon put in place a process toward ratification but not without strenuous fights to obtain the required unanimity.

3.2 The Fight in the Brussels IGC

Angela Merkel, the German Chancellor, was able to forge a compromise that essentially preserved the text adopted in Brussels in 2004 precisely because of its focal point qualities (all accounts indicate that she knew that any modification would open an unending discussion about other points requiring change) in the Council meeting she led in the same city in 2007. In addition, educated from the French and Dutch referendum experience, she produced a strategy for adoption that avoided referendums as much as possible.

In her efforts to have the same text accepted, she entered into serious conflict with the Polish leadership, who wanted to preserve the voting rules of Nice and, in the absence of these rules, advocated the adoption of the "square root" rule produced by the power index literature. The "square root" rule was supported by many EU academics (e.g. Hosli and Machover 2004; Kauppi and Widgrén 2004), some of whom urged EU member states in 2004 to adopt the proposal in an open letter, signed by 47 scholars (Open Letter 2004). As these academics claimed, the Swedish government had already proposed such a solution since 2000. Figure 2.11 captures the essence of this government conflict.

In this figure, I present the population size of the EU countries, their voting weight according to the Nice Treaty, and the approximation of these weights by a linear and a square root function. It is clear that for Poland (as well as Spain) the Nice rules produce significantly better results than the square root rule, which is better than the linear function. For Germany it is exactly the opposite: the linear function is the best, followed by the square root rule, and last is the Nice Treaty. The source of the conflict between Germany and Poland is obvious on the basis of this figure.

This conflictual situation was magnified by the fact that Poland, being in favor of the status quo, could block the whole procedure, and Germany, by virtue of being the President of the EU at the time, was responsible for the meeting's agenda. As Figure 2.11 indicates, the conflict could not be more pronounced. The figure also suggests that the situation would have been substantially different if another country with less clearly pronounced preferences over the alternatives (say one of the other big countries, France or Italy or the UK) or one more sympathetic to the Polish point of view (say a Scandinavian country) had occupied the Presidency.

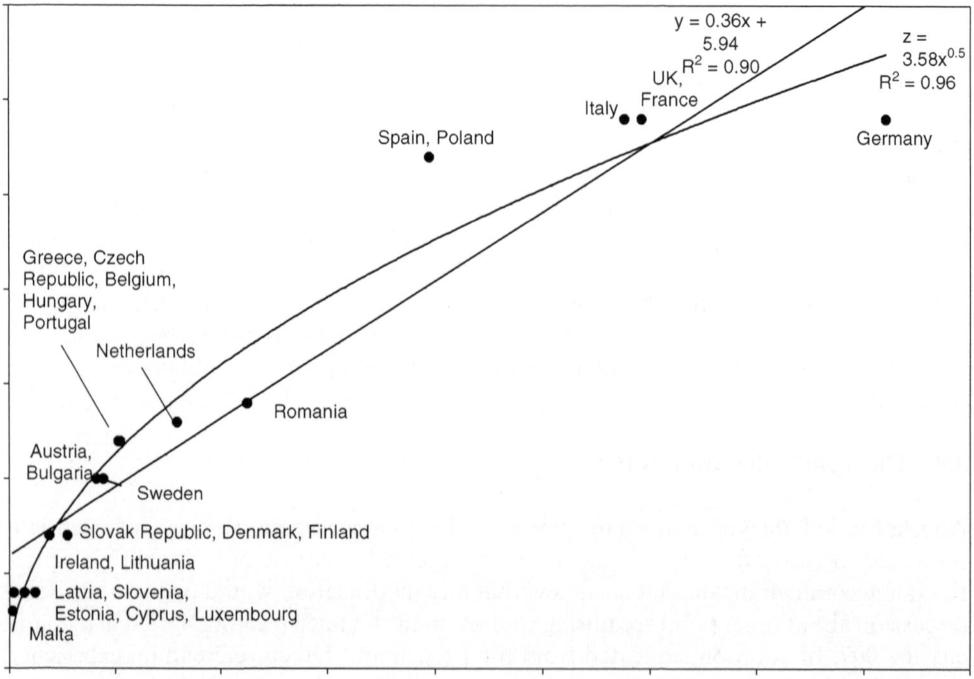

Figure 2.11 Population and voting power of EU countries with linear and square root approximations

4 DISCUSSION OF THE UNION'S ACHIEVEMENT

This chapter has argued that the Convention presidency created institutional means of agenda control. This factor was key in overcoming the plausible possibility of no agreement among European political elites. The ensuing convoluted process of IGCs and failed referendums on the Constitution highlight two questions. First, why do political elites have a different attitude than the masses towards the EU Constitution? Second, how was the adoption of the Constitution worked out so smoothly, while the ratification process was derailed? The answers to both these questions are related.

First, the difference between elites and the masses in their response to the Constitution can be explained by reference to the reversion point. The constitutional process specifies that whenever an agreement cannot be reached the European Union reverts to the previous ratified agreement. This statement implies that if the EU Constitution is not adopted, the EU reverts to the Nice Treaty. This outcome had been unacceptable for European elites for quite a while. This is the reason for the decision to move to a constitutional convention. The Nice Treaty rules along with the expansion of the EU to 25 (and now 27) countries would make political decisionmaking next to impossible in the EU. This is the reason that the process of revision was initiated and concluded among elites. However, the masses had a different point of view. Whether it was fear of foreigners, or bureaucracies (both France and the Netherlands), or inflationary currency (the

Netherlands) or fear of weakening of the welfare state (France), the masses were rejecting the EU Constitution not because of a comparison with the alternative (the Nice Treaty) but because of consequences irrelevant to the Constitution. Indeed, adoption or rejection of the Constitution has no effect on inflation, or foreigners, or the welfare state. It does have an impact on bureaucracies (Tsebelis 2005) but exactly in the opposite to the feared direction. It is the rejection of the Constitution that is more likely to lead to more bureaucracy. So, it is the lack of comparison of the effects of the Constitution relative to the status quo at the level of the masses that most likely generated the negative referendum outcomes.

Strange as it may seem, the answer to the second question, why the Constitution was adopted painlessly but had difficulty being ratified, is to a large extent the same. It is precisely because elites were aware of the alternative that they were eager to adopt a new constitution. What this study points out is that, in addition to this understanding that agreement was imperative, the European Convention came to a conclusion *because* the Praesidium under the leadership of Giscard had a unified conception and exercised all its agenda-setting powers: the ones attributed to them by the Convention mandate as well as the ones generated on their own through the procedures of their own making (the elimination of amendments, the iterated agenda-setting process, and the absence of voting). But the most important moment of the Convention was Giscard's refusal to reintroduce the Nice institutions for debate (and the replacement of the amendment agenda by the sequential agenda).

Understanding that the adoption of a constitution was an exceptional event made possible by the combination of a very creative, consistent, and overpowering agenda-setting process and the impasse created by the status quo (Nice Treaty) explains how we came to an EU Constitution, and how difficult it was to move away from the document. And this realization may be helpful when Europeans contemplate counterfactuals to the institutional treaty that was eventually adopted in Lisbon.

In conclusion, Valéry Giscard d'Estaing and the Praesidium of the Convention deserve credit for leading the Convention to an outcome that simplified the previous treaties, was internally consistent, and produced institutions that can function for an enlarged EU. However, they were unable to anticipate the rejection of their text at the hands of Dutch and French voters because these rejections were, to a large extent, unrelated to the content of the Convention's work. There was no indication during their drafting of the constitutional text that so many referendums would be called, let alone any indication of the lens through which voters would make their decisions about the constitution.

The inability to rely on voters to decide on EU referendums on the basis of European issues led to the decision of Angela Merkel to bypass voters altogether and return to the traditional intergovernmentalist approach. Merkel and her team were able to overcome serious objections in the Brussels Intergovernmental Conference and impose the only natural set of focal EU institutions on all participants. Her task was made easier by the rise of a new government of Spain that did not align with Poland for a return to Nice. However, it was still a Herculean task: I have demonstrated that Poland had very good reasons to insist on Nice and was aided by the unanimity requirement; I have demonstrated that most small-size countries would prefer a "square root" solution for a weighted voting rule in the Council. Yet, Merkel constructed the necessary coalition and used the appropriate arguments to unite the EU around the only possible focal point.

The fact that this focal point was also Germany's most preferred outcome made the completion of her task sufficiently urgent to press for staying with the earlier compromise.

Let us assume for the moment the counterfactual: that a country preferring the "square root" solution or one more or less indifferent between the various weighting schemes happened to occupy the EU Presidency at the time. In this situation the EU focal point of the Convention document was not supported strongly by the President's country interests. It would be difficult to imagine that under these circumstances the Presidency would place EU interests ahead of the national preferences, and the most likely outcome would have been survival of Nice, or at best adoption of the "square root rule," if the Presidency in this case was able to close off renegotiation of other issues. In addition, Merkel was a credible and respected politician; one can easily imagine that the situation would have easily resulted in an impasse with a less skilled or respected politician (Berlusconi?) at the helm, whether from a big country or from a small one. So, even if only one of these necessary (and jointly sufficient) conditions had been absent we would have moved to a situation where the Nice Treaty would have likely survived for the foreseeable future.

This chapter has demonstrated the divergence between the strategic calculations of EU elites and the gut reaction of EU publics, which was resolved in favor of the elite point of view, in two steps: first the elimination of referendums which threatened to derail the unification process, and second the reintroduction of the Brussels compromise as the only focal point of EU integration. If either of these steps had not been possible, the Nice institutions would have almost assuredly survived and no reform would have been possible.

EU institutions are very difficult to modify for two reasons. First, because they require exceptionally high majorities (unanimity in IGCs and very high qualified majorities even in legislative procedures); second, because the preferences of the different countries are highly divergent. These are the reasons that they have remained stable for decades despite the series of conferences aimed at modifying them.

The last sequence of constitutional modifications was successful because these obstacles were bypassed. First, instead of using the Nice Treaty as the default solution (which would have guaranteed its eternal preservation) Giscard was able to remove it from the table (as I demonstrated in the second section) and produce his own default solution. Second, this substitution of the default solution enabled the institutional solution he produced to have remarkable survival capacities. It was only slightly modified in a six-year process where most of the relevant national actors were replaced by their successors or their opponents. Yet, all of these actors understood very well that the only possible solution was in the neighborhood of Giscard's proposal. So they kept the tatonnement process: they eliminated the obstacles that were incompatible with the process (referendums) and modified slightly the solutions to satisfy marginal objections (tatonnement with the Irish referendum) so that the institutional solution became viable. Table 2.1 showed how this process worked: a big departure from Nice (because of Giscard's substitution of the default alternative) and small modifications subsequently (because of tatonnement around Giscard's proposal).

What is important to understand is that the same conditions that for so long had generated the inability to make significant changes to EU institutions (from Rome to Nice) were put in place for a different default solution (the Convention proposal) and gave it the same survival properties.

REFERENCES

BBC News (2000) "Blair hails Nice success." 11 December 2000. Available at *news.bbc.co.uk/2/hi/uk_news/1065039.stm*. Retrieved 27 October 2010.

Closa, Carlos (2004) "The Value of Institutions: Mandate and Self-mandate in the Convention Process." *Politique européenne* 2: 7–20.

de Witte, B. (2001) "The Nice Declaration: Time for a Constitutional Treaty of the European Union?" *International Spectator* 36 (1): 21–30.

European Convention (2003) "Summary of Plenary Meeting on 15 May 2003." Available at http://register.consilium.eu.int/pdf/en/03/cv00/cv00748en03.pdf.

Galloway, David (2001) *The Treaty of Nice and Beyond: Realities and Illusions of Power in the EU*. Sheffield: Sheffield Academic Press.

Hosli, Madeleine O. and Moshe Machover (2004) "The Nice Treaty and Voting Rules in the Council: A Reply to Moberg (2002)," *Journal of Common Market Studies* 42 (3): 497–521.

Huber, John D. and Charles R. Shipan (2002) *Deliberate Discretion? The Institutional Foundations of Bureaucratic Autonomy*. Cambridge: Cambridge University Press.

Kauppi, Heikki and Mika Widgrén (2004) "What Determines EU Decision Making? Needs, Power or Both?" *Economic Policy* 19: 221–66.

König, Thomas and Thomas Bräuninger (2004) "Accession and Reform of the European Union: A Game-Theoretical Analysis of Eastern Enlargement and the Constitutional Reform." *European Union Politics* 5 (4): 419–39.

Magnette, Paul (2001) "Appointing and Censuring the European Commission: the Adaptation of Parliamentary Institutions to the Community Context." *European Law Journal* 7 (3): 292–310.

McCubbins, Mathew D., Roger G. Noll and Barry R. Weingast (1987) "Administrative Procedures as Instruments of Political Control." *Journal of Law, Economics, and Organization* 3 (2): 243–77.

McCubbins, Mathew D., Roger G. Noll and Barry R. Weingast (1989) "Structure and Process, Politics and Policy: Administrative Arrangements and the Political Control of Agencies." *Virginia Law Review* 75 (2): 431–82.

Moe, Terry M. (1990) "Political Institutions: The Neglected Side of the Story." *Journal of Law, Economics, and Organization* 6: 213–53.

Moe, Terry M. and Michael Caldwell (1994) "The Institutional Foundations of Democratic Government: A Comparison of Presidential and Parliamentary Systems." *Journal of Institutional and Theoretical Economics* 150: 171–95.

Moravcsik, Andrew (2006) "What Can We Learn from the Collapse of the European Constitutional Project?" *Politische Vierteljahresschrift* 47 (2): 219–41.

Open Letter to the Governments of the EU Member States (2004). Available at http://www.esi2.us.es/~mbilbao/pdffiles/letter.pdf.

Rasch, Bjørn Erik (2000) "Parliamentary Floor Voting Procedures and Agenda Setting in Europe." *Legislative Studies Quarterly* 25: 3–23.

Santoni, Michele and Francesco Zucchini (2004) "Does Policy Stability Increase the Constitutional Court's Independence? The Case of Italy during the First Republic (1956–1992)." *Public Choice* 120 (3–4): 439–61.

The Economist (2003) "Brussels Breakdown." Available at http://www.economist.com/realarticleid.cfm?redirect_id=2300460. Retrieved 27 October 2010. First published 18 December 2003.

The Economist (2005) " The Europe that Died." Available at http://www4.economist.com /research/articlesBySubject/display.cfm?id=&startRow=379&endrow=393&type=country&subject=France.

Times Online (2008) "Irish Voters Sign Death Warrant for EU's Lisbon Treaty." Available at http://www.timesonline.co.uk/tol/news/world/ireland/article4134077.ece.

Tsebelis, George (1994) "The Power of the European Parliament as a Conditional Agenda-setter." *American Political Science Review* 88: 128–42.

Tsebelis, George (2002) *Veto Players: How Political Institutions Work*. Princeton: Princeton University Press and Russell Sage Foundation.

Tsebelis, George (2005) "Agenda Setting in the EU Constitution." Paper presented at the Domestic Structures and European Integration Conference, Brussels.

Tsebelis, George (2006) "The European Convention and the Rome and Brussels IGCs: A Veto Players Analysis." In Thomas König and Simon Hug (eds), *Preference Formation and European Constitution-building: A Comparative Study in Member States and Accession Countries.* ECPR/Routledge.

Tsebelis, George (2008) "Thinking about the Recent Past and the Future of the EU." JCMS lecture. *Journal of Common Market Studies* 46 (2): 265–92.

Tsebelis, George and A. Kreppel (1999) "Coalition Formation in the European Parliament." *Comparative Political Studies* 32 (8): 933–66.

Tsebelis, George and Jeannette Money (1997) *Bicameralism*. Cambridge and New York: Cambridge University Press.
Tsebelis, George and S.O. Proksch (2007) "The Art of Political Manipulation in the European Convention." *Journal of Common Market Studies* 45 (1): 157–86.
Tsebelis, George and Xenophon Yataganas (2002) "Veto Players and Decision-Making in the EU after Nice: Policy Stability and Bureaucratic/Judicial Discretion." *Journal of Common Market Studies* 40 (2): 283–307.
Yataganas, Xénophon (2001a) "The Treaty of Nice: The Sharing of Power and the Institutional Balance in the EU – A Continental Perspective." *European Law Journal* 7 (3): 242–91.
Yataganas, Xénophon (2001b) "Delegation of Regulatory Authority in the EU: The Relevance of the American Model." Jean Monnet Working Paper 3/01.

3 EU decision making and the allocation of responsibility

*Manfred J. Holler**

1 ON POLITICAL RESPONSIBILITY

When, on 25 March 1957, the Treaty of Rome was signed creating the European Economic Community (EEC) of The Six, the legislative and executive power was installed in the Council of Ministers ("the Council" in what follows). The voting weights were four votes each for the larger countries France, Italy, and West Germany, two votes each for Belgium and the Netherlands, and one vote for Luxembourg. Given the differences in size of the various countries, irrespective of whether measured by population or total GDP, it seemed that Luxembourg was highly overrepresented. However, a qualified majority rule of 12 votes was prescribed and, given this quota, Luxembourg had no say in cases that were submitted to a formal vote. For the given vote distribution w = (4, 4, 4, 2, 2, 1) and the decision rule d = 12, its a priori voting power was zero.

Can we conclude that the citizens of Luxembourg were not responsible for what happened in the EEC? Perhaps not, because in practical terms decisions by the Council relied on a full consensus, and the unanimity rule assigns to Luxembourg the same amount of voting power as it assigns to France, Italy or West Germany. However, could Luxembourg afford to say no if the five other EEC members said yes? Hardly![1] Does this imply that the government and the citizens of Luxembourg were not responsible for what happened in the EEC? Who is responsible for EU decision making: the Council, the Commission, the European Parliament (EP), the voters who selected the members of the EP or the voters who selected the members of their national governments, directly or via a parliament, the members of the national parliaments and their party peers who decide on government coalitions, the national governments that are represented in the Council, or the politicians, voters and bureaucrats who, in the past, designed the rules and defined the objects of today's decision making in the EU? What follows if we can answer this question and allocate responsibility to particular institutions and their members? What is responsibility?

The model underlying the following analysis starts with a simple relationship between actions (A) and outcomes (O). In our context, actions A are the result of collective

* Acknowledgements to Marko Ahteensuu, Richard Baldwin, Leonidas Donskis, Gianfranco Gambarelli, Nicola Maaser, Chell Mann, Jacek Mercik, Jacques Pelkmans, Sina Rummelhagen, Philipp Schliffke, Johannes Schwarze, Izabella Stach, George Tsebelis and Giuliana Zibetti

[1] The abstention of France could bring the working of the Council to a halt. In 1965, due to disagreements between Charles de Gaulle and the Commission's agriculture proposals, France boycotted all meetings of the Council, bringing work to a halt until the dispute was resolved the following year by the so-called Luxembourg compromise.

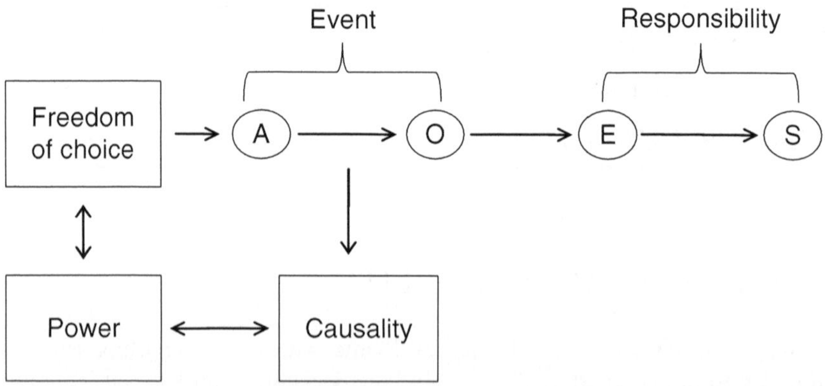

Note: A = action; O = outcome; E = evaluation; S = sanction, accountability

Figure 3.1 The power–responsibility scheme

decision making and outcomes O can be public, merit, or private goods – however, our focus will be on public goods. We identify A with decision making, a perhaps heroic assumption, given bureaucratic impediments, on the one hand, and the sometimes overly optimistic view on feasibility, on the other. The inputs in decision making are power (P), i.e. the potential to act, and freedom of choice (F), i.e. the set of alternatives that is available to choose from. Responsibility is embedded in the evaluation (E) of O and the possibility to sanction (S), honor or punish, A and therefore the choice and decision making that resulted in A. Thus, E and S represent responsibility in our model. (See Figure 3.1.)

This model and its analysis is motivated by the expectation (or hope) that the allocation of responsibility to individual decision makers will improve choices. This necessitates to clarify the causation that links actions A to outcomes O and also to relate causality to individual decision makers. The latter is solved by linking decision making to power P and freedom of choice F; both serve as a proxy of free will, which completes the responsibility model in the case of individual decision making. The hypothesis underlying this chapter is that under a huge pile of provisos we can specify the causal impact of an individual decision maker in a collective decision process by P and thus measure his or her responsibility by P and E. The expectation is that the allocation of responsibility will improve decision making just as the assignment of property rights can improve the allocation of goods. However, quite similar problems exist in the case of collective decision making as in the provision of public goods.

The discussion and conceptualization of these problems with reference to EU decision making is the core of this chapter. Section 3 presents some key results of applying the voting power approach to the European Parliament, the Council of Ministers, and codecision making involving both institutions. In Section 4, the close relationship between freedom of choice and voting power is elaborated using formal models to represent both concepts. The focus will be on the Public Good Index of power. With the help of a similar model the close relationship between power and causality can be demonstrated. This is shown, with a focus on the NESS concept of causality, in Section 5. These sections offer material that should be of interest also from a methodological point of view. Section 6 will integrate these building blocks and relate them to reponsibility. The next section, i.e. Section 2, contains an overview of the various problems embedded in the power–responsibility hypothesis with focus on EU decision making and a further illustration of the responsibility model presented in this chapter. This section can be read as an extended introduction or as a summary note.

In the sequel the reader will repeatedly find references to power measures, more specifically to the Banzhaf index, the Shapley–Shubik index and the Public Good Index (PGI). This is not the occasion to discuss these measures in detail, but a short introduction could be of help to those readers who have had as yet no experience with these measures. All three are based on the concept of a swing (or critical) player, i.e. a player that can turn a winning coalition into a losing one and a losing coalition into a winning one.

In its normalized form, the Banzhaf index of player i, β_i, is equal to the number of coalitions that have i as swing player divided by the total number of swing positions in the (voting) game, summed over all players (voters). The PGI differs from the Banzhaf index inasmuch as only minimum winning coalitions (MWCs) are considered. S is an MWC if $S\backslash\{i\}$ is a losing one, for all $i \in S$; i.e. all players of an MWC have a swing position. The PGI of player i, labelled h_i, counts in how many MWCs i is a member and divides this sum by the sum of all swing positions the players have in the all MWCs of the game.

The Shapley–Shubik index is slightly more complicated as it takes the orderings of players in a coalition into consideration. The swing player metamorphoses into a pivot that turns a losing coalition into a winning one, taking the sequence of coalition members into account. The index value for player θ_i counts the number of pivot positions of i in the voting game under consideration and divides this number by the number of all permutations that can be formed out of the n players of the game, i.e. n!

Below are some simple examples that illustrate the Banzhaf index and the PGI and their applications. Applications of the Shapley–Shubik index are also discussed. For those readers who want to learn more about these measures a substantial amount of literature is available that deals with power measures. Felsenthal and Machover (1998) is definitively the most substantial text in this area. However, in what follows we will not presuppose an intimate familiarity with these measures.

2 RESPONSIBILITY, CAUSATION AND POWER

Definitions of responsibility often include a moral component referring to duties, guilt, blameworthiness, or even shame. This is especially the case when it comes to collective responsibility.[2] So far the EU is hardly an institution that arouses moral sentiments despite its decision making on immigration, environmental standards, and security policy, areas in which moral norms seem to be highly relevant. In general, however, questions of efficiency are brought forward when it comes to EU decision making, either defined as straightforward economic efficiency and international competitiveness or combined with the more sophisticated problem of balancing the preferences of the citizens of its member states.

---

2 See the contributions published in May and Hoffman (1991).

The latter is an issue of preference aggregation and will be only briefly discussed in this chapter. The responsibility notion of this chapter focuses on an evaluation of decision making and its outcome. It implies that sanctions or, more generally, accountability will be demanded if the evaluation indicates poor performance. If there is a causal relationship between decision and outcome, then the assignment of responsibility seems to be straightforward and sanctioning only an issue of power. If there is a power to sanction, then performance can be expected to improve or to be even optimal (in some sense). This is the case of liability and tort law. Both assume causal relationships. However, EU decisions are collective choices. The choices may still be evaluated by their outcomes. However, the allocation of responsibility to individual decision makers and the assignment of responsibility and accountability (e.g. sanctions) is not obvious as there is no straightforward causality that links the outcome of collective decision making to the individual decision maker. It is not clear how responsibility can improve the decision making process without solving these problems.

A first approach to an appropriate solution suggests allocating responsibility in accordance with the power of the individual decision entity (see Holler 2007). In the case of the Council, such an entity is the national government that represents a particular member state. Below we will discuss several studies that measure the power of the national representation in the Council. The results, the power distributions in the Council, could serve as a first approach to allocating contributions to the EU budget or CO_2 emission rights within the Union.

The agents who select these governments, i.e. voters, are secondary decision makers. Their impact on the outcome of the Council decisions is much more difficult to evaluate and so far only very stylized designs have been studied, e.g. the Penrose square root rule, which is supposed to guarantee the equal a priori voting power of every EU citizen in the decision making of the Council. One of the problems with the Penrose square root rule is that it does not guarantee that citizens have equal power when it comes to selecting their national governments and thus may not ensure the representation of their preferences in the Council. The British first-past-the post system does not even guarantee that a clear majority of votes will lead to a majority of seats in the Westminster Parliament. On the other hand, proportional representation often necessitates coalition formation and a coalitional compromise in policy making, which is also the case in EU decisions. Voters who voted for party A, and against the competing party B, often are frustrated by finding A and B in the same government coalition after the election. In such cases it is rather difficult to trace the link between the voters' preferences and the political outcome.

In general, on the EU level, the power structure is even more complex than on the national level, as the EP and the Commission also have a say in decision making, and EP members seem to be cross-pressured by national and ideological interests, the latter deriving from their party affiliations. In what follows I will consider this relationship in a very stylized way without going into institutional and legal details that underlie the structure of this relationship. Tsakatika (2008) identifies three institutional requirements for political responsibility: accountability, openness and identifiability. He concludes that in the EU there is a "responsibility deficit" across all three dimensions but especially concerning accountability and identifiability. The latter, he argues, is a result of the complexity of power relations in EU decision making, which hinders the identification of the agent responsible for a given political outcome. Interestingly, this conclusion relates power and responsibility – two concepts that are not always seen in close relationship with each other. Thus, it seems to be an adequate point of departure to study the power structure of this organization. In what follows, some tools will discussed and illustrated which should help to create a legal framework such that political or economic responsibility works.

In a democratic system, political responsibility functions to legitimate rulings through voting and to sanction poor performance by voting for an alternative. This however can only work if the legal system allows for political competition. Elections (and voting) are the standard tools to implement political competition. However, countervailing power, the control of one decision making institution by another and the need for a bargaining solution, is another mechanism that implements competition and allows for political responsibility. This is about checks and balances. In a democratic society this mechanism involves representation and, again, voting as a means of selection but also of sanctioning. Liability derives from legal responsibility and accountability presumes a straightforward causal relation. Both do not directly apply to EU decision making as it concerns the legislative institution itself and involves collective choices.

EU policy, also due to its historical background, has a strong impact on the economic performance and the structuring of the private economic sector. With reference to EU standardization politics, I will argue below that the EU tends to shift duties and solutions to the private sector when political responsibility becomes a burden. Political responsibility is traded with economic responsibility. The idea of economic responsibility by and large coincides with the invisible hand: economically inefficient projects get punished by deficit and perhaps bankruptcy, while efficient projects are profitable, successful and will multiply as long as there is demand. The market mechanism takes over responsibility. But where are the sanctions on the designers of the market if market performance is poor? As noted by Adam Smith, self-interest and the invisible hand only "frequently" promote the interest of the society (Smith 1776–77 [1981]: 456).

In Goerke and Holler (1998),[3] we argued that the New Approach to European Standardization (NAES), laid out in the Commission's Green Paper of October 1990, was a means of the EU authority to get rid of the responsibility of European standardization, a project that looked unprofitable from a political point of view. NAES stipulates that, in general, standards will no longer be decided upon by the Commission in conjunction with the Council. Instead, the Commission is meant to establish standards (a) with the help of European standardization bodies, (b) via providing direct or indirect incentives to companies which should apply standards and should contribute to the financing of the standardization process, and (c) with the support of the national standardization bodies. The mutual recognition (MR) of national regulations on product specifications and of decisions of the European Court of Justice (ECJ) concerning the goods market can be regarded as an implication of NAES.

It could be argued that by renouncing the "Old Approach" that relied on detailed harmonization, the Commission has shed its influence on standardization in Europe to a large degree and has handed over its responsibilities to fairly independent bodies such as the CEN (Comité Européen de Normalisation), CENELEC (Comité Européen de Normalisation Electrotechnique) and ETSI (European Telecommunications Standards

[3] See also Holler (2012) for a recent discussion.

Institute).[4] The introduction of MR is a further step in this direction. In Goerke and Holler (1998), taking a public choice perspective, we asked why the Commission should have engineered this deprivation of formal power in European standardization. Why does the Commission rely on the interaction of nominally independent agents in organizing European standardization when it seems a relevant hypothesis to assume that these agents act, at least predominantly, in their own interest or in the interest of those whom they are funded by? Is MR an adequate instrument to bring the internal goods market closer to efficiency despite the self-interested agents in the standardization game? Does regulatory competition work the same as competition on goods markets is supposed to work? Does it enhance efficiency?

Or is NAES just an instrument of the EU authorities, the Commission and the Council, to dispose of the responsibility for European standardization – and also to avoid explicit conflicts due to vested interests? If so, then the introduction of MR can be viewed as a means of obfuscation in this policy arena. Government politicians could be at a disadvantage in popularity and lose votes on the national level if they are held responsible for the standardization policy of the Commission and the Council, especially if the resulting harmonization is felt to be tremendously inflexible and biased in favor of some (interest) groups in the population. The Old Approach, based on detailed (technical) standardization, was not very popular, sometimes even subject to satire and jokes, and it was rather costly. In comparison, it appears that MR obfuscation policy works properly. On the one hand, it seems to give back some regulatory power to national institutions; on the other, it seems not only to favor the market of regulations but also to support competition between the regulators and even in the internal goods market. But these effects are far from obvious. For instance, in a recent publication, Kerber and van den Bergh (2008) argued that MR leads to a number of inconsistencies: instead of preserving decentralized regulatory powers and supporting regulatory competition, MR is primarily a path to convergence and rather rigid harmonization. On the other hand, Pelkmans (2012: 363) concludes: "Mutual recognition is a great invention of the EU." Regulatory MR "has been very successful over time. . . The combination of an even more effective approach to existing barriers and an intrusive and targeted pre-emption policy for future ones has effectively spared the single goods market from destructive erosion." In Pelkmans (2007: 699), he observes that MR "is rightly applauded as an ingenious innovation by economists, lawyers and political scientists alike." But Pelkmans also talks of disillusions. He points out that "in actual practice, when shipments arrive at a border or in harbours, civil servants or inspectors will typically focus on the detailed specifics in their *national* laws, presumably that is even their routine instruction or impulse" (Pelkmans 2012: 348). This procedure may create substantial transaction costs and a high degree of uncertainty.

The relationship of responsibility and obfuscation needs further discussion, also with respect to EU decision making.[5] However, to some extent, legal and political

---

[4] With respect to EU members, the distribution of voting weights in CEN and CENELEC is identical with the Council; however the decision rule requires acceptance by 71 percent, *abstentions not being counted.*

[5] For the public choice approach to obfuscation, see Magee et al. (1989), Magee (1997) and the various contributions in Breton et al. (2007).

responsibilities can be substituted by economic responsibility if market participants act accordingly. Glazer et al. (2010) and Kanniainen and Pietarila (2006) present models that demonstrate that oligopolies take environmental protection, sound personnel policy, or avoidance of child labor into consideration if some consumers are willing to pay a higher price for "good products" – and other consumers imitate them. Of course, often there are problems of asymmetric information that undermine the willingness to pay for higher quality. Moreover, the functioning of such mechanisms is rather constrained when goods are public and decisions are made by collectivities: EU authorities should not rely on moral persuasion if they are looking for an efficient policy outcome.

3 VOTING POWER IN EU DECISION MAKING

There are numerous studies that analyze the power distribution in the Council. This of course is partly due to changes in the vote distribution in the course of the EU enlargement, but also because the Council was and still is the most important decision body in the EU. Moreover, EU legislative decisions have become more and more important over time, covering a growing domain of legislative policy within the realm defined by its member states. Power studies of potential vote distributions and alternative decision rules were presented as arguments in the theoretical and political discussion shaping the Council. The power analysis of the Council also served as an illustration and test of the applied measure. Below we will discuss some examples.

The Commission constitutes the EU executive body. Over the years it has gained the status and form of an EU government. One of its important functions is to introduce proposals into the EU legislative process. As such it may serve as gatekeeper, and this is how it is modeled in the power analysis.[6]

The decision rule of the EP is simple majority voting, while rather sophisticated qualified majority rules have been implemented for the Council over the years. This has consequences not only for the decision making of the individual institutions but also for the public debate of the decision rules and seat distributions, as well as the power relations of the EP and the Council when both exercise legislative functions on the EU level. The latter case is discussed in the context of codecision. First, however, we will briefly look into the power relations of the EP and the Commission considered separately.

3.1 The European Parliament

Over recent years, with the extension of the application of codecision, the analysis of the EP in the EU legislative process has gained importance. However, there are still relatively few studies that analyze the power distribution in the EP.[7] The problem is that the EP

[6] See, e.g., Steunenberg (2001) and the further elaboration of this model in Holler and Napel (2007).

[7] A recent collection of papers, edited by Cichocki and Zyczkowski (2010), contains several contributions on power allocation in the European Parliament. The focus of this volume is on a "system of equal influence of the citizens in the EU", which is evident from the title of the contribution delivered by the editors.

members have a national and ideological (i.e. party) affiliation and it depends on the issue under consderation whether the one or the other dimension becomes prominent. With reference to the national dimension, an earlier study by Holler and Kellermann (1977) analyzed the effect of a change of the vote distribution that preceded the first direct election to the EP in spring 1978. The application of the Shapley–Shubik index showed that there were no changes in the a priori voting power although the shares of representatives of the various member countries changed. The direct election promised that the EP would have during the next three decades a more substantial impact than it then had.

Because of the direct election, however, it seems that the ideological affiliation of the EP members and their voters has become stronger and stronger. In a more recent study of the EP, Nurmi et al. (2007) tried to answer the question whether it makes sense for a supporter of a smaller party group to vote for his or her first preference or to cast a strategic vote in favor of one of the bigger party groups. An application of the Banzhaf index shows that it does not disadvantage a voter who prefers a smaller party to follow his or her preferences and vote for it or its candidates. Here it is assumed that party groups are the prime movers in the EP and both the representatives and the voters are interested in ideological positions and the policies that derive from these positions.

The enlargement of the EU necessitates an apportionment of EP voting rights to the newcomers. The standard procedure takes into account the size of the population and tries to guarantee the representation of the major political parties of each country.[8] This covers the national and ideological dimension identified above. Bertini et al. (2005) propose to restructure the distribution of EP seats according to not only population sizes but also economic performance as measured by GDP. They suggest a formula that is based on the Banzhaf index and thus incorporates the potential to form a winning coalition, i.e. a priori voting power. Applying this to Europe of the 27 they show that, with the exception of Italy, all countries have their maximum power value if they either are represented in accordance to population or, alternatively, by GDP. The authors do not give a definitive method for allocating seats. Their intention was to build up scenarios to understand which EU country would have advantages if we take into account only GDP, only population, or a linear combination of the two. Taking into account GDP only, the analysis shows that Germany should have 24.35 percent of the seats, France 16.38 percent, Italy 13.42 percent, and so on. This percentage for Italy will decrease if a higher weight is given to the population. It will fall to 12 percent if only population is taken into consideration. The situation for Poland is quite different: there will be 1.8 percent of seats to it if the apportionment is based on GDP and 8.04 percent if it is based on population.

However, seat shares are a poor proxy for a prior voting power. Applying the Banzhaf index, Bertini et al. (2005) show that the maximum power for Italy is 12.09 percent. It was not obtained in accordance with the maximum number of seats (13.42 percent), but through a linear combination $S = 0.8P + 0.2G$ where P and G represent "population" and "GDP," respectively. This linear combination should be Italy's preferred method for assigning seats among EU member countries. However, in this case Italy would have only 12.28 percent of the seats. For the corresponding voting game its Banzhaf index shows a

8 Today the EP has 736 members. There are 96 members elected by German voters. The voters of Cyprus, Estonia, Luxembourg and Malta are represented by six members each.

maximum. (Note that all other EU member states prefer a different apportionment rule than Italy.)

This result indicates that having more seats does not always mean having more power. Here the nonmonotonicity is due to the multi-dimensionality of the reference space for the seat apportionment. Individual voters also face the multi-dimensionality of the EP, but in general they are not informed about individual decisions of the EP and the decisions of their representatives. (This holds even for students of political sciences.) Elections to the EP are often used as by-elections sanctioning the performance of the political parties on the national level. Voters "do not reward parties for good performance, or punish them for bad performance. Instead, they mainly serve as vehicles for voters to express their satisfaction or frustration with the parties in their national parliament" (Kaniovski and Mueller 2011: 62). Thus the political responsibility mechanism does not work for the EP and its members. However, the stronger the involvement of the EP in EU decision making and the more important EU decision making is for the political performance on the national level, the more sophisticated the selection of candidates should be that the political parties offer for the EP. So far EP membership seems to mainly function as a traineeship for more influential positions on the national level, or as a reward to deserving party activists.

3.2 The Council of Ministers

The recent history of the shaping of the Council is highlighted by the Nice Treaty of 2001 and the Brussels agreement of 2004–the latter was designed as part of the Treaty establishing a constitution for Europe. The discussion was about the proposed seat distributions, on the one hand, and the decision rules, on the other. In accordance with the Treaty of Nice each EU member state is assigned a voting weight which to some degree reflects its population. With the sum of the weights of all 27 member states being 345, the Council adopts a piece of legislation if

(a) the sum of the weights of the member states voting in favor is at least 255 (which is approximately a quota of 73.9 percent);
(b) a simple majority of member states (i.e. at least 14) vote in favor;
(c) the member states voting in favor represent at least 62 percent of the overall population of the European Union.

The distribution of weights shows, to pick out some prominent features, an equal distribution of 29 votes to the four larger EU member states, Germany, France, the UK, and Italy, and 4 votes for each of the member states at the opposite end of the scale: Latvia, Slovenia, Estonia, Cyprus and Luxembourg. Malta with a weight of 3 and population of about 400,000 concludes the scale. Note that Germany, with a population of about 82.5 million, and Italy, with a population of 57.7 million, have identical voting weights. The voting weights are monotonic in population size, but obviously this monotonicity is "very" weak.

For a proposal to pass, all three of these conditions must be satisfied. However, a careful analysis shows that condition (a) is the most significant one. In fact, Felsenthal and Machover (2001) demonstrate that the probability of forming a coalition which meets condition (a) but fails to meet one of the other two is extremely low. Therefore, the "triple majority rule" implied by the Nice Treaty boils down to a single rule. Condition (b) was meant to balance the rather unbalanced representation of the German population, implied by the equal seat share with France, Italy and the UK, but has in general no effect on the Council's decisions.

Given the shortcomings of the voting rule of the Treaty of Nice a revision did not come as a surprise.[9] According to the Brussels agreement of 2004, the Constitutional Treaty, the Council takes its decisions if two criteria are simultaneously satisfied:

(a) at least 55 percent of EU member states vote in favor;
(b) these member states comprise at least 65 percent of the overall population of the EU.

A major defect of the Nice voting rule seems to be the high probability that no decisions will be taken and the status quo prevails, i.e. in the low decision making efficiency as measured by the Coleman power of a collectivity to act. This measure, also called passage probability, represents the probability that the Council would approve a randomly selected issue, where random means "that no EU member knows its stance in advance and each member is equally likely to vote for or against it" (Baldwin and Widgrén 2004: 45). It is specified by the proportion of winning coalitions assuming that all coalitions are equally likely. For the Treaty of Nice rule this measure is 2.1 percent only, while for the Constitutional Treaty it is 12.9 percent. However, Baldwin and Widgrén (2004) demonstrate that, with no substantial change in the voting power of the member state, the Treaty of Nice system can be revised so that its low decision making efficiency increases significantly. Thus, the difference in effectiveness does not necessarily speak for the Constitutional Treaty rule. But perhaps fairness does.

Condition (b) of the Constitutional Treaty implies that the voting weights applied are directly proportional to the population of the individual member states. At a glance this looks like an acceptable rule, representing the "one man, one vote" principle. However, it caused an outcry in those countries that seem to suffer by the redistribution of a priori voting power implied in the substitution of the "triple majority rule" of the Treaty of Nice by the "double majority rule" of the Constitutional Treaty – also referring to a violation of the "one man, one vote" principle. For instance, Slomczynki and Zyczkowski (2007a, b) point out that the larger and the smaller countries will gain power should the double majority rule of the Constitutional Treaty prevail, while the medium-sized countries, especially Poland and Spain, will be the losers in comparison to the voting power implications of the Treaty of Nice. (But obviously the Council's voting system of the Treaty of Nice was considered defective.)

Both the Treaty of Nice and the Constitutional Treaty imply voting rules that are based on a compromise between the two principles of equality of member states and equality of citizens. The double majority rule emphasizes these principles. Large states gain from the direct link to population, while small countries would derive disproportionate power from the increase in the number of states needed to support a proposal. The combined

[9] Illuminating historical details about the decision making that led to the Treaty of Nice and the Constitutional Treaty of 2004 are described in Baldwin and Widgrén (2004). Obviously, the authors had some inside knowledge.

effect reduces the a priori voting power of the medium-sized countries. More specifically, Germany will gain by far the most voting power under the Constitutional Treaty rule, giving it 37 percent more clout than the UK, while both countries have equal voting power in accordance to rule (a) of the Treaty of Nice. Moreover, the Constitutional Treaty rule will make France the junior partner in the traditional Franco-German alliance, which may lead to severe tensions in this relationship.

Obviously, there are substantial differences between the two schemes discussed, and their application to EU decision making might have substantial and unwarranted consequences. Moreover, there are conflicts of interests made obvious by the analysis of voting power. In order to lessen these conflicts, Slomczynki and Zyczkowski (2007a, b) propose an allocation of seats and power that they call the "Jagiellonian compromise," named after their home university at Krakow. The core of this compromise is the square root rule, suggested by Penrose (1946). This rule is meant to guarantee that each citizen of each member state has the same power to influence EU decision making.[10] Applied to the two-tier voting problem of the Council (i.e. voting in the member states at the lower level and in the Council at the upper level), it implies choosing the weights that are proportional to the square root of the population. What remains to be done is to find a quota (i.e. decision rule) such that the voting power of each member state equals its voting weight.

For smaller voting bodies the latter generally cannot be achieved when applying one quota only;[11] however, the EU has a sufficiently large number of members that this equality can be duly approximated. Slomczynki and Zyczkowski (2007b) give an "optimal quota" of 61.6 percent for the EU of 27 member states. Interestingly, the optimal quota decreases with the size of the voting body.[12]

A further expansion of EU membership (e.g. the admission of Turkey) does not comprise a challenge to the square root rule. The adjusted seat distribution will take care of (the square root of) the additional population share, by redistributing seats or by adding more seats to the Council, and the quota will be revised so that the a priori power is as equal as possible to the seat distribution. This is why Slomczynki and Zyczkowski (2007a, b) suggest not fixing the quota in a new constitutional contract but only prescribing the procedure, i.e.

(a) that the voting weights attributed to each member state are proportional to the square root of the population;
(b) that a decision is taken if the sum of the weights of the members that vote yes exceeds the quota $q = (1+1/\sqrt{M})/2$, where M represents the number of member states.

---

[10] Of course, in all practical terms, this probability is zero. Therefore, the norm of equal power cannot be justified on the basis of potential influence. However, fairness could be a better explanation: individual agents might be powerless, but they do not envy each other.

[11] See Berg and Holler (1986) and Holler (1985).

[12] This is immediate from the approximation of the optimal quote q given in Slomczynki and Zyczkowski (2007a). For a voting body of M voters it is: $q = (1+1/\sqrt{M})/2$. For the EU of 25 member states the optimal quote was 62 percent. (See Slomczynki and Zyczkowski (2007b). Compare Slomczynki and Zyczkowski (2006).)

The choice of the optimal quota guarantees that the Council's decision making efficiency of the square root system is always larger than 15.9 percent. This is larger than calculated for the Constitutional Treaty, and far more than promised by the Treaty of Nice rule. Slomczynki and Zyczkowski (2007b) point out that the efficiency of the square root system does not decrease with an increasing number of members states, whereas the efficiency of the double majority rule does.

Gros et al. (2007: 2) observe that it "is widely assumed that the insistence of the Polish government on the square root approach is motivated by the desire to increase its voting power." However, Gros et al. argue that their figures show

> that this will not necessarily be the case. Poland is in general unlikely to gain a lot from the square root approach because it is nearly a big member state: 21 member states are smaller than Poland, and only 5 are larger. Any formula that gives more (relative) weight to smaller member countries is thus likely to affect Poland in a similar way as the other large member countries. (ibid.)

When we discuss schemes of qualified majority, seat distributions, and weighted voting, we should keep in mind that there are still substantial areas of Council decisions that are subject to unanimity, e.g. foreign and security policy. Moreover, even when the qualified majority rule applies, the Council does not always make use of it, but searches for unanimous agreement if the policy implementation needs the support of all member states, and it does not vote, against particular member states that are crucial to the success of the policy. Why, then, is voting power so important? Kauppi and Widgrén (2004, 2007) show that the distribution of voting power in the Council can explain most of the allocation of the EU budget. They conclude that power indices

> do a good job of capturing the actual distribution of power among EU members. Of course, one cannot directly verify the accuracy of such indices since it is impossible to directly measure power. Instead, we evaluate whether our power measures help us understand the "footprints" that the exercise of power leaves in the data. The idea is simple. Since all nations would welcome more spending in their nation and all would resist a cut in spending, the EU budget allocation across members is one manifestation of power that is both observable and quantifiable. (Kauppi and Widgrén 2004: 224)

Their analysis leads them to the conclusion that a major part of the Council decisions can be explained by power politics. The pure Shapley–Shubik index of a priori voting power explains 70 percent of the EU budget allocation. The modified Shapley–Shubik index, taking care of relatively stable cooperation structures in the EU such as the Franco-German axis, accounts for over 90 percent of the variation in budget shares.

One might be tempted to use the budget shares as a proxy for voting power and responsibility for EU policy. If we discuss the results of Kauppi and Widgrén with respect to responsibility, we have to take into consideration that the contributions to the EU budget are approximately 1 percent of GDP of the EU member countries; it is, in other words, a flat tax.[13] There are good arguments to take the economic potential of membership into account

---

[13] In a private e-mail communication (26 September 2010) Richard Baldwin added, "There is some gaming with the UK rebate, but basically they decided to stick with the flat tax and haggle over the expenditure." And he continued, "a more complex 'tax' system could produce

when it comes to deciding what the EU can do. One might argue that here task responsibility is necessary to define and expand what an agent, here the EU, can do. It specifies "whose job it is to see to it that certain tasks are performed and certain things are accomplished" (Goodin 1998: 150).[14] But political responsibility is quite different when it derives from voting power as a result of the Treaty of Nice or the Constitutional Treaty. The analysis of Bertini et al. (2005) demonstrates that voting power varies substantially depending on whether we take GDP (and thus contributions to the EU budget) or population as the determinant for seat allocation. As already noted, Poland will be allocated 1.8 percent of seats in the EP if the apportionment is based on GDP and 8.04 percent if it is based on population. The corresponding power values are 1.79 percent and 7.93 percent. Of course, this result is also valid for the Council under the apportionment rules. The fact that Bertini et al. apply the Banzhaf index while Kauppi and Wigrén's argument rests on the Shapley–Shubik index does not dwarf the gap that exists between a responsibility that refers to economic resources, on the one hand, and to population, i.e. voters, on the other. For a large number of players, and 27 is such a large number, these indices show very similar values.

3.3 EU Codecision

There is still a puzzle to solve: why does the allocation of the budget follow national voting power distribution in the Council, as demonstrated by Kauppi and Widgrén, while annual spending plans are negotiated between the EP and the Council on the basis of a proposal by the Commission? The EP is organized along ideology based party factions and members of the EP are said not to follow narrowly defined national interests. Is the Council the stronger institution although both institutions are meant to have equal influence on the budget?

Napel and Widgrén (2006) analyze the power relations of the Council and the EP in the EU legislation under the codecision procedure as a noncooperative game; i.e. both institutions are assumed to act strategically. Their results are that (a) the procedure favors the status quo and (b) the Council has a stronger a priori influence on the outcome than the EP. Both results are due to the qualified majority rule of the Council (whereas the EP only applies simple majority voting). Thus the low decision making efficiency of the Council, discussed above, carries over to the codecision procedure.

At some stage of the sequential game that the Council and the EP play in the model of Napel and Widgrén, Conciliation Committees enter the arena. Such a committee is composed of the representatives of EU member states – at the time of the study these numbered 25 – representing the Council and a delegation of EP members of the same

---

manipulation by the member states (they already do this with the VAT contribution) that would waste a lot of time and effort on all sides."

[14] For a discussion and application of Goodin's task responsibility, see King (2006). This concept is closely related to Miller's remedial responsibility: "To be remedially responsible for a bad situation means to have a special obligation to put the bad situation right, . . . The problem is to find a principle, or set of principles, for assigning such responsibilities which carries moral weight, so that we can say that agents who fail to discharge their remedial responsibilities act wrongly and may properly be sanctioned" (Miller 2001: 454). In this chapter we also look for principles but in the case of EU decision making we should neither rely on moral weight and nor wait for bad situations.

size. It is interesting to note that here the Union of States principle reflected in rule (b) of the Treaty of Nice determines the representation of the Council. This is generally not taken into consideration when the a priori voting power distribution in the Council is analyzed as a weighted voting game. On the other hand, Napel and Widgrén have, in addition to making use of stylized procedural rules that determine the strategies of the players, made rather crude assumptions on the preferences of the players, i.e. the Council, the EP and the Conciliation Committees, to get a full description of a game model. The individual members of the Council and the EP, also when they are members of a Conciliation Committee, are assumed to have single-peaked preferences. Of course, the latter is a strong assumption, given that many EU policies have a strong distributional character and thus are prone to cyclical majorities and unstable voting outcomes. The fact that we cannot observe a high degree of instability, resulting in prevalent revisions of decisions, seems to be the result of excessive logrolling. The Franco-German alliance is a manifestation of such a policy.

3.4 Power Measures in the EU

As Leech (2003: 485) summarises:

> An understanding of where power lies requires us to take account of many relevant factors: the political complexions of governments, the Paris–Bonn axis, the commonality among the Benelux countries, the Nordic or Mediterranean members, the small states versus the large states, new Europe versus old Europe, the Eurozone, etc. . . . But from the point of view of the design of the formal voting system in a union that is expanding with the admission of new members being quite a normal process, it would clearly be inappropriate to base constitutional parameters like voting weights on such considerations. That might lead to, for example, allocating France smaller voting weights because otherwise its tendency to vote with Germany would give it more power, and the UK larger weight because of its tendency to independence. That would appear arbitrary and would fail to provide a guide for what the votes of new entrants should be. Far better to allocate the voting weights on the basis of general philosophical principles that can be seen to apply equally to all countries and citizens, to new members as well as old ones.

Leech (ibid.) concludes: "A priori power indices are useful in this."

As demonstrated in Napel and Widgrén (2006), there could be other ways for achieving a better understanding of power relations in the EU. In general, power indices are inadequate for forecasting a particular result, as decisions are driven by preferences (and ideologies). But they seem appropriate behind a Napel and Widgrén (2006) veil of ignorance when the agents and their preferences are not yet determined or when the particular preferences of the agents should not matter, as in the analysis of the functioning of institutions like the Council and the EP.

4 FREEDOM OF CHOICE AND POWER

There seems to be an intuition that directly links power to responsibility. However, power is a colorful concept. Above it was more or less defined on the notion of potential influence, i.e. the number of swing positions a player controls. If we accept this notion then we can conclude that power is what the power indices measure. But is it power that makes us responsible or is it the freedom of choice that seems to go with it that is the source of responsibility? If you have no alternatives to choose from, how can you be responsible? Can you have power without freedom of choice? If we can demonstrate that freedom of choice can be fully represented by power, then some of these questions might no longer be relevant. This, however, requires us first to clarify what we mean by freedom of choice and how we measure it. The latter is important as our power concept is based on measuring.

4.1 A Conceptual Framework of Measuring Freedom

The following conceptual framework concurs with Pattanaik and Xu (1990). X is the set of opportunities. Z is the power set of X. It has X, ∅ and all A, B $\subseteq$ X as its elements. *R* is the *freedom of choice relation* such that, for all A, B $\in$ Z, A*R*B expresses: "The degree of freedom of choice of A is at least as large as the degree of freedom of B." That is, *R* is a binary relation with respect to the opportunity sets in Z. In what follows we look at three specifications of R which are $R_{\#}$, R_{α}, and $R\subseteq$,

The *R* relation supports the definition of two other relations, *I* and *P*. (i) If A*R*B and B*R*A, then A*I*B: "The degree of freedom of choice of A is as large as the degree of freedom of B." This is the equality relation of freedom of choice. (ii) If A*R*B and *not* B*R*A, then A*P*B: "The degree of freedom of choice of A is larger than the degree of freedom of B." This is the strict freedom of choice relation.

The similarity to the definition of preference relations is obvious. However, freedom of choice does not consider preferences. In fact, there are no agents to whom preferences can be assigned. There are however concepts of freedom of choice that identify the value of a choice set with its "best" element. Such an approach presupposes preferences. There might even be a straightforward relationship between an individual i's preferences and i's freedom of choice, *R*, which is of interest when studying decision making. *R* could have an impact on i's wellbeing in addition to the choice as such; i.e. it could be an argument of i's utility function. Is there a preference for freedom of choice? Or, *R* could be assumed to augment social welfare; e.g. cultural diversity is considered an asset. Moreover, *R* could be of interest if preferences are not fixed (or given) when A, B $\subseteq$ X are offered, and alternatively, *R* could be of interest if A, B $\subseteq$ X are fuzzy and their elements are not fully fixed. (See Foster 2010.)

4.2 A Cardinality Measure of Freedom of Choice: $R_{\#}$

Pattanaik and Xu (1990) propose three properties (axioms) that uniquely characterize the binary freedom of choice relation *R* on opportunity sets that are elements of Z, given x, y $\in$ X.

Property 3.1 (Simple anonymity) *For all x, y in X,* $\{x\}I\{y\}$.

This property expresses indifference between *no choice* situations.

Property 3.2 (Simple strict monotonicity) *For all distinct x, y* $\in$ *X,* $\{x, y\}P\{x\}$.

This property compares a choice and a *no choice* situation.

Property 3.3 (Simple independence) For all $A, B \in Z$ and all $x \in X \setminus (A \cup B)$ follows $[ARB \Leftrightarrow A \cup \{x\} RB \cup \{x\}]$.

Property 3.3 implies that the existence of alternative x has no impact on how we rank A and B with respect to freedom of choice; i.e. the R ranking of A and B is *independent* of whether there is an alternative x or not. Does this make sense?

Pattanaik and Xu (1990) prove that the only specification of R that satisfies these properties is the counting relation $R_{\#}$: the degree of freedom of choice of A is at least as large as the degree of freedom of B, if the number of elements in the set A is at least as large as the number of elements in set B; i.e. $AR_{\#}B \Leftrightarrow |A| \geq |B|$.

There are a series of arguments that question the above axioms and the result that Pattanaik and Xu derived. Here is a short list:

(1) $R_{\#}$ ignores the preferences of the individuals to whom the set of alternatives are allocated.
(2) $R_{\#}$ ignores complementary and substitutional relationships among the alternatives (as it assumes "strict" independence).
(3) $R_{\#}$ does not take account of differences in value (prices) between elements of X.
(4) $R_{\#}$ ignores the *capability* of the decision maker to make use of the various alternatives in X.[15]

4.3 The α-Ordering and Inclusion

A further elaboration of the freedom of choice concept that takes care of the above critical arguments seems to be a straightforward project. Klemisch-Ahlert (1993) defines an ordering R_α such that for all A, B $\in$ Z,

$$AR_\alpha B \Leftrightarrow \sum_{x \in A} \alpha(x) \geq \sum_{x \in B} \alpha(x) \quad (3.1)$$

In (3.1) α is a mapping that assigns a weight $\alpha(x) > 0$ to every x in X. More specifically, α maps the elements of the set X into a finite space of positive and finite real numbers. We can think of α representing a pricing function, but this is only a thought experiment, because prices do not exist or are not considered relevant for measuring freedom of choice.[16] Alternatively, we can think of α representing social values that result from empathy and face-to-face social interaction, "washed up on the beach along with the human race by the forces of biology and social evolution" as proposed by Binmore (1998: 9). Of course, the choice of α can reflect legal constraints and priorities. Or, it could express the political salience of the various alternatives in the

[15] Argument (4) is due to Sen (1985); it triggered a substantial discussion. In a recent OPHI Working, Foster (2010) incorporates capabilities into the axiomatic freedom of choice approach. The result "can be viewed as providing the theoretical basis for empirical measures of capabilities" (Foster 2010: 3).

[16] If prices exists and are considered relevant then we could simply compare budget sets for measuring freedom of choice. See Screpanti (2006, 2009) for such an application.

perception of the voters and the eyes of the media. In this case, it might be highly relevant for defining the freedom of choice of EU politicians and perhaps even more so for the national governments.[17] The manipulation of salience, i.e. salience policy, can be a rather successful political tool. Can we interpret the New Approach on European standardization with its reference to mutual recognition, noted above, as an intentional shifting of salience?

An ordering which satisfies (3.1) is called an α-ordering. The α-ordering R_α satisfies *Properties 3.2 and 3.3.*; however, it satisfies *Property 3.1* only if $\alpha(x) = \alpha(y)$, *which is in general not the case*. As a consequence Klemisch-Ahlert (1993) introduced

Property 3.4: *For all x, y in X,* $\{x\}R\{y\} \Leftrightarrow \alpha(x) \geq \alpha(y)$.

Then she demonstrated that R_α satisfies Properties 3.2, 3.3, and 3.4 if condition (3.1) applies. In general, there are many α-orderings that satisfy these properties. Can we propose conditions such that (3.1) holds, irrespective of the specification of α?

Klemisch-Ahlert (1993) shows that if we cannot exclude any particular α-ordering, only constrained by $\alpha: X \to]0,\infty[$, then we can compare freedom of choice with respect to A and B only if B is a subset of A or A is a subset of B, or both; i.e. if there is *inclusion*. The inclusion ordering $R\subseteq$ is defined as:

For all A, B $\in$ Z and B $\subseteq$ A $\Rightarrow$ A$R\subseteq$B.

If this relationship applies, then we have $\Sigma_{x\in A}\alpha(x) \geq \Sigma_{x\in B}\alpha(x)$ and condition (3.1) holds.

$R\subseteq$ is the inclusion relation of freedom of choice. It defines an incomplete ordering as many choice sets cannot be compared with respect to this relation. The inclusion relation is also relevant for the interpretation of power measures. In fact, we will demonstrate a close correspondence between freedom of choice and power as measured by the Public Good Index.

4.4 Power, the PGI and $R_{\#}$

In what follows, we will restrict ourselves to voting power: this is the kind of power that seems to be quantifiable. Perhaps this is the reason why it dominates the power discussion in the EU. It is defined as the impact an individual voter (or bloc of voters) has on the outcome of a vote where the outcome is defined as winning or losing, i.e. as satisfying a given decision rule d (e.g. a majority quota q) or not. If N is the set of voters (agents, players, decision makers) and S is a subset of N, then S is a winning coalition if it satisfies d and it is a losing coalition if not. If S is a winning coalition and S\{i} is a losing one, then i has a swing – and exerts power. Similarly, i has a swing if S is losing and S ∪ {i} is winning.

[17] In fact, politicians might have an interest to shape the α-function. For the public choice theory of political salience, see Schofield (2009).

If S is a winning coalition we assign the value of 1 to it, v(S) = 1; if S is losing then we assign the value of 0, v(S) = 0. This defines a simple game which is the standard model of a voting game.

When it comes to Europe, we are hardly ever interested in who forms a winning coalition, but in what decision is made. Of course, this decision is the result of coalition formation. But what seems to matter is the outcome, and not who supported it. If we think of EU policies, then many possible outcomes have properties that define a (pure) public good: non-exclusion and non-rivalry in consumption. This is one of the arguments why we apply the Public Good Index (PGI) to discuss voting power and relate it to freedom of choice: we consider the set of minimum winning coalitions (MWCs) and count how often i has a swing. Note that each member of an MWC has a swing; i.e. there are no surplus players in S if S is an MWC.

For illustration and further discussion, let us assume a voting body, i.e. a weighted voting game $v = (d, w)$ with a decision rule d = 51 and distribution of voting weights $w = (w_1, w_2, w_3, w_4, w_5) = (35, 20, 15, 15, 15)$. Thus we have $v° = (51; 35, 20, 15, 15, 15)$ for the voting body where N = {1, 2, 3, 4, 5} is the set of players. The set of MWCs is:

$$M(v°) = \{\{1, 2\}, \{1, 3, 4\}, \{1, 3, 5\}, \{1, 4, 5\}, \{2, 3, 4, 5\}\}$$

In order to get the corresponding values of the PGI, we count the number of coalitions in $M(v°)$ that have player i as a member, i.e., the decisiveness c_i, and divide this number by the sum of all c_i −values (which is 15 for the above game). As a result we get the PGI.

$$h° = h(v°) = (4/15, 2/15, 3/15, 3/15, 3/15).$$

We see that $h°$ violates local monotonicity: although player 2 controls more voting weight than player 3 (or 4 and 5, respectively), the power value of player 2 is smaller. This is possibly the case because the game is not decisive; i.e. it could well be that votes split into equal shares of 50 and no winning coalition prevails.[18]

Now let us assume that each coalition in $M(v°)$ represents a different policy, i.e. public good, so that, in the end, player 1 controls a set A = {a, b, c, d} and player 2 controls a set B = {a, e}. If we conclude that the power of player 1 is larger than the power of player 2, then this strictly parallels the conclusion that the freedom represented by A is larger than the freedom represented by B and there $AR_{\#}B$ and, even more specifically, $AP_{\#}B$.

The formal equivalence of the measuring of power and freedom of choice, when the latter is related to $R_{\#}$, should not come as a surprise since both the PGI and the Banzhaf index (as well as the Shapley–Shubik index) are counting indices as classified in Malawski (2004). However, in the next section it will be demonstrated that an equivalence relation to the freedom of choice relation *R*Í can be formalized for the PGI.

4.5 The R⊆-equivalence of PGI-ordering

We can formalize the PGI as

[18] For a discussion of nonmonotonicity, see Section 5 below.

$$h_i(v) = \frac{c_i}{\sum_{i \in N} c_i}$$

where c_i, as defined above, is the number of decisive sets (i.e. MWCs) that have i as a member. Let us define the sum of all decisive positions in a game as $\Sigma_{i \in N} c_i = c(v)$ and let $M_i(v)$ express the set of all MWCs that have i as a member. Then PGI-monotonicity is defined as follows. Given $M_i(u) \supseteq M_i(v)$, a solution f on the set of all simple games satisfies PGI-monotonicity if, for any pair of simple games u and v,

$$f_i(u)c(u) \geq f_i(v)c(v) \tag{3.2}$$

for all player $i \in N$ holds. Alonso-Meijide et al. (2008) show that the PGI is the only index that satisfies PGI-monotonicity, symmetry, null player, and efficiency.[19] That is, we can specify f by h and substitute, in (3.2), f_i by h_i.

Of course, the ordering that derives from a direct application of PGI-monotonicity is incomplete as there are many games u and v such that $M_i(u) \supseteq M_i(v)$ does not apply. However, PGI-monotonicity allows us to discuss the problems as follows:

(1) Can we conclude from $M_i(u) \supseteq M_i(v)$ that i has at least as much freedom of choice in game u as in game v?
(2) Can we conclude from $M_i(u) \supseteq M_j(u)$ that i has at least as much freedom of choice in game u as j?
(3) Can we conclude from $h_i(u) \geq h_j(u)$ that i has at least as much freedom of choice in game u as j?

Note if $h_i(u) > h_i(v)$, then, in accordance with $R_{\subseteq}$, we conclude that game u contains more freedom of choice than game v for agent i if $M_i(u) \supset M_i(v)$ and $M(u) \subseteq M(v)$ hold. Moreover, if $h_i(u) > h_i(v)$, then, in accordance with $R_{\#}$, we conclude that game u contains more freedom of choice than game v for agent i if $c_i(u) > c_i(v)$ and $c(u) \leq c(v)$ hold. Of course, $M(u) \subseteq M(v) \Rightarrow c(u) \leq c(v)$, but the reverse does not "necessarily" hold.

5 COLLECTIVE CHOICE, POWER AND CAUSALITY

The specification of causality in the case of collective decision making with respect to the individual agent cannot be derived from the action and the result as both are determined by the collectivity. They have to be traced back to decision making. However, collective decision making has a quality that differs substantially from individual decision making. For instance, an agent may support his favored alternative by voting for another alternative or by not voting at all. Nurmi (1999, 2006) contains a collection of such "paradoxes."

These paradoxes tell us that we cannot derive the contribution of an individual to a particular collective action from the individual's voting behavior. Trivially, a vote is not a contribution, but a decision. Resources such as voting power, money, etc. are potential

[19] See Alonso-Meijide et al. (2008) for definitions.

contributions and causality might be traced back to them if collective action results. As a consequence, causality follows even from votes that do not support the collective action. This is reflected in everyday language when one simply states that the Parliament has decided, when in fact the decision was made by a majority smaller than 100 percent. We say the EU has decided even when there was strong, but not decisive, resistance in the EP and only a qualified majority in the Council agreed. But how can we allocate causality if it is not derived from decisions?

5.1 The Potential to Act

Imagine a five-person committee N = {1, 2, 3, 4, 5} that makes a choice between the two alternatives x und y. The voting rule specifies that x is chosen if either (i) 1 votes for x or (ii) at least three of the players 2–5 vote for x. Let us assume that all individuals vote for x. What can be said about causality? Clearly this is a case of over-determination and the allocation of causation is not straightforward. The action of agent 1 is an element of only one minimally sufficient coalition, i.e. decisive set, while the actions of each of the other four members are in three decisive sets each. If we take the membership in decisive sets as a proxy for causation, and standardize such that the shares of causation add up to one, then vector

$$h^\circ = \left(\frac{1}{13}, \frac{3}{13}, \frac{3}{13}, \frac{3}{13}, \frac{3}{13}\right)$$

represents the degrees of causation.[20] Braham and van Hees (2009: 334), who introduced and discussed the above case, conclude that "this is a questionable allocation of causality." They add that "by focusing on minimally sufficient coalitions, the measure ignores the fact that anything that players 2–5 can do to achieve x, player 1 can do, and in fact more – he can do it alone."

Let us review the above example. Imagine that x stands for polluting a lake. Now the lake is polluted, and all five members of N are under suspicion for having polluted it. Then h° implies that the share of causation for 1 is significantly smaller than the shares of causation of each of the other four members of N. If responsibility and perhaps punishment follow causation then the allocation h° seems highly pathological. As a consequence Braham and van Hees propose to apply the weak NESS instead of the strong one, i.e. not to refer to decisive sets, but to consider sufficient sets instead and count how often an element i of N is a necessary element of a sufficient set (i.e. a NESS).[21] Taking care of an adequate standardization so that the shares add up to 1, we get the following allocation of causation:

---

[20] An alternative measure of "degree of causation" and responsibility is introduced in Chockler and Halpern (2004). It builds on contingency: if a candidate wins an election with 11–0 then a voter who voted for this candidate is less responsible for the victory than if the candidate had won 6–5, but still the voter is responsible under the counterfactual contingency that there could be a 6–5 vote. Similarly, Felsenthal and Machover (2009) allocate responsibility after the decision is made and known.

[21] For a discussion of the NESS test, see Braham (2005, 2008) and Braham and Holler (2009). This literature refers to earlier work by Wright (1985, 1988).

$$b° = \left(\frac{11}{23}, \frac{3}{23}, \frac{3}{23}, \frac{3}{23}, \frac{3}{23}\right).$$

The result expressed by $b°$ looks much more convincing than the result proposed by $h°$, does it not? Note that the b-measure and h-measure correspond to the Banzhaf index and the PGI, respectively, and can be calculated accordingly.

So far the numerical results support the weak NESS test and thus the application of the Banzhaf index. However, what happened to alternative y? If y represents "no pollution" then the set of decisive sets consists of all subsets of N that are formed of the actions of agent 1 and the actions of two out of agents 2, 3, 4, and 5. Thus the actions of 1 are members of six decisive sets while the actions of 2, 3, 4, and 5 are members of three decisive sets each. The corresponding shares are given by the vector

$$h^* = \left(\frac{1}{3}, \frac{1}{6}, \frac{1}{6}, \frac{1}{6}, \frac{1}{6}\right).$$

Obviously, h^* looks much more convincing than $h°$ and the critical interpretation of Braham and van Hees does no longer apply: agent 1 cannot bring about y on its own, but can cooperate with six different pairs of other agents to achieve this goal.

Note that the actions (votes) bringing about x represent an improper game – two "winning" subsets can exist at the same time[22] – while the determination of y can be described as a proper game. However, if there are only two alternatives x and y then "not x" necessarily implies y, irrespective of whether the (social) result is determined by voting or by polluting. The h-values indicate that it seems to matter what issue we analyze and what questions we raise while the Banzhaf index with respect to y is the same then for x: $b° = b^*$.

The formal rules of EU decision making seem to guarantee properness, and thus the strong NESS test and the PGI might be adequate instruments. However, as discussed above, decision making efficiency is more likely to be a problem as the corresponding game often lacks decisiveness.

5.2 The Challenge of Nonmonotonicity

Whether we should apply h or b, or a third alternative, to measure causation is still an open question, and one this chapter will not answer. However, if we want to relate responsibility to power then the nonmonotonicity, i.e. the violation of local monotonicity, that represents the strong NESS test of the PGI is quite a challenge: if the collective choice is made through voting then it is not guaranteed that a voter with a larger share of votes has at least as much responsibility for the collectively determined outcome as a voter with

---

22 Note that the result x implies the possibility of over-determination. Wright (1985) has identified two types of over-determination: *duplicative* and *pre-emptive* causation. "A case of duplicative causation is one in which two similar and independent causal processes $C1$ and $C2$, each of which is sufficient for the same effect E, may culminate in E at the same time" (Braham and Holler 2009: 149). This applies to x, the case of pollution.

a smaller share. If we review the discussion of voting weights in the EU Council then we might wonder.

From the above example we can learn that nonmontonicity might indicate that we asked the wrong question: is the responsibility with respect to keeping the lake clean or is it with polluting and then perhaps sharing the costs of cleaning it? Felsenthal and Machover (1998: 221ff) argue that any a priori measure of power that violates local monotonicity is "pathological" and should be disqualified as serving as a valid yardstick for measuring power. In Holler and Napel (2004a, 2004b), we argue that the PGI shows nonmonotonicity (and thus confirms that the measure does not satisfy local monotonicity) if the game is not decisive, as the weighted voting game $v° = (51; 35, 20, 15, 15, 15)$ discussed in Section 4.4 demonstrates, or is improper and therefore indicates that perhaps we should worry about the design of the decision situation. The more popular power measures, i.e. the Shapley–Shubik index and the Banzhaf index, satisfy local monotonicity and thus do not indicate any particularities if the game is not decisive or is improper. Interestingly, these measures also show a violation of local monotonicity if we consider a priori unions, and the equal probability of permutations and coalitions, respectively, does no longer apply. The concept of a priori unions or pre-coalitions is rather crude because it implies that certain coalitions will not form at all, i.e. have a zero probability of forming.[23]

Note since the PGI considers MWCs only, this is formally equivalent to putting a zero weight on coalitions that have surplus players. Is this the ("technical") reason why the PGI may show nonmonotonicity? However, instead of accepting the violation of monotonicity, we may ask for what decision situations the PGI guarantees monotonic results – this may help to design adequate voting bodies. In Holler et al. (2001), the authors analyze alternative constraints on the number of players and other properties of the decision situations. For example, it is obvious that local monotonicity will not be violated by any of the known power measures, including PGI, if there are n voters and $n-2$ voters are dummies. It is, however, less obvious that local monotonicity is also satisfied for the PGI if one constrains the set of games so that there are only $n-4$ dummies. A hypothesis that needs further research is that the PGI does not show nonmonotonicity if the voting game is decisive and proper and the number of decision makers is lower than six.[24]

To conclude, the PGI and thus the strong NESS concept may produce results that are counterintuitive at first glance. However, in some decision situations they seem to tell us more about the power structure and the corresponding causality allocation than the Banzhaf index and the corresponding weak NESS concept do.

6 THE POWER–RESPONSIBILITY SCHEME SUMMARIZED

The conclusion of the above exercise is that reponsibility can be allocated in relation to power. This scheme takes care of both causality and freedom of choice. One of the

[23] See Alonso-Meijide and Bowles (2005) for examples of voting games with a priori unions and Holler and Nurmi (2010) for a discussion.

[24] Perhaps this result also holds for a larger number of decision makers but I do not know of any proof. For a related discussion and the introduction of weighted monotonicity, see Alonso-Meijide and Holler (2009).

implications is that we can link the concepts of freedom of choice and power to responsibility because membership of controlling coalitions can be interpreted as a proxy of causality and the responsibility of the individual decision maker for the social outcome.

There are immediate theoretical applications for this measure of responsibility. In particular, this approach can be seen as an alternative to welfare calculation and utility maximization, which seem to dominate the law and economics literature. The approach to responsibility that is suggested here accounts for the observation that people often compare social states and social systems with respect to the degree of freedom and the distribution of power and responsibility independent of preferences and welfare calculations. It also takes care of theoretical arguments which suggest that power and responsibility should be evaluated without reference to preferences.[25] The binding nature of law is not because it matches the agent's preferences but because it concurs with the agent's capacity to fulfill an obligation. In fact, the capacity to act creates the obligation and the related freedom of choice is the basis of the corresponding responsibility to which the law refers.

However, who is and who can be made responsible in the case of EU decision making? In the political arena of mass democracy the individual voter's causality and concomitant responsibility is difficult to quantify, so is his or her potential of political sanctioning. For an individual voter the implementation of responsibility via voting is hardly possible. First, his or her impact is negligible – and this leads to the paradox of voting and the hypothesis of expressive behavior.[26] Second, as e.g. demonstrated in Nurmi (1999, 2006), there are all kind of traps and intricacies – euphemistically labeled paradoxes - that make voting a rather unreliable instrument, at least if there are more than two alternatives.

To conclude, if the collectivity, the State, makes irresponsible choices then the responsibility of a voter cannot be derived from his vote, because, in general, a single vote has no causal effect on the outcome no matter whether the square root rule is applied to the allocation of votes or not. This is how collective responsibility comes into play implying that every member of a collectivity is responsible for what the collectivity does or fails to do, irrespective of the member's contribution to the decision that underlies the collectivity's behavior. This results in responsibility via membership. It raises the question of what the relevant collectivity is and how we can choose membership. When it comes to the State as the agent of one's country, the question is do we have a choice?

Owing to the EU, the potential of mobility has substantially increased and "voting with one's feet" looks like a possible option. If you are not satisfied with your government you can choose another member country for your residence. (Note that, in general, you have no voting rights in your new country as long as you do not become one of its citizens.) However, in practical terms David Hume's verdict still holds for a large share of the EU population as the low mobility within the EU shows:

> Can we seriously say, that a *poor peasant* or artizan has a free choice to leave his country, when he knows no foreign language or manners, and lives from day to day, by the small wages which

---

[25] See Braham and Holler (2005a, 2005b) and Napel and Widgrén (2004, 2005) for opposing views on the relationship of power and preferences. (For a comment, see Holler and Nurmi 2010. Compare Holler and Widgrén 1999.)

[26] For the "possible irresponsibility" of expressive voting, see Hillman (2010).

> he acquires? We may as well assert, that a man, by remaining in a vessel, freely consents to the dominion of the master; though he was carried on board while asleep, and must leap into the ocean, and perish, the moment he leaves her. (Hume 1777 [1985]: 475)

Still, mobility in the EU is an important issue and might be highly relevant for assigning responsibility. But this has to be studied in another paper. Another string of arguments that deserve further discussion derives from the precautionary principle (Ahteensuu 2011): if we cannot solve the problem of responsibility then, one might argue, the corresponding decision should not be made.[27] If we apply this principle to today's situation, then a severe lack of "necessary" decisions could be the consequence. The precautionary principle and it consequences could motivate rethinking political responsiveness. A more substantial participation of the EP, also balancing its power with the Council (e.g. by reducing the qualified majority quota of the latter[28]) could be a first step to establishing political responsibility. Another possible means to increase citizen participation and thus enhance the potential of political responsibility could be the direct election of the representatives that the member countries assign to the Commission.

In the Republic of San Marino, every six months, the proportionally elected multiparty Council selects two captains to be the heads of state. These Capitani Reggenti are chosen from opposing parties so that there is a balance of power. They serve a six-month term, and a subsequent re-election is not possible. Once their six-month term is over, citizens have three days in which to file complaints about the captains' activities. If they warrant it, judicial proceedings against the ex-head(s) of state can be initiated.[29] Should the European Court of Justice evaluate the policies of the Council and the EP? Perhaps impartial commenting could help to make voters more aware of EU decision making and thus increase political responsibility. However, there have to be more effective ways for the voter to hold his or her representatives accountable than to vote every four years, if responsibility is to work.

REFERENCES

Ahteensuu, M. (2011): *The Precautionary Principle in Environmental and Health Risk Governance: A Philosophical Analysis*. Munich: Oldenbourg.

Alonso-Meijide, J.M. and Bowles, C. (2005): "Power indices restricted by a priori unions can be easily computed and are useful: A generating function-based application to the IMF." *Annals of Operations Research*, 137, 21–44.

Alonso-Meijide, J.M. and Holler, M.J. (2009): "Freedom of choice and weighted monotonicity of power." *Metroeconomica* 60(4), 571–83.

---

[27] This presents a slight modification (or an extension) of the common understanding of the precautionary principle which calls for early measures to avoid and mitigate environmental damage and health hazards in the face of scientific uncertainty. (See Ahteensuu 2011.) The relevant kinds of uncertainties are concerned not only with the causal link between an action (or a decision) and an effect, but also with the inability to assign responsibility.

[28] This follows from Napel and Widgrén (2006) discussed in Section 3.3.

[29] The practice of multiple heads of state and the frequent elections of the heads of state are derived directly from the rules that governed the Roman Republic. See Machiavelli's *Discorsi* for an involved analysis of the Roman Republic.

Alonso-Meijide, J.M., Casas-Mendez, B., Holler, M.J. and Lorenzo-Freire, S. (2008): "Computing power indices: multilinear extensions and new characterizations." *European Journal of Operational Research* 188, 540–54.

Baldwin, R. and Widgrén, M. (2004): "Winners and losers under various dual majority rules for the EU's Council of Ministers." In Wiberg, M. (ed.), *Reasoned Choices: Essays in Honor of Academy Professor Hannu Nurmi on the Occasion of his 60th Birthday*, Turku: Digipaino, 42–92; also CEPR Discussion Paper No. 4450, June 2004.

Berg, S. and Holler, M.J. (1986): "Randomized decision rules in voting games: a model of strict proportional power." *Quality and Quantity* 20, 419–29.

Bertini, C., Gambarelli, G. and Stach, I. (2005): "Apportionment strategies for the European Parliament." In Gambarelli, G. and Holler, M.J. (eds), "Power measures III." *Homo Oeconomicus* 22: 589–604. Munich: Accedo Verlag.

Binmore, K. (1998): *Game Theory and the Social Contract*, Volume II: *Just Playing*. Cambridge, MA, and London: The MIT Press.

Braham, M. (2005): "Causation and the measurement of power." In Gambarelli, G. and Holler, M.J. (eds), *Power Measures III.*" *Homo Oeconomicus* 22: 645–53. Munich: Accedo-Verlag.

Braham, M. (2008): "Social power and social causation: towards a formal synthesis." In Braham, M. and Steffen, F. (eds), *Power, Freedom, and Voting: Essays in Honour of Manfred J. Holler*. Berlin and Heidelberg: Springer, 1–21.

Braham, M. and Hees, M. (2009): "Degrees of causation." *Erkenntnis* 71, 323–44.

Braham, M. and Holler, M.J. (2005a): "The impossibility of a preference-based power index." *Journal of Theoretical Politics* 17, 137–57.

Braham, M. and Holler, M.J. (2005b): "Power and preferences again: a reply to Napel and Widgrén." *Journal of Theoretical Politics* 17, 389.

Braham, M. and Holler, M.J. (2009): "Distributing causal responsibility in collectivities." In Gekker, R. and Boylan, T. (eds), *Economics, Rational Choice and Normative Philosophy*. London and New York: Routledge, 145–63.

Breton, A., Galeotti, G., Salmon, P. and Wintrobe, R. (eds) (2007): *The Economics of Transparency in Politics* (Villa Colombella Papers). Aldershot: Ashgate Publishing.

Chockler, H. and Halpern, J.Y. (2004): "Responsibility and blame: a structural-model approach." *Journal of Artificial Intelligence Research* 22, 93–115.

Cichocki, M.A. and Zyczkowski, K. (eds) (2010): *Institutional Design and Voting Power in the European Union*. Farnham, UK and Burlington, VT, USA: Ashgate.

Felsenthal, D. and Machover, M. (1998): *The Measurement of Voting Power. Theory and Practice, Problems and Paradoxes*. Cheltenham: Edward Elgar.

Felsenthal, D. and Machover, M. (2001): "The Treaty of Nice and qualified majority voting." *Social Choice and Welfare* 18, 431–64.

Felsenthal, D. and Machover, M. (2009): "A note on measuring voters' responsibility." *Homo Oeconomicus* 26, 259–71.

Foster, J.E. (2010): "Freedom, opportunity and wellbeing." In Oxford Poverty & Human Development Initiative (OPHI), Working Paper No. 35.

Glazer, A., Kanniainen, V. and Puutvaara, P. (2010): "Firms' ethics, consumer boycotts, and signalling." *European Journal of Political Economy* 26, 340–50.

Goerke, L. and Holler, M.J. (1998): "Strategic standardization in Europe: a public choice perspective." *European Journal of Law and Economics* 6, 95–112.

Goodin, R. (1998): "Social welfare as a collective social responsibility." In Schmidtz, D. and Goodin, R. (eds), *Social Welfare and Individual Responsibility*. Cambridge: Cambridge University Press.

Gros, D., Kurpas, S. and Widgrén, M. (2007): "Weighting votes in the Council: towards a 'Warsaw compromise'?" In VOX: Research-based policy analysis (20 June), 1–5.

Hillman, A. (2010): "Expressive behavior in economics and politics." *European Journal of Political Economy* 26, 403–18.

Holler, M.J. (1985): "Strict proportional power in voting bodies." *Theory and Decision* 19, 249–58.

Holler, M.J. (2007): "Freedom of choice, power, and the responsibility of decision makers." In Josselin, J-M. and Marciano, A. (eds), *Democracy, Freedom and Coercion: A Law and Economics Approach*. Cheltenham: Edward Elgar, 22–45.

Holler, M.J. (2012): "Efficiency or obfuscation? Comment on 'Mutual recognition' by Jacques Pelkmans." In Behrens, P., Eger, T. and Schäfer, H.-B. (eds), *Ökonomische Analyse des Europarechts*. Tübingen: Mohr Siebeck, 367–75.

Holler, M.J. and Kellermann, J. (1977): "Power in the European Parliament: what will change?" *Quality and Quantity* 11, 189–92.

Holler, M.J. and Napel, S. (2004a): "Local monotonicity of power: axiom or just a property." *Quality and Quantity* 38, 637–47.

Holler, M.J. and Napel, S. (2004b): "Monotonicity of power and power measures." *Theory and Decision* 56, 93–111.
Holler, M.J. and Napel, S. (2007): "Democratic decision procedures, stability of outcome, and agent power, with special reference to the European Union." In Pardo, J.C. and Schwartz, P. (eds), *Public Choice and the Challenges of Democracy*. Cheltenham: Edward Elgar, 220–34.
Holler, M.J. and Nurmi, H. (2010): "Measurement of power, probabilities, and alternative models of man." *Quality and Quantity* 44, 833–47.
Holler, M.J. and Widgrén, M. (1999): "Why power indices for assessing European Union decision-making?" *Journal of Theoretical Politics* 11, 321–30.
Holler, M.J., Ono, R. and Steffen, F. (2001): "Constrained monotonicity and the measurement of power." *Theory and Decision* 50, 385–97.
Hume, D. (1777): *Essays: Moral, Political and Literary*, reprinted (1985). Indianapolis: LibertyClassics.
Kaniovski, S. and Mueller, D.C. (2011): "How representative is the European Union Parliament?" *European Journal of Political Economy* 27, 61–74.
Kanniainen, V. and Pietarila, E. (2006): "Corporate social responsibility: can markets control?" *Homo Oeconomicus* 23, 153–79.
Kauppi, H. and Widgrén M. (2004): "What determines EU decision making? Needs, power or both?" *Economic Policy* 19: 221–66.
Kauppi, H. and Widgrén, M. (2007): "Voting rules and budget allocation in an enlarged EU." *European Journal of Political Economy* 23, 693–706.
Kerber, W. and van den Bergh, R. (2008): "Mutual recognition revisited: misunderstandings, inconsistencies, and a suggested reinterpretation." *Kyklos* 61, 447–65.
King, P. (2006): "What do we mean by responsibility? The case of UK housing benefit reform." *Journal of Housing and the Built Environment* 21, 111–25.
Klemisch-Ahlert, M. (1993): "Freedom of choice: a comparison of different rankings of opportunity sets." *Social Choice and Welfare* 10, 189–207.
Leech, D. (2003): "The utility of the voting power approach." *European Union Politics* 4, 234–42.
Magee, S.P. (1997): "Endogenous protection: the empirical evidence." In Mueller, D.C. (ed.), *Perspectives on Public Choice: A Handbook*. Cambridge: Cambridge University Press.
Magee, S.P., Brock, W.A. and Young, L. (1989): *Black Hole Tariffs and Endogenous Policy Theory*, Cambridge: Cambridge University Press.
Malawski, M. (2004): "'Counting' power indices for games with a priori unions." *Theory and Decision* 56, 125–40.
May, L. and Hoffman, S. (eds) (1991): *Collective Responsibility: Five Decades of Debate in Theoretical and Applied Ethics*. Savage, MD: Rowman & Littlefield.
Miller, D. (2001): "Distributing responsibility." *Journal of Political Philosophy* 54, 437–46.
Napel, S. and Widgrén, M. (2004): "Power measurement as sensitivity analysis – a unified approach." *Journal of Theoretical Politics* 16, 517–38.
Napel, S. and Widgrén, M. (2005): "The possibility of a preference-based power index." *Journal of Theoretical Politics* 17, 377–87.
Napel, S. and Widgrén, M. (2006): "The inter-institutional distribution of power in EU codecision." *Social Choice and Welfare* 27, 129–54.
Nurmi, H. (1999): *Voting Paradoxes and How to Deal with Them. Berlin*, Heidelberg and New York: Springer.
Nurmi, H. (2006): *Models of Political Economy*. London and New York: Routledge.
Nurmi, H. and Hosli, M.O. (2003): "Which decision rule for the future Council?" *European Union Politics* 4, 37–50.
Nurmi, H., Raunio, T. and Helin, J. (2007): "The best represented voters in Europe: an a priori voting power analysis of the 2004 elections for the European Parliament." *Homo Oeconomicus* 24: 485–500.
Pattanaik, P. K. and Xu, Y. (1990): "On ranking opportunity sets in terms of freedom of choice." *Recherches Economique de Louvain* 56, 383–90.
Pelkmans, J. (2007): "Mutual recognition in goods: on promises and disillusions." *Journal of European Public Policy* 14, 699–716.
Pelkmans, J. (2012): "Mutual recognition: rationale, logic and application in the EU internal goods market." In Behrens, P., Eger, T. and Schäfer, H.-B. (eds), *Ökonomische Analyse des Europarechts*. Tübingen: Mohr Siebeck, 341–65.
Penrose, L.S. (1946): "The elementary statistics of majority voting." *Journal of the Royal Statistical Society* 109, 53–7.
Schofield, N. (2009): *The Political Economy of Democracy and Tyranny*. Munich: Oldenbourg-Verlag.
Screpanti, E. (2006): "Progressive taxation and the distribution of freedom." *Metroeconomica* 57, 1–12.
Screpanti, E. (2009): "A quasi-natural measure of choice freedom for budget- and time-constrained opportunity sets." *Metroeconomica* 60, 715–23.

Sen, A. (1985): *Commodities and Capabilities*. Oxford: Oxford University Press.
Slomczynski, W. and Zyczkowski, K. (2006): "Penrose voting system and optimal quota." *Acta Physica Polonia* B 37, 3133–43.
Slomczynski, W. and Zyczkowski, K. (2007a): "From a toy model to the double square root voting system." *Homo Oeconomicus* 24, 381–99.
Slomczynski, W. and Zyczkowski, K. (2007b): "Jagiellonian compromise: an alternative voting system for the Council of the European Union," http://chaos.if.uj.edu.pl/~karol/pdf/JagCom07.pdf.
Smith, A. (1776–77): *An Inquiry into the Nature and Causes of the Wealth of Nations*, reprinted in Campbell, R.H. and Skinner, A.S. (eds), (1981) *Glasgow Edition of the Works and Correspondence of Adam Smith*, vol. II. Indianapolis: LibertyClassics.
Steunenberg, B. (2001): "Enlargement and institutional reform in the European Union: separate or connected issues?" *Constitutional Political Economy* 12, 351–70.
Tsakatika, M. (2008): *Political Responsibility and the European Union*. Manchester: Manchester University Press.
Wright, R. (1985): "Causation in tort law." *California Law Review* 73, 1735–1828.
Wright, R. (1988): "Causation, responsibility, risk, probability, naked statistics, and proof: pruning the bramble bush by clarifying the concept." *Iowa Law Review* 73, 1001–77.

4 Can member state liability for the infringement of European law deter national legislators?

*Hans-Bernd Schäfer**

1 INTRODUCTION

Legislative injustice originates when a legal norm does not conform to higher-ranking law, if the legislative body through its actions or lack of action has precipitated or extended an illegal condition. For most legal orders state liability for legislative injustice does not exist or it exists only in rare and exceptional cases. The most important exception to this is EC law. Through a series of wide-reaching decisions, the European Court of Justice (ECJ) established liability for harm in the case that a national law of a member state violates EC law and an individual's right is violated.[1]

The ECJ has justified its innovative decisions in particular to give full effect to European law.[2] It created an instrument for European citizens that should lead to a more effective implementation of EC law within the member states and provide incentives to legislators in the member states to conform to EC law. The focus of this chapter is to examine whether and to what extent this goal can be achieved by state liability for infringement of European law by legislators in member states.

The economic analysis of the incentives of liability for legislative acts of EU member states which violate superior law is undeveloped to date. Lee, who uses the concept of external effects, comes to an optimistic conclusion, which is however not supported by the reasoning in this chapter: "the temptation of national authorities to make decisions which benefit their own national economies at the expense of other Member States will be kept in check, and only those measures which are, on balance, beneficial for the Union

* The analytical part of the chapter is partly from a working paper "State Liability for Legislative Injustice" (2009) written in cooperation with Vincy Fon (George Washington University). I thank Thomas Eger, Michael Fehling, Friedrich Schoch Ariel Porat, Sharon Hannes and Michael Trebilcock for valuable comments. All errors are mine.

[1] W. Van Gerven, "Non-Contractual Liability of Member States, Community Institutions and Individuals for Breaches of Community Law with a View to a Common Law for Europe", 1 *M.J.* 6 (1994). W. Van Gerven, "Bridging the Unbridgeable: Community and National Tort Laws After *Francovich* and *Brasserie*," 45 *I.C.L.Q.* 507 (1996). For a comprehensive overview, see Peeka Aalto, *Public Liability in EU Law, Brasserie, Bergadern and Beyond*, Oxford: Hart Publishing (2011).

[2] "The Court argued that the full effectiveness of Community law would be impaired if individuals were unable to obtain redress when their rights were infringed by a Member State's breach of Community law. The ECJ found that in cases of infringement of directly effective Community law, the right to reparation [was] the necessary corollary of the direct effect." See M.G. Puder (2000) "Phantom Menace or New Hope: Member State Public Tort Liability After the Double-Bladed Light Saber Duel", 33 *Vand. J. Transnat'l L.* 311.

as a whole will be undertaken."[3] Cohen questioned such optimism in an earlier article on state liability, which however is not related to the problem of legislative injustice: "None the less the critical assumption behind such recommendations [of state liability] is that the government reacts to liability rules as a private actor would."[4] This observation, which Cohen related to wrongful acts of government officials, is even more important when the majority of a parliament makes the wrongful acts. Cohen goes even so far as to question the rationale of state liability in general: "We might better direct our efforts to designing effective 'political' markets instead of attempting to use economic signals to influence state and bureaucratic action."[5] Dari-Mattiacci et al. attribute different functions to state liability, but remain skeptical about the deterrence effects, as taxpayers have to pay and the principal and agent chains between them and the actors, whose behavior liability should improve, are too long.[6]

The economic analysis in this chapter is based on the insight that the models used in civil law to determine the liability for damages are not applicable. Firstly, parliaments are neither profit-maximizing companies nor utility-maximizing individuals. Rather the effect of liability on majority decisions in parliament must be analyzed on the basis of preferences of the members of Parliament. Secondly, this chapter operates on the premise that contrary to the models in civil liability, an efficiency analysis in terms of "wealth maximization" is not suitable. EU law is not based on the efficiency of allocation alone as an ethical maxim, but instead is based on a multitude of differing principles that are partially but not completely efficiency oriented. In an economic analysis of state liability for violating superior European law the question is not whether liability increases wealth but instead how suitable it is to help superior European law succeed and to eliminate unlawful national laws. Therefore, we are not talking about efficiency but about the effectiveness of liability in regard to the assertion of European law.

The chapter contains two main sections. Section 2 describes the judge-made liability rules for the infringement of European law, which might lead to damage awards if a law in a member state violates European law. Section 3 analyzes the effects of this form of liability on the voting behavior of members of national parliaments and asks whether the liability leads to fewer violations of European law by national laws of member states. The most important result of the study is the realization that the compensation for damages in the full amount of damages is not an optimal deterrence. The deterrence resulting from liability can fail, thus leaving the number of illegal national laws which violate European law unaffected. Ultimately, it can even lead to perverse incentives. The main observation

---

3 An exception is stated by Ian B. Lee (1999), "In Search of a Theory of State Liability in the European Union", The Jean Monnet Center International and Regional Economic Law and Justice, NYU, http://centers.law.nyu.edu/jeanmonnet/papers/99/990909.html. However this article does not go beyond the works of Calabresi and Posner in the 1970s. This would however lead to a wrong analysis, as the deterrence effects of state liability on the decisions of a parliament must be modeled in a different way as the liability of a utility-maximizing individual or a profit-maximizing firm.

4 D.S. Cohen (1990), "Regulating Regulators: The Legal Environment of the State," 40 *U. Toronto. L.J.* 213–70.

5 Ibid., p.270.

6 G. Dari-Mattiacci, Nuno Garoupa and F. Gomez-Pomar (2010), "State Liability", *European Review of Private Law*, 18 (4).

which drives this result is the fact that more state liability for the losers of national regulations which violate European law reduces civil engagement and lobbyism against such laws and consequently the costs for members of parliament to pass such laws.

2 MEMBER STATE LIABILITY FOR LEGISLATIVE INJUSTICE IN EC COUNTRIES

The EC treaty does not stipulate state liability when a member state violates EC law. The liability for legislative injustice has been created solely through judicial interpretation. In *Francovich and Bonifaci v. Italy* (1991),[7] the ECJ decided that a directive was not implemented in a timely manner by Italian legislators, triggering a claim for damages when an individual's rights are violated. The legal consequence is full compensation for damages, not an award below the actual damage suffered as often awarded under national state liability laws, which for example often does not cover lost profits. Moreover, liability is triggered by the violation of any individual right without any privilege of the right of private property over other rights.[8] The introduction of these liability rules by the ECJ is explicitly teleological. The laws of the EC should become "completely effective"[9] and liability for legislative injustice expressively serves this purpose.

An extension of *Francovic* is *Brasserie du Pêcheur*, in which a French brewery brought a claim against the German government. The company could not export its beer to Germany, as it did not comply with the purity requirements laid down by German law. In a 1987 judgment the European Court of Justice held that this prohibition was contrary to the principle of free movement of goods enshrined in the treaty.[10] The damage suffered by the plaintiff was, thus, caused by the import ban on beer not brewed according to German legal standards. The French company sought damages for losses of 1.8 million DM suffered between 1981 and 1987. If these damages had been granted, all other non-German producers of beer would have had strong incentives to claim similar compensation.[11] In the cases *Brasserie du Pêcheur v. Germany* (1996) and *Faktortame* (1996)[12] the ECJ decided that a law in a member state that violates EU treaties likewise triggers a claim for damages if the violation interferes with individual rights and the breach of EC law is "sufficiently serious." In *Brasserie du Pêcheur* liability was the consequence of a legislative *omission* (to uplift the import ban) and in *Factortame* of a legislative *act*. Jurisdiction has

---

[7] Cases C-6/90 and C-9/90, *Francovich and Bonifaci v. Italy* [1991] ECR I-5357.

[8] Nikolaou, Evangelos (2005), "From Francovich to Köbler and Beyond: The Evolution of a State Liability Regime for the European Community." LL.M. thesis, the University of Helsinki, https://oa.doria.fi/bitstream/handle/10024/2969/fromfran.pdf?sequence=2, R. Treinz Staatshaftung für Verletzungen primären Gemeinschaftsrechts durch die Bundesrepublik Deutschland, EuZW 1993, S. 599–605.

[9] *Francovich*, a.a.O.32

[10] Case 178/84, *Commission v. Germany* (1987) E.C.R. 1227 ('Reinheitsgebot').

[11] This section is taken from R. Van den Bergh and Hans-Bernd Schäfer (2000), "Member States Liability for Infringement of the Free Movement of Goods in the EC: An Economic Analysis," *Journal of Institutional and Theoretical Economics*, 156: 382–95.

[12] Joined cases C-46 and 48/93, *Brasserie du Pêcheur SA v. Germany* and *R. v. Secretary of State for Transport, ex parte Factortame Ltd. and others*, [1996] ECR I-1029.

been expanded to include flawed decisions made by members' courts that violate primary or secondary EC law. Since then, the ECJ has taken several decisions and refined state liability for the infringement of European law by the legislation of a member state: *British Telecom*,[13] *Hedley Lomas*[14] and *Dillenkofer*.[15]

In the case of *Köbler v. Austria* (2003), liability for legislative injustice was extended to court decisions in as far as they obviously infringe European law. This extension was motivated by the need to establish a liability rule which works equally in different member countries. As the same problem might be decided by the legislator in one member state and by courts in another member state, the exclusion of court decisions violating EC law would lead to different liability regimes in different countries.

Just as primary legal protection by way of an injunction is independent of the negligence of the legislator, so is the secondary legal protection by way of damage compensation. However, the issue of fault enters the law through the back door, because a violation of the law must be "sufficiently serious" to trigger liability. In the case of court decisions only an obvious violation triggers liability. Therewith courts can, for example, verify if the legislator in the member state was aware that the law clearly violated EC law and still passed it, if the legal situation was not clear, or if the violation against EC law as determined by the ECJ can be viewed as a surprising decision.[16] Important to determining the extent of the liability claim is that the ECJ allows the defense of comparative negligence. For example, whoever knowingly accepts an illegal state of affairs over years cannot later enforce his claim for full damages. The damage award can be reduced by a percentage.

These decisions of the ECJ were so far-reaching and expanded Community law so much into spheres which had been regarded as off limits that they caused angry critiques, especially from European governments. One scholar even called this a "quiet revolution." Especially Germany and Britain criticized the "judicial activism." The UK government even tried to initiate a change of the treaty and proposed that the member states should limit member state liability for breaches of EC law, however without avail. The UK was not alone but was far from securing the unanimous consent of all EU member states necessary to change the treaties. A more subtle but – at least in the short run – more effective reaction was the tendency of some national courts in EC member states to not adjust internal procedures to give the EC law the full effect, which makes a damage claim long, costly and uncertain. Even though the late transformation of EC directives is widespread and commonplace the number of cases until 1998 was quite low, generally less than five in Belgium, France, Germany, Ireland, Italy, the Netherlands, Sweden, and the UK and not even one in Austria, Denmark, Finland, Greece, Portugal, and Spain.[17] The dilatory

---

[13] Case C-392/93, *The Queen v. H. M. Treasury, ex parte British Telecommunications plc*, 1996 E.C.R. I-1631, [1996] 2 C.M.L.R. 217.

[14] Case C-5/94, *The Queen v. Ministry of Agriculture, Fisheries and Food, ex parte Hedley Lomas (Ireland) Ltd.*, 1996 E.C.R. I-2553, [1996] 2 C.M.L.R. 391.

[15] Joined Cases C-178/94, C-179/94, C-188/94, C-189/94 & C-190/94, *Dillenkofer v. Germany*, 1996 E.C.R.I-4845, [1996] 3 C.M.L.R. 469.

[16] D.J. Meltzer (2006), "Member State Liability in Europe and the United States," *I-CON*, 4 (1) 39–83, p. 47. Harlow, C., "*Francovich* and the Problem of the Disobedient State," 2 *E.L.J.* 199 (1996). Hervey, T.L., "*Francovich* Liability Simplified," 26 *Indust. L.J.* 74 (1997).

[17] J. Tallberg (2000), "The Anatomy of Autonomy: An Institutional Account of Variation in Supranational Influence." *JCMS: Journal of Common Market Studies*, 38 (5), 843–64.

attitude of some courts in member states led to reaction of the ECJ. In *Traghetti del Mediterraneo SpA*[18] the ECJ specified the conditions for member state liability and made especially clear that courts in member states cannot exclude liability.

3 ECONOMIC ANALYSIS OF THE DETERRENCE EFFECT OF STATE LIABILITY ON LEGISLATORS

The following analysis of member state liability assumes that a national legal norm has been struck down by the ECJ. It asks whether member state liability for any person whose rights were infringed leads to fewer new and eliminates more existing national legal norms which violate European law.

Typically – but not necessarily – the illegal laws are those catering to special interest groups. Such laws are always justified with public interest goals such as consumer protection, product safety, environmental protection or public health. In reality there is often a small advantage but the laws cut severely into the four freedoms as stipulated in the European treaties. They generate high profits for individual groups or economic sectors at the expense of the general public. The ECJ can strike down such laws, in particular when they violate the principle of proportionality.

The following analysis differs from the economic analysis of civil liability on two counts. First it models the behavior of legislators and not of profit-oriented companies or companies that minimize costs. Secondly, it is not about whether liability increases the wealth of a nation by increasing the efficiency of allocation. Instead the liability rule will be exclusively judged by whether the superior European law can assert itself more effectively against national law with member state liability than without.

This section is divided into two subsections. In the first subsection, it is assumed that superior law – the treaties, directives and regulations – cannot be modified. Based on this premise, it is examined how liability for legislative injustice influences the decision-making process of legislators. In the second subsection it is assumed that legislators can modify the superior law when they have to assume that the national law will otherwise be declared void and state liability is triggered therewith. This possibility to change superior law might also change the incentives for the legislator provided by the threat of liability.

First a single-chamber parliament is analyzed in which the majority of its members pass a law. The analysis first abstracts from the existence of parties that use party discipline to keep its members of parliament in line. It presupposes that every parliament member makes his decision based on his personal benefits from the enactment of the law. The chamber has n members (MPs). Every MP has a personal net advantage of $g_i (i = 1, 2, \ldots n)$ by the passing of a law. It can be either positive, zero or negative. This benefit arises from factors that can positively or negatively influence the re-election, extension of power, or career of the MP. All MPs are ranked in descending order according to their personal advantage that is achieved by the passing of the bill.

---

[18] Case C-140/09, *Fellimento Traghetti del Mediterraneo SpA v. Presidenza del Consiglio dei Ministri.*

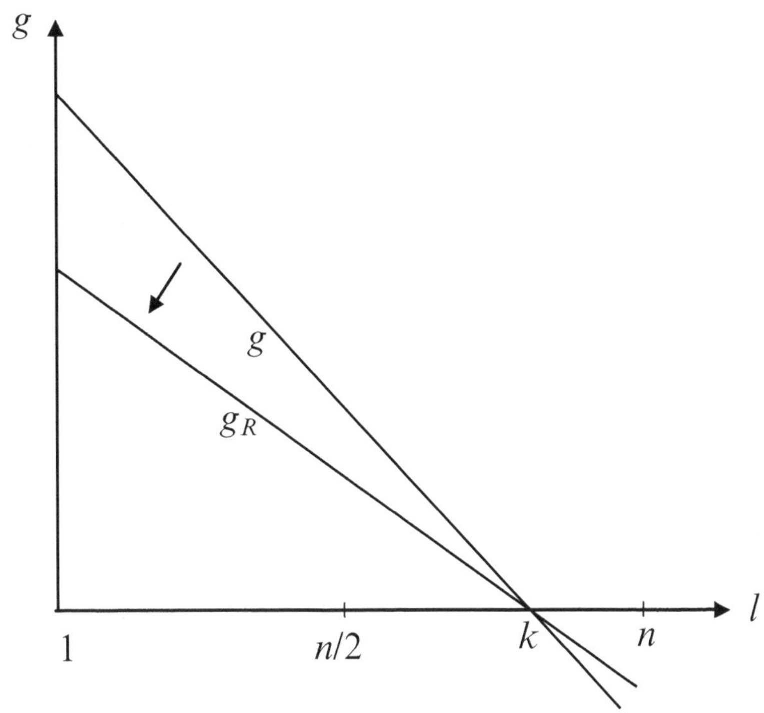

Figure 4.1 *Laws violating European law with and without jurisdiction of the ECJ*

This section works with the premise that the members of a national parliament or government have no influence on the superior European law, which therefore is assumed to be unchanging. First it is examined under which conditions a law which violates the European law is passed, if the ECJ had (counterfactually) no power to strike down national law. Then the voting behavior of the legislators is examined under the premise of judicial review without member state liability. State liability for legislative injustice is then examined as to whether it reduces the number of unconstitutional laws.

3.1 Legislation without Judicial Review or Member State Liability

The n members of parliament (MPs) are displayed on the horizontal l-axis of Figure 4.1 and the personal net gain of an MP is measured on the vertical axis. I represents the i-th MP starting with the first MP (I = 1). Since the legislators are ranked according to their personal net gains from the law, the first MP has the highest and the n-th MP the lowest personal net gain (g_i) from the proposed legislation. It is possible for MPs to have the same personal gain from the proposed legislation. For this reason $g(I)$ does not have to be strictly decreasing. To simplify the graph though, it is assumed that the personal net gain functions $g(I)$ are strictly decreasing.

This simplifying assumption implies that there is only one marginal MP with zero personal gain from the legislation (the k-th MP). Graphically, k is uniquely determined as the horizontal intercept of the personal net gain curve $g(I)$. For every MP who is ranked before k, the personal net gain is positive; these k MPs would vote for the proposed legislation. The remaining n–k MPs, those ranked after the k-th MP, have a personal loss and would vote against the legislation. Without courts to repeal illegal legislation and/or to determine if a law is illegal, the k MPs would vote for the law and the n–k MPs would vote against it. Therefore, k is the marginal voter for the proposed bill, when there is no court with the power to strike it down. For the bill to be passed, it is necessary and sufficient for k to be greater than $n/2$. In this case each bill that violates European law would be passed as if European law did not exist. Only the advantages from signaling and reputation could – as in international law – reverse this result. They are however outside the scope of this chapter.

3.2 Judicial Review by the European Court of Justice and Member State Liability

After a bill is passed, a citizen can bring a suit to the the ECJ for a judicial review. The court investigates whether the law violates European law. In that case the court repeals the law ex nunc.

Now consider the impact of judicial review on the voting behavior of the MPs if no liability exists. Although the MPs know that the ECJ would likely declare the bill invalid eventually, they also know that it will often take years for the Court to reach a decision. This implies that the gains (losses) from the legislation are not likely to become zero. The number of periods of personal gains or losses is reduced as a consequence of judicial review. It is reasonable to assume that if an MP enjoys a personal net gain (loss) in one period from the special legislation, the MP remains a gainer (loser) in other periods as well. That the total private net gain (loss) from the legislation will end after the legislation is declared a violation of EC law means that the private gain (loss) for every MP from the special interest legislation is smaller than when there is no judicial review.

Specifically, for each of the MPs ranked before the marginal k-th voter, the personal net gain remains positive though smaller than in the case without judicial review. The MP continues to vote for the bill. For each initial detractor of the proposed bill who suffers personal net losses without judicial review the loss is also reduced with judicial review, but a loss remains. This MP continues to vote against the bill. Thus, with the additional constraint of judicial review, there is – under this condition – no change in the voting behavior among the MPs. Graphically, judicial review induces a counter-clockwise rotation of the personal net gain curve g (without judicial review) around the horizontal intercept at k. In Figure 4.1, g_r represents the personal net gain curve for the legislation with judicial review. As long as gainers from the special legislation without judicial review remain gainers for a certain number of periods until the judicial review has found the legislation unconstitutional, the voting behavior in parliament does not change with the introduction of judicial review.

The unchanged voting behavior of MPs derives from the assumption that judicial review reduces the gains and losses from voting for the bill but does not reverse gains into losses and vice versa. Each winner from the legislation will remain a winner and each loser will remain a loser.

This outcome is however not necessary. The power of the court to strike down national legislation weakens civil engagement and lobbyism of potential losers against a law that infringes European law, as it might be less costly to go to court after the law was passed than to fight politically against the law. This would reduce the loss – or increase the gain – for an MP from an unconstitutional law, as the pressure group influence on him weakens. If this effect of judicial review is higher than the effect from the reduction of benefits from the legislation, it becomes unclear what the effect on the net gain of the MP is. Even a perverse effect might result. Some MPs who would vote against the law without judicial review might be for it with judicial review. Only if this perverse effect can be disregarded will the introduction of judicial review have either no or – via the reputation mechanism – a desired deterrence effect.

3.3 Unconstitutional Bills with Judicial Review and State Liability

Liability leads to more frequent litigation, because the claimant can not only block the encroachment of the state on his rights, but can also sue for damages. The expected gain from a legal action is higher with judicial review plus damage compensation than without a damage claim. The number of claims against the state will increase. With the damage award the courts will eliminate more illegal bills than without. However, by the same token lobbyism and civil engagement against unconstitutional laws will be discouraged. The net effect on the number of laws in member states and their undesired effects that violate European law is not clear.

How does state liability for laws in member states which infringe European law influence the voting behavior of members of parliament? Does it lead to fewer unconstitutional bills of member state countries? In the following section we assume that

- each MP knows that the bill violates European law;
- the state whose parliament passed the bill is liable in damages. This compensation for damages will have to be borne by the state whose parliament has caused the damage. The total budget of the state will then be reduced if the tax rate remains constant.

Liability impacts the personal gains of members of parliament (g_i) from passing the bill in two ways.

The total budget of the state will be reduced and the budget constraint for the parliament tightens as a consequence of state liability. Every member of the parliament knows that the tightened budget imposes a private cost on him, regardless of whether he had a large or a small private gain or even a personal loss from the unconstitutional legislation.[19]

The reduction of governmental services is not the only effect of liability in comparison to no state liability. When citizens that were damaged by the unconstitutional bill are compensated for losses, they are less motivated to try to prevent an unconstitutional law from being enacted and to use their political clout to prevent that. The introduction of

[19] Alternatively one can assume that taxes are increased, which would again impose a loss on every MP, because the taxes do not result in better government services.

liability could even lead to the paradoxical reaction of legislators voting for an unconstitutional bill which would not receive a majority otherwise. The legislator knows that no one will protest too loudly in his district, because the losers from the bill know that they will be compensated for their loss if an unconstitutional bill is passed. This effect may be possibly larger than the losses that members of parliament suffer from the reduction of governmental services as a consequence of liability. Paradoxically the introduction of state liability for legislative injustice could even increase the number of legislators that vote for an unconstitutional bill.

In contrast to a situation in which the ECJ can strike down unconstitutional bills but not award damages, the changes in voting behavior are therefore based on two factors:

(1) the reduction of governmental services at a constant tax rate either maintains or reduces the gain for each legislator from an unconstitutional bill;
(2) the compensation for damages increases the gain for some of the legislators from the unconstitutional bill and does not reduce the gain for any of legislators because civil engagement and pressure groups are weakened.

Therefore it is doubtful that liability for legislative injustices always shifts the gain curve $g(I)$ downwards and ensures therewith that some of those legislators that would vote for the bill without liability change their preferences with liability and vote against the bill.

3.3.1 Liability increases the number of legislators that vote for an unconstitutional bill

Here is a vivid example. Lawmakers decide on a licensing provision that – until it is repealed by the court – leads to monopoly prices for privileged insiders. We assume that without the threat of liability claims, there is no majority for the bill because political pressure against the bill is high. If potential competitors are awarded full compensation for damages resulting from being disadvantaged, the number of legislators that plan on voting for the bill can actually increase. Those who are disadvantaged might not exercise their political clout against the bill, because they expect full compensation. When only a handful of legislators will support the draft because of the reduced pressure from those disadvantaged by it, liability might cause the law to be passed, when it would not have been passed without liability. Therefore it is possible that a bill which violates superior law receives more votes under state liability than if the same bill were only subject to judicial review without state liability. Liability creates a perverse incentive in this constellation.

3.3.2 Liability decreases the number of legislators that vote for the unconstitutional bill

If one disregards these perverse effects, the marginal k-th MP and possibly some MPs who gain without state liability may now turn losers under the threat of state liability if they vote for the bill. These MPs are likely to be the voters with only a small gain from the legislation which violates EU law if no liability exists. With judicial review but no state liability they would gain from the bill; with state liability they become losers if they still vote for the bill and winners if they vote against the bill. Some legislators who under a system without liability would have voted for legislative injustice now vote against the bill.

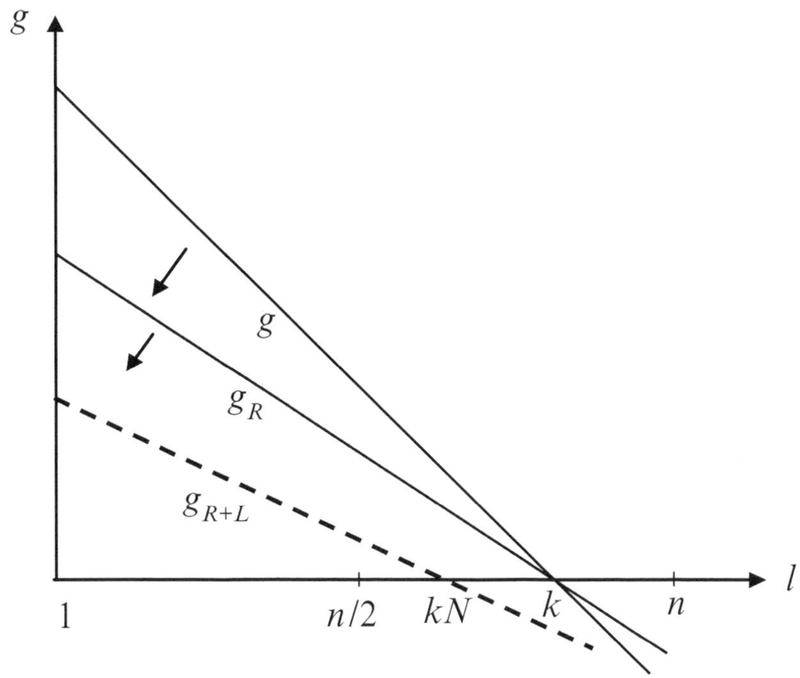

Figure 4.2 Judicial review and member state liability

Graphically, this implies a shift of the profit curve $g(l)$ g_r to g_r+_l, in which $r+l$ represents a legal system under which the court can repeal the illegal law as well as force the state whose parliament enacted it to pay damages. It is important to note that the damage award must not lead to the same personal loss for every legislator. Therefore the curve g_r+_l does not preserve the ranking of legislators like curve g and g_r. The curve g_r does not shift parallel to the bottom because of liability. The points of the new curve g_r+_l in Figure 4.2, however, must be either lower than the old (g_r) for each point or at least at the same value.

Some legislators who would have voted for the bill without liability now reject it. When one designates the new marginal voter in parliament as kN and $k\text{N}<k$, then the number of legislators that oppose the draft of the bill increases by $k-k$N.

In Figure 4.2 kN is larger than $n/2$. In that case the bill which violates European law continues to garner majority support in spite of the threat of liability for the state. However, when kN is smaller than $n/2$, then the bill will lack majority support and the threat of liability stops the bill. It is possible that some unconstitutional bills with a slight majority vote without state liability will not gain majority approval with state liability. In general, the introduction of liability for legislative injustice cannot completely stop the enactment of illegal laws.

Proposition 1 Member state liability for the infringement of European law increases the expected gains for the claimant from a lawsuit against the government. It increases the number of lawsuits and more unconstitutional laws will be repealed.

Proposition 2 *Member state liability for the infringement of European law can either increase, decrease or keep constant the net gain of a legislator from the enactment of a law which violates EC law. The same holds for the number of legislators that vote for such a bill. This can either change or maintain the majorities in parliament. Therefore the relevance and even the direction of the effect of member state liability on the number of laws violating EC law is unpredictable.*

3.4 Member State Liability with Legal Uncertainty

Up until now the presumption was made that members of parliament are aware of the legal or illegal status of the draft in question. This is not always the case. Often members of parliament do not and cannot know if they are enacting an illegal law, because only after a lengthy procedure will the courts decide on the matter. Until then the legal status of the law remains unclear.

When this happens, we assume that each MP assigns the same positive probability to the event that the bill be judged as constitutional (q) or unconstitutional ($1-q$). The expected gain for each MP is then the probability weighted average of his net gain (g_1) if the law does not violate European law and his net gain (g_2) if the bill violates European law.

This leads to the following observation.

For some legislators the bill causes a positive expected gain and for others a loss, independent of whether it violates EC law. There is no effect of liability on the voting of these legislators.

For some MPs however the bill causes a gain if it is in line with the constitution but a loss under legal uncertainty. Therefore these MPs would vote for the bill if it clearly would not violate European law and vote against it under the condition of legal uncertainty. Only for this group of MPs can liability serve as a deterrence mechanism.

An MP belonging to this group will be deterred by the liability threat, when the expected losses from an illegal law $(g_{2,r+l})(1 - q) < 0$ are higher than the expected gains from a law that does not violate European law $(g_{1,r+l})q > 0$. The indices *1, 2* denote "violating European law" and "not violating European law", or

$$(g_{2,r+l})(1 - q) + (g_{1,r+l})q < 0.$$

Liability for legislative injustice with legal uncertainty works as a deterrent if for more than $k-n/2$ MPs this condition holds. In all other cases it does not have any effect.

With legal uncertainty for the legislator the deterrence effect – if there is one – decreases with the probability that the law does not violate European law and is always smaller than under legal certainty; that is, when the MPs know that the bill is illegal.

In turn it is not possible to say what the deterrence effect for state liability is. It increases with the probability that judicial review strikes down the law ($1-q$) and the losses that the MP would expect to suffer in the event that the bill in a member state which violates EC law would be enacted. This result does not even take into account the possibility of perverse effects.

4 RELAXING ASSUMPTIONS

4.1 Political Parties and a Two-chamber System

The previous analysis assumed autonomous decision-making powers of MPs and a one-chamber system. What changes without these two assumptions?

In a party system like in Europe, MPs vote according to the party line. Thereby the analysis is transferred from parliament to the party fraction. In a two-party system the draft of the bill must gain the majority of the votes within the governing fraction. The marginal voter, whose gain from the legislation is zero must have a ranking that lies over half of the fraction members. Therewith the analysis remains basically the same and does not change the results.

In a multiple party system the draft must receive the majority in every governing fraction. The analysis remains the same. The result changes in that the deterrence of liability for legislative injustice only needs to work for members of one of the fractions to prevent the bill from being enacted. In a ruling coalition the likelihood of deterrence therefore increases with the number of parties which form the coalition.

The same holds true for a two-chamber system when the bill requires the approval of both chambers. Deterrence only needs to work in one chamber in order to prevent the bill from becoming law.

If one regards perverse effects of liability as an exception it is likely that the deterrence effect of liability increases with the number of parties supporting the government and with the number of chambers which the bill has to pass.

4.2 State Liability with the Possibility to Change Superior Law

So far we have assumed that a decision of the court to uplift a law and to grant damage compensation for legislative injustice has no effect on legislative activity. Legislators make no attempt to change the superior law. This leads to reduced governmental services or the increase of taxes. However the incentives of member state liability change when the legislator can change the constitutional law, e.g. by changing the European treaties.

A court with the power to repeal laws and even grant damage compensation for legislative injustice must therefore be prepared for its decisions to be counteracted by parliament through fresh legislation and in the case of the EU through changing the treaty or secondary law. The treaty can only be modified unanimously. In each country there must be a majority in the national parliament to change the treaty to counteract the decision of the ECJ. Major changes even require a referendum in some member states. This is extremely unlikely and most probably only hypothetical. Unlike a national constitutional court, the ECJ hardly has to worry about its decisions being overturned by fresh legislation when they are based on the treaties.

It might be easier to change European secondary law, because the Lisbon treaty introduced more majority decisions in the European Council, which finally decides on regulations and directives. However the co-decision procedure makes most secondary law dependent not only on a vote of the European Council but also on the European Parliament, which is another hurdle and makes fresh legislation again less likely.[20] A formal aspect is also important. Neither the European Parliament nor the European Council is entitled to initiate fresh legislation. Only the Commission has the proposal right. This might not rule out initiatives from member countries, but any of them has to get support by the Commission for a formal initiative to change the law.

5 CONCLUSION

The effect of member state liability for the infringement of European law on the decision making of member state parliaments is unambiguous neither in its relevance nor even in its direction. Liability can provide incentives to pass fewer or more bills which violate European law or to delay the transformation of European law into national law. Liability can lead to more laws in member states which violate European law as the victims of such laws have fewer incentives for civil engagement and lobbyism and might put less pressure on the legislator to avoid enacting such laws. Then the introduction of liability would have undesirable consequences. Even if such an effect is excluded, liability can remain ineffective if it does not lead to a change in the preferences of a sufficiently large number of MPs and a change of the majority. Theoretical reasoning on the effect of member state liability for the infringement of EC law therefore does not lead to the result that member state liability for infringement of EC law leads to a full effect of European law.

20 S. Hagemann and B. Hoyland (2010), "Bicameral Politics in the European Union," *Journal of Common Market Studies*, 48 (4) 811–33.

5 Subsidiarity for a changing union

Emanuela Carbonara, Barbara Luppi and Francesco Parisi

1 THE SUBSIDIARITY PRINCIPLE

While the concept of subsidiarity reached political prominence in the twentieth century, it is as "old as European political thought" (Carrozza, 2003, p. 38). According to Millon-Delsol (1992), the concept of subsidiarity can be traced back to classical Greece. In *Politics*, Aristotle conceived of society as an interconnected system of associations, with each association required to perform specific tasks and provide for its own needs.[1] In the middle ages, Thomas Aquinas renewed the concept of subsidiarity in *Summa Theologica* (1274). Aquinas and subsequent authors of the medieval scholasticism school viewed subsidiarity as being built upwards from the person and his autonomy. Subsidiarity was, therefore, the ordinating principle of the relationships between communities in society. Each community (for example, a family) should be allowed to contribute to the public good without interference from other communities or their ruling institutions and, at the same time, receive aid when it needs it.

Politicians and political theorists such as Althusius, Montesquieu, Locke, Tocqueville and Abraham Lincoln have used the concept of subsidiarity in their work (Carozza, 2003). In the nineteenth century, political theorists invoked the concept of subsidiarity as a balancing criterion to bridge the opposing aspirations of those who advocated for decentralized markets and those who believed in centralized planning.[2] Subsidiarity offered a viable criterion to avoid the totalitarian solutions advocated by those two extreme views of society. The Catholic Church renewed its interest in the idea of subsidiarity and started applying the concept to social life in the latter part of the nineteenth century. In 1891, Pope Leo XIII included the subsidiarity principle in his encyclical "*Rerum Novarum*," claiming that:

> Whenever the general interest or any particular class suffers, or is threatened with harm, which can in no other way be met or prevented, the public authority must step in to deal with it

and the intervention's limits

> must be determined by the nature of the occasion which calls for the law's interference – the principle being that the law must not undertake more, nor proceed further, than is required for the remedy of the evil or the removal of the mischief. (Leo XIII, 1891, pp. 250–51)

[1] See Millon-Delsol (1992, pp. 18–30, 37–47) for a comprehensive history of the emergence and development of the concept of subsidiarity.

[2] Subsidiarity was viewed as an instrument to limit the irreversible process of progressive centralization, known as Popitz's law (Popitz, 1927).

The idea of subsidiarity evolved significantly into a political principle in the late 1930s. In the encyclical "*Quadragesimo Anno*" (1931), Pius XI wrote:

> The supreme authority of the State ought, therefore, to let subordinate groups handle matters and concerns of lesser importance, which would otherwise dissipate its efforts greatly. Thereby the State will more freely, powerfully and effectively do all those things that belong to it alone because it alone can do them: directing, watching, urging, restraining, as occasion requires and necessity demands. Therefore, those in power should be sure that the more perfectly a graduated order is kept among the various associations, in observance of the principle of "subsidiarity function" . . . the more faithfully this subsidiarity principle function is followed and a graded hierarchical order exists among the various associations, the greater also will be both social authority and social efficiency, and the happier and more prosperous too will be the condition of commonwealth.

Pius XI emphasized the importance of non-interference of the state. He argued that civil society should attempt to reach a cooperative balance with the state, provided that limits are set on centralized authority and various social groups are protected from the state's failures. Pius XI's reformulation served as a starting point for the subsequent applications of the subsidiarity principle.

The principle of subsidiarity gained increasing political and legal prominence when the European Union adopted it as one of its central constitutional principles. The following section provides a brief history of events leading to the adoption of subsidiarity as a constitutional principle of the European Union in the Maastricht Treaty in 1992.

2 SUBSIDIARITY AS A CONSTITUTIONAL PRINCIPLE OF THE EUROPEAN UNION[3]

Federal governments and unions of states face the fundamental task of allocating the creation and enforcement of policy to either federal (central) government or local governments. Within the European Union (EU), subsidiarity is intended to prescribe the allocation of competences at the central (European Union) or local (member states) level and to 'balance' the European Union's powers at the central level with the member states' powers at the local level.

Prior to recognition of the subsidiarity principle, the distribution of powers between the Community and the member states represented one of the most delicate and contentious political issues in the European Union. Since the creation of the European Economic Community in 1958, member states' political actors were critical of what they perceived to be an irreversible process of centralization of competences at the Community level. Although, in theory, the transfer of competences from member states to the Community could only take place through conferral within the limits of the competences conferred by the member states to attain the Community objectives set out in Articles 2 and 3 of the

---

[3] For a more extensive historical and legal analysis of the principle of subsidiarity, see Carbonara et al. (2009). For a study of the European Union from a comparative and constitutional perspective of federalism, see Vibert (1995), Wechsler (1954), Weiler (1985, 1991) and Weiler and Trachtman (1996).

1958 Treaty of Rome (i.e. the creation of a common market and the harmonization of related policies), competences were often reallocated outside the original scope as a result of political considerations. Everling (1997) and Carbonara et al. (2009) provide a number of examples of reallocation of competences that were hardly warranted by the original treaty provisions, ranging from aids or levies to regulation of product quality and special monetary systems. Political pressures towards centralization found little constraint from within the Community laws and procedures.[4]

The 1986 Single European Act expanded the scope of the Community action to new fields (such as research, finance, economic convergence, social policy and the environment) and raised the member states' concerns about new waves of centralization. Several intergovernmental conferences addressed these concerns and eventually laid the foundations for the Maastricht Treaty, redefining the boundaries of the enlarged political, economic and monetary union. The member states' concerns were addressed in these intergovernmental conferences with a discussion of possible rules that could provide a more effective constraint to new centralization proposals. Among these rules, subsidiarity played an important role as a potential constraint against unwarranted centralization. The subsidiarity principle was formally adopted in 1992 by the Treaty of the European Union (Treaty of Maastricht, signed on 7 February 1992, entered into force on 1 November 1993). The December 1992 Edinburgh summit further stressed the critical role of subsidiarity, requiring all institutions of the Union to use a test of subsidiarity as a condition precedent to their policy action, giving the European Court of Justice the role of guidance and adjudication to ensure compliance with subsidiarity.[5]

The subsidiarity principle is currently included in Article 5 of the consolidated version of the Treaty Establishing the European Community, which states:

> The Community shall act within the limits of the powers conferred upon it by this Treaty and of the objectives assigned to it therein. In areas which do not fall within its exclusive competence, the Community shall take action, in accordance with the principle of subsidiarity, only if and in so far as the objectives of the proposed action cannot be sufficiently achieved by the Member States and can therefore, by reason of the scale or effects of the proposed action, be better achieved by the Community. Any action by the Community shall not go beyond what is necessary to achieve the objectives of this Treaty.

The subsidiarity principle also plays a prominent role in the draft of the proposed European Constitution, under Article 9, which states that the principles of subsidiarity and proportionality govern the use of Union competences. Paragraph 3 of Article 9 further specifies that

> under the principle of subsidiarity, in areas which do not fall within its exclusive competence the Union shall act only if and insofar as the objectives of the intended action cannot be sufficiently achieved by the Member States, either at central level or at regional and local level, but can rather, by reason of the scale or effects of the proposed action, be better achieved at Union level.

---

[4] Article 308 of the EC Treaty allowed the Council to self-authorize reallocations of competences based on its own determination of whether those competences were necessary to achieve one of the Community's objectives.

[5] For an account of the instrumental and political use of subsidiarity as a political banner to assuage the concerns of the Euro-skeptics, see Bermann (1994, p. 332) and Marquardt (1994).

Despite the prominence of subsidiarity in the European constitutional framework, the European Union has struggled with the interpretation and implementation of this principle. At the 1992 Edinburgh Summit, the European Council provided some clarification of the meaning and modes of application of subsidiarity, specifying that action at the central level should be carried out only upon evidence of clear benefits of scale or effectiveness compared with the independent action of member states. In that context, the Council further stressed that the European Union's centralization decisions should be supported by qualitative or quantitative analyses showing the comparative advantage of the Union in carrying out specified competences (Marquardt, 1994). As pointed out by Estella (2002, p. 103), Provision 3 of the Protocol 30 annexed to the European Union Treaty reinforced the legal dimension and binding force of the subsidiarity principle as a dynamic principle regulating the exercise of competences already attributed to the Community, allowing action to be taken or restricted according to the evolution of circumstances. The reference to cost–benefit analysis and to the dynamic nature of subsidiarity created more questions than answers. Despite various attempts to clarify the meaning of comparative advantage in the context of subsidiarity, the implementation of the subsidiarity principle remains obscure and in need of formal guidelines in the opinion of both scholars and policymakers. As van den Bergh (1997) points out, the existing legal guidelines lack formalization and leave skeptism regarding the subsidiarity test's real utility in providing an effective constraint on centralization.[6] Absent a formalization of the subsidiarity test, the European Court of Justice faces unavoidable difficulties in assessing the qualitative and qualitative merits of a case on the ground of subsidiarity in a substantive judgment.[7]

Subsidiarity is also one of the key concepts of the 2009 Treaty of Lisbon, which implements an *early warning system*, enabling national parliaments to vigilate on the correct application of the subsidiarity principle. According to the early warning system, national parliaments can file objections if they believe that EU legal initiatives violate the subsidiarity principle. If the majority of national parliaments agree on the violation and the Commission does not change the proposed law, the European Parliament and the Council could terminate its consideration, on the grounds of breach of subsidiarity (see Kiiver, 2008). Such procedure undoubtedly strengthens the role of subsidiarity in the European Union and is designed to limit the danger of excessive centralization. However, when it comes to the definition of subsidiarity, the Lisbon Treaty still refers to Article 5 of the Treaty of Maastricht and sheds no further light on the possible formulation of a viable subsidiarity test. As such, the Lisbon Treaty seems to suffer from the same limitations that affected the failed Constitution.

---

[6] As pointed out by van den Bergh (1997): "Because law on its own does not provide sufficiently accurate and reliable standards for evaluating the effects of legal rules, economic theory must be incorporated into the legal analysis. . . . The wording of Article 5(2) itself invites an economic analysis: to justify the exercise of powers by European Community institutions 'the scale or effects of the proposed action' must be taken into account. This formulation allows for the consideration of scale economies and externalities; both factors are powerful efficiency arguments in favor of centralization."

[7] Provision 13 of Protocol 30 of ECT states that "compliance with the principle of subsidiarity shall be reviewed in accordance with the rules laid down by the Treaty". The European Court of Justice therefore plays a critical role bearing the responsability of "ensuring that in the interpretation and application of the EC Treaty the law is observed." EC Treaty, art. 164.

In the following section, we will survey the existing economic models of subsidiarity and examine the extent to which these formalizations may provide a valuable guidance for the implementation of the subsidiarity test and for the understanding of the limits of subsidiarity as a principled constraint on centralization.

3 ECONOMIC MODELS OF SUBSIDIARITY

The subsidiarity principle's underlying rationale lies in the fundamental principle of constitutional design: competences should be allocated to the level of government that can best exercise them. The efficiency with which a level of government can carry out a given competence determines its fitness under the subsidiarity principle. The idea of allocating competences on the basis of a test of efficiency is not novel. For example, Tiebout (1956) characterized the economic conditions needed for efficient provision of public goods by a decentralized federal government. Bewley (1981) formalized Tiebout's insights, pointing out the impact of interregional (or interjurisdictional) spillovers on the efficiency of a decentralized federal government. In the presence of economic interdependencies across regions (or jurisdictions) and free mobility of citizens, the provision of public goods at the local level may be inefficient due to a high level of competition across regions. A number of authors have examined the impact of federalism on the efficient provision of a public good by an elected central planner in the presence of interjurisdictional spillovers.[8]

The subsidiarity principle tackles the fundamental question of allocation of competences between federal governments relative to their comparative advantage in carrying out such competences. Centralization is warranted only if it is allowed to capture efficiencies beyond what member states or individuals could achieve by acting at the local level.[9] According to Inman and Rubinfeld (1998, p. 545),

> subsidiarity is a principle of governance designed to give meaning to the divisions of power and responsibility between the central government and constituent states in a federal system. The principle seeks to allocate responsibilities for policy formation and implementation to the lowest level of government at which the objectives of that policy can be successfully achieved.

Inman and Rubinfeld (1997) identify three alternative concepts of federalism: centralized federalism, decentralized federalism and democratic federalism. Efficient allocation of power is the hallmark of economic federalism analysis.[10] The overarching principle

---

8 See Oates (1999) for an extensive discussion on federalism, Musgrave (1997) on the efficiency of federalism in the presence of fiscal competition and Feldstein (1997) for an application to the monetary union. More generally, see Pelkmans (2006) for a practical proposal for the implementation of the subsidiarity test.

9 See Edwards (1996), Flaherty and Lally-Green (1996), Tabellini (2002) and Alesina and Wacziarg (1999) for the legal and economic debate on the subsidiarity principle.

10 See also Inman and Rubinfeld (2002). For additional economic analysis of federalism from a public choice, game theoretical and political economy perspective, see Tullock (1969), Breton and Scott (1978), Cooter and Drexl (1994), Frey and Eichenberg (1996), Besley and Coate (1997), La Porta et al. (1999), Schmid-Lübbert and Schäfer (2003), Sinn (1994) and Streit and Mussler (1994), Vaubel (1994a, 1994b). For a textbook survey of additional legal material see Stephan et al. (2003).

"prefers the most decentralized structure of government capable of internalizing all economic externalities" (Inman and Rubinfeld, 1997, p. 45). Only when two governments can provide services with the same efficiency will economic federalism consider other factors like political participation or protection of individual rights. As Oates (1972) formulized, the central government provides for those public services distinguished by significant externalities involving spatially dispersed population, while local governments provide those public services for which such spillovers are limited or absent. The principle of economic federalism assigns power to the central government when competiton between jurisdictions produces inefficiencies.

As Inman and Rubinfeld point out, for most economists a strong central government is the default choice to achieve efficiency. However, the principle conceived in such a narrow way has had limited success in achieving efficiency. "The primary weakness of the principle of economic federalism has been to advocate the central government as the only institution best able to provide pure public goods and correct interjurisdictional externalities" (Inman and Rubinfeld, 1997, pp. 47–8).

The federalism concepts proposed by Inman and Rubinfeld (1997) can be formalized into three alternative forms of subsidiarity tests. The subsidiarity test can be carried out directly by the central government ("centralized subsidiarity test") or individually by member states under a unanimity rule ("decentralized subsidiarity test") or majority rule ("democratic subsidiarity test").

In this section, we apply a formalization of the subsidiarity test to a situation in which central and local governments are trying to decide whether to reallocate some governmental functions from the local to the central level. The subsidiarity test evaluates the benefits and the costs of reallocating a given activity from local to central governments. In a simplified economic framework, the test consists of applying a cost–benefit analysis to assess the optimal level of allocation of a given activity.

Consider a Union constituted by N member states, which plans to centralize k activities (or policy functions). In the case where the governmental activities remain allocated at the local (or member state) level, the country i in the Union chooses a level of public good denoted by g_i^{*L} associated with a welfare level equal to $W_i(g_i^{*L})$. If the policy functions are allocated at the central (or Union) level, each country i in the Union will receive a level of public good denoted by g^{*C} (decided at the Union level), with an associated level of welfare equal to $W_i(g_i^{*L})$.

The formalization of the subsidiarity test is illuminating because outcomes are likely to differ under the three forms of the test in the presence of heterogeneity of preferences across the states.

First, centralized or economic federalism "prefers the most decentralized structure of government capable of internalizing all economic externalities, subject to the constitutional constraint that all central government policies be decided by an elected or appointed 'central planner'" (Inman and Rubinfeld, 1997, p. 45). The case of centralized federalism can be regarded as a test of centralized subsidiarity, where the test is performed at the central level.

Analytically, the subsidiarity test can be written as follows:

$$W^U(g^{*C}) \geq \sum_{i=1}^{N} W_i(g_i^{*L}).$$

According to the centralized test of subsidiarity, centralization will be implemented only when the aggregate welfare of the Union improves; i.e. when the welfare of the Union associated with a level of governmental activity g^{*C} decided at the central level is higher than the sum of the welfare of the single member state at the local level of governmental activity g_i^{*L} independently chosen at the country level.

It is important to note that the centralized test of subsidiarity does not take into account the individual welfare of member states pre- or post-centralization. On the contrary, it evalutes only aggregate welfare, which implies that a single member state could be worse off under centralization. Nonetheless, the subsidiarity test would be passed and centralization would occur if the aggregate welfare of the Union improves.

Inman and Rubinfeld (1997) identified the so-called "cooperative federalism" or decentralized federalism as the second form of federalism, according to which all policy functions are initially allocated at the local level and the member states must choose whether to transfer a bundle of the governmental competences to a central government. This principle "prefers the most decentralized structure of government capable of internalizing all economic externalities, subject to the constitutional constraint that all central government policies are agreed to unanimously by the elected representatives for each of the lower-tier governments" (Inman and Rubinfeld, 1997, p. 48).

Member states perform the test associated with a decentralized federalism at the local level and require unanimous consent of all member states in the Union for centralization to occur.[11]

The decentralized subsidiarity test for country i takes the following form:

$$W_i(g^{*C}) \geq W_i(g_i^{*L})$$

and centralization will take place only under the requirement that the subsidiarity test has been satisfied for each member state in the Union, i.e. for $i = 1, \ldots, N$. Under this so-called unanimity rule, the subsidiarity test has to be passed by all member states, i.e. for all $i = 1, \ldots, N$, otherwise the competences will be kept at the local level.

The subsidiarity test may require a majority rule instead of unanimity. In Inman and Rubinfeld (1997), "democratic federalism" allocates powers among the various levels of government on the basis of a majority rule.

Democratic federalism prefers "the most decentralized structure of government capable of internalizing all economic externalities, subject to the constitutional constraint that all central government policies are agreed to by a simple (51 percent) majority of elected representatives from lower-tier governments" (Inman and Rubinfeld, 1997, p. 50).

The democratic subsidiarity test must be satisfied for the majority of member states in order to obtain a majority vote in favor of centralization. Under the median voter theorem (Downs, 1957), the subsidiarity test should take into consideration the median

[11] As pointed out by Carbonara et al. (2009), the "early warning mechanism" proposed by the European Commission on 10 May 2006 represents a move towards a form of unanimity or decentralized federalism. This mechanism would render national parliaments "subsidiarity watchdogs," by allowing them to raise objections to EU legislative proposals on grounds of subsidiarity. See also Cooper (2006).

member state (denoted with m). The democratic subsidiarity test takes the following form:

$$W_m(g^{*C}) \geq W_m(g_m^{*L})$$

Centralization will occur only if the welfare of the median member state is higher when the competences are allocated at the central level rather than at the member state level.

Each subsidiarity test may have a different impact on the process of centralization and the optimal allocation of competences. The three tests can serve in an economic model of federalism to illustrate the process of progressive centralization triggered by these principles.

As shown by Carbonara et al. (2009), the practical effects of the alternative forms of subsidiarity on the degree of centralization decision depend on the distribution of preferences across member states in the Union. In the presence of the states' heterogeneity of preferences, outcomes under the decentralized subsidiarity test may differ from those reached under the centralized test. The centralized subsidiarity test passes every time the decentralized subsidiarity test is satisfied for all member states. Intuitively, if centralization improves each country's welfare in the Union, then it must be true that the aggregate benefits outweigh the aggregate costs of centralization. Note however that the opposite is not necessarily true. Satisfaction of the centralized subsidiarity test does not necessarily imply satisfaction of the subsidiarity test at the country level for all member states.

The democratic subsidiarity test may conflict in some situations with the centralized subsidiarity test. The satisfaction of the centralized subsidiarity test does not imply satisfaction of the democratic subsidiarity test in the presence of a skewed distribution of preferences. Given that centralization will occur if the subsidiarity test is satisfied for the median member state, manipulation of the cost and benefit of centralization for the median state can have important effects. Alternative cost-sharing rules do not yield the same centralization decision because they may have different effects on the placement of the median state's preferences. As shown by Carbonara et al. (2009), a decentralized subsidiarity test leads to less centralization than the other two forms of subsidiarity. Instead, the effects of centralized and democratic subsidiarity on the equilibrium level of centralization vary according to the placement of the median state's preferences relative to the average preferences of all states.

4 SUBSIDIARITY FOR A CHANGING UNION

Recent economic and legal literature examines extensively the idea of subsidiarity as an instrument for achieving an optimal level of centralization of policy responsibilities. A number of economic works investigate how the subsidiarity principle could be formalized to provide a practical guideline for governmental action. The law and economics literature focuses on the trade-offs between the costs and benefits of centralization (Alesina et al., 2005a; Carbonara et al., 2009; Parisi and Fon, 2009), on the role of subsidiarity in addressing situations with economies of scale and cross-border externalities (Schaefer,

2006), and on the effects of subsidiarity compared with the alternative of using fixed competence catalogues (Kirchner, 1997).[12]

This section builds on the existing literature by presenting a simple model of policy allocation that illustrates the main arguments regarding the debate on the adoption of the subsidiarity principle. A single federal government (or a union of states like the European Union) consists of N member states. Federal and state governments engage in the provision and performance of a policy function. The welfare function for a member state i, $i = 1, \ldots, N$ from public spending is:

$$\alpha_i H(g_i) - g_i \tag{5.1}$$

where $H(g_i)$ is the i-th state's total benefit from the provision of policy functions (with $H_g(\cdot) > 0$ and $H_{gg}(\cdot) \leq 0$) and g_i represents total public spending in the provision of the policy function. The parameter α_i differs across countries and measures how much a country values public spending. It is distributed in the population of member states. The parameter α for each member state is public information and assumes values over the interval $[\alpha^{MIN}, \alpha^{MAX}]$.[13]

Using this simple framework, we model the decision to allocate policy responsibilities either at a local or central level according to the subsidiarity principle. The federal government and its member states have to decide whether policy responsibilities should be allocated to the federal government (centralization) or to the local level.

When a policy responsibility is allocated at the local level, each member country decides how much to invest in that particular area and maximizes the utility function (5.1) with respect to g. The first order condition for the policy function therefore is:

$$H_g^L = \frac{1}{\alpha_i} \tag{5.2}$$

The formula g_i^{*L} denotes the expenditure of country i for the public good in a decentralized setting, where local governments sets the level of public expenditure. Equation (5.2) defines an implicit function $g^{*L}(\alpha_i)$ for member state i. Intuitively, the higher the appreciation for the policy function is, the higher α_i, and the public expenditure for the policy function.

Those in favor of centralization and harmonization argue that allocating policy responsibilities to the central level results in economies of scale and positive externalities, which increase the efficiency of providing that specific function (Schäfer, 2006). The concept of economies of scale is often used loosely in this context to include benefits from coordination that are more readily obtained through centralized policy responsibilities and harmonization.

---

[12] The effects of the application of subsidiarity are examined in a number of fields: see Devine et al. (1996) for the impact on competitiveness and industrial policies, with a particular focus on SME. See Fourage (2004) for impact on social reform and poverty.

[13] A country may value public spending in all areas in different ways. Analytically this would imply that each country i has a different α_{ij} for each policy function, $j = 1, \ldots, M$. For simplicity we assume a constant value of the parameter α_i across policy functions.

For example, Alesina et al. (2005a) characterize the benefit of centralization as the possibility of exploiting economies of scale. They characterize the costs of centralization as the result of the heterogeneity of preferences across the member states: one size does not necessarily fit all.[14] When balancing the benefits resulting from economies of scale with the varying preferences of the citizenry, the optimal degree of centralization should ensure that all activities where preferences are homogeneous – thus ensuring the predominance of economies of scale – should be carried out at the central level. On the other hand, all activities with high heterogeneity of preferences should be carried out at the local level.

Alesina et al. (2005a) model the benefits of centralization as spillovers from public spending. Formally, when decisions on a certain policy area are allocated at the federal level, welfare from public spending on that area for each country i becomes:

$$\alpha_i H\left(g_i + \beta \sum_{j=1, j \neq i}^{N} g_j\right) - g_i \tag{5.3}$$

where $\beta \in [0, 1]$ measures the size of the spillover effects on public spending.

The 1994 report prepared for the Steering Committee on Local and Regional Authorities[15] raised a similar consideration, in which subsidiarity was linked to three grounds of efficiency, one of which was the notion of "proximity." Proximity refers to the advantage of a lower level of government to be more familiar, at a lower cost, with people's preferences, hence having a comparative advantage in supplying rules and governmental services at the local level.

In a rigid union (Oates, 1972), in which every member state has to adopt the same policy, the median voter theorem applies and the first order condition of the median member state in the union, denoted by m, becomes:

$$H_g^C(g_m[1 + \beta(N - 1)]) = \frac{1}{\alpha_m[1 + \beta(N - 1)]} \tag{5.4}$$

Alesina et al. (2005a) show that the equilibrium expenditure of public goods in a rigid union, denoted as g_i^{*C}, increases with the preference for the public good exhibited by the median voter α_m. At the same time, the equilibrium expenditure of public goods decreases with the number of member states N and the size of the spillover β increases, if the elasticity of the marginal utility of the public good is higher than one.[16]

The subsidiarity principle can be interpreted as a form of flexibility of the union. Alesina et al. (2005a) model the subsidiarity principle to allow the Union to complement the expenditure of the public good at the country level with the Union's additional

---

14 See Easterly and Levine (1997) and Alesina et al. (1999) for a discussion on preference heterogeneity in the presence of ethnic divisions. See Mazzaferro and Zanardi (2008) for the impact of preference heterogeneity on centralization.

15 See Delcamp (1994), Report on "Definition and limits of the principle of subsidiarity," Council of Europe, Steering Committee on Local and Regional Authorities n. 55, p. 26.

16 The non-monotonicity of the size of the public good expenditure can be explained by the presence of a substitution and an income effect.

expenditure.[17] At equilibrium, the median and all member states with weaker preferences choose a zero additional expenditure of the public good, while the member states with preferences higher than the median country have a positive expenditure of the public good at the country level. Alesina et al. (2005a) show that in the presence of the subsidiarity principle, the Union chooses an aggregate provision of the public good lower than the one chosen by a rigid union. The subsidiarity principle should be applied when there is a strict majority rule in the Union with a fixed number of member states. The expected result is that all the members of the Union with preferences weaker than the median country will spend less than a rigid union, and will benefit from the additional positive spillovers created by those countries with preference higher than the median voter. Additionally, the median member of the Union cannot be worse off, since it can always replicate the expenditure chosen in case of a rigid union.

In a related paper, Alesina et al. (2005b) provide empirical evidence on the expansion of the policy-making role of the European Union in the period between 1971 and 2000. The evidence shows that the range of competences attributed to the European Commission, the Parliament, the Court of Justice and, more generally, the central governmental level has expanded significantly, "far away from the EEC's original mandate," which only established a free market zone and harmonized trade policy (ibid., p. 276). In the European Union, the process of allocating policy responsibilities has been drawn away from the optimal balance of economies of scale and the heterogeneity of preferences identified by the economic analysis discussed above.

The centralization of policy functions may, however, introduce diseconomies of scale if union membership becomes too widespread. As opposed to the phenomenon pointed out by Alesina et al. (2005a), spillovers can decrease in the number of countries and even become negative. This implies that diseconomies of scale could occur beyond a certain size of the union, at least for certain policy functions. For instance, consider two related policy functions like financial regulation and its enforcement. While financial regulation likely yields positive and possibly increasing spillovers as the number of harmonizing countries increases, enforcement can become very expensive and ineffective when a unique central authority must monitor an increasing number of countries.[18]

In the analysis, redistribution of policy functions across countries in the union does not play a role in the determination of g_i^{*C}. This implies that the allocation of costs among member states does not affect the decision of whether to provide more or less than in the decentralized equilibrium. Things change substantially when decisions are made locally by a democratic majority.

Carbonara et al. (2009) characterize the optimal allocation of policy functions in multi-level governments, focusing on the interplay of economies of scale, economies of scope, and heterogeneity of preferences.[19] Their analysis unpacks the loaded concept

---

[17] Alesina et al. (2005a) set a two-stage game model, where the member state chooses in stage 1 the expenditure of the public good at the local level, and the Union chooses a complementary expenditure in stage 2.

[18] The economic model can be extended to capture the possibility of having diseconomies of scale, once the government reaches and exceeds its optimal size.

[19] The authors do not examine the role of spillover effects in the demand of public goods. Spillover effects are analytically equivalent to the economies of scale.

of "comparative advantage of the central government" and provides an economic framework for the subsidiarity test.[20] With respect to the previous economic analysis, Carbonara et al. (2009) examine the role of economies of scope that exist "when there is an advantage in administering or producing sets of services within the same governmental unit rather than each service separately" (ibid., p. 748).

The introduction of economies of scope in the standard economic framework creates a potential "lumpiness" or non-linearity into the subsidiarity decision. Positive economies of scope change how the optimal centralization decision under subsidiarity should be made. In the presence of positive economies of scope, moving an important service to the central government, without its productive counterpart, may reduce the efficiency performance of overall government. This implies that centralization decisions under subsidiarity should be made globally by examining all combinations of services and not simply by making assignments separately, service by service, as is typically done to reallocate governmental competences.

Analytically, the welfare function for a member state i, $i = 1, \ldots, N$ from public spending is:

$$\alpha_i H(g_i) - C(g_i) \tag{5.5}$$

where $H(g_i)$ is the i-th state's total benefit from the provision of policy functions, $C(g_i)$ the cost function of the local government. g_i represents total public spending in the provision of M policy function[21] and is denoted as a vector of the M public spending of state i on each policy j, i.e. $g_i = [g_{i1}, \ldots, g_{ij}, \ldots, g_{iM}]$.

In the setting described, a bundle of k functions may be allocated at central level, where $k \leq M$. In case of economies of scope between policy function j and z, the marginal cost of implementing policy function j decreases if policy function z is realized at the same governmental level (either central or local).

Carbonara et al. (2009) show that the presence of economies of scale with no economies of scope at both central and local levels leads to a subsidiarity test favoring centralization, if the Union has a sufficiently large cost advantage with respect to member states.[22] Consistently with Alesina et al. (2005a), the allocation of competences at the central level is desirable if centralization yields sufficiently lower per-unit costs to compensate for the loss due to the heterogeneity of states' preferences. The level of centralization attained does not depend on whether centralization proceeds stepwise ($k = 1$), wholesale of all competences ($k = M$) or with any intermediate bundling of centralized competences ($1<k<M$).

The presence of the economies of scope introduces room for lock-in effects in the

---

20 Carbonara, Luppi and Parisi (2009) adopt a dynamic framework, where the structure of costs evolves according to previous centralization decisions. On the contrary, the frameworks of the previous literature have been static with a fixed structure of costs over time.

21 Public spending has to be intended in a broad sense as investment in a given policy area. For instance, lawmaking and the production of regulations can be included as intances of public spending and, more specifically, are also public goods.

22 The member state has a cost advantage with respect to the Union if the marginal cost of providing the j-th function at local level is lower than that of the Union.

centralization process. Lock-in effects may be observed when the process of centralization is stalled at a local rather than global optimum and may prevent reaching the efficient level of centralization. Consider the limiting case of no economies of scale. The subsidiarity test may favor the allocation of competences at the central level if the economies of scope at the central level prevail over those at the local level.[23] Lock-in effects may arise due to the fact that, unlike economies of scale, economies of scope at the central (or local) level grow larger as additional functions are centralized (or decentralized). The Union will benefit from larger economies of scope when all functions are concentrated at central level. The same reasoning applies for the individual member state when all functions are left at the local level. This implies that the subsidiarity test most likely fails to centralize, all other things equal, when functions are transferred in a stepwise fashion, $k = 1$. As pointed out by Carbonara et al. (2009), states suffer the highest loss in terms of forgone economies of scope when centralization starts and the first functions are moved to the central level. This occurs more frequently in the early stages of centralization. To the contrary, if a sufficient number of functions are bundled together when transferred to the central level, the economies of scope at the central level could become strong enough to satisfy the subsidiarity test.[24] The presence of economies of scale reinforces this result. Additionally, the subsidiarity test could favor centralization even if the economies of scope at the local level prevail over those at the central level, due to a cost advantage at the central level.[25]

The timing in the application of subsidiarity plays a critical role in the process of allocation of competences. Problems of excessive centralization may be observed when subsidiarity is introduced after an initial phase of centralization. The subsidiarity test may have perverse effects, favoring further centralization rather than limiting it, with path-dependent effects on later centralization decisions.

The puzzling increase in centralization after the adoption of the subsidiarity principle can be explained starting from the observation that the effects of subsidiarity are possibly reversed if the test is introduced after several functions are previously centralized. As pointed out by Carbonara et al. (2009), in the short term the subsidiarity principle may actually accomplish its stated goal, but we conclude that in the long run the subsidiarity principle may actually lead to further centralization. This was the situation in the European Union, where the subsidiarity principle was formally adopted after several important functions had already been allocated at the central level through political decision-making and without a blueprint for expansion.

These results suggest that currently subsidiarity should play an extended role as a corrective judicial instrument rather than a preventive governmental guideline. Estella (2002,

---

23 Carbonara et al. (2009) show that prevailing economies of scope at the central level are a necessary but not a sufficient condition for satisfaction of the subsidiarity test in the presence of economies of scope.

24 Lock-in effects can be observed for intermediate bundling of centralized functions $k<M$, but not in the case of wholesale centralization, $k = M$. The lock-in effect is decreasing in k.

25 Carbonara et al. (2009) show that in the presence of economies of scale and economies of scope at both central and local level, a necessary but not sufficient condition for centralization is the presence of larger economies of scope at the central level.

p. 141), however, notes that the "juridification" of subsidiarity has not triggered much use of subsidiarity as a "justiciable" principle by the European Court of Justice.[26]

Our argument, consistent with the findings of Estella, is that the effectiveness of subsidiarity as a preventive governmental guideline has been detrimentally affected by the timing of its implementation. The economies of scope of previously centralized functions attract further competences at the central level. This suggests that the late implementation of subsidiarity led to the reduced effectiveness of this principle both as a procedural guideline for governmental action and as a corrective judicial principle. The true bite of subsidiarity could be ensured by allowing the application/use of subsidiarity as a justiciable principle to challenge the centralization of competences that took place prior to the "juridification" of subsidiarity in the Maastricht Treaty. The scope and power of subsidiarity could be further promoted, allowing its application to bundles of already centralized competences. This would avoid the lock-in effect that may be caused by scope economies within bundled competences.

The possibility of a retroactive application of the subsidiarity test to previously centralized functions has been made possible by Provision 3 of the Amsterdam Treaty (Protocol No. 30 of the ECT introduced by the Amsterdam Treaty). Provision 3 allows the subsidiarity principle to be applied to the exercise, as opposed to the attribution, of community competences (Estella, 2002, p. 103). This implies that subsidiarity could allow community actions to be restricted or discontinued when they are no longer consistent with the criteria of subsidiarity. As pointed out in the previous analysis, the problem of excessive centralization can be effectively corrected by using subsidiarity to revisit previous centralization decisions, with the possible decentralization of already centralized competences. The extent to which this retroactive application of subsidiarity represents a politically viable option and will be effectively carried out under the Amsterdam Treaty remains to be seen. The existing law and economics analysis will hopefully provide some guidance for the prospective and retrospective application of subsidiarity in a changing European Union.

REFERENCES

Alesina, Alberto and Romain Wacziarg (1999), "Is Europe Going Too Far?" 51 (1) *Carnegie-Rochester Conference Series on Public Policy*, 1–42.

Alesina, Alberto F., Ignazio Angeloni and Federico Etro (2005a), "International Unions," 95 *American Economic Review*, 602–15.

Alesina, Alberto, Ignazio Angeloni and Ludger Shucknecht (2005b), "What Does the European Union Do?" 123 *Public Choice*, 275–319.

---

[26] Bermann (1994, p. 336) suggests that lawmaking institutions within the Community are better equipped to assess the comparative advantages of proposed legislations. This argument suggests that subsidiarity's prevalent role should be that of scrutinizing proposed interventions prior to enactment. Subsidiarity can be recast from a jurisdictional principle (which rules over the allocation of competences between the central authority and member states) to a procedural principle, which provides the legislative authority with the guidelines to manage the inquiry regarding whether an action should be warranted at the central or member state level. See Estella (2002, pp. 104–36) for a clarification on the distinction between material subsidiarity and procedural subsidiarity.

Alesina, Alberto, Reza Baqir and William Easterly (1999), "Public Goods and Ethnic Divisions," 114 (4) *Quarterly Journal of Economics*, 1243–84.

Aquinas, Thomas (1274), *Summa Theologica*, English translation, 2nd revised edition (1920) (Fathers of the English Dominican Province, transl.), Benziger Bros.

Bermann, George A. (1994), "Taking Subsidiarity Seriously: Federalism in the European Community and the United States," 94 *Columbia Law Review*, 331–456.

Besley, Timothy and Stephen Coate (1997), "An Economic Model of Representative Democracy," 112 *Quarterly Journal of Economics*, 85–114.

Bewley, Truman (1981), "A Critique of Tiebout's Theory of Local Public Expenditures," 49 *Econometrica*, 713–39.

Breton, Albert and Anthony Scott (1978), *The Economic Constitution of Federal States*, University of Toronto Press.

Carbonara, Emanuela, Barbara Luppi and Francesco Parisi (2009), "Self-Defeating Subsidiarity," 5 *Review of Law and Economics*, 741–83.

Carozza, Paolo G. (2003), "Subsidiarity as a Structural Principle of International Human Rights Law," 97 *American Journal of International Law*, 38–79.

Cooper, Ian (2006), "The Subsidiarity Early Warning Mechanism: Making It Work," *Intereconomics*, 254–57.

Cooter, Robert and Drexl, Josef (1994), "The Logic of Power in the Emerging European Constitution: Game Theory and the Division of Powers," 14 *International Review of Law and Economics*, 307–26.

Delcamp, Alain (1994), "Definition and Limits of the Principle of Subsidiarity," Council of Europe, Steering Committee on Local and Regional Authorities, Report no. 55.

Devine, Pat, Yannis Katsoulacas and Roger Sugden (eds) (1996), *Competitiveness, Subsidiarity and Industrial Policy*, London: Routledge.

Downs, Anthony (1957), *An Economic Theory of Democracy*, New York: Harper and Row.

Easterly, William and Ross Levine (1997), "Africa's Growth Tragedy: Policies and Ethnic Divisions," *Quarterly Journal of Economics*, November, 1203–50.

Edwards, Dennis J. (1996), "Fearing Federalism's Failure: Subsidiarity in the European Union," 44 *American Journal of Comparative Law*, 537.

Estella, Antonio (2002), *The EU Principle of Subsidiarity and its Critique*, Oxford: Oxford University Press.

Everling, Ulrich (1997), "Constitutional Problems of the European Union – A Lawyer's View," in Dieter Schmitchen and Robert Cooter (eds), *Constitutional Law and Economics of the European Union*, Cheltenham: Edward Elgar Publishing, Chapter 10.

Feldstein, Martin (1997), "The Political Economy of the European Economic and Monetary Union: Political Sources of an Economic Liability," 11 (4) *Journal of Economic Perspectives*, 23–42.

Flaherty, John P. and Maureen E. Lally-Green (1996), "The European Union: Where is it Now?" 34 *Duquesne Law Review*, 923–8.

Fourage, Didier (2004), *Poverty and Subsidiarity in Europe*, Cheltenham: Edward Elgar Publishing.

Frey, Bruno S. and Reiner Eichenberger (1996), "FOCJ: Competitive Governments for Europe," 16 *International Review of Law and Economics*, 315–27.

Inman, Robert P. and Daniel L. Rubinfeld (1997), "Rethinking Federalism," 11 (4) *Journal of Economic Perspectives*, 43–64.

Inman, Robert P. and Daniel L. Rubinfeld (1998), "Subsidiarity and the European Union," in Peter K. Newman (ed.), *The New Palgrave Dictionary of Economics and the Law*, 545–51.

Inman, Robert P. and Daniel L. Rubinfeld (2002), "Subsidiarity, Governance and EU Economic Policy," *CESifo Forum*, 4/2002, Munich.

Kiiver, Philipp (2008), "The Treaty of Lisbon, the National Parliaments and the Principle of Subsidiarity," *Maastricht Journal of European and Comparative Law*, 15, 77–83.

Kirchner, Christian (1997), "Competence Catalogues and the Principle of Subsidiarity in a European Constitution," 8 *Constitutional Political Economy*, 71–87.

La Porta, Rafael, Florencio Lopez-de-Silanes, Andrei Shleifer and Robert Vishny (1999), "The Quality of Government," 15 (1) *Journal of Law, Economics and Organization*, 222–97.

Leo XIII (1891), *Rerum Novarum*: Encyclical Letter on Capital and Labor, 15 May.

Marquardt, Paul D. (1994), "Subsidiarity and Sovereignty in the European Union," 18 *Fordham International Law Journal*, 616–36.

Mazzaferro, Carlo and Alberto Zanardi (2008), "Centralisation versus Decentralisation of Public Policies: Does the Heterogeneity of Individual Preferences Matter?" 29 (1) *Fiscal Studies*, Institute for Fiscal Studies, 35–73.

Millon-Delsol, C. (1992), *L'Etat Subsidiare: Ingerénce et Non-Ingerénce de l'Etat: Le Principe de Subsidiarité aux Fondements de l'Histoire Européenne*, Paris: PUF

Musgrave, Richard A. (1997) "Devolution, Grants, and Fiscal Competition," 11 (4) *Journal of Economic Perspectives*, 65–72.

Oates, Wallace E. (1972), *Fiscal Federalism*, New York: Harcourt Brace Jovanovich.
Oates, Wallace E. (1999), "An Essay in Fiscal Federalism," 37 (3) *Journal of Economic Literature*, 1120–49.
Parisi, Francesco and Fon, Vincy (2009), *Sources of Law: The Economics of Lawmaking*, Oxford: Oxford University Press.
Pelkmans, Jacques (2006), "An EU Subsidiarity Test is Indispensable," *Intereconomics*, 249–54.
Pius XI (1931), *Litterae Encyclicae Quadragesimo Anno*.
Popitz, Johannes (1927), "Der Finanzausgleich," *Handbuch der Finanzwissenschaft*, vol. 2, Tübingen: J.C.B. Mohr, 338–75.
Schäfer, Wolf (2006), "Harmonization and Centralization versus Subsidiarity: Which Should Apply Where?" *Intereconomics*, 246–9.
Schmid-Lübbert, Stefanie and Hans-Bernd Schäfer (2003), "The Constitution of the European Union," in C.K. Rowley and F. Schneider (eds), *Encyclopedia of Public Choice*, Springer.
Sinn, Hans-Werner (1994), "How Much Europe? Subsidiarity, Centralization and Fiscal Competition," 1 (41) *Scottish Journal of Political Economy*, 85–107.
Stephan, Paul, Francesco Parisi and Ben Depoorter (2003), *The Law and Economics of the European Union*, Newark, NJ: Lexis Publishing.
Streit, Manfred and Mussler, Werner (1994), "The Economic Constitution of the European Community: From Rome to Maastricht," 5 *Constitutional Political Economy*, 319–53.
Tabellini, Guido (2002), "The Assignment of Tasks in an Evolving European Union," CEPS policy briefing 10, CEPS, Brussels.
Tiebout, Charles M. (1956), "A Pure Theory of Local Expenditures," 64 (5) *Journal of Political Economy*, 416–24.
Tullock, Gordon (1969), "Federalism: Problems of Scale," 6 *Public Choice*, 19–29.
van den Bergh, Roger (1997), "The Subsidiarity Principle and the EC Competition Rules: The Costs and Benefits of Decentralization," in Dieter Schmitchen and Robert Cooter, *Constitutional Law and Economics of the European Union*, Cheltenham: Edward Elgar Publishing.
Vaubel, Roland (1994a), "The Political Economy of Centralization and the EC," 81 *Public Choice*, 151–90.
Vaubel, Roland (1994b), "The Public Choice Analysis of European Integration, a Survey," 10 *European Journal of Political Economy*, 227–49.
Vibert, Frank (1995), *Europe: A Constitution for the Millenium*, Cheltenham: Edward Elgar Publishing.
Wechsler, Herbert (1954), "The Political Safeguards of Federalism: The Role of the States in the Composition and Selection of the National Government," 54 *Columbia Law Review*, 543–60.
Weiler, Joseph H.H. (1985), "Alternatives to Withdrawal from an International Organization: The Case of the European Economic Community," 20 *Israel Law Review*, 282–98.
Weiler, Joseph H.H. (1991), "The Transformation of Europe," 100 *Yale Law Journal* 2403–83.
Weiler, Joseph H.H. and Joel P. Trachtman (1996), "European Constitutionalism and Its Discontents," 17 *Northwestern Journal of International Law and Business* 354.

PART 2

BASIC FREEDOMS

6 Mutual recognition: economic and regulatory logic in goods and services

*Jacques Pelkmans**

1 INTRODUCTION AND PURPOSE

Mutual recognition (MR) is one of the most appreciated innovations of the EU. The idea is that one can pursue market integration, indeed 'deep' market integration, while respecting 'diversity' amongst the participating countries. Put differently, in pursuing 'free movement' for goods in the EU internal market and hence going beyond merely removing tariffs and quotas, mutual recognition facilitates free movement by disciplining the nature and scope of 'regulatory barriers', whilst allowing some degree of regulatory discretion for the EU Member States. Compared with alternative options of 'deepening' market integration, this solution is attractive and, in principle, welfare increasing. Mutual recognition might also be appreciated because, in avoiding EU regulation, it tends to limit centralisation, while facilitating 'regulatory competition' between Member States and, possibly, lowering the costs of the incredible regulatory heterogeneity business faces in the EU internal market. Nevertheless, mutual recognition is many things to many people.[1] The present contribution will not cast the net so wide. The focus will be on the successful and far-reaching examples of the EU internal market for goods and services.

The chapter attempts to explain (1) the rationale and logic of mutual recognition in the EU internal goods market (Section 2), (2) its working in actual practice in the EU for more than 25 years, culminating in a qualitative benefit/cost analysis (Section 4) and (3) its recent improvement in terms of 'governance' in the so-called 2008 Goods Package (Section 5), thereby ameliorating the benefits/costs ratio. Lest it be forgotten, mutual recognition in the EU ought to be applied both to existing national regulation and *new* national regulation emerging from the Member States. For the latter, the EU has created an intrusive mechanism which has successfully protected the internal goods market from

* The author is indebted to Thomas Eger for suggestions as well as to the participants of the Hamburg workshop preparing the Handbook. Of course, all errors and omissions are mine.

[1] In the literature one finds that MR is a rule about conflicts of law between two or more countries, or a rule of choice concerning what country law applies, or, simply (functional) 'equivalence', or, a form of 'decentralized policing'. Authors distinguish 'pure', 'rootless' and 'managed' MR from (just) 'recognition', to mention only some examples.

MR can be very limited in scope, too, and this might not always be appreciated. Thus, WTO promotes mutual recognition agreements (MRAs) but all they do is to underpin MR solely for conformity assessment of a trading partner's technical requirements of a good (for purposes of im/export). The disappointment about making MRAs work effectively in world trade, despite their limited scope, can be better understood when understanding how the EU has solved quality requirements and mutual trust in this sensitive domain. However, this is a very demanding regime, perhaps too intrusive for many WTO partners. See e.g. Section 5 and the references there.

serious erosion over time (Section 3). Where possible and useful, this chapter will refer to notions sometimes seen, particularly by economists, as closely related to mutual recognition such as regulatory competition and 'better' regulation. The scant economic theory of MR is summarised in Box 6.1 in Section 4. It will be shown that mutual recognition, rather than being inspired by academic theory, has emerged from the profound frustrations in EU circles about the first two decades of the internal market. Sections 6 and 7 attempt to extend the analysis to services. The former will show how the application of MR has spilled over from goods to services markets, culminating in the debate about a horizontal liberalisation directive (the Bolkestein draft of 2004) and the later services directive 2006/123. The meaning for the internal services market is not yet fully clear as will be shown. Section 7 will briefly set out MR as applied in vertical (i.e. sectoral) services directives, with some examples. Section 8 concludes.

2 RATIONALE AND LOGIC OF MUTUAL RECOGNITION

2.1 The Fundamental Problem

The EU first established a customs union in the period 1958–68. Internally, it implies 'free trade', the removal of all tariffs and quotas. Further deepening of goods market integration is required by the treaty because, unlike the WTO, the treaty incorporates the obligation to establish 'free movement'. Free movement implies the 'right' for EU economic agents to move goods (or services, as the case might be) into any national market in the EU, that is, to have unhindered market access. This concept is therefore much more radical than free trade as such. That right overrides the powers of EU Member States to put in place or maintain any access barrier, except if and insofar as the treaty specifies such instances or allows for certain derogations of free movement.

In more general economic parlance, free movement goes beyond free trade in that non-tariff barriers are forbidden or made irrelevant. Radical as that certainly is, free movement is not unlimited or unconditional. Simplifying, Member States may have two types of non-tariff barriers: those that *cannot* be justified by market failures or exceptions to the internal market (such as national security or public order) and those that *can* be justified. The design of the treaty, subsequent case law and secondary legislation (like directives) should effectively eliminate the former, sooner or later. But what about the latter? In traditional thinking, there are three ways of addressing 'justified' national interventions in their markets causing access barriers: national treatment, prohibitions and harmonisation.[2] Each one has drawbacks. If one wishes to protect the national regulatory autonomy (perhaps assuming that national regulation and other interventionism faithfully expresses the preferences of voters in a representative democratic system and these ought to be respected), the solution is to apply 'national treatment'. This means that EU Member States would allow 'free' movement of goods (and services) if the providers comply with the rules of the destination (host) country. Discrimination is forbidden in this approach.

---

[2] See e.g. Schmidt (2007) and Schmidt (ed.) (2007) for elaboration; see also various contributions in Kostoris Padoa Schioppa (ed.) (2005).

This approach would imply, at best, a very truncated instance of 'free movement'. Economically, it would lead to major trading costs incurred before having market access, due to costs of adaptation; indeed, the tariff equivalents of such costs may well imply a significant degree of factual protection from exposure to competitive imports from other EU countries. The EU internal market would largely remain fragmented except for goods (and services) which are not or only lightly regulated. Apart from non-discrimination in e.g. host country regulation, it differs little from (free) trade under the WTO. In other words, if one really wants 'deep' market integration, the national regulatory autonomy will have to be compromised to some degree.

In traditional thinking, there are two ways of compromising national regulatory autonomy for the purpose of 'free movement': prohibitions and 'harmonisation'. When prohibiting all regulatory or other non-tariff barriers in the EU, even when 'justified' by (say) market failures, welfare is bound to fall. The whole point of subjecting markets to regulation in the event of market failures is to prevent sub-optimal functioning of markets. The costs of not-overcoming market failures vary enormously, dependent on the issue and the kind of market failure, so it is hard to generalise. However, the very purpose[3] of the EU and a properly functioning internal market as its principal means is to stimulate higher productivity increases and more economic growth, which is inconsistent with an approach of all-out prohibitions lowering welfare over a broad spectrum of applications. Indeed, an internal market with many market failures is pointless.

This leaves a third way: harmonisation. The origin of the term reflects a sophisticated response to the fundamental problem of 'deep' market integration. The term used to refer to the idea that national regulation of the Member States would need to be 'brought into harmony' in such a way that 'free movement' could be accomplished without all the costs of adaptation, etc. The English treaty term 'approximation' similarly expresses this idea. However, in the early history of the EU, harmonisation degenerated into full uniformity due to mistrust (or bargaining tactics, under veto threat) of Member States and the initial refusal to accept the full consequences of 'deep' market integration, including some degree of regulatory adaptation. Harmonisation became excessively detailed and 'heavy', causing high costs of (EU) regulation, and without any cost/benefit analysis. Nowadays, there is a far greater awareness of the need to make 'proportionate' (EU) regulation, e.g. no more than necessary for the market failure. Today, the European Commission is held to subject every proposal to strict Regulatory Impact Assessment.[4] The lesson of four decades of (EU) harmonisation is that one has to find a suitable balance between, on the one hand, not suppressing the preferences of the (or some) Member States too much (as this may be welfare decreasing) and, on the other hand, avoiding overly costly common regulation by incorporating each and every specific element of national (often diverse) rules, prompting 'regulatory failure'.

The treaty incorporates all three options (see below Section 2.2). There is a general

[3] Other than the broader political considerations of post-war peace and being a 'Community of values'.

[4] This is a subject of its own. See, for the detailed Guidelines of the Commission, http://ec.europa.eu/governance/impact/docs_en.htm. For a very careful evaluation of the Commission impact assessments since 2003, see the report by the EU Court of Auditors, 2010, http://eca.europa.eu/portal/pls/portal/docs/1/5372733.pdf.

prohibition of what one might call regulatory barriers, but with derogations, as well as a broad harmonisation provision. National treatment might apply as well, once derogations of free movements can be invoked, and if these derogations are not disciplined in other ways by case law. However, usually, one should expect that derogations will prompt proposals for harmonisation of some kind. Certainly in goods, few areas are left where derogations have remained without eventually having resulted in harmonisation (or at least attempts at it). In other words, national treatment is no longer of much significance when speaking about free movement. But it ought to be noted that, in services, the mode of 'establishment' is far more important than free movement (due to the need to satisfy clients' preferences of proximity of providers and of building relations of trust). In establishment, national treatment (host country rules) makes more sense and normally causes fragmentation less easily. Thus, such national treatment is typically disciplined by general regulatory principles under the treaty (including non-discrimination in a wide sense) and sometimes by basic common rules, leaving scope for local variation and discretion.

After some 20 years of building the EU internal (goods) market, the balance between the three options and the results for free movement looked anything but promising. To put it simply, a huge number of regulatory barriers were still in place because the general prohibition was undermined by countless derogations, invoked by Member States almost without discipline, whilst harmonisation proved costly and very slow (also due to vetoes). It is against this background that MR as an innovation has to be understood. First, the CJEU interpretation of the prohibition was significantly tightened from a narrow legalistic to a more economic interpretation of what a (regulatory) barrier is. This meant that the burden of proof for Member States of what is a justified barrier was made more difficult – it had simply been too easy before. Second, the CJEU imposed a duty on Member States to 'think internal market', so to say, and not solely national. The criterion became '*equivalence*'. Even if derogations were justified by overcoming market failures, this would not automatically mean that imports could be blocked. As it turned out, numerous instances appeared to exist where other Member States acted very similarly in response to the same market failures. If such national responses were 'equivalent' in terms of avoiding the market failure(s), neither harmonisation nor the refusal of market access would be justified. Free movement ought to be allowed, even if the details of national laws were distinct, as long as their objectives of e.g. protecting consumer or workers were 'equivalent'. A fourth option had been born, mutual recognition, not undermining national regulatory autonomy, nor leading to harmonisation, yet 'deepening' market integration.

2.2 Case Law on the Fundamental Trilemma and Mutual Recognition

This section will discuss the same fundamental problem in the context of the treaty as well as CJEU case law, explaining in greater detail the logic of MR.

As noted, the three options (before MR emerged) can be found in the treaty. The second option – prohibition of 'other' barriers – is laid down in Arts 34 and 36, TFEU. Art. 34 TFEU is not merely about forbidding quotas but also about 'all measures having equivalent effect' (to quantitative restrictions). If all 'other barriers' would fall under this term, an all-out prohibition would amount to a revolutionary amputation of national regulatory autonomy, making it impossible to uphold the Member States' obligations (often in their constitutions) with respect to a number of risks such as safety and health

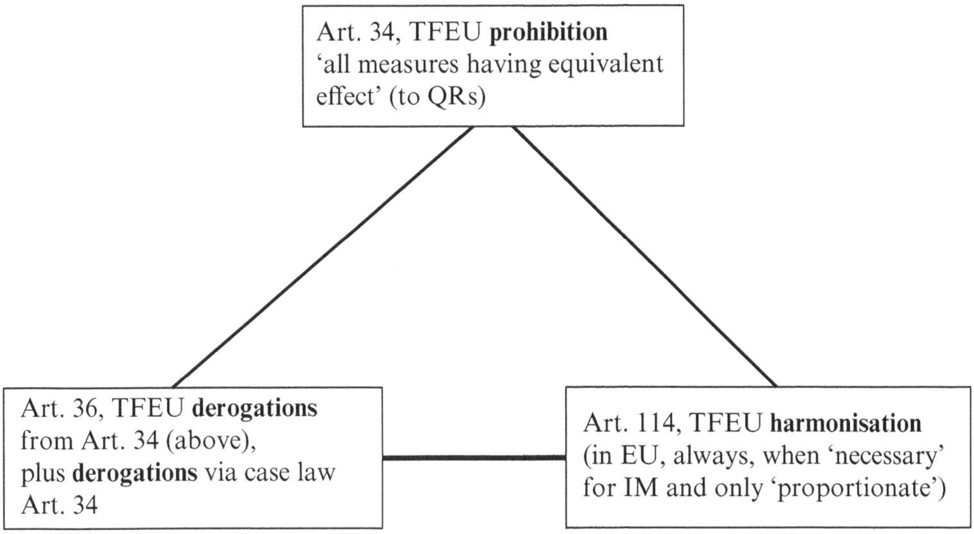

Note: QR = quantitative restriction; IM = internal market.

Figure 6.1 EEC's free-movement-of-goods trilemma

aspects of goods. Such aspects can credibly relate to market failures. Therefore, in the light of the first option – respect for national regulatory autonomy, hence, national treatment – the CJEU was initially very prudent in its case law on Art. 34, TFEU, leaving ample scope for 'justified' exceptions for Member States. Moreover, and hardly surprising, Art. 36 TFEU comprises a series of derogations e.g. about health and intellectual property rights.[5] As to the third option – harmonisation – Art. 114, TFEU (Art. 95, EC) forms the legal basis for 'approximation' for purposes of 'the establishment and functioning of the internal market'. Figure 6.1 visualises the 'trilemma' of the EU in effectively realising and guaranteeing 'free movement of goods'.

Mutual recognition has emerged from the tensions, problems and profound dissatisfaction in combinating these three fundamental treaty provisions. Putting it simply, the Union was caught in a seemingly impossible trilemma: Art. 34 could not be relied on in a blanket form as this would erase the capacity of Member States to regulate, if only for correcting or overcoming market failures; Art. 36 could not be relied on too much either since this would make a mockery of the common market idea, with more holes than a good Emmenthaler cheese; but Art. 114 was not a panacea either as it would imply building a vast EU regulatory regime over many decades, amounting to a drastic de facto centralisation, with all the costs that this would entail. Moreover, the decision-making (in the Council in the 1970s) ex Art. 114 was still under veto and the mistrust amongst Member States as well as vis-à-vis the Commission was such that EU rules were only acceptable to all if no discretion for escape or disguised protectionism would remain (the

[5] Art. 34 TFEU was Art. 28, EC and Art. 30, EEC; Art. 36, TFEU was Art. 30, EC and Art 36, EEC. These texts were never amended.

so-called Old Approach, going into extreme detail and with full technical specifications). So, when harmonisation *was* decided under unanimity, it was bound to generate excessive regulatory costs and – due to veto tactics and resistance to specific aspects which were left out for political reasons – relatively minor (net) benefits, while requiring disproportionate efforts by EU bodies, and fuelling considerable discord. Risking regulatory failure with net benefits so small (or even negative) and going at snail's pace, this approach to harmonisation would never accomplish the internal goods market.

In order to appreciate the CJEU case law from which mutual recognition emerged, one has to understand this trilemma but also remember the difference between the treaty concept of 'free movement' and free trade. Had the Rome treaty relied on free trade, mutual recognition might never have been invented or at best in an intolerably crippled version.[6] Free movement is much more compelling than free trade[7] as it forces the country into a different position: the *right* of market access (here: inside the EU) is not negotiable but *guaranteed as such to economic agents*, and the country can only deviate by explicit derogations as specified in the treaty or CJEU case law.

Thus, free movement needs to be ensured by stringent prohibitions of the panoply of regulatory barriers. Otherwise, it would degenerate into free trade inside the EU customs union. In the early days, Art. 34, TFEU was legalistically interpreted: the term 'measures with an equivalent effect' did not catch anywhere near the number and types of 'regulatory barriers' required to render free movement economically meaningful in the internal goods market. Once the CJEU understood that free movement requires an 'economic' interpretation of this prohibition (rather than a formal and too literal one), it ruled in *Dassonville* (case C-8/74) that such measures (i.e. what we call 'regulatory barriers') refer to trading rules 'capable of hindering, directly or indirectly, actually or potentially, intra-Community trade'. Such a formula is capable of covering practically all regulatory obstacles. This strict prohibition is balanced by derogations for Member States, which need to be *respected* at EU level.

However, the Commission's 'guardian' role and the CJEU case law also have the effect of *disciplining* the recourse to such derogations in terms of scope and interpretation, otherwise they would undermine the accomplishment of free movement. Mutual recognition is one critical principle disciplining the derogations of Member States, so that free movement (often) prevails.

This discipline emerged with the *Cassis de Dijon* (C-120/78) case law, leading to mutual recognition (MR). See also Figure 6.2. Following logically from *Dassonville*, the CJEU first defines what is now called the 'origin principle': 'Member States must allow a product lawfully produced and marketed in another Member State into their own market.' Member States can block imports or condition them but only if 'justified' (the derogations listed in Art. 36, TFEU, and the case law, based on the rule of reason, on Art. 34, TFEU itself). As noted above, the issue is how to respect *and* discipline the recourse to these derogations. Case law since *Cassis de Dijon* does both(!) by asking

---

6 An insightful elaboration of how far one might go under free trade is provided by Sykes (1995). Under free trade, a country agrees not to impose tariffs and quotas and can bind itself under a treaty but remains autonomous otherwise. Such (mainly regulatory) autonomy can be further constrained in limited ways under the WTO. See e.g. Weiler (2005); Sykes (1995); Trachtman (2007).

7 Parts of the following and Figure 6.2 are adopted, with changes, from Pelkmans (2007a).

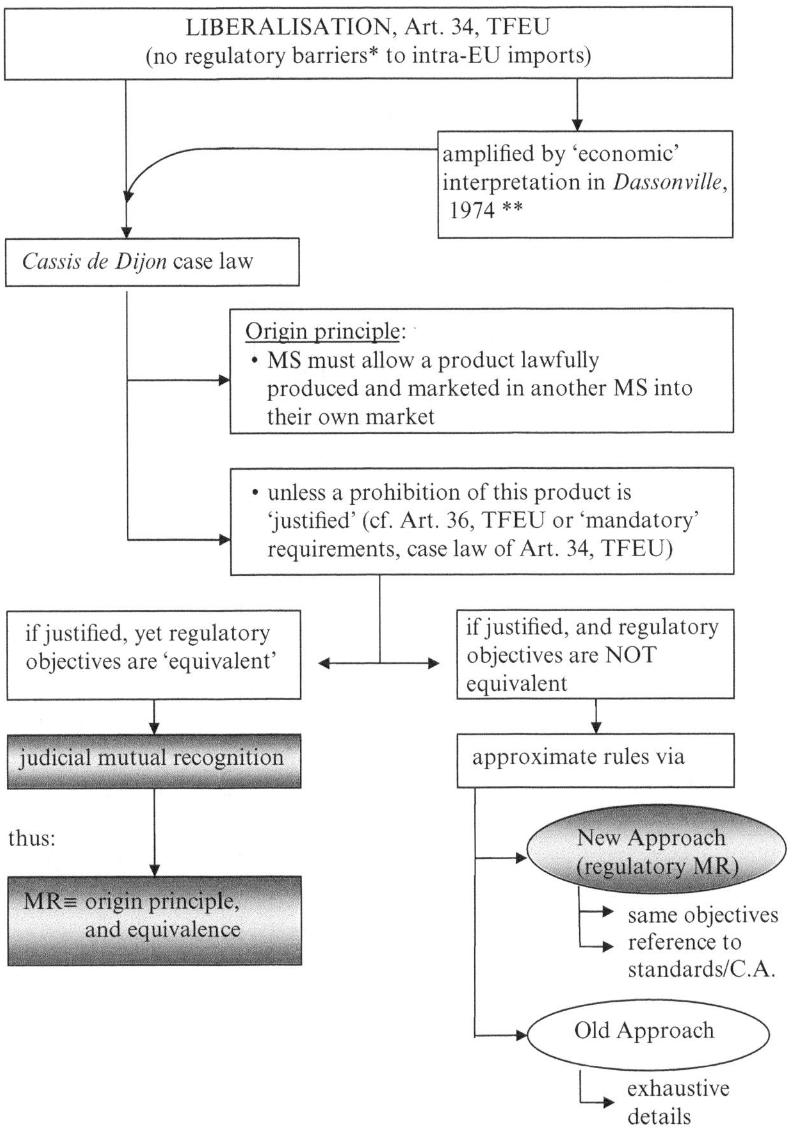

Notes:
* Art. 34, TFEU speaks of 'measures having an equivalent effect' to 'quantitative restrictions'. Since *Dassonville*, this is tantamount to regulatory barriers.
** What we call 'regulatory barriers' are defined by the CJEU as 'all trading rules enacted by MS which are capable of hindering, directly or indirectly, actually or potentially, intra-Community trade'.
C.A. = conformity assessment MS = Member States

Source: Pelkmans (2007a) (as adapted)

Figure 6.2 Logic of Mutual Recognition goods

whether a formally justified recourse to derogations really matters for the risks consumers or workers run in the internal market.[8] The overwhelming majority of the exceptions invoked relate to what could be called 'SHEC'-type regulation, that is, related to objectives of Safety, Health, Environment or Consumer protection.[9] SHEC regulation is in essence 'risk regulation'. If the risk reduction aimed for by SHEC objectives is similar between two or more Member States, the regulatory objective is essentially the same (equivalent), and a good can be freely imported without affecting the regulatory preferences of the importing EU country. If equivalent, CJEU case law says that the derogation cannot be invoked. After all, the effect in terms of risks to consumers, workers, etc. is then similar so that the barrier cannot be justified. The importing Member State ought to 'recognise' that the regulatory regime of the exporting Member State does not increase risks in an appreciable way. In so doing, the CJEU implies that MR amounts to the combination of the *origin principle* and *equivalence*. This is *'judicial mutual recognition'* (bottom-left boxes in Figure 6.2).

If *not* equivalent, the derogations do apply and the only way to restore free movement is 'approximation'. However, even here MR can (and did) lead to a highly significant simplification. Thus, the New Approach is based on directives where the joint definition of regulatory (SHEC) *objectives* is what matters in the text. Once objectives are commonly defined, the lack of equivalence is by definition removed and can no longer be a reason to hinder intra-EU imports. The Old Approach (mainly developed before *Cassis de Dijon*), by contrast, harmonises by attempting to unify almost all technical aspects of (SHEC) regulation, including extremely detailed technical specifications, testing, approvals, inspection and certification. This is unnecessarily costly and rigid. It is also exceedingly difficult to accomplish in Council decision-making and far more difficult still in a Council where Member States were insisting on veto power. The quality of this overly specific and detailed regulation suffered for the simple reason that 'bad regulation' with superfluous or excessively costly requirements would be forced into EU law via the use of veto power. The Old Approach also violates any respect for diversity, even where it would have been possible.[10]

The Old Approach can only be justified economically in cases of extreme risks where uncertainty is potentially too costly: the high costs of extreme specification are

---

[8] Note that this test can be regarded as an early manifestation of a shift from form-based legalistic justifications to effects-based economic approaches, as is now customary in e.g. EU competition law.

[9] The notion of SHEC is a simplification but it catches the large bulk of regulatory issues related to MR. It is also relevant in services, be it that investor/saver protection should be added as a special case (see Section 7). In Art. 36, TFEU the key references are to health and safety and possibly elements of environmental policy. The rule-of-reason case law ex Art. 34, TFEU explicitly underpins environmental and consumer protection. All other justifications are either of trivial importance (e.g. arts trade) or relate to IPRs. For legal analysis, see Barnard (2007, Chapters 6, 7 and 19) and Weiler (2005).

[10] For details, see Atkins (1997). See Pelkmans (1987) for the many drawbacks of the Old Approach. Typical examples of this approach are the 23 tractor directives, the 1973 chocolate directive (meanwhile revised considerably), several other prescriptive food directives, the more than 50 car and car components directives enacted during the 1970s and 1980s (also revised since then), chemicals and pharmaceuticals regulation.

overcompensated by the benefits of avoiding unacceptable risks. The New Approach is a lot easier to negotiate since it is predominantly about regulatory *objectives*. There is, in addition, a learning process among the Member States precisely because they cannot normally fall back on specific technical solutions, driven by engineers, but have to focus on risks, risk reduction and (much less restrictive) performance requirements.

Thus, with the New Approach, the market failures are addressed whilst the costs of EU regulation fall considerably compared with the Old Approach. The New Approach is therefore not synonymous with MR but the underlying thinking is closely related, which is why it can be referred to as *'regulatory mutual recognition'*. This phrase refers to the common definition of regulatory objectives in a light directive.[11] The absence of further technical details implies that different technical requirements are subject to MR. The sensitivity of this type of risk regulation is such that both Member States (e.g. inspectors where relevant) and business are in need of far greater practical guidance about what exactly is 'recognised' in markets; after all, one light directive might refer to many thousands of quite distinct goods. Indeed, in actual practice, when shipments arrive at a border or in harbours, civil servants or inspectors will typically focus on the detailed specifics in their *national* laws, presumably that is even their routine instruction or impulse. This problem turned out to be paramount for the practical working of judicial MR (see below), though barely realised at first. In regulatory MR it was addressed rightaway. Since the New Approach was regulatory in nature and an alternative to the Old Approach, all stakeholders immediately realised that the specifics – no longer incorporated in law as in the Old Approach – had to be known for producers in other ways, before actual production would take place.

Thus, in the New Approach, the common objectives in light directives are complemented by 'reference to standards'. A carefully structured regime of 'co-regulation' has been set up which develops (voluntary) European technical standards on the basis of 'mandates' issued by the European Commission, in turn derived from the SHEC objectives in the relevant directive(s). Market participants, and not Eurocrats or national civil servants, develop standards for the EU. The Commission recognises these standards (if a correct follow-up of the mandate, hence, serving SHEC objectives for the EU) and, after official publication, business can rely on them for intra-EU free movement.[12] This regime is much appreciated because it provides business with guidelines and certainty. European standards incorporated in a regulatory MR regime are also attractive because they do remain voluntary. In case a company is innovative and creates novel aspects or techniques or uses new materials not foreseen in a European standard, the new good can be tested directly (and certified) on its compliance with the SHEC objectives in the relevant directive(s).

---

[11] A typical case is the toys directive 88/378/EEC, recently revised as directive 2009/48/EC of 18 June 2009. An extremely broad application is the machines directive 98/37/EC covering more than 40 000 types of machines.

[12] This is legally referred to as the 'presumption of compliance'. For European business, this is cost saving in terms of information and incentivising in terms of legal certainty. Companies, when making technical products, will have few difficulties in following European performance standards in their in-factory manuals. If done faithfully, the goods will then enjoy intra-EU market access, without the need to master complex EU case law.

Unlike in the Old Approach, innovation is not throttled, for two reasons: (i) performance standards are expected and they provide a lot of room for product differentiation and innovation[13] and (ii) a company is, even with the flexible performance standard, still free to construct 'around' the standard (though it needs to acquire certification from a so-called Notified Body, assigned to fulfil these tasks).

In short, as Figure 6.2 sets out, 'judicial mutual recognition' amounts to the origin principle in its pure formulation, together with equivalence of existing regulatory objectives of Member States, whereas its main alternative, 'regulatory MR', consists of the common regulation of SHEC objectives, together with mutual recognition of all the specific technical requirements in national laws facilitated by recognised European performance standards. In both approaches, the quite sensational result is that existing technical details in national laws, supposedly to be enforced by the responsible inspectors or civil servants, *cannot* be used to block intra-EU imports, except if those goods do not comply with recognised European standards or clearly violate SHEC objectives themselves.

2.3 A Digression on How MR Case Law Works

In stylising the MR case law with Figure 6.2, the logic of focusing on equivalent objectives stands out. The objectives reflect the market failures to be overcome, providing justified reasons to regulate in the first place. In an economic perspective, this is what matters. However, European lawyers would probably find such a presentation of the CJEU case law wanting. Although there can be no doubt that the CJEU has emphasised time and again that Member States ought to think and act in terms of equivalence in a number of ways, there are also numerous CJEU cases about restrictions of the free movement of goods where equivalence considerations are absent. Does that imply that MR is not relevant i.e. Figure 6.2 would not apply? The answer is that restrictions may be declared illegal under EU law for many other reasons, which, in standard case law proceedings, tend to be verified *before* arriving at an equivalence test. See Figure 6.3. If a Member State claims that its restrictions of free movement are 'justified' (see the upper left box) by derogations, routine case law will first test these derogations against a number of core principles and conditions of EU law arising from the treaty or case law itself (see central box). The most prominent one is non-discrimination on grounds of nationality (Art. 18, TFEU), on the basis of which the CJEU has developed strict and extensive case law ever since the outset of the EU. Member States have learned, by now, to avoid discrimination in goods markets but this has taken decades and remains less than perfect. If a restriction is caught as discriminatory, it is illegal and no equivalence test is needed.

The second condition is spelled out in modern regulatory parlance: proper risk assessment (i.e. science based by independent experts and in tune with internationally expected rigour in analysis). The idea is that, since SHEC is risk regulation, the risk(s) have to be underpinned by state-of-the-art scientific analysis, as the basis for risk-reducing national regulation, in order to be evaluated by the CJEU. In cases of 'disguised' protectionism, this test is an effective way to reveal that restrictions of free movement based on national

[13] Indeed, the use of (prescriptive, hence, restrictive) design standards has to be justified. The result is that they have become exceedingly rare nowadays.

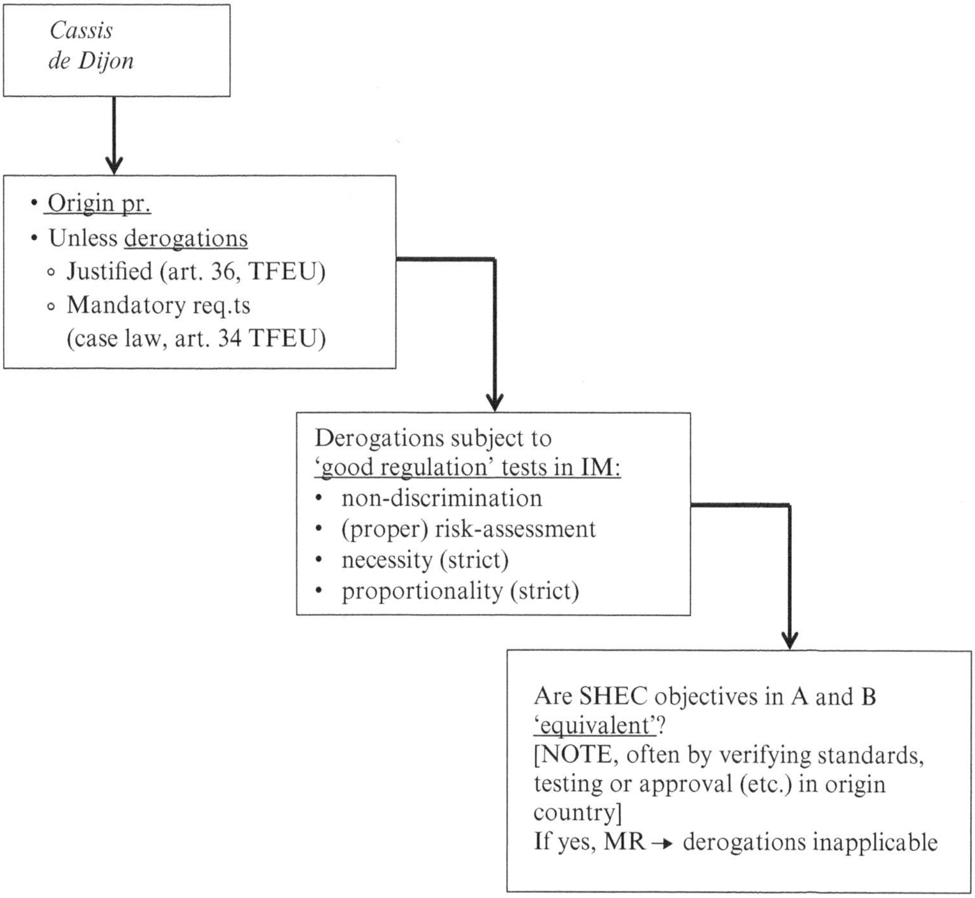

Figure 6.3 Mutual Recognition: CJEU analysis in goods

regulation do not offer consumers or workers any (greater) protection in terms of SHEC. Initially, systematic risk assessment was not practised in Europe (except in e.g. pharmaceuticals) and ad-hoc testimonies by scientists in court would accomplish analogue results.[14]

Third, the 'necessity' test aims to verify that regulatory interventions by the EU country are 'necessary' given the risk reduction preferences. The CJEU tends to assume a strict position. It might also verify whether the measures are actually suitable to bring down the risks to the desired level. Finally, and decisive in numerous cases, the CJEU applies a 'proportionality' test in an ever stricter fashion over time. Narrowly conceived, proportionality is equated with 'no more than necessary' in order to achieve the regulatory objective. In many cases the CJEU could avoid having to render a judgment on

[14] Example: in the nisine case (*Koninklijke Kaasfabriek Eyssen*, Case 53/80 [1981] E.C.R. 409) the Netherlands was allowed to keep its restrictive approach to nisine as an additive to cheese only after scientific testimonies on the possible hazards and risks turned out to be split, and the country got the benefit of the doubt.

national objectives (expressing national preferences) by focusing solely on the relation between instruments and objective(s). In particular, the restrictive effect on free movement (hence, the costs inflicted on actual or potential competitors from other Member States) can often be avoided or reduced by other regulatory options. More widely conceived, the CJEU has insisted that Member States take into account the internal market context of their measures, i.e. imposing a duty on (a) Member State(s) to cooperate in pre-empting regulatory barriers. This is a critical step towards MR. Altogether, these four tests (in the central box of Figure 6.3) can be said to amount to 'good regulation principles in an internal market context'. Adhering to those principles already reduces the restrictions on free movement of goods a great deal. In other words, besides the national economic benefits of 'good regulation', the static and dynamic benefits of actual and potential cross-border competition in the internal goods market can be enjoyed as well.

Following these tests, one can shift to the third box in Figure 6.3: the question of 'equivalence'. In principle, this is about equivalence of objectives but, in actual practice, it usually takes the form of practical verification of instruments reflecting these objectives. Thus, the CJEU has a long track record in prohibiting identical testing in the destination country compared to proven tests in the origin country. Similarly, verifications can refer to (European or equivalent national) standards, (type) approvals, certification or inspection reports. In this operational approach, this test comes very close to the duty, sometimes imposed as a result of the proportionality test, of Member States to work together in a spirit of avoiding barriers when equivalence renders them superfluous.

3 PREVENTING NEW REGULATORY BARRIERS FROM ARISING

MR, whether judicial or regulatory, pays attention to the *stock* of regulatory barriers in the internal goods market. But focusing on the stock is rather narrow-minded. Perhaps it is too little realised but Member States have grown into genuine 'regulatory machines'. The painstaking case law based on MR and the enormous European standardisation work linked to the New Approach – no matter how helpful – completely ignore that Member States tend to create a steady flow of *new* regulatory barriers year after year. In the days of unanimity, given a very low speed of harmonisation removing barriers, the Commission began to fear that the fragmentation of the internal goods market was increasing, not decreasing. Even before the EU would succeed in its rethink of the method of harmonisation (the New Approach), a mechanism was set up to ensure that the flow of *new* national regulation would be subjected to a kind of MR, and, thus, would not add new restrictions of free movement.

It is possible to show convincingly that the internal goods market would long have been hopelessly constricted if the EU had not introduced an amazingly tough control and correction system for new national legislation in process.[15] This system is based on ideas underlying MR, topped up by an intrusive and stringent notification system (with tough

[15] The Mutual Information Directive 98/34 (before 83/189/EEC), recently amended as directive 2006/96/EC, OJEU 2006, L 363, p. 81. The Committee is still called the 98/34 Committee.

sanctions in case of non-notification, emerging from firm rulings by the CJEU), close monitoring by the Commission of failures to notify, detailed scrutiny of draft laws of Member States by a special Committee chaired by the Commission, and – most remarkable of all – automatic or semi-automatic suspension of the national legislative process for periods varying from 3 months to as much as 18 months, dependent on the need for remedies and their nature. This chapter is not the place to discuss all the features of the regime[16] but it is difficult to overestimate its merits.

What matters for present purposes is how central MR is to the remedies sought. The basic requirement for these (new) national regulations is that there be explicit and clear clauses on MR or 'equivalence'. After all, regulations where Member States still have regulatory autonomy (in goods) must be in the 'non-harmonised area'[17] and that is *where MR ought to apply*. Such clauses can be attached to the objectives or the technical standards referred to. Reference to standards becomes more effective over time as CEN and CENELEC[18] increasingly write standards which, by definition, are valid for all EEA countries, Turkey (due to the customs union with the EU), Switzerland (due to bilateral agreements) and several other European countries. In a rising number of instances, such standards may be identical with world standards.[19] When world standards are used in such instances, MR extends to imports from third countries if adherence to these standards is ensured by credible conformity assessment. The large majority of national draft laws passing the 98/34 Committee either contain equivalence clauses by now or are adjusted after insistence by the committee (Pelkmans et al., 2000). If the enacted laws, later, do not have such clauses, they infringe EU law, and are unenforceable against intra-EU imports. The conclusion is that the regime, backed up by significant resources and efforts as well as by strict CJEU rulings, forms a powerful and credible agent for mutual recognition to be maintained and to become more 'visible' for business over time.

The numbers are impressive. Between 1988 and 1998 the total number of national notifications was about 5000 and the trend was upward (Pelkmans et al., 2000, p. 274). In the period 1999 to 2005, the annual rate was close to 600 a year and moved up once the new Member States came in (Pelkmans, 2007a, p. 707). The 'comments' and so-called 'detailed opinions' from other Member States and the Commission during those seven years suggest that some 2100 national draft laws were suspected to cause barriers in future. This staggering quantity of national regulations and decrees, if gone unchecked,

---

16 See Pelkmans et al. (2000) for an extensive explanation and discussion of this control mechanism.

17 If an issue is subject to harmonised EU regulation, Member States lose their regulatory autonomy.

18 These two and ETSI (telecoms and internet standards) are the three European standardisation bodies, linked to the New Approach and other EU regulatory initiatives via Memoranda of Understanding.

19 CEN, CENELEC and ETSI have agreements (e.g. the Dresden and Vienna ones) with ISO and IEC as well as the ITU which facilitate the fullest possible use of world standards when writing European standards. In reality, it is often the other way around: European standards are quite often used as (a basis for) world standards. The EU is far more active than e.g. ANSI, the American Standards body in ISO, in world standardisation. For example, according to Renda and Schrefler (2006), 27 per cent of CEN standards reflect ISO standards and 57 per cent of CENELEC standards is identical to IEC standards. See also WTO (2005).

would have made a mockery of the internal goods market.[20] The newest report[21] shows an average of 663 notifications for the years 2006 to 2008 (so, almost 2000 such draft laws for about one-third of the goods traded in the EU!). The Commission and Member States reacted 1215 times to these notifications, with 'detailed opinions' (where the suspicion of emerging barriers is strong) totalling no less than 321! What would have become of the single goods market without MR as the basis for this procedure?

4 BENEFITS AND COSTS OF EU MUTUAL RECOGNITION UNTIL 2008

It is insightful to subject MR in goods to a benefit/cost analysis. This is done in Table 6.1 and briefly elaborated in the text of the present section.[22] There are many benefits to MR, whether judicial or regulatory. Table 6.1 suggests three categories of benefits. First of all, there are regulatory benefits, in the sense of 'better regulation'. If MR is purely judicial, Member States' autonomy with respect to regulatory objectives is retained due to their 'equivalence', even though free movement prevails. If MR is regulatory, Art. 114/3 TFEU prescribes a high level of protection (typically, in SHEC-type risk regulation), so that there can be no race to the bottom via bargaining. Moreover, there will be a bias against regulatory failure of Member States because technical specifications (which might lead to overregulation) are no longer in directives, whilst the technical standards referred to are based on performance criteria rather than design (i.e. prescriptive detail).

Second, strategic benefits relate to the deepening and quality of the internal market. If MR is judiciary, the breakthrough was and is that free movement prevails whereas it was hindered or blocked before. It accomplishes this without adding any EU regulation; that is, it avoids centralisation. Moreover, judicial MR disciplines Member States' overregulation, since their rules cannot stop intra-EU imports originating from regimes with lighter rules (as long as the objectives are equivalent). Finally, judicial MR forms the basis for 'regulatory competition' without a race to the bottom which goes further than MR in a static sense.[23] If MR is regulatory, the deepening of the internal market is accelerated

[20] That Member States are regulatory machines is realised even better if one knows that these new regulations relate to only one-third of all goods traded in the EU. Some 50 per cent fall under harmonised rules (hence, Member States can no longer enact alone in these areas) and some 20 per cent are unregulated goods markets.

[21] See COM (2009)690 of 21 December 2009, The operation of directive 98/34 from 2006 to 2008, and COM Staff Document SEC (2009) 1704 on the same date.

[22] This section, including Table 6.1, is adapted from Pelkmans (2007a), with relatively minor changes.

[23] See Sun and Pelkmans (1995) for an elaborate assessment of the conditions for regulatory competition in the EU internal market for goods to occur, and improve welfare, with a case study in goods and one in services. It is crucial to first realise that regulatory competition in the internal market can only work if equivalence of objectives is ensured; that is, if MR applies. If not, Member States will tend to invoke the derogations and intra-EU trade will be impeded. However, this invocation is only legal if based on a market failure, usually a problem of SHEC, in turn based on a credible risk asssessment with scientific evidence. Thus, minuscule residues of catalysers for large-scale beer brewing as well as preservatives (when beer travels long distances) violate the German beer purity law, but have no consequences for health or safety. Thus, whilst Germany can maintain

Table 6.1 Benefits and costs of mutual recognition

Types of benefits	Judicial MR	Regulatory MR	Types of costs	Judicial MR	Regulatory MR
regulatory	autonomy of MS retained for objectives	common SHEC objectives ensured bias against 'regulatory failure'	information	MR 'invisible' for economic agents, except at high costs (w/o clear MR clauses) even if info is collected, many 'grey areas'; uncertainty (e.g. case law) for business and MSAU no rule book imposed on MSAU	some modest uncertainty, if European standards are lacking or innovation is used
strategic	free movement prevails over-regulation of MS disciplined basis for regulatory competition w/o race to the bottom no (add'l.) EU rules	internal market deepening accelerated over-regulation MS & EU disciplined only minimal (extra) EU rules	transaction	monitoring extremely costly, evidence anecdotal at best When MSAU refuse, reputation and waiting costs, little (EU) help (except SOLVIT) assuring rights for business unattractive, costly and slow	regulatory & standardisers' networks monitor and solve, partly (with delays)
economic welfare	pro-competitive	pro-competitive	compliance	unknown, possibly serious costs for existing rules	

Notes:
MS = Member States; MSAU = MS Authorities.
N.B. This table merely assesses MR of *existing* rules (i.e. Section 2 and not Section 3 of this chapter).

its beer purity law for domestic producers, that law cannot be a reason to stop the import of beer from other Member States. It does not follow, however, that beer brewers located in Germany are immediately and powerfully exposed to price competitive imports of 'other' EU beer. Beer distribution in German pubs is entirely in the hands of local breweries and, more often than not, Germans stick to beer made according to the purity law. What one observes is some marginal penetration in supermarkets (bottles/cans) and patrol stations along highways and its pro-competitive impact is probably modest. Therefore, regulatory competition should be subjected to a careful industrial economic analysis before jumping to conclusions about the removal of local (over?) regulation prompted by local industry 'suffering' from local rules stricter than rules in other Member States. Stronger, the larger German breweries do not have to apply the purity law to exports (which for some of them are their lifeline of business) and therefore remain competitive in the internal market.

because lengthy negotiations can be avoided (especially blockages on technical details) and agreement on goals is far easier. This is so because ministers in the Council and MEPs are not hindered by a lack of technical expertise or deep asymmetries of information when it comes to setting regulatory objectives, instead of an ocean of technical detail. After 1985, when the Council began to apply qualified majority voting, agreement became relatively easy to accomplish. Furthermore, regulatory MR disciplines overregulation at both levels of government, since the focus is on objectives and the reliance on European performance standards reduces considerably the scope for idiosyncratic (or protectionist?) specifics. Regulatory MR does add EU rules but minimally so, and drastically less than the Old Approach would do.

The third benefit concerns economic welfare, which is what the internal market is all about: MR is pro-competitive, if not strongly pro-competitive at times, compared with its alternatives, albeit that strategic quality games cannot be excluded (given that equivalence of objectives is to be satisfied). Box 6.1 elaborates on the scarce economic analysis available in the literature.

With this litany of advantages, MR seems almost too good to be true. Indeed, this is how, naively, MR is often portrayed among economists. Unfortunately, there is an inclination to neglect the considerable drawbacks of MR in actual practice, both for business and authorities, whether EU or national. It is important to appreciate the costs of MR for business and authorities.

Table 6.1 distinguishes three types of costs. First, information costs, which are especially large for judicial MR. After all, MR is 'invisible' to economic agents, unless specific laws contain clear equivalence clauses, be it on objectives or standards. What economic agents 'see' are the requirements in local laws. Since judicial MR is developed in CJEU case law, numerous businesses have no idea about MR or that it might matter to them, let alone that companies would know how to verify whether it is applied to their goods. One costly consequence of this ignorance is that many SMEs fail to consider MR and thus either refrain from exporting to countries, or do export but after costly adaptations, which is exactly what MR aims to avoid. For companies which do know about MR, the costs of verifying whether MR would apply to their goods can be high and/or lead to uncertainty. In addition, there are costs because of 'grey areas' about when 'equivalence' applies, both for business and the authorities, even when national authorities do act in a spirit of MR. Unfortunately, the lack of a 'rule book' for MR, in particular for national inspecting agencies or other officials, causes most civil servants not to act in that spirit; rather, they often attempt to enforce local rules. The Commission has gradually come to realise the downside of judicial MR and issued reports and soft guidelines; it has also greatly improved the information on its (TRIS) website,[24] promoted seminars and launched a special campaign for the new Member States. Vis-à-vis business this is unlikely to help much because many SMEs tend to ignore such general campaigns. For officials the utility is greater. For regulatory MR, information costs are far lower.

Second, transaction costs are also substantial for judicial MR. However, hard evidence

---

24 The TRIS website provides information on the removal or prevention of regulatory (mainly technical) barriers to free movement. See http://ec.europa.eu/enterprise/tris/index_en.htm.

BOX 6.1 MUTUAL RECOGNITION AND ECONOMIC WELFARE

Despite the appreciation for mutual recognition that economists often show, there is scant economic analysis in the literature. A number of case studies for the Cecchini report (esp. MAC Group, 1988) and for the Monti ex-post-1992 report (esp. Atkins, 1997) comprise fairly careful cost estimates of the failure to apply mutual recognition. Anecdotal and qualitative evidence about similar instances can also be had from UNICE (2004) and EFTA (2008).

There are scattered attempts to develop economic theory but it is disjointed and no 'body' of economic analysis is available yet. One 'strand' which has received some attention is based on the cost-increasing effect of regulatory barriers rendering market entry more difficult. Abraham (1991) shows graphically and for homogeneous goods that, dependent on the costs of adjustment to enter national markets inside the internal goods market, the latter may well remain effectively fragmented, with permanent price disparities. The Old Approach, with vetoes, is likely to prompt calls for a level playing field, which is bound to push up the overall EU level of regulation and thereby 'raising rivals' costs', in turn significantly reducing the competitive threat for the least competitive country. Mutual recognition would thus be clearly pro-competitive. Falvey (1989) and Abraham (1991) consider SHEC regulations as 'quality signalling'. With mutual recognition, consumers in the high-price country have an information problem: they might distrust the low price as a signal of lower quality. This is likely to induce the low-price exporters to invest in reputation building (e.g. voluntary certification) or to undertake to systematically test and certify their goods in compliance with standards from the high-cost country. Perhaps unexpectedly, this leads to what Vogel (1995) has observed and called 'trading up', a convergence to higher quality levels between trading countries. Theoretically more sophisticated but even further removed from the practice of MR in the EU is Lutz' (1996) model of vertical product differentiation. He shows, under restrictive assumptions, that mutual recognition can generate a higher economic welfare than both no regulation and full harmonisation. But the case is not a general one, e.g. his model can even produce the result that entry deterrence can be achieved by strategically choosing quality. Yet another study by Suwa-Eisenmann and Verdier (2002) introduces a political support function (only having regard to the producer interest). With distinct institutional capacities, implicit regulatory protection inside the Union can emerge. Finally, Felbermayr and Jung (2008) introduce technical barriers and mutual recognition in the new trade models with heterogeneous firms. The authors are interested in unravelling the effects of e.g. mutual recognition on industry productivity but strictly within the rigour of this new family of models. One result, based on a calibrated version of their model, is that lower technical barriers (so not necessarily mutual recognition only) lead to reallocation of market shares from more to less productive firms.

about transaction costs is scattered and/or anecdotal, with little idea of how representative these data are, as the Commission cannot monitor judicial MR. Case studies indicate that, in particular, SMEs are deterred by actual transaction costs as well as by uncertainty. The deterrent effect is greatest when Member States' authorities routinely refuse market access if a good does not match local technical requirements. Imposing withdrawal implies a loss of reputation for the company at stake. This is followed by waiting costs, which can only be reduced drastically if bilateral cooperation between Member States is quasi-automatic or the Commission intervenes. Waiting costs can be sensitive if time-to-market matters a lot in sales and marketing. The recent SOLVIT voluntary cooperation procedures[25] are beginning to help fill this gap.

Furthermore, business is often hesitant to ensure its rights under Community law. One reason is that future business in the destination country ought not to be jeopardised. Besides, the pursuit of one's rights under Community law is very slow and costly. Business often rightly notes that legal progress about free movement should not be achieved by it but should be reasonably guaranteed by the system.[26] It is striking that these costs are arising, in part, from the absence of networking between Member States and sound investment in bilateral cooperation inside the Union. The contrast with regulatory MR is significant. In sectors covered by the New Approach, regulatory and standardisers' networks broadly monitor, contacts are not anonymous, occasional network meetings take place and some problem solving does occur, albeit with delays. As a result, ensuring one's rights is rarely necessary.

Third, compliance costs typically exist when judicial MR fails; under regulatory MR they are exceptional. However, there is no reliable evidence on compliance costs.

Until 2008, MR in the EU goods market was therefore characterised by multiple and substantial benefits and a number of costs which, for business, tended to accumulate to often deterrent levels. There are also costs for national authorities when they enforce rules in the spirit of MR. The disturbing conclusion, at least for judicial MR, is that the very companies relying on MR in the internal market are hardly 'protected' by its regime. The incentives were in some ways *perverse* and they will have to be altered into positive

---

[25] SOLVIT is an on-line problem-solving network of national officials, coordinated by the Commission. It tackles complaints about the misapplication of internal market (and other EU) law by public authorities but without legal proceedings, in a period of no more than ten weeks. In September 2006, SOLVIT claimed a success rate of 75 per cent of cases solved 'informally', a clear incentive to use it, although some Member States leave their SOLVIT units understaffed, thereby frustrating the process. Some 16 per cent of the cases are about market access of goods. See http://ec.europa.eu/solvit/site/index_en.htm.

[26] The frustrations about the practical problems or indeed neglect of MR were so strong that European business began to turn away from MR. A first manifestation of this turn-around can be found in the Molitor report (1995) and the UNICE (1995) regulation report. With a delay the Commission started to recognise these issues, once it moved away from a narrow case-law based mindset about MR. See COM(1999)299 of 16 June 1999, on MR in the internal market, and COM(2002)419 of 23 July 2002, the second bi-annual report on MR. Examples were published in the Internal Market Scoreboard no. 10 of May 2002. How deep business frustration ran, however, is clear from UNICE (2004) under the telling title: 'It's the internal market, stupid!', with many examples of neglect or misapplication of MR. Indeed, it appears from interviews of businesses having relied on MR that 'firms find themselves unwillingly appointed as guardian of the Treaty (here, free movement under MR), chasing violations at their own costs' (Pelkmans, 2005, p. 123).

ones for judicial MR to engender the much-wanted benefits for the Union. The picture for regulatory MR is far brighter.

5 RESTORING MUTUAL RECOGNITION INCENTIVES UNDER PROPER EU GOVERNANCE

For about a decade, the Commission and stakeholders[27] have cooperated in relative tranquility in order to introduce appropriate 'governance' systems ensuring that MR would work much better in the single market. The outcome[28] consists of three pieces of EU legislation: one on the application of MR by Member States and the obligations of companies (Regulation 764/2008), and two on overcoming the imperfections of the New Approach (Regulation 765/2008 and Decision 768/2008).[29]

After a brief note on the latter two pieces of EU legislation, the focus will be on MR regulation 764/2008. The accreditation and market surveillance regulation 765/2008 addresses four concerns of the New Approach: accreditation, market surveillance, import controls and CE marking (which indicates conformity with EU law and the referred European Standards). None of these affect the fundamental link between the New Approach and MR (the agreement on common objectives, hence equivalence) but two of them are relevant for secondary instances of MR in the New Approach. The first one is concerned with the MR of certificates issued by Notified Bodies (EU approved certification bodies), which is extremely convenient for European business. It turned out that not all Notified Bodies had been subjected to strict eligibility criteria by 'their' Member States and this has led to various problems and a lack of credibility. With a new, permanent, high-quality European system of accreditation as well as peer review, the consistent and high degree of credibility of Notified Bodies will be ensured. With respect to CE marking, consumers and their associations have often complained about confusion with other marks, the evasion of the manufacturers' responsibility (in the value chain) and unreliable self-certification (hence, sticking on a CE mark) in the case of certain imports. Regulation 765/2008 tackles these problems and tightens import controls.[30]

The mutual recognition regulation 764/2008 constitutes a response to the numerous complaints and criticisms about the factual working of MR 'on the ground' (see

---

[27] Including European business, standardisation bodies, testing and certification bodies (including Notified Bodies, assigned by the EU to execute conformity assessment under the New Approach), accreditation networks in Europe, consumers, the EU Economic and Social Committee as well as Council working groups and the IMCO Committee of the European Parliament.

[28] The so-called 2008 Goods Package, also referred to as the New Legislative Framework.

[29] Reg. 764/2008 (the mutual recognition regulation) of 9 July 2008 laying down procedures relating to the application of certain national technical rules to products lawfully marketed in another Member State and repealing Decision 3052/95/EC, in OJEU of 13 August 2008, L 218, pp. 21–9; Reg. 765/2008 (the accreditation and surveillance regulation) of 9 July 2008 setting out the requirements for accreditation and market surveillance relating to the marketing of products and repealing Reg. (EEC) 339/93 in OJEU of 13 August 2008, L 218, pp. 30–47; Decision 768/2008/EC of 9 July 2008 on a common framework for the marketing of products, and repealing Council Decision 93/465/EEC in OJEU of 13 August 2008, L 218, pp. 82–128.

[30] For details, see Pelkmans (2009).

Section 4). The purpose of the regulation is to significantly reduce the various costs of MR to European business and, in so doing, enhance the internal market benefits. It does this via two routes: (a) information obligations (e.g. on technical requirements in rules for the relevant goods) are imposed on EU countries in order to help EU-based companies intending to access the local market as well as administrations of other Member States; (b) a detailed specification of how a correct application of MR brings with it extensive procedural safeguards, such that the burden of proof of not granting MR is essentially on the importing Member State. The first track lowers or eliminates the information costs so that companies merely incur the ordinary business risks when accessing a national market in the EU: good for them and good for (actual or potential) competition in the single market as a whole. The second track respects the national regulatory autonomy and the public interest pursued via regulation (as the MR case law does as well), but *imposes disciplines* on the Member States in shifting the burden of proof for not respecting MR, even when goods have already been marketed elsewhere in the internal market, onto those authorities. The required proof is subjected to EU rules which protect the companies against arbitrary or too hastily decided barriers. Moreover, the rules impose transparency and facilitate appeal. For all these reasons, the regulation is a genuine relief for business, in particular SMEs. Table 6.2 summarises the key provisions.

The information obligations for Member States have to be organised structurally via so-called 'contact points', behind which a system has to be set up making it possible to access and provide highly specialised technical information (what laws and decrees? what (national or European) standards? what institutions involved?).

Such information has to be given for free (as a right) and within two weeks. The back-up system has to dispose of sufficient means in order to be capable of delivery throughout the year. The 27 contact points are expected to be in touch with one another routinely (a new electronic system might be set up for that purpose) so as to make MR work much better and without much ado. This should be an effective underpinning of mutual trust, indispensable for smooth MR. A further 'service' to European business is the Commission announcement of a list of goods falling under MR, in eurospeak the 'non-harmonised sector'. Meanwhile, a first version of such a list has become available but it is not improbable that improved and refined lists will follow in the future since the identification of exactly what does and does not fall under MR is not always easy.[31]

The reversal of the burden of proof is new but can, in fact, be traced back to an Interpretative Communication on the case law on MR in 2003.[32] The procedures are

---

[31] This only goes to show that, in some cases, European business was, and to some extent still is at times, uncertain about the relevance of MR to their products. The list can be found at http://ec.europa.eu/enterprise/intsub/a12/.

[32] Interpretative Communication on easier access for goods, practical application of the MR principle, in OJEC C 265 of 4 November 2003, in which also many instances of improper conduct by national authorities are discussed, showing the necessity of the reversal for business. The reader should also realise that the CJEU is wary of employing the term 'mutual recognition', even though it is the very source of the idea. However, in the Pre-amble of Reg. 764/2008, the term MR is employed without reservation.

Table 6.2 Mutual recognition regulation 764/2008

Procedural safeguards for mutual recognition via
- Information obligations to companies from other Member States (entrants)
- Proper application of mutual recognition

Mutual recognition and reversal of the burden of proof
- ***purpose:*** Member States have the burden of proof for non-conformity in case the product has already been lawfully marketed elsewhere in the EU
- (Art. 4) economic operator provides information (on request of the EU country of destination) about the properties of the product and the lawful marketing (earlier, elsewhere in the EU)
- Mutual recognition of the certification by accredited bodies (Reg. 765/2008)
- (Art. 6) various procedural safeguards for a company about to access the market of Member State X, in the event X wants to prohibit the product (written, technical or scientific evidence, on the basis of the 'essential requirements' [CJEU language for regulatory objectives], etc.)
- plus a period of 20 days, no temporary suspension during procedures (except for 'serious risk'); failing a response within 20 days, access granted automatically
- appeal possible

General
- deals with 'technical rules' not harmonised at EU level
- specific exceptions and 'general prohibitions' (public morality or security, e.g. weapons)

Information obligations (Member St. & COM)
- ***purpose*** is to reduce information costs drastically and, in so doing, facilitate the exploitation of free movement and MR
- accessibility of national technical rules (esp. for SMEs)
- system of 'contact points' (see item 29, preamble); info free, within 15 days, sufficient means, explicit reference to SOLVIT
- Commission draws up indicative, non-exhaustive list of products falling under the 'non-harmonised sector'

plus: electronic system for exchange of technical information between contact points of the Member States [encouragement, not compulsory]

N.B. In force as from 13 May 2009

prescribed in considerable detail and ensure that a company is not left in limbo: suspension of the import is not allowed unless there is a 'serious risk' and long delays (beyond a total of 40 days) will result in automatic market access. One does not need to read more than the UNICE reports (1995, 2004), the two Commission communications on MR of 1999 and 2002 (COM(1999)299 and COM(2002)419) and the Interpretative Communication to appreciate what a great difference the reversal implies for European business: apart from the psychological effect, Member States will be forced to alter their administrative conduct at all levels and firms will be able to enforce their rights under much greater legal certainty and with lower costs, if any.[33]

It is important to underline that nothing in these procedures affects the SHEC objectives of national regulations. If there is a genuine issue of non-conformity, the Member State has every right to take the good from the market and the Commission will normally support that. Finally, a subtle difference between Reg. 764/2008 and the previous rules consists in the MR of certificates. From now on, this general term covers voluntary certification as well (that is, outside the New Approach and therefore possibly of relevance to (unharmonised) national regulation). For business, this is an efficiency improvement since companies often insist on testing other properties than the EU SHEC requirements (for example, durability or consistent quality, especially for components). More often than not, Member States refused to recognise such voluntary certification done elsewhere where it mattered for their national requirements.

It would seem that the MR regulation has rightly been applauded as the appropriate 'governance' to make MR work as intended, thereby deepening the internal market for goods whilst improving its effective functioning.

6 MUTUAL RECOGNITION IN SERVICES: HORIZONTAL LIBERALISATION

Negative and positive market integration in services has always fallen behind the deepening of the internal market in goods; it has also been less wide in scope and less firm. It is only in the last two decades that the CJEU and, more hesitantly, the EU legislator have begun to address the barriers in earnest. In the context of the present chapter, the focus will merely be on aspects relevant to MR, thereby inevitably leaving out many other interesting elements needed for a fuller appreciation of the gradual emergence of a functioning internal services market. The present section will discuss what is called 'horizontal services liberalisation': the achievement of free movement and the effective exercise of the right of establishment in sectors which are regulated only relatively lightly. The term suggests that the EU legislator (Council and EP) would not need to regulate or perhaps only with 'minimum harmonisation'. The CJEU should be able to ensure these economic freedoms, possibly with MR as well. Section 7 will briefly discuss MR in (vertically) regulated services such as financial services, transport and professional services.

CJEU case law in services is complicated and, at times, confusing.[34] The following cannot be but a stylised presentation of its logic. The CJEU has gradually tightened its rulings with the effect of disciplining more effectively national services regulation in the internal market. It is useful to keep Figure 6.3 (on goods) in mind because the analogy with services is close. If we ignore the objective of investor and saver protection – which falls under vertical regulation of financial markets anyway, hence not under horizontal

[33] More examples of problems caused by Member States are found in Atkins (1997) and in Pelkmans (2005).

[34] The reader is referred to surveys such as Andenas and Roth (eds) (2001), Hatzopoulos and Do (2006), Hatzopoulos (2008), Maydell (2008), Snell (2008), Barnard (2008) and Klamert (2010).

liberalisation – the objectives Member States pursue in national services regulation amount to SHEC. But this is not nearly as clear cut as it is in goods, and case law also goes beyond SHEC. In the treaty section on services, there is no article comparable to Art. 36, TFEU (identifying specific derogations); in the treaty section on establishment, Art. 52, TFEU only specifies derogations on the general grounds of 'public policy, public security or public health'. Provisions on the economic freedoms are similar to that on goods (i.e. Art. 34, TFEU), without employing the convoluted wording 'measures with an equivalent effect to . . . quantitative restrictions'. Art. 56, TFEU states that 'restrictions on freedom to provide services within the Union shall be prohibited'. It is the same in Art. 49, TFEU: 'restrictions on the freedom of establishment of nationals of a Member State in the territory of another Member State shall be prohibited'. Establishment is also subject to 'national treatment' (Arts 49, 54 and 55, TFEU). If derogations to the free movement of services are applied, non-discrimination is compulsory (Art. 61, TFEU). Note that all these provisons have never been revised since 1957.

In case law on services, the lack of detail in the treaty has had two crucial consequences, apart from an initial hesitation on the part of economic agents to challenge restrictions imposed by Member States. First, hindering or blocking free movement of services or establishment was initially assessed by the CJEU with a view to direct or indirect discrimination. One might say that national services regulation was gradually 'cleansed' of discriminatory provisions, a much needed but nonetheless modest achievement.[35] Second, with almost no specifications on possible derogations, a body of 'rule of reason' justifications was built up, regarded as 'imperative reasons relating to the public interest' or, much the same, 'imperative requirements in the general interest'.[36] Over time, the list has become quite long and the wording is often rather general.[37] One may indeed argue on the grounds of legal certainty or for the deepening of the internal services market that the treaty ought to be revised, yielding more specific guidance, and/or secondary EU law be enacted (in other words, a more active and agile EU legislator, creating legitimacy for the rules and unburdening the CJEU of such creative constructions). Sooner or later, a more sweeping approach was bound to emerge since early case law kept numerous barriers in place. In order to understand the essence of the greater determination since the beginning of the 1990s, two modes of disciplining national regulation are important: disciplining 'restrictions' and the 'country-of-origin-principle'. The first one has become more prominent since the *Saeger* ruling (1991) and also plays a role in the services directive 2006/123, whereas the second one is employed in the e-commerce directive, the TV without frontiers directive and the Bolkestein draft directive.

---

[35] Note that, in exceptional instances, and based on a strict CJEU interpretation, discriminatory provisions may be justified for 'public policy, public security or public health' under Art. 52, TFEU.

[36] The first formulation can be found in e.g. Case C-58/98 *Corsten* [2000] ECR I-0000 para. 35; the second in e.g. Case C-55/94 *Gebhard* [1995] ECR I-4165 para. 39.

[37] Known as the 'general good' approach framed in very broad objectives, and subsequently assessed strictly, it includes e.g. intellectual property, consumer protection, protection of workers, conservation of national heritage, sound administration of justice, cohesion of the tax system, requirements of road safety, the financial balance of the social security system and language requirements (for dentists, in the interest of patients). The reader will observe that many of these are inspired by the approach in goods.

The *Saeger* ruling[38] sharpens CJEU case law by employing language reminiscent of *Dassonville*: 'Art. [now 56, TFEU] . . . requires . . . the abolition of any [non-discriminatory] restriction . . . liable to prohibit or otherwise impede the activities of a provider of services established in another Member State where he lawfully provides similar services'. Wording like 'less advantageous' or 'more difficult' has also been used. Observe that this ruling disciplines restrictions but does not go as far as *Cassis de Dijon*, where the origin principle is first pronounced. Nevertheless, the difference is slim because 'otherwise impede' or 'more difficult' casts the net very wide indeed. Both in *Cassis de Dijon* (see Figure 6.2) and in *Saeger*, it is really the justified derogations which matter, but the set of derogations in services seems larger. Subsequent case law (and to some extent, even earlier) strictly analyses the application of derogations, in analogy with the central box in Figure 6.3. If non-discriminatory, measures have to be necessary,[39] proportionate ('not go beyond what is necessary')[40] and, what comes close to the same thing, 'it must not be possible to obtain the same result by less restrictive rules'.[41]

In a third step (in analogy with Figure 6.3, bottom-right box), the CJEU tests for a simple form of MR via explicit proofs such as (identical) tests on standards, licensing and its conditions or approvals in the EU country of establishment of the provider. Rather than MR of precise 'objectives', the CJEU refers to the 'public interest' as pursued in the country of origin. Thus, the treaty freedom to provide services 'may be restricted only by rules justified by the public interest . . . in so far as that interest is not safeguarded by the rules to which the provider of such a service is subject in the Member State where he is established'.[42] In the *Mediawet* case[43] the Court held that restrictions of the freedom to provide services are prohibited 'if the requirements embodied in that legislation are already satisfied by the rules imposed on those persons in the Member State in which they are established'. In a simpler form, e.g. by forbidding duplication of tests or a new certificate of solvency[44] or guarantees already furnished by the provider in his home country,[45] this MR test goes back three decades. The main effect of the gradual sharpening and widening of this MR test during the 1990s and later was to stimulate economic agents to reveal (by going to court) the many restrictions they were subjected to. The increasing awareness of a thick and very wide web of restrictions in the internal services market eventually led to the 2002 Commission Report[46] on those barriers, as a stepping stone to the draft Bolkestein directive.[47]

The underlying conviction of the Bolkestein draft was that case law would not suffice

---

38 Case C-76/90 [1991] ECR I-4221.

39 In *Saeger*, the CJEU speaks of 'objectively necessary'; in Case C-222/95 *Parodi* [1997] ECR I-3899, para. 31, the wording is 'indispensable for attaining the objective pursued'.

40 For example, in Case C-424/97 *Haim* [2000] ECR I-0000 para. 60 and many other ones.

41 Case C-288/89 *Mediawet* I [1991ECR I-4007 para. 15.

42 From Case C-355/98 *Commission vs. Belgium* [2000] ECR I-1221, para. 37. Similar wording can be found in the *Saeger* case and many other cases.

43 Case C-288/89 *Mediawet* [1991] ECR I-4007, para. 13.

44 In the German insurance cases: Case C-205/84 *Commission vs. Germany* [1986] ECR 3755, para. 37].

45 Case C-279/80 *Webb* [1981] ECR 3305, para. 20.

46 COM (2002) 441 of 30 July 2002, The state of the internal market for services.

47 COM (2004) 2 of 13 January 2004, Proposal for a directive on services in the internal market.

to establish a well-functioning internal market for services and that the EU legislator had to act firmly. The 'restrictions' approach was replaced by the more radical origin principle (= CoOP) in Art. 16: 'Member States shall ensure that providers are subject only to the national provisions of their Member State of origin which fall within the coordinated field.' This 'field' was widely drawn[48] and the origin country was to be responsible 'for supervising the provider and the services provided by him, including services provided by him in another Member State' (Art. 16/3). Given the CoOP, the design of the directive consisted in accompanying it with a complicated list of various types of derogations and, in a few instances, harmonisation (in consumer protection, simplification of 'red tape' and two black lists, one for free movement restrictions and one for restrictions of the right of establishment). Realising that the CoOP and its supervision provisions would require a high degree of mutual trust between Member States, far-reaching provisions about administrative cooperation between EU countries were introduced by organising the allocation of supervisory tasks, exchange of information and mutual assistance.[49] The economic impact of the CoOP in this design hinges critically on (a) whether EU countries impose sufficiently different regulatory requirements on the services falling within the coordinated field (if not different, MR would do; if different or revised to lower them in some countries, the question becomes whether market failures will be re-introduced, hence, the public interest would be harmed, without having a duty to harmonise); (b) the number and importance of the derogations specified in the directive (indeed, such a radical approach forms a standing invitation to lobbies or Member States to insert more derogations, which is exactly what happened). On the first point, based on Kox and Lejour (2005)'s regulatory heterogeneity index for intra-EU services, De Bruijn et al. (2007) show that the CoOP as originally envisaged in the draft would significantly reduce intra-EU regulatory heterogeneity for intra-EU services trade. Since such heterogeneity entails fixed entry costs for providers for each Member State of destination, the fall of the index due to the CoOP yields extra trade growth and jobs. On the second point, once derogations multiply, the relevant 'field' shrinks to services with relatively few serious obstacles and the CoOP largely loses its purpose. It also matters what eventually happens with these derogations. In one politically prominent but economically minor instance, cross-border health services, a separate vertical directive has been proposed[50] and adopted after much debate by the European Parliament on 19 January 2011. Other specific draft directives are likely to follow (e.g. on security services).

There are many reasons why the Bolkestein strategy failed and a modest reformulation of Art. 16 was opted for. The reader is referred to the literature.[51] But two considerations

---

[48] Art. 16/2 stated 'national provisions relating to access to and the exercise of a service activity, in particular those requirements governing the behaviour of the provider, the quality or content of the service, advertising, contracts and the provider's liability'.

[49] The draft also encouraged the drawing up of EU-wide 'codes of conduct', provisions which survived the turbulent legislative process all the way to directive 2006/123. For the meaning of such provisions, see Delimatsis (2010).

[50] COM (2008) 414 of 2 July 2008, Proposal for a directive on the application of patients' rights in cross-border health care. This draft directive remains rather close to established case law.

[51] See the references in note 34 and e.g. Nicolaidis and Schmidt (2007), Pelkmans (2007b) and Chang et al. (2010).

are worth mentioning here. One is whether the CoOP in the Bolkestein draft was really identical to that introduced in a few previous directives (see also Klamert, 2010). Art. 3/2 of the e-commerce directive[52] stipulates that 'Member States may not . . . restrict the freedom to provide information society services from another Member State'. Clearly, this is not identical to the Bolkestein draft: dependent on the derogations, this is a narrower or wider application of the restrictions approach. Similarly, in the TV directive, now revised as the Audiovisual Media Services directive,[53] Art. 2a sets out the so-called 'country of transmission' principle: Member States ' shall ensure freedom of reception and shall not restrict retransmissions . . . of audiovisual services from other Member States'. Again, some derogations follow, of course. Apart from the legal issue of national courts having to interpret the rules of origin countries under the Bolkestein formulation, and *not* in the two directives quoted here, one wonders whether a far-reaching degree of discipline of restrictions is economically very different from a CoOP approach with (too) many derogations.

The second consideration is about the derogations in the Bolkestein draft. Apart from derogations due to sectoral regulation and other enumerated instances, one would expect the derogations that have emerged from case law on services to be respected. However, this was not the case: no reference or explicit summary was included, which left the very general derogations based on public policy, public security or public health from the treaty as the *only* ones applicable. This caused a lot of consternation: can secondary EU law override case law (normally, not) and, just as important, does all this imply that this case law did not refer to market failures and, hence, had always been unjustified? However, if both these questions were answered in the negative, the economic meaning of the CoOP would be curtailed and a degree of legal uncertainty would not help the internal market. MR does not entail these problems because of the basic idea of 'equivalence'. However, MR beyond what case law in services had achieved would almost certainly require minimum harmonisation in a range of services, going against the very idea of horizontal liberalisation.

Directive 2006/123 removed the CoOP from the draft and replaced it with a restatement of the treaty rules and *some* case law. Art. 16/1 says that 'Member States shall respect the right of providers to provide services in a Member State other than in which they are established . . . [and] . . . ensure free access and free exercise of a service activity within its territory'. Restrictions are subject to non-discrimination, the necessity test and the proportionality test, as in case law. After specifying a blacklist of seven restrictive measures, Art. 16/3 is now explicit on the derogations from the treaty (public policy, security or health) and adds two: environment and employment conditions (including collective agreements). This is remarkable, to say the least. In a clause merely (re)stating the freedom to provide services in the internal market (and not the CoOP), a huge list of established case law derogations are simply left out. Some of these are dealt with by the blacklists of restrictions on free movement (Art. 16/2) and on establishment (Art. 14),

---

52 Directive 2000/31/EC, OJEU L 178/1 of 17 July 2000.

53 Directive 2007/65/EC of 11 Dec. 2007, amending Directive 89/552/EEC, OJEU of 18 Dec. 2007, L 332/27. Note that para. 27 of the Pre-amble says that the CoOP should remain the core of the directive.

but otherwise this set-up is simply aggravating legal uncertainty. The hope is that the extensive screening of national (and local!) regulation up to 2008 inclusive, together with the 'mutual evaluation' between Member States conducted in 2010, has done away with most of the reasons why, once, the case law was developed.[54] Finally, it is regrettable that Art. 16/1 does not explicitly mention a basic form of MR, namely, in close cooperation with other Member States, the duty to verify provisions in EU countries of origin as well as their supervision. There are different ways of specifying this duty, the most rigorous one being the analogy with Figure 6.4 on the mutual recognition directive for goods, assigning the burden of proof to the Member State where the service is provided. A partial compensation of this omission is found in the provisions on administrative cooperation, going much further than CJEU case law. Arts 28 and 29 of the directive are useful in underlining the cooperative obligations of the country where the provider is established. Called 'mutual assistance', it goes some way towards MR. This is going to be supported by the (electronic) Internal Market Information system (for the national officials), which has meanwhile begun to operate for a number of internal market purposes. What is lacking in these two articles is an emphasis on the *duty* of the country where the service is provided to verify details in the origin country and find them wanting, with a formal reasoned decision and appeal options, before imposing restrictions in the first place. That obligation would render it similar to the measures in Figure 6.4 ensuring MR for goods.

7 MUTUAL RECOGNITION IN EU SECTORAL SERVICES REGULATION

The present section will briefly describe the application of MR in sectoral EU services regulation. In financial markets, transport and professional services, MR has assumed meanings and forms somewhat distinct from horizontal MR. Financial market liberalisation and EU regulation (as well as supervision) have gone through four stages.

The first stage only concerned the right of establishment, took place during the 1970s and hardly induced cross-border intra-EU financial market liberalisation. During the EC1992 process, the free movement of services was tackled in a novel way. With exchange restrictions removed by 1988, the financial markets regime built by 1992 consisted mainly of directives ensuring 'sound' financial institutions such as banks, insurance companies and investment houses (merchant banks), based on solvency requirements, capital requirements, avoiding large exposures to single companies (or countries), etc. Market

---

[54] In its report on mutual evaluation, the Commission holds that Member States, alone, together and with the Commission, have achieved a lot: 'a major step forward in terms of removing barriers and the modernisation/simplification of legislation. Hundreds of discriminatory, unjustified or disproportionate requirements existing throughout the EU have been abolished in important service sectors such as retail, the services of the regulated professions, the construction sector, the tourism or business sector. This has been carried out via more than 1000 implementing laws . . . Many Member States have also set up specific mechanisms to prevent new barriers from emerging in the future', COM(2011) 20 of 27 Jan. 2011, Towards a better functioning Single Market for services – building on the results of the mutual evaluation process of the Services directive, p. 4. For details, see the extensive survey of all Member States in SEC(2011)102 of 27 Jan. 2011, Accompanying Document (to COM(2011) 20).

players' trust (including consumers') in the soundness of such institutions is critical: they themselves cannot verify that and this asymmetry of information is so important that it can be paralysing for the internal financial markets. Once such institutions are very big, contagion might also occur and in that event financial stability might be impaired. Hence, for micro and macro economic reasons, the EU had to arrange common minimum rules on supervision, too. The novel aspect was the move from host to home country control (of the supervision of banks, etc.). It works as follows. The home country of a bank (where the headquarters is established) is obliged to supervise, following the EU rules, and cooperate in a joint EU Committee of national supervisors; in order to establish and maintain mutual trust, information (on those banks, etc.) will flow freely and fully in the Committee whenever needed. Based on these provisions, the bank receives a kind of 'EU passport' to do business anywhere in the EU, and if that is done with subsidiaries, the supervision of the home country is 'mutually recognised' by the host country of the subsidiary.

During the second stage, the services as such in the four financial markets (banking, insurance, investment services and asset management) were usually not EU regulated, with the exception of consumer credit and mutual funds.

The third stage consisted of the EU Financial Services Action Plan (2000–05) with a major upgrading programme in 43 Directives and Regulations, mainly on wholesale markets, whilst tightening investment services, with far less host country control, a protectionist legacy of national stock exchanges[55] and, again, institutions. This time, much greater attention was paid to detailed risk assessment of many specific financial products.[56] As we now know, the basics (e.g. on capital requirements) were far too lax, however, and have been tightened after the financial crisis. No less than three successive capital requirement directive upgrades are being legislated over 2010 and 2011. Moreover, several financial players were unregulated (e.g. equity and hedge funds; credit agencies, which turned out to have been influenced by conflict of interest), a number of new financial products (e.g. CDS) contained huge and hidden risks and the EU supervision cooperation failed hopelessly.

The fourth stage (since 2008) is repairing these flaws and omissions with a flurry of new EU legislation as well as (slightly more centralised) common supervision in the European System of Financial Supervisors, plus a new body for permanent surveillance of financial stability (the European Financial Stability Board). Whether this is going to be sufficient is as yet unclear. The much greater emphasis on risk assessment (see e.g. the Solvency II insurance directive with thousands of pages of applications at the third level of implementation, to be available by 2012) and the much-needed centralisation for 50 or more European (rather than national) banks would seem to be inevitable for sound functioning of financial markets in Europe and for trust of market players to return.

The form and details of MR in financial markets require a high degree of mutual trust,

---

[55] Especially the MIFID directive: Directive 2004/39/EC, OJEU L 145/1 of 30 April 2004. See e.g. Casey and Lannoo (2006).

[56] In the so-called Lamfalussy procedures, levels 2 and 3 would regulate numerous risk assessment models or methods. This was also linked to practical aspects of Basel II (on capital requirements). Thus, again, the products themselves were not regulated, but now their risks were addressed, technically.

not least because during the financial crisis it turned out that national supervision had been too lax and cooperation between national supervisors was deficient, to the point of breaking down when it mattered most. Greater centralisation in combination with stricter (and more uniform) EU rules seems to be the only way to ensure renewed mutual trust, but, ironically, that also leaves less scope for MR.

In transport services, regulation is more limited, that is, mainly safety rules for transport equipment, environmental rules and minimum qualifications of firms and persons providing services (as well as strict rules for working hours while flying, riding or driving). Again, licensing and supervision of safety and environment is national (although the latter can of course be randomly inspected by other Member States) and mutually recognised. In this sector, the MR system seems to work well. This is a major achievement. The treaty calls for a common transport policy but this has anything but the characteristics of a heavy, imposing set of rules and prescriptions.[57] Quite the contrary, focusing on essential regulation only and combined with MR of home-country control, a relatively smooth and highly competitive single transport market has emerged. Only for rail freight is progress being slow.

In professional services, the rules are national. More often than not, these rules are a mix of public regulation and private codes of conduct, with internal sanctioning regimes for purposes of reputation and consumer trust. Because of this mix, it is exceedingly hard to unravel the possibly anti-competitive elements from the ones justified by market failures. This is rendered even more difficult by the nature of these services consisting of 'experience' goods (but not always with repeat purchasing) or 'credence goods' with strong asymmetries of information. Following the powerful Europeanisation of business, professional services are much more active across borders than one or two decades ago and therefore less resistant to a gradual Europeanisation of codes of conduct. Still, codes as well as national regulation frequently maintain idiosyncratic characteristics which tend to segment the internal market and render cross-border services expensive or impossible. The sector has long attempted to apply MR to its diplomas. Art. 53, TFEU has employed the term 'mutual recognition' for this purpose ever since the Rome treaty. At first, this MR lacked any credibility, due to a lack of trust, a lack of willingness on the part of providers (presumably, a protection of 'their' markets) and a lack of demand from European business. What was practised boiled down to 'maximum harmonisation' in endless negotiations, resulting in a throttling of free movement or establishment. Since 1989 an new approach reflects a MR spirit, which has culminated in an overarching directive 2005/36.[58] It is based on an 'equivalence' approach, promotes more automatic recognition as well as simplification of red tape and organises stronger inter-Member State cooperation. A recent evaluation demonstrates the many lingering difficulties of various forms of recognition under the directive.[59] Diploma recognition is of course only one amongst several reasons why the internal market of professional services does not easily open up. The example of accountancy services, whether by persons or firms, is perhaps

57 In the late 1960s and 1970s, however, some EU countries were insisting on such an approach.

58 On the recognition of professional qualifications, OJEU L 236 of 23 September 2005.

59 Meeting report, Evaluation of directive 2005/36/EC, 13 Sept. 2010, with annexes including comments from professionals themselves, on website DG Markt, European Commission, Markt-D4/IW D(2010) 361557, http://ec.europa.eu/internal_market, go to professional qualifications.

exemplary of the deep-rooted obstacles which have to be overcome. MR could never be expected to accomplish this without many other routes.[60]

8 CONCLUSIONS

Mutual recognition is a great invention of the EU. However, before it works *beyond* some obvious instances of disguised protectionism,[61] MR requires considerable refinement. The EU has gradually developed judicial and regulatory MR in goods. The latter, in the forms of the New (and Global) Approach and the new (more horizontal) food legislation after 1985, has been very successful over time. The 2008 Goods Package contains what can be held to be the completion of a system grown deeper and wider over more than two decades, with solid underpinning of mutual trust via accreditation in an EU-wide network and other improvements, not least at the EU external border. A remarkable, though little known, track in regulatory MR is the prevention of *future* regulatory barriers arising in the internal goods market. The combination of an ever more effective approach to existing barriers and an intrusive and targeted pre-emption policy for future ones has effectively spared the single goods market a process of destructive erosion.

Judicial MR in goods has long remained somewhat problematic. It has worked quite well in the food sector but only very selectively in other areas. Business criticism in the 1990s was often bitter because the legal tradition of basing everything on case law completely ignored the day-to-day reality of cross-border market access in the EU.[62] Three types of costs were incurred by European business, severely discouraging the exploitation of MR (and hence losing a good deal of the potential benefits for the internal market). Once the Commission began to realise this, it started to complement a steady stream of infringement procedures with the building of MR governance together with the Member States and many stakeholders. The new governance edifice was accomplished in a decade via a highly consensual approach. Reg. 764/2008 on (judicial) MR was packaged together with the betterment of regulatory MR (see above). The new governance of judicial MR drastically reduces these costs and gives far-reaching legal certainty, inter alia via a reversal of the burden of proof for non-conformity of goods already allowed on the market in other Member States. With also the high-quality, yet competitive, system of certification over the entire EU and the expected consolidation of the Notified Bodies, market access in goods regulated only at the national level will significantly further improve and this should incentivise, in particular, SMEs keen (but deterred in the past) to operate in a range of countries in the single market.

In services, MR has assumed different forms. Therefore, it is hazardous to generalise. As far as horizontal services liberalisation is concerned, case law on the freedom to provide services in the internal market has long remained shallow. Over time, a

---

60 See e.g. Philipsen (2009) for an overview of the economics of accounting regulation in OECD countries, with much attention to the EU case. See also Delimatsis, (2010).

61 Remember the typical cases of Cassis de Dijon, Italian pasta of durum wheat, a Dutch refusal to import certain types of German bread, the French prohibition of aspartam in light-cola, etc.

62 One phrase used being that MR is 'a phantom in the court room'.

stepwise logic comparable to (horizontal) goods liberalisation as in Figure 6.3 was developed. However, based on the inevitability of creating a philosophy of the (EU) 'general good', given the absence of any specification in the treaty, CJEU case law built up a huge list of 'rule-of-reason' derogations, in turn disciplined (as in goods) by non-discrimination, necessity and proportionality. A modest form of MR was added, by insisting that provisions, guarantees, approvals, testing or licensing conditions in the EU country of origin had to be verified first. However, with an enormous increase in CJEU cases during the late 1990s and the five years thereafter, it became clear that barriers in the internal market for services were far too numeous and restrictive for this case law to be effective.

The Bolkestein draft directive responded to this observation by a design centred on the origin principle, applied more radically than before in some other directives. This failed in a highly turbulent process of legislation. Directive 2006/123 would seem to be modest in its core Art. 16, but upon further reflection this is not clear at all. The directive has removed the 'general good' derogations in a single stroke, except environment. It is now unclear what the status of these derogations will be, although it would be remarkable if the CJEU would revise its case law following this piece of secondary legislation. If these derogations still apply, Art. 16 means little. Moreover, many sectoral derogations were included in the text of the directive itself, shrinking the scope of the directive to relatively unproblematic areas. The directive is still valuable, if only because of the two blacklists (for services and establishment restrictions), the points of single contact for business and the elaborate administrative cooperation stipulated (a soft form of MR). However, MR could have been pushed much further, in that provisions similar to the MR Regulation in goods (Figure 6.4) – in particular, a duty on the country where the services are provided to assume the burden of proof based on verification in the origin country, with reasoned decisions and appeal options – should have been included. Still, the mutual evaluation between the Member States has proven to be remarkably sucessful and has led to countless instances of removing barriers.

Finally, some attention is paid to MR in sectoral services regulation. In financial services and in transport, it is not the services which tend to be regulated but the firms or market institutions providing services. It is the supervision of these provisions which is mutually recognised (home-country control and an EU passport for establishment). The high degree of mutual trust of this approach necessitates tight cooperation, if not some centralisation, of the organisation. In transport, this seems to work, with less centralisation in road haulage and more in air transport and rail. In financial services, several stages in building EU financial markets have not prevented the financial crisis. It has revealed that further tightened and tougher rules with respect to risk management are badly needed. Also, better common supervision is a conditio sine qua non for MR to be applied in a credible fashion. For professional services, the relevance of MR relates to diplomas. After fake attempts to apply MR (realising 'maximum harmonisation' in endless negotiations, without much hope of any economic impact for cross-border services), a more MR-driven approach has been built up since 1989, culminating in an overarching 2005 directive. However, to make this work effectively remains exceedingly hard. It might well be indispensable that EU-wide codes of conduct (also encouraged in the 2006 services directive) and further harmonisation be accomplished, possibly aided by EU competition policy, before genuine MR in this domain works.

REFERENCES

Abraham, F. (1991), 'Building blocks of Europe's single market', *Tijdschrift voor Economie en Management*, 36(4), 395–416.
Andenas, M. and W.H. Roth (eds) (2001), *Services and Free Movement in EU law*, Oxford: Oxford University Press.
Atkins, W. (1997), *Technical Barriers to Trade*, study for the single market review (3) 1, Luxembourg, Office for Official Publications of the EU.
Barnard, C. (2007), *The Substantive Law of the EU*, 2nd edn, Oxford: Oxford University Press.
Barnard, C. (2008), 'Unravelling the services directive', *Common Market Law Review*, 45(2), 323–94.
Casey, J.P. and K. Lannoo (2006), 'The MIFID revolution: a policy view', *Competition and Regulation in Network Industries*, 1(4), 515–35.
Chang, M., D. Hanf and J. Pelkmans (2010), 'The services directive: Trojan Horse or White Knight?', *Journal of European Integration*, 32(1), 97–114.
de Bruijn, R., H. Kox and A. Lejour (2007), 'Economic benefits of an integrated European market for services', *Journal of Policy Modeling*, 30(2), 301–19.
Delimatsis, P. (2010), 'Thou shall not . . . (dis)trust: codes of conduct and harmonisation of professional standards in the EU', *Common Market Law Review*, 47(4), 1049–87.
EFTA (2008), 'Study on certification and marks in Europe', Brussels, January, http://www.efta.int/content/publications.
Falvey, R. (1989), 'Trade, quality reputations and commercial policy', *International Economic Review*, 30(3), 607–22.
Felbermayr, G. and B. Jung (2008), 'Sorting it out: technical barriers to trade and industry productivity', FIW Working paper no. 14, Vienna (WIFO, WIIW, WSR).
Hatzopoulos, V. (2008), 'Legal aspects of the internal market for services', in J. Pelkmans, D. Hanf and M. Chang (eds), *The EU Internal Market in Comparative Perspective*, Brussels and New York: PIE Lang.
Hatzopoulos, V. and U. Do (2006), 'The case law of the ECJ concerning the free provision of services 2000–2005', *Common Market Law Review*, 43(4), 923–91.
Klamert, M. (2010), 'Of empty glasses and double burdens: approaches to regulating the services market a propos the implementation of the services directive', *Legal Issues of Economic Integration*, 37(2), 111–32.
Kostoris Padoa Schioppa, F. (2005), *The Principle of Mutual Recognition in the European Integration Process*, Basingstoke: Palgrave Macmillan.
Kox, H. and A. Lejour (2005), 'Regulatory heterogeneity as an obstacle for international services trade', CPB Discussion Paper 49, The Hague, CPB, www.cpb.nl.
Lutz, S. (1996), 'Trade effects of minimum quality standards with and without deterred entry', CEPR Discussion Papers no. 1384, April, London.
MAC Group (1988), 'The costs of non-Europe in the foodstuffs sector', *Research on the costs of non-Europe*, Basic Findings (background to the Cecchini report), Vol. 12, Part A, Luxembourg: OOPEC.
Maydell, N. (2008), 'The services directive and existing Community law', in F. Breuss, G. Fink and S. Griller (eds), *Services Liberalisation in the Internal Market*, Vienna and New York: Springer.
Molitor, B. et al. (1995), 'Report of the group of independent experts on legislation and administrative simplification', European Commission, COM (1995) 228 of 21 May.
Nicolaidis, K. and S. Schmidt (2007), 'Mutual recognition on trial: the long road to services liberalisation', *Journal of European Public Policy*, 14(5), 717 ff.
Pelkmans, J. (1987), 'The new approach to technical harmonisation and standardisation', *Journal of Common Market Studies*, 25(3), 249–69.
Pelkmans, J. (2005), 'Mutual recognition in goods and services: an economic perspective', in F. Kostoris Padoa Schioppa (ed.), *The Principle of Mutual Recognition in the European Integration Process*, Basingstoke: Palgrave Macmillan, pp. 85–128.
Pelkmans, J. (2007a), 'Mutual recognition in goods, on promises and disillusions', *Journal of European Public Policy*, 14(5), 699–716.
Pelkmans, J. (2007b), 'Deepening services market integration: a critical assessment', *Romanian Journal of European Affairs*, 7(4), 5–31.
Pelkmans, J. (2009) (in Dutch), 'The 2008 Goods Package: useful deepening of the internal market', *SEW-Tijdschrift voor Europees en Economisch recht* (Review for European and Economic Law), 57(11), 429–42.
Pelkmans, J., E. Vos and L. di Mauro (2000), 'Reforming product market regulation in the EU: a painstaking, iterative two-level game', in G. Galli and J. Pelkmans (eds), *Regulatory Reform and Competitiveness in Europe*, Cheltenham: Edward Elgar, Vol. 1, pp. 238–91.
Philipsen, N. (2009), 'Background note on competition and regulation in auditing and related professions',

in *OECD Policy Roundtable on Competition and Regulation in Auditing*, December, Paris, OECD DAF/COMP(2009)1, pp. 11–48.
Renda, A. and Schrefler, L. (2006), 'European standardisation, current issues and expected progress', Briefing Note to the IMCO of the European Parliament, February, Brussels, CEPS.
Schmidt, S.K. (2007), 'Mutual recognition as a new mode of governance', in S.K. Schmidt (ed.), 'Mutual Recognition as a New Mode of Governance', *Journal of European Public Policy*, 14(5) (Special Issue).
Snell, J. (2008), 'Freedom to provide services in the case law and in the services directive: problems, solutions and institutions', in U. Neergaard, R. Nielsen and L. Roseberry (eds), *The Services Directive – Consequences for the Welfare State and the European Social Model*, Copenhagen: DJOF Publishing.
Sun, J.M. and J. Pelkmans (1995), 'Regulatory competition in the internal market', *Journal of Common Market Studies*, 33(1), 67–90.
Suwa-Eisenmann, A. and Vredier, T. (2002), 'Reciprocity and the political economy of harmonisation and mutual recognition of regulatory measures', CEPR Discussion Paper no. 3147, London, January.
Sykes, A. (1995), *Product Standards for Internationally Integrated Goods Markets*, Washington DC: Brookings Institution.
Trachtman, J. (2007), 'Embedding mutual recognition at the WTO', *Journal of European Public Policy*, 14(5), 780–99.
UNICE (1995), *Releasing Europe's Potential through Targeted Reform*, Brussels.
UNICE (2004), *It's the Internal Market, Stupid!*, a company survey on trade barriers in the EU, Brussels, Internal Market Working Group.
Vogel, D. (1995), *Trading up: Consumer and Environmental Regulation in a Global Economy*, Cambridge, MA: Harvard University Press.
Weiler, J. (2005), 'Mutual recognition, functional equivalence and harmonisation in the evolution of the European common market and the WTO', in F. Kostoris Padoa Schioppa (ed.), *The Principle of Mutual Recognition in the European Integration Process*, Basingstoke: Palgrave Macmillan.
WTO (2005), 'Trade, standards and the WTO', in *World Trade Report 2005*, Geneva, pp. 29–169.

7 The law and economics of the free movement of persons in the European Union

*Herbert Brücker and Thomas Eger**

1 INTRODUCTION

After the failure of the European Defence Community and the European Political Community in 1954 the six founding members of the European Economic Community decided to relaunch European integration on an *economic* basis. The core of this integration is the establishment of a Common Market without barriers to the free movement of goods, services, persons, and capital. The idea was to redress the fragmented goods and factor markets in Europe and to increase economic growth by improving the division of labour and specialisation among the Member States (Eichengreen 2007, 163 ff.; Gillingham 2003, 34 ff.).

The free movement of persons, one of the four 'fundamental freedoms', was originally strongly linked to economic activity. According to the traditional Harris–Todaro (1970) approach, economically active persons migrate if the expected income gains from migration exceed the migration costs. These costs are complex (for details see e.g. Straubhaar 2002; Trachtman 2009). They consist, for example, of the direct cost of changing residence and the utility loss from abandoning social contacts in the country of origin, as well as the time and effort required to establish new contacts in the country of destination, the time and effort required to learn a new language if necessary and to adapt to a different culture, the additional cost of finding an appropriate school for the children, lower pensions for people who have changed their countries of residence during their economically active period more frequently, and so on. To a considerable extent, governments have erected legal barriers to the free movement of persons so as to be able to monitor foreigners who intend to reside or work in the respective countries. The provisions on the free movement of persons that are part of the Treaties since the Treaty of Rome (1957) aim at removing these legal barriers in order to reduce migration costs.

As long as income differences between countries reflect differences in labour productivity, the private motive to migrate improves the overall allocation of labour, since the production loss in the country with net emigration is overcompensated by the production gain in the country with net immigration. Even though there are winners and losers of migration, the gains to the winners are larger than the losses to the losers. The more legal barriers are removed and the lower migration costs, the higher total production will be in all countries concerned. However, this is not necessarily the case when we take into account that

* We wish to thank Nuno Garoupa, Clemens Buchen, Dominique Demougin, Jerg Gutmann, Jarek Kantorowicz, Roya Sangi, Sönke Häseler and the participants of the Law and Economics Workshop in Haifa for valuable comments. Thanks also go to Linda Albertsen for proofreading and technical assistance.

the migration of labour force will actually be induced by differences in net compensation in the broadest sense, i.e. gross compensation minus all kinds of taxes and contributions plus all kinds of social benefits such as children's allowances, housing subsidies, unemployment relief, means-tested benefits, free access to education and so on. In this case, fewer legal barriers and lower migration costs may under certain circumstances reduce total production in the countries concerned; i.e. the gains to the winners are smaller than the losses to the losers. Thus, whether the net benefit of migration is positive remains an empirical question.

Primary law[1] grants workers,[2] self-employed persons[3] and the providers and receivers of services[4] free market access in all Member States of the European Union. The articles regarding workers, self-employed persons and services are guided by some common principles (Barnard 2010, 223 ff.). First of all, restrictions on entry into and residence in a territory of Member States can only be justified by reference to one of the derogations explicitly mentioned in the Treaty (public policy, public security and public health), provided the restriction is proportionate and does not violate fundamental human rights. Secondly, all the articles concerned prohibit discrimination on the grounds of nationality – subject to the public policy, public security and public health derogations and the public service exception.

Since the end of the transition period for the free movement in 1968, there have been two tendencies in the legal treatment of the free movement of persons – initiated mainly by secondary legislation[5] and by European Court of Justice (ECJ) case law, but also by primary law. On the one hand, there is a tendency, especially from ECJ case law, to replace the narrow concept of the prohibition of discrimination on grounds of nationality by the much broader concept of the prohibition of discriminatory and non-discriminatory obstacles to free movement. On the other hand, one can observe a continuous extension of the principle of free movement of persons from exclusively economically active persons to the inclusion of non-economically active persons and towards the general concept of European citizenship.

The removal of more and more legal obstacles to the free movement and the extension of the principles of free movement from the economically active to the economically non-active population raise two questions from an economic perspective:

1. To what extent has the elimination of legal obstacles to labour mobility increased the efficiency of labour allocation within the EU?
2. Has the elimination of legal obstacles to the free movement of non-economically active persons negatively affected the allocation of labour and the stability of the Member States' social insurance systems?

---

1 Primary law is the supreme source of law in the European Union. It consists of the founding Treaties establishing the European Union, the major Treaties amending the EU, the Protocols annexed to those Treaties and additional Treaties making changes to specific sections of the founding Treaties.

2 Free movement of workers, ex Articles 39–42 TEC, since 1 December 2009, Articles 45–8 Treaty on the Functioning of the European Union (TFEU).

3 Freedom of establishment, Articles 49–54 TFEU (ex Articles 43–8 TEC).

4 Freedom to provide and receive services, Articles 56–62 TFEU (ex Articles 49–55 TEC).

5 Law made by the European Union institutions in exercising the powers conferred on them by the Treaties is referred to as secondary legislation. Secondary legislation consists of the legal acts listed and defined in Article 288 TFEU, i.e. regulations, directives, decisions, recommendations and opinions.

Despite the continuous removal of legal barriers to the mobility of workers and other persons, the level of labour mobility across the 15 Member States of the European Union (EU-15) has been modest for long periods of time. This can be traced back inter alia to the facts that income levels between the EU-15 countries are relatively similar and that there are still many bureaucratic hurdles to the mobility of persons in the EU (European Commission 2010). For our analysis, we therefore also draw on evidence from the recent Eastern enlargement round of the EU. The high income differentials between the incumbent and the new Central and Eastern European Member States have created substantial migration incentives, which in turn enable us to analyse the economic consequences of free movement in a case where labour mobility is particularly relevant.

The Accession Treaties which the EU concluded with the new Central and Eastern European Member States provided for transitional arrangements for the free movement of labour. These arrangements allow the EU-15 countries to postpone the opening of their labour markets according to the '2 + 3 + 2' formula. This formula entitles the EU-15 countries to restrict access to their labour markets initially for a two-year period and, by a simple declaration, for another three years. Finally, the transitional arrangements can be extended by another two years if either the equilibrium in the labour market is seriously distorted or if free labour mobility threatens to cause severe distortions. In the first phase, only Ireland, Sweden and the United Kingdom opened their labour markets for workers from the eight new Central and European Member States which joined the EU on May 2004 (NMS-8). During the second phase, starting in 2006, all other EU-15 countries, except Austria, Belgium, Denmark and Germany, granted free access to their labour markets. In the final phase (2009–11), only Austria and Germany continued to restrict access to their labour markets for workers from the new Member States. The freedom of establishment, which includes also the right to self-employment, was already granted in all Member States since the beginning of the enlargement in 2004. The freedom of service provision, which also includes the posting of workers, was also already granted in 2004 with the notable exceptions of Austria and Germany. These two countries were entitled to protect 'sensitive' branches such as construction and cleaning services according to the '2 + 3 + 2' formula.

A similar '2 + 3 + 2' scheme for the free movement of persons was applied when Bulgaria and Romania joined the EU in 2007. In the initial phase (2007–09), only Finland and Sweden allowed open access to their labour markets, followed by Greece, Spain, Portugal and Denmark in the second phase.

The chapter is structured as follows. First, we discuss the two main tendencies in the legal treatment of the free movement of persons in further detail: in the following section we show how secondary legislation and ECJ case law have been used to remove step by step even non-discriminatory obstacles to the free movement of persons; thereafter, the focus is placed on legal developments that weaken the link between the right of free movement of persons and economic activity. Second, we scrutinise the empirical evidence as to whether the removal of barriers to the free movement of persons actually raised mobility within the EU, whether workers' mobility has increased the efficiency of resource allocation, and, hence, European income levels, and whether EU immigrants have created a burden for the welfare systems in the countries of destination.

Due to the restriction in scope, we will omit asylum policy and the evolution of the legal treatment of third-country nationals (see the excellent overview by Barnard 2010, 519–56).

2 FROM THE PROHIBITION OF DISCRIMINATION TO THE PROHIBITION OF OBSTACLES TO FREE MOVEMENT

Direct discrimination on the grounds of nationality is clearly prohibited by the Treaty. According to Article 45 (2) of the Treaty on the Functioning of the European Union (TFEU) (ex Article 39 (2) EC) any discrimination based on nationality between the *workers* of the Member States as regards employment, remuneration or other conditions of work and employment is prohibited. Since 1974, the Court has clarified that Articles 39, 43 and 49 EC (now Articles 45, 49, and 56 TFEU) have vertical[6] as well as horizontal[7] direct effect. That means individuals can rely on these articles not only in actions against the state but also in actions against other private actors. Consequently, the prohibition of discrimination holds not only for national laws but also for private collective agreements, such as the nationality clauses by the International Cycling Union,[8] the UEFA's transfer rules and nationality clauses,[9] and even discriminatory entry requirements by individual companies.[10] Article 45 (3) TFEU (ex Article 39 (3) EC) specifies the principle of free movement by granting workers certain rights, such as the right to accept offers of employment, to move freely within the territory of Member States for this purpose, to stay in a Member State for purpose of employment, and to remain in the territory of a Member State after employment in this state. Further details of these rights were originally regulated by three acts of secondary legislation: Regulation 1612/68, which elaborates on the equal treatment principle and sets out many of the substantive rights and entitlements of workers and their families; Directive 68/360, which regulates the formalities and conditions of entry and residence of workers and the self-employed and their families; and Regulation 1251/70, which protects the right of workers and their families to remain in the host state (after retirement of the worker, permanent incapacity to work, and so on). These secondary measures have been partially replaced by the Citizens' Rights Directive 2004/38. Direct discrimination of workers on the grounds of nationality can be justified only in two ways: either on grounds of public policy, public security and public health (Article 45 (3) TFEU) or because of employment in the public service where the provisions of Article 45 do not apply (Article 45 (4) TFEU).

The *freedom of establishment* (Articles 49–55 TFEU) concerns self-employed persons as well as companies.[11] According to the ECJ the self-employed, unlike workers, work 'outside a relationship of subordination, they bear the risk for the success or failure of their employment, and they are paid directly and in full' (Barnard 2010, 295). Article 49 TFEU includes the right 'to take up and pursue activities as self-employed persons and to set up and manage undertakings . . . under the conditions laid down for its own nationals by the law of the country where such establishment is effected'.[12] The article thus prohibits

---

6 Case 167/73 *Commission v. France* [1974] ECR 359; Case 41/74 *Van Duyn* [1974] ECR 1337.

7 Case 36/74 *Walrave and Koch* [1974] ECR 1405.

8 Case 36/74 *Walrave and Koch* [1974] ECR 1405.

9 Case C-415/93 *Bosman* [1995] ECR I-4921.

10 Case C-281/98 *Angonese* [2000] ECR I-4139.

11 We will focus in this chapter on self-employed persons and neglect companies.

12 Article 49 TFEU applies both to primary establishment, where an individual leaves the home state to set up a permanent establishment in another Member State, and to secondary

discrimination on the grounds of nationality (equal treatment principle). The requirement of equal treatment refers to the right of access to self-employment ('right to take up activities') and the exercise of activities as a self-employed person ('right to pursue activities'). These rights are specified by Directive 73/148/EEC, which requires Member States to abolish restrictions on the movement and residence of nationals wishing to establish themselves in another Member State, to provide services in another Member State or to enter another Member State to receive services. Moreover, Directive 75/34 refers to the right to remain permanently in a Member State after having been self-employed there. These directives have recently been replaced by the Citizens' Rights Directive 2004/38, as far as the freedom of establishment is concerned. Of significant importance are the directives on harmonising or mutually recognising the national education and qualification requirements that must be met to pursue an economic activity or profession in another Member State. Initially, from the 1960s, the Community followed a harmonisation approach which focused on specific sectors of economic or professional life, so as to obtain agreement from all Member States on the minimum standard of training and education needed for a qualification in a specific field ('vertical approach'). Since this approach proved to be very difficult and time consuming, the European Commission initiated in the 1980s a change from harmonisation in detail to the principle of mutual trust ('horizontal approach'), which was inspired by the development of ECJ case law regarding the free movements of goods.[13] Pursuant to this new approach, three important directives were enacted between 1989 and 1999.[14] They have been updated and consolidated by Directive 2005/36/EC on the recognition of professional qualifications. Direct discrimination against self-employed persons on the grounds of nationality can be justified either on grounds of public policy, public security and public health (Article 52 TFEU) or because the activity is connected with the exercise of official authority (Article 51 TFEU).

There is a thin line between the *freedom to provide services* (Articles 56–62 TFEU) on the one hand and the freedom of establishment or of free movement of workers on the other. The distinction between 'establishment' and 'services' is made on the basis of duration, i.e. the permanent versus temporary stay of the provider of the service in another Member State. The distinctive feature between 'workers' and 'services' is supervision: i.e. under the free movement of workers the employees work under the supervision of the company in the host state; under the freedom to provide services the posted workers are supervised by the company in the state of origin. The original idea, which was to treat the freedom to provide services in the same way as the free movement of goods and to apply the 'principle of origin', was modified by the Posted Workers Directive 96/71/EC and the Services Directive 2006/123/EC.[15]

---

establishment, where an individual maintains the establishment in the home state while setting up and maintaining a second establishment.

[13] Mutual recognition of product standards, according to Case 120/78 *Cassis de Dijon* [1979] ECR 649.

[14] Directive 89/48 on the mutual recognition of higher education diplomas and certificates; Directive 92/51 on the mutual recognition of diplomas and certificates awarded after a post-secondary education course of at least one year's duration; Directive 99/42 on all other sectors and professions that were covered only by vertical directives.

[15] However, in the recent cases of *Viking* and *Laval* the ECJ deemed industrial action taken by

The ECJ clarified in several judgments that the Treaty prohibits not only direct but also indirect discrimination. This refers to national measures that put the same burden in law, but a different burden in fact, on nationals from other Member States, such as requirements concerning residence, language, particular qualifications and licences that are typically satisfied by nationals but not by migrants. In *Sotgiu*, where the German Postal Services increased the separation allowance paid to workers employed away from their place of residence within Germany but not for those workers whose residence at the time of their initial employment was situated abroad, the ECJ made clear: 'The rules regarding equality of treatment . . . forbid not only overt discrimination by reason of nationality but also all covert forms of discrimination which, by the application of other criteria of differentiation, lead in fact to the same result.'[16] Another example of indirect discrimination of workers is *Allué and Coonan* where Italian law limited the duration of employment contracts between universities and foreign language lecturers, whereas other employees typically faced no limitation of their employment period. Since only 25 per cent of foreign language lecturers were Italian nationals, the ECJ considered the law to be indirectly discriminatory without justification.[17] In *Vlassopoulou*, the ECJ observed indirect discrimination against a self-employed person. German authorities refused a Greek lawyer, who was registered with the Athens Bar and had practised German law for several years in Germany, admission to the Bar on the grounds that she had not passed the relevant German examinations. The ECJ stated that 'even if applied without any discrimination on the basis of nationality, national requirements concerning qualifications may have the effect of hindering nationals of the other Member States in the exercise of their right of establishment'.[18] However, the ECJ concluded that national authorities could still refuse foreign lawyers admission to the Bar where practical and other experience was not deemed to be a sufficient substitute for the national examinations.

With respect to the free movement of workers, the ECJ made the step from the prohibition of discrimination to the prohibition of (even non-discriminatory) obstacles to free movement in *Bosman*.[19] Here the ECJ judged that the UEFA transfer rules, which used to require football clubs hiring players from other clubs to pay transfer fees to the old club after the contract with the player expired, were capable of impeding free movement of workers and breached Article 39 EC (now Article 45 TFEU) – even though these rules did not directly or indirectly discriminate on grounds of nationality.

The ECJ followed the same approach with respect to the freedom of establishment. In *Gebhard*[20] a German national, who had obtained a German law degree, started practising as a *Rechtsanwalt* in Germany and worked for about ten years with a Milan law firm, opened his own chamber in Milan, started using the title *avvocato* and employed a number

---

trade unions, in order to enforce the terms and conditions of employment of the country of destination, to hinder the freedom of establishment or the freedom to provide services, respectively: Case C-438/05 *International Transport Workers' Federation v. Viking Line* [2007] ECR I-10779; Case 341/05 *Laval un Partneri Ltd v. Svenska Byggnadsarbetareförbundet* [2007] ECR I-11767.

16 Case 152/73, *Sotgiu v. Deutsche Bundespost* [1974] ECR 153, para 11.

17 Case 33/88 *Allué and Coonan v. Università degli Studi di Venezia [1989] ECE 1591.*

18 Case C-340/89 *Vlassopoulou v. Ministerium für Justiz* [1991] ECR I-2357.

19 Case C-415/93 [1995] ECR I-4921.

20 Case C-55/94 [1995] ECR I-4165.

of Italian *procuratori*. He was then suspended by the Milan Bar for using the title *avvocato* without being registered. The ECJ used this case as an occasion to formulate general principles regarding all basic freedoms. National measures liable to hinder or render less attractive the exercise of the fundamental freedoms guaranteed by the Treaty must fulfil four conditions: (1) they must be applied in a non-discriminatory manner; (2) they must be justified by mandatory requirements in the general interest; (3) they must be suitable for securing the attainment of the objective which they pursue; (4) they must not go beyond what is necessary in order to attain it. Regarding the specific problem of Gebhard the Court confirmed that qualification requirements must be in principle complied with, but that national authorities should also take into account relevant experience.

Since *Gebhard* it has become clear that the ECJ will apply the principles developed in *Dassonville*[21] and *Cassis de Dijon*[22] with respect to the free movement of goods to all basic freedoms, including the free movement of persons: (1) national measures that directly discriminate on grounds of nationality constitute a breach of the Treaty if they cannot be justified by the express derogations; (2) indirectly discriminatory or non-discriminatory national measures that establish obstacles to the free movement (of persons) violate the Treaty if they cannot be justified by the express derogations or by mandatory requirements in the general interest or if they are not proportional. The Court has already recognised many 'mandatory requirements' such as professional rules intended to protect the recipients of a service; protection of workers; consumer protection; guaranteeing the quality of skilled trade work and protecting those who have commissioned such work; ensuring the balance between sports clubs; prevention of social dumping and unfair competition; prevention of abuse of free movement of services; avoiding disturbances on the labour market; social protection of workers with respect to, for example, social security provision; combating illegal employment; preserving the system of administration of justice; the coherence of a scheme of taxation; the effectiveness of fiscal supervision; the need to ensure the effective collection of income tax, and preventing wholly artificial arrangements aimed solely at escaping national tax normally due; preserving the financial balance of a social security scheme; controlling costs, and preventing a waste of financial, technical, and human resources; the obligation of solidarity (Barnard 2010, 512–16).

Differences between national pension systems or the specific design of rent formulas may also constitute (discriminatory or non-discriminatory) obstacles to the free movement of workers. If mobile workers have to expect lower pensions than immobile workers the incentive to work in other Member States will be reduced (Fenge and von Weizsäcker 2009). Similar problems arise with the other elements of the social security system, such as health insurance, unemployment insurance, family benefits and others. These potential obstacles to the free movement of workers were already addressed in 1971 by Regulation 1408/71, which provides for some coordination of Member States' social security systems with respect to migrant workers. The coordination is characterised by four principles: (1) aggregation of all claims from different countries; (2) exportability, i.e. if somebody is entitled to a cash benefit from one country, he or she may generally receive it even if living in a different country; (3) equal treatment, i.e. migrant workers have the same

---

21 Case 8/74 [1974] ECR 837.
22 Case 120/78 [1979] ECR 649.

rights and obligations as domestic workers; (4) prevention of overlapping benefits, i.e. at any moment in time a migrant worker is covered by the legislation of one and only one country, which is determined by the social security institutions (and not by the worker's choice); this is typically the country of employment, in the case of posted workers the country of origin (with some exceptions). Regulation 1408/71 and application regulation 574/72 have been amended several times and continuously elaborated by ECJ case law. They were recently replaced by regulation 883/2004 (amended by regulation 988/2009) and its application regulation 987/2009, which extend the scope of application of the principles and entered into force on 1 May 2010. A far-reaching change concerns the central principle of equivalence, which was introduced by the new Article 5 and requires equal treatment of benefits, income, and facts or events with respect to their legal effects by all Member States.[23]

To summarise: during the past 50 years, many legal barriers to the free movement of labour within the EU have been abolished. The question arises to what extent this development has contributed to an efficient reallocation of labour among the Member States, given that language barriers, cultural differences and red tape continue to exist, that it is ex ante far from clear which restrictions to the free movement of persons will be honoured or sanctioned by the ECJ and that the income differences among the Member States are – at least for the EU-15 – not overly large.

3 THE EROSION OF THE LINK BETWEEN THE RIGHT OF FREE MOVEMENT AND ECONOMIC ACTIVITY

Originally, the right of free movement of persons was restricted to economically active individuals. As a consequence of ECJ case law and the development of primary and secondary legislation, the link between the right of free movement and economic activity has eroded in two respects:

- The equal treatment principle has been applied to more and more categories of people who are not engaged in an economic activity.
- The application of the equal treatment principle is no longer restricted to access to and the terms and conditions of employment, but has been extended to social and tax benefits.

Let us start with the first point. In the 1960s, secondary legislation began to specify the details of the right of free movement. Directive 64/221/EEC concerns restrictions on entry and residence of workers and their families on the grounds of public policy and public security. It requires that restrictions on the grounds of public policy 'must be based exclusively on the personal conduct of the individual concerned'.[24] Regulation 1612/68 elaborates on the equal treatment principle and sets out many of the substantive rights and entitlements of workers, including prospective workers and those who were employed

---

[23] For a recent overview see Jorens (ed.) (2010).

[24] Article 3 (1) of Directive 64/221; now Article 27 (2) of Directive 2004/38.

but are no longer working, and their families. Directive 68/360 regulates the formalities and conditions of entry and residence of workers and their families. Regulation 1251/70 protects the right of workers and their families to remain in the host state after retirement, as a consequence of permanent incapacity to work, and so on. Similar rights were granted to the self-employed.[25] All these rights were directly or indirectly connected to economic activity. Family members, irrespective of their nationality, owned derivative rights, dependent on the work of the bread-winner. Since then, the ECJ has extended the notion of 'family member' from spouses, children and economically dependent parents and parents-in-law to divorced spouses and unmarried companions (Menéndez 2009, 7; Schütz et al. 2004, 655 ff.).

The ECJ has given the term 'worker' a broad meaning. In *Lawrie-Blum*[26] the Court described the essential feature of an employment relationship: a worker provides services for, and receives remuneration from, another person, who in turn supervises the worker. This includes, for example, part-time workers, apprentices, professional football players, and prostitutes. An important question is to what extent the principles of free movement of workers apply also to persons who are in the process of qualifying for a profession. While Article 7(3) of Regulation 1612/68 already provided that workers from other Member States shall 'have access to training in vocational schools and retraining centres' under the same conditions as national workers, the ECJ started in *Gravier*[27] to define 'vocational training' broadly and included also general forms of education, such as university studies (Barnard 2010, 288; Schütz et al. 2004, 629 ff.; Strumica 2006, 739 ff.). The Belgian imposition of a university enrolment fee exclusively on foreign students was considered an impermissible form of discrimination on the grounds of nationality in access to vocational training. Some years later, in *Brown*[28] and *Lair*,[29] the ECJ clarified that the equal access right under Article 12 EC refers to registration and tuition fees only, not to maintenance grants.

Already in 1989, the ECJ made reference to the tourists' right to receive services[30] in order to weaken the link between equal treatment of migrant persons and economic activities. In *Cowan*[31] a British tourist was attacked and robbed outside a métro station in Paris. The French authorities refused his application for criminal injuries compensation from public funds because he was neither a French national nor resident in France. The Court said: 'When Community law guarantees a natural person the freedom to go to another Member State, the protection of that person from harm in the Member State in question, on the same basis as that of nationals and persons residing there, is a corollary of that freedom of movement.'[32]

In the early 1990s, the Community adopted three directives that conferred a general right of movement and residence on non-economically active persons, provided they had

---

25 Directives 73/148 and 75/34.
26 Case 66/85 [1986] ECR 2121.
27 Case 293/83 [1985] ECR 593.
28 Case C-197/86 [1988] ECR 3205.
29 Case C-39/86 [1988] ECR 3161.
30 Recognised in the joint cases 286/82 & 26/83 *Luisi and Carbone* [1984] ECR 377.
31 Case 186/87 [1989] ECR 195.
32 Para. 17.

sufficient subsistence resources and health insurance.[33] The decoupling of free movement from economic activity culminated with the Treaty of Maastricht (1992/1993) in the recognition of the status of 'citizen of the Union' for all nationals of the Member States: 'Every citizen of the Union shall have the right to move and reside freely within the territory of the Member States, subject to the limitations and conditions laid down in this Treaty and by the measures adopted to give it effect' (Article 21 TFEU). The introduction of a European citizenship can be interpreted as a change in paradigm, from a narrow focus on economic activity to a broader one which takes into account also those forms of mobility of persons that are not induced by economic motives (Wollenschläger 2009, p. 21). This development has been confirmed and consolidated by the Citizens' Rights Directive 2004/38, which repeals and replaces previous secondary legislation aimed at facilitating the free movement of economically active persons.[34] This directive confirms and extends the right of free movement essentially in the following way:[35]

- For stays *up to three months*, the only requirement on Union citizens is that they possess a valid identity document or passport.
- The right of residence for *more than three months* remains subject to certain conditions: applicants must be either engaged in an economic activity or they must have sufficient resources and health insurance to ensure that they do not become a burden on the social services of the host Member State during their stay. A residence permit is no longer required, instead there is a simplified procedure of issuing a registration certificate.
- After a *five-year* period of uninterrupted legal residence Union citizens acquire the right of permanent residence in the host Member State.

However, it should be mentioned that the implementation of the 'Citizens' Rights Directive' in the Member States remains far from perfect, as many documents prove.[36]

Since the late 1990s, in a number of cases, the ECJ has been using the opportunity to combine the principles of citizenship (now Article 21 TFEU) and equal treatment (now Article 18 TFEU) to extend the right of free movement beyond the sphere of economic activity. A particularly interesting application is equal treatment with respect to social

---

[33] Council Directives 90/364/EEC on the rights of residence for persons of sufficient means ('playboy directive'), 90/365/EEC on the rights of residence for employees and self-employed persons who have ceased their occupational activity, and 90/366/EEC on the rights of residence for students, which was repealed and replaced by Directive 93/96/EEC. See Barnard (2010, 224 f.) and Schütz et al. (2004, pp. 633f.).

[34] Directives 64/221, 68/360, 72/194, 73/148, 75/34; the three Residence Directives from the 1990s: 90/364, 90/365, 93/96; and Articles 10 and 11 of Regulation 1612/68 (provisions on family rights).

[35] For more details see Barnard (2010, 424–61).

[36] Report from the Commission to the European Parliament and the Council on the application of Directive 2004/38/EC on the right of citizens of the Union and their family members to move and reside freely within the territory of the Member States, COM (2008) 840 final; Horizontal Synthesis report on the Implementation of Directive 2004/38/EC, submitted by Milieu Ltd. (Belgium) and Europa Institute, University of Edinburgh, available at http://ec.europa.eu/justice/doc_centre/citizenship/movement/doc/horizontal_synthesis_report_en.pdf (last accessed on 10 June 2011).

benefits (Barnard 2010, 282–8). Article 7 (2) of Regulation 1612/68 already postulates that migrant workers will enjoy the same social (and tax) benefits as national workers.

In *Martinez Sala* (1998)[37] a Spanish woman who used to work between 1976 and 1989, with some interruptions, for various employers in Germany became unemployed and received financial assistance from public funds. Since 1984 she had faced difficulties renewing her residence permit. She did, however, obtain a receipt for her application and was therefore lawfully resident in Germany. Because of the missing valid residence permit, the German authorities refused her request for child allowance. The ECJ ruled that Mrs Sala was a European citizen under Article 18 EC (now Article 21 TFEU), which requires equal treatment under Article 12 EC (now Article 18 TFEU), and concluded that the requirement by the German authorities to present a valid residence permit in order to receive child allowance was a breach of Community law.

In *Baumbast*[38] a German national and his Colombian wife had established residency some time ago in the United Kingdom and lived there together with their common child (of German and Colombian nationality) and a daughter from the wife's previous marriage. Since Mr Baumbast worked for a British company, all family members obtained a residence permit valid until 1995. After 1993, Mr Baumbast became self-employed and thereafter depended on social welfare from time to time. Mrs Baumbast's application in 1995 for indefinite leave of residence was denied by the British authorities. The ECJ decided, for the first time, that Article 18 (1) EC (now Article 21 (2) TFEU) has direct effect on granting a right of residence and that not only Mr Baumbast, who no longer qualified as a worker under Community law, but also his wife, a non-Community national, and his children had a right of residence. This right is not unlimited, but, when balancing the right of residence against the legitimate interests of the Member States, the core content of the right and the principle of proportionality have to be taken into account (Menéndez 2009, 12 ff.; Strumica 2006, 718 f.).

Martinez Sala and *Baumbast* are leading cases with an important impact on subsequent case law. Even though European citizens still do not have the same rights of residence as nationals of the Member States, the personal scope of the right of free movement 'extends to "supranational citizens", who may be economically inactive but at least have stable social links and bounds with the Member States on account of previous legal residence' (Menéndez 2009, 24). One important implication of this case law is that 'supranational citizens' are now entitled to have access to non-contributory social benefits (ibid., 18).

The Courts emphasised the significance of the citizenship provisions again in *Grzelczyk*.[39] Mr Rudy Grzelczyk, a French national, relocated to Belgium in order to study sports at the University of Louvain-la-Neuve. During the first three years, he financed his study by part-time work. In the fourth year, however, he was going to prepare for the exams. For this reason, he was no longer able to engage in part-time work and therefore applied to the Belgian authorities for public assistance benefits (the 'minimex'). The application was refused on the grounds that he was neither Belgian nor a migrant worker. First of all, the ECJ ruled that Article 12 EC on non-discrimination (now Article

[37] Case C-85/96 [1998] ECR 2691.
[38] Case C-413/99 [2002] ECR I-7091.
[39] Case C-184/99 [2001] ECR I-6193.

18 TFEU), which has to be read in conjunction with Article 18 EC on the citizens' right to move and reside freely (now Article 21 TFEU), is applicable. Since migrants, but not Belgian nationals, must be 'workers' to be entitled to 'minimex', the Belgian law breaches Community law. Secondly, the Court had to clarify whether the student was entitled to reside in Belgium. The Students' Directive 93/96 made the students' right of residence for a period longer than three months dependent on a declaration by the students that they have sufficient resources to support themselves. According to the ECJ, the truthfulness of this declaration is to be assessed only at the time when it is made. When the student's financial situation changes over time and he or she becomes a temporary burden on public funds, the host state is not allowed to automatically withdraw a student's residence permit or refuse to renew it. A certain, but limited, degree of financial solidarity among the states is unavoidable. The more a person in need is integrated into the society of a foreign Member State, the more this person can reasonably expect support from the tax-financed public funds of this state.[40] The question arises whether Union citizenship established a 'door opener' to the Member States' social insurance systems (Hilpold 2008, 28 ff.).

The decoupling of equal treatment from economic activity has been further affirmed in *Trojani*.[41] Mr Trojani, a French national, in 2000 moved to Belgium where he claimed to have worked temporarily. In 2002 he became involved in a reintegration programme of the Salvation Army, which provided him with board, lodging and some pocket money in return for various jobs amounting to about 30 hours a week. His application for the minimum subsistence allowance ('minimex') was denied by the Belgian authorities on the grounds that he was neither Belgian nor a worker under Community law. The Court said that even though Mr Trojani could not derive the right to reside in Belgium from Article 18 EC (now Article 21 TFEU), he was still lawfully resident in Belgium according to domestic law, since he held a residence permit issued by the Belgian authorities. As a citizen of the Union, he could rely on equal treatment according to Article 12 EC (now Article 18 TFEU) even with respect to social benefits. Of course, the Member States are allowed to terminate a residence permit, in particular to stop social welfare tourism. However, the termination must not come automatically, and it must be proportionate (Barnard 2010, 444 f.; Strumica 2006, 720 f.; Hilpold 2008, 32 f.).

In some recent cases, the Court has decided that the principle of equal treatment is binding not only for the migrants' host states but also for their home states. In *D'Hoop*[42] a Belgian national who had completed her secondary education in France returned to Belgium, where she completed her university education. Her application to the Belgian authorities for a tide over allowance, a type of unemployment benefit to support young people between the end of education and their first job, was rejected on the ground that she did not complete her secondary education in Belgium. The Court said: 'By linking the grant of tide over allowances to the condition of having obtained the required diploma in Belgium, the national legislation thus places at a disadvantage certain of its nationals

---

40 In *Bidar* (Case C-209/03 [2005] ECR I-2119) the Court explicitly stated that the degree of financial solidarity with nationals of other Member States should depend on the degree of integration of the students into the society of that state, indicated, e.g., by the period of residence.

41 Case C-456/02 [2004] ECR I-7573.

42 Case 224/98 [2002] ECR I-6191. For further cases see Barnard (2010, 446 f.); Wollenschläger (2009, 39 f.).

simply because they have exercised their freedom to move in order to pursue education in another Member State.'[43]

To summarise: by combining Union citizenship (now Article 21 TFEU) and non-discrimination (now Article 18 TFEU) the European Court of Justice has facilitated access to non-contributory social benefits even for non-economically active migrants. The question arises whether or to what extent this development induces 'social welfare tourism' by non-economically active persons and thereby interferes with the Member States' ability to provide tax-financed social services.

4 HOW RELEVANT IS THE REMOVAL OF BARRIERS TO THE MOBILITY OF WORKERS AND NON-ACTIVE PERSONS?

Although the removal of barriers to the mobility of the economically active and non-active population in the EU and EEA is different from all other modes of regional economic integration in the world, the level of internal migration in the EU is modest. As of 2008, about 11.3 million persons or 2.3 per cent of the current 27 EU Member States' population have been citizens of other EU Member States. That is slightly less than one-third of the foreign population in the EU-27. In the EU-15 countries, the share of the population from other EU countries is, at about 3 per cent, somewhat higher. The shares in the ten new Central and Eastern European Member States are negligible (Table 7.1).

Before the EU's Eastern enlargement, the share of citizens from other EU Member States in the foreign population of the EU had declined continuously due to converging per capita income levels in the EU-15. Given the substantial income differences between the EU-15 and the NMS-8, the number of foreign residents from the latter region in the EU-15 has increased from about 0.9 million persons in 2003 to almost 2.1 million persons in 2009, in other words by 1.3 million persons in the first six years after the start of the EU Eastern enlargement. During the same period of time, the population from Bulgaria and Romania (NMS-2) has increased by about 1.6 million. Before the financial crisis, net immigration from the NMS-8 to the EU-15 amounted to about 250 000 persons p.a. As a consequence of the crisis, this figure declined to half of that in 2009.

According to recent forecasts, the foreign population from the NMS-8 in the EU-15 will, presuming a recovery of the European economies, increase by another 2.3 million to 4.4 million persons by 2020, and the population from the NMS-2 by another 1.7 million to 4.0 million persons (Brücker et al. 2009b). Thus, under the assumption that the stock of migrants from the other EU Member States remains largely constant, the foreign population from the EU Member States will increase by another 4 million persons to 15.3 million persons in 2020, so that the share of citizens from other EU Member States in the population of the EU-27 will be about 3.1 per cent in 2020.

The modest share of EU-15 foreigners in the EU population and the increasing share of NMS-8 foreigners in the EU-15 can be attributed to differences in per capita income levels. As Table 7.2 shows, per capita income levels of the EU-15 are relatively similar; if we exclude the outliers Luxembourg and Portugal, the gross national income (GNI) per capita levels

---

[43] Para. 34.

Table 7.1 Population in the EU-27 by nationality status, 2008

	Total population	Non-nationals		Citizens of other EU Member States		Citizens of non-EU countries	
	thousands	thousands	% of pop.	thousands	% of pop.	thousands	% of pop.
Austria	8319	835	10.0	290	3.5	545	6.6
Belgium	10667	971	9.1	659	6.2	312	2.9
Bulgaria	7640	24	0.3	4	0.0	21	0.3
Cyprus	789	125	15.9	81	10.3	44	5.6
Czech Republic	10381	348	3.3	132	1.3	216	2.1
Denmark	5476	298	5.5	93	1.7	205	3.7
Estonia	1341	229	17.1	8	0.6	221	16.5
Finland	5300	133	2.5	47	0.9	86	1.6
France	63753	3674	5.8	1283	2.0	2391	3.8
Germany	82218	7255	8.8	2516	3.1	4740	5.8
Greece	11214	906	8.1	158	1.4	748	6.7
Hungary	10045	177	1.8	101	1.0	76	0.8
Ireland	4401	554	12.6	392	8.9	162	3.7
Italy	59619	3433	5.8	934	1.6	2498	4.2
Latvia	2271	415	18.3	8	0.3	408	17.9
Lithuania	3366	43	1.3	3	0.1	40	1.2
Luxembourg	484	206	42.6	177	36.6	29	6.0
Malta	410	15	3.8	8	2.0	7	1.8
Netherlands	16405	688	4.2	263	1.6	425	2.6
Poland	38116	58	0.2	25	0.1	33	0.1
Portugal	10618	446	4.2	116	1.1	331	3.1
Romania	21529	26	0.1	6	0.0	20	0.1
Slovak Republic	5401	41	0.8	26	0.5	15	0.3
Slovenia	2026	69	3.4	4	0.2	65	3.2
Spain	45283	5262	11.6	2113	4.7	3149	7.0
Sweden	9183	524	5.7	241	2.6	284	3.1
United Kingdom	61176	4021	6.6	1615	2.6	2406	3.9
EU-27	**497431**	**30779**	**6.2**	**11302**	**2.3**	**19476**	**3.9**
Other EEA:							
Norway	4737	266	5.6	138	2.9	128	2.7
Switzerland	7593	1602	21.1	968	12.7	634	8.3

Source: Eurostat Population Statistics, online, Luxembourg, download: 23 November 2010.

measured at purchasing power standards range from 86 per cent of the EU-15 average in Greece to 121 per cent in the Netherlands. At current exchange rates, the gross hourly wages and salaries range from about 40 per cent of the EU-15 average in Greece and Portugal to 166 per cent in Denmark, but most countries are in a range of 80 to 120 per cent. Compared with global differences in wages and GNI per capita levels, these are relatively small income differences, which do not motivate mass labour mobility given the high costs of migration. As a consequence, within the EU-15, the distribution of the foreign population from other EU-15 countries largely reflects income differences which go back to the era of guest worker recruitment in the late 1960s and early 1970s. Within the EU-15, the overwhelming share

Table 7.2 GNI per capita, hourly gross wages and salaries and net migration in the EU, the other EEA and the candidate countries, 2007

	GNI per capita at PPS[1]		GNI per capita		Hourly gross wages and salaries[2]		Net migration[3]	
	in EUR	in % of EU-15	in EUR	in % of EU-15	in EUR	in % of EU-15	in 1000	rate per 1000
Austria	31 400	114f	32 400	112[f]	15.00	103	29	3.59
Belgium	29 900	108	31 500	109	17.53	120	53	5.12
Denmark	31 400	114	42 500	147	24.23	166	10	1.87
France	27 700	100	29 900	103	17.58	121	90	17.24
Finland	29 600	107	34 000	117	15.46	106	11	0.18
Germany	28 600	104	29 700	102	16.56	114	26	0.31
Greece	23 800	86	20 000	69	5.71	39	40	3.62
Ireland	31 000	112	36 500	126	17.55	121	69	16.93
Italy	25 100	91	25 700	89	9.86	68	377	6.56
Luxembourg	56 300	204	60 400	208	25.25	173	5	11.81
Netherlands	33 300	121	34 800	120	17.71	122	−26	−1.59
Portugal	17 600	64	14 700	51	6.72	46	26	2.48
Spain	25 200	91	22 800	79	10.88	75	605	14.17
Sweden	31 300	113	37 100	128	17.68	121	51	5.65
United Kingdom	29 400	107	33 400	115	16.84	116	214	3.57
EU-15	**27 600**	**100**	**29 000**	**100**	**14.56**	**100**	**1580**	**4.12**
Cyprus	22 100	80	19 200	66	8.28	57	6	7.26
Malta	18 700	68	12 800	44	7.27	50	1	2.49
Czech Republic	18 700	68f	11 500	40[f]	3.71	25	35	3.40
Estonia	16 700	61	10 900	38	3.51	24	0	0.12
Hungary	14 800	54	9300	32	4.16	29	21	2.11
Latvia	13 900	50	8000	28	2.92	20	−2	−1.06
Lithuania	14 300	52	9300	32	2.95	20	−5	−1.41

Poland	12900	47	7700	27	3.34	23	−36	−0.95
Slovak Republic	16400	59	9800	34	3.42	24	4	0.72
Slovenia	22000	80	16300	56	8.31	57	6	3.14
NMS-8	**14700**	**53**	**9000**	**31**	**3.65**	**25**	**23**	**0.31**
Bulgaria	9300	34	3700	13	1.11	8	−34	−4.35
Romania	9600	35[f]	5400	19[f]	1.76	12	−100	−4.61
NMS-2	**9400**	**34**	**5000**	**17**	**1.60**	**11**	**−134**	**−4.54**
NMS-10	**13200**	**48**	**7800**	**27**	**3.03**	**21**	**−111**	**−1.08**
EU-25	**25600**	**93**	**25900**	**89**	**12.74**	**88**	**1470**	**3.02**
EU-27	**24600**	**89**	**24600**	**85**	**12.12**	**83**	**1477**	**3.03**
Iceland	32000	116	46900	162	n.a.	n.a.	5	n.a.
Norway	45700	166	60400	208	26.14	179	24	n.a.
Switzerland	34700	126	41500	143	22.59	155	37	n.a.
Albania	n.a.	n.a.	n.a.	n.a.	n.a.	n.a.	−20	−6.43[4]
Bosnia-Herzegovina	n.a.	n.a.	n.a.	n.a.	n.a.	n.a.	8	2.05[4]
Croatia	13900	50[f]	8600	30	n.a.	n.a.	7	1.64
Macedonia	7300	26[f]	2700	9[f]	n.a.	n.a.	−1	−0.26
Serbia-Montenegro	n.a.	n.a.	n.a.	n.a.	n.a.	n.a.	−20	−2.45[4]
Turkey	10500	38[f]	6500	22[f]	n.a.	n.a.	−3	−0.04
CAND-6	**10600**	**38**	**6500**	**22**	**n.a.**	**n.a.**	**−28**	**−0.30**

Notes:

1 Purchasing power parity standards (Eurostat estimate).
2 2006: Hourly labour cost according to Eurostat.
3 2005.
4 2005 (World Development Indicators, 2007).
f forecast.

Sources: GNI and hourly labour costs: Eurostat; net migration: Eurostat, supplemented by WDI. Authors' own calculations and presentation.

of the foreign population from other EU Member States originates from Portugal, Greece, Italy and Spain, i.e. countries which were characterised by relatively low income levels compared with the countries in western and north-western Europe in the 1960s and 1970s, or, as in the case of Italy, by substantial regional income differences within countries.

Still, the level of labour mobility within the EU is fairly low compared with large countries with similar income differences: only about 1 per 200 workers change residence between EU countries p.a. compared with 5 between the states of the USA. The elasticity between the migration rate and the difference in income levels among countries of the EU can be estimated at between one-fifth and one-third of that among the states of the USA (Boeri et al. 2002; Barro and Sala-i-Martin 1991, 2004; Decressin and Fátas 1995; Puhanyi 2001). It is important to note in this context that these figures also mirror the extremely low levels of regional labour mobility across regions within the EU Member States: despite substantial differences in wages and unemployment rates, e.g. between the southern and northern regions of Italy, between Flanders and Wallonia in Belgium or between Eastern Germany and the industrial strongholds in the South of Germany, regional migration figures look modest. The low migration across European countries reflects a large number of barriers and red tape: language and cultural barriers, the lack of recognition of educational degrees, the limited portability of pension claims, high transaction costs in the housing markets, rigid labour market institutions with low job-turnover, to name only some of the most important obstacles to labour mobility.[44] Comparable barriers are much lower or altogether absent in the US.

The rather low labour mobility within the Common Market generally hinders the adjustment to structural shocks and labour market imbalances across the EU. Note that regional labour mobility plays a key role in absorbing labour market shocks in the US: as Blanchard and Katz (1992) have demonstrated in an influential study, regional labour mobility eliminates regional differences in unemployment rates triggered by structural shocks. Regional labour mobility is certainly too low in the EU to play the same role there, which creates problems not least for structural adjustment in the Eurozone.

This does not imply however that the legal provisions on the free movement of labour do not play a role in facilitating the mobility of labour and other persons in the EU. This can be illustrated by the recent EU Eastern enlargement. The findings of Brücker et al. (2009a, 2009b) suggest that the free movement has triggered substantial migration from the new Member States into the old EU countries compared with third countries with similar income levels. They use a model which explains the stock of migrants as a percentage of the sending country population by economic variables such as differences in income and employment rates, as well as by institutional variables which affect the mobility of workers and other persons. Inter alia, these institutional variables capture the migration conditions for EU citizens, for citizens of countries for which transitional arrangements apply and for third-country nationals. Institutional variables enter the model both as level variables and as interaction terms with the income and employment variables. This allows the authors to identify the impact of institutions on countries which are characterised by different economic conditions (see Box 7.1).

44 The recent EU Citizenship Report identifies numerous obstacles that still impede de facto the free movement of persons within the EU (European Commission 2010).

BOX 7.1 ASSESSING THE IMPACT OF FREE MOVEMENT ON MIGRATION STOCKS

Consider the following simple migration model in the Harris–Todaro (1970) tradition. The level of migration is determined by income expectations in the respective locations, which in turn are a function of the wage and the employment rate. Under the assumption that individuals are heterogeneous regarding their preferences or productivity, the equilibrium stock of migrants is then a log-linear function of the income level and the employment rate. This also holds true if we consider that migration is temporary (Brücker and Schröder, 2011).

Institutions affect migration stocks both directly and indirectly: via the intercept and via the slope parameters of other explanatory variables such as income levels and employment rates. We therefore specify the long run migration function as

$$mst_{fit} = \alpha'\mathbf{x}_{ft} + \beta'\mathbf{x}_{it} + \gamma'\mathbf{z}_{fit} + \eta'(\mathbf{z}_{fit} \times \mathbf{x}_{ft}) + \lambda'(\mathbf{z}_{fit} \times \mathbf{x}_{it}) + \varepsilon_{fit} \qquad (7.1)$$

where mst_{fit} denotes the migration stock from country i to foreign country f at time t, $\mathbf{x}_{ft}$ denotes a vector of explanatory variables in destination country f, $\mathbf{x}_{it}$ a vector of explanatory variables in sending country i, $\mathbf{z}_{fit}$ a vector of institutional variables which characterise migration conditions between sending country i and destination f, $\mathbf{z}_{fit} \times \mathbf{x}_{ft}$ and $\mathbf{z}_{fit} \times \mathbf{x}_{it}$ interaction terms, which capture the impact of institutional conditions on the slope parameters of the model, α, β, γ, η and λ vectors of coefficients. The error term ε_{fit} is specified as a one-way error component model with country-specific fixed effects. We estimate the model in dynamic form as a structural adjustment model which considers one lag of the dependent variable.

As explanatory variables we consider GDP per capita as a proxy for the wage level and the employment rate in the destination and sending countries, which determines the probability of employment in the respective locations. Dummy variables capture the following institutional regimes affecting migration conditions: free movement within the EU and the European Economic Area (EEA), transitional arrangements for free movement, guest worker agreements between relevant EU Member States and sending countries, third-county migration conditions (e.g. those in place for Turkey and Maghreb countries), and the emigration restrictions in place for countries under the iron curtain. Beyond that we consider wars, dictatorship and the Freedom House political rights and civil rights index as institutional variables. Note that geography and other constant factors affecting migration, such as language, are captured by country-specific fixed effects.

Using the coefficients on the institutional variables and the interaction terms enables us to identify the impact of institutions on the scale of migration. Reporting the estimation results is beyond the scope of this chapter (cf. Brücker et al. 2009b). Note that in this model free movement has a different impact on the scale of migration depending on the income level and the employment rates. For a ratio of the income level of the EU-15 to the sending country of 2:1 – which corresponds to the average income difference between the EU-15 and the NMS-8 – the model predicts a long-run equilibrium stock of migrants of 4.5 per cent of the sending countries' population to the EU-15 under free movement. By contrast, the predicted stock is below 1 per cent under the institutional conditions for third-country nationals. In this back-of-the-envelope calculation we have applied averages of country-specific fixed effects for the NMS-8.

Note that the specification of the migration equation in the form of a stock model has important implications. As Brücker and Schröder (2012) demonstrate, equilibrium between migration stocks and explanatory variables such as the income differential emerges in a temporary framework with heterogeneous agents, i.e. individuals who differ in their preferences or productivity. Eventually, an equilibrium is achieved where the benefits from migration equal its costs for the marginal individual. In this equilibrium, the net migration rate becomes zero. The model is in accordance with the experience of the EU's southern enlargement in the 1980s inasmuch as net migration flows did not increase after the introduction of free movement despite substantial income differences because the main receiving countries had already accumulated a large stock of migrants. By contrast, this was not the case when the EU opened its labour markets for the Central and Eastern European Member States.

Needless to say, every migration estimate suffers from serious data limitations. Not all EU countries provide satisfactory accounts of migration stocks, so that in some important destination countries the data have to be derived from household surveys such as the Eurostat Labour Force Survey. Moreover, different national legislation affects the naturalisation rate of migrants in different ways, which may distort stock figures. Further, the concept of nationality differs also across countries, making it impossible to harmonise the data completely. In addition, no distinction is made between persons who actually migrated and non-nationals who were born in the host country. Finally, border commuters, i.e. persons who are nationals and resident in one state but work in another one, are not captured by the data.[45] The estimates therefore must be understood as an indication of the magnitudes involved, not as an accurate forecast.

The findings suggest that the free movement of workers and other persons has a substantial impact on migration: For a ratio of the income levels between the EU-15 and the sending countries of 2:1 – which corresponds to the current income differences between the EU-15 and the NMS-8 countries – the model predicts a long-run stock of migrants of 4.5 per cent of the sending countries' population if the rules of free movement apply.

[45] Their estimated number in the EU (including EEA and EFTA) is 780 000, mainly concentrated in the area of Central-Western Europe. See Scientific Report on the Mobility of Cross-Border Workers within the EU27/EEA/EFTA Countries, Final Report presented to the European Commission by MKW Wirtschaftsforschung GmbH and Empirica Kft., Munich/Sopron, 2009, available at http://www.mkw-gmbh.de/fileadmin/templates/mkw-gmbh/publications/MKW_workers_mobility.pdf (last accessed on 10 June 2011).

By contrast, for the same income difference, the model predicts only a stock of 1 per cent of the population of the sending countries if the rules for third-country nationals apply (Box 7.1).

Altogether, although cross-country migration is relatively low in the EU, it is fair to state that the free movement of workers and the provisions for the mobility of the non-active population have a substantial impact on mobility compared with the third-country counterfactual – at least in the case where income differences are as substantial as between the EU-15 and the new Central and Eastern European Member States.

5 DOES THE FREE MOVEMENT OF WORKERS INCREASE EUROPEAN INCOME LEVELS?

The rationale for the free movement of workers is that it increases the productive use of labour, and, hence, per capita income levels in the integrated area. Textbook models of labour migration predict, under the assumptions of fixed capital stocks and otherwise closed economies, that labour migration reduces wages and increases capital income in the receiving countries, while the converse holds true for the sending countries. Moreover, in the receiving countries, the total factor income of the native population increases, while that in the sending countries declines (see e.g. the seminal paper by Berry and Soligo 1969). Real world economies are much more complex. Labour is heterogeneous, so that some groups of labour which are net substitutes to migrants tend to lose in the receiving countries while others which are net complements tend to win. Moreover, if wage rigidities exist, the immigration of labour can increase unemployment if migrants raise labour supply in segments with low labour market flexibility (e.g. of unskilled workers), or reduce it, when labour supply is increased in flexible segments (Brücker and Jahn 2011). As a consequence, the total factor income of the population in the receiving countries may decline if immigration increases unemployment substantially (Boeri and Brücker 2005; Wagener and Eger 2009).

Finally, the assumption of fixed capital stocks is extremely unrealistic. As Kaldor (1961) has already demonstrated, the capital–output ratio is constant over time. This has far-reaching implications for the economic consequences of migration. If the capital–output ratio is constant, the productivity-adjusted labour intensity remains constant as well. Thus, the capital stock adjusts completely to labour supply shocks, at least in the long run, such that aggregate wages and other factor prices remain constant. There is empirical evidence that the adjustment of capital stocks is fast (e.g. Ottaviano and Peri 2006), so that it is rather likely that migration will affect different groups in the labour market, but not aggregate wages and employment opportunities.

In order to analyse the economic consequences of labour migration in the EU, we focus here on a simulation of the effects of labour mobility in the context of the EU's Eastern enlargement (see Brücker et al. 2009a; Baas et al. 2007). The simulation is based on a structural model whose coefficients are estimated empirically. Since European countries are characterised by high and persistent unemployment the model is based on a setting with imperfect labour markets.

More specifically, the model presented here follows the literature in assuming that identical firms produce a variety of a composite output good under monopolistic competition, which allows us to derive an aggregate production function. Similar to Borjas (2003) and Ottaviano and Peri (2006) we employ a nested production function with constant elasticity of substitution which distinguishes labour by education, work experience and immigrants and natives. The model considers three education groups, four groups by work experience, and native and foreign workers, which gives 24 groups in the labour market. Although a simplification, this approach has the advantage that it enables us to analyse the labour market impact of migration for different groups of workers in detail. Alternatively, one could consider a sectoral approach which addresses the implications of immigration for different branches of the economy; however, this would preclude an in-depth analysis of the impact for different groups of workers. In the context of the EU's Eastern enlargement the second approach has been also applied by Baas et al. (2007), as well as by Baas and Brücker (2008). Since the findings in these studies resemble by and large those of the aggregate production function approach we do not report them here.

An important feature of the model is that it incorporates wage rigidities via a wage-setting curve (Layard et al. 2005), which states that wages tend to decline with an increasing unemployment rate, albeit imperfectly. Consider an economy where wages are fixed by collective agreements between trade unions and employer federations. In this case the wage falls with increasing unemployment, but not necessarily in proportion. Alternative wage-setting mechanisms such as efficiency wages or shirking models yield similar results. In the empirical analysis the model allows for the elasticities of the wage-setting curves to differ across different segments of the labour market. Thus, different degrees of wage flexibility, e.g. in the segments of high and low skilled workers, are considered. Once wages are fixed, the so-called 'right-to-manage' assumption is applied, i.e. at given wages firms adjust employment in a way such that profits are maximised. Consequently, the employment level can fall below the full employment level depending on the wage. Finally, the model lets the capital stock adjust to the increasing supply of labour. The long-run simulations presented below are based on the assumption that the capital–output ratio remains constant (complete adjustment), while we assume in the short-run simulations that the capital stock is fixed. For a brief presentation of the model see Box 7.2; for further technical details see Brücker and Jahn (2011).

As outlined above, the impact of migration depends largely on the structure of the labour supply shock. For example, unemployment may increase if immigration occurs in labour market segments with sticky wages, while the converse holds true if the labour supply is increased in segments with flexible wages. Interestingly enough, the findings of Brücker and Jahn (2011) indicate that wage flexibility is particularly high for younger workers and in both the highly and the less skilled segments of the labour market. It is thus worthwhile to look not only at the skill structure of the migrant workforce but also at their age structure if we want to learn something about wage and employment effects.

Table 7.3 presents the skill and age structure of NMS-8 migrants compared with the native working age population in the EU-15 and selected immigration countries. Compared with the native population, immigrants from NMS-8 evidently have a lower share in the less-skilled labour market segment (without vocational training), a higher one in the medium skill segment (vocational training) and a slightly lower one in the high education segment (university or similar education degrees). However, the figures must be taken with a grain of salt, given that educational degrees tend to be reported below their true levels if immigrants are employed below their skill levels. This is also an issue

BOX 7.2 THE EFFECTS OF LABOUR MOBILITY UNDER IMPERFECT LABOUR MARKETS

European labour markets are characterised by persistent unemployment which is caused inter alia by institutional rigidities such as collective bargaining and employment protection. Addressing the economic effects of migration in a model with perfect labour markets is thus misleading. The impact of migration is therefore analysed in a model with collective bargaining, where wages respond to an increase in the unemployment rate, albeit imperfectly (cf. Brücker and Jahn (2011) for details).

Consider an economy with i types of labour and j identical firms which produce under monopolistic competition with labour and capital a variety of an aggregate output good. The aggregate production function of the economy is given by $Y = G(\mathbf{L}, K)$, where Y is the aggregate output good, and $\mathbf{L} = [L_1, L_2, \ldots, L_i, \ldots L_n]$ a vector of labour inputs. For employment, $L_i \leq N_i$ holds in all segments of the labour market i, i.e. it is smaller than or equal to the total labour force N_i, where the vector $\mathbf{N} = [N_1, N_2, \ldots, N_i, \ldots N_n]$. Total labour supply is given by

$$N_i = \overline{N}_i + \gamma_i M, \quad \sum_i \gamma_i = 1, \tag{7.2}$$

where N_i is the total labour force and $\overline{N}_i$ the native labour force in segment i, M the total migrant influx and γ_i the share of workers of type i among the migrant inflow.

Wages and labour demand are determined sequentially. In the first stage wages are fixed, e.g. in a collective bargaining process. It is assumed that wages decline in the unemployment rate, but not necessarily perfectly. This gives for the wage in each segment of the labour market

$$w_i = f_i(u_i), \quad f_i' \leq 0, \quad \forall i, \tag{7.3}$$

where the unemployment rate is defined as $u_i = 1 - L_i/N_i$. The wage-setting function f_i determines the flexibility of the labour market. Once the wage is fixed, firms choose employment levels to maximise profits. Under monopolistic competition the profit-maximising wage level is given by

$$w_i = \nu^{-1} Y_{L_i}, \quad \forall i, \tag{7.4}$$

where the mark-up factor $\nu = (1 - 1/\eta)^{-1}$ is derived from product demand. The price of the output good has been normalised without loss of generality to 1.

Applying the implicit function theorem to

$$\Omega_i(\mathbf{L}, M) \equiv \nu^{-1} Y_{Li}(\mathbf{L}, K(\mathbf{N}(M))) + f_i(u_i(L_i, N_i(M))) = 0, \quad \forall i, \tag{7.5}$$

yields for the employment response

$$\frac{d\mathbf{L}}{dM} = \left(\frac{\partial v^{-1}\mathbf{Y}_L}{\partial \mathbf{L}} - \frac{\partial \mathbf{f}}{\partial \mathbf{u}}\frac{\partial \mathbf{u}}{\partial \mathbf{L}}\right) \times \left(\frac{\partial \mathbf{f}}{\partial \mathbf{u}}\frac{\partial \mathbf{u}}{\partial \mathbf{N}}\frac{d\mathbf{N}}{dM} - \frac{\partial v^{-1}\mathbf{Y}_L}{\partial K}\frac{\partial K}{\partial \mathbf{N}}\frac{d\mathbf{N}}{dM}\right), \tag{7.6}$$

and for the wage response

$$\frac{dw}{dM} = \frac{\partial v^{-1}\mathbf{Y}_L}{\partial \mathbf{L}}\frac{d\mathbf{L}}{dM} + \frac{\partial v^{-1}\mathbf{Y}_L}{\partial K}\frac{\partial K}{\partial \mathbf{N}}\frac{d\mathbf{N}}{dM}. \tag{7.7}$$

Four things are noteworthy about equations (7.6) and (7.7). First, if the elasticity of the wage-setting functions with respect to the unemployment rates converges to minus infinity, then $d\mathbf{L}/dM \rightarrow d\mathbf{N}/dM$ and immigration has no impact on unemployment. This corresponds to the case with perfectly flexible labour markets. Secondly, if the elasticity of the wage-setting function and the capital stock do not adjust to the increasing labour supply, then employment remains unchanged and unemployment increases in lockstep with labour supply. This corresponds to the case of absolutely inflexible labour markets as in the famous Harris and Todaro (1970) model. Thirdly, if capital stocks adjust completely to the increase in labour supply, neither aggregate wages nor the aggregate unemployment rate change as a consequence of immigration. This is the case if the capital–output ratio remains constant (Ottaviano and Peri 2006). Since this is the case at least in the long term (Kaldor 1961), this assumption is applied in the long-run simulations. Fourth, the effects for the individual groups in the labour markets depend on the elasticities of the wage-setting curves and the elasticities and cross-elasticities of labour demand, which are in turn determined by the production function. Thus, the exact impact of immigration on labour markets depends on the structure of the labour supply shock and is an empirical question.

In our empirical application we distinguish the labour force by education, work experience and natives/foreigners. More specifically, Baas et al. (2007) distinguish three education groups, four groups of work experience and native and foreign workers by citizenship in their empirical analysis, to which we refer in the text. This gives 24 groups in the labour market. Production technologies are specified in the form of a nested constant elasticity of substitution (CES) technology and the elasticities of the wage-setting functions are estimated separately.

if education levels are self-reported, as in case of Labour Force Survey data which are used here.

The difference between the immigrant and the native population is more striking with respect to the age structure: 63 per cent of the immigrant population belongs to the young age group, compared with only 34 per cent of the native population. Thus, immigration from the NMS-8 has a substantial impact on the age structure of the workforce (Table 7.3).

Analogously, emigration changes factor proportions in the sending countries. Table 7.4 presents the education and the age structure of the emigrant population from the

Table 7.3 Education and age structure of NMS-8 immigrants in the EU-15, 2007

	Austria		Germany		United Kingdom		EU-15	
	NMS-8	natives	NMS-8	natives	NMS-8	natives	NMS-8	natives
	Share of NMS-8 and native working-age population in per cent							
Low education	7.7	16.1	19.8	13.5	12.4	22.9	16.9	27.2
Medium education	67.8	65.9	53.3	60.5	76.0	44.9	60.8	45.4
High education	24.4	18.0	26.9	26.0	9.5	31.5	21.5	27.2
15–34 years	36.8	35.5	48.7	30.3	86.0	34.5	63.0	33.9
35–49 years	38.8	45.3	36.5	44.9	11.2	39.3	26.8	42.2
49–64 years	24.4	19.2	14.9	24.8	2.9	26.3	10.2	23.9

Note: The working-age population is defined as the population between 15 and 64 years of age. Low education is defined according to ISCED 0–2, medium education as ISCED 3 and high education according to ISCED 5–6. Missing information in the LFS data suggests that education levels of the NMS population are underestimated.

Source: Authors' compilation based on Brücker et al. (2009a) and the Eurostate LFS.

Table 7.4 Education and age structure of NMS-8 emigrants in the EU-15, 2007

	Poland		Czech Republic		Hungary		NMS-8	
	emigrants	stayers	emigrants	stayers	emigrants	stayers	emigrants	stayers
	Share of NMS-8 and native working-age population in per cent							
Low education	17.6	22.4	13.9	14.5	8.4	21.3	16.9	9.1
Medium education	60.0	68.4	48.3	79.7	65.0	65.3	60.8	69.6
High education	21.7	9.2	35.6	5.8	26.6	13.4	21.5	21.3
15–34 years	64.7	22.4	65.4	14.5	43.4	21.3	63.0	37.7
35–49 years	27.2	68.4	21.5	79.7	33.4	65.3	26.8	40.0
49–64 years	8.1	9.2	13.1	5.8	23.4	13.4	10.2	22.4

Note: The category emigrants refers to the emigrant population of the respective country or the NMS-8 in the EU-15. The category stayers refers to the native population staying in the respective country or the NMS-8. All other categories are defined as in Table 7.3.

Source: Authors' compilation based on LFS data and on Brücker et al. (2009a).

NMS-8 into the EU-15 compared with the native population staying behind in the NMS-8 and selected sending countries there. In all of the three major sending countries – Poland, the Czech Republic and Hungary – the emigrants' education level is well above that of the native population which stays behind. In particular, the share among the

Table 7.5 Sectoral breakdown of NMS-8 and total employees in the United Kingdom and Germany, 2010

Sector	Unted Kingdom		Germany	
	NMS-8	all	NMS-8	all
	Share of sector in per cent of total employees			
Agriculture, forestry, fishing	1.6	1.6	4.5	0.7
Mining	0.0	0.3	0.1	0.3
Manufacturing industries	19.1	10.8	17.6	22.9
Energy, water	0.9	0.0	0.7	1.7
Construction	6.2	7.6	5.9	5.6
Trade and repair	16.1	14.1	12.5	14.7
Transport and communication	11.3	6.4	8.0	8.1
Hotels and restaurants	15.4	4.5	9.1	2.9
Finance and insurance	2.4	4.0	1.3	3.7
Real estate	15.9	13.0	0.8	0.8
Public sector, defence	1.0	6.9	1.7	6.1
Education	1.8	10.4	3.6	4.1
Health and social services	6.7	13.2	13.4	12.6
Other public and private services	2.0	6.9	18.8	15.6
Private household services	0.6	0.2	2.2	0.1
Exterritorial organisations	0.0	0.1	0.1	0.1

Source: Authors' compilation based on German and UK Labour Force Survey data and Baas and Brücker (2010).

skill groups with a university or similar degree (ISCED 5+6) is about twice as high as among the stayers. The same does not hold true for the NMS-8 aggregate. This reflects a composition effect, i.e. countries with a relatively less skilled population send more migrants than those with a higher share of skilled individuals. Moreover, the emigrant population is much younger than the native population in the sending countries – the share of young people is disproportionally large among the emigrant population. Thus, East–West migration in the context of EU enlargement has not only involved a loss of skilled individuals but also contributed to the ageing of the workforce in the sending countries (Table 7.4).

It is not only the skill and age structure of migration which affects the sending and destination countries' economies and their labour markets. A concentration of migrants in certain sectors may also have other implications. Table 7.5 presents a sectoral breakdown of the migrant workforce from the NMS-8 in Germany and the UK compared with the total employment breakdown. There is no uniform pattern between the two main destination countries of NMS-8 migrants in the EU-15. In the UK, NMS-8 migrants are disproportionally represented in hotels and restaurants, manufacturing industries, and transport and communication. In Germany we find particularly high shares in hotels and restaurants, agriculture and other public and private services. Interestingly, the shares in construction are similar to those of natives and also private household services do not play a particularly large role. However, these figures refer

Table 7.6 Simulation of the macroeconomic impact of migration from the NMS-8 into the EU-15, 2004–07

	Change of labour force	GDP		GDP per capita		Factor income per native		Unemployment		Wages	
		Short-run	Long-run	Short-run	Long-run	Short-run	Long-run	Short-run	Long-run	Short-run	Long-run
	Changes in per cent (unemployment rate: changes in percentage points)										
AT	0.42	0.31	0.34	0.00	0.02	0.12	0.15	0.02	0.02	−0.02	0.00
BE	0.22	0.11	0.17	−0.08	−0.02	0.01	0.07	0.07	0.05	−0.04	0.00
DE	0.10	0.04	0.10	−0.03	0.02	−0.01	0.04	0.03	0.01	−0.03	0.00
DK	0.23	0.13	0.20	−0.08	−0.01	0.00	0.07	0.02	0.00	−0.05	0.00
ES	0.19	0.03	0.11	−0.08	−0.01	−0.04	0.04	0.05	0.02	−0.04	0.00
FI	0.09	0.03	0.08	−0.06	−0.01	−0.02	0.04	0.03	0.01	−0.03	0.00
FR	0.01	0.01	0.01	0.00	0.00	0.00	0.00	0.00	0.00	0.00	0.00
GR	−0.01	0.00	−0.01	0.01	0.00	0.00	−0.01	0.00	0.00	0.00	0.00
IE	4.87	0.80	2.93	−2.07	−0.02	−0.77	1.31	0.87	0.37	−1.61	0.00
IT	0.11	0.04	0.08	−0.03	0.01	0.00	0.04	0.02	0.01	−0.03	0.00
LU	1.00	0.81	1.13	0.23	0.55	0.34	0.65	0.12	0.05	−0.25	0.00
NL	0.14	0.09	0.12	−0.03	−0.01	0.02	0.04	0.02	0.01	−0.02	0.00
SE	0.38	0.25	0.33	−0.01	0.07	0.05	0.12	0.05	0.03	−0.06	0.00
UK	1.28	0.50	0.89	−0.28	0.10	−0.05	0.34	0.21	0.11	−0.29	0.00
CZ	−0.08	−0.07	−0.11	0.01	−0.03	0.01	−0.03	−0.02	0.00	0.03	0.00
EE	−0.21	−0.09	−0.19	0.12	0.02	0.12	0.02	−0.04	0.00	0.06	0.00
HU	−0.44	−0.34	−0.49	0.10	−0.04	0.10	−0.04	−0.04	0.00	0.11	0.00
LT	−1.14	−0.55	−1.15	0.61	−0.01	0.61	−0.01	−0.32	−0.01	0.31	0.00
LV	−0.43	−0.26	−0.46	0.17	−0.03	0.17	−0.03	−0.09	0.00	0.12	0.00
PL	−1.77	−0.88	−1.94	0.90	−0.18	0.90	−0.18	−0.59	0.03	0.43	0.00
SI	0.26	0.15	0.21	−0.10	−0.05	−0.10	−0.05	0.02	0.00	−0.04	0.00
SK	−1.34	−0.53	−1.51	0.82	−0.18	0.82	−0.18	−0.55	0.00	0.43	0.00
EU-15[1]	**0.36**	**0.13**	**0.26**	**−0.09**	**0.03**	**−0.02**	**0.10**	**0.06**	**0.02**	**−0.09**	**0.00**
NMS-8	**−1.16**	**−0.52**	**−1.10**	**0.65**	**0.05**	**0.65**	**0.05**	**−0.42**	**−0.02**	**0.25**	**0.00**
Total	**0.11**	**0.11**	**0.20**	**0.11**	**0.20**	**0.16**	**0.25**	**−0.03**	**0.00**	**−0.07**	**0.00**

Note: [1] Without Portugal.

Source: Authors' estimates and simulations.

to official employment only and by definition do not cover irregular or unregistered employment relations.

Table 7.6 presents the key findings on the macroeconomic impact of migration from NMS-8 into the EU-15 in the context of the EU's Eastern enlargement. The simulations use the actual migration figures from the NMS-8 by education and age groups during the years 2004–07. During the 2004–07 period, the labour force of the EU-15 has increased through immigration from the NMS-8 by 0.36 per cent, while that of the NMS-8 has declined by 1.16 per cent. Since skill-downgrading, i.e. employment below education levels, might be a problem for the analysis, the education figures have been adjusted in the receiving countries using information on the occupational status of immigrants which is provided by the Labour Force Survey.

The simulation results are summarised in Table 7.6. They indicate that GDP in the enlarged EU increases by 0.11 per cent in the short run and, after the adjustment of the capital stock, by 0.2 per cent in the long run. While the aggregate GDP of the sending countries declines by 0.52 per cent in the short run and by 1.1 per cent in the long run, that of the EU-15 increases by 0.13 per cent in the short run and by 0.26 per cent in the long run. This is not surprising since the NMS-8 lose a substantial part of their workforce, which causes a decline in output even if the capital stock remains fixed. In the long term the adjustment of the capital stock has a multiplier effect: the smaller workforce in the NMS-8 reduces the real return on capital so that both domestic and international investors reduce their investment until the capital–output ratio and, thus, the real return on capital reach their pre-migration levels. For the receiving countries the converse holds true: returns on capital increase in the short term so that investment increases until the pre-migration capital–output ratio is restored.

GDP per capita increases in the sending countries in the short term due to the higher capital intensity of production and is slightly reduced in the receiving countries. However, this effect is very small in the destination countries since the migrants are younger on average and therefore more likely to be employed than the native population in the receiving countries, so that their GDP per capita increases at least in the long term when the capital stock has adjusted due to higher participation in the labour force.

The factor income of the native population, i.e. the wage sum and the sum of capital returns, falls moderately in the EU-15 by 0.02 per cent but increases in the long run by 0.1 per cent. The initial decline is triggered by the slight increase in the unemployment rate in the short term (0.06 percentage points), which almost disappears in the long term. By contrast, the unemployment rate declines substantially in the NMS-8 by 0.42 percentage points in the short term, but only modestly in the long term. Due to the adjustment of capital stocks, the long-term impact on wages is zero as expected. In the short term, wages decline moderately in the EU-15 and increase in the NMS-8.

Altogether, the simulation results suggest that even if we consider imperfect labour markets we may expect aggregate gains from the free movement of labour from a European perspective. There are two main sources of these gains. First, the movement of labour from low to high income countries increases the productive use of labour and, hence, output and aggregate income levels. Second, there is a short-term gain if labour emigrates from regions with relatively high unemployment rates, which is the case in the context of the EU's Eastern enlargement. As a consequence, the aggregate unemployment rate in the EU declines, which generates a second benefit. However, since labour markets adjust over time, these gains disappear in our simulations in the long term, so that the aggregate unemployment rate reverts to its original level.

The aggregate GDP gain of 0.2 per cent looks small at first glance. However, since we consider here only labour migration of 0.36 per cent of the labour force in the receiving countries, the figure is not really small. Aggregating over the entire EU, the total gain from the 2003–07 migration amounts to 24 billion euros in 2007. Note that these gains accrue annually. Moreover, according to the estimates of Brücker et al. (2009b), only between one-third and half of the migration potential from the NMS-8 has been realised by 2007. Thus, we can expect an annual long-term gain of between 48 and 72 billion euros from the free movement of labour for the EU-27.

6 DO EU IMMIGRANTS CREATE A FISCAL BURDEN FOR THE WELFARE STATE?

In political as well as in scholarly discussions there is some concern that immigrants, especially those from the new Central and Eastern European Member States, will negatively affect the generous social welfare programmes in the destination countries. Empirically, this problem can be addressed from two different but interrelated perspectives. First of all, one must analyse whether immigrants are over-represented among the pool of welfare recipients and whether their average receipt of welfare transfers is above or below the corresponding figures for natives. Secondly, it has to be investigated whether differences between immigrants and natives can be attributed to observable individual and household characteristics. If the observed characteristics fail to explain the observed differences in the reliance on the welfare system, these differences can be labelled 'residual welfare dependency', i.e. immigrants would, *ceteris paribus*, be more likely than natives to receive some form of welfare transfer. However, even if immigrants do not behave differently from natives, countries with generous welfare systems may tend to attract those immigrants who are eligible to receive welfare transfers, and this would put pressure on the welfare system itself (Sinn 2003).

Several studies on Europe and the US provide evidence that the immigrant population is over-represented among the pool of non-contributory welfare recipients, notably social assistance recipients, although for some – but not all – European countries those differences can be explained by differences in socio-economic characteristics (Barrett and McCarthy 2008; Boeri 2006; Hansen and Lofstrom 1999). As these programmes are non-contributory, a relatively high take-up rate may generate pressure on the fiscal budget, although the overall fiscal impact of immigration is still uncertain (Auerbach and Oreopoulos 1999). However, social assistance is often the main source of income for those migrants who are not entitled to contributory benefits (e.g. unemployment benefits, pensions) since they have not accumulated enough work experience in the host country to be eligible for social insurance. The most important contributory system is the pension system in most countries. Due to the favourable age structure and the discrimination of pension systems against brief contribution periods, migrants are usually net contributors to this type of social benefit. As a consequence, some studies find that there are substantial net fiscal gains from immigration for the welfare system in receiving countries even though the migrant population pays lower taxes and faces a higher unemployment risk than natives. These gains are expected to increase as populations age (Bonin et al. 2000; Bonin 2002, 2006).

A recent study (Boeri and Monti, 2009; Brücker et al. 2009a) provides some further insights on this issue. Based on data collected from the European Survey on Income and Living Conditions (EU-SILC) between 2004 and 2006, it focuses on the potential welfare dependency of immigrants from the new Eastern European Member States (for a description of the study see Box 7.3). This survey does not disclose information about the interviewees' citizenship or the country of birth. However, it provides a rough distinction between immigrants from EU-25 countries and those from other countries, which is useful in our context since it provides a hint as to whether EU regulations such as the equal treatment provision affect the welfare dependency of EU immigrants differently from that of third-country nationals. Note that meanwhile a substantial number of

BOX 7.3 ANALYSING THE IMPACT OF IMMIGRATION ON WELFARE DEPENDENCY

Boeri and Monti (2009) provide an analysis of the welfare dependency of EU-25 immigrants and extra-EU immigrants compared to the native population based on the 2004–06 waves of the EU-SILC dataset. Following the public finance literature, they distinguish between contributory benefits (e.g. pensions, unemployment benefits) and non-contributory benefits (e.g. social assistance). In their descriptive analysis they calculate the coefficients

$$\frac{R_{M_i}}{M_i} - \frac{R_N}{N} \tag{7.8}$$

and

$$\frac{B_{M_i}}{M_i} - \frac{B_N}{N}, \tag{7.9}$$

where R_{Mi} and R_N denote the number of immigrants and natives, respectively, who take up welfare benefits, B_{Mi} and $B_{N.}$ denote the amount of benefits which immigrants and natives, respectively, take up, M_i the number of immigrants from i (i is either an EU-25 country or an extra-EU country), N the number of natives. A positive coefficient in equation (7.8) thus indicates that the welfare take-up rates are higher among the migrant population than in the native population, while the converse holds for a negative coefficient. Analogously, a positive coefficient in equation (7.9) indicates that the average amount of benefits a migrant receives is higher than that of natives, while a negative coefficient indicates the opposite. As outlined in the text, EU-25 and non-EU-25 immigrants have lower contributory take-up rates and on average receive lower contributory welfare benefits than natives. EU-25 immigrants are also under-represented with respect to non-contributory benefits in most EU-15 countries, while extra-EU immigrants are over-represented in this welfare category.

The differences in welfare dependency between migrants and natives might be caused by observable human capital and household characteristics such as age, education, the number of children, etc., or by the migrant status itself. The latter effect is called 'residual dependency'. Boeri and Monti (2009) run a standard Probit model of the form

$$\Pr(Y = 1|\mathbf{X}) = \varphi(\mathbf{X}'\beta), \tag{7.10}$$

where Pr denotes the probability of welfare take-up, $\mathbf{X}$ a vector of explanatory variables, β the corresponding vector of coefficients and $\varphi(.)$ the cumulative distribution function of the standard normal distribution. The model controls for sex, age, age squared, education, number of children, household size, house ownership and some regional characteristics. The residual dependency effect is identified via a migrant dummy.

> The findings of Boeri and Monti (2009) indicate that immigrants are less likely to receive contributory benefits if we control for individual and household characteristics in most EU countries. The result for Germany contradicts earlier findings in the literature (Barrett and McCarthy 2008). The findings are less homogeneous with respect to non-contributory benefits. Immigrants from EU-25 countries are less or equally likely to receive non-contributory benefits in most EU-15 countries with the exception of Germany and Luxembourg. However, there is a residual welfare dependency for non-contributory benefits of extra-EU immigrants in Belgium, Finland, France, Germany and the Netherlands.
>
> For details see Boeri and Monti (2009).

EU immigrants originate from the new Member States: according to national statistics, immigrants from countries that joined the EU in 2004 represent 53 per cent of total immigration from the EU-25 in Greece, 47 per cent in Finland, 43 per cent in Ireland and 35 per cent in Austria. Furthermore, the report shows that immigrants from the new Member States are similar to immigrants from other Member States with respect to their educational achievements (Boeri and Monti 2009).

With respect to *contributory benefits*, such as pensions and unemployment insurance, the share of migrants from EU-25 to EU-15 countries who receive this sort of transfer, is lower – and in most cases significantly so – than the corresponding share of natives; and the average transfers migrants receive is significantly below the average transfers to natives. A broadly similar picture emerges also for extra-EU immigrants. One should, however, bear in mind that the under-representation of immigrants among the pool of recipients of contributory benefits does not per se entail that immigrants provide a positive contribution to European pension systems, which are under strain from the ageing population. For instance, the under-representation could be due to the migrants' choice to return to their home countries upon retirement to enjoy the higher local purchasing power of their pensions; this entails that any data that capture only residents fail to account for the share of contributory benefits that is paid to past immigrants. Moreover, there is no capitalisation of future claims against the pension system.

With respect to *non-contributory benefits*, such as public assistance benefits and family allowances, the picture which emerges from descriptive statistics is quite different. It shows a pronounced divide between migrant households from the EU-25 and from extra-EU countries. In most destination countries, EU-25 migrant households are also under-represented among the recipients of non-contributory benefits. More specifically, Luxembourg is the only EU-15 country where immigrant households from EU-25 countries are over-represented among welfare recipients when we focus on non-contributory benefits alone, while in all other countries, including Austria, Finland, Greece and Ireland, where the share of migrants from the new Member States is the highest, the share of recipients among immigrant households is either not significantly different or even below the corresponding share for native households. When looking at the average transfers received rather than at the share of the recipients, the picture is more complex, as there are six EU-15 countries where immigrant households from the EU-25 countries receive significantly higher non-contributory benefits than native households do: in the Netherlands and the United Kingdom, the difference exceeds 1000 euro per year. Conversely, immigrant households from other countries tend to be over-represented in most destination countries – with Greece representing the sole significant exception among EU-15 countries – in the pool of recipients of non-contributory transfers.

Consequently, descriptive statistics suggest that – at least with respect to immigrants from EU-25 countries – there is little or no evidence that immigrants are over-represented in the pool of welfare recipients, which holds for contributory as well as for non-contributory benefits. Moreover, the available evidence does not suggest that the principle of equal treatment and other privileges granted to EU citizens compared with third-country nationals have affected the welfare dependency of these groups. If there is a difference, then non-EU immigrants are more likely to receive welfare.

The descriptive statistics may conceal substantial differences in human capital and household characteristics, as well as behavioural differences between migrants and natives. In order to disentangle these two effects – the observable characteristics such as age and number of children from the behavioural differences – Boeri and Monti (2009) conduct a multivariate analysis at the country level. Applying a standard probit model which explains welfare take-up by gender, age (and its square), marital status, number of children and household members, educational level and income before transfers, they identify the behavioural differences between migrants and natives by a dummy variable.

With respect to *contributory benefits*, the dummy variable for immigrants from EU-25 countries is either not significantly different from zero or negative and highly statistically significant. With respect to *non-contributory benefits* the estimates suggest that in seven EU-15 countries immigrant households from EU-25 countries have a lower probability of receiving non-contributory benefits once other relevant confounding factors are controlled for; for some countries, such as Ireland and Sweden, being an immigrant household reduces, *ceteris paribus*, the estimated probability of receiving transfers by more than 15 percentage points (see Box 7.3 for details).

To summarise, the evidence from the EU-SILC data does not support widespread public concerns that immigrants are exploiting the welfare state in destination countries, even in the stricter sense of 'residual welfare dependency' embedded in the multivariate analysis.

A special problem refers to the free mobility of students. When universities (e.g. in Austria) are financed by taxes and are not allowed to discriminate against applicants from other Member States (e.g. Germans), taxpayers' willingness to finance universities might be (dramatically) reduced. However, this argument is only valid if the students return to their home countries or move to other countries. If they stay in the country of destination and contribute to the tax system later, there might be a net fiscal gain since the destination country has financed only a part of the public education expenses. In both cases there are spill-over effects across countries which might have a detrimental impact on the incentives to invest in public education. This problem is however beyond the scope of this chapter (for details see Ringe 2009).

7 CONCLUSIONS

In this chapter, we have discussed how the European legislators and the European Court of Justice have over the past 50 years removed more and more legal barriers to the free movement of labour within the Community and have facilitated access even of non-economically active migrants to non-contributory social benefits of the Member States. Even though the level of internal migration in the EU is still modest, empirical evidence confirms that this policy has a positive overall effect on efficiency and social welfare, with specific consequences for the sending and the receiving countries.

First, the free movement of workers and the provisions for the mobility of the non-active population have a substantial impact on mobility compared with the third-country counterfactual – at least when income differences are as substantial as between the EU-15 and the NMS-8.

Second, there is no support for the widespread public concern that the removal of impediments to the free movement of labour will lead to a mass inflow of unskilled workers from the NMS-8 to the EU-15. Instead, immigrants from the NMS-8 countries have a lower share in the less-skilled labour market segment (without vocational training), a higher one in the medium skill segment (vocational training) and a slightly lower one in the high education segment (university or similar education degrees), compared with the native population. Regarding the age structure, the share of younger immigrants (15–34 years) from the NMS-8 is much larger than the share of the young age group in the native working-age population.

Third, especially from the perspective of Poland, the Baltic countries, Bulgaria and Romania, East–West migration in the context of EU enlargement has not only involved a loss of many skilled individuals but also contributed to the ageing of the workforce in these sending countries.

Fourth, as our simulations demonstrate, labour migration has contributed to a small but visible increase in the aggregate GDP of the entire EU, where the GDP gains of the receiving countries in the EU-15 countries exceed the losses in the sending countries of the NMS-8 or the NMS-10. Interestingly enough, GDP per capita increased in the receiving countries not least as a consequence of the NMS immigrants' higher labour force participation. In the long run, GDP per capita increases in the sending and in the receiving countries.

Fifth, the impact of immigration on the welfare state in the receiving countries is ambiguous. With respect to contributory benefits, such as pensions and unemployment insurance, the share of EU immigrants in the EU-15 who receive this sort of transfer is lower – and in most cases significantly so – than the corresponding share of natives, and the average transfer migrants receive is always significantly below the average transfer to natives. In most destination countries, EU immigrant households are also under-represented among the recipients of non-contributory benefits, such as public assistance benefits and family allowances. Looking at average transfers the picture is more complex as there are six EU-15 countries where immigrant households from the EU-25 countries receive significantly higher non-contributory benefits than native households. In sum, there is no support for the widespread concern among the public that immigrants tend to exploit the welfare state in the destination countries.

REFERENCES

Auerbach, A.J. and P. Oreopoulos (1999), 'Analyzing the Fiscal Impact of U.S. Immigration', *American Economic Review* 89 (2): 176–180.

Baas, T. and H. Brücker (2008). 'Macroeconomic Consequences of Migration Diversion – a CGE Simulation for Germany and the UK', IAB-Discussion Paper 03/2008.

Baas, T. and H. Brücker (2010), 'Macroeconomic Impact of Eastern Enlargement on Germany and UK – Evidence from a CGE Model', *Applied Economics Letters* 17 (2): 125–8.

Baas, T., H. Brücker, A. Hauptmann, and E. J. Jahn (2007), 'The Macroeconomic Consequences of Labour Mobility', IAB-Deliverable 4.

Barnard, C. (2010), *The Substantive Law of the EU: The Four Freedoms*, third edition, Oxford: Oxford University Press.

Barret, A. and Y. McCarthy (2008), 'Immigrants and Welfare Programmes: Exploring the Interactions between Immigrant Characteristics, Immigrant Welfare Dependence and Welfare Policy', IZA-Discussion Paper 3494, Bonn.

Barro, R. and X. Sala-i-Martin (1991), 'Convergence across States and Regions', *Brookings Papers on Economic Activity* (1): 107–82.

Barro, R. and X. Sala-i-Martin (2004), *Economic Growth*, second edition, Boston, MA: MIT Press.

Berry, R.A. and R. Soligo (1969), 'Some Welfare Aspects of International Migration', *Journal of Political Economy*, 77 (5): 778–94.

Blanchard, O.J. and L. Katz (1992), 'Regional Evolutions', *Brookings Papers on Economic Activity* (1): 1–75.

Boeri, T. (2006), 'Migration Policy and the Welfare State.' Paper prepared for the conference Reinventing the Welfare State, March, The Hague.

Boeri, T. and H. Brücker (2005), 'Why are Europeans so Tough on Migrants?', *Economic Policy* 20: 631–703.

Boeri, T. and P. Monti (2009), 'The Impact of Labour Mobility on Public Finances and Social Cohesion', IAB-Deliverable 5.

Boeri, T., G. Hanson and B. McCormick (2002), *Immigration Policy and the Welfare System*, Oxford: Oxford University Press.

Bonin, H. (2002), 'Eine fiskalische Gesamtbilanz der Zuwanderung nach Deutschland', *Vierteljahreshefte zur Wirtschaftsforschung* 71 (2): 215–29.

Bonin, H. (2006), 'Der Finanzierungsbeitrag der Ausländer zu den deutschen Staatsfinanzen: eine Bilanz für 2004', IZA-Discussion Paper No. 2444.

Bonin, H., B. Raffelhüschen and J. Walliser (2000), 'Can Immigration Alleviate the Demographic Burden?', *Finanz Archiv* 57: 1–21.

Borjas, G.J. (2003), 'The Labour Demand Curve is Downward-Sloping: Reexamining the Impact of Immigration on the Labour Market', *Quarterly Journal of Economics* 118 (4): 1335–74.

Brücker, H. and E.J. Jahn (2011), 'Migration and Wage-setting – Reassessing the Labour Market Effects of Migration', *The Scandinavian Journal of Economics* 113 (2): 286–317.

Brücker, H. and P.J.H. Schröder (2012), 'International Migration with Heterogeneous Agents: Theory and Evidence from Germany, 1967–2009', *The World Economy* 35 (2): 152–82.

Brücker, H., et al. (2009a), 'Labour Mobility within the EU in the Context of Enlargement and the Functioning of the Transitional Arrangements: Final Report', IAB-Final Report.

Brücker, Herbert, A. Damelang and K. Wolf (2009b), 'Forecasting Potential Migration from the New Member States into the EU-15: Review of Literature, Evaluation of Forecasting Methods and Forecast Results', Nürnberg: IAB-Deliverable 3.

Coldron, K. and L. Ackers (2009), 'European Citizenship, Individual Agency and the Challenge to Social Welfare Systems: a Case Study of Retirement Migration in the European Union', *Policy & Politics* 37 (4): 573–89.

Decressin, J. and A. Fátas (1995), 'Regional Labour Market Dynamics in Europe', *European Economic Review* 39 (9): 1627–57.

Eichengreen, B. (2007), *The European Economy since 1945*, Princeton: Princeton University Press.

European Commission (2010), 'EU Citizenship Report 2010: Dismantling the Obstacles to EU Citizens' Rights', COM (2010) 603 final.

Fenge, R. and J. von Weizsäcker (2010), 'Public Pension Systems and Distortions of Intra-EU Mobility: the Lodge Test', *Journal of Pension Economics and Finance* 9 (2): 263–75.

Gillingham, J. (ed.) (2003), *European Integration 1950–2003: Superstate or New Market Economy?*, Cambridge: Cambridge University Press.

Hansen, J. and M. Lofstrom (1997), 'Immigration and Welfare Participation: Do Immigrants Assimilate Into or Out-of Welfare?', IZA Discussion Paper No. 100.

Harris, J. and J. Todaro (1970), 'Migration, Unemployment and Development: A Two-Sector Analysis', *American Economic Review*, 126–42.
Hilpold, P. and G. Roth (2008), 'Unionsbürgerschaft und Bildungsrechte oder: Der EuGH-Richter als "Künstler"' in *Der EuGH und die Souveränität der Mitgliedstaaten: Eine kritische Analyse richterlicher Rechtsschöpfung auf ausgewählten Rechtsgebieten*, G.H. Roth and P. Hilpold (eds) Vienna, pp. 11–55.
Jorens, Y. (ed.) (2010), '50 Years of Social Security Coordination: Past–Present–Future', Luxembourg: European Union. Report of the conference celebrating the 50th Anniversary of the European Coordination of Social Security, Prague 7–8 May 2009.
Kaldor, N. (1961), 'Capital Accumulation and Economic Growth', in F.A. Lutz and D.C. Hague (eds), *The Theory of Capital*, New York: St. Martins.
Layard, R., S. Nickell and R. Jackman (2005), *Unemployment: Macroeconomic Performance and the Labour Market*, Oxford: Oxford University Press.
Menéndez, A.J. (2009), 'European Citizenship after Martinez Sala and Baumbast: Has European Law Become More Human but Less Social?', ARENA Working Paper (online) No. 11, June, http://www.sv.uio.no/arena/english/research/publications/arena-publications/workingpapers/working-papers2009/WP11_09_Online.pdf, accessed July 2011.
Ottaviano, G.I.P. and G. Peri (2006), 'Rethinking the Effects of Immigration on Wages', NBER Working Paper No. 12497.
Puhanyi, P.A. (2001), 'Is Labour Mobility an Adjustment Mechanism for Euroland? Empirical Evidence for Western Germany, France, and Italy', *German Economic Review* (2): 127–40.
Ringe, D. (2009), 'Tuition Fees and Equal Access to Higher Education in Germany and the EU: An Analysis from a Law and Economics Perspective', Dr. rer. pol. diss., University of Hamburg, http://ediss.sub.uni-hamburg.de/volltexte/2009/4266/pdf/Ringe2009TuitionFeesAndEqualAccessToHigherEducation.pdf, accessed July 2011.
Schütz, H.-J., T. Bruha and D. König (2004), *Casebook Europarecht*, Munich: Beck.
Sinn, H.W. (2003), *The New Systems Competition*, Oxford: Blackwell.
Straubhaar, T. (2002), *Migration im 21. Jahrhundert: Von der Bedrohung zur Rettung sozialer Marktwirtschaften?*, Tübingen: Mohr Siebeck.
Strumica, F. (2006), 'Citizenship and Free Movement: European and American Features of a Judicial Formula for Increased Comity', *Columbia Journal of European Law* 12 (3): 713–49.
Trachtman, J.P. (2009), *The International Law of Economic Migration: Toward the Fourth Freedom*. Kalamazoo: Upjohn Institute.
Wagener, H.-J. and T. Eger (2009), *Europäische Integration: Wirtschaft und Recht, Geschichte und Politik*, Munich: Vahlen.
Wollenschläger, F. (2009), 'Die Unionsbürgerschaft und ihre Dynamik für den Integrationsprozess jenseits des Marktes', *Zeitschrift für europarechtliche Studien* (1): 1–52.

PART 3

CORPORATION LAW AND CORPORATE GOVERNANCE

8 Corporate governance in Europe: foundations, developments and perspectives

Patrick C. Leyens

1 FOUNDATIONS OF CORPORATE GOVERNANCE IN EUROPE

Corporate governance in Europe looks back on a long history. From the beginnings of corporate law the owners of stock corporations experienced what became known through Berle and Means in 1932 as the problem of separation of ownership and control.[1] Already the governance problems of the Dutch East India Company,[2] founded in 1602 as the first listed company in Europe, had led to the installation of an early form of a supervisory board.[3] In the second half of the 20th century corporate governance became a research discipline of its own. Its core question concerns the relative importance of factors which influence managerial behaviour and align it to the interests of shareholders or stakeholders.[4] A truly international and increasingly interdisciplinary debate has detected the building blocks of corporate governance inside and outside the company:[5] the board, labour, financial intermediaries, capital markets and corporate finance, disclosure and information intermediaries as well as lenders.[6] The perhaps most important finding is that the relative importance of these building blocks needs to be determined according to path dependencies, which include legal as well as socio-economic factors.[7]

The European Action Plan 2003 on the modernisation of company law and enhancement of corporate governance[8] illustrates that corporate governance has become a key

---

1 A. Berle and G. Means, *The Modern Corporation and Private Property*, New Brunswick, 1991 (reprint 1st edn, 1932). On the separation of ownership and control cf. also E.F. Fama and M.C. Jensen, 26 *J. L. & Econ.*, 301 (1983).

2 E. Gepken-Jager, G. van Solinge and L. Timmerman (eds), *VOC 1602–2002 – 400 Years of Company Law*, 2005.

3 E. Gepken-Jager, in *VOC 1602–2002* (supra n. 2), pp. 41, 56. See also P. Frentrop, *A History of Corporate Governance 1602–2002*, 2003, pp. 49, 62.

4 K.J. Hopt, 59 *Am J. Comp. L.* 1, 6 et seq. (2011).

5 For international ground work R. Kraakman et al., *The Anatomy of Corporate Law*, 2nd edn, 2009. For the current state of research in the United States see L.A. Bebchuk and M.S. Weisbach, 23 *Rev. Fin. Stud.* 939 (2010) and further contributions to the special issue.

6 K.J. Hopt et al. (eds), *Comparative Corporate Governance: The State of the Art and Emerging Research*, 1998.

7 L.A. Bebchuk and M.J. Roe, 52 *Stan. L. Rev.* 127 (1999); W.W. Bratton and J.A. McCahery, 38 *Colum. J. Transnat'l L.* 213 (1999); M.J. Roe, *Political Determinants of Corporate Governance*, Oxford 2003. On the implications for the internationalisation of the law L.A. Bebchuk and A. Hamdani, 157 *U. Pa. L. Rev.* 1263 (2009). Cf. also infra Section 3, n. 121

8 Commission of the European Communities, Communication from the Commission to the Council and the European Parliament of 21 May 2003, 'Modernising Company Law and

issue of European integration.[9] To mark only two developments at the outset, the Statute of the European Company 2001 (Societas Europaea) introduced a first genuine corporate form which provides a board model option. This option is accompanied by flexible ways of employee participation which allow to accommodate for legal and socio-economic differences within the Member States.[10] Another development concerns best practice standards, which have been triggered by the so-called 'comply or explain approach'.[11] Since 2006 listed companies have been obliged to state their compliance with a national corporate governance code or to explain their possible non-compliance.[12] In essence, this marks a trend towards a more capital market based approach in line with the European Takeover Directive of 2004.[13]

To a large extent corporate governance reforms are scandal driven.[14] The unexpected downfall of the US-American energy provider Enron in 2001[15] was felt as a shock also for the other side of the Atlantic. As a reaction the European Commission appointed the High Level Group of Company Law Experts.[16] Its recommendations to tighten the corporate governance framework strongly inspired the above-mentioned Action Plan of 2003.[17] The recent financial market crisis led to the European Commission's Green Paper on the 'Corporate Governance in Financial Institutions' of 2010,[18] which proposes specific governance rules especially for banks.[19] The current reform agenda is formulated in the subsequent Green Paper on improvements of the EU corporate governance framework of 2011.[20]

Enhancing Corporate Governance in the European Union – A Plan to Move Forward', COM (2003) 284(01) final.

9 For a comprehensive treatment of integration issues cf. H.-J. Wagener and T. Eger, *Europäische Integration*, 2nd (edn), 2009.

10 Council Regulation (EC) No. 2157/2001 of 8 October 2001 on the Statute for a European Company (SE), O.J. L 294/1 of 10 November 2001, Art. 39 para. 5 and Art. 43 para. 4. On the S.E. in detail K.J. Hopt, M. Menjucq and E. Wymeersch (eds), *La Société Européenne, organisation juridique et fiscale, intérêts, perspectives*, 2003.

11 Directive 2006/46/EC of 14 June 2006, O.J. L 224/1 of 16 August 2006, Article 46a, para. 1, lit. a, b.

12 See K.J. Hopt et al., *European Corporate Governance in Company Law and Codes*, Report Prepared for the European Corporate Governance Conference, Riv. Soc. 2005, 534, 550.

13 Directive 2004/25/EC of 21 April 2004 on takeover bids, O.J. L 142/12 of 30 April 2004. On takeover law in the UK P.L. Davies, *Gower and Davies' Principles of Modern Company Law*, 8th edn, 2008, para. 28–1 et seq.

14 L. Enriques and P. Volpin, 21 *J. Econ. Persp.* 117 (2007); J. Hill, in G. Ferrarini et al. (eds), *Reforming Company and Takeover Law*, 2004, p. 225.

15 J. Armour and J.A. McCahery (eds), *After Enron*, 2006.

16 High Level Group of Company Law Experts, 'A Modern Regulatory Framework for Company Law in Europe', November 2002 (chaired by Jaap Winter).

17 Supra n. 8.

18 European Commission, 'Corporate Governance in Financial Institutions and Remuneration Policies', Green Paper, 2 June 2010, COM(2010) 284 final.

19 For an assessment of corporate governance failures see the High Level Group on Financial Supervision in the EU, Report, 25 February 2009 (chaired by Jacques de Larosière), p. 29, nos. 110 et seq.

20 European Commission, 'The EU Corporate Governance Framework', Green Paper, 5 April 2011, COM(2011) 164 final.

This survey addresses selected legal developments with a view to foundations and perspectives of interdisciplinary research on corporate governance. To start with, the most important institution of internal corporate governance is the board of directors (Section 2.1). Ownership structures matter for defining the specific control problems and specific types of investors – especially large or institutional investors – perform different monitoring tasks (Section 2.2). The services of information intermediaries – especially auditors, rating agencies and financial analysts – strengthen the monitoring power of capital markets but conflicts of interest and oligopolistic intermediary structures reveal partly unresolved regulatory challenges (Section 2.3).

2 DEVELOPMENTS AND KEY ISSUES OF REGULATION

2.1 The Board of Directors

2.1.1 Board model options

The relationship between shareholders and managers is best described as a contingent long-term contract, which is incomplete due to unknown future developments within a complex environment.[21] Agency theory sees the task of the manager agents in a continuous alignment of the company's business activity to the preferences of the holders of corporate control rights – i.e. in a share-value oriented system – to the interests of the shareholders. The shareholder principals, however, are unable to identify whether the business outcomes are the result of their manager agents' endogenous activity or of exogenous circumstances, e.g. stock price movements that generally affect the industry sector. To be operative over time, furthermore, the incomplete agency contract between shareholders and managers must leave a considerable freedom of business discretion to the managers. This business discretion is the cause of most principal–agent problems.[22] It follows that the main concern for internal corporate governance arrangements is to safeguard care and loyalty in the use of business discretion by managers.

The internationally predominant one-tier board is characterised by an accumulation of management and supervisory tasks within one single company organ, the board of directors. The UK Cadbury Code 1992,[23] however, has led to a de facto division of responsibilities of the one-tier board.[24] One-tier boards of major companies are composed of a considerable number of non-executive directors who assume prime responsibility for the supervision of executive decision making at board level.[25] This division of management

---

21 M.C. Jensen and W.H. Meckling, 3 *J. Fin. Econ.* 305 (1976); J. Tirole, 'Corporate Governance', 69 *Econometrica* 1 (2001); O.E. Williamson, 'Corporate Governance', 93 *Yale L. J.* 1197 (1984).

22 W.A. Klein and J.C. Coffee, *Business Organization and Finance*, 2004, p. 123; M. Ruffner, *Die ökonomischen Grundlagen der Publikumsgesellschaft*, 2000, p. 135 f.

23 A. Cadbury, Report of the Committee on the Financial Aspects of Corporate Governance, London, 1992.

24 P. Davies, in G. Ferrarini et al. (eds), *Reforming Company and Takeover Law*, 2004, pp. 183, 193.

25 Higgs Review, Final Report, January 2003, http://www.ecgi.org.

and supervisory tasks is known from the two-tier structure which is prescribed by law in Germany, where the so-called *Aufsichtsratsmodell* requires a supervisory board as a second organ of a stock corporation.[26]

The Draft 5th Directive 1991 sought to prescribe the two-tier model for all companies based in a European Member State.[27] The directive never came into force. Instead of full harmonisation the Action Plan 2003 envisages a choice between the two board models.[28] This choice already exists for the Societas Europaea[29] and it is also known to some Member States, e.g. Belgium, Denmark, Finland, France, Luxembourg and the Netherlands.[30] Italian law and Portuguese law, for example, provide for even more board model options.[31] For those who advocate factual convergence of board structures, introducing a board model option does not make much of a difference to the status quo. Especially, English company law appears to be flexible enough to allow shareholders a definition of the board directors' responsibilities in such a way that there are few differences compared with a two-tier structure.[32]

In essence, board model options are a question of transaction governance. In theory shareholder choices should follow the same rules as applicable to the choice between discrete contract, hybrid or cooperation (to use Oliver Williamson's terminology).[33] In France, around 20 per cent of the mostly large and internationally active CAC-40 companies have opted for the two-tier model.[34] The Netherlands shows similar results.[35] Swiss law prescribes a two-tier model for banks and insurance companies.[36] It seems to be premature though to conclude that two-tier structures are chosen by private parties or by regulators where a strong supervisory function is needed. The internationally prevailing predominance of the one-tier structure rather indicates that both board models can be successfully used to overcome agency problems.

A recent study on the Societas Europaea revealed that two-tier structures are preferred where the national law prescribes labour co-determination on board level.[37] Co-determination is especially strong in Germany, where half of the supervisory board seats of major companies must be given to worker representatives.[38] Giving employees

---

26 P.C. Leyens, 4 *Kyoto J. L. Pol.* 17, 21 (2007).

27 For details see S. Grundmann, *European Company Law*, 2nd edn, 2012, section 12. pp. 247 et seq.

28 Commission of the European Communities (supra n. 8), p. 17. The Action Plan follows closely the recommendations of the High Level Group of Company Law Experts (supra n. 16), Recommendation III.9, p. 59.

29 Supra n. 10 and accompanying text.

30 K.J. Hopt, 59 *Am. J. Comp.* 1, 19 (2011).

31 K.J. Hopt and P.C. Leyens, *ECFR* 2004, 135, 156 on France and Italy in comparison to England and Germany. On board model options in Portugal see J. Fedtke and A. Rathenau *RIW* 2006, 734.

32 P.C. Leyens, in *Festschrift Hopt*, 2010, pp. 3135, 3140 et seq.

33 O.E. Williamson, 22 *J. L. & Econ.* 233 (1979).

34 K.J. Hopt and P.C. Leyens, *ECFR* 2004, 135, 156.

35 K.J. Hopt, 59 *Am. J. Comp.* 1, 22 et seq. (2011).

36 K.J. Hopt, 59 *Am. J. Comp.* 1, 21 (2011).

37 H. Eidenmüller, in A.M. Pacces (ed.), *The Law and Economics of Corporate Governance*, pp. 82, 88; comment by P.C. Leyens, id., p. 117.

38 S. Grundmann (supra n. 27), section 12, pp. 262 et seq.

voice on the day-to-day business decisions can be difficult to accept from the viewpoint of shareholders and accordingly it is not surprising that a two-tier structure is more frequently chosen to prevent this result.

A more general conclusion seems to be that board model choices depend on an interplay of considerations including transaction governance. They take into account legal institutions such as mandatory co-determination or perceived expectations of capital markets. Accordingly, board model choice is a path dependent decision to a certain degree.[39] However, there is no evidence available that regulators have a better estimate as to the board model that best fits the governance of a specific private transaction. Accordingly, the burden of proof seems to be on those who advocate mandatory law instead of party autonomy and board model options.

2.1.2 Independence of board directors

Independence at board level has become the new paradigm in the debate on internal corporate governance in Europe and internationally.[40] As an implementing measure of the Action Plan 2003, the European Commission published its 'Recommendation on the role of non-executive or supervisory directors of listed companies and on the committees of the (supervisory) board' in 2005.[41] Whilst for the board a sufficient number of independent directors is recommended, the audit, nomination and remuneration committees should be composed of a majority of independent directors. The use of a non-binding 'recommendation' illustrates a shift away from earlier attempts to full harmonisation and marks a new focus on best practice standards applicable to both one-tier and two-tier board structures.

The movement towards stronger independence standards has been strongly triggered by the code movement in the United Kingdom. Early criteria as set out by the Cadbury Code 1992[42] were somehow circular: 'they should be independent of management and free from any business or other relationship which could materially interfere with the exercise of their independent judgement'.[43] The Combined Code 1998, which built on the Cadbury Code, appreciated that independence could hardly be defined in a way which covers all possible circumstances. The United Kingdom Corporate Governance Code 2010 follows its predecessor and stipulates a list of negative criteria indicating a lack of independence but leaves the final decision on whether a director is deemed to be independent to the board.

The European Commission has adopted this approach and its Recommendation 2005 almost literally resembles the wording of the criteria known from the United Kingdom.[44]

---

[39] See P.L. Davies, 2 *ICCLJ* 435 (2001) on the one-tier board and M. Lutter 2 *ICCLJ* 423 (2002) on the two-tier board.

[40] Comprehensive analysis of the United States J.N. Gordon, 59 *Stanford L. Rev.* 1465 (2007).

[41] European Commission Recommendation of 15 February 2005 on the role of non-executive or supervisory directors of listed companies and on the committees of the (supervisory) board, O.J. L 52, 25 February 2005, p. 51.

[42] Full texts of the corporate governance codes are collected by the European Corporate Governance Institute; cf. http://www.ecgi.org.

[43] Cadbury Report, supra n. 23, para. 4.12.

[44] European Commission Recommendation 2005, supra. n. 41, Annex II.

The criteria show that conflicts of interest can derive not only from financial hold-ups, as in case of a controlling shareholder whose representatives would be deemed non-independent. Conflicts of interest can also derive from rather behavioural aspects, as in the case of a former executive officer. In fact, it is hardly imaginable that a former chief executive officer (CEO) could act with the necessary degree of independence and actively promote investigations of wrong strategic decisions or accounting malpractices when possible failures lie in his previous term of office.

In light of the spirit of the Recommendation 2005 the explicit exemption of worker representatives from the list of negative criteria can only be understood as a political compromise.[45] This becomes even clearer with a view to the accounting failures which stand in the background of the aim to strengthen independence at board level. Independent directors are less bound to the company and should accordingly be less reluctant to timely disclose accounting fraud or a forthcoming corporate collapse. It is true that employees have a strong interest in preventing a corporate collapse in the long run. It is a demanding expectation though that a workforce representative actively engages in investigations of severe failures although the own human capital and that of the election body is strongly bound to the company and would be lost immediately upon public awareness of a major accounting failure.

2.1.3 Composition of board committees

The three main committees of the board recommended by the European Commission in 2005 are thought to account for the most important responsibilities of the board, i.e. nomination, remuneration and auditing. This identification of main responsibilities is in line with basic findings of the principal–agent theory. In essence, the nomination task helps to evade the adverse selection problem before contract conclusion, remuneration for incentive compatible agency contracts supports the alignment of time and risk preferences and, last not least, auditing stands for overcoming information asymmetries that arise after conclusion of the agency contract.[46]

The Green Paper of the European Commission 2011 focuses on possible ways to improve professional diversity at board level.[47] This is a reaction to the recent financial crisis revealing evident failures of non-executive directors who did not understand, challenge or veto the decisions of executive directors to engage into complex high-risk transactions. The overall challenge remains unchanged, i.e. finding a balance between directors who have profound knowledge from inside the company and others who are independent and, at the same time, motivated enough to challenge e.g. the views of former executive directors or representatives of controlling shareholders. It is clear that independence to a considerable extent goes hand in hand with a lower information level. On the one hand, former executives, controlling shareholders and – e.g. in Germany – workforce representatives lack independence. On the other hand, they are aware of information which an independent third person might not have or will not be able to process effectively.

So far, the rationale of group decision making remains widely unnoticed in the debate

45 K.J. Hopt, *ZIP* 2005, 461. See also P.C. Leyens, 4 *Kyoto J. L. Pol.* 17, 28 (2007).

46 For details see P.C. Leyens, *Information des Aufsichtsrats*, 2006, p. 26 et seq.

47 European Commission (supra n. 20), p. 5 et seq.

about the right proportion of independent directors on the board.[48] To understand its fruitfulness one might look at the incentives of the better informed non-independent directors when independent directors are in the minority. Incentives to share information are low because non-independent directors can simply outvote their less informed colleagues. Conversely, independent directors have low incentives to critically challenge existing views as a board decision will probably not be accounted to them but to the majority vote of their non-independent counterparts.[49] Joint liability of all board members might increase participation incentives in such situations but cross-country studies show that non-executive directors are scarcely held financially responsible in court.[50]

When independent directors are in the majority the assessment is different: non-independent directors cannot outvote a majority of independent directors. Accordingly, to achieve a certain decision they need to share their information through explaining, discussing and convincing their independent colleagues. Conversely, independent directors understand that decisions will be traced back to their own majority vote and that they need to actively search for information.

Against this background it seems that the European Commission Recommendation 2005 is right in proposing a majority of independent directors, at least for the three main committees of the board. Sufficient expertise in each committee can be achieved with a view to the specific committee task. For example, the so-called Modernised Audit Directive[51] 2006 now requires companies of public interest, especially listed companies, to set up an audit committee and to appoint at least one member with competence in accounting and/or auditing. Task specific qualification requirements could also be a way ahead for the composition of risk committees discussed in the European Commission's Green Paper 2010 on financial institutions.[52]

2.2 Shareholders

2.2.1 Relevance of ownership structures

The classic paradigm of the 'Berle and Means corporation'[53] is based on the assumption of dispersed ownership and rational control apathy of shareholders.[54] Collective action by dispersed shareholders is impeded by prohibitively high coordination costs (collective action problem). In addition, individual control efforts, although having collective effect, remain uncompensated by the group (free riding). Accordingly dispersed shareholders prefer exit over voice and managerial discipline is mainly executed by market forces, especially the market for corporate control.

---

[48] On the state of the discussion S.M. Bainbridge, 55 *Vand. L. Rev.* 1 (2002).

[49] K.J. Hopt, 59 *Am. J. Comp.* 1, 36 (2011) on other incentive factors such as pay and time.

[50] B. Cheffins, B. Black and M. Klausner, 11 *Europ. Fin. Management* 153 (2005); B. Cheffins and B. Black, 84 *Texas L. Rev.* 1385 (2006); M. Roth, 8 *J. Corp. L. Stud.* 337 (2008).

[51] Directive 2006/43/EC of the European Parliament and of the Council of 17 May 2006 on statutory audits of annual accounts and consolidated accounts, amending Council Directives 78/660/EEC and 83/349/EEC and repealing Council Directive 84/253/EEC, O.J. 2006 L 157/87, Art. 41 para. 1.

[52] European Commission (supra n. 18), p. 11 et seq., specific question no. 1.6.

[53] Supra n. 1.

[54] References supra n. 21.

This paradigm has never been fully applicable to continental Europe.[55] Ownership structures in the European Member States are less dispersed than in the US, semi-dispersed (especially in the United Kingdom)[56] or rather concentrated (especially in Belgium, Germany, Italy and Sweden).[57] The corporate governance problem for countries with concentrated ownership lies in protecting the minority shareholders against expropriations by the majority.[58] There exist different legal institutions to balance out conflicts between minority and majority shareholders. In the European Union a common approach towards conflicts between minority and majority shareholders in corporate groups has not been found yet, although the expropriation risks are most obvious where cash flows can be diverted from subsidiaries to parent companies.[59]

Recently, also studies on ownership structures in the United States have argued that controlling shareholders are found more often than generally assumed.[60] This is a chance for a renewed transatlantic dialogue on corporate governance.

2.2.2 Monitoring by large investors

The general control apathy hypothesis[61] does not hold for an investor who owns a considerable or even controlling amount of shares. For such large investors the cost and benefit assessment of voice versus exit differs from that of dispersed shareholders. According to many studies a robust empirical relation can be found between the existence of large shareholdings and corporate performance.[62] The explanations differ. Arguably one reason is that large investors have a stronger voice and that – under certain conditions – they exercise it to bring about changes in internal corporate governance.[63] Another explanation is that takeovers are more profitable for shareholders who already own a large block of shares.[64]

Not only a large or controlling shareholding but also a cumulative role as a lender can give monitoring incentives. This is in line with experiences, for example in Germany, where the 'Rhenish Capitalism' with its strong role of banks is said to have helped in the process of reconstructing Germany post-WWII.[65] The so-called 'German Inc.', however,

---

55 B. Cheffins, 83 *Bus. Hist. Rev.* 443 (2009) asks 'Is Berle and Means a Myth?' Cf. also J. Hill, *Seattle U. L. Rev.* 1005 (2010). Comprehensive discussion in F. Barca and M. Becht (eds), *The Control of Corporate Europe*, 2001.

56 B. Cheffins, in J.A. McCahery et al. (eds), *Corporate Governance Regimes: Convergence and Diversity*, 2002, p. 147.

57 For an overview on shareholder structures and market capitalisation see S. Grundmann (supra n. 27), p. 276, para. 489 et seq.

58 R. Kraakman et al. (supra n. 5), p. 89 et seq.

59 Comprehensive analysis of the legal issues by the Forum Europaeum Konzernrecht, 1 *EBOR* 165 (2000).

60 C.G. Holderness, 22 *Rev. Fin. Stud.* 1377 (2009).

61 For details see supra section 2.2.1.

62 R. Morck, A. Shleifer and R.W. Vishny, 20 *J. Fin. Econ.* 293 (1988).

63 For surveys see D. Del Guercio and J. Hawkins, 52 *J. Fin. Econ.* 293 (1999); S. Gillan and L.T. Starks, 19 *J. App. Corp. Fin.* 55 (2007).

64 A. Shleifer and R.W. Vishny, 94 *J. Pol. Econ.* 461 (1986). See also S.J. Grossman and O.D. Hart, 11 *Bell J. Econ.* 42 (1980).

65 H. Baum, in K.J. Hopt et al. (eds), *Corporate Governance in Context: Corporations, States and Markets in Europe, Japan, and the US*, Oxford, 2005, p. 3.

was a trade-off between the benefits of a strong voice of influential large shareholders or stakeholders and attracting international investors. Around 2000 the erosion of the 'German Inc.'[66] started with sales of equity holdings by banks and a reduced presence of bank representatives on supervisory boards.[67] Further steps followed with sales of cross-holdings by DAX-30 firms.

This development has certainly decreased conflicts of interest but it also embodies the danger that the national corporate governance system is left in a vacuum, if market forces, especially the market for corporate control, are not yet fully developed.[68]

2.2.3 Voice by institutional investors

Institutional investors, such as pension funds, are normally more diversified than large investors and hence less susceptible to conflicts of interest. This is one of the arguments why they could serve as a collective action mechanism overcoming rational control apathy of dispersed shareholders. With a view to Germany their monitoring could also fill gaps which are caused by the described changes of the national corporate governance system.[69]

A single institutional investor normally does not hold a large percentage of the stock of one company. In many countries, however, the overall share of institutional investors in corporate ownership amounts e.g. up to 44.4 per cent in the United Kingdom or even up to 70 per cent in some German companies.[70] The internal policies of institutional investors include provisions to reconsider their investment or even to automatically withdraw their funds if important variables change, especially in case of a credit rating downgrade. Their professional personnel continuously monitor corporate performance and also collect information on the corporate governance of issuers. This explains why in turn the management of any issuer continuously monitors investment or disinvestment signals sent by institutional investors and why vivid investor relations are maintained.

It could be expected that the influence of institutional investors on business decisions is lower than that of a large investor.[71] Some evidence exists, though, that US companies are prepared to make relatively small changes such as having a shareholder vote before adopting 'blank-check preferred stock', or nominating women or minority representatives as members of the board of directors.[72] It has been questioned whether these

---

66 P. Zumbansen, 3 *German L. J.* (2002), available at <http://www.germanlawjournal.com>.

67 See P.O. Mülbert, in K.J. Hopt et al. (eds), supra n. 6, p. 445.

68 H. Baum (supra n. 65), p. 19; R.H. Schmidt, in J.P. Krahnen and R.H. Schmidt (eds), *The German Financial System*, 2004, p., 386, 417.

69 T. Baums, R.M. Buxbaum and K.J. Hopt (eds), *Institutional Investors and Corporate Governance*, Berlin, 1994; W. Gerke, M. Bank and M. Steiger, 'The Changing Role of Institutional Investors', in G. Ferrarini, K.J. Hopt and E. Wymeersch (eds), *Capital Markets in the Age of the Euro*, 2002, p. 357; G.P. Stapledon, *Institutional Shareholders and Corporate Governance*, 1996.

70 The presence of institutional investors in Germany is limited to some companies; cf. DAI Factbook 08.7/GB 1 on the UK (date: 2006) and 0.8–5–1 on Germany (date: 2009).

71 On large investors see section 2.2.2.

72 W.T. Carleton, J.M. Nelson and M.S. Weisbach, 53 *J. Fin.* 1335 (1998) base their study on letters exchanged between the Teachers Insurance and Annuity Association–College Retirement Equities Fund (TIAA-CREF), which is a large US pension fund, and companies. They argue for an informal influence of institutional investors on corporate governance through private negotiations.

observations can be generalised.[73] However, it has been argued that around 90 per cent of the abnormal returns brought in by Hermes, one of the leading institutional investors in the United Kingdom, are due to its influence on corporate decision making rather than stock picking.[74]

The findings above indicate that institutional investors are indeed able to exercise monitoring power. However, their rather silent behaviour on excessive risk taking before the recent financial crisis has led the European Commission to the conclusion that institutional investors probably aggravate short-termism in capital markets.[75] Short-sighted management decisions lead to a sub-optimal use of corporate resources for short-term effects while the same resources could be used more profitably in the long run (Myopia problem).[76] Some causes of short-termism can be tackled by rule setting on internal corporate governance, e.g. by provisions on the structuring of remuneration schemes or the prohibition of certain value destroying takeover defences.

Other causes relate to external corporate governance and it seems that the functioning of markets is less easily addressed by regulation. With a view to institutional investors, the European Commission argues that short-termism is encouraged by adverse remuneration structures for the managers of institutional investment funds.[77] If the asset management contract values individual performance on creating small short-term profits higher than a better long-term result it might well be a consequence that managers of institutional investors will amplify herd behaviour, contribute to pro-cyclical movements of the market and accelerate possible downward spirals.

Already the High Level Group of Company Law Experts,[78] later also the Action Plan 2003[79] and now the Green Papers 2010 and 2011[80] have argued to enact a European-wide duty of institutional investors to disclose their investment policies. Enhanced transparency will certainly contribute to a more careful market assessment of the reasons for disinvestment decisions taken by institutional investors. Voice, however, is more expensive than exit. Despite single examples like the one of Hermes, it seems that fund managers will be reluctant to participate actively in management decisions of a single company. The large number of equity holdings maintained by a fund due to its diversification obligation underlines this estimation; e.g. a fund in the United States might have around 5000 stock holdings only in the home market.[81] Using the resources for voice might even carry dangers of being sued for breach of fiduciary duties.[82] Accordingly, it is doubtful whether

---

73 L.A. Bebchuk and M.S. Weisbach, 23 *Rev. Fin. Stud.* 939, 942 (2010).

74 M. Becht et al., 22 *Rev. Fin. Stud.* 3093 (2009), base their study on data between 1998 and 2004 made available by Hermes, the fund manager owned by the British Telecom Pension Scheme, which is well known for its activism.

75 European Commission (2011, supra n. 20), para. 2.3.1 (p. 12) and (2010, supra n. 18), para. 3.5 (p. 8).

76 Ruffner (supra n. 22), p. 349 et seq.

77 Supra n. 75.

78 High Level Group (supra n. 16), item III.7, recommendation III.7 (p. 56).

79 European Commission (2011, supra n. 20), para. 3.3.1 (p. 12).

80 Supra n. 75.

81 S.C.Y. Wong, 25 *Butterworths J. Int'l Banking and Fin. L.* 406 et seq. (2010). See already H. Fleischer, *ZGR* 2011, 155, 162, notes 53 et seq.

82 J.M. Mendoza, C. van der Elst and E.P.M. Vermeulen 7 *S. C. J. Int'l L. & Bus.* 1, 32 (2011).

it can be generally expected from institutional investors that they value voice over exit and contribute to a more sustainable use of corporate resources by the management of issuers.

In the United Kingdom the new Stewardship Code 2010[83] requires institutional investors to state their compliance with seven general principles of good conduct.[84] A code might address some important general issues such as conflicts of interest and it can be a valuable back-up of a disclosure duty, as discussed above.[85] Still, a meaningful effect on the behaviour of fund managers depends on the business case and more precisely on the costs of voice versus exit. Whilst a comply-or-explain approach for issuers[86] arguably serves to enhance trust in corporate governance, the public will positively value compliance with a stewardship code probably only in as far as compliance becomes a proxy for attracting higher amounts of client funds.

More importantly, the growing awareness of the role of institutional investors touches a general question of corporate governance, i.e. to what extent legislation should address not only the companies' management but also market actors with a view to strengthening their function as monitors for corporate governance. This question is a paradigm for the interplay between internal and external corporate governance mechanisms. It has received most attention regarding information intermediaries, as discussed in the following subsection.

2.3 Information Intermediaries

2.3.1 Auditors, rating agencies and financial analysts

In theory, information intermediaries such as auditors, rating agencies and financial analysts, are meant to play an important role for detecting corporate failures. Accordingly, they can contribute to the managers' choice of sustainable corporate governance arrangements.[87] Unexpected corporate breakdowns and, most recently, their failure to detect early the disastrous risk management of financial institutions indicates that expectations were too high and that the interplay between companies and information intermediaries needs further analysis.[88]

---

83 Financial Reporting Council, The UK Stewardship Code, July 2010.

84 The Principles of the Code (n. 83) state that institutional investors should: 'publicly disclose their policy on how they will discharge their stewardship responsibilities, have a robust policy on managing conflicts of interest in relation to stewardship and this policy should be publicly disclosed, monitor their investee companies, establish clear guidelines on when and how they will escalate their activities as a method of protecting and enhancing shareholder value, be willing to act collectively with other investors where appropriate, have a clear policy on voting and disclosure of voting activity, report periodically on their stewardship and voting activities'.

85 On the pros and cons B. Cheffins, 73 *Modern L. Rev.* 1004 (2010); J.M. Mendoza, C. van der Elst and E.P.M. Vermeulen, 7 *S. C. J. Int'l L. & Bus.* 1, 32 (2011). In German K.U. Schmolke, *ZGR* 2007, 701, 719 et seq. and recently H. Fleischer, *ZGR* 2011, 155, 162 et seq.

86 Cf. supra n. 11 and accompanying text.

87 For a functional overview see 'Financial Intermediary' by P.C. Leyens, in J. Basedow, K.J. Hopt and R. Zimmermann (eds), *Max Planck Encyclopedia on European Private Law*, forthcoming.

88 On the United States J.C. Coffee, *Gatekeepers*, 2006.

The statutory auditor has been the subject of lively discussion.[89] Capital markets rely on the auditor report certifying the soundness of corporate accounting, which in turn provides the issuer's management with incentives to use proper accounting techniques in order to avoid a qualification of the report. To perform its statutory task the auditor collects sensitive information about corporate practices, including risk management and other aspects of corporate governance. This leads to a double role of the auditor for corporate governance. In addition to the verification service provided to the market the auditor serves as the most important source of information independent from management that is required for a strong monitoring by non-executive or supervisory directors.

European legislation has continuously tried to improve the reliability and the scope of the statutory auditors' assessment of the annual accounts.[90] Legislative measures reach back to the Fourth Council Directive 1978 stipulating European requirements on the annual accounts of companies. The Modernised Audit Directive[91] 2006 sets rules on approval and registration and it also covers independence requirements. In line with the general trend in European company law it distinguishes between (simple) entities and public-interest entities like listed stock corporations, banks and insurance companies. Public-interest entities have to adhere to higher standards regarding financial disclosure and corporate governance in general. For that reason the directive obliges the board of such companies to set up an audit committee which supervises the accounting process and the effectiveness of internal controls. Perhaps the most important effect of this legislation is that it enhances the channels of information flows between the auditor and internal supervisors of management.[92]

Altogether, the achievements of the past mitigate – but certainly do not free the public from – the so-called 'expectation gap' which exists between correctly understanding the statutory audit as a guarantee for accurate accounting and the misled perception of a guarantee for sound corporate governance in general. Safeguarding sound corporate governance is the task of the (supervisory) board of directors.

The recent crisis underlined that the audit report is only part of a wider set of intermediary control mechanisms. Generally, rating agencies and financial analysts also help to route information between issuers and investors. Information intermediaries verify available information, evaluate it in line with macroeconomic developments and supply missing information. Their services facilitate private transactions and possibly augment the information efficiency of the financial market as a whole.

Regulatory problems – not only for auditors but also for other information intermediaries – especially concern safeguarding the independence of the intermediary's judgement.[93] A paradigmatic problem concerns services combinations. In line with

---

[89] K. Cearns and E. Ferran, 8 *JCLS* 191, 197 et seq. (2008) on developments in Europe and the UK.

[90] On the state of European legislation see the entry 'Auditor' by P.C. Leyens, in *Max Planck Encyclopaedia of European Private Law* (supra n. 87).

[91] Cf. supra note 51.

[92] Cf. P.C. Leyens, 4 *Kyoto J. L. Pol.* 17, 24 (2007). In detail P.C. Leyens (supra n. 46), p. 201 et seq.

[93] P.C. Leyens, 11 *JCLS* 33, 43 (2011).

economic research, legislation has tried to tackle the so-called 'low-balling' problem.[94] 'Low-balling' means that an intermediary decreases the degree of scrutiny with a view to subsequently attract counselling engagements with the same issuer at more profitable terms. Originally the idea was developed with a view to auditors but it equally connects, for example, to rating agencies. Both the Modernised Audit Directive and the Regulation on Credit Rating Agencies 2009[95] include restrictions on services combinations. This leads to a long-expected convergence in the legislation on auditing and ratings. Similarly, financial analysts' conflicts of interest have been addressed in a Communication of the European Commission to the European Council in 2006[96] and it remains to be seen whether – or rather when – financial analysts will come into the regulatory focus again.[97] For auditors the debate goes on and the European Commission's Green Paper 'Audit Policy: Lessons from the Crisis of 2010'[98] now also envisages a mandatory external rotation of the auditor after a maximum length of engagement, e.g. eight years.[99]

It is widely agreed that information intermediaries and possibly some other actors like the already discussed institutional investors have considerable influence on the overall chances and costs of companies to participate in equity and also in debt markets (gatekeeping function).[100] Extant research has helped to identify common legal principles for information intermediaries as known e.g. from concepts such as contract and trust law.[101] Building on those findings the next challenge is to integrate the gatekeeping function into a coherent regulatory concept that allows to substitute or reduce direct interference with party autonomy.

Due to their statutory mandate, auditors already form part of a regulatory reliance concept. Similarly, credit ratings are used to define the amount of regulatory capital banks have to keep for certain financial engagements.[102] This role of rating agencies, of course, has been severely criticised, as the agencies reacted much too late in the recent financial crisis. Conversely, the agencies have been heavily criticised for their immediate downgrade of states in the current sovereign debt crisis. It seems that a more refined approach towards regulatory reliance on information intermediaries needs to cope especially with two pivotal issues touched on in the following subsections.

---

94 L. DeAngelo, 3 *Journal of Accounting and Economics* 113 (1981).

95 Regulation (EC) 1060/2009 on credit rating agencies of 16 September 2009, O.J. L 302/1 of 17.11.2009.

96 European Commission, Investment research and financial analysts, COM(2006) 789 final, 12 December 2006.

97 On conflicts of interest of financial intermediaries C. Kumpan and P.C. Leyens, *ECFR* 2008, 72, 90 ff.

98 European Commission, 'Audit Policy: Lessons from the Crisis', Green Paper, COM(2010) 561 final, 13 October 2010, p. 11, 13, specific question no. 18.

99 The proposal of a cooling-off after eight years has been formulated by the Max Planck Institute Working Group (W. Doralt et al.), Max Planck Private Law Research Paper No. 10/24, 8 December 2010, available at SSRN: http://ssrn.com/abstract=1723039, p. 7, recomm. 3.4.

100 On gatekeeping R.H. Kraakman, 2 *J. L. Econ. & Org.* 53–104 (1986). Liability aspects are also discussed by F. Partnoy, 79 *Wash. U. L. Q. 491* (2001); A. Hamdani, 77 *S. Cal. L. Rev.* 53 (2003).

101 K.J. Hopt, in G. Ferrarini et al. (supra n. 14), p. 51, 67.

102 Cf. the 'Rating Agency' by P.C. Leyens, in *Max Planck Encyclopedia on European Private Law* (supra n. 87).

2.3.2 The market for information intermediation

Intermediary information on international firms naturally does not stop at national borders. In a cross-border context, a high standardisation in procedures of analysis and formats of information provides quality which pays. This economic rationale might explain the strong accumulation of market power in some of the information intermediary industries, especially the highly concentrated markets for statutory audits and credit ratings of international firms, and to a lesser extent also the concentration of financial analyst services at major banks.[103]

In the auditing industry we find – after the breakdown of Arthur Andersen in the aftermath of the Enron debacle of 2001 – only four top auditing firms. At the same time capital markets require at least *four* kinds of services: statutory audit, auxiliary services on the preparation of annual accounts, transaction advice including tax assessment and peer review in court or elsewhere.[104] Due to conflicts of interest these services should not be provided in combination by one auditing firm to a single client. Accordingly, the downfall of just one additional firm out of the remaining top-four group could cause severe disturbances of the information services structure in global capital markets. The consequences could be even more tempered in the rating market which so far has been divided between only two major and one smaller agency.[105]

The European Commission Recommendation of 2008[106] has proposed caps for auditor liabilities, which have been greatly diverse throughout Member States.[107] Early attempts reach back to a Green Paper of 1996,[108] the original draft of the Fifth Council Directive[109] and the first draft of the statute for the Societas Europaea 1970.[110] Liability caps are an important device also for opening the market to new auditing firms and increasing competition for quality. More far-reaching measures such as divesture orders have not yet been discussed in detail for the auditing or the rating sector. This could become part of the agenda especially if another auditing firm or one of the major rating agencies falls down.

2.3.3 Issuer pays vs investor pays

The degree to which capital markets can rely on information provided by intermediaries depends on whether that information is independent from what the issuers provide.[111]

---

103 For details cf. P.C. Leyens, 11 *JCLS* 33, 53 (2011).

104 J. Bigus and R.-C. Zimmermann, 12 *Int'l J. Auditing* 159 (2008).

105 Standard & Poor's, Moody's, and the smaller Fitch.

106 O.J. 2008 L 162/39. See comment on consultation by W. Doralt et al., 67 *Cambridge L. J.* 62 (2008).

107 For an overview cf. 'Auditor' by P.C. Leyens, in *Max Planck Encyclopedia on European Private Law* (supra n. 87).

108 European Commission, 'The Role, the Position and the Liability of the Statutory Auditor within the European Union', Green Paper, O.J. 1996 C 321/1.

109 European Commission, Proposal for a Fifth Directive on the Coordination of Safeguards which, for the Protection of the Interests of Members and Outsiders, are Required by Member States of Companies within the Meaning of Article 59, Second Paragraph, with Respect to Company Structure and to the Power and Responsibilities of Company Boards, O.J. 1972 C 131/49, Art. 62.

110 European Commission, Proposal for a Council Regulation Embodying a Statute for the European Company, O.J. 1970 C 124/1, Art. 209.

111 P.C. Leyens, 11 *JCLS* 33, 35 et seq. (2011).

Whilst the 'low-balling' problem describes incentives resulting from a service combination, the problems resulting from the financing of intermediary services by issuers (issuer pays model) are prevalent even when only one type of service is offered. Especially, rating agencies have been harshly criticised for their failures to accurately detect the risks of financial institutions in the recent crisis. Similar criticism was raised earlier when investment grade ratings had been published only very shortly before the downfall of Enron in 2001. It is clear that conflicts of interest play a role and that those conflicts can be aggravated by the issuer pays model.

The legal framework for ratings has been considerably tightened by the European Regulation of 2009,[112] which in large part replaced the self-regulatory approach taken by the IOSCO Code of Conduct.[113] The new legislation, however, has also introduced a duty of investors to disclose the outcome of a privately solicited rating. Consequently, a privately solicited and *privately paid-for* rating becomes a public good.[114] At its 68th meeting, in 2010, the German Jurists Association[115] argued to remove the disclosure duty in order to improve the incentives for private investors to solicit ratings.[116] The private solicitation of a rating creates a contractual relationship exposing rating agencies to liability risks towards their contractual partner. The incentives to sue for a breach of contract are high when adverse investment decisions are based on an incorrect rating.[117] This increase in liability risks will possibly strengthen incentives to provide accurate information and the expectation is that – even if not published – privately solicited ratings and issuer-solicited ratings will conform rather than differ.

It remains a task for the future to identify possible measures which could further alleviate the dangers of conflicts of interests deriving from the issuer pays model. Comparing the possible complementing measures found for the treatment of different types of intermediary services could be a first step.[118] For example, the strong responsibility, qualification and independence requirements of an audit committee diminish the possibilities of management to exercise pressure on the auditor. Similarly, it could be a task for an independent committee of the (supervisory) board to mandate or, at least, to oversee the mandating and performance of rating agencies.

3 PERSPECTIVES FOR LAW AND ECONOMICS RESEARCH

The European corporate governance debate today shows an almost unique openness to economic research and the dialogue between law and economics has been considerably

---

112 Supra n. 95.

113 Revised version: International Organization of Securities Commissions, Code of Conduct Fundamentals for Credit Rating Agencies, May 2008.

114 Id., Art. 10 para. 1 sentence 2.

115 For reports in German see P.C. Leyens, AnwBl 2010, 584 (analysis); *JZ* 2011, 418 (resolutions); K.J. Hopt and P.C. Leyens, *SZW* 2011, 198 (summary, incl. posposals).

116 For details see D. Zimmer, in *Verhandlungen des Deutschen Juristentages*, 2010, p. G 5, 75 et seq. 80.

117 Possible complementary measures which were not discussed by the German Jurists Association relate to liability exclusion clauses or mandatory self-retainers.

118 See P.C. Leyens, 11 *JCLS* 33, 51 et seq. (2011).

fostered within all – only eclectically treated – areas discussed above. Whilst in its beginnings the modern corporate governance debate mostly comprised institutional economics, in the late 1990s the interdisciplinary debate was shaken up by a series of cross-country comparisons published by La Porta and others.[119] In essence, these studies argued that the success of national economies could be regressed to the existence of some specific legal institutions of investor protection. Today it seems to be accepted that the authors went too far in their main finding that a better performance is more likely to be achieved by a common law than by a civil law system.[120] Some of the weaknesses in the used dataset certainly could have been avoided by a more thoroughly undertaken legal comparative work.[121] At the time of publication, however, the reaction of the European legal academia was somewhat low-voiced.[122] Ever since the awareness for the influence of and also for critical assessments of 'numerical comparisons' has grown.[123] Needless to state that adjudicators, regulators and legal researchers need to distinguish between anecdotal and statistical evidence and be aware of whether studies claim causality against mere correlation. In total, the debate on corporate governance in Europe illustrates a growing offer and demand for law and economics research, most probably without dangers of a 'lemon market'.

---

[119] See, e.g. R. La Porta et al., 61 *J. Fin.* 1–32 (2006); 106 *J. Polit. Econ.* 1113 (1998).

[120] Id.; cf. also P.G. Mahoney, 30 *J. Legal Stud.* 503 (2001), who claimed a renaissance of Hayek's views on different levels of property rights protection in common and civil law countries. For a renewed new attempt see J. Armour et al., *Brigham Young U. L. Rev.* 1435 (2009).

[121] On the elusive quest of global corporate governance standards see L.A. Bebchuk and A. Hamdani, 157 *U. Pa. L. Rev.* 1263 (2009) with response by K.J. Hopt, 158 *U. Penn. L. Rev.* (PENNumbra) 27 (2009) from a European perspective.

[122] Cf. R. Michaels, 57 *Am. J. Comp. L.* 765 (2009).

[123] For shortcomings and improvements on anti-director rights indices H. Spamann, 23 *Rev. Fin. Stud.* 467 (2010).

PART 4

PRIVATE LAW

9 Private law I: tort

*Michael G. Faure**

1 INTRODUCTION

In this chapter I will address the way in which the EU has dealt with one particular aspect of private law, namely tort law, from the perspective of economic analysis of law. When referring to EU law the crucial question (and the one that this chapter will deal with) is obviously to what extent harmonisation or centralisation of decision making to the central (EU) level may be indicated.

The approach I will follow is the one of the economics of federalism. The economics of federalism seems to be a particularly appropriate way of looking at harmonisation efforts in Europe because the European Commission has been using economic arguments to justify its harmonisation efforts for some time. More specifically, the argument has been long advanced that a harmonisation of law, including private law, is necessary in order to harmonise the conditions of competition within Europe. One aspect of this chapter is an analysis of whether this 'economic' argument for the harmonisation of the conditions of competition is indeed a valid economic justification for harmonisation. Moreover, applying the economics of federalism to the harmonisation of private law within Europe also has the advantage that a balanced view of the need to harmonise private law can be presented. Indeed, economic analysis does not come up with black and white statements in favour of or against harmonisation, but allows balanced criteria to be advanced on the basis of which those areas and topics which may be good candidates for harmonisation are indicated.

Of course the reader should be aware that applying the economics of federalism to the harmonisation issue means that I will only provide 'one view of the cathedral'.[1] Moreover, the harmonisation issue is addressed only from an economic angle in this chapter. Although I have argued above that I think economics can provide an interesting contribution to the harmonisation debate, I want to repeat that I realise that this really is just one view of the cathedral. One may indeed well argue that there may be other, non-economic, arguments for a harmonised legal system, such as the belief that this will lead to a higher degree of protection than Member States would achieve when using national law. But even if non-economic arguments are advanced to justify European harmonisation, it seems important that in future European documents these reasons are clearly explained within the scope of the subsidiarity principle. Indeed, the legal framework to deal with harmonisation questions is presented by the subsidiarity principle, which is still incorporated in the Lisbon Treaty.[2]

* I am grateful to Jorge Alberto Fierro Abella and to Hans-Bernd Schäfer for useful comments on an earlier version of this chapter.

1 Paraphrasing the words of Calabresi and Melamed (Calabresi and Melamed 1972).

2 This can now be found in Art. 3b of the Treaty on the Functioning of the European Union (TFEU) and reads as follows: 'Under the principle of subsidiarity, in areas which do not fall within

Increasingly, many initiatives are taken to achieve a European harmonisation in the field of private law. Private initiatives constitute, for example, the European Group on Tort Law, which drafted principles of European tort law in 2005 (see Jansen 2001; Spier and Haazen 1999). This is an academic exercise addressing the common roots of tort law in various laws of Member States, more comparable to the American restatement. However, one particular initiative goes much further. It is a major project concerning a European Civil Code, supervised by Prof. Christian von Bar von Osnabrück. His ideas led to the drafting of a so-called Draft Common Frame of References (DCFR) (Von Bar et al. 2008). This is, according to some, nothing less than a draft of a European Civil Code and has also been financially supported by the European Commission. It gave rise to many critical reflections, especially as far as the ambitions of this document are concerned (see e.g. Eidenmuller et al. 2008a, 2008b). A particularly strong reaction followed by the well-known comparative lawyer Pierre Legrand, who pointed to the impossibility of legal transplants (more particularly between the common law and the civil law) (Legrand 1997) and who published an article with the meaningful title 'Antivonbar' (Legrand 2008).

Since many other contributions to this book deal at a more general level with the economic foundations for centralisation within the EU, I will only briefly focus on the traditional arguments in favour (or against) harmonisation of tort law. I will do so by on the one hand examining in general whether economics holds that a particular topic would deserve harmonisation and, if so, to what extent. On the other hand I will also examine to what extent particular issues in tort law (mostly product liability and environmental liability) have been harmonised within European law to date and whether this harmonisation fits into the economic framework. To the extent that the latter is not the case it will be examined whether there are alternative explanations for the harmonisation.

The structure of this chapter is as follows: after this introduction, the economic criteria for (de)centralisation in general will be briefly summarised (Section 2). Then these criteria are applied to tort law by focusing more specifically on the economic reasons for centralisation (Section 3). I then turn to some policy aspects of the harmonisation of tort law, by addressing it from an interest group perspective (Section 4). A few concluding remarks will be formulated in Section 5.

2 ECONOMIC STARTING POINT: RESPECT FOR VARYING PREFERENCES

2.1 Tiebout

The question of whether regulation should be promulgated at a central (European or federal) level or at a more decentralised level (or, to generalise, what kind of regulation should be set at which level) has been addressed in the economics of federalism. The

---

its exclusive competence, the Union shall act only if and in so far as the objectives of the proposed action cannot be sufficiently achieved by the Member States, either at central level or at regional and local level, but can rather, by reason of the skill or effects of the proposed action, be better achieved at Union level.'

starting point for the analysis is usually Tiebout's theory about the optimal provision of local public goods (Tiebout 1956; for a discussion see Rose-Ackerman 1992). Tiebout argued that when people with the same preferences cluster together in communities, competition between local authorities will, under certain restrictive conditions, lead to allocative efficiency. If there are, for example, in one community citizens who greatly prefer sporting facilities and in another a majority of citizens with a preference for opera, the first community will probably construct sporting facilities, whereas the second may build an opera house. If someone living in the second community preferred sporting facilities to the opera house, he could then move to the first community, which apparently provides services more to his tastes. The idea is that well-informed citizens will move to the community that provides the local services that are best adapted to their personal preferences. Through this so-called 'voting with one's feet', competition between local authorities will lead citizens to cluster together according to their preferences (compare Mueller 1997). In practice, it is clear that different communities do indeed offer a variety of different services. The idea is that the citizen can have an effect on this provision of local public goods either by influencing the decision making (vote) or by moving (exit).

2.2 Competing legal orders

This basic idea applies not only to community services but also, for example, to fiscal decisions (Inman and Rubinfeld 1994) and environmental choices (Oates and Schwab 1988). In addition, this idea of citizens moving to the community that provides services which best correspond with their preferences can also be applied with respect to legal rules. Thus, it has been argued by Van den Bergh that competition between legislators will lead to legal systems competing with each other to provide the legislation that corresponds best to the preferences of the citizens. Ogus also argues that the various lawmakers in the nation states will create a competitive market for the supply of law (Ogus 1999, 2001). The idea therefore is that in an optimal world citizens will cluster together in states that provide legal rules that correspond to their preferences. Well-informed citizens who are dissatisfied with the legislation provided could move (voting with their feet) to the community that provides legislation that corresponds best to their preferences. This idea, assuming that different legal systems offer different legal rules to satisfy the demands of the citizens, thus explains the variety and differences between legal systems (Van den Bergh 1998, 134; 2000, 437–9). Moreover, it also shows that differences between the various legal rules of different countries should not necessarily be judged negatively, as is often the case in Europe today. The idea of competing legal systems can probably best be seen 'in action' in private international law where actors can choose the legal system that best suits their needs in a choice of law regime.[3] Frey and Eichenberger have proposed an extreme form of this competition between legal orders by suggesting the emergence of functional overlapping competing jurisdictions (FOCJs), whereby citizens could choose

---

[3] Although the choice for a particular legal regime may not always be related to the quality of the legal system but, say, to the quality of the court or arbitration system. The latter explains, according to Ogus, the popularity of English law in choice of law clauses in contracts (Ogus 1999, 408).

different governmental authorities for different functions of government (Frey 1996; Frey and Eichenberger 1996, 335; Casella and Frey 1992, 639).

This system, assuming that competition between legal orders leads to allocative efficiency in the provision of legal rules, works only if certain conditions are met. One condition is that citizens have adequate information on the contents of the legal rules provided by the various legislators, in order to be able to make an informed choice. In addition, exit is often costly, so people may stay even if the (legal) regime does not best suit their needs.[4] Moreover, a location decision is obviously made under the influence of a set of criteria, in which the legal regime may not be decisive.[5] Usually the job location and residence are so important that in reality people are left with little choice (Rose-Ackerman 1992). Finally, as I will discuss below, this system of competition between legal orders works only if the decisions in one legal order have no external effects on others.

2.3 Bottom-up federalism

In economic literature, the Tiebout model is used to argue that, from an economic point of view, decentralisation should be the starting point, since competition between legislators will lead to allocative efficiency. Van den Bergh also uses his theory to provide criteria for centralisation/decentralisation within the European Union. Taking Tiebout as a starting point and assuming that competition between decentralised legislators will lead to an optimal provision of legal rules, the crucial question is: why centralise? Van den Bergh criticises that part of the European legal literature which seems to focus on the question why there should be decentralisation (referred to by Van den Bergh as 'top down federalisation'). According to economic theory, that is the wrong question. Starting from Tiebout's model, there is reason to believe in what Van den Bergh calls a 'bottom up federalisation', assuming that in principle the local level is optimal, since the local level has the best information on local problems and on the preferences of citizens. Decision making should be moved to a higher level only when there is a good reason.[6] Economic theory has indeed suggested that there may be a variety of reasons why the local level is not best suited for taking decisions and that there are occasions when central decision making can lead to more efficient results.

These basic economic ideas show that economists are traditionally sceptical concerning the virtues of harmonisation. Whereas lawyers may consider differences between legal systems as problematic, the starting point for the economists is that differences are as such not bad, on the condition that these differences between legal systems also reflect varying preferences of citizens.[7] This seems at first blush to contrast with the increasing tendency amongst lawyers to strive for a general harmonisation of tort law. In this respect one can,

---

4 As Ogus states, there should be no barriers to the freedom of establishment and to the movement of capital (Ogus 1999, 407). For these conditions, see also Van den Bergh (2000, 438).

5 That is one of the reasons why Frey and Eichenberger argue in favour of FOCJ: the choice for one legal or institutional regime should not be exclusive; there may be 'overlapping' jurisdictions depending upon the different functions (Frey and Eichenberger 1996, 316–18).

6 A major supporter of this 'presumption in favour of decentralisation' is Revesz (see Revesz, 2000a, 2000b).

7 This idea is also to be found in the work of many lawyers. See in this respect Smits (2002a).

for example, point to the principles of European tort law drafted by the European Group on Tort Law (European Group on Tort Law 2005).[8] Also the Draft Common Frame of Reference (DCFR) prepared by the study group on a European civil code contains a book on non-contractual liability arising out of damage caused to another (Von Bar et al. 2008).[9] These initiatives show a strong belief of some lawyers in the virtues of harmonisation of tort law. This contrasts with the economic approach that takes decentralisation with rule making respecting the preferences of citizens as a starting point and only pleads in favour of centralisation when particular criteria are met.

3 CRITERIA FOR CENTRALISATION OF TORT LAW

3.1 Transboundary Externalities

3.1.1 General: centralisation!

The Tiebout argument in favour of competition between local communities obviously works only if the problem to be regulated is indeed merely local. Once it has been established that the problem to be regulated has a transboundary character, there may be arguments to be made in favour of centralisation. First, there is an 'economies of scale' argument to shift powers to a higher legal order that has competence to deal with the externality over a larger territory. This corresponds with the basic insight that if the problem to be regulated crosses the borders of competence of the regulatory authority, the decision-making power should be shifted to a higher regulatory level, preferably to an authority which has jurisdiction over a territory large enough to deal with the problem adequately (Ogus 1999, 414; Kimber 1995, 1; Esty 1996, 625; Rose-Ackerman 1992, 164–5). 'Economic theory provides a straightforward but unrealistic answer to regional problems: draw "optimal" jurisdictional boundaries' (Rose-Ackerman 1995, 38). This 'economics of scale' argument is thus related to the argument that transaction costs will be lower if regulation is made at the higher level.[10] There is, however, another argument in favour of centralisation which relates to the fact that in cases of transboundary externalities states would have no incentive to impose stringent regulations upon their own citizens if the consequences of harmful actions were only felt outside their own territories. Moreover, victims in states that incur pollution may experience considerable problems in filing transboundary lawsuits for environmental pollution cases, as a result of which transboundary harm will often not be internalised (Faure and Betlem 2008, 133–8). Transboundary externalities thus may create inefficiencies in the absence of central regulation.[11]

This argument in favour of centralisation could thus play a role with respect to

---

[8] For a critical evaluation see Van den Bergh and Visscher (2006).

[9] For a critical evaluation see Eidenmüller et al. (2008a). The same article has been published in English in Eidenmüller et al. (2008b). See also Jansen (2007). See also the contributions in Schulze et al. (2008).

[10] It is thus related to the 'transaction costs' argument, to be discussed below.

[11] See, for the 'interstate externalities' and 'economies of scale' justifications for centralisation, Revesz (2000b, 67).

transboundary torts. Thus, many have proposed central decision making in the areas of environmental liability, since this area of private law is typically transboundary.[12] However, this externality argument obviously cannot provide a general justification for the harmonisation of rules of tort law as long as accidents are confined within national borders. Moreover, even with these typical transboundary torts one should not move too hastily to centralisation, since there may be remedies within national law as effective in dealing with these transboundary problems.

Moreover, Van den Bergh has demonstrated that in some cases, more particularly in the area of private law, European law cannot be considered an effective remedy to the interstate externality problem (Van den Bergh 1998, 143). In some cases European law goes further than is necessary to cure transboundary externalities; in other cases less comprehensive legal instruments than total harmonisation could be used to remedy the problem (Van den Bergh 1998, 144–5). There is, in other words, always the risk that the cure may be worse than the disease. The first issue relates to the fact that European directives often cover both local and community-wide problems, such as pollution, without making a distinction between regional and interstate pollution (Van den Bergh 1999, 10). The second point is that in some cases transboundary externalities may also be internalised by national law. The simple fact of transboundary effects is therefore not sufficient to justify European law making (Van den Bergh 1998, 144–5). Nevertheless, there certainly may be cases where one could hold that decentralised legal rule making would not be able to remedy the transboundary externality.

This shows indeed that in cases of transboundary torts there may be an argument in favour of centralisation, but only if there is a serious risk that nation states would be able to externalise harm, in other words if the nation states were able to throw the negative effects of their own actions on the shoulders of their neighbours (Faure and Betlem 2008, 133–8; Faure 2010, 383–7). Moreover, European harmonisation would then have to be limited to transboundary torts. The 'transboundary externality' argument indeed provides no justification for a harmonisation of tort law which merely deals with 'national torts'. Finally, it would have to be clear that national legal remedies cannot provide an adequate answer to the problem posed by interstate torts.

3.1.2 Examples

Although the risk of transboundary externalities may in principle constitute an important argument in favour of harmonisation of tort law, it is doubtful that this argument can justify harmonisation in some of the areas on which the EU has been active, more particularly environmental and product liability. To some extent a harmonisation of the rules concerning environmental liability took place via the Directive on Environmental Liability.[13] It is doubtful whether the 'transboundary externality' argument could be used as a justification for the way in which the EU harmonised environmental liability for the simple reason that the directive largely applies to damage to biodiversity and for example

[12] See for an extensive discussion of the arguments in favour of centralisation, applied to environmental liability, De Smedt (2007).

[13] Directive 2004/35/CE on environmental liability with regard to the prevention and remedying of environmental damage. For an economic analysis of the application of the subsidiarity principle to environmental liability see De Smedt (2007).

to soil pollution, which is not necessarily transboundary. Although the risk of cross-border externalities was used by the European Commission to justify European action, the literature was critical of this justification since the directive also applies to local pollution (Faure and De Smedt 2001; Bergkamp 2000, 107). The transboundary character of environmental damage could lead to a 'transboundary only' regime which would only apply to interstate pollution and not to local pollution.[14] In a document preceding the Environmental Liability Directive, the so-called White Paper on Environmental Liability, the European Commission rejected this argument since it feared that a European regime which would be applicable only to transboundary harm would create an undesirable discrimination between transboundary and local pollution.

Similar problems arise with respect to another domain that has been harmonised at the European level, namely product liability. The risk of an externalisation of harm to other legal systems would only arise if consumers would have no possibility of filing a law suit against manufacturers located abroad that would have marketed harmful products under the protection of their 'lenient' national product liability law. This is, however, not a very realistic scenario since manufacturers remain liable in export markets and within the EU citizens have the possibility to sue manufacturers for harm that is suffered in another country. In sum, the mere fact that different states within the EU would hold different preferences with respect to product liability and that hence different regimes would exist can as such hardly be considered an argument in favour of harmonisation as long as states are not capable of externalising harm to victims in third countries. This they cannot do as long as manufacturers remain liable in countries where they export their products, whereby the law in the victim state will apply.[15]

Thus, even though at first blush the transboundary character of externalities may seem an important argument in favour of centralisation of tort law, the concrete examples of the product liability and environmental liability directives make clear that in these particular cases it is doubtful whether this argument could provide an economic justification for centralisation at the European level.

3.2 The Race for the Bottom

3.2.1 General: a risk of destructive competition

There may be an economic argument for centralisation, in that there is a risk that a 'race for the bottom' would emerge between countries to attract foreign investments. As a result of this, prisoner's dilemmas could arise, whereby countries would fail to enact or enforce effective legislation. Centralisation can be advanced as a remedy for these prisoner's dilemmas. This 'race for the bottom' argument could in theory play a role in the case of product safety[16] and environmental production. It would mean that local governments would compete with lenient safety standards to attract industry (Rose-Ackerman 1992, 166–70). The result would be an overall reduction of standards below efficient

---

[14] This had also been suggested by Van den Bergh (1998, 143–5).

[15] In other words: protecting manufacturers through lenient product liability law would make no sense for national states since manufacturers remain liable in export markets. See further on this Faure (2000).

[16] For a detailed discussion of this argument, see Esty and Geradin (1998, 16–19).

levels. This should correspond with the traditional game theory result that prisoner's dilemmas create inefficiencies.

The 'race for the bottom' argument has had supporters as well as opponents in North American scholarship. Law and economics scholars tend to stress the benefits of competition between states and point out the dangers of centralisation (Revesz 1992; Revesz 1996), whereas some legal scholars tend to attach more belief to the race-for-the-bottom rationale for centralisation (see Esty and Geradin 1997, 1998).

This 'race for the bottom' argument has not as such been explicitly discussed in the European legal debate. It only shows up in the argument that the conditions of competition should be harmonised. That will be discussed below. From an economic perspective the race for the bottom is only a rationale for centralisation if it can be established that states could attract industry with lenient tort rules (Van den Bergh 2000, 445). Let us examine, on the basis of an example, whether that is a realistic scenario.

3.2.2 Example: environmental liability

From an economic perspective, differences in the conditions of competition only pose a problem if it is clear that environmental costs would be considerably different between the Member States and that these differences would lead to the relocation of firms to the Member State with the lowest standards. In that case, the so-called 'race for the bottom' argument, in environmental cases referred to as the 'pollution haven' hypothesis, might be an argument in favour of centralisation.[17] The question therefore arises whether there is empirical evidence that states can indeed attract industry by lenient environmental standards.

Empirical evidence to uphold this 'race for the bottom' rationale is rather weak. Repetto argues that pollution control costs are only a minor fraction of the total sales of manufacturing industries (Repetto 1994). Moreover, Jaffe et al. (1995) argue that empirical evidence shows that the effects of environmental regulations are 'either small, statistically insignificant or not robust to tests of model specification'. However, Esty and Geradin argue that the stringency of environmental regulations might have some effect on new firms in their decision to locate for the first time (Esty and Geradin 1998, 12–15), but that this will not induce existing firms to relocate. They equally argue that other criteria such as tax levels, public services and the unionisation of the labour force have a much more significant impact on the location decision than environmental regulation. Recently, this empirical evidence has been somewhat contradicted by Xing and Kolstad (1995), who argue that the laxity of environmental regulations in a host country is a significant determinant of foreign direct investment by the US chemical industry. The more lax the regulations, the more likely the country is to attract foreign investment, so Xing and Kolstad argue. Although this somewhat weakens the evidence presented by Jaffe et al. as far as the location of new firms outside the US is concerned, it does not contradict their finding that existing firms will not relocate solely because of the stringency of environmental regulations.

---

[17] Although Esty and Geradin have rightly pointed out the fact that a whole variety of legal instruments exist which may remedy the problem, whereby the total harmonisation of standards would be the most far reaching (Esty and Geradin 1997, 282–94).

Arguments against the 'race for the bottom' rationale for central environmental regulation have also been formulated with respect to the American example. Many scholars (Pelzman and Tideman 1972; Elliott et al. 1985), among them Revesz (1992, 1996) in particular, have argued that this 'race for the bottom' argument finds no support in existing models of interjurisdictional competition.[18] In addition, Revesz stresses that central standard setting would not be an effective response to the race-for-the-bottom problem, since the local communities concerned would have other means to attract industry if they wished (relaxation of regulatory controls in other areas). Revesz has encountered opposition, especially from Esty (1996), but he has provided a powerful reply to his critics (Revesz 1997).

This material, therefore, weakens the prisoner's dilemma argument. Moreover, it has also been argued that, as far as environmental standards are concerned, it is not at all clear that there will be a race for the bottom. There is also some evidence that Member States do in fact strive for high environmental standards, even if this puts extra costs or burdens on their industries. Some countries may therefore be more involved in a race for the top instead of a race for the bottom.[19] One could also question whether European law is at all able to remedy a real race-for-the-bottom risk, given the enforcement deficit.

3.3 Harmonisation of Marketing Conditions

3.3.1 General: no!

This 'race for the bottom' argument, that competition among jurisdictions for economic activity will be 'destructive', corresponds – to some extent – with the European legal argument that the creation of harmonised conditions of competition is necessary to avoid trade distortions. This argument has traditionally been used to harmonise legislation of the Member States in a variety of areas. Simply stated, the argument is that complying with legislation imposes costs on industry. If legislation is different, these costs will therefore differ as well and the conditions of competition within the common market will not be equal. The argument apparently assumes that total equality of conditions of competition is necessary for the functioning of the common market. 'Levelling the playing field' for European industry is the central message.

There are, however, some problems with this traditional European argument which in fact claims that any difference in legislation between the Member States might endanger the conditions of competition and therefore justifies harmonisation of legal rules. The latter argument seems particularly weak (Spier and Haazen 1999, 478). From an economic point of view, the mere fact that conditions of competition differ does not necessarily create a race-for-the-bottom risk. There can be differences in marketing conditions

---

[18] See for a similar conclusion with respect to natural resource legislation Johnston (2003), who argues that regulatory centralisation may be just as tragic for natural resources as the regime of local control that it is designed to replace.

[19] See Van den Bergh et al. (1996, 141–2). Ogus argues that there may be benefits to firms of being located in a high standard Member State, since this may generate technological improvements and thus competitive advantages; that may explain the race for the top (Ogus 1999, 415). See, generally, Vogel (1995, 13–14).

for a variety of reasons, and if the conditions of competition were indeed totally equal, as the argument assumes, there would also be no trade.

Also, Europe has developed an elaborate set of rules which guarantee – *inter alia* – a free flow of products and services[20] and thus contribute to market integration without the necessity of harmonising all rules and standards.[21] In this context, the case law of the European Court of Justice with respect to the free movement of goods versus environmental protection springs to mind. This shows that the goal of market integration can be achieved through (other) less comprehensive instruments than total harmonisation (Esty and Geradin 1997, 296–9; Ogus 1994, 177–9) which can remove barriers to trade just as effectively. Hence, one should make a distinction between the political ideal of creating one common market in Europe on the one hand and the (economic) 'race for the bottom' argument on the other hand.[22]

It should be stressed that although the European argument that markets will be distorted without the harmonisation of the conditions of competition is constantly repeated in a stereotypical way, its validity is hardly ever questioned. The argument as it is usually presented in Europe cannot be fitted into the economic criteria for centralisation, since it suggests that removing any difference in legal systems would be necessary to cure the 'race for the bottom' risk, which is supported neither by economic theory nor by empirical evidence. Also, even if one were to take the (political) 'common market' goal as a starting point and private law were to be harmonised on that ground, this would still not create a level playing field since differences in, for example, energy sources, access to raw materials and atmospheric conditions would still lead to marketing conditions that favour trade (Van den Bergh 1999, 6).

There is, in addition, a strong counter-argument, in that there are many examples showing that economic market integration is possible (without the distortions predicted by the 'race for the bottom' argument) with unstandardised legal orders. Public choice scholars have often advanced the Swiss federal model as an example where economic market integration goes hand in hand with differentiated legal systems (Frey 1994). It is apparently possible to create a common market without the total harmonisation of all legal rules and standards. That is not to say that there may not be other arguments in favour of the harmonisation of tort law in Switzerland. Notably the 'reduction of transaction costs' argument – to be discussed below – may well constitute a powerful reason to prefer one Federal Swiss tort law instead of 26 different cantonal systems. Therefore, clear steps towards harmonisation of private law can be seen in Switzerland as well (Wininger 2001; Koziol 1996). Note, however, that this is not because harmonisation would be necessary to make market integration possible.

---

20 See articles 34–7 of the Treaty on the Functioning of the European Union (the 'old' articles 30–36).

21 See generally on the potential conflict between free trade and environmental protection, Esty (1999).

22 See also Richard Revesz, who equally argues that these are separate points which should be distinguished (Revesz 2000a, 19).

3.3.2 Example: product liability

The harmonisation of the 'conditions of competition' argument has obviously played an important role in the area of product liability, and it has even been used explicitly as one of the rationales for the European Product Liability Directive. In the product liability debate one could often hear the traditional argument that uniform rules in Europe are necessary to guarantee the free movement of goods within the EC. What can be said about this argument?

A difference should probably be made in this respect between product safety standards on the one hand and product liability rules on the other hand. It could be argued that differences in product safety standards may indeed endanger interstate trade. Therefore, rules with respect to – *inter alia* – a free flow of products and services may certainly contribute to the European goal of market integration. The Product Safety Directive 52/59 of 29 June 1992 aims clearly at removing differences in safety standards, since the Commission considers that these differences might endanger the establishment of the internal market. The preamble reads:

> Whereas it is important to adopt measures with the aim of progressively establishing the internal market over a period expiring on 31 December 1992; whereas the internal market is to comprise an area without internal frontiers in which the free movement of goods, persons, services and capital is ensured;
> Whereas some Member States have adopted horizontal legislation on product safety, imposing, in particular, a general obligation on economic operators to market only safe products;
> Whereas those legislations differ in the level of protection afforded to persons;
> Whereas such disparities and the absence of horizontal legislation in other Member States are liable to create barriers to trade and distortions of competition within the internal market. . .

Where the preamble to the Directive of 29 June 1992 on general product safety therefore clearly states that disparities and the absence of horizontal legislation in other Member States are liable to create barriers to trade and distortions of competition within the internal market, this is probably true. However, the question arises whether the goal of market integration can only be achieved by means of such a comprehensive instrument as total harmonisation and more particularly the question arises whether this may justify the harmonisation of rules of private law, such as product liability. Indeed, the political goal of market integration may justify the need for some rules aiming at the reduction of trade restrictions and may justify a minimum harmonisation of product safety standards. In that respect the directive on general product safety in fact only provides for a general obligation to place only safe products on the market, but safety standards may still be drawn up in the Member State in which the product is in circulation or may rely on codes of good practice, which need not necessarily be European.[23]

Ogus is relatively enthusiastic about these product safety directives, precisely because the harmonisation is limited to 'essential safety requirements'. To meet these requirements the Member States can still use their national standards, whereby voluntary standards set by expert committees will allow for an easy mutual recognition. The approach chosen in the product safety directives therefore even promotes competition between different national and European standards systems, so Ogus holds (Ogus 1994, 177–9).

---

[23] See article 4 (2) of the Directive 92/59 of 29 June 1992 on general product safety.

The goal of 'levelling the playing field' is much more apparent in the Product Liability Directive. That directive is clearly justified on the ground that differing liability rules in the Member States would hamper the conditions of competition. The considerations preceding the directive read:

> Whereas approximation of the laws of the Member States concerning the liability of the producer for damage caused by the defectiveness of his products is necessary because the existing divergences may distort competition and affect the movement of goods within the common market.

The weakness of this argument is that it assumes that differences in marketing conditions are always and necessarily a problem for the creation of a common market. Conditions of competition are obviously never equal, as the 'levelling the playing field' argument assumes. In the ideal case of totally equal market conditions, there would be no trade. This political goal of market integration may moreover be questioned on economic grounds.[24] In addition, one should realise that even if product liability law were totally harmonised in Europe, this would still not create a level playing field, since differences in, for example, energy sources, access to raw materials and atmospheric conditions would still lead to market conditions that divert trade (Van den Bergh 1999, 6).

Finally, the question can be asked whether the European Product Liability Directive, as it has been drafted, can indeed achieve a total harmonisation of marketing conditions. It is in fact very unlikely that this is the case.[25] Indeed, according to article 13 all the different, already existing, product liability laws remain in effect, which means differences that already exist will remain unchanged. In addition, at many points the directive itself refers to national legislation; for example, with respect to the rights of contribution or recourse (articles 5 and 8.1), non-material damage (article 9), the suspension or interruption of the limitation period (article 10.2) and nuclear accidents (article 14). It should also be mentioned that in three cases the directive expressly allows the Member States to derogate from the provisions of the directive – namely liability for primary agricultural products, liability for development risks and the introduction of a financial limit on liability. Moreover, the directive cannot of course bring any harmonisation for all the product accidents to which it does not apply, because of limitations in the definitions of 'product', 'producer' and 'damage'. Many notions in the directive are also unclear and can give rise to interpretation problems.[26] These problems might lead to different interpretations of the provisions of the directive by the legislator and courts of the different Member States.

Since it is clear that this Product Liability Directive cannot approximate to the Member States legislation, it has been suggested that this could only be used as an argument to give the EC competence in this matter.[27] For all these reasons some authors qualify the directive itself as a defective product (Storm 1985).

The Product Liability Directive still relies highly on national law and can for that

---

[24] See for a critical analysis Van den Bergh (1999).

[25] Almost all authors agree on that point. See Duintjer Tebbens (1986, 373–4); Storm (1985, 245); Van Wassenaer van Catwijck (1986, 81) and Martin Casals and Solé Feliu (2001).

[26] Consider the defect notion in article 6, which might have different interpretations.

[27] Article 100 of the EEC treaty indeed gave legislative competence to the community in order to harmonise the different legislations of the Member States. It was, however, heavily debated

reason never lead to a 'levelling of the playing field' or a 'harmonisation of marketing conditions'. This example of the European Product Liability Directive therefore nicely shows that the harmonisation of the 'conditions of competition' argument is not a useful basis for European action towards centralisation of tort law.

3.4 Reduction of Transaction Costs

3.4.1 General: if possible, yes!

From an economic perspective, probably the most important argument for a harmonisation of tort law (for issues that are not transboundary) is that such a harmonisation could lead to a reduction of administrative costs.[28] One could indeed easily argue that in Europe today many liability rules exist which may in fact reflect similar values and preferences, but are technically different as a result of the differences in underlying doctrines and the legal techniques used. If it were possible to have uniform liability rules which do indeed reflect similar values and preferences at relatively low costs this should indeed be considered an important advantage. This is of course the leading thought behind many initiatives which have been developed by academic tort lawyers in Europe who examined whether it is possible to proceed to a harmonisation of tort law.[29]

Many of these harmonisation projects are undertaken by academic lawyers who examine the existing differences between tort rules in the legal systems and try to find the largest common denominator. Such an approach, looking for a common denominator on the basis of comparative legal studies and of case law,[30] seems far more promising than the approach followed by the European Commission so far. The 'top-down' approach of the European Commission, forcing Member States to implement European legislation as laid down in directives, has not proven to be very successful, especially in the area of private law. The approach chosen by the various academic study groups seems much more aimed at a search for a *ius commune* in tort law. Hence, their search for the common roots of the tort law systems in Europe can be considered a 'bottom-up' approach.

The advantage of the work of the study groups is that most of this work is also based on a specific conceptual idea of tort law. On that basis the different groups formulate proposals for the various areas of tort law as a more or less coherent framework. A major disadvantage of the European approach today is that one has the impression that the Commission at one moment presents a European Product Liability Directive, then thinks it might be a good idea to work on the liability for services and the next

whether this article 100 was an appropriate basis on which to ground the legislative power of the EC with respect to product liability (see Krämer 1986, 274–5).

28 A somewhat related argument deals with economies and diseconomies of scale in administration. See in that respect Rose-Ackerman (1992, 165–6).

29 Within the scope of this chapter it is obviously not possible to mention all the projects that aim to achieve a harmonisation in the area of tort law (see Jansen 2001). A European group on tort law, coordinated by Prof. Helmut Koziol (of Vienna) developed principles of tort law. See Spier and Haazen (1999). Another initiative is the major project concerning the European Civil Code supervised by Prof. Christian von Bar (from Osnabrück). See for their view on the issue of harmonisation of tort law Von Bar (2000a). In 2008, his ideas were laid down in the Draft Common Frame of Reference, discussed above.

30 For comparisons of tort rules on the basis of case law see Van Gerven et al. (1998, 2000).

morning considers a directive on environmental liability. If one sees the approaches followed in these different European initiatives it becomes clear that they are so different that a fundamental vision on the function and goals of tort law seems to be absent.[31] An approach aimed at a lowering of administrative costs whereby a largest common denominator would be sought, respecting differences between national values and preferences, would also have the advantage that an almost traditional hostility against the Europeanisation of tort law could be more easily overcome. Indeed, it is clear that the resistance to harmonisation will be much stronger when national legal systems have to give up national rules which are strongly rooted in national values or tradition. This may be totally different if the national rules are replaced by another rule which is formulated in a technically different way but still reflects the same values and preferences. If one therefore accepts that the opportunities for harmonisation (from the perspective of lowering administrative costs) should especially be seen where preferences do not differ, but only legal techniques are different, the economic approach to tort law can be very helpful to achieve this goal. Indeed, as has been explained above, the economic analysis of tort law has the advantage of focusing on functions and goals of tort law and, hence, enables the study of tort law at a higher level of abstraction.[32] Thus this higher level of abstraction, essential for the economic analysis of tort law, may well enable the focus on the common roots between the various legal systems. Hence, the economic approach to tort law can provide an important contribution to the search for a *ius commune* of tort rules in Europe. Now that specific harmonization attempts have seen the light, more particularly the principles of European tort law and the DCFR, economic analysis could also be used (and has also been used) to critically evaluate whether the search for these principles constitutes the right path to harmonisation.[33]

Whether the harmonisation attempts will be successful in the long run is hard to predict today. Some scholars are very pessimistic and stress the differences between the legal systems (and legal cultures) in Europe to argue that these will inhibit a harmonisation of private law (Legrand 1997, 111; 2008). From an economic perspective one can easily argue that many legal rules often serve the same goal and could therefore be harmonised, certainly if only the legal techniques used differ and not the underlying values and preferences (Van den Bergh 2007a). However, in some cases these differences can be rooted so deeply in the legal cultures and traditions that the costs of harmonisation could be extremely high, maybe even prohibitive.[34] In addition, the administrative costs of harmonisation need to be taken into account. These also include implementation costs. These costs refer to existing differences between national jurisdictions when interpreting a common text. The larger the differences between the legal systems of the Member States are, the higher obviously these implementation costs may be. From an economic

---

[31] That was an important point of criticism of the current European tort law as developed by the European Commission. See Koziol (2001, 32–3) and Widmer (1999, 99). See also Koziol (2008).

[32] This is also suggested by Van den Bergh and Visscher (2006).

[33] For a critical economic analysis of the principles of European tort law see Van den Bergh and Visscher (2006). For a critical analysis of the tort roles in the DCFR see *inter alia* Eidenmüller et al. (2008a, 2008b).

[34] See in this respect the interesting observations by Majone (2008) as well as Van Dam (2007).

perspective it can be held that the argument of harmonisation based on the potential reduction of administrative costs (through a simplification by uniform legal rules) is of course valid only when the marginal costs of this harmonisation are indeed lower than the marginal benefits of such a unification.[35]

3.4.2 Example: product liability

The transaction costs argument may play an important role in justifying the coordination of product safety standards to prevent states from hindering the free flow of products and services (Vogel 1995, 52–5). Indeed, some cooperation between states seems necessary if a product is mass produced and internationally distributed to avoid interstate trade being hampered as a result of varying national product safety standards (Schwartz 1996, 924–5). Also in international trade law it is well known that divergent health, safety and related regulatory standards between countries of origin and countries of destination, especially in cases where these standards are more stringent than in the countries of destination, provoke allegations by the countries of origin that they are subject to discrimination in the countries of destination. Harmonisation is therefore certainly useful to avoid pointless incompatibilities which do not reflect different preferences (Trebilcock and Howse 1999). These transaction costs arguments do therefore apply in the field of economic regulation and product safety. Therefore, the Directive on General Product Safety, taken in the framework of the 1992 programme to establish the internal market, may well be considered an instrument which saves transaction costs (Van den Bergh 1998).

The question, however, arises whether these transaction costs savings as a result of harmonised rules can also be expected for product liability. One could argue that a manufacturer which markets its products across the whole of Europe would, in the absence of harmonisation, need specialised legal counsel in every state and that its insurance underwriters would have to calculate the liability exposure separately in accordance with each state's product liability law (Ackerman 1996). This argument, however, neglects the fact that there is a benefit in differentiated liability rules that reflects varying preferences. These benefits can again be the same as in the general setting of tort law (e.g. referring to differences in the level of non-pecuniary losses, but also in the contents of the liability rules). Moreover, the costs of harmonisation in the field of tort law (which is so rooted in legal culture) may be huge and the alleged transaction costs savings may be less than expected. Indeed, even in the case of a harmonised legal rule, manufacturers would still need local counsels to bring their case to court. Accordingly, economies of scale under a harmonised rule would probably be insignificant.[36]

Above we looked more closely at the Product Liability Directive and argued that, given its dependence on national law, it can never lead to a harmonisation of marketing conditions. Hence it has not been able to create the legal certainty required, reducing transaction costs for manufacturers.[37] The Product Liability Directive in fact adds a layer

---

[35] See in this respect also Van den Bergh (1998, 146–8).

[36] So Ackerman (1996, 453, note 135). See similarly for the European Product Liability Directive Faure (2002, 111–30).

[37] Van den Bergh rightly points to a lot of interpretation problems in the European Product Liability Directive, which backs up the conclusion that the transaction cost savings may be small,

of complexity to the labyrinth of conflicting standards of liability. It can therefore never lead to uniformity or a lowering of transaction costs (Ackerman 1996, 454).

3.5 Minimum Level of Protection

3.5.1 General: doubtful

We will now leave the economic criteria for harmonisation and address whether other, non-economic, arguments can be advanced in favour of the harmonisation of tort law. Some may indeed argue that it is not economic arguments that demand the harmonisation of tort law in Europe but, for example, the desire to provide a minimum level of protection to accident victims in the whole of Europe.

At first sight this idea of guaranteeing a minimum quality to European victims of accidents sounds appealing. However, one should then realise that, as will be argued below, a minimum level of protection may be imposed upon citizens, even if this would not correspond with their preferences. This amounts to paternalism. Moreover, if that were a political desire it would of course have been far more important to provide, for example, minimum social security, basic health care and harmonisation in the area of minimum wages. Those areas are traditionally still very sensitive and related to national sovereignty and Europe has not intervened in them yet. It would therefore be rather strange to harmonise tort law on the basis that European citizens should receive adequate protection, when such a minimum protection is not provided for more basic needs.

Moreover, it is questionable whether tort law itself is an appropriate instrument to provide this minimum level of protection. The human rights arguments for harmonisation may be quite valid, but it can hardly be seen how these could be applied to the area of tort law.[38] Other instruments, based on the European Convention on Human Rights, would be more appropriate to provide this minimum level instead of the top-down harmonisation approach followed by the European Union.

3.5.2 Example: non-pecuniary losses

There are probably areas in tort law where the differing preferences are much stronger than the reduction of transaction costs benefits. The example of the amounts awarded for non-pecuniary losses may provide an illustration. Many have argued that there are still considerable differences between the Member States in that respect (Van Dam 2006, 322). However, it is relatively difficult to argue that these differences themselves lead to huge economic problems. One could argue that these differences reflect differing national preferences and therefore there seems to be no point in favour of harmonisation in this area. In this case the differences are probably not just differences in legal technique and can therefore not be reduced to pointless incompatibilities. It is therefore difficult to see any transaction costs benefit from harmonisation there, whereas the disadvantages (in terms of not respecting national preferences) under harmonisation would be huge. From

---

simply because a full harmonisation of the rules of private law is apparently difficult to achieve (Van den Bergh 1998, 146–7).

[38] Unless the principle of equality is used as a justification for the harmonisation of tort law. See Spier and Haazen (1999, 479–80).

an economic perspective there would thus not be an argument to harmonise, say, the specific amounts awarded in the various cases of non-pecuniary losses.

Serious differences indeed still exist, both with respect to the question whether some victims (and their relatives) are entitled to compensation for non-pecuniary losses, but also as far as the amounts awarded are concerned.[39] Some have therefore argued that it is unacceptable that within Europe a victim who, for example, suffers the loss of an arm would receive less in, say, Portugal than in, say, Germany. They implicitly argue that there is no reason to treat those victims differently and that the call for harmonisation of the amounts awarded for non-pecuniary losses is justified.[40]

What can, again, be said about this argument from an economic perspective? *First* differences in amounts awarded for non-pecuniary losses are certainly not pointless, but may reflect differing preferences of the citizens in the various states. In this respect one should, *second*, also remember that Coase taught that every increase in protection can always be passed on via the price mechanism (Coase 1960). In other words if, for example, in the area of product liability, one would argue that the Portuguese should pay higher amounts for non-pecuniary losses for victims of product accidents, this would lead to an increase in prices. Indeed, the manufacturer will add the additional damage costs to the price of the products. The effect therefore is that consumers pay a higher price for the protection awarded. It may well be that consumers in Portugal are not willing to pay this higher price. A European intervention forcing all Europeans to come up to, say, the German level would therefore amount to paternalism.

Some argue that given the increasing mobility in Europe today, it cannot be understood why, say, a German professor would receive less for his pain and suffering if he were to have an accident in Portugal rather than in Germany (Magnus and Fedtke 2001). That fact is, again, hardly an argument in favour of harmonisation. Indeed, the fact that the Portuguese would choose a lower level of damage awards for pain and suffering than the Germans reflects differing preferences. There is no reason why the Portuguese would – paternalistically – have to come up to the German level, just to please German tourists. The latter can, moreover, being aware that they will not enjoy the same level of protection abroad as in Germany, seek additional protection – if they desire so – in the form of a voluntary first party insurance. Such insurance for tourists is widely available on the market. The mere fact of tourism and mobility can therefore hardly be considered as an argument in favour of harmonisation.

Contrary to what is sometimes assumed, there may be hence very clear reasons why some countries have lower or higher levels of compensation for non-pecuniary losses than others. If this corresponds to differing preferences, one can, at least from an economic perspective, see no need for a general harmonisation merely based on the reason that the existence of such differences is 'unjust'.[41] The example, again, shows that harmonisation cannot be addressed in black and white statements. Some issues may be harmonised at relatively low costs, whereas other costs (which are closely related to preferences) can

---

39 For an overview of the current differences between the Member States as far as the amounts awarded for pain and suffering are concerned see Rogers (2001).

40 This argument is made by Magnus & Fedtke (2001) and in Magnus (2002); also compare Magnus (1995).

41 For a similar analysis, see Hartlief (2002a).

be differentiated. In the area of compensation for non-pecuniary losses harmonisation[42] could lead to a paternalistic measure and to disrespect for the preferences of citizens. Even a call for the need to provide the same minimum protection to all accident victims within Europe can hardly justify such a paternalistic measure. However, with this statement and the reference to the need for providing a basic level of victim protection we have left the area of economics. Indeed, the reader should recall once more that in this chapter I have only provided 'one view of the cathedral'.

It is indeed still thinkable that other, non-economic reasons would be advanced to argue that a harmonisation of e.g. pain and suffering would still be necessary in Europe, for instance to guarantee the minimum level of protection to all European victims. Those who would advance this argument should, however, realise that Europe today does not provide such a minimum protection to accident victims either. Social security is indeed to an important extent not yet harmonised. Also the compensation after industrial accidents or occupational diseases can still be very different between the Member States. If one would therefore argue that a minimum level of protection of accident victims is necessary, it seems more indicated to focus on those areas first instead of pleading for a harmonisation of compensation for non-pecuniary losses.

4 POLICY ASPECTS

4.1 General

The result of applying economic criteria to the question of whether tort law should be harmonised is that there would only be arguments in favour of centralised European rule making (1) if inefficiencies were created by national tort law so that damage could be externalised to other countries or (2) if it could be established that states would attract industry by their lenient tort law standards. The latter is, however, unlikely since states would, on the contrary, be more likely to enact legislation to protect victims of accidents within their own jurisdiction with high standards. However, there might be transaction costs savings if European intervention were able to create legal certainty and achieve full harmonisation. Other arguments, such as the need to create a 'level playing field' or 'the harmonisation of marketing conditions' cannot, at least from an economic perspective, justify centralisation.

Looking more specifically at the Product Liability Directive and comparing this with the criteria for centralisation we can conclude as follows:

1. The EC Product Liability Directive is not able to correct the risk of interstate externalities caused by product damage, if such a risk already exists.
2. There is no empirical evidence of a risk that states could attract manufacturers with lenient product liability legislation (the directive would only apply to manufacturers). On the contrary, there might be a risk of a race for the top, protecting national victims of product-related accidents.

---

[42] See also Hartlief (2002a, 2002b).

3. The Product Liability Directive, given its high reliance on national law, can never lead to a 'levelling of the playing field' or a 'harmonisation of marketing conditions'.
4. The Product Liability Directive, which in fact adds an additional layer of complexity to the labyrinth of conflicting standards of liability, does not lead to uniformity or a lowering of transaction costs (Ackerman 1996, 454).

A similar conclusion could probably also be reached as far as another piece of European tort law is concerned, namely the Environmental Liability Directive.

4.2 Public Choice Considerations

A question which obviously cannot be avoided when inefficiencies are found is whether this can be explained on the basis of public choice theory. Indeed, one notices that many of the harmonisation efforts do not fit into the economic theory of centralisation and would hence, at least from an economic perspective, not be considered as promoting social welfare. If a certain legislative action cannot be said to promote public interest, public choice scholars would ask the question whether the legislation favours special interest groups.[43] Of course, one can generally hold that the lack of transparency at the European level is a highly useful cover for lobbying activities. In fact, the desire to create a European liability regime sometimes simply serves the interests of industry and is the result of lobbying.

Some have argued that the comparative lawyers themselves can be considered to be a lobby group. Harmonisation efforts will undoubtedly serve their interests since harmonisation requires knowledge of the various legal systems that need to be harmonised. A call for harmonisation does undoubtedly create a demand for comparative lawyers and may hence serve their interests.[44]

It is of course also possible that the demand for a unified tort law would come from insurance companies. From their perspective, decentralisation of tort law may impose costs upon them; hence, one could expect that also (liability) insurers would lobby in favour of a harmonisation of tort law.

Finally, in the context of public choice analysis, one should obviously also mention the interests of the European bureaucracy itself. Until 1985 Europe had done relatively little as far as the harmonisation of private law was concerned (because differing legal cultures hampered it). Maybe a European Product Liability Directive, although it did not fulfil the economic criteria for centralisation, might have served the interests of the Brussels bureaucracy to show that Europe could bring about a piece of legislation in an area which is considered important by many lawyers and is moreover very sensitive to public opinion. Hence, the fact that the Commission wanted, for example, a European Product Liability Directive may to some extent also simply have been due to the prestige that this directive, as one of the first in the area of private law, would give the European Commission.

---

[43] For a discussion of harmonisation efforts in Europe from a public choice perspective, see Van den Bergh (1998, 148–51; 2000, 448–51) and Revesz (2001).

[44] See Ogus (1999, 405; 2001, 28–32), as well as Van den Bergh (2000, 449).

4.3 Example: Environmental Liability

We concluded that relatively few economic arguments can be found to justify centralisation in the area of environmental liability. This was only justified by transboundary pollution and even then the question arose whether the same result could not be reached through different, less extensive legal instruments than total harmonisation.

Nevertheless, there seemed to be strong forces striving for a European environmental liability regime, at least for damage to biodiversity. This resulted in the Environmental Liability Directive.[45] To some extent this can still be explained on public interest grounds, since also non-economic, ecological arguments could be advanced, in favour of a minimum quality of restoration for polluted soils. However, public choice scholars have taught that there is always a risk that regulation in fact serves the interests of particular pressure groups.[46]

Indeed, another non-economic reason why the European Union would like to harmonise liability legislation can be found in public choice theory. With respect to environmental standard setting, intensive rent-seeking behaviour by interest groups can be identified. European industries may be confronted at state level by 'green' non-governmental organisations (NGOs), whereas these countervailing powers might have less force in Brussels. Moreover, the lack of transparency in the decision-making process will stimulate European industries to engage in serious lobbying.

The lobbying does not necessarily have to result in lower environmental standards. In particular cases, special interest groups representing industry might, understandably, lobby in favour of harmonisation at a higher level of environmental protection (Esty and Geradin 1997, 303). Interest groups in areas that are already heavily regulated may have incentives to extend their strict (national) regulations to the European level, forcing foreign competitors to follow the same strict regulation to which they already comply. The result is that industry will lobby to erect barriers to entry. In addition, green NGOs will be pleased with this lobby and will obviously support the demand to transfer strict national standards into a European standard.[47] Thus, industries in heavily regulated (and probably polluted) areas can (supported by green NGOs) force their very stringent standards upon their (southern) competitors, although these Member States probably would not need these stringent standards if the policy goal were only one of reaching a uniform level of environmental quality.

Thus it becomes clear that the 'harmonisation of conditions of competition' argument is used to serve the interests of industries in heavily regulated areas by erecting barriers to entry. Hence, environmental law can be used to limit market entry and environmental law is abused to serve private interest goals. This leads to the conclusion that the 'harmonisation of conditions of competition' argument, as presented in European rhetoric, can be problematic, from both the economic and ecological points of view, and in fact serves

---

45 See Directive 2004/35/EC of 21 April 2004 on environmental liability with regard to prevention and remedying of environmental damage. For a comment see the contributions in Betlem and Brans (2006).

46 For a public choice analysis of (de)centralisation of environmental law see Ferejohn (2000).

47 These 'alliances' between environmentalists and domestic producers are also discussed in Vogel (1995, 52–5).

the interests of industrial groups in heavily regulated areas.[48] It can actually be in their interest that 'conditions of competition' are harmonised.

It is not clear yet whether the recent harmonization efforts with respect to environmental liability should be considered as an attempt by interest groups to create barriers to entry. One could still run the risk that industry in Member States with stringent soil sanitation would strive for centralisation, thus creating a barrier to entry for competitors from countries where these strict standards do not yet apply. It is too early to assess whether the desire to create a European environmental liability regime in fact serves the interest of industry. One should, however, always be aware of the fact that the risk, that centralisation may be abused to create barriers to entry, may always appear in any attempt towards centralisation.

5 CONCLUDING REMARKS

Today there is undoubtedly a general trend among academic lawyers in favour of the harmonisation of tort law in Europe (Jansen 2001; Koziol 1996; Magnus 1995; Nieuwenhuis 1998). Symptomatic in this respect are major projects such as those focusing on a European civil code. This chapter has used the economic analysis of law to focus on one specific aspect of the harmonisation debate, the question of whether there should be any harmonisation of tort law at all and, if so, in what areas.

The starting point of economic analysis is seemingly different from the one often heard in the European debate (Ott and Schäfer 2003; Smits 2002b, 2002c, 2002d). Economists do stress that differences as such are not a bad thing at all, provided that those differences also reflect the differing preferences of citizens.[49] If that is the case, the starting point is that these differences should be respected and that they may even contribute to an increased quality of the legal system because legal systems will compete to provide the best legal order to their citizens. Of course, some may argue that it is questionable whether the fact that in Portugal, say, lower amounts are awarded for pain and suffering than in Germany does really reflect the preferences of Portuguese citizens. Even if one does doubt the ability of the national legislator or judge to adequately take into account the preferences of citizens, there is still no reason to assume that Europe would do a better job in that respect. Why would the European bureaucrats in Brussels be better able to know what the preferences of the Portuguese are than the Portuguese would be to find this out for themselves? To assume so is a paternalistic and dangerous argument. Legislation that allows for different national preferences will, moreover, have the advantage that it will lead to competition between legal orders.

However, it was equally indicated that in some cases this basic idea of competition between legal orders may not provide optimal outcomes. The economic literature

---

48 This is not to say that there is no risk of regulatory capture resulting in inefficient standards at the level of the Member States; compare (in the US context) Rose-Ackerman (1992, 166 and 173). However, in Europe, it is especially the untransparent Brussels bureaucracy which is feared from a public choice perspective.

49 Some lawyers also follow this line of reasoning. See e.g. Smits (2000, 43), who presents 'In praise of Diversity'.

makes clear that there may be an argument in favour of harmonisation where transboundary externalities exist, but this does not justify a total harmonisation of tort law. It merely calls for a regulation of transboundary accidents at the centralised level. The other economic argument in favour of harmonisation is the risk of destructive competition, also referred to as the 'race for the bottom'. However, it seems very unlikely that within the European context states will compete in order to attract industry with lenient tort laws. There is no empirical evidence at all that currently European Member States would have engaged in such a race for the bottom with an inefficient tort law. It is much more likely that a race for the top would take place, since states would probably prefer to protect those of their national citizens who might also suffer accidents.

The traditional 'economic' European argument – that harmonisation of the conditions of competition is necessary in order to create a level playing field – was critically discussed and rejected as being wrong. This argument has been used for a long time in Europe. To some extent this was understandable, since the argument for the 'harmonisation of marketing conditions' was necessary to give Europe competencies in specific matters. However, it is very doubtful whether such harmonisation of marketing conditions is desirable, since this could justify a (largely unnecessary) harmonisation of all sorts of legal rules, because all kinds of legislation could arguably have an influence on marketing conditions. The initiatives that Europe has taken so far with respect to tort law have not proven to be a major success. All legal writers agree, for example, that the European Product Liability Directive could never lead to the harmonisation of marketing conditions. Moreover, the European directives generally seem to have the problem that they follow a 'top-down' approach, whereby the European regime is mandatorily imposed upon the Member States, sometimes as an additional layer of protection, such as in the case of the European Product Liability Directive. This should lead to a critical review of the harmonisation efforts undertaken by the European Commission. Unfortunately, the Commission seems only interested in promoting further harmonisation instead of focusing on less (and maybe better) harmonisation.[50]

It is important to stress that from an economic perspective probably the most important reason in favour of centralisation of tort law is the potential for reducing transaction costs. To some extent one can certainly argue that various tort rules in the Member States reflect similar preferences and only differ as a result of differing legal techniques. If it were possible to align rules of tort law that reflect similar preferences, this could certainly be considered a gain. That is precisely the approach chosen in a variety of (mostly privately initiated) academic projects on harmonisation of tort law. In most of these projects the academics involved analyse the existing differences between the various aspects of tort law in the Member States and try to find a common denominator. This approach seems to be more promising than that chosen by the European Commission. That top-down approach of imposing directives on Member States has so far not been very successful. The approach chosen by the academic groups focuses on the search for a *ius commune* and can therefore be called 'bottom-up'. If these groups succeed in showing that some differences are merely of a technical nature and can thus be regarded as pointless incompatibilities, which do not touch upon or relate

50 See Green Paper on liability for defective products (COM (1999) 396 final).

to differing preferences, then this harmonisation approach of searching for a common denominator may well prove to be more successful than the approach chosen by the European Commission so far.

Whether these groups will be successful is obviously difficult to predict. Some have stressed the importance of legal tradition and legal principles. Indeed, from an economic perspective one can easily argue that different legal rules sometimes serve the same purpose and thus could easily have been harmonised. However, in some cases these are so heavily rooted in differing legal cultures and traditions that the costs of harmonisation may be huge, some would argue even prohibitive.[51] From an economic perspective one can obviously merely state that harmonisation based on a potential for the reduction of transaction costs makes sense only if the marginal costs of this harmonisation effort are indeed lower than the marginal benefits of unification.

Economics can provide a few guidelines to these unification groups as far as the topics and methods of harmonisation are concerned.

First, it seems important primarily to focus on those areas of tort law where preferences apparently do not differ. One could think of the choice between a strict liability regime on the one hand and negligence/fault on the other hand. If it could be established that the legal systems largely agree on the area where a strict liability regime should be applied, then one could argue that the differences in form are merely technical and do not reflect varying preferences, so that that would be a good candidate for harmonisation.[52]

The same could be argued, for example, concerning the weighing of interests the judge has to undertake in a negligence case when he has to establish a standard of care for a particular behaviour and when the wrongfulness of the behaviour of the defendant has to be established. If the research showed that, although the wordings and principles are dramatically different, the underlying methodology is similar, harmonisation might be possible.[53] However, the way in which a judge in a particular legal system will fulfil this duty of care may again be strongly linked to differing preferences. Thus it would be possible, to be specific, to indicate that whatever methods judges use to establish negligence in a particular case, it may still be possible that, say, in a medical malpractice case the appropriate care required from a physician in Portugal may well be different from the care required from a physician in Germany.[54] This shows that it may be possible to call for centralisation, but that this centralisation should not necessarily be equated with harmonisation.[55] The previous example shows that it

---

51 That point has especially been made by Legrand (1997, 111).

52 I certainly do not want to argue that there are no differences between the Member States as far as the cases are concerned to which a strict liability rule applies. Some might argue that the differences, say, between France and the United Kingdom in that respect are huge (for an overview, see Koch and Koziol (2002), Van Gerven, Lever and Larouche (2000, 467–687) and Von Bar (2000b, 333–432)). The point is only made that if there were – factual – agreement, say, on the strict liability of the guardian of a dangerous installation, this would mean that preferences on that point do not appear to differ.

53 See on that point generally, Koziol (1998) and for a comparison of the wrongfulness concept in Austria and Germany, Koziol (2001) and Lewisch (2001), as well as Van Dam (2000, 143–50).

54 Comparative research has indicated that this is indeed the case. See Faure and Koziol (2001).

55 This was correctly argued in the context of environmental liability by Arcuri (2001).

would, for example, be possible to centralise the way judges deal with the negligence standard, but this could be combined with a differentiated application of the duty of care in specific cases.[56]

One should probably be very careful to strive for harmonisation in those areas of tort law which are indeed clearly linked to national preferences and values. This is probably the case for the issue of compensation for non-pecuniary losses. Here one should be very careful in calling for harmonisation (Hartlief 2002a). First of all, the benefits of harmonisation in that area should be made clear; second, it is very likely that the costs of harmonisation would be huge; and, third, harmonisation in those cases could lead to a paternalistic measure and to disrespect for the preferences of citizens. Even a call for the need to provide the same minimum protection to all accident victims within Europe can hardly justify such a paternalistic measure.

The future of European tort law at this moment is rather uncertain. At the time of writing it is not known what will happen with this DCFR. Some scholars, more particularly Smits (2002a, 2002b, 2002c) have pleaded in favour of a multi-layered approach whereby European law (thus possibly the DCFR) would merely constitute a 28th option from which potential parties could choose. In this optional approach the DCFR would not be imposed top-down, but could be opted for by interested parties. At this stage it is unknown whether this will be a politically feasible option.

The conclusion at the normative level, however, should not necessarily be that there is no need for any European action at all with respect to tort law.[57] However, the Commission still seems to be stuck in the old jargon of the 'harmonisation of conditions of competition', whereas that seems to be a weak reason for harmonisation. There may be other, non-economic, reasons to justify harmonisation. But then these goals and expectations should be spelled out more specifically. Even those who dream of a European tort law as a political ideal can still benefit from economic analysis. Economics can help to show whether the methods of harmonisation chosen in a particular case can lead to the goals advertised. Moreover, those who blindly follow an unbalanced harmonisation dream should also be aware of the fact that in some cases they may (probably unknowingly) be instruments in the hands of powerful lobby groups who can benefit from harmonisation. In this respect the important lesson from the public choice school, that whenever inefficient regulatory measures are enacted there is usually a special interest group that benefits from this action, should not be forgotten.

---

[56] See, however, Koziol (2001, 33), who argues that a harmonisation effort would not suffice with mere vague notions whereby the normative choices in specific cases would be left to the national legislators or judges. Spier and Haazen (1999, 484) also see this problem where they argue 'the use of standards as a smoke-screen for deep disagreement creates a false consensus'.

[57] Compare Spier and Haazen (1999, 477): 'Nor is convergence or unification of private law ever strictly speaking necessary . . . If we favour convergence of European private law, we deem it simply *desirable*, perhaps highly desirable, but nothing more.' This desirability of the harmonisation of private law in Europe is, however, highly criticised – *inter alia* – by Smits (2001, 73).

REFERENCES

Ackerman, R. (1996), 'Tort law and federalism: whatever happened to devolution?', *Yale Law and Policy Review* (YLPR), 453.
Arcuri, A. (2001), 'Controlling environmental risk in Europe: the complementary role of an EC environmental liability regime', *Tijdschrift voor Milieuschade en Aansprakelijkheidsrecht* (TMA), 37–45.
Bergkamp, L. (2000), 'The White Paper on Environmental Commission's liability: a weak case for an EC strict liability regime', *European Environmental Law Review* (EELR), 105–14.
Betlem, G. and Brans, E. (eds) (2006), *Environmental Liability in the EU: The 2004 Directive Compared with US and Member State Law*, London.
Calabresi, G. and Melamed, D. (1972), 'Property rules, liability rules and inalienability: one view of the cathedral', 86 *Harvard Law Review* (HLR), 1089–1129.
Casella, A. and Frey, B. (1992), 'Federalism and clubs: towards an economic theory of overlapping political jurisdictions', 36 *European Economic Review* (EER), 639–46.
Coase, R.H. (1960), 'The problem of social cost', *Journal of Law and Economics* (JL & Econ), 1–44.
De Smedt, K. (2007), *Environmental Liability in a Federal System: A Law and Economics Analysis*, Antwerp: Intersentia.
Duintjer Tebbens, H. (1986), 'De Europese Richtlijn Produktaansprakelijkheid', *Nederlands Juristenblad* (NJB), 369–74.
Eidenmüller, H., Faust, F., Grigoleit, H-Chr., Jansen, N., Wagner, G. and Zimmermann, R. (2008a), 'Der gemeinsame Referenzrahmen für das europäische Privatrecht. Wertungsfragen und Kodifikationsprobleme', *Juristenzeitung* (JZ), 529–50.
Eidenmüller, H., Faust, F., Grigoleit, H-Chr., Jansen, N., Wagner, G. and Zimmermann, R. (2008b), 'The Common Frame of Reference for European Private Law – policy choices and codification problems', 28 *Oxford Journal of Legal Studies* (OJLS), 659–708.
Elliott, E.D., Ackerman, B. and Millian, J. (1985), 'Towards a theory of statutory evolution: the federalization of environmental law', *Journal of Law, Economics & Organization* (JLEO), 313–40.
Esty, D. (1996), 'Revitalizing environmental federalism', 95 *Michigan Law Review* (MiLR), 570–653.
Esty, D. (1999), 'Economic integration and the environment', in Vig, N. and Axelrod, R. (eds), *The Global Environment: Institutions, Law and Policy*, 190–209.
Esty, D. and Geradin, D. (1997), 'Market access, competitiveness, and harmonization: environmental protection in regional trade agreements', 21 *Harvard Environmental Law Review* (HELR), 265–336.
Esty, D. and Geradin, D. (1998), 'Environmental protection policies and international competitiveness: a conceptual framework', *Journal of World Trade* (JWT), 5–46.
European Group on Tort Law (ed.) (2005), *Principles of European Tort Law: Text and Commentary*, Vienna: Springer.
Faure, M. (2000), 'Product liability and product safety in Europe: harmonisation or differentiation?', 53 *Kyklos*, 467–508.
Faure, M. (2002), 'Productaansprakelijkheid in België en Europa: quo vadis?', in Dirix, E. et al. (eds), *Liber Amicorum Jacques Herbots*, Deurne, 111–30.
Faure, M. (2010), 'Globalization and multi-level governance of environmental harm', in Faure, M. and Van der Walt, A. (eds), *Globalization and Private Law: The Way Forward*, Cheltenham: Edward Elgar, 383–425.
Faure, M. and Betlem, G. (2008), 'Applying national liability law to transboundary pollution: some lessons from Europe and the United States', in Faure, M. and Song, Y. (eds), *China and International Environmental Liability: Legal Remedies for Transboundary Pollution*, Cheltenham: Edward Elgar, 129–91.
Faure, M. and De Smedt, K. (2001), 'Should Europe harmonise environmental liability legislation?', *Environmental Liability* (Env. Liability), 217–37.
Faure, M. and Koziol, H. (eds) (2001), *Cases on Medical Malpractice in a Comparative Perspective*, Vienna: Springer.
Ferejohn, J. (2000), 'The political economy pollution control in a federal system', in Revesz, R., Sands, P. and Stewart, R. (eds), *Environmental Law, the Economy and Sustainable Development*, Cambridge: Cambridge University Press, 96–103.
Frey, B. (1994), 'Direct democracy: politico-economic lessons from Swiss experience', *American Economic Review* (AER), 338–42.
Frey, B. (1996), 'FOCJ: Competitive governments for Europe', *International Review of Law and Economics* (IRLE), 315–27.
Frey, B. and Eichenberger, R. (1996), 'To harmonise or to compete? That's not the question', *Journal of Public Economics* (JPub.E), 335–49.
Hartlief, T. (2002a), 'Comments on Magnus, U., "Towards European Civil Liability"', in Faure, M., Schneider,

H. and Smits, J. (eds), *Towards a European Ius Commune in Legal Education and Research*, Antwerp: Intersentia, 225–30.
Hartlief, T. (2002b), 'Op weg naar een Europees aansprake lijkheidsrecht?', *Tijdschrift voor Privaatrecht* (TPR), 945–53.
Inman, R. and Rubinfeld, D. (1994), 'The EMU and fiscal policy in the New European Community: an issue for economic federalism', 14 *International Review of Law and Economics* (IRLE), 147–61.
Jaffe, A., Peterson, S., Portney, P. and Stavins, R. (1995), 'Environmental regulation and the competitiveness of US manufacturing: what does the evidence tell us?', 33 *Journal of Economic Literature* (JEL), 132–63.
Jansen, N. (2001), 'Auf dem Weg zu einem Europäischen Haftungsrecht', *Zeitschrift für Europäisches Privatrecht* (ZeuP), 30–65.
Jansen, N. (2007), 'Traditionsbegründung im europäischen Privatrecht: Zum Projekt eines "gemeinsamen Referenzrahmens"', in Eger, T. and Schäfer, H.-B. (eds), *Ökonomische Analyse der Europäischen Zivilrechtsentwicklung*, Tübingen: Mohr-Siebeck, 74–110.
Johnston, J.S. (2003), 'The tragedy of centralisation: the political economics of American natural resource federalism', 74 *University of Colorado Law Review* (UCLR), 487–649.
Kimber, C. (1995), 'A comparison of environmental federalism in the United States and the European Union', 54 *Maryland Law Review* (MaLR), 1658–90.
Koch, B.A. and Koziol, H. (eds) (2002), *Unification of Tort Law: Strict Liability*, The Hague/London/New York: Kluwer Law International.
Koziol, H. (1996), 'Das niederländische BW unter der Schweizer Entwurf als Vorbildes für ein künftiges europäisches Schadenersatzrecht', *Zeitschrift für Europäisches Privatrecht* (ZeuP), 587–99.
Koziol, H. (ed.) (1998), *Unification of Tort Law: Wrongfulness*, The Hague/London/New York: Kluwer Law International.
Koziol, H. (2001), 'Ein Europäisches Schadenersatzrecht – Wirklichkeit oder Traum', *Juristiche Blätter* (JBL), 29–38.
Koziol, H. (2008), 'Rechtsvereinheitlichung auf europäischer Ebene aus privatrechtlicher Sicht', in Faure, M.G., Koziol, H. and Puntscher-Riekmann, S. (eds), *Vereintes Europa – Vereinheitliches Recht?*, Vienna: Verlag der Österreichischer Akademie der Wissenschaften, 47–56.
Krämer, L. (1986), *EEC Consumer Law*, Brussels: Story-Scientia, 274–5.
Legrand, P. (1997), 'The impossibility of legal transplants', *Maastricht Journal of European and Comparative Law* (MJECL), 111–24.
Legrand, P. (2008), 'Antivonbar', *Journal of Comparative Law* (JCL), 1(1), 13–39.
Lewisch, P. (2001), 'A comparison of the negligence concept of the German BGB and the Austrian ABGB in an economic perspective', paper presented at the Annual Conference of the European Association of Law and Economics, Vienna, September.
Magnus, U. (1995), 'European perspectives of tort liability', *European Review of Private Law* (ERPL), 427–44.
Magnus, U. (2002), 'Towards European civil liability', in Faure, M., Schneider, H. and Smits, J. (eds), *Towards a European Ius Commune in Legal Education and Research*, Antwerp: Intersentia, 205–24.
Magnus, U. and Fedtke, J. (2001), 'German Report on non-pecuniary loss', in Rogers, H.W.V. (ed.), *Damages for Non-pecuniary Loss in a Comparative Perspective*, 109–28.
Majone, G. (2008), 'Unity in diversity: European integration and the enlargement process', *European Law Review* (ELR), 33, 457–81.
Martin Casals, M. and Solé Feliu, J. (2001), 'Responsabilidad por productas en España y (des)armonizacion Europea', 4 *Revista de responsabilidad civil y seguros*, 1–17.
Mueller, D.C. (1997), 'Federalism and the European Union: a constitutional perspective', 90 *Public Choice* (PC), 255–80.
Nieuwenhuis, J.H. (1998), 'Wat is een onrechtmatige daad? Europese perspectieven', *RMThemis*, 242–8.
Oates, W. and Schwab, R. (1988), 'Economic competition among jurisdictions: efficiency enhancing or distortion inducing?', 35 *Journal of Public Economics* (JPub.E), 333–54.
Ogus, A. (1994), *Regulation: Legal Form and Economic Theory*, Oxford: Clarendon Press.
Ogus, A. (1999), 'Competition between national legal systems: a contribution of economic analysis to comparative law', *International & Comparative Law Quarterly* (ICLQ), 405–18.
Ogus, A. (2001), 'The contribution of economic analysis of law to legal transplant', in Smits, J. (ed.), *The Contribution of Mixed Legal Systems to European Law*, Antwerp: Intersentia, 27–37.
Ott, C. and Schäfer, H.-B. (2003), 'Die Vereinheitlichung des Europäischen Vertragsrechts: Ökonomische Notwendigkeit oder akademisches Interesse?', in Ott, C. and Schäfer, H.-B. (eds), *Vereintheitlichung und Diversität des Zivilrechts in transnationalen Wirtschaftsräumen*, 203–36.
Pelzman, S. and Tideman, T. (1972), 'Local v. national pollution control: note', *American Economic Review* (AER), 959–63.
Repetto, R. (1994), 'Trade and sustainable development', UNEP, *Environment and Trade Series*.

Revesz, R. (1992), 'Rehabilitating interstate competition: rethinking the race for the bottom rationale for federal environmental regulation', *New York University Law Review* (NYULR), 1210–54.
Revesz, R. (1996), 'Federalism and interstate environmental externalities', *University of Pennsylvania Law Review* (UPLR), 2341–416.
Revesz, R. (1997), 'The race for the bottom and federal environmental regulation: a response to critics', *Minnesota Law Review* (MinLR), 535–64.
Revesz, R. (2000a), 'Environmental regulation in federal systems', in Somsen, H. (ed.), *Yearbook of European Environmental Law* (YEEL), Oxford: Oxford University Press, 1–35.
Revesz, R. (2000b), 'Federalism and environmental regulation: an overview', in Revesz, R., Sands, P. and Stewart, R. (eds), *Environmental Law: The Economy and Sustainable Development*, Cambridge: Cambridge University Press, 37–79.
Revesz, R. (2001), 'Federalism and environmental regulation: a public choice analysis', *Harvard Law Review* (HLR), 553–641.
Rogers, H.W.V. (ed.) (2001), *Damages for Non-Pecuniary Loss in a Comparative Perspective*, Vienna: Springer.
Rose-Ackerman, S. (1992), *Rethinking the Progressive Agenda: the Reform of the American Regulatory State*, New York: Free Press.
Rose-Ackerman, S. (1995), *Controlling Environmental Policy: The Limits of Public Law in Germany and the United States*, New Haven, CT: Yale University Press.
Schulze, R., Von Bar, C. and Schulte-Mölke, H. (eds) (2008), *Der Akademische Entzurf für einen gemeinsamen Referenzrahmen: Kontroversen und Perspektiven*, Tübingen: Mohr-Siebeck.
Schwartz, G. (1996), 'Considering the proper federal role in American tort law', 38 *Arizona Law Review* (ALR), 924–5.
Smits, J. (2000), *The Good Samaritan in European Private Law*, Deventer.
Smits, J.M. (2001), 'Waarom harmonisering van het contractenrecht (via beginselen) onwenselijk is', *Contracteren*, 73–4.
Smits, J. (2002a), 'The future of European contract law: on diversity and the temptation of elegance', in Faure, M., Smits, J. and Schneider, H. (eds), *Towards a European Ius Commune in Legal Education and Research*, Antwerp: Intersentia, 239–56.
Smits, J. (2002b), 'On successful legal transplants in a future Ius Commune Europaeum', in Harding, A. and Örücü, E. (eds), *Comparative Law in the 21st Century*, London, 137–54.
Smits, J. (2002c), 'Toward a multi-layered contract law for Europe', in Grundman, S. and Stuyck, J. (eds), *An Academic Green Paper on European Contract Law*, The Hague, 387–98.
Smits, J. (2002d), 'The harmonisation of private law in Europe: some insights from evolutionary theory', 31 *Georgia Journal of International and Comparative Law* (GJICL), 79–99.
Spier, J. and Haazen, O.A. (1999), 'The European Group on Tort Law ("Tilburg Group") and European principles of tort law', *Zeitschrift für Europäisches Privatrecht* (ZeuP), 469–93.
Storm, P. (1985), 'Een gebrekkig product', *Maandblad voor Ondernemingsrecht* (TVVS), 241–6.
Tiebout, C.M. (1956), 'A pure theory of local expenditures', *Journal of Political Economy* (JPE), 415–24.
Trebilcock, M. and Howse, R. (1999), 'Trade liberalization and regulatory diversity: reconciling competitive markets with competitive politics', 6 *European Journal of Law and Economics* (EJLE), 21 and 30.
Van Dam, C.C. (2000), *Aansprakelijkheidsrecht: Een grensoverschrijdend handboek*, The Hague.
Van Dam, C. (2006), *European Tort Law*, Oxford: Oxford University Press.
Van Dam, C. (2007), 'European tort law and the many cultures of Europe', in Wilhelmsson, T. et al. (eds), *Private Law and the Many Cultures of Europe*, Alphen aan den Rijn: Kluwer Law International, 57–80.
Van den Bergh, R. (1998), 'Subsidiarity as an economic demarcation principle and the emergence of European private law', 5 *Maastricht Journal of European and Comparative Law* (MJECL), 129–52.
Van den Bergh, R. (1999), 'Economics in a legal strait-jacket: the difficult reception of economic analysis in European law', paper presented at the workshop Empirical Research and Legal Realism: Setting the Agenda, Haifa, 6–9 June.
Van den Bergh, R. (2000), 'Towards an institutional legal framework for regulatory competition in Europe', 53 *Kyklos*, 435–66.
Van den Bergh, R. (2007a), 'The uneasy case for harmonising consumer law', in Heine, K. and Kerber, W. (eds), *Zentralität und Dezentralität von Regulierung in Europa: Schriften zu Ordnungsfragen der Wirtschaft*, Stuttgart, 186–95.
Van den Bergh, R. and Visscher, L. (2006), 'The principles of European tort law: the right path to harmonisation?', 14 *European Review of Private Law* (ERPL), 511–43.
Van den Bergh, R., Faure, M. and Lefevere, J. (1996), 'The subsidiarity principle in European environmental law: an economic analysis', in Eide, E. and Van den Bergh, R. (eds), *Law and Economics of the Environment*, Oslo: Juridisc Forlag, 121–66.
Van Gerven, W., Lever, J. and Larouche, P. (2000), *Cases, Materials and Texts on National, Supranational and International Tort Law*, Oxford: Hart Publishing.

Van Gerven, W., Lever, J., Larouche, P., von Bar, Ch. and Viney, G. (1998), *Cases, Materials and Texts on National, Supranational and International Tort Law: Scope of Protection*, Oxford: Hart Publishing.
Van Wassenaer van Catwijck, A.J.O. (1986), 'Produktaansprakelijkheid', in *Serie Praktijkhandleidingen*, Zwolle, 81.
Vogel, D. (1995), *Trading Up: Consumer and Environmental Regulation in the Global Economy*, Cambridge, MA: Harvard University Press.
Von Bar, C. (2000a), 'Konturen des Delikt-rechtskonzept der Study Group on a European Civil Code', *Zeitschrift für Europäisches Privatrecht* (ZeuP), 515–32.
Von Bar, C. (2000b), *The Common European Law of Torts*, vol. II, Oxford: Oxford University Press.
Von Bar, C., Clive, E. and Schulte-Nölke, H. (eds) (2008), *Principles, Definitions and Model Rules of European Private Law: Draft Common Frame of Reference (DCFR)*, Sellier: Munich.
Widmer, P. (1999), 'Die Vereinheitlichung des Europäischen Schaden-ersatzrechts aus der Sicht eines Kontinental Europäers', *Revue Hellénique de Droit International* (RHDI), 52, 99.
Wininger, B. (2001), 'L'architecture de l'Avant-projet de loi sur la responsabilité civile', *Revue de Droit Suisse* (RDS), 299–326.
Xing, Y. and Kolstad, C.D. (1995), 'Do lax environmental regulations attract foreign investment?', 16-95 Working Paper in Economics, University of California.

10 Private law II: contract

*Fernando Gomez**

1 INTRODUCTION

Under the heading "European private law" very different phenomena are grouped together. One may use the term to refer to the emergence and affirmation, mostly in the last couple of decades, of an important set of legal rules created by European institutions that would belong to what most would characterize as private law in the ordinary sense of the term in most legal systems. We find EU legislative action in areas of company law (probably the first to be set in motion), tort law (product liability, environmental liability, some areas of liability insurance), contract law (consumers' rights and protection in multiple kinds of contractual transaction between consumers and firms), IP (copyright and related rights, trademarks and, to a lesser extent, patents), unfair competition law (advertising, commercial practices of firms *vis-à-vis* consumers) and also in private international law (the important Rome I and Rome II regulations, for instance).

The bulk of these initiatives – though not all – have been undertaken under the umbrella of common market powers and policies of the EU. This would come as no surprise, because among the fundamental reasons for the existence of the European Union, and among the major sources of policies and activities, the establishment and implementation of an open common European market is for sure one of them.[1] The notion of what constitutes the internal market makes it almost self-evident the existence of a close link between this goal and source of policies and private law rules. The concept of the internal market is stated in art. 26 of the Treaty on the Functioning of the European Union (former art. 14 of the EC Treaty), according to which:

> 1. The Union shall adopt measures with the aim of establishing or ensuring the functioning of the internal market, in accordance with the relevant provisions of the Treaties.
> 2. The internal market shall comprise an area without internal frontiers in which the free movement of goods, persons, services and capital is ensured in accordance with the provisions of the Treaties.

One may also use the term European private law to label – perhaps a bit loosely – the diverse range of efforts, initiatives, networks and groups that have flourished within the European legal academic community in recent years in order to promote the study and further the analysis of private law rules, and specially in contract law and contract-related

* I am grateful to participants at a Workshop in the University of Hamburg for their comments, to the Spanish Ministry of Innovation and Science for financial support, and to Marian Gili and Laura Alascio for excellent research assistantship.

[1] See, for the theoretical and empirical importance of common market policies in the EU, Alberto ALESINA, Ignazio ANGELONI, and Ludger SCHUKNECHT, "What does the European Union Do?," 123 *Public Choice* (2005), p. 275.

consumer law, in the European context, both EU-originated rules, and national rules of the Member States.[2] Some, or even most of these groups, also advocate for an enhanced level of harmonization and uniformity of core areas of private law, and more specifically, contract law, among European legal systems, even though the core function of all those efforts and initiatives has been essentially academic in spirit.

I will not deal further with the two notions of European private law just described. Although one could – and maybe even justly so – criticize certain normative content or technical decisions of the EU lawmakers in certain directives, or even challenge the opportunity or the legal basis in EU constitutional law of some private law rules adopted by the EU, I take – or assume, at least – both notions to be fundamentally sound in inspiration, and positive in effects. In any case, apparently they are not at this moment seriously or widely questioned either in theoretical or in practical terms.

The notion of European contract law, though, has a more ambitious – even menacing, to some – dimension: a trend towards increased – from its current levels, already the product of decades of EU legislative activity in promoting rules that approximate legal systems – harmonization of contract law[3] across European legal systems, eventually leading to a true and perfect unification in the final stage of the process.

The most recent and significant milestone in this trend is the DCFR. The Principles, Definitions and Model Rules of European Private Law, known as the Draft Common Frame of Reference (DCFR), constitute the impressive output of an important academic and legal endeavour in the field of private law and, in particular, of contract law,[4] in the European context. The DCFR is not easy to characterize. It is intended to be, its name proclaims, a frame of reference for thinking, legislating and applying private law. It is also meant to be a toolbox, as the European Commission has often – for obvious reasons of political caution – labelled it. In fact, in the DCFR there are probably many – and not all of them mutually compatible – goals to be pursued, and many functions that it is forced to perform.

Although largely academic in inspiration and spirit, and almost entirely in its manufacture, the DCFR is not the typical academic product: it is not a commentary, treatise,

---

[2] See, for a detailed summary of all those initiatives and processes, Francisco J. INFANTE RUIZ, "Entre lo político y lo académico: un Common Frame of Reference de derecho privado europeo," *InDret* (2008), available at www.indret.com, with many detailed references. For the most recent developments, see Walter DORALT, "Strukturelle Schwächen in der Europäisierung des Privatrechts – Eine Prozessanalyse der jüngeren Entwicklungen," Max Planck Private Law Research Paper No. 10/17 (2010).

[3] Despite the frequent use of the term "private law" in this chapter, harmonization efforts and proposals do not affect, or only in a narrow way, some of the major areas of private law, such as property – with the exception of those sub-areas more closely linked to contracts, such as security interests as rights *in rem* – family, and wills, trusts, and estates. In fact, EU harmonization of private law is most directly associated with contract law and, to a lesser extent, with tort law.

[4] Although the DFCR covers ground beyond contract law, and emphatically defends the choice of broad coverage (see pp. 23 and following of the Introduction to the DCFR, Outline Edition), the fact is that both quantitatively and qualitatively the bulk of the DCFR is contract law. For the idea that the contract law portion of the DCFR does not need the remainder of the DCFR content, see Stefan GRUNDMANN, "Grand European *Code Napoléon* or Concise Uniform Contract Law? Defining the Scope of a Common Frame of Reference," in Alessandro Somma (ed.), *The Politics of the Draft Common Frame of Reference*, Wolters Kluwer Law&Business (2009), p. 22.

collection of essays or papers devoted to European Private law. It is a body of proposed model rules, accompanied by a set of standard terms, or definitions, to facilitate its comprehension, use and application. Rules, with or without the addition of "model," are intended to eventually govern real-world behaviour of individuals or firms, either directly, as an immediate source of legal rules, or indirectly, by the influence they can exert upon real-world lawmakers in the drafting of rules that will directly govern the behaviour of economic agents in society. At least the indirect regulatory role through the EU or national law-makers is explicit in the DCFR.[5]

In addition, the European Commission appears to have taken very seriously the importance of the DCFR not only as a toolbox but also as the basis of legislative action at the EU level that would result in some degree of harmonization of the current legal diversity in private law across Member States. Although the exact features and scope of that action are still undecided, the Commission has established an Expert Group[6] to work over the DCFR in order to produce a streamlined text, and has launched a consultation concerning the possible alternative ways in which such text could be used.[7]

The phenomenon of European harmonization of private law, and more specifically, contract law, has attracted the attention of those interested in the economic basis and the economic effects of lawmaking, and has already been extensively analyzed from an economic perspective.[8] This chapter does not purport to offer a complete and exhaustive

---

[5] See Hugh BEALE, "The Future of the Common Frame of Reference," *European Review of Contract Law* (2007), p. 260.

[6] Commission Decision of 26 April 2010 (2010/233/EU) setting up the Expert Group on a Common Frame of Reference in the area of European Contract Law (OJ L 105, 27.4.2010). It should be noted that I am a member of that Expert Group, although the opinions expressed in this chapter are strictly individual, and unrelated to the membership in that Group, and thus not necessarily shared by the other group members, or by the European Commission.

[7] See Green Paper from the European Commission on policy options for progress towards a European Contract Law for consumers and businesses, of 1 July 2010 (COM (2010) 348 final). The policy options spelled out in the Green Paper are the following: (a) the publication on the web of non-binding model contract rules which could be used in the Single Market; (b) a toolbox for current and future EU lawmakers; (c) a Contract Law Commission Recommendation that would call on EU Member States to include the European contract law instrument into their national legal systems; (d) an optional European Contract Law instrument, which could be freely chosen by consumers and businesses in their contractual relations as an alternative to the existing national contract laws for cross-border contracts, or also for domestic contracts; (e) harmonization of national contract laws by means of an EU Directive; (f) full harmonization of national contract laws by means of an EU Regulation; (g) the creation of a full-fledged European Civil Code, replacing all national rules on contracts.

[8] See Gerhard WAGNER, "The Economics of Harmonization: the Case of Contract Law," 39 *Common Market Law Review* (2002), p. 995; Michael FAURE, "How Law and Economics May Contribute to the Harmonization of Tort Law in Europe," in Reinhard ZIMMERMANN (ed.), *Grundstrukturen des Europäischen Deliktsrechts*, Nomos Verlagsgesellschaft (2003), p. 31; Helmut WAGNER, "Economic Analysis of Cross-Border Legal Uncertainty – The Example of the European Union," in Jan Smits (ed.), *The Need for a European Contract Law: Empirical and Legal Perspectives*, Europa Law Publishing (2005), p. 27; Roger VAN DEN BERGH and Louis VISSCHER, "The Principles of Tort Law: The Right Path to Harmonization?," *European Review of Private Law* (2006), p. 511; Nuno GAROUPA and Anthony OGUS, "A Strategic Interpretation of Legal Transplants," 35 *Journal of Legal Studies* (2006), p. 339; Wolfgang KERBER and Stefan GRUNDMANN, "An Optional European Contract Law Code: Advantages and Disadvantages," 21 *European Journal of Law and Economics*

economic analysis of all dimenions involved in the process of building a European contract law, or the outcome of such a process. It does not even attempt to present a comprehensive survey of the economic dimensions or factors that play an important role in evaluating harmonization of European private law. This chapter simply aims to present the economic dimensions that seem to be particularly relevant for assessing the current harmonization of European contract law, and to evaluate its likely effects, relating it to the existing literature – and criticisms – of an economic orientation, and with the help of my previous contributions on these matters.

The structure of this chapter will be as follows. Section 2 will discuss some of the major economic arguments raised against legal harmonization processes based on conscious coordination of legal orders, or imposed by political mandates at higher territorial levels of lawmaking, two dimensions that can cogently be considered to be taking place in the current EU harmonization exercise, highlighting some of their weaknesses as applied to European contract law. Section 3 will examine how the European harmonization process can be characterized, in terms of its lawmaking, as essentially amounting to re-codification, and the economic disadvantages that may arise from that characterization, in spite of the benefits that could also evolve. Section 4 will present the shortcomings of the current European harmonization of Contract law concerning the lack of adequate recognition of the importance of a clear theoretical starting point for the behavior of the agents subject to contract law. Section 5 addresses a crucial issue of the entire process from an economic perspective, namely, what are the desirable substantive rules, provided laws should be harmonized across legal systems, while not being built from scratch, but over pre-existing national, and eventually EU, rules. Section 6 takes up a problem closely connected to the one just described. In the European process, it is fiercely debated whether harmonized rules should entirely replace, set a floor to, or perfectly co-exist with the national rules that predated harmonized ones. This is the theoretical debate underlying the controversies about maximum and minimum harmonization.[9] This section

(2006), p. 215; Helmut WAGNER, "Costs of Legal Uncertainty: Is Harmonization of Law a Good Solution?," Working Paper, University of Hagen Department of Economics (2007); Fernando GOMEZ, "The Harmonization of Contract Law through European Rules: A Law and Economics Perspective," *European Review of Contract Law* (2008), p. 89; Filomena CHIRICO, "The Function of European Contract Law: An Economic Analysis," Working Paper, Tilburg Institute of Law and Economics (2008); Willem H. VAN BOOM, "Harmonizing Tort Law: A Comparative Tort Law and Economic Analysis," Rotterdam Institute of Private Law, Working Paper Series, available at www.ssrn.com; Francesco PARISI and Vincy FON, *The Economics of Lawmaking*, Oxford University Press (2009), p. 51; Fernando GOMEZ, "The Empirical Missing Links in the Draft Common Frame of Reference," in Cafaggi and Micklitz (eds), *European Private Law After the Common Frame of Reference*, Edward Elgar (2009), p. 101; the different contributions on the content of the DCFR in Gerhard WAGNER (ed.), *The Common Frame of Reference: A View from Law and Economics*, Sellier (2009), and in Filomena CHIRICO and Pierre LAROUCHE, *Economic Analysis of the DCFR*, Sellier (2009); Fernando GOMEZ, "Some Law and Economics of Harmonizing Private Law," in Hartkamp et al. (eds), *Towards a European Civil Code*, 4th edn, Kluwer Law International (2010), p. 401; Fernando GOMEZ, "The Economics of Harmonized Law-Making in Private Law: Mechanisms, Modes and Standards," in Brownsword et al. (eds), *Foundations of European Private Law*, Hart Publishing (2011).

9 See, below, text and note 57 for references on the current controversy surrounding the maximum harmonization character of the Commission's Proposal on a Directive on consumer rights.

provides a summary of the results of a formal economic inquiry into the matter.[10] Section 7 briefly concludes.

2 SOME ECONOMIC CRITICISMS OF THE EUROPEAN HARMONIZATION PROCESS IN CONTRACT LAW: AN UNNECESSARY AND UNDESIRABLE PROCESS

This section will not re-examine many of the criticisms that have been raised with regard to harmonization of contract law in Europe understood as a conscious process of political adoption of some EU-wide body of rules in this area. Many of them have been offered from the viewpoint of law and economics, although critical views have also been expressed from other perspectives while bearing in mind very different considerations to economic efficiency.[11]

I have discussed several benefits and costs of the harmonization of European contract law elsewhere,[12] so I will not develop a broad and comprehensive presentation of potential disadvantages here.

This section merely aims to present in a different light what I take to be the two major critical positions, from an economic standpoint, over the current process of harmonization of contract law in Europe, namely that the EU process under way is substantially unnecessary in view of its economic effects, on the one hand, and that it is essentially undesirable, on the other, for its implications and effects. These criticisms are not as forceful as one may imagine at first blush, both on theoretical and on empirical grounds.

This view, however, should not imply that the ongoing harmonization exercise of contract law in Europe is flawless, a kind of admirable exercise that should by all means succeed. I remain highly skeptical about the ultimate soundness of the process, and about the good that may result from its most probable outcome, but I think it pays to clarify the real force of some of the objections thrown upon it. Actually, the next section will expand on some of the most critical dimensions of the European harmonization process in contract law.

The main thrust of the argument holding that the harmonization process is unnecessary has two components. The first one is that the transaction costs raised by legal diversity and fragmentation in Europe are not too significant or, at least, are not as significant as the pro-harmonization rhetoric, and the mantras concerning the obstacles to

---

10 Fernando GOMEZ and Juanjo GANUZA, "Optimal Standards for European Consumer Law: Maximum Harmonization, Minimum Harmonization, and Coexistence of Standards," Working Paper, UPF Department of Economics and Business (2010).

11 See, from social justice and other perspectives, the contributions in Alessandro Somma (ed.), *The Politics of the Draft Common Frame of Reference*, Wolters Kluwer Law&Business (2009).

12 See Fernando GOMEZ, "The Harmonization of Contract Law through European Rules: A Law and Economics Perspective," *European Review of Contract Law* (2008), p. 89; Fernando GOMEZ, "Some Law and Economics of European Private Law Harmonization," in Edwin Hondius et al. (eds) *Towards a European Civil Code*, 4th ed., Kluwer Law International (2010).

the European single market, may suggest. Some critics of the harmonization process in contract law point out that there is little or no evidence of the importance of the costs of legal diversity for active cross-border trade,[13] and even if there may be some costs associated with diversity, economic agents can overcome the barriers at reasonable cost.[14] This leads to a – shared by many – second component of the superfluity critique, namely that the rules of private international law and choice of law – now exemplified in Europe by the Rome I Regulation, and earlier by the Rome Convention – are able to carry the weight in removing or weakening the disruptions to international exchanges and interactions that may be caused by legal diversity.[15]

Goods, services, capital, and also persons move across national borders, in Europe as elsewhere, typically through economic interactions that are not free from the reach of legal rules and regulations. Cross-border transactions involving the provision of goods and services, and the investment of capital, are governed by the laws and regulations contained in the different national legal orders involved. For sure, the fragmentation and disparity of legal systems can be, to some extent, alleviated through adequate choice of law rules that may determine the application to the transaction at hand of the rules of a single legal order, or at least determine which subsets of rules of different legal orders will be governing the transaction.

But even the most intelligently designed rules on choice of law are unable to remove all the obstacles and transaction costs that legal fragmentation may erect in the way of cross-border trade and unified markets. It is clear, however, that choice of legal order by the parties to the transaction is not always to be expected, and cannot provide in all circumstances the desired outcome. There are, undoubtedly – natural or man-made – costs linked to that choice that may sometimes – even often – be high enough to prevent adequate choice and the positive consequences from it.

One source of such costs may be that, in the production and distribution of goods and services, the relevant choice of action for firms frequently has to be made before any anticipated choice of legal order by the parties to the transaction can effectively be made, let alone the outcome of such choice can be made known to the firm. This scenario is particularly likely with respect to goods and services produced for mass consumer markets, in which safety, quality, and other features of the product or service are subject to legal and regulatory standards which cannot be reasonably tailored to the possibly divergent requirements of the various legal orders that may be involved, when prospective buyers that can profitably be served by the firm are located in different jurisdictions, and the outcome of the choice of law cannot be confidently anticipated by the producer. Sometimes, it is possible to defer to a later stage production decisions that are affected by legal rules and regulations, such as packaging (contents, language, information to

---

13 Roger VAN DEN BERGH and Louis VISSCHER, "The Principles of Tort Law: The Right Path to Harmonization?," *European Review of Private Law* (2006), pp. 514–15.

14 Gerhard WAGNER, "The Economics of Harmonization: the Case of Contract Law," 39 *Common Market Law Review* (2002), p. 1014.

15 The potential and effectiveness of choice of law rules is emphasized by Giesela RÜHL, "International Transactions: Plurality of Law, and Constitutional Uncertainty: Conflicts of Laws Revisited," Working Paper, Humboldt University, Berlin (2009); Eirin O' HARA and Larry RIBSTEIN, *The Law Market*, Oxford University Press (2009).

be included), which can be undertaken locally in each national market, but usually at a cost. For other dimensions of goods and services, this possibility may simply be technologically unfeasible or economically prohibitive.

Another source of such costs hindering effective choice of law is the lack of information by buyers, and specially consumers, who will be at best ill-informed about the content, let alone the likely advantages for them, of alternative legal or regulatory standards in other foreign legal orders. The incentives to learn and become informed are commonly very weak, particularly in one-shot transactions, and often the reputation of the foreign producer of goods and services will not suffice to dispel the doubts that many consumers may reasonably have about the standards in a different legal system. Moreover, in the field of consumer markets, mistakenly or not, existing EU legal rules severely restrict the choice of governing law, and substantially subject the transaction to the law of the home country of the consumer in a way that is hard to modify.[16]

From the previous analysis, it seems highly unlikely that, given these costs and constraints for effective choice, choice of law rules, even the most efficient ones that could be imagined, would be able to eliminate the transaction costs arising from legal diversity. Consequently, parties intending to transact across national borders (firms willing to serve several national markets; consumers willing to be served by sellers in foreign countries, who may be hesitant to be subject to a foreign law) will face significant costs.

As to the empirical relevance of those costs, it is true that there is not an overwhelming body of evidence on the actual impact and magnitude of the costs of legal diversity for cross-border activities and trade. The study commissioned by the EU on the matter was indicative of the relevance, but not totally conclusive about the magnitude of costs at stake, and the same would be a good characterization of other surveys.[17]

There is some important evidence, however, that cannot be discarded as providing clear illustration, to say the least, of the importance of legal diversity as a source of transaction costs. Clermont and Eisenberg[18] convincingly show how foreign plaintiffs need to present stronger cases to win in US courts. And, more directly relevant to the European context, den Butter and Mosch[19] find in an empirical study that similarity of legal systems may be able to produce roughly 50–80 percent more cross-border trade, using data of 25 OECD countries. Most recently, Turrini and van Ypersele[20] estimate that legal similarity can increase trade among OECD countries by up to 65 percent, controlling for transportation costs, common culture and language, and similar factors.

In sum, transaction costs from legal fragmentation do not seem to be so negligible (in fact, probably they are likely to be not negligible at all, both for theoretical and for

---

[16] See art. 6 of EC Regulation of 17 June 2008, on the law applicable to contractual obligations (Rome I Regulation).

[17] See Stefan Vogenauer and Stephen Weatherill, *The Harmonisation of European Contract Law: Implications for European Private Laws, Business and Legal Practice*, Hart Publishing (2006).

[18] See Kevin Clermont and Theodor Eisenberg, "Xenophilia in American Courts," 109 *Harvard Law Review* (1996), p. 1120.

[19] See Frank den Butter and Robert Mosch, "Trade, Trust, and Transaction Costs," Tinbergen Institute Working Paper No. 2003-082/3 (2003).

[20] See Alessandro Turrini and Tanguy van Ypersele, "Legal Costs as Barriers to Trade," Center for Economic Policy Research Discussion Paper Series, No. 5751 (2006), p. 20.

empirical reasons), and choice of law rule, however helpful, cannot carry the weight to reduce them significantly.[21] Thus, the basis for the argument of harmonization being unnecessary may well not be as strong as it seemed, although it is true that it would be naïve to think that reduction of legal disparity, helpful as it may be, will be a magical solution for barriers to cross-border trade, since many other factors would persist, making those transaction costs relatively high.[22] But it would be a question of assessing the marginal benefits – the reduction, even if not dramatic, in transaction costs – with respect to the marginal costs of the harmonization.

The undesirability argument essentially emphasizes the serious disadvantages of harmonization as a stifling and paralyzing phenomenon, especially when it is imposed by superior political fiat that wants to impose uniformity over diversity, but also when countries play cooperative coordination games trying to reduce disparities across legal systems and unifying legal solutions for a given area of the law. These features characterize the EU-sponsored process in contract law, which contains collaborative inputs from Member States, and which may end up being adopted at the EU level, and thus, to a greater or lesser extent, imposed upon the national legal orders.

According to the view that bringing together the existing content of legal rules across countries seriously stifles learning and experimentation by lawmakers and legal systems, harmonization would reduce, and even suffocate, the sources of improving the efficiency of existing legal solutions.[23] Harmonization would also stifle competition among legal systems, and thus destroy the environment best conducive to efficient legal outcomes, which is that of healthy competition by lawmakers in order to better tailor rules to the preferences of the "clients" of the rules.[24]

---

21 See, for an argument about the importance of legal diversity for transaction costs in cross-border trade, from a legal perspective, Stefan LEIBLE, "Was tun mit dem Gemeinsamen Referenzrahmen für das Europäische Vertragsrecht? – Plädoyer für ein optionales Instrument," *Betriebsberater* (2008), p. 1469.

22 See Gary Low, "The (Ir)Relevance of Harmonization and Legal Diversity to European Contract Law: A Perspective from Psychology," *European Review of Private Law* (2010), p. 288, with arguments from experimental psychology and behavioral economics, emphasizing the relative unimportance of legal diversity in this domain.

23 See Larry RIBSTEIN and Bruce KOBAYASHI, "An Economic Analysis of Uniform State Laws," 25 *Journal of Legal Studies* (1996), pp. 140–41; Anthony OGUS, "Competition between National Legal Systems: A Contribution of Economic Analysis to Comparative Law," 48 *International and Comparative Law Quarterly* (1999), p. 415; Helmut WAGNER, "Economic Analysis of Cross-Border Legal Uncertainty – The Example of the European Union," in Jan SMITS (ed.), *The Need for a European Contract Law: Empirical and Legal Perspectives*, Europa Law Publishing (2005), p. 38; Roger VAN DEN BERGH and Louis VISSCHER, "The Principles of Tort Law: The Right Path to Harmonization?," *European Review of Private Law* (2006), p. 517; Helmut WAGNER, "Costs of Legal Uncertainty: Is Harmonization of Law a Good Solution?," Working Paper, University of Hagen Department of Economics (2007), p. 5; Giesela RÜHL, "International Transactions: Plurality of Law, and Constitutional Uncertainty: Conflicts of Laws Revisited," Working Paper, Humboldt University, Berlin (2009), p. 14.

24 See Roger VAN DEN BERGH, "Towards an Institutional Legal Framework for Regulatory Competition in Europe," 53 *Kyklos* (2000), p. 435; Michael FAURE, "How Law and Economics May Contribute to the Harmonization of Tort Law in Europe," in Reinhard ZIMMERMANN (ed.), *Grundstrukturen des Europäischen Deliktsrechts*, Nomos Verlagsgesellschaft (2003), pp. 47–9; Roger VAN DEN BERGH and Louis VISSCHER, "The Principles of Tort Law: The Right Path to

Both theory and evidence would suggest, at least in my view, the opportunity to reassess the true weight of these two shortcomings of harmonization. The experimentation argument would emphasize that different jurisdictions with diverse substantive legal rules may reciprocally learn from the failures, the weaknesses, but also from the successes of alternative and different regimes, so that the costs of designing more efficient rules will be reduced. By eliminating diversity, which would be a precondition for comparatively assessing the merits of diverse solutions to the same set of problems, harmonization destroys legal experimentation. The interest of lawmakers in different jurisdictions in learning from the experiences of others is an empirical matter; on a theoretical basis there is no reason to assume among lawmakers widespread and ample intellectual curiosity, and interest in the experiences of foreign systems. In fact, it is reasonable to anticipate that important variation across jurisdictions is very likely to be present in reality regarding this feature of the lawmakers' mindset.

One important weakness in the argument is that it assumes that harmonization will be complete both in terms of substance of the rules and in terms of geographical coverage of the harmonized outcomes. Both assumptions, and especially the second, are very likely not to hold. The fact that, say, EU countries harmonize their substantive legal rules in a given area, such as contract law or consumer law, does not mean that all jurisdictions in the world will follow and will adopt that solution: Asian, North and South American, and other jurisdictions will still offer diverse legal solutions to the same set of problems, and thus learning and experimentation may still be possible. In fact, the level of experimentation may increase, if the harmonization process steers interest towards the consequences in the real world of the harmonized legal outcomes and, thus, draws attention to the importance of that matter. Moreover, even disregarding other solutions in different jurisdictions not affected by harmonization, the assessment and evaluation of the effects of the adopted harmonized rules need not cease after harmonization. Again it is an empirical question, but it may well be the case that the effort to continuously or, at least, periodically estimate the actual effects of the harmonized regime increases over the level that predated the harmonization process.

A related but somewhat different point would be that even if the effects of the rules are assessed with the same intensity, changing the harmonized set of rules will be more costly, and thus the learning process will provide less tangible results after legal harmonization. At an abstract level, there is nothing that should lead us to think that modifying the harmonized rule (an EU rule, for instance) is typically more costly than modifying the set of heterogeneous legal solutions (of the Member States).

Harmonization?," *European Review of Private Law* (2006), pp. 519–20. Some views of what is taken to be desirable and healthy competition in the construction of European contract law do not focus on competing national legal orders, but on competing views and ideas about the form and content of the European rules: Stefan GRUNDMANN, "Grand European Code Napoléon or Concise Uniform Contract Law? Defining the Scope of a Common Frame of Reference," in Somma (ed.), *The Politics of the Draft Common Frame of Reference*, Wolters Kluwer Law&Business (2009), p. 37. These views about a spontaneous process in which uncoordinated and probably selfish actions by the players in the game produce the social good are a form of the classical "invisible hand" type of argument, no doubt widely appealing to economists and economically oriented lawyers given its historical pedigree (Adam Smith, Hayek). For an analysis of the – strict – conditions of the working of these arguments in legal policy matters, see Adrian VERMEULE, "The Invisible Hand in Legal and Political Theory," 96 *Virginia Law Review* (2010), p. 1417.

It may well be true that the former is the case, but it need not be. For instance, if harmonization has taken place through a uniform rule adopted at a higher level of government, there is no reason to think that it will always be more difficult or costly to change a given law at the higher political level than at the lower one. Which one would be more costly depends on many conditions and factors, constitutional and political variables playing a large role presumably. For instance, it is very hard to generally determine whether it is easier to alter a rule in a European directive or in a civil code of a given European country. Some argue, correctly at a general level of analysis, that it is more cumbersome, slow and costly to change the median legislative provision in the European Acquis (due to procedural costs and costs of reaching the required minimum consensus and agreement among Member States to pass the legislation) than to amend the median law in the legal system of a Member State. But civil codes, where one typically finds the core rules of contract law, are not ordinary laws, at least not in terms of the time, effort and cost of modifying them. Civil codes are typically stable bodies of rules, which countries and legal communities change only reluctantly, and not too often, as the experience of most European countries clearly illustrates. The question whether it would be easier to reform them or to amend an existing European rule on these matters may not receive the same answer as with other kinds of rules.

Additionally, the ability and the ease with which legal systems may adapt a rule to new sets of circumstances, and to technological, economic, and social changes, is very important for lawmaking and its impact on social welfare. But this variable – adaptability – is, I would argue, more connected to the mode of making law – rules vs standards, codified rule vs case law – than to the harmonized or heterogeneous content of the rule. As I will argue in Section 3 below, it may speak against harmonization, but in its version of codification or re-codification of more flexible modes of lawmaking.

In sum, it does not seem that the learning and experimentation argument can be deemed decisive against harmonization, either in its coordination or in its politically imposed versions.

Concerning the argument that legal harmonization represses healthy competition among lawmakers and, thus, interferes with a competitive process that would eventually lead to rules that would perfectly match the preferences of their addressees, we are also somewhat more skeptical than most who have looked upon the matter from a law and economics perspective. I will not fully pursue the matter here, but I will try to outline how the theoretical conditions for efficient regulatory competition and the empirical knowledge concerning the efficiency of regulatory "races" across jurisdictions may weaken the persuasive force of the arguments against harmonization based on market competition among lawmakers.

First, the theoretical assumptions that underlie the result of efficient regulatory competition, both in the initial model of mobility of individuals[25] and in the model of mobility of capital,[26] are numerous and very stringent concerning the goals of lawmakers, the

---

[25] See the initial and pioneering contribution on competition in local public goods provision by Charles Tiebout, "A Pure Theory of Local Expenditures," *Journal of Political Economy* (1956), p. 416.

[26] See Wallace Oates, *Fiscal Federalism*, Harcourt Brace Jovanovich (1972).

informational requirements, the policy instruments, the distribution of costs and benefits, and more. It appears unlikely that they will all hold in most real-world circumstances in which jurisdictions and lawmakers adopt measures and rules.[27]

Second, although the empirical evidence concerning whether the presence of competitive sources of rules and regulations does actually benefit or harm the feasibility of efficient outcomes in the affected population is not unidirectional, some of the most recent evidence, at least in the environmental sphere, should lead us to be even more cautious and less cavalier with respect to the possibility of finding actual cases of races to the bottom that, in the end, are hurtful for social welfare. Whereas the earlier literature on regulatory competition in environmental standards did not find conclusive evidence of an erosion of standards due to regulatory competition,[28] some of the recent evidence seems to point in the opposite direction.[29]

Again, none of this is decisive or entirely carries the day in the debate. Indeed, one should look to further evidence to estimate the empirical relevance of the potentially efficient and inefficient consequences of regulatory competition, in the environmental area as well as in other sectors. Also, new theoretical work may uncover some dimensions that may reveal lower levels of costs or of benefits resulting from regulatory competition.[30]

---

[27] For the Tiebout kind of "voting with the feet" – either physically or virtually – models, see Gerhard WAGNER, "The Economics of Harmonization: the Case of Contract Law," 39 *Common Market Law Review* (2002), p. 1007. For fiscal federalism models, see Arik LEVINSON, "Environmental Regulatory Competition: A Status Report and Some New Evidence," 56 *National Tax Journal* (2003), pp. 94–5. In both cases, the contrast between the exacting set of assumptions for regulatory competition leading to optimality and the likely characteristics of the settings in which lawmakers, however well-intention they may be, have to operate casts some doubt on the implementability of optimal results through competition of lawmakers and regulators. For the specific case of corporate law, see Oren BAR-GILL, Michal BARZUZA and Lucian BEBCHUK, "The Market for Corporate Law," *Journal of Institutional and Theoretical Economics* (2006), p. 134; Fernando GOMEZ and Maribel SAEZ, "Competition, Inefficiencies and Dominance in Corporate Law," *Journal of Institutional and Theoretical Economics* (2006), p. 161. Of course, the preceding argument does not imply that regulatory competition is inexistent, or is doomed to failure, simply that it is not very likely to be expected in the real world as a mechanism to implement socially optimal outcomes.

[28] See for instance, John LIST and Shelby GERKING, "Regulatory Federalism and Environmental Protection in the United States," 40 *Journal of Regional Science* (2000), p. 453. Most of this evidence is aptly reviewed, with an eye on the harmonization debate, in Michael FAURE, "How Law and Economics May Contribute to the Harmonization of Tort Law in Europe," in Reinhard ZIMMERMANN (ed.), *Grundstrukturen des Europäischen Deliktsrechts*, Nomos Verlagsgesellschaft (2003), p. 47 and following.

[29] See Randy BECKER and Vernon HENDERSON, "Effects of Air Quality Regulations on Polluting Industries," 108 *Journal of Political Economy* (2000), p. 379; Michael GREENSTONE, "The Impacts of Environmental Regulations on Industrial Activity: Evidence from the 1970 and 1977 Clean Air Act Amendments and Census of Manufactures," 110 *Journal of Political Economy* (2002), p. 1175; Per FREDRIKSSON and Daniel MILLIMET, "Is There a 'California Effect' in US Environmental Policymaking?," 32 *Regional Science and Urban Economics* (2002), p. 101; Arik LEVINSON, "Environmental Regulatory Competition: A Status Report and Some New Evidence," 56 *National Tax Journal* (2003), p. 98. For a survey of the recent evidence, see Arik LEVINSON, "pollution haven hypothesis," in Steven DURLAUF and Lawrence BLUME (eds), *The New Palgrave Dictionary of Economics*, Macmillan (2008).

[30] See Juanjo GANUZA and Fernando GOMEZ, "Soft Negligence and the Strategic Choice of Firm Size," 40 *Journal of Legal Studies* 2 (2011), showing how when potential injurers – for

The presence of this positive evidence of actual inefficiencies should make us less confident that the regulatory competition argument is a winning card against EU harmonization of contract law.

3 EUROPEAN PRIVATE LAW HARMONIZATION AS RE-CODIFICATION

There are, however, some important features of the current process of harmonizing European contract law that should, in my view, raise more concern. I would like to pursue two issues here: first, its likely re-codification effect, and the problems this may bring that one may call epistemic; second, the lack of convincing and conscious starting points in terms of the behavioral regularities of contracting parties.

Let me start with the first question. Regardless of the specific content of the legal rules involved, if one takes a set of model rules such as the ones in the DCFR as the image of what one would expect as the outcome of harmonization, it seems clear that it resembles to a large extent a code of broad legal rules governing central areas of private law such as contract and tort. This codification of contract and tort law, or re-codification, at least for most legal systems which already have civil codes covering these fields, is problematic.

The reason for this attitude does not lie in a belief in the general efficiency of the common law as such, or in faith in any uniform superiority of judge-made law over legislation, or even over codification as the quintessence of systematic and abstract legislative mode of making law. In fact, I remain very skeptical about the soundness of the broad statement that the common law is overall efficient as a set of legal rules – as I would also be unmoved to accept a similar claim about any other legal order at such broad level of analysis.

Even the new and more sophisticated versions of the evolutionary characterization of case law decision making,[31] which model judge-made rules as a continuous process of court decisions over time, in which the biases of the individual judges tend to be reciprocally washed out, and which lead legal rules to approximate, at least probabilistically, more efficient and predictable outcomes, are subject to very stringent assumptions, some of them overtly implausible, taking legal orders and the entire evolution of rules over time in a global fashion, as these models typically do.[32]

---

instance, firms that may cause environmental harm – may choose their levels of assets and may become insolvent, if legal systems use standards of behaviour that adapt to the actual levels of assets, they have less incentive to lower assets, and also cause lower levels of harm, which means that decentralized choice of standards will be less harmful.

[31] Obviously, judge-made law is not synonymous with common law, and statute law is not synonymous with civil law, given that there is a substantial component of statutory law in common law legal orders, and the reverse in civil law systems. With this in mind, however, I will loosely use "common law" and "judge-made" interchangeably in the following discussion, given that I will not be determining the relative efficiency of real-world legal systems belonging to one or the other tradition. On these distinctions, see Nuno GAROUPA and Carlos GOMEZ, "The Syndrome of the Efficiency of the Common Law," University of Illinois College of Law Working Paper (2009).

[32] See Nicola GENNAIOLI and Andrei SHLEIFER, "The Evolution of Common Law," 115 *Journal of Political Economy* (2007), p. 43; Nicola GENNAIOLI and Andrei SHLEIFER, "Overruling and the

I am also equally unconvinced by the literature, essentially of empirical bent, trying to show the superior economic performance of societies that possess a legal system of common law origin, with respect to those originating in the civil law tradition, and especially those founded on the French legal system taken after the legal transformation produced by the codification in the early 19th century.[33]

My somewhat critical stance towards the current process of private law harmonization in the form of codified statutory law covering the core of contract and tort law, is not based, thus, on a general preference for judge-made law over statutes in all areas of the law, nor does it derive from a general distrust of codes as modes of designing and formulating legal rules by legislatures.[34]

The point is more modest in scope and reach. It is simply that contract law is a legal field in which the most important features with respect to lawmaking seem to better correspond to the comparative advantages of judge-made law over statute law, and particularly over abstract rules aspiring to universal, or quasi-universal, application. This point, thus, does not necessarily extend to the entire reach of a legal system. But contracts are highly context-dependent with respect to the desirability of the available legal solutions, and seem to require open-textured conditions of application in order to fit the legal consequence properly with the circumstances present in a given setting. Additionally, the adaptation to new contingencies and to modifications in the environment in which the rules have to determine the behavioural incentives seems to be an important element in the picture.

Rules in contract law should not be fact-invariant, or circumstance-invariant. Continuous and adaptive rule-making that is jointly supplied with adjudication, responsive to the particular circumstances of the economic interaction at hand, seems a more desirable rule-making option than setting uniform binding abstract principles and rules requiring uniform outcomes across diverse economic circumstances and scenarios – or at least with an important element of circumstance invariance – which is linked to the idea of a contract law code.

Instability of the Law," 35 *Journal of Comparative Economics* (2007), p. 35; Giacomo PONZETTO and Patricio FERNANDEZ, "Case Law versus Statute Law: An Evolutionary Comparison," 37 *Journal of Legal Studies* (2008), p. 379. For the implausibility of an overall satisfaction of the conditions for efficient evolution, see Adrian VERMEULE, *Law and the Limits of Reason*, Oxford University Press (2009), p. 118.

[33] See, for a survey of this literature on the economics of legal origins by the pioneers of this field, Rafael LA PORTA, Florencio LOPEZ-DE-SILANES, and Andrei SHLEIFER, "The Economic Consequences of Legal Origins," 46 *Journal of Economic Literature* (2008), p. 285. The debate generated in different disciplines (finance, comparative economics, economic growth, legal history, comparative law) has been more than ample, and even a summary would be beyond the scope of this chapter. For this summary, see Nuno GAROUPA and Carlos GOMEZ, "The Syndrome of the Efficiency of the Common Law," University of Illinois College of Law Working Paper (2009) and references therein.

[34] It can be argued that early 19th-century codification in continental Europe, and especially in France and other countries that followed her lead, was an adaptive response to the conditions of the judiciary and the political preferences of legislatures at that time: see Benito ARRUÑADA and Veneta ANDONOVA, "Judicial Cognition and Market Order," 4 *Review of Law and Economics* (2008), p. 665; Benito ARRUÑADA and Veneta ANDONOVA, "Common Law and Civil Law as Pro-Market Adaptations," 26 *Washington University Journal of Law & Policy* (2008), p. 81.

The latter properties appear to fit substantially better the judge-made law model of producing legal rules. This mode of lawmaking is, even for cognitive and psychological reasons, more contextual and circumstance-attentive than statutory law, is able to better mirror the differences in factual content, is more modest and less intrusive in the use of legal consequences, and is parsimonious, but continuous, in adapting to the emergence and change of factual settings.[35] All these seem attractive features for lawmaking in contract. Even some of the usually identified shortcomings of judge-made lawmaking, such as the inability to cope with sudden and radical changes in circumstances requiring rapid modified legal response,[36] are not so relevant when one thinks of contracts, and even in the contingencies in which swift legal innovation is called for, reliance in judge-made law does not prevent legislatures from stepping in and introducing rapid and abrupt changes when the pace in the change of events so requires.

But wait a minute. Are not the majority of European jurisdictions under regimes of contract law contained precisely in civil codes? Would it then make a difference to replace the old national codes with a new European one? Whatever its appearance, however, contract law in Europe is now *de facto* judge-made law, even in the countries possessing civil codes. One reason for this feature is that the many written rules in contract law in the codes[37] all tend – though not always, for sure – to be old rules, in the sense of rules that have been around for some time, and often for a very long time, in a given legal system. In some countries, they are directly or indirectly from the codification period, and even their substantive content may be traced back to the 19th or 18th century, to *ius commune*, or to Roman law. That gives them, regardless of their textual appearance as more or less precise propositions, a relevant degree of open-textured character, and typically invites or allows more creative (or more aggressive, if one prefers) and less formalistic interpretive strategies, at least in view of the need to take into account the passage of time and the necessary adjustment to new circumstances. New written laws, and particularly a new code, would, with high likelihood, invite a more formalistic and automatic application of the new provisions in the code, with less reflection about the economic circumstances of application.

Of course, my previous argument is simply a conjecture. I do not have theoretical or

---

[35] See Jeffrey RACHLINSKI, "Bottom-Up versus Top-Down Lawmaking," 73 *University of Chicago Law Review* (2006), p. 933; Jeffrey RACHLINSKI and Cynthia FARINA, "Cognitive Psychology and Optimal Government Design," 87 *Cornell Law Review* (2002), p. 549. Even if courts enjoy cognitive and epistemic advantages in settings such as those associated with contracts and torts, and even if they may exploit better than other types of lawmakers some well-known cognitive abilities of the human brain, such as categorization and pattern-recognition, it does not mean that courts are cognitively optimal lawmakers, or that they should always and for all fields of the law be preferred to legislatures for epistemic reasons: Frederick SCHAUER, "Do Cases Make Bad Law?," 73 *University of Chicago Law Review* (2006), p. 883; Adrian VERMEULE, *Law and the Limits of Reason*, Oxford University Press (2009), p. 123 and following.

[36] See Giacomo PONZETTO and Patricio FERNANDEZ, "Case Law versus Statute Law: An Evolutionary Comparison," 37 *Journal of Legal Studies* (2008), p. 403 and following; Adrian Vermeule, *Law and the Limits of Reason*, Oxford University Press (2009), pp. 109–10.

[37] See, for this difference in profusion of legal provisions on contract and tort law in civil codes, and the changes over time, Francesco PARISI and Vincy FON, *The Economics of Lawmaking*, Oxford University Press (2009), p. 25 and following.

empirical proof of the consquences I have anticipated. Moreover, it is true that the creation of common codified rules – abstract, almost by their very nature – may also bring benefits. First, it may update and improve the quality of the capital stock of legal knowledge, bringing some desirable renovation to sets of concepts and rules that are dated in many European legal systems. And this will bring savings in legal learning costs for all agents involved, the contract parties and also those in charge of running the legal system dealing with contracts. The larger geographical and cultural reach of the newly created legal rules may also reinforce the network externality dimension that legal notions and rules undeniably possess.

Despite these potential advantages, and despite the actual level of quality of the new – or newly formulated at least – European rules, I still see re-codification from the European harmonization process leading to a set of more formalistic and less context-dependent legal solutions. As I have tried to argue, this would likely fit worse the needs of legal governance of contracts. And this effect is likely to dominate, or at least to be of substantial importance.

In sum, for reasons linked to the epistemics of lawmaking in what would be the core of harmonization of contract law in Europe, a note of caution about the mode of lawmaking seems important from an economic viewpoint.

4 THE LACK OF CLEAR BEHAVIORAL MODELS ON CONTRACTING BEHAVIOR

The second important issue is of a different nature. Contract law, as any other area of the legal system, tries to affect, in the desired direction, the behavior of those subject to its rules. Thus, in order to give adequate structure and content to a new set of rules at the European level that will have some influence on European citizens and firms, one would need some estimate of how the latter would likely respond to the rules. This estimate, in turn, requires some kind of – at least implicit – model of how firms and individuals behave in the contracting sphere and whether this model seems to be sufficiently confirmed by the available empirical evidence of actual behavior by contracting parties or other agents in a similar situation.

In this respect, the current process, both the EU political inspiration – although this comes as no surprise – and the work of the experts behind the DCFR, seems to be lacking both in terms of a clear expression of the models that will guide the estimates about the likely effects of the newly adopted rules and in the empirical validity of those models.

For instance, a substantial part of the harmonization effort will affect contracts between firms and consumers. Some sort of general understanding of consumer behavior must underlie the choice among different regulatory alternatives (in terms of general or individualized information disclosure, of cooling-off periods, of enforceability of penalty terms, just to mention a few examples).

Neither the Commission documents nor the DCFR contain an explicit or implict reference to the need to take into account some model of behavior expected from the agents subject to the principles and rules. A plausible one, and even a likely one, given the good reception that such accounts of human behavior have encountered among many lawyers on the other side of the Atlantic, is that of behavioral economics, or behavioral law and economics. The approach adopted in the DCFR does not make direct reference to it, nor is it even traceable that it generally underlies the choices made by the drafters, even when paternalist policies are proposed.

The most theoretically oriented (and, as it turns out, also the most empirically oriented) among the drafters of a new body of principles and rules in contract law could have tried to find such a model of human reaction to law and legal institutions in the extensive experimental literature by psychologists and economists showing that human beings, when making choices of very diverse nature and scope, are subject to a number of behavioral biases. In laboratory settings it has been well documented that some phenomena[38] repeatedly appear in observed behavior. People seem to show bounded rationality, that is, limited capacity to acquire and process information, as revealed by the use of cognitive heuristics that can lead to judgment errors, such as hindsight bias (attaching over-dimensioned likelihoods to events that have actually occurred), the availability heuristic (excessive reliance on easily available data) and the representative bias (excessive representativeness of small samples). Other important expressions of bounded rationality experimentally identified have to do with time inconsistency or hyperbolic discounting (too little weight of future and uncertain events) and over-optimism on the part of the agents (underestimation of probabilities of bad outcomes affecting them). There are other sources of departure in observed behavioral responses from the axioms of expected utility in the neoclassical sense, such as loss aversion (the overweight awarded to losses from the starting point as compared with missed opportunities to gain), the endowment effect (valuation of an asset depending on the set of entitlements known by the agent), and the *status quo* bias (reluctance to alter the existing state of the world due to attaching some unidentified intrinsic value to it).

To formulate a model, however, even a model that is evidence-based and not merely speculative, is not enough. To be taken seriously for policy-making, and for legal policy-making even more, this model has to be confirmed by evidence. Even if one takes the magnitude and relevance of the experimental findings relative to those behavioral biases for granted, as I do,[39] there is – at least at the present state of knowledge – no good reason to adopt as a general model of consumer behavior – or contracting behavior more generally – the one based on biased and bounded rationality, instead of the rationality model commonly used by economics and by law and economics.

The reasons for this – at least provisory – skepticism are of a varied nature. First, because it is one thing to identify some bias in a laboratory setting, even repeatedly, but a very different one to test the statistical significance of such bias on real-world markets

---

38 See, among many surveys helpful for legal audiences, Cass Sunstein (ed.), *Behavioral Law and Economics*, Cambridge University Press (2000); Christine JOLLS and Cass SUNSTEIN, "Debiasing through Law," *Journal of Legal Studies* (2006), p. 199.

39 Albeit not all do, even among experimental economists: Elizabeth HOFFMAN et al., "Preferences, Property Rights and Anonymity in Bargaining Games," *Games and Economic Behavior* (1994), p. 346; Charles PLOTT and Kathryn ZEILER, "The Willingness to Pay–Willingness to Accept Gap, the Endowment Effect, Subject Misconceptions and Experimental Procedures for Eliciting Valuations," *American Economic Review* (2005), p. 530.

using rigorous empirical techniques. And even if the empirical tests do not confirm the implications of the rationality assumption, this by itself is not an empirical confirmation of the behavioral account, given that the data may be influenced by some other unobserved variable.

Several empirical studies have tested some of the implications of bounded rationality models of consumer behavior in different settings, and have not found empirical support for the hypothesis based on the pervasive presence of certain behavioral biases in such consumer markets:[40] credit card markets, testing for (i) evidence of highly borrowing consumers paying higher interest rates but enjoying low introductory teaser rates;[41] (ii) the true causal factor behind the correlation between credit card debt and filings for personal bankruptcy;[42] (iii) the factors explaining the "borrow high lend low" puzzle;[43] standard form contracts, and testing for evidence of competitive pressures decreasing quality of non-salient or hidden terms;[44] allocation of shelf space in supermarkets, and testing whether it is a result of manipulation by retailers of cognitive biases afflicting consumers, or else responds to manufacturer margins for different lines of products;[45] choice of calling plans when different pricing options are introduced.[46]

There are, of course, a number of serious empirical studies showing how data on actual behavior in a given consumer market seem to give support to the presence of a certain behavioral bias as an important factor behind observed patterns of market behavior. Among others, such studies include evidence with respect to: (i) credit card markets and hyperbolic discounting;[47] (ii) fitness club markets and time-inconsistent preferences

---

[40] A good summary of such studies, in Joshua WRIGHT, "Behavioral Law and Economics, Paternalism and Consumer Contracts: An Empirical Perspective," *New York University Journal of Law & Liberty* (2007), p. 470.

[41] See Tom BROWN and Lacey PLACHE, "Paying with Plastic: Maybe Not so Crazy," *University of Chicago Law Review* (2006), p. 77, finding no evidence of hyperbolic discounting.

[42] See Todd ZYWICKI, *Bankruptcy and Personal Responsibility: Bankruptcy Law and Policy in the Twenty-First Century*, Yale University Press, (2007).

[43] The puzzle refers to the observation that many people borrow on their credit cards – at high interest rate – while holding positive balances on their accounts – yielding no or little interest: David GROSS, and Nicholas SOULELES, "Do Liquidity Constraints and Interest Rates Matter for Consumer Behavior? Evidence from Credit Card Data," *Quarterly Journal of Economics* (2002), p. 149; Nadia MASSOUD, Anthony SAUNDERS and Barry SCHOLNICK, "Who Makes Credit Card Mistakes?," University of Alberta and NYU Working Paper (2006), find that traditional demographic (age, educational level, country of origin if immigrant) and economic variables (income) seem to be the major factors explaining the puzzle, and not intrinsic human biases.

[44] See Florencia MAROTTA-WURGLER, "What's in a Standard Form Contract: An Empirical Analysis of Software License Agreements," *Journal of Empirical Legal Studies* (2007), p. 677.

[45] See Benjamin KLEIN and Joshua WRIGHT, "The Economics of Slotting Contracts," *Journal of Law and Economics* (2007), p. 421.

[46] See Eugenio MIRAVETE, "Choosing the Wrong Calling Plan? Ignorance and Learning," *American Economic Review* (2003), p. 297.

[47] See David GROSS and Nicholas SOULELES, "Do Liquidity Constraints and Interest Rates Matter for Consumer Behavior? Evidence from Credit Card Data," *Quarterly Journal of Economics* (2002), p. 149; Haiyan SHUI and Lawrence AUSUBEL, "Time Inconsistency in the Credit Card Market," University of Maryland Working Paper (2004); Stephan MEIER and Charles SPRENGER,

with unsophisticated consumers who cannot self-realize their own time inconsistency;[48] (iii) internet purchases of computer equipment using price search engines and consumer myopia concerning hidden terms and attributes.[49]

The sensible response to this apparently conflicting set of pieces of evidence is not to weigh it in a sort of purely quantitative fashion, but to conclude, at least tentatively, that the evidence is still inconclusive regarding the real-world impact in consumer markets of many of the behavioral biases present in laboratory settings. Arguably it should lead us to consider that there is no single answer empirically satisfactory for the entire range of biases and for the entire set of circumstances and markets in which consumers may exhibit those biases.

The second reason lies in the power of learning. Consumers and non-professional contracting parties in general, as human beings, are often not fully rational, are in fact clouded by cognitive and other biases that lead them to make mistakes, not only in laboratories and experiments conducted by researchers but also in real life and concerning actual market interactions. People learn from their prior mistakes, however, because they possess good feedback mechanisms that allow them to be aware of the consequences of mistakes, and induce them to avoid the same errors in later rounds of trade or future market interactions. Given that their own pockets – sometimes, their own life and limb – are at stake, the incentives to draw lessons from past mistakes and to improve performance in later transactions are powerful and effective.[50] The likelihood of learning taking place and being effective in eliminating the negative consequences of bounded rationality features is greater the more standardized the product or service (thus allowing learning not only from past own experience but also from other consumers' experience) and the higher the routine nature of the transaction. Learning by consumers is important not just for the empirical relevance of behavioral biases in consumer markets but also for the normative consequences of the observed level of their presence: if learning is to be expected, the benefits of a regulatory or legal intervention in the relevant market are lower, for a given initial level of biased behavior among consumers. Although conceptually different from learning, other kinds of consumer reactions to biases, such as developing personal rules to guide behavior precisely to counteract the former, may also lead to results that resemble those of learning.[51]

There is a substantial amount of empirical evidence showing that consumers learn from mistakes and improve their behavior in a wide range of consumer markets: credit card

---

"Impatience and Credit Behavior: Evidence from a Field Experiment," Federal Reserve Bank of Boston Working Paper (2006).

48 See Stefano DELLA VIGNA and Ulrike MALMENDIER, "Paying not to Go to the Gym," *American Economic Review* (2006), p. 694.

49 See Glenn ELLISON and Sara ELLISON, "Search, Obfuscation, and Price Elasticities on the Internet," MIT Department of Economics Working Paper (2004).

50 See Richard EPSTEIN, "Behavioral Economics: Human Errors and Market Corrections," *University of Chicago Law Review* (2006), p. 111; Richard EPSTEIN, "The Neo-classical Economics of Consumer Contracts," *Minnesota Law Review* (2008), p. 803.

51 See Roland BENABOU and Jean TIROLE, "Willpower and Personal Rules," *Journal of Political Economy* (2004), p. 848; Dilip SOMAN and Amar CHEEMA, "When Goals are Counterproductive: The Effects of Violation of a Behavioral Goal on Subsequent Performance," *Journal of Consumer Research* (2004), p. 52.

markets,[52] video rental markets,[53] telephone markets.[54] Still, of course, learning may take time, and may be costly, so I do not imply that consumer learning is a magic formula that would always restore markets to the functioning that full rationality and full information would characterize. In fact, it is clear that firms can interfere with the learning processes of consumers through several means, and they would do so when it is in their interest to pursue that strategy, and the environment is able to sustain such shrouding behavior by firms. For instance, they can hide and make less accessible the elements of the transaction which consumers are more likely to be misled about; they can create artificial non-standardization and product multidimensionality to retard and increase learning costs; they can engage in bundling to discourage learning and comparison shopping; they can engage in loss-leader tactics. Even in a non-bounded rationality environment, firms may engage in some of these tactics, to increase consumer search costs, but behavioral biases and learning may provide them with additional reasons for them. In sum, consumer learning does not eliminate the relevance of behavioral biases for consumer markets, but definitely recommends a more parsimonious attitude towards their magnitude and effects, and undermines a broad and indiscriminate translation of the experimental findings of the behavioral law and economics literature into a general model of consumer behavior, let alone contract behavior by all individuals.

The preceding discussion shows that in order to adopt far-reaching legal rules that would significantly affect the behavior of individuals and firms, consumers and professionals, in a myriad of settings and market and non-market interactions, as is foreseen in the current harmonization exercise of European contract law, we would be better off, in theoretical terms, by having clear starting points in terms of our general understanding of how agents will act under legal rules. And that there is a growing, though far from complete, amount of empirical literature on real-life contracting behavior that we need to consider in order to confirm the choice of general model, and the likely effects of the legal measures. The EU legislator would ignore these considerations at the peril of the welfare of European contracting parties.

5 THE OPTIMAL CONSTRUCTION OF HARMONIZED EUROPEAN STANDARDS IN CONTRACT LAW

As most literature on European contract law summarized in the previous pages shows, most of the debate, either from a law and economics perspective or from other perspectives (political science, constitutional law or comparative law), on the process of

---

52 See Sumit AGARWAL et al., "Do Consumers Choose the Right Credit Contracts?," Federal Reserve Bank of Chicago Working Paper (2006); Sumit AGARWAL et al., "Stimulus and Response: The Path from Naïveté to Sophistication in the Credit Card Market," NYU Stern School of Business Working Paper (2007).

53 See Peter FISHMAN and Devin POPE, "The Long-Run Effects of Penalizing Customers: Evidence from the Video-Rental Market," University of California at Berkeley Department of Economics Working Paper (2005).

54 See Eugenio MIRAVETE, "Choosing the Wrong Calling Plan? Ignorance and Learning," *American Economic Review* (2003), p. 297.

constructing a significant body of European contract law has focused on the pros and cons of the idea of harmonizing contract law across European countries through the use of European legislative tools.

From a normative standpoint, the "whether" question is not the only relevant one. The "how" question is equally important, maybe even more, on second reflection. And not just in the implementation phase but also as a crucial element to informedly answer the "whether" puzzle: when one cannot find a way to build harmonized standards that seems promising or convincing enough, one would be reasonably inclined to answer the "whether" question in the negative.

Given the setting in which the harmonization of European contract law takes place, which necessarily has to be built largely upon the pre-existing and diverse national rules (already harmonized EU law would not be comprehensive enough), to properly determine the content of the harmonized standard becomes a crucial issue, if we want the exercise to improve social welfare in European societies, and not to be just a challenging intellectual subject for academic lawyers. For instance, should the new harmonized European standards and rules for the protection of one class of contracting parties (consumers, let us say) simply reflect the current minimum level of protection contained in the directives already in force, when they exist, or should they correspond to the minimum, to the average, or to the maximum levels of consumer protection now observed in the different national legal systems?

Surprisingly, the question of what factors one should take into account when building harmonized standards has not received a lot of theoretical attention either in the legal or in the economic literature. There is, to be sure, a very large legal and economic literature concerned with determining regulatory standards for consumer protection and in other areas of regulation, but the relationship to an explicit harmonization process seems to be lacking in the literature. In the remainder of this chapter I will summarize the theoretical arguments that I have elaborated elsewhere.[55]

With social welfare in mind, it is very likely that the largest advantage of building and establishing harmonized legal standards of behavior for contracting parties, in Europe as in other areas of the world, is essentially to reduce the transaction costs in cross-border commercial activity, and thus to enlarge economic welfare arising from those increased economic interactions that cross national borders. This may be specially true in the European context, since other obstacles (tariffs, regulatory measures with equivalent effect) have been eliminated, and one of the major policy goals is to ensure a free area of trade and movement of goods, services, capital and people.

To be sure, there are costs involved when aiming at reducing transaction-costs through legal harmonization, both in the process of designing the standards as well as when enforcing such harmonized standards. These costs may well outweigh the benefits, so that the adoption of harmonized standards may reduce welfare, and not increase it, over the pre-existing scenario of diverse legal regimes. But the positive effect, if any, of harmonized standards materializes through increased trade (which of course includes a reduction in

---

[55] Juanjo GANUZA and Fernando GOMEZ, "Optimal Standards for European Consumer Law: Maximum Harmonization, Minimum Harmonization, and Coexistence of Standards," UPF Department of Economics and Business Working Paper (2010).

the costs of all activities related to trade, and also the increase in the contract surplus from the interaction) by firms and consumers.

The thrust of the theory on building harmonized standards for economic transactions is that constructing optimal harmonized standards to induce trade across national borders essentially depends on the technologies: the cost functions of the firms that will produce the goods and services, on the one side, and the preferences of the populations in the countries that build the unified standards, on the other. That is, the definition of the harmonized standards of behavior in European contract law should consider the distribution of the costs of providing the products and services (not just the material costs of production, but any cost necessary to ensure the actual and satisfactory delivery of the product or service to the consumer) across the various European countries; it should also consider the distribution of the societal preferences of consumers in the various Member States over the relevant issue affected by the behavior that would be subject to the legal rule or standard, be it the safety of the product sold, the length of the seller's contractual warranty, or the level of detail on the content of the contract boilerplate clauses to be communicated in advance of the conclusion of the contract. In short, optimal standards should be based on the firm's available technology and on the preferences of those of those societies that might be harmonizing their laws.

It is of course true that weighing the effects of the considerations of the technologies and the societal preferences is a difficult exercise, and probably cannot be carried out in a detailed or specific way for many relevant areas of contract law, or any other law for that matter. Despite these obstacles to implementing the theoretical proposal on how to build harmonized standards, the basic idea remains an important theoretical guidance, because it clearly points to the factors that an exercise in harmonizing rules and standards in contract law should consider essential, even flawed full information about those factors is not available in many, even in most, circumstances. Moreover, technology and costs for firms and consumer preferences are crucial, but so too is their mutual correlation, or lack thereof. It can be shown that whether the parameters concerning technologies and social preferences for consumer protection are correlated or independent, and in the former case, the sign of the correlation determines whether the optimal harmonized standard falls between the pre-existing national standards, equals highest standard, or even, counter-intuitively, exceeds even the toughest national standard.

In order to better understand and assess the construction of the optimal harmonized standards, it is worth starting by considering what the optimal standard would be situation of no cross-border trade between the countries involved. For simplicity, let us assume that the number of countries is just two, although the theory could be extended to any larger number of countries and legal systems.

In a situation of autarky, lawmakers in each country would ideally set the legal standards governing the relevant problem (let us say, the extent of consumer rights *vis-à-vis* the seller in a given setting or contract) by looking at how costly compliance with the legal standard would be for the firms in the country, and how much and how strongly consumers in that country prefer to enjoy the set of rights corresponding to that level of legal protection. If lawmakers in the national legal systems are benevolent and well-informed – and let us assume them to be that way, at least to compare their ideal standards with the ideal harmonized ones – they will come up with the best standards for each country, optimally balancing the costs for firms and the preferences of the consumers.

Imagine, then, that in order to allow trade to happen between the countries, so that the more efficient firms from one country – assume that these firms enjoy a cost advantage due, for example, to their technological development – can participate in the foreign market, it is necessary to build a single legal standard for both countries, because otherwise firms could not show that they are complying with the relevant legal requirements. The reasons for this "accreditation of compliance" obstacle may be manyfold in practice, but in order to better grasp the effects of the different alternatives it is helpful to think that without some kind of common harmonized rule or standard, it is infinitely costly to show compliance with the relevant authorities of the foreign – to the firm – country, and/or to the foreign consumers. The next step is then to ask how this unified standard should be constructed and how it would compare to the pre-existing national standards.

As was the case with national standards, the best way to handle the matter is to look at costs and preferences, now, due to the single and unified nature of the relevant legal standards, for the aggregate of both countries – which now will become one single market in terms of the legal requirements and accreditation of the compliance with them, and thus in terms of the firm that will serve consumers in both countries. We have to take into account the preferences in each country, weighted by the population in both of them, in order to get the aggregate magnitude.

The relationship between this new, harmonized standard and its national predecessors gives rise to different scenarios. We have essentially three of these.

First, the single harmonized rule can fall between the requirements established by the two pre-existing national ones: if country **A** had standard **h**, and country **B** had standard **l**, being **h** > **l**, the new unified standard would be:

$$\mathbf{m}, \text{ with } \mathbf{h} > \mathbf{m} > \mathbf{l}.$$

This intermediate standard would be desirable when country **A** and country **B** have similar firms in terms of costs and technologies, but the preferences are quite different in one and the other country, and also when the country with the more efficient firms (**A**, in our example) also has consumers with stronger preferences for a higher legal standard. In both cases, the adequate harmonized standard falls between the requirements established by intermediate one between the national standard of the two countries.

Second, the optimal unified standard can also coincide with the tougher of the pre-existing national standards, in the somewhat unusual case in which countries had consumers with the same preferences regarding the level of protection, but one country has more efficient firms. If this was the case, if **A** had standard **h** and **B** had standard **l**, the optimal harmonized standard **m** would equal **h**, that is:

$$\mathbf{h} = \mathbf{m} > \mathbf{l}.$$

Third, the more interesting and also the more counterintuitive case would be one where the two countries differ regarding firms' costs and consumers' preferences, so that the country with the more efficient firms (assume it is **B**) would have consumers with weaker preferences for higher legal standards than those of country **A**. Then, if **A** had standard **h** and **B** had standard **l**, the optimal unified standard **m** could be intermediate, but it could also be higher than **h**, if the population of country **A** where sufficiently large compared with the population of country **B**. That is, in this third scenario in which the preferences of contracting parties and the costs of the firms complying with legal standards are independent or positively correlated, the harmonized standard **m** could be:

$$\mathbf{h} > \mathbf{m} > \mathbf{l} \text{ or } \mathbf{m} > \mathbf{h} > \mathbf{l}.$$

In other words, if the small country had the more efficient firms, and the larger country had the consumers who cared more about their legal rights, it would be possible to expect an efficient unified standard that could be tougher than any of the pre-existing national ones.

A natural corollary of the preceding analysis is that if one is concerned about reaching efficient solutions in building harmonized legal standards, the lawmaker's task is not an easy one, since the details of the relationship between the costs for firms and the preferences of consumers are crucial for reaching the optimal level of unified legal rules and standards.

6 FULL HARMONIZATION, MINIMUM HARMONIZATION AND CO-EXISTENCE OF STANDARDS

The basic theory outlined in the previous section implicitly assumes that harmonization for the purposes of improving cross-border trade requires strictly unified standards across the countries involved in the harmonization process. This is, of course, not necessarily true, and is even probably untrue in many, if not most, circumstances. Countries could build harmonized standards to facilitate trade, but these do not need to replace entirely the pre-existing national standards.

In fact, whether a new, harmonized standard would co-exist or not, and under what conditions, with the national standard is a crucial choice in the entire harmonization exercise, and one which does not have a straight-forward theoretical solution.

In EU law, this matter presents itself as the choice between full harmonization and minimum harmonization. As is well known, in the context of the new directive on consumer rights, proposed by the European Commission,[56] there has been heavy criticism in academic circles against the intention expressed in the initially proposed new directive to make it a full harmonization directive, which would imply that pre-existing national standards – including those more protective of consumers – would be entirely abrogated by the new legislation, and the introduction or adoption in the future of national rules departing either way – either increasing or decreasing the level of consumer protection – from the harmonized ones would also be entirely ruled out.[57]

---

[56] See Proposal of 8 October 2008 for a Directive on consumer rights, COM (2008) 614 final.

[57] See for a collection of these criticisms addressed to the full harmonization approach in this area, Michael Faure, "Towards a Maximum Harmonization of Consumer Contract Law?," in *Maastricht Journal of Transnational and International Law* (2008), p. 440; Peter Rott and Evelyn Terre, "The Proposal for a Directive on Consumer Rights: No Single Set of Rules," in *Zeitschrift für Europäisches Privatrecht* (2009), p. 460; Hans.-W. Micklitz and Norbert Reich, "*Crónica*

Under minimum harmonization, the harmonized standard, as has mostly – though not always – happened in the past with EU directives in consumer law, sets a mandatory floor in the relevant variable, parameter or behavior, allowing the Member States to keep, or to create in the future, more exacting standards for protecting consumers, but wiping out pre-existing lower national standards, and preventing those lower standards from being adopted in the future. Under full harmonization, the harmonized standard entirely displaces and eliminates the national standards, pre-existing or future, regardless of whether they are higher or lower than the harmonized one.

In theoretical terms, however, it must be noted that minimum harmonization is not at all equivalent to pure co-existence of standards, harmonized and national. Under minimum harmonization, standards lower than harmonized ones are automatically eliminated and replaced by harmonized standards, and countries with a higher standard are allowed not only to keep applying but also essentially to ignore the harmonized standard, since firms operating in that national market would be forced to comply with the stricter national standard. Thus, under minimum harmonization, unless there is some possibility of entry into the markets with standards that are different from and stricter than, those mandated by the national authorities of the firm, there would be no new cross-border trade.

It would be possible, however, to complement minimum harmonization with some possibility of entry, if firms using a standard that was at least as high as the national standard would be allowed to participate in that market. This would be a kind of imperfect or asymmetric "country of origin" regime that would allow cross-border trade only under standards that are higher than that of the import country, but not the reverse. Additionally, the complement to minimum harmonization may take the form of a full "country of origin" or "mutual recognition" principle which would allow firms from other countries (remember, now operating under a standard that is at least as high as the minimum harmonized standard) to enter the national markets of countries with higher standards, yet not complying with these higher standards of the receiving country, but only with at least the harmonized level.

In pure co-existence (or competition between national standards and the harmonized one, if one prefers to frame the case in this way) the harmonized standard would not replace the existing ones, regardless of whether they were higher or lower than

---

de Una Muerte Anunciada: The Commission Proposal for a Directive on Consumer Rights," *Common Market Law Review* (2009), p. 471; Simon WHITTAKER, "Unfair Contract Terms and Consumer Guarantees: The Proposal for a Directive on Consumer Rights and the Significance of Full Harmonization," in *European Review of Contract Law* (2009), p. 223; Christian TWIGG-FLESSNER and Daniel METCALFE, "The Proposed Consumer Rights Directive – Less Haste, More Thought?," in *European Review of Contract Law* (2009), p. 368; Jan SMITS, "Full Harmonization of Consumer Law? A Critique of the Draft Directive on Consumer Rights," *European Review of Private Law* (2010), p. 9; Gary LOW, "The (Ir)Relevance of Harmonization and Legal Diversity to European Contract Law: A Perspective from Psychology," *European Review of Private Law* (2010), p. 288; Martin EBERS, "De la armonización mínima a la armonización plena: la propuesta de Directiva sobre derechos de los consumidores," *InDret* (2010); Marco LOOS, "Full Harmonization as a Regulatory Concept and its Consequences for the National Legal Orders: The Example of the Consumer Rights Directive," Centre for the Study of European Contract Law, University of Amsterdam Working Paper 2010/03 (2010).

the harmonized level.[58] Again, two versions of co-existence are theoretically possible, depending on whether the choice to adopt the harmonized set of standards is given to the governments or to the contracting parties themselves. Some argue that the latter would be equivalent to granting the choice to the firms who will be subject to them in their operations, since consumers would have no meaningful way to influence the firms' decision.[59] Although it is not as obvious as it may seem that consumers would "never" have a say in the choice of one or the other set of rules, for the purposes of the analysis it does not hurt to assume that firms can decide to comply with the European or their national body of rules – or both, depending on the target market, if using both sets is feasible in technological and economic terms (something that will be considered below). For our theoretical analysis it is possible to disregard the legal complexities behind an EU optional set of rules in contract law and the technically – in the legal sense – hard relationship between national mandatory rules and the Rome I Regulation.[60]

In the first case, to have some bite in improving cross-border trade,[61] this harmonized optional standard should allow firms from the country adopting the harmonized level to be able to enter, under the harmonized standard, the national markets of other countries who have not adopted it. Otherwise, in the setting of our basic model, no country would have an incentive to adopt the harmonized standard.

The option to select the harmonized set of rules may be given to the firms themselves (or to the parties, through choice of law in the contract, but analytically both possibilities are very similar in our economic model of harmonization), who may decide to operate under their national standard or under the harmonized standard (or under both, if that is technologically and materially feasible). Again, if the standard is to have some bite in cross-border transactions, the firms using the harmonized standard would be allowed to enter any national market, regardless of the level of the national standard in place in such

---

[58] The model of co-existence and choice between harmonized rules and national rules is argued forcefully by Wolfgang KERBER and Stefan GRUNDMANN, "An Optional European Contract Law Code: Advantages and Disadvantages," 21 *European Journal of Law and Economics* (2006), p. 215; Stefan GRUNDMANN,"European Contract Law of What Colour?," in *European Review of Contract Law* (2005), p. 184. For a specific version of co-existence, in the area of B2C e-commerce (the so-called "Blue-button" proposal) see Hans SCHULTE-NÖLKE, "EC Law on the Formation of Contract – From the Common Frame of Reference to the Blue Button," in *European Review of Contract Law* (2007), p. 333. Against the possibility of co-existence, arguing that it would eliminate all the benefits that may ensue from harmonization, Walter DORALT, "An Optional Contract Law for Europe? Rote Karte oder grünes Licht für den Blue Button," Max Planck Private Law Research Paper No. 10/16 (2010).

[59] Walter DORALT, "An Optional Contract Law for Europe? Rote Karte oder grünes Licht für den Blue Button", Max Planck Private Law Research Paper No. 10/16 (2010).

[60] See, for a more detailed presentation of these complexities, Aurelia COLOMBI CIACCHI, "An Optional Instrument for Consumer Contracts in the EU: Conflict of Laws and Conflict of Policies," in Alessandro Somma (ed.), *The Politics of the Draft Common Frame of Reference*, Wolters Kluwer Law&Business (2009), p. 3.

[61] Remember, if no discernible effect over cross-border transactions takes place as a consequence of the harmonization process, this will be essentially moot, and thus essentially a waste of resources and energy, unless there are other benefits of an entirely different kind (intellectual spillovers over national legal orders, increased sense of a common destiny and even identity, and so on) which are beyond the scope of our economic theory of harmonization of legal rules, and whose magnitude, and even existence, is very hard to assess.

market. This model would correspond essentially to the "Optional Instrument" considered as Option 4 in the Green Paper from the European Commission on policy options for progress towards a European contract law for consumers and businesses, of 1 July 2010, and also to the "blue button" proposal that some have advocated for.[62]

How do these different ways to arrange the relationship between the harmonized standard and the national ones fare comparatively in terms of their effects on the level of the harmonized standard, on the level of cross-border trade and, ultimately, on social welfare?

The first and basic observation that will be apparent from the analysis that will follow is that the choice of harmonization model (full, minimum, co-existence) matters for the determination of the level of the harmonized standard. This implies that one cannot treat the issue of the substantive level and content of the harmonized rules and standards separately from the question of whether these harmonized rules will constitute a new full harmonization regime or a minimum harmonization regime or will co-exist alongside the existing national rules. They are distinct questions, but the answer to the second one conditions the first in a decisive way.

Full harmonization is analytically one of the simpler cases. In fact, it corresponds to the basic model of optimal harmonized standards outlined above in Section 5. What was summarized there with respect to optimal unified rules exactly matches the outcomes of full harmonization when the lawmaker responsible for the harmonized standards tries to reach the most efficient results, given the full harmonization regime.

Under minimum harmonization,[63] one needs to consider three different accompanying scenarios. The first one is that in which the adoption of a harmonized set of rules does not imply any opening up of markets for firms that do not use the national standard, which, by definition, has to be higher than the harmonized one – lower national standards have been superseded by the European standards. That is, national markets remain entirely separated. If this is the environment, then, optimal harmonized standards should correspond to the lowest pre-existing national standards, and in fact the entire harmonization exercise is useless. It is thus important to emphasize that the economic benefits of harmonizing rules and standards in contract law require as a necessary condition some opening of national markets for entry of foreign firms, otherwise the efficiency gains will not arise, since national markets would still be served by local firms, and for this scenario

---

62 See note 58 above.

63 Under full or maximum harmonization, given that the harmonized standard wipes out entirely the national ones, there is no room for strategic reactions by the national lawmakers in view of the new harmonized rules. Under minimum harmonization, however, given that only standards that are lower than the level imposed by the harmonized rules are eliminated, but higher ones remain always possible, national lawmakers could increase the existing standards in order to countereffect the harmonizing – and market-opening – effects of the agreed standards. If these reactions are possible, then the lawmaker in charge of the harmonization exercise should take this into account and react accordingly at the time of building the harmonized standards. In order to simplify the analysis, I do not allow for this possibility, even if not discarding the plausibility of this complication, and even its empirical relevance. It should be pointed out, however, that this opportunity for strategic behavior by national lawmakers that minimum harmonization allows for would be a comparative disadvantage of minimum harmonization versus full harmonization and pure co-existence, where there is no room for these undesirable maneuvers by national lawmakers.

the diversity of national standards – reflecting the underlying actual diversity in consumer preferences and firms' costs in satisfying legal requirements – constitutes a superior policy option.

The second one is that of partial entry of foreign firms into national markets: foreign firms using a standard that is at least as high as the national standard would be allowed to enter the national market. That is, when minimum harmonization is combined with the possibility of entry of standards that are at least as high as the national standard, there is some chance of entry by the more efficient firms from other countries into the markets of other states. Here, let us also assume that firms may operate under two different sets of rules, their own national standards and the new harmonized ones, serving, for instance, their national market under the pre-existing – and higher than the harmonized one – national standard and the foreign market under the new harmonized set of rules. I will later discuss the relevance of this assumption for the comparison between the different harmonization regimes.

What are the results in this setting of minimum harmonization with partial entry under higher standards? As under full harmonization, there are two interesting cases. In the first, the country with more efficient firms (**A**) (with the notation used in the previous section) also has consumers with stronger preferences for a higher legal standard. Here, minimum harmonization with partial entry would require a harmonized standard that is lower than that under full harmonization in the same case. At the same time welfare in both countries would be higher than with full harmonization: the efficient firms from country **A** would serve the markets of both country **A** and country **B**, but the first market (**A**) under the pre-existing national standard of **A**, and the second market (**B**) under the new harmonized intermediate – but lower than the equivalent standard under full harmonization – standard.

In the second case, the two countries are diverse in firms' costs and consumers' preferences, so that the country with more efficient firms (**B**) has a consumer population with weaker preferences for higher legal standards than that of country **A**. Now, under minimum harmonization with partial entry – only of higher standards – the optimal harmonized standards can be very low or very high, depending on whether the gains from cross-border trade are low or high. Here, there is no easy comparison with the outcomes under full harmonization, although the intermediate standards under maximum harmonization are no longer desirable, and the optimal harmonized standards are either very low – inducing no increased entry of the efficient firms into foreign markets – or very high – with opposite effects.

The third major scenario under minimum harmonization is that in which minimum harmonization is combined with the complete effects of the country of origin principle. The harmonized standard with the minimum harmonization effect actually eliminates the lower pre-existing standards, but the country of origin principle with full effect would allow firms to enter a foreign market under their own national standards – all of them equal to or higher than the harmonized level, by definition of minimum harmonization – and this possibility of entry will be true even if those standards are lower than the level required by national law of the country where consumers are located, the receiving or importing country.

When minimum harmonization is coupled with full country of origin, the more interesting cases are again the two mentioned above. In the first of them, namely when the country with the more efficient firms (**A**) is the one with consumers showing stronger preferences for a higher legal standard, the level of the harmonized standard and the outcomes in terms of trade exactly mirror those under minimum harmonization with partial entry. In the second case (**B**, the country with the more efficient firms, with consumers with weaker preferences for a higher legal standard than that of the other country), the introduction of the full country of origin principle improves the performance of minimum harmonization in terms of opening trade, as one would expect, and allows higher levels of welfare. Now, in this case, minimum harmonization with complete country of origin effect allows for intermediate harmonized standards and, simultaneously, allows that more efficient firms from the country with the pre-existing lower standard enter the market of the other country, a possibility that did not exist under minimum harmonization with only partial entry. These increased opportunities, in turn, expanding the range of optimal standards, allow us to obtain the welfare gains of increased cross-border trade with less distortion in the satisfaction of consumers' preferences for the level of protection in the country that adopted the lower pre-existing standard.

Finally, let us now turn our attention to the option of the regime characterized by the co-existence of (harmonized and national) standards. Again, let us first assume that firms may operate under two different sets of standards and rules, their own national ones and the harmonized ones, although later it will be shown how significant are the consequences of modifying this important assumption for the outcomes of a harmonization process.

In this setting, the performance of the co-existence regime is excellent. It is always as good as minimum harmonization in many cases, and in the remaining important case, namely where the country with more efficient firms is also that with a population of consumers with lower valuation of the protection provided by higher legal standards, it outperforms minimum harmonization in any of the versions that have been explored above. In other words, it performs better than minimum harmonization, either uncoupled or coupled with partial entry or with full country of origin principle. The reason is that in this case the optimal harmonized standard under co-existence of harmonized and national standards allows the more efficient firms to be fully able to serve all markets: the market with the pre-existing lower standard will be served with that national standard, and the other market – that of the country with a previous higher standard – will be served with the harmonized standard, which will be exactly tailored for the consumers' preferences of that country, given that it is being served by the more efficient foreign firms.

In fact, it can be shown that, under the above-explained assumption that firms are able to operate subject to more than one standard, a regime of co-existence of harmonized and national standards leads, if the lawmaker establishing the national standards strives for efficiency, to the first-best solution for consumers and firms in all affected countries.[64]

To sum up the relative advantages and disadvantages of the various alternative regimes organizing the harmonization of rules in contract law (and in other areas as well, since the theoretical issues are likely to be similar), it is possible to conclude that full harmonization has the potential to produce significant gains in terms of reduction of legal obstacles

[64] See, for details, Juanjo GANUZA and Fernando GOMEZ, "Optimal Standards for European Consumer Law: Maximum Harmonization, Minimum Harmonization, and Coexistence of Standards," UPF Department of Economics and Business Working Paper (2010).

to cross-border trade, since the elimination of legal diversity is radical and complete.[65] Maximum harmonization, however, forces important welfare sacrifices in terms of the appropriate matching of the level of the standard to the local preferences of the affected countries and societies, since all of them are subject to the same level of protective rules, disregarding the maybe importantly divergent preferences across countries over the issues subject to the harmonized rules.

Thus, the existence of several standards – which will fall short of true full harmonization – may improve welfare since they allow for a better match between consumer preferences and the level of the standard, even if they sometimes fail to realize the full potential gains from trade across national borders. That is, it may be better to allow some barriers to cross-border trade to remain in place as a consequence of legal diversity, in favor of better adapting the standards to which products and services should be subject to social preferences on consumer protection. It is true, though, that softer forms of harmonization, such as minimum harmonization, unless one wants them to be entirely moot in showing some significant effect on improving cross-border trade activity, need to be supplemented by measures that guarantee some entry by the more efficient firms into the markets of other countries. That is, softer forms of harmonization require that the national standards do not remain entirely entrenched, and the markets continue to be totally separated.

Accordingly, a complete or at least an attenuated version of the country of origin principle would allow for this improvement in cross-border trade – although to a lower extent than full harmonization, but with better outcomes in terms of respecting variety in societal preferences for the level of legal standards.

Minimum harmonization, however, may not be the optimal regime even if one is very concerned with preserving a good match between the level of standards and the preferences of the citizens in each country. There may be even greater potential welfare gains in allowing that national and harmonized standards coexist, that is, in using an even softer approach than minimum harmonization. Thus, harmonized rules and standards in European private law could be thought of as instruments to be deployed alongside existing national standards, and not replacing even the standards that are lower than the harmonized one, at the same time allowing the most efficent firms to exploit the gains from cross-border trade, given that, at least arguably, the harmonized standards could be able to overcome the existing barriers preventing active transactions serving consumers across national borders, while simultaneously being respectful of the real diversity in Europe, in terms of the preferences and the basic economic conditions of the societies in which the rules are to be applied. Indeed, when firms are flexible enough in their technologies and

---

[65] This is probably an exaggeration, since even under full harmonization of a given area of the law, however ample this may be (such as private law), many important features and properties of the national legal systems will remain separate and diverse (procedures, courts, legal culture and tradition, and so on). This will obviously reduce the positive impact of full harmonization in promoting cross-border transactions. See, for this and similar arguments, Fernando GOMEZ, "The Harmonization of Contract Law through European Rules: A Law and Economics Perspective," *European Review of Contract Law* (2008), p. 89; Gary Low, "The (Ir)Relevance of Harmonization and Legal Diversity to European Contract Law: A Perspective from Psychology," *European Review of Private Law* (2010), p. 288.

cost functions to be able to operate under more than one set of standards, this regime allowing perfect co-existence of standards, national and harmonized (European, in our case), is the best strategy to go ahead with harmonization.

It must be clearly underlined, though, that the advantage of the co-existence approach to harmonization crucially depends on the assumption already mentioned several times in this section, namely that firms are not forced (for technological, economic or other reasons) to provide goods and services only and solely subject to one single set of rules. If this assumption is not met, and firms can only do business under one single set of legal rules and standards, one is squarely back in front of the fundamental dilemma of harmonization as an instrument to reduce transactions costs in cross-border transactional activity, namely the trade-off between gains from trade and the matching of legal rules and standards to societal preferences and local conditions.

One could argue, however, that in the different areas of the law directly affecting contracting and cross-border trade, it is possible to distinguish between two kinds of rules and standards. Some – let us say, safety requirements of products, standards determining quality levels in goods and services – impact the behavior and decisions of the agents in a kind of durable or rigid way, so that it is difficult to act and serve markets under more than one set of rules and standards. For instance, economies of scale probably make it too expensive to build a production plant with diverse production chains depending on the standard of the market in which the goods will be sold. Other rules and standards may have little or no impact on the fixed costs of the firm, and may affect behavior only after the fundamental production decisions have been taken, allowing the firm to tailor the product or service to more than one governing standard. Plausibly a large part of traditional contract law may fall into the second category, because firms, even with the same product and service for all markets, may be able to adjust the terms of the contract with the other party to the requirements of diverse national or harmonized contract law rules and standards. Probably this would not cover the entire area of contract law, but arguably a major portion of it. This sub-set of contract law rules would be a natural candidate for harmonization in the form that I have labeled co-existence of standards and that the European Commission and others refer to as an optional contract law instrument.

At a general level, the fundamental dilemma between lower transaction costs in cross-border trade and satisfaction of local preferences and conditions does not have a general theoretical answer. It brings to the forefront, however, the choice between full harmonization as the most powerful engine to ensure gains from trade, and co-existence of standards as the mode of harmonization that better serves to preserve and satisfy variety in societal preferences over the substance and of legal rules and level of standards. Minimum harmonization, although being sometimes more appealing than maximum harmonization, would be dominated by the softer and looser approach of allowing full co-existence of national and harmonized standards, regardless of their relative levels.

7 CONCLUSIONS

EU or European contract law is a multi-faceted notion, evoking different phenomena, some even affecting what has been the past impact – large, by all means – of EU law-making powers upon the private laws of Member States. Undeniably, some different developments are under way, which shows a purposeful process of reducing legal diversity across European countries in order – among other reasons of a different kind – to strengthen a true and active pan-European market for firms and consumers. Most reactions to this current process, both from a legal and from an economic perspective, have focused on the desirability of the process itself. This is, no doubt, an important question, and we have reassessed in this chapter some of the economic criticisms raised against European harmonization of contract law, finding that the force of many of them is probably less than commonly considered. The re-codification element of the current harmonization exercise and the lack of clear models of behavior of the agents subject to the new rules seem to me to be more troublesome from a law and economics perspective than what is usually acknowledged.

Additionally, a crucial issue appears to have been almost completely overlooked by EU institutions, and by both lawyers and economists dealing with harmonization of contract law in Europe, and this is the "how" question, at least in a theoretical way. I present here the sketch of a theory of optimal decision making in a harmonization process, a theory that extends to the various modes and regimes to organize the position of harmonized rules and standards and the national standards of the countries affected by such harmonization. The costs for the firms (the agents, in general, be they firms or not, although the most natural setting is that of firms) subject to the standards and the preferences in the different societies regarding the substance and level of rules and standards are the key factors to take into account when designing harmonized rules. The choice of harmonization regime, that is, whether the outcome should be full harmonization, minimum harmonization or simply a co-existence of a new harmonized standard with the old national sets of rules, has been shown to be decisive for the substantive decisions over the standards.

The choice among regimes, moreover, should try to effectively reduce barriers for cross-border commercial activity, while at the same time preserving the alignment between the substantive standards actually applied in the different countries and the societal preferences in each of them. Without a clear positive impact on cross-border trade, the harmonization exercise would largely remain a pure intellectual enterprise, however fascinating it may be for its own sake.

PART 5

CONSUMER PROTECTION

11 The evolution of consumer protection in the EU

*Fabrizio Cafaggi and Antonio Nicita**

1 INTRODUCTION

Consumer protection law in Europe is not a clear or unique set of rules.[1] Rather, it refers to a broad range of areas which focus on specific purposes covered by different legislations and regulations, such as unfair and deceptive advertising, outright fraud, consumer credit, warranty transactions, as well as consumers' switching costs in network industries and so on. This wider production of rules is further complicated by the circumstance that European regulations have proceeded parallel to uncoordinated initiatives by national governments and parliaments. Today, a comprehensive multi-level approach to consumer law is still missing and the protection of consumers' interests is fragmentated into many sectoral regulations, which nonetheless increasingly recur, in their regulatory design, to enforcement devices borrowed from other areas, such as contract law.[2]

The evolution of the European approach to consumer protection could be fixed by two milestone dates in 1975 and 1992.[3] In 1975, the Council of the European Union issued a preliminary program for a consumer protection and information policy, by outlining five basic areas of consumer rights: (a) the right to protection of health and safety; (b) the right to protection of economic interests; (c) the right to redress; (d) the right to information and education; and (e) the right of representation (the right to be heard).[4] In 1992, the Maastricht Treaty, amending the Treaty establishing the European Economic Community with a view to establishing the European Community, clearly stated, in Art. 3, that the activities of the Community shall include "a contribution to the strengthening of consumer protection." Interestingly, the 1992 Maastrich Treaty introduced for consumers a separate "activity" with respect to those, equally mentioned in the same article, aimed at "the elimination, as between Member States, of customs duties and quantitative restrictions on the import and export of goods, and of all other measures having equivalent effect"; at implementing "a common commercial policy" and an "internal market characterized by the abolition, as between Member States, of obstacles to the free movement of goods, persons, services and capital"; and at enforcing "a system ensuring that competition in the internal market is not distorted." In this respect, thus, "the strengthening of consumer protection" was clearly imagined as a distinct, at least partially, aim of the European Community relative to sectoral regulation or even competition policy, to

* This chapter has been written in the framework of a research project, supported by Scuola Superiore della Pubblica amministrazione, on transnational governance by contract.

1 See F. Cafaggi, Introduction, *Making European Private Law*, Edward Elgar, 2008, pp. 4–6.

2 Cafaggi and Micklitz, *New Frontiers of Consumer Protection*, Intersentia, 2009, pp. 21–2.

3 See Ewoud Hondius, "The notion of consumer: European Union versus Member States," in *Sydney Law Review* Vol. 28: 89, 2006.

4 *Official Journal* [1975] EU C 92/1.

the aim of completing the European internal market. The original emphasis was put on the consumer "protection" rather than on consumer welfare or on fulfilling the goals of competition policy.[5]

The legal basis for European intervention has been primarily approximation of laws rather than the specific provision of consumer protection. The rationale for introducing consumer legislation was related not only to increasing consumer protection but also to creating an integrated European market. This approach has emphasized the regulatory nature of legislation instead of the welfare approach typical of Member States (MS). Thence the resulting multi-level structure was not inspired by homogeneous approaches and rationales and, as a consequence, it has been subject to tensions reflected in the "dialogue" between national courts and the ECJ. In the first stage, directives were deployed with minimum harmonization standards. Later either for legislative choice or the Court's interpretation, there has been a shift towards complete harmonization.

From a law and economics perspective, as we will argue below, this notion of consumer "protection" raises several puzzles as it is not clear "who" the consumer is, to whom such a protection would be granted, to what extent, and by which means. Indeed, the purpose of protecting consumers *under any circumstance* may well interfere with free market dynamics. The traditional idea that the consumer is, by definition, a "weak contracting party" to be protected, under any circumstance, in free market exchanges against parties with "asymmetric" bargaining power may even contrast with the notions of the competitive markets mechanism, economic efficiency and consumer welfare, which at the same time evolved over the years as the core of European competition and liberalization policies. The tension between consumer protection and competition policy at the European level partly mirrors the one between the evolution of an European approach towards a unified and harmonized framework and national resistances on maintaining local traditions.

In this chapter we first address some law and economics puzzles behind the notion of consumer protection (Section 2) and the relationship between consumer law and competition policy (Section 3). We finally focus on the evolution of the regulatory function of EU consumer law and conclude (Section 4).

2 THE LAW AND ECONOMICS OF CONSUMER PROTECTION: FROM OLD ISSUES TO NEW FRONTIERS

The fundamental question that the law and economics approach may raise with respect to consumer protection is whether we need a specific legislation in favor of consumers,

---

[5] See Fernando Gomez Pomar, "EC Consumer Protection Law and EC Competition Law: How Related are They? A Law and Economics Perspective" 8 (InDret Working Paper No. 113, 2003); John Vickers, "Economics for Consumer Policy," British Academy Keynes Lecture, October 2003; Roger J. van den Bergh, "Competition Law and Consumer Protection Legislation," in *Economic Analysis of Law: A European Perspective*, A. Hatzis ed., 2003, Edward Elgar; Katalin Judit Cseres, *Competition Law and Consumer Protection*, Kluwer Law International, European Monographs 49, The Hague 2005; Mark Armstrong, "Interactions between Competition and Consumer Policy," *Competition Policy International Journal*, vol. 4, 2008.

rather than referring to standard remedies in contract law, property law and tort law or even antitrust law.[6]

The traditional starting point for a specific rationale in protecting "the consumer" relies on the "subjective conditions" under which a contractual decision is made. Subjective conditions may refer both to the circumstances under which the consumption decision is made (for example door-to-door selling) and to the "identity" of the consumer (vulnerable or even "credulous" consumer).

The point is that under the above circumstances the consumer might be forced to make a choice she would not be willing to make under a different initial condition; for instance, when a sufficient time has elapsed between the seller's proposal and the conscious buyer's final decision (so as to prevent the seller's undue pressure on the buyer's freedom to choose) or when the buyer has had the opportunity to have access to the relevant information needed in order to make the "correct" choice.

The weakness of this argument, which has been traditionally raised in the legal realm, is that of regarding the consumer to be protected as being, by definition, a "weak" party in an "unequal bargaining" situation.[7]

2.1 The Consumer as the Weak Bargaining Party

This notion of a "weak consumer" raises nonetheless some economic puzzles. According to the conventional economic approach, the "weaker" party in a bargaining situation does not necessarily need any particular form of protection from the point of view of economic efficiency. Indeed, if there are gains from trade, any surplus sharing is efficient ex post, even under "unequal" bargaining. The asymmetric bargaining power would generate distributional consequences, rather than affecting trading efficiencies. Any form of protection would thus be driven by distributive concerns, rather than by the purpose of enhancing efficiency.[8] The notion of the weaker bargaining party is indeed rather different under the economic perspective as the weaker party is simply the one obtaining a smaller share of the bargaining surplus, due to a number of features, such as the parties' degree of impatience and the level of outside options.[9] Moreover, the final outcome may also depend on the structure of the bargaining procedure, as in many bargaining situations being a *proponent* or a *responder* may affect the surplus

---

[6] F. Cafaggi, "The Making of European Private Law," p. 294, in F. Cafaggi and H.M. Watt, *Making European Private Law: Governance Design*, Cheltenham, Edward Elgar, 2008.

[7] Hugh Beale, "The Inequality of Bargaining Power," 6 *Oxford Journal of Legal Studies* 123 (1986); Spencer Nathan Thal, "The Inequality of Bargaining Power Doctrine – The Problem of Defining Contractual Unfairness," 8 *Oxford Journal of Legal Studies* 17 (1988); Hans-W. Micklitz, "The New German Sales Law: Changing Patterns in the Regulation of Product Quality," 25 *Journal of Consumer Policy* 379, 386–9 (2002).

[8] Gillian Hadfield, Robert Howse and Michael J. Trebilcock, "Rethinking Consumer Protection Policy: Remarks to the University of Toronto Faculty of Law" (20 June 1996); Stefan Haupt, "An Economic Analysis of Consumer Protection Law," 4 *German Law Journal*, 1137–64 (2003); Fernando Gomez Pomar, *supra* note 5.

[9] Martin J. Osborne and Ariel Rubinstein, *Bargaining and Markets*, Academic Press, San Diego, 1990.

sharing.[10] However, it should be noticed that the weaker party in a bargaining game will always get at least her outside option and the consumer "loss," in this respect, is always an "opportunity" loss which refers to the potential gains from trade, if there is a minimum level of competition.

Suppose that a seller and a buyer are involved in a bargaining situation in which they have to set a price p in order to split the gains from trade $(v - c)$, where v is the consumer willingness to pay and c is the cost of delivery. Let us assume that some asymmetry (degree of patience, outside options) characterizes the parties' bargaining power. If the "winner" is the buyer, the price set will approach the cost of delivery, $p \geq c$, and the "rent" extracted by the buyer will be equal to $v - p > 0$. The seller will then be the weaker party, but he will never obtain less than c. Thus, the seller will take the minimum amount of the potential gains from trade, but will never incur a loss (as would be the case, should the seller be forced to sell at a price lower than the delivery costs).

From the conventional economic perspective, this means that, whatever is the price set by the parties' bargaining, the bargaining will be efficient, even when "unequal," provided that the actual price falls in the range of value between the buyer's maximum willingness to pay and the seller's delivery costs.

2.2 Bargaining Power versus Market Power

Furthermore, this economic argument is independent of the structure of the market (monopolist, oligopolist or competitive). The structure of the market may certainly affect the parties' bargaining power, but as long as the price falls within the range of values defining the gains from trade it will not affect the efficiency feature of the economic exchange. Thus, a monopolistic seller may well fix a price equal to the consumer's maximum willingness to pay, extracting all the potential rent from that exchange, and still perform an efficient contract, relative to that buyer. The efficiency consequences of a monopoly on the market are independent of that single bargaining.

The monopoly inefficiency refers to the "other" potential contracts, involving customers with a willingness to pay higher than the cost of delivery, that are truncated by the monopoly pricing. Thus the "contractual efficiency" of the single bargaining between a monopolistic seller and a buyer is one thing, and the "market efficiency" of the monopoly configuration, which refers to the contracts that the monopolist will not sign, rather than to those signed, is another. Indeed, in the extreme case of a perfect discriminating monopoly, each single buyer will be a "weak" party, paying a price equal to her willingness to pay, but nonetheless each contract will be efficient according to the conventional definition and the market configuration will be efficient as well (as there will be no buyer, having a willingness to pay higher or equal to the cost of delivery, who will not have the opportunity to sign a contract with the monopolist).

That said, from the conventional perspective, the problem of consumer protection will thus refer, rather than to the ex post consequences of an "unequal" bargaining, to the ex ante or "initial conditions" of exchange, which turned out to be somewhat "vitiated"

---

10 Martin J. Osborne and Ariel Rubinstein, *supra* note 9.

and might have induced the consumer to behave under a "regret" assumption. However, it is important to stress that what the consumer should regret, in this respect, is not the outcome of an efficient contract, i.e. the final split of the gains from trade, but rather the fact of having been forced to sign an *inefficient* contract. In other words, consumer protection matters from the perspective of economic efficiency as long as this form of protection inhibits the emergence of inefficient contracts, rather than the economic consequences of unequal bargaining power over efficient contracts.

Protecting a consumer against his initially "wrong" decision is then efficient, as long as his ex post, "correct" valuation, v^*, of the received economic proposal falls below the price initially paid, $p°$. This means that at the price paid, $p°$, there was not a potential gain on the buyer's side, being $(v^* - p°) \leq 0$. Thus, in this situation, a gain from trade is efficient only if the price paid falls within the range of values $(v^* - c)$, c being the marginal cost of delivery.

Then the traditional legal justification for consumer protection, which relies on the idea that the monopoly power of huge companies should be restricted as consumers are (always) economically inferior to producers and traders,[11] should be more cautiously evaluated on strictly efficiency grounds.

The conventional approach would suggest to apply a *rule of reason* to specific circumstances in which the "initial conditions" are vitiated due to some subjective feature affecting the consumer's choice. As Iain Ramsay[12] outlined, this means departing from the mainstream notion of perfectly rational agents and investigating the specific circumstances which affect individual behavior, first of all the relevance of informational asymmetries,[13] but also the way in which information is framed, as well as agents' ability to fully understand, independently of the amount of information received, the consequences of their choices, due to their limited knowledge, as in the case of many financial choices, or to the limited time to evaluate experience or credence goods.

In the above cases, standard-form contracts, mandatory legal warranties, and cooling-off periods may correct, under given conditions,[14] contractual failures.

2.3 The "Fundamental Transformation" in After-markets

An interesting case refers to information that normally is available only after the contract is signed and that raises lock-in situations.[15] These are sometimes referred in the economic literature as "after-market" outcomes: once a contract is signed and eventually a product

---

[11] Stefan Haupt, *supra* note 8.

[12] Ian Ramsay, "Consumer Protection," in Peter Newman (ed.), *The New Palgrave Dictionary of Economics and the Law*, vol. I, Macmillan, London (1998), p. 412.

[13] Fernando Gomez Pomar, *supra* note 5.

[14] Stefan Haupt, *supra* note 8; Pamaria Rekaiti and Roger van den Bergh, "Cooling-Off Periods in the Consumer Laws of the EC Member States: A Comparative Law and Economics Approach," 23 *Journal of Consumer Policy* (2000), 371, at 373.

[15] See J. Vickers, *supra* note 10; Joseph Farrell and Paul Klemperer, "Coordination and Lock-In: Competition with Switching Costs and Network Effects," in *Handbook of Industrial Organization*, Volume 3, 2007, Elsevier, pp. 1967–2072.

or service delivered, the consumer is locked-in for all the problems that may arise (i.e. repairs, maintenance, assistance and so on) and that the consumer was not able to fully consider or even expect at the moment of the purchase.

As the consumer is locked-in, his outside options are reduced ex post and consequently the seller may impose a take-it-or-leave-it offer in the "secondary market" of the supplementary services tied with the original product or service. In a sense, the seller will be a monopolist in the after-market and may extract the full quasi-rent from the buyer (hold-up).

In our view, in this situation the traditional correspondence between the consumer's weaker bargaining power, on the one side, and the seller's "monopolistic" power, on the other, may hold. But this is true only because it is the result of a "fundamental transformation"[16] from the ex ante market exchange to the ex post after-market hold-up.

As a consequence, when the ex post quasi-rent lost by the consumer in the after-market is large enough to outweigh the ex ante gains from trade, an inefficient contract will result, and this leads us back to the case of the "regret" assumption, as the full ex ante consideration of overall prices would have induced the buyer not to sign the contract in the first instance.

Two crucial questions then arise. Is a "specific" regulation needed to cope with these "contractual failures" or can the market mechanism "autonomously" solve it? Should any form of regulation be applied to any consumer, even a sophisticated one, or shall we distinguish among a group of consumers, on the one side, and according to the specific content of the contract, on the other?

The answer to the first question depends on the point at which we start our analysis. Several scholars have argued that learning, reputation and word of mouth in the long term will correct the inefficient outcomes, under any market structure, as "good sellers" will be willing to signal their superior quality and buyers will be willing to pay for it.[17] The Smithian "invisible hand" will thus correct short-term inefficiencies, without any regulatory intervention. However, the paradox with the assumption of self-correcting markets is that some parties have to be damaged in the first instance in order to induce virtuous behavior on the other side of the contract. In the absence of any safeguard, some "efficient consumers" (i.e. those having a willingness to pay higher than or equal to the potential contractual price) may simply decide not to start a bargaining in the first instance, due to a lack of protection. Indeed, this will be a standard market failure, calling for "some" regulation.

On the other side, regulation could lead to a false positive, when sophisticated consumers receive "too much" protection. Indeed this would mean interfering with a potential efficient bargaining, affecting the default option of the protected party vis-à-vis the counterpart. In turn, this may adversely affect the incentives of the non-protected party to even

---

[16] Oliver Williamson (1985), *The Economic Institutions of Capitalism*, Free Press.

[17] Sanford Grossman, "The Informational Role of Warranties and Private Disclosure of Product Quality," 24 *Journal of Law and Economics* (1981), p. 461; Alan Mathios, "The Impact of Mandatory Disclosure Laws on Product Choices: An Analysis of the Salad Dressing Market," 43 *Journal of Law and Economics* (2000), pp. 658–60.

start a bargaining process. In this case we will have the opposite result of a "regulatory failure" due to an excess of protection.

2.4 Market Failure or Regulatory Failure?

As Stefan Haupt has outlined,[18] there are many domains of European consumer law which raise several concerns in this respect. Mandatory disclosure of information[19] may play a crucial role in some areas (consumer credits,[20] insurance,[21] time-sharing,[22] distance contracts[23]) but disclosure law might be superfluous when unfavorable information is easily available or when private informed sellers maintain strong incentives to reveal it.[24] Standard-form contracts may serve well in some circumstances, when search costs are prohibitive, when there is bounded rationality or even when there is a risk of consumer confusion due to information overload. However, standardization may also inhibit efficiency enhancing contractual autonomy for those sophisticated consumers who are capable of selecting the information they need. On the other side, in oligopolistic markets, standardization may adversely enforce collusion among competitors, acting as a facilitating practice. Finally, mandatory cooling-off periods, as those granted by the doorstep selling directive[25] and the distant selling directive,[26] may increase incentives for the purchasing of credence and experience goods, but they may raise ex post opportunistic behavior by hit-and-run consumers, decreasing sellers' incentives to invest.[27]

---

[18] Stefan Haupt, *supra* note 8.

[19] See, for instance, Council Resolution of 14 April 1975 on a preliminary programme of the European Economic Community for a consumer protection and information policy, O.J. EC 1975 C 92/1; Council Resolution of 19 May 1981 on a second programme of the European Economic Community for a consumer protection and information policy, O.J. EC 1981 C 133/1; Council Resolution of 23 June 1986 concerning the future orientation of the policy of the European Economic Community for the protection and promotion of consumer interests, O.J. EC 1986 C 167/1.

[20] EC Directive 87/102 relating to the approximation of the laws, regulations and administrative provisions of the Member States concerning consumer credit, O.J. 1987 L 42/48, amended by EC Directive 90/88, O.J. 1990 L 61/14 and in O.J. 1998 L 101/17.

[21] EC Directive 92/96 of 10 November 1992 on the coordination of laws, regulations and administrative provisions relating to direct life assurance and amending EC Directives 79/267 and 90/619 (third life assurance Directive), O.J. 1992 L 360/1

[22] EC Directive 94/47 on the protection of purchasers in respect of certain aspects of contracts relating to the purchase of the right to use immovable properties on a timeshare basis, O.J. 1994 L 280/83.

[23] EC Directive 97/7 on the protection of consumers in respect of distance contracts, O.J. 1997 L 166/19.

[24] Roger J. van den Bergh, *supra* note 5.

[25] EC Directive 85/577 to protect the consumer in respect of contracts negotiated away from business premises, O.J. 1985 L 372/31.

[26] EC Directive 97/7 on the protection of consumers in respect of distance contracts, O.J. 1997 L 166/19.

[27] Hans-Peter Schwintowski, "Contractual Rules Concerning the Marketing of Goods and Services – Requirements of Form and Content versus Private Autonomy," in Stefan Grundmann, Wolfgang Kerber and Stephen Weatherill (eds), *Party Autonomy and the Role of Information in the Internal Market*, Walter de Gruyter, Berlin–New York (2001), p. 331, at p. 346.

As a consequence, from a law and economics perspective, it seems that the question of consumer protection should always be addressed under a narrow path neighboring on two opposite risks: market failure and regulatory failure.

3 TOWARDS THE "EMPOWERED CONSUMER": A UNIFYING PERSPECTIVE?

The evolution of consumer law, especially in Europe, has revealed how the above dichotomic distinction between regulatory and market solutions to consumer protection became rather misleading in the last decades.

One of the reasons lies in what has been termed "consumer activism," i.e. an active consumer's behavior which, by affecting market outcomes, may positively align agents' incentives in such a way as to reduce "inefficient contracts," increasing consumer welfare. The surrounding idea is that the market mechanism can correct "contractual failures" also through consumer empowerment, i.e. through a "light" regulatory design aimed at enhancing the market discipline device provided by consumer choice. An "active" consumer is one able to gain access to the relevant information, to sanction inefficiencies through exerting "exit" choices and to coordinate collective actions so as to faster reach socially desired outcomes.

The empowerment of consumers is pursued in the European Union through a progressive regulatory shift from standards to a new regulatory function of contractual rules and remedies and through a complementary role of public and private enforcement. This process is particularly appreciable in sector specific legislations, both at the European and the national levels, ranging from financial to telecom, from energy and gas to transport, from payment systems to media and so on.

The last release of the OECD's indicators of entry barrier reduction shows that, on average, in almost all network industries, European countries are today aligned towards the highest value of the indicator measuring the removal of barriers to entry.[28] This result was driven by a mass of European directives and national legislation that, within a regulatory framework based on independent authorities and on a pervasive role of antitrust law,[29] have successfully liberalized access to essential facilities,[30] enhancing downstream competition.

However, while the supply side of liberalization policies registered a remarkable success in terms of entry barrier reduction, the demand side of market openness is still in its infancy. As the last release of the Eurobarometer on consumers' satisfaction shows, contract conditions and the affordability of the services' prices in network industries still

---

[28] Filippo Belloc and Antonio Nicita, "The Political Determinants of Liberalization: Do Ideological Cleavages Still Matter?" in *International Review of Economics*, 2011

[29] David Levy-Faur, "The Governance of Competition: the Interplay of Technology, Economics, and Politics in the Making of the European Union Electricity and Telecom Regimes," *Journal of Public Policy*, Vol. 19, No.2, 1999, pp. 175–207.

[30] Angelo Castaldo and Antonio Nicita, "Essential Facility Access in Europe: Building a Test for Antitrust Policy," *Review of Law and Economics*, Berkeley Press, 3:1, 2007.

show large variations across countries. Moreover, network industries rank in the lowest positions in terms of consumers' satisfaction.

The lesson to be derived from this result is that the removal of entry barriers is a necessary but not a sufficient condition for reaching a substantial market openness. A paradigm shift from supply-side liberalizations to demand-side consumer-based regulatory policies is needed in order to provide consumers with an actual empowerment. By enhancing consumers' mobility among providers and access to relevant information, the effective mechanism of competition may then complete, on the demand side, the liberalization process.

As Ennis and Heimler[31] have pointed out, focusing on "demand-side elements can yield substantial benefits to consumers, especially by changing the elasticity of residual demand faced by individual firms. Small changes in switching costs, search costs, or the number of 'elastic' consumers can have large beneficial impacts on equilibrium outcomes".

In recent years, consumer empowerment has received growing attention from the European Commission in several domains. Sectoral regulation, also at the national level, has increasingly recurred to contractual law provisions as the privileged means for implementing consumer empowerment. This is not to say that standard consumer protection measures, such as those against duress and undue pressure, pre-purchase information, undue post-purchase surprise, misleading advertising, and so on, lose their centrality and function. Rather they are increasingly coupled with policies based on the regulatory function of contract law in order to enhance consumer wefare, through consumer activism and the disciplinary device of the resulting competitive mechanism.

In this respect, as we outline in the next section, the recent evolution of the European approach to consumer protection goes hand in hand with the enforcement of competition policy.

4 CONSUMER AND COMPETITION POLICIES IN THE EU: TRADE-OFFS AND COMPLEMENTARITIES

Competition and consumer law interplay in different ways in highly competitive and non-competitive markets.[32] Traditionally, some tensions between the consumer and competition policies have been outlined, particularly in those areas characterized by a high innovation rate and/or price and quality discrimination, to the extent that mandatory rules may prevent efficient investments.

Nowadays, several authors have acknowledged that consumer and competition policies are much more complements than substitutes as they both serve the purpose of completing the European internal market.[33] This is particularly true today, as the mentioned

[31] Ennis, E. and Heimler, A., "Promoting Competition on the Demand Side" (2004), SSRN Working Paper.

[32] Fabrizio Cafaggi and Hans-W. Micklitz, *Administrative and Judicial Enforcement in Consumer Protection: The Way Forward*, 2008.

[33] See Fernando Gomez Pomar, "EC Consumer Protection Law and EC Competition Law: How Related are They? A law and economics perspective" 8 (InDret Working Paper No. 113, 2003); John Vickers, "Economics for Consumer Policy," British Academy Keynes Lecture,

paradigm shift towards consumer empowerment would enhance the mechanism of competition.

There are nonetheless some issues that we would like to briefly address in order to clarify what are, in our view, the specific domains of the two policies.

Competition policy is not against monopoly. A de facto monopoly configuration will be opposed by European antitrust law only when it is reached through anti-competitive agreements or opportunistic mergers among rivals. Beside that, only the abuse of a dominant position is deemed anti-competitive. When a monopoly or a dominant position is reached through external growth in the market, it might be the result of competition in and for the market, pursued by a more efficient firm relative to rivals. Thus, as anticipated in the previous sections, a monopoly configuration might be associated with efficient contracts even if it generates a "market inefficiency" as some efficient exchanges will occur. However, the inefficiency of a monopoly configuration should be correctly compared not with the mainstream benchmark of perfect competition but rather with the level of "workable competition," which depends on the specific characteristics of the relevant market.

The economic analysis of competition law has induced many antitrust authorities to progressively shift the application of Arts 101 and 102 of the Treaty, from *per se rule* to *rule of reason*. An example concerns the adoption of discriminatory practices by a dominant firm. Art. 102 says that any abuse of a dominant position "shall be prohibited as incompatible with the common market insofar as it may affect trade between Member States." Such abuse may consist in

> directly or indirectly imposing unfair purchase or selling prices or other unfair trading conditions; limiting production, markets or technical development to the prejudice of consumers; applying dissimilar conditions to equivalent transactions with other trading parties, thereby placing them at a competitive disadvantage; making the conclusion of contracts subject to acceptance by the other parties of supplementary obligations which, by their nature or according to commercial usage, have no connection with the subject of such contracts.

As we have argued in the previous section, many forms of price discrimination, including bundling and tie-in, enacted by a dominant firm may increase, under given conditions, consumer welfare as, under price discrimination, a larger number of potentially efficient exchanges will occur in the market, relative to the non-discrimination case.

However, price discrimination induces a departure from standard-form contracts and its main consequence is that of treating a distinct group of consumers in a different way. As we have noticed in the previous section, the efficiency enhancing nature of consumers' discrimination practices is independent of the distributional consequence of each specific contract signed between the monopolist and each consumer in the market.

In the extreme case of a perfectly discriminating monopolist, the monopolist will extract all the rent from each single buyer, but nonetheless the discrimination will lead

---

October 2003; Roger J. van den Bergh, "Competition Law and Consumer Protection Legislation," in *Economic Analysis of Law: A European Perspective*, A. Hatzis (ed.), 2003, Edward Elgar; Katalin Judit Cseres, *Competition Law and Consumer Protection*, Kluwer Law International, European Monographs 49, The Hague, 2005; Mark Armstrong, "Interactions between Competition and Consumer Policy," *Competition Policy International Journal*, vol. 4, 2008.

to the same efficiency level of perfect competition, as all the potential efficient exchanges will be made. Of course, under price discrimination some consumers will be worse off but some others will be better off, with potentially undesirable distributional consequences.

In this respect, protecting "the" consumer is meaningless, as each consumer will have a different willingness to pay. A discriminating monopolist will enhance the overall consumer welfare as more buyers will be able to buy the product, relative to the case of non-discrimination. The consequence of this reasoning is that we should look at the specific condition of the market before concluding against price discrimination by a dominant firm.

This conclusion clearly contrasts with the traditional view that depicts the consumer as the weak party in a contract against a party with market power. In some cases, then, imposing standard-form contracts or inhibiting discrimination may reduce market efficiency and thus decrease the welfare of those "efficient consumers" whose willingness to pay is above the cost of delivery but below the monopolist price under no discrimination.

In some other circumstances, prohibiting price discrimination may enhance consumer welfare. This is the case when, for instance, price discrimination by a dominant firm is functional to target competitors in some areas. In this case, the dominant firm fixes lower prices in areas open to competition and raises the prices in those areas where the monopoly is safe. Here "discrimination" serves the purpose of enacting an exclusionary practice to the detriment of consumer welfare, when as efficient or more efficient competitors are excluded from the market.

The above example shows that the economic assessment of an anti-competitive behavior relies on the specific characteristics of the market, on the level of actual and potential competition and the effects generated on the market by the behavior of the dominant firm. In this respect the "rule of reason" approach of competition law might contrast with the provisions of consumer law, as the latter are generally less "elastic" to the specific conditions of the relevant market.

On the other hand, there are inefficient configurations that cannot be faced by competition law but which, nonetheless, would need some protection. These are, for instance, the cases in which ex ante competitive markets may generate some "abuse of economic dependence" ex post in the after-market due to lock-in effects. As we have outlined in the previous section, these are the circumstances in which once a contract is signed and eventually a product or service delivered, the consumer is locked-in for all the problems that may arise (i.e. repairs, maintenance, assistance, and so on) and that the consumer was not able to fully consider or even expect at the moment of the purchase. As this outcome might be generated even in an ex ante competitive market, the antitrust law will not be able to oppose it as an abuse of dominant position.

The evolution of antitrust law, in the US and in the EU, has clearly outlined that rational consumers should be able to anticipate after-market lock-in. Thus, unless this lock-in is generated by an ex ante dominant firm, it is deemed not deserving an antitrust intervention. Here, there is then a potential for consumer protection which is complementary to antitrust law, as it covers, and prevents, some potential contractual inefficiency that antitrust law is not able to solve.

A similar argument could be raised for all those contractual rules, imposed by non-dominant firms, that increase switching costs (breach penalties, technological lock-in, exclusivity clauses) without any economic justification.

In other words, since there could be some contractual inefficiencies even in competitive markets without a dominant firm, consumer law can contribute to solving these inefficiencies in a proper way when competition law could not. The same holds for situations characterized by oligopoly or collective dominance, when firms' alignment is the result of firms' rationality rather than the outcome of an anti-competitive agreement. In all these cases, consumer law can efficiently be a complement of competition law, provided that its provisions do not weaken the mechanism of competition to the detriment of consumer welfare. Thus consumer protection policies need to internalize the current and future level of competitiveness in their design.

5 THE RISE OF THE REGULATORY FUNCTION OF EUROPEAN CONSUMER LAW?

European consumer protection has been evolved over time according to three interdependent processes or "movements," both at the national and at the European level: (i) the increasing regulatory function of private law, (ii) the "constitutionalization" of private law and (iii) the "multi-level system" of private law. Each of these "movements" outlines a partially overlapping process which actually led to an unresolved fragmentation of the several tools designed for "consumer protection," raising inevitably some tensions among the many purposes behind it.

Traditionally, civil codes in European states have been based on the principle of private autonomy of the parties. According to some authors,[34] this was mainly the result of the application of the liberal "freedom-to-choose" paradigm to contracts. The 1929 world economic crisis generated a first "regulatory response," through the introduction of some rules defining public law constraints on parties' contractual autonomy. After World War II, mandatory rules for consumer protection, together with the design of competition law rules, have been introduced in some MS, starting a process which has steeply increased over the years and that has been defined as "the regulatory function of private law."[35]

This regulatory function could be defined as "the ability of private law instruments, in particular contract, torts and property, to address market failure,"[36] beside other distributive functions. This "process" has been mainly driven by a progressive shift from standard "command and control" regulation to "incentive regulation," under the impulse of the European Commission.

There are at least three economic rationales behind this phenomenon. The first relies on the idea that the proper design of economic incentives tends to induce more "efficient"

34 See M. Freedland, "Private Law, Regulation and Governance Design and the Personal Work Contract," in F. Cafaggi and H.M. Watt, *Making European Private Law*, p. 231.

35 See K. Cseres, "Governance Design for European Private Law: Lessons from the Europeanisation of Competition Law in Central and Eastern Europe," p. 142; H. Collins, "Governance Implications for the European Union of the Changing Character of Private Law," p. 276; F. Cafaggi, "The Making of European Private Law," p. 294; all in F. Cafaggi and H.M. Watt, *Making European Private Law*.

36 See F. Cafaggi and H.M. Watt, *Making European Private Law*.

decisions by economic agents, when the relevant information is privately owned and decentralized "in the market." For instance, "green taxes" or "tradable permits for pollution" allow producers to strategically adapt to environmental targets in a more efficient way than standards would do, precisely because they induce efficient "self-selection" in the market.

The second economic rationale refers to the minimization of transaction costs, in the form of both monitoring and enforcement costs, as regulators often do not have, at least in due time, all the relevant information to take proper decisions and, consequently, their enforcement role could be undermined by the time needed to monitor behaviors, collect information, and take final decisions. Transaction costs held by regulators may then generate adverse incentives by reducing the level of overall deterrence.

A third economic rationale could be referred to the "maturity" of market openness, for instance in the case of network industry liberalizations. As we have previously outlined, while liberalizations initially focus on the reduction of barriers to entry, acting selectively on the supply side, the ex post "success" of liberalization, in terms of market competition, crucially depends on the demand side, i.e. on consumer empowerment and mobility among providers. As consumers may face high transaction costs to coordinate their behavior in the market, private law tools may provide a powerful set of instruments to efficiently align incentives on both sides of the market.

Several EC Directives network industries (in telecommunications, gas and electricity, banking, among others) converge in identifying fundamental principles which should govern the contractual relationship between incumbents owning essential facilities and new entrants on the one side, and between providers and consumers on the other. Consumers should be able to freely choose and change their providers. This leads to obligations concerning transparency of information in contractual terms, right of withdrawal without penalty, compensation and refund, meeting of "declared" minimum quality standards, virtually no charge for changing supplier, and elimination of the exclusivity clause, even de facto as in the case of the English clause.

This fundamental shift, from "command and control" regulation to "incentive regulation," has another pervasive consequence. When a violation of contractual rules occurs, the enforcement domain also includes private enforcement.

These ambiguities in the notion of the "consumer" and the nature of his "protection" were maintained and even accrued as the European approach to consumer protection co-evolved with national legislations under an uncoordinated regime. Indeed, EU consumer law has evolved as a multi-level regime where a few areas of consumer law emerged as a separate body in the early 1970s in some MS. Legislation was introduced in France, the UK and Germany in several fields, among which was contract law concerning unfair contract terms.[37] These approaches were rather different: while consumer law in Germany and to some extent in France was conceived as part of welfare law and the protection of the weaker party constituted the primary objective, the UK had since the outset a mixed approach combining welfare and regulatory functions. MS have been displaying a strong level of public regulation, featuring a collective judicial enforcement model, predominantly based on public institutions (ombudsmen, consumer agencies) or private

---

37 In Germany in 1976, in the UK in 1977, in France in 1978.

organizations (consumer associations). European legislation on consumer protection has focused primarily on substantive law, leaving MS the task of providing for effective enforcement. This choice has been partly influenced by lack of competence and by the principle of procedural autonomy.

The emergence of EU consumer law occurred in the late 1970s but the acquis grew substantially only in the second half of the 1980s and in the 1990s. Traditionally the acquis does not encompass consumer legislation in regulated markets. However a significant body of consumer law has been introduced in sector specific legislation ranging from finance to telecom, from energy and gas to transport, from payment systems to media. This means that understanding the evolution of consumer protection in the EU requires nowadays a broader approach, with a look at the acquis that has emerged in regulated markets.[38]

There has been an evolution also in relation to modes of enforcement. In the first stage the majority of MS opted for judicial enforcement. Lately both the EU approach and the MS attitudes have changed, shifting from private to public enforcement. These changes have reinforced the institutional change quite clear in consumer protection in regulated markets where regulators have taken over substantial implementation power and the role of courts has shifted from enforcement to judicial review. Today even in general consumer protection the role of regulators at MS level is stronger. Some states have given consumer protection competence to competition authorities (Italy); others have created independent regulatory agencies (the Netherlands); others have kept the competence within the executive. There is a clear correlation between the regulatory function of consumer regulation and the institutional changes just described, suggesting the inadequacy of courts to implement regulatory objectives.

The broadening of the "consumer acquis" has had a clear impact on national legal systems. The principle of procedural autonomy allows MS to choose within certain limits the modes of implementation of the acquis. Essentially two different legislative strategies have been adopted to implement EU legislation: separation and integration. Some countries have adopted a consumer code separate from civil and commercial codes (France, Spain, Italy and some eastern European countries). Separation has also been the perspective of the Scandinavian countries. Integration between consumer legislation and general civil and commercial law is the German example, with the BGB Modernisierung of 2001.[39]

MS legislative choices not only have a systematic impact but also reflect two different philosophies of market design. The separation from a regulatory perspective emphasizes specific regulatory needs for consumer transactions and harms which would not be necessary for business-to-business relationships. The integration strategy suggests on the contrary that similar regulatory objectives characterize both B2B and B2C relationships.

These differences have today an impact on how the European policies are implemented at national level and partially undermine the harmonization project and its regulatory objectives.

---

[38] See F. Cafaggi, Introduction, in *Making European Private Law*, 2008, p. 289ff.

[39] See F. Cafaggi, RTDPC 2008.

PART 6

LAW ENFORCEMENT

12 An economic analysis of legal harmonization: the case of law enforcement within the European Union

*Nuno Garoupa**

1 INTRODUCTION

Legal harmonization in the European Union is presented by many of its supporters and enthusiasts as economically justified. Paradoxically, legal economists are quite skeptical about the overall economic advantages of harmonization and unification. There is now a vast economics literature looking at the multiple determinants of legal convergence. The more detailed and more realistic are the models, the more skeptical the literature is about legal harmonization.

Law enforcement has not been immune to the legal harmonization discussion. The economics literature has not attracted so much attention. Nevertheless, in the same vein, legal economists are not convinced by the superiority of coordination over decentralized enforcement. For example, the externalities in the market for criminal law are self-evident. However, the centralized solution is not immune to agency costs. The extent to which the benefits of internalizing externalities outweigh these agency costs is much less obvious.

Harmonization of law enforcement is pursued in the European Union within the former Third Pillar, now absorbed into the consolidated European Union structure under the Treaty of Lisbon. Established under the Maastricht Treaty (1993), the former Third Pillar essentially covered asylum and immigration policies (transferred to the First Pillar under the Treaty of Amsterdam, 1999), rules concerning external borders and customs, coordination of legal policies in relation to illicit drugs, international fraud, terrorism, organized crime and judicial cooperation. Certain European agencies were created in this context, for example, Eurojust (2002) and Europol (1999). Special mechanisms were developed such as the European Arrest Warrant.

The approach taken by the European Union has not been unproblematic. The European Arrest Warrant, for example, has raised concerns in terms of different law enforcement policies. This mechanism can only be activated for the purpose of criminal prosecution and enforcing certain sentences; it cannot be used for police investigation. However, different models concerning prosecution and judicial oversight have been at the heart of the debate over the adoption of a harmonized arrest warrant. Initially only Belgium, Denmark, Finland, Ireland, Portugal, Spain, Sweden and the United Kingdom accepted the mechanism with effect from January 2004. Other Member States joined in

* The author is grateful to Manfred Holler and the participants at the Hamburg meeting for helpful suggestions. Roya H. Samarghandi has provided superb research assistance. The usual disclaimers apply.

November 2004. Italy did not implement the mechanism until April 2005 since there was concern on how this legal instrument would be used. There are around 13,500 of these warrants issued per year.

Similarly, in the area of human rights, the enforcement by the ECJ of general principles of law derived from the European Convention on Human Rights (now formally binding on the European Union under the Treaty of Lisbon) effectively harmonized minimum guarantees in criminal prosecution and trial. With all Member States being members of the European Convention on Human Rights and subject to the jurisdiction of the European Court of Human Rights, we could be tempted to think that legal harmonization promoted by the European Union in this context has been of marginal importance. However, we can immediately consider the importance of the UK Human Rights Act 1998 to recognize that preferences concerning the enforcement of human rights tend to vary across Member States, even if only slightly.

Cooperation in criminal matters, at the level of enforcement agencies and judicial matters, is aimed at a more effective fight against crime. The final goal of such European policy is to enhance deterrence and legal compliance, reducing crime rates and the costs of fighting crime. Strictly speaking, the Third Pillar does not impose an extensive legal harmonization in the area of criminal law, but effectively pushes Member States in such a direction. In this context, the Schengen Agreements offer a good example to discuss the economic arguments for and against legal harmonization.

In March 1995, the Schengen Agreement became operational, after being beset for a long time by technical problems and by political uncertainty, particularly in France. The Agreement, signed in June 1985 by Germany, Belgium, France, Luxembourg, and the Netherlands, gave concrete form to the gradual elimination of checks at their common borders. Italy joined the Agreement in November 1990, Portugal and Spain in June 1992, Greece in November 1992, Austria in April 1995, and Denmark, Finland, Iceland, Norway, and Sweden in December 1996. The Agreement aimed at creating a common territory without internal border controls. It provided for the cooperation of law enforcement authorities, particularly as regards drugs and firearms. Controversially, it created an information exchange system relating to wanted persons and objects within an international database. It provided for the harmonization of the rules governing the crossing of the common external frontiers, visa policy and the issuing of visas (including the creation of a uniform visa), conditions of entry, and residence of foreigners in the common territory. It also contained rules on asylum applications (complemented by the Dublin Convention of 15 June 1990) and on extradition. The Schengen Agreement was complemented by the Implementing Convention, signed in June 1990 and effective from September 1993 for the original five Member States, and from March 1994 for Portugal and Spain. The complementary convention was intended to accompany the elimination of internal borders with measures and arrangements aimed at ensuring security.

The United Kingdom and Ireland decided not to join these Agreements. One of the arguments behind their decision was the need to keep border controls and checks to deter crime. The United Kingdom, and to a lesser extent Ireland, considered that the freedom of movement of persons provided by European Union law could only apply to nationals of the countries of the European Union. In that sense, the Schengen Agreement was not a natural consequence of European law. The cooperation arising out of Schengen, therefore, was developed on the fringe of the European Community.

The status of the Schengen Agreement changed in 1999 with the Treaty of Amsterdam. It was integrated into the new Treaty, thus becoming part of the *acquis communautaire*. The United Kingdom and Ireland kept their opt-outs for essentially the same reasons as explained before.

By virtue of being part of the Treaty of Amsterdam, the Schengen Agreement lost its treaty status and is now subject to change by the European Union legislative procedure. At the same time, the new Members of the Union joined the Schengen Agreement at accession. With effect from May 2004, the Czech Republic, Estonia, Hungary, Latvia, Lithuania, Malta, Poland, Slovakia and Slovenia joined the Schengen Area. Switzerland joined in October 2004. As to Bulgaria and Romania, although they formally joined the Schengen Area in January 2007 after accession to the Union, it was not effective until March 2011. The same applies to Liechtenstein, who joined in February 2008, but not with effect until 2011. Finally, the legal status of Cyprus in the Schengen Area has been complicated because of the political situation in the island.

Meanwhile, both the United Kingdom and Ireland have changed their initial skeptical position. The United Kingdom asked for formal participation in certain areas of cooperation on law enforcement in May 1999, effective since 2004. Ireland asked for a similar role in February 2002, but it is still not effective.

This chapter explores the interaction between the economic advantages of legal harmonization and the economics of law enforcement. The Schengen Area largely provides for incremental harmonization, if not selected unification, of criminal law enforcement across the European Union. Is there an economic rationale? Can we frame the discussion in the context of the trade-off between reducing transaction costs and satisfying local preferences? These are the questions addressed in this chapter.

The chapter is organized in the following way. In Section 2, I discuss the general costs and benefits of legal harmonization. In Section 3, I address the economics of law enforcement in this context. Section 4 concludes the chapter.

2 THE COSTS AND BENEFITS OF LEGAL HARMONIZATION[1]

The European Union is a hybrid jurisdiction subject to a potential harmonization or unification pattern of legal development.[2] The main economic benefit of harmonization is the reduction of transaction costs that facilitates market integration, exchange of goods and services, and economic growth. Notwithstanding, the satisfaction of local preferences as embodied by the different legal cultures and legal orders is impossible with further integration of legal norms. In fact, comparativists have emphasized that, albeit possible incremental convergence of legal systems, they are irremediably inconsistent.[3]

A naïve view of legal harmonization focuses only on the potential reduction of transaction costs. Legal economists have recognized that changing legal regimes

---

[1] This section deeply relies on Garoupa and Gómez Ligüerre (2012).

[2] The use of the word "hybrid" is provocative in this context. European Union law is enforced by civil law and common law courts.

[3] See, among others, Pierre Legrand (1996, 1997, 1999).

has important disadvantages in the context of legal transplants.[4] Following the economics literature on the subject, the list of possible costs from harmonizing should include:

1. Direct costs imposed on some Member States from acquiring information, importing new rules and introducing new practices, and interpreting and applying them.[5] These costs seem less significant when civil law has prevailed in most Member States, but could be high in areas of the law with high variance. Examples include the areas of the law covered by the Draft Common Framework of Reference (DCFR) and human rights.
2. Rent-seeking or entrenchment costs from those who plausibly lose from changing legal rules (long-entrenched interests) and are willing to waste resources to avoid those changes (e.g. lawyers or the bar association).[6] These costs could have been reduced more recently as the European Union has forced competition in the legal profession and other related services (mainly since the Establishment Directive in 1998).[7]
3. Indirect costs due to the potential loss of legal coherence, consistency, network effects and potential development of contradictions and instability within the emergent law.[8]
4. Private legal order costs incurred by limiting individual benefits from opting-out of the current legal order or developing third-party arrangements, that is, by imposing public adjustment of the law, which is an imperfect substitute for private adjustment (assuming that existing arrangements allowed for such adjustment).[9] In our analysis, allowing European Union law to coexist with national law could increase flexibility if it facilitates the malleability of the legal system.
5. Lack-of-innovation costs since systems without local variations are less likely to innovate and adjust to dynamic preferences.[10] Jurisdictional competition is the main source of legal innovation. A reduction of jurisdictional competition has a long-term impact on the overall quality of the legal system.
6. Subsequent costs of adjustment and administrative costs on the production of more law when transplants deviate from original national law.[11] In particular, the costs of legal transposition and enforcement could be relevant when different languages and legal cultures are forced to coexist.
7. Potential costs caused by coordination failure due to the presence of strategic externalities or the public good nature of transplanting.[12] This could be a significant problem if harmonization is left to be completed by the market.

---

4 See Garoupa and Ogus (2006).
5 Ibid.
6 Ibid. See also Ogus (1999).
7 See, for example, Gromek-Broc (2002).
8 See Garoupa and Ogus (2006). See also Ogus (2002).
9 Ibid.
10 Ibid.
11 See Grajzl and Dimitrova (2009).
12 See Garoupa and Ogus (2006) and Carbonara and Parisi (2009).

8. Domestic transaction costs resulting from harmonization and legal unification.[13] Although these costs could be relevant given the entrenchment of national law, they should be less significant than in a situation of pure legal transplanting from a different jurisdiction given the ongoing pluralism of European law.

After reviewing all the possible costs from legal harmonization, the conclusion can only be that it is unlikely that all areas of the law should be targeted. The net benefit of legal harmonization is expected to vary, depending on the legal determinants and the economic context. At the same time, the net benefit from legal harmonization heavily depends on the initial conditions, that is, how different jurisdictions are before the process of harmonization takes place.

In fact, preferences have to be considered against the list of costs and benefits from harmonization. Preferences (understood as legal culture, tradition, and social inclination for a particular legal family) are the standard explanation for the prevalence of different legal systems.[14] In the legal transplant literature, the traditional argument is that cultural, political, and social preferences might explain why jurisdictions do not switch their legal regime.

Transaction costs have to be traded against local preferences. The conditions under which harmonization is efficient are likely to be satisfied for certain areas of the law and unsatisfied for other areas of the law. Areas of the law that facilitate jurisdictional exchange of goods and services are more likely to satisfy the conditions for efficient legal harmonization. Areas of the law that are of little significance for jurisdictional exchange of goods and services are less likely to satisfy those conditions. Inevitably the mere recognition that harmonization reduces transaction costs is a flawed economic argument to support its efficiency.

3 THE ECONOMICS OF HARMONIZING LAW ENFORCEMENT

3.1 Basic Model

In a previous article,[15] I have discussed the Schengen Agreement in the context of the market for narcotics. My argument was that the Schengen Area could be seen as the response to a standard market failure. There are obvious geographic externalities on the market for narcotics. Individuals can move and choose where to trade, buy and consume narcotics. They can also decide in which jurisdictions to commit the crimes that will provide them with the means to acquire drugs. Profits made in the market for narcotics can travel to different jurisdictions. Inevitably law enforcement policies in one jurisdiction will have significant spillover effects on neighboring jurisdictions. Jurisdictions respond to other jurisdictions in terms of enforcement policies.

---

13 See Garoupa and Ogus (2006) and Carbonara and Parisi (2007).

14 See, among others, *supra* note 3.

15 Garoupa (1997).

Therefore, coordination of law enforcement policies can potentially internalize these externalities.

However, there are two main drawbacks. Preferences concerning the regulation of the market for narcotics could vary (and they do vary, with the Netherlands being the usual outlier). A coordinated solution is likely to require some jurisdictions to implement law enforcement policies that are not their most preferred. These jurisdictions can still be better off by joining the union (because the potentially second-best coordinated solution could be better than the uncoordinated solution), but face serious domestic pressure given the divergence of preferences. There are important costs in controlling and enforcing true coordination. There are standard agency costs that could be enhanced if there are asymmetries of information.

Another problem is the potential existence of free-riding and consequent distribution of costs. Although the coordinated solution could improve the overall welfare of the union, some jurisdictions might need to be subsidized to enter the union while others should be taxed. Administering such complex institutional arrangements is not easy.

In the simple economic model, assume that expected sanctions are the same but the particular combination of probability and severity of punishment differs. Suppose the probability is harmonized targeting an intermediate value (for example, the simple average of both probabilities). The immediate consequence is that one jurisdiction will have a higher expected sanction (hence, fewer criminals) than the other jurisdiction. Given the local preferences concerning crime rates, sanctions have to be adjusted, with further costs in terms of enforcement policies. Alternatively, if sanctions cannot be adjusted, each jurisdiction faces pressure to cheat on harmonization and apply the former probability of punishment.

As I have explained before, it is well known in economics that a cooperative solution asserts a larger surplus than a non-cooperative solution in the presence of important externalities. Clearly one important determinant of the cooperative solution is the spill-over effect; the more interdependent are jurisdictions (the lower are criminal displacement costs), the more likely is the success of such a solution. Within the Schengen Area, this observation suggests that islands or countries with geographical discontinuities within the union have less to gain. This could explain the degree of skepticism exhibited by the United Kingdom and Ireland.

The elimination of internal borders favors jurisdictional criminal mobility. In the economic model, rational offenders will commit their offenses where the marginal cost of one more offense is lower. This marginal cost is determined by law enforcement policies and displacement costs. This effect should lead to competition among the different jurisdictions to have a tougher law enforcement policy in order to avoid immigration of offenders. This competition produces a waste of resources because each jurisdiction ignores the loss of welfare on other jurisdictions. Therefore, a cooperative solution internalizes this externality.

However, some observations should be taken into account when implementing a cooperative solution. On one hand, some countries may be worse off in a cooperative solution. On the other hand, there are incentives to serious "free-ride behavior." In fact, an important point is to understand why countries have different policies before harmonization. According to the rational theory of law enforcement, there are three possible explanations: (a) different individual preferences with respect to committing an offense,

(b) different wealth distribution, (c) different enforcement technology. Even if the first two explanations are possibly true, I suggest the third explanation is the one that should be attended to. A cooperative solution does not affect the first two observations, but plays an important role in the discussion of the third.

Technological differences across the European Union could be explained by the difficulty of police bureaucracies in adjusting to changes. Cooperation could lower adjustment costs by making access to new technologies easier, providing more information, or creating internal incentives for police bureaucracies to be more flexible. In the future, jurisdictional cooperation could create competition between police bureaucracies across the European Union, making them more efficient.

A related problem is the eventual conflict between the supranational structure (Europol) and the local bureaucracies. Currently, there is no strict hierarchy of different enforcement agencies. National police forces keep the monopoly in many areas, including the direction and control of operations that take place within their jurisdiction. Jurisdictional overlap is effectively reduced to a small set of areas, essentially working groups. The existence of "free-riding" could support the creation of a supranational structure, making relevant policy decisions at a supranational level and enforcing decisions on its members. However, this benefit must be compared with the cost of federalizing police bureaucracies within the European Union.

The effects of the Schengen Area on criminal activities are still an open empirical question. As to the actual effect of jurisdictional cooperation and coordination, it will take quite a while to assess this question since most of it has been at the level of working groups, with a possible exception of the common visa policy. As to the elimination of internal borders, the issue of criminal mobility is certainly there. Most Member States have complained more than once about the conditions at their borders. However, quite realistically speaking, most criminal organizations have considerable money and are in a position of taking full advantage of communication facilities, independent of border controls.

Although my original paper focuses on the market for narcotics, a similar reasoning could be developed for visa policy, control of common external frontiers, organized crime, or more generally to any criminal activity with a serious jurisdictional spillover effect.[16] The main implication of the economic model is that not all jurisdictions should join the union and coordinate law enforcement policies. There could be two main reasons. First, preferences over law enforcement are too different. Second, the net burden of financing the coordinated solution falls excessively on a particular jurisdiction. I argued that we could understand the British and Irish opt-outs in this light. The later developments of the Schengen Agreement have largely confirmed my analysis.

More recent contributions in the application of jurisdictional competition to the criminal law market are also important.[17] These contributions frame the criminal law market from the perspective of jurisdictions that want to avoid immigration of crime but could welcome the financial gains obtained by such activities.[18] There are two possible

---

[16] See Monheim-Helstroffer and Obidzinski (2010).

[17] For the general literature, see O'Hara and Ribstein (2009).

[18] I follow here the work by Teichman (2005, 2006) and Teichman and Broude (2009).

consequences. A race to the top happens when every jurisdiction invests excessively in enforcement to have the highest probability and severity of punishment, and therefore displace crime. Another version of the same could be each jurisdiction reducing the quality of its criminal justice system so as to secure convictions more easily and therefore displace crime. Overall, crime rates might be reduced, but jurisdictions either waste resources (achieve deterrence at an excessively high cost) or reduce the quality of their criminal justice system.

A race to the bottom takes place when every jurisdiction reduces barriers to investing illegal gains obtained in other jurisdictions. The direct effect of weaker regulations is not surprising. Crime rates will go up and more illegal gains will be generated.

Both races, to the top and to the bottom, are clearly inefficient. However, there is no guarantee that a centralized solution would immediately solve the problem. Presumably a centralized solution would impose a common enforcement policy that eliminates these races. However, the incentives to deviate from the coordinated solution are high. Central solutions could be unstable and difficult to manage. Finally, there are further potential inefficiencies derived from asymmetric information.

3.2 Tax Evasion

A consequence of harmonization of fiscal policy in the European Union is the need for coordination of enforcement policies against tax evasion. Therefore, a European effort to control and reduce tax evasion is an important area of research. The problem of tax compliance concerns equity and efficiency at the same time. It can be approached from different perspectives: public finance and tax harmonization, law enforcement, design of European tax authorities, labor supply, or a combination of all of these. Our direct concern is enforcement measures.

The economic model predicts that sanctions should be large and the probability of auditing low. It is well known that the empirical adherence is not high. With respect to the European context, it is of particular interest to explore the diverse psychological, moral, and social influences. Also of importance is the relationship between tax bureaucracies, judicial authorities and European institutions.

A first observation is that the free movement of people and capital has not pushed governments to adopt similar enforcement policies across Europe. One possible explanation is competition between Member States to attract capital gains that have evaded taxation elsewhere. Another explanation is a rent-seeking one. Those who can take advantage of the current loopholes are precisely those who have more influence in policy-making, those who can easily move capital across Europe.

A second observation is that tax compliance seems to be higher in Northern Europe than in Southern jurisdictions. Such a fact is a consequence of different audit programs, enforcement policies and also social norms. Diverse social norms are important because it will be difficult to change them in a top-to-bottom policy as harmonization of tax compliance precludes this.

An important factor is the taxpayer's perception of the fairness of the tax burden and the degree of satisfaction with the government. Clearly taxpayers across Europe differ with respect to fairness perception and satisfaction. Also the "democratic deficit" of the European Union could reduce shame and guilt from non-compliance. A European tax compliance policy should start with governments sharing information and training truly European tax practitioners, making detection and compliance easier. It is likely that sharing information would help governments detecting "ghosts" more than tax evaders.

In my view the fundamental problem with enforcement of tax compliance in Europe (and not in the US) is the diversity and complexity of rules. Enforcement measures are difficult to design when even enforcers are bewildered by the complexity.

3.3 EU Corruption

Corruption is becoming an important issue in the context of the European Union. Within the rational theory, corruption is a natural consequence of over-regulation in Europe. There is a public monopoly of law enforcement and a clear tendency for the use of public administrative agencies. Most European public agencies are centralized and monopolistic bureaucracies rather than competitive and open structures. Control mechanisms are usually very weak and judicial review of agency action is mild. It is not surprising that corruption emerges.

An important research area is how much over-regulation in Europe is caused by rent-seeking making corruption endogenous. That of course is a consequence of weak political control mechanisms and a lack of financial and procedural accountability. There are three areas that the European Union should target to reduce corruption. First, enforcement policies should be designed to deter corruption and severely punish corrupt bureaucrats, in particular at the top of the European bureaucracy. Second, salaries and wages to bureaucrats and enforcers should be high to increase the opportunity cost of corruption. Finally, European bureaucracies should be redesigned to be competitive, open, with clear financial and procedural accountability. Judicial as well as political review and control is important to enforce anti-corruption measures.

The situation within the European Union is complex given the different social norms concerning "corruption." For example, while in Southern Europe it seems to be a common and accepted practice that bureaucrats accept Christmas presents from potential interested parties, such practice is not admissible in Northern Europe. The absence of strong uniform social norms concerning "corruption" implies that deterrence and enforcement must be primarily enhanced by law. However, such harmonization of practices has to recognize the inevitable costs of violating local norms.

4 CONCLUSIONS

This chapter has reviewed the general costs and benefits of legal harmonization. I have discussed them in the context of law enforcement, in particular the Schengen Area. I have pointed out that the economics literature is skeptical about the efficiency of legal harmonization. It seems clear that without empirical analysis it will not be possible to settle these questions.

An important conclusion of the economic analysis is to expose flawed arguments popularized by non-economists on the efficiency of legal harmonization. The reduction of transaction costs in order to facilitate exchange of goods and services or the benefits produced by enforcement policy coordination *per se* cannot be taken as an indication of economic efficiency. They are one significant element in the equation, but they have to be compared with important agency costs.

REFERENCES

Carbonara, Emanuela and Francesco Parisi (2007), "The Paradox of Legal Harmonization," 132 *Public Choice* 367–400.

Carbonara, Emanuela and Francesco Parisi (2009), "Choice of Law and Legal Evolution: Rethinking the Market for Legal Rules," 139 *Public Choice* 461–92.

Garoupa, Nuno (1997), "Optimal Law Enforcement and the Economics of the Drug Market: Some Comments on the Schengen Agreements," 17 *International Review of Law and Economics* 521–35.

Garoupa, Nuno and Carlos Gómez Ligüerre (2012), "The Efficiency of the Common Law: The Puzzle of Mixed Legal Families," forthcoming in *Wisconsin International Law Journal*.

Garoupa, Nuno and Anthony Ogus (2006), "A Strategic Interpretation of Legal Transplants," 35 *Journal of Legal Studies* 339–63.

Grajzl, Peter and Valentina Dimitrova (2009), "The Choice in the Lawmaking Process: Legal Transplants vs. Indigenous Law," 5 *Review of Law and Economics* 615–60.

Gromek-Broc, Katarzyna (2002), "The Legal Profession in the European Union – a Comparative Analysis of Four Member States," 24 *Liverpool Law Review* 109–30.

Legrand, Pierre (1996), "European Legal Systems Are Not Converging," 45 *International and Comparative Law Quarterly* 52–81.

Legrand, Pierre (1997), "Against a European Civil Code," 60 *Modern Law Review* 44–63.

Legrand, Pierre (1999), *Fragments on Law-as-Culture* (Open Library).

Monheim-Helstroffer, Jenny and Marie Obidzinski (2010), "Optimal Discretion in Asylum Lawmaking," 30 *International Review of Law and Economics* 86–97.

Ogus, Anthony (1999), "Competition Between National Legal Systems: A Contribution of Economic Analysis to Comparative Law," 48 *International and Comparative Law Quarterly* 405–18.

Ogus, Anthony (2002), "The Economic Basis of Legal Culture: Networks and Monopolization," 22 *Oxford Journal of Legal Studies* 419–34.

O'Hara, Erin and Larry Ribstein (2009), *The Law Market* (Oxford University Press).

Teichman, Doron (2005), "The Market for Criminal Justice: Federalism, Crime Control, and Jurisdictional Competition," 103 *Michigan Law Review* 1831–76.

Teichman, Doron (2006), "Decentralizing Crime Control: The Political Economy Perspective," 104 *Michigan Law Review* 1749–62.

Teichman, Doron and Tomer Broude (2009), "Outsourcing and Insourcing Crime: The Political Economy of Globalized Criminal Activity," 62 *Vanderbilt Law Review* 796–848.

13 Private enforcement of antitrust law

Roberto Pardolesi

1 THE EUROPEAN SETTING

Private enforcement of antitrust law in Europe is still looking for its identity.

Competition law was originally developed as an administrative tool, "a means for the state to intervene in market processes in order to achieve public goals," following an approach dating back to the 1890s in Vienna and coherent with the received continental wisdom that a discipline intended to bar distortions of the market did not belong to the realm of private law, so that it could not be applied in regular courts (Gerber, 2009).

Actually, whether private enforcement was entitled, or not, to play a role – albeit nominal – in the European Union under the 1957 Treaty of Rome is an unsettled issue: with the exception of para. 3, the original version of Article 101 and the whole Article 102 TFEU have always been directly applicable in Member States. But it is certain that in the "formative era" competition law kept being centered exclusively upon public decision-making: it was for the administrative authorities to take action against the evils of cartels and monopolies. Since 1973, however, the Commission has repeatedly expressed the view that private actions can provide a useful complement to its role as public enforcer. Yet, for many ensuing years it has even been unclear whether individuals harmed by a breach of European competition rules have any right to claim damages: so entrenched was the reliance on the public nature of the machinery entrusted with the application of competition law!

The European Court of Justice's 2001 decision in *Courage v. Crehan* finally erased any doubt:

> The full effectiveness of Article [101 TFEU] and, in particular, the practical effect of the prohibition laid down in Article [101] (1) would be put at risk if it were not open to any individual to claim damages for loss caused to him by a contract or by conduct liable to restrict or distort competition. Indeed, the existence of such a right strengthens the working of the Community competition rules and discourages agreements or practices, which are frequently covert, which are liable to restrict or distort competition. From that point of view, actions for damages before the national courts can make a significant contribution to the maintenance of effective competition in the Community.[1]

Regulation 1/2003 introduced a change of paradigm in the enforcement of European competition rules permitting the substitution of decentralized and private enforcement for centralized and public enforcement of Articles 101 and 102 TFEU. The Regulation envisaged enforcement not only by national competition authorities but also through litigation between private parties before the national courts. However, the determination

[1] Judgment of 20 September 2001, case C-453/99, [2001] ECR I-6297.

of appropriate remedies and procedures for claiming damages still lies within the competence of each Member State. Therefore only the requirements of equivalence (the rules are to be not less favorable than those governing similar domestic actions) and effectiveness (the rules should not render practically impossible or excessively difficult the exercise of rights conferred by Community law) restrict Member States' discretion.

2 A METHODOLOGICAL CAVEAT

Before going any further, it deserves clarifying that the notion of private enforcement of competition law should consider, *inter alia*, (and focus predominantly on) the attempts to persuade private parties to the use of compensatory awards to take private law actions in defense of public law goals in cases brought by individuals.[2] Given that available resources for enforcing the relevant provisions are scarce, the efforts of antitrust institutions (the Commission and national competition authorities (NCAs)) might be exhausted long before getting to the desired level of protection of unrestricted competition. This is why fostering the award of a financial benefit on individuals on proof of anticompetitive conduct has come to be seen as a possibly precious aid for achieving compliance with the antitrust law.

As a consequence, the notion of private enforcement assumes some kind of deviation from the general discipline, in order to incentivize judicial initiatives of private parties. This happens, for instance, in the US, where incentives to bring civil suits were already introduced in Section 4 of the Clayton Act, with the provision of treble damages, including court costs and attorney's fees.[3] A somewhat analogous move was forecast by the European Commission in the 2005 Green Paper, avowedly pursuing the objective of incentivizing potential claimants through minimization of costs and maximization of benefits, obtained by the proposed introduction of double damages for cartels. In the ensuing debate, however, the "penalty" flavor of the project was dropped, due to the resistance of most stakeholders; coherently, the term "private enforcement" disappeared, surrogated by the more neutral slogan of "full compensation," according to the general rules of tort law.

As of now, then, European law does not contemplate any consistent proxy of a specific regime shaped for the goal of promoting private initiatives against breach of competition law. This being the framework, it is to be recognized that, from a legal point of view, the

---

[2] This way of approaching the problem assumes an already working division of labor between public authorities (which, as will be seen, have traditionally taken the lead in Europe) and private parties, elaborating on the opportunity to redefine their respective responsibilities. For an "unbiased" analysis of the reasons for choosing in the vacuum (a process likely to end up with "the search for a second-best solution . . . requiring complex considerations of various criteria as well as being dependent on the factual context of regulation"), cf. Klöhn (2010).

[3] Not surprisingly, where diverse interests surface, the preferred reaction is de-trebling of damages: see, for a telling illustration, the Standards Development Organization Advancement Act of 2004, Pub. L. No. 108–237 (de-trebling, as well as relief from joint and several liability, was also granted, but on entirely different grounds, to cooperators of the public enforcer by the Antitrust Criminal Penalty Enhancement and Reform Act of 2004 (ACPERA), extended for an additional year in 2009).

European debate about private enforcement of antitrust law boils down to the product of an optical distortion, consisting of looking at a (peculiar) case of tort liability through the lens of another discipline: it is as though one would ask, with regard to road traffic regulated by public provisions, which role is to be assigned to lawsuits filed by pedestrians injured by speeding drivers. In principle, a private right of action for recovering damages does stand on its own. The possibility that, while vindicating her own interest, the plaintiff contributes to the public enforcement of competition law is a side-effect, unrelated to the grounds for awarding compensation. Monopoly conduct or cartel agreements may cause prejudice for buyers: say, as a minimum, in the form of an overcharge.[4] If the legal prerequisites for filing a damages suit are fulfilled, the claim will thus proceed under every antitrust sky. As remarked by Komninos (2008), there is no hierarchical relationship between the initiative of a public body charged with the task of enforcing antitrust law and private plaintiffs invoking pecuniary redress. While public enforcement is undertaken by specifically entrusted authorities that apply the relevant rules vertically to economic operators, civil litigation takes place horizontally between individuals in the framework of a civil process, in which the parties advance independent claims stemming from a violation of their interests as consumers or competitors. Needless to say, the violation consists of an infringement of antitrust law: but, again, the reason for awarding protection lies in the harm produced by the illegal conduct.

As usually occurs whenever an infringement of a public law, in and of itself susceptible of triggering some sort of administrative or criminal sanction, determines also some loss for an individual, the two trajectories remain conceptually autonomous: a feature that is preserved even where the pre-existence of an administrative ruling influences heavily the practical viability of a private action. Yet, it is obvious that remedies in the context of private litigation also serve the public interest in maintaining effective competition in the market. This circumstance does not mean that tort law, when referred to prejudice provoked by an anticompetitive behavior, becomes a province of antitrust enforcement.

The alternative, then, is not whether there ought to be private redress in addition to public enforcement, since, on this count, the answer can only be positive. The crucial question dwells, instead, on the role to be assigned to the private side of antitrust litigation: since the door of damages actions is open, it appears of utmost importance to establish how much private litigation should exist in this area. Put differently, the main concern focuses on the many obstacles that hinder the practical feasibility of judicial redress for individuals harmed by anticompetitive conduct. In Europe those obstacles look almost insurmountable, so that private antitrust damages actions have been confined to the margin of the overall picture. The recent impetus toward enhanced private enforcement aims at removing, or at least reducing, these obstacles, in order to achieve better standards of corrective justice and, as a consequence, a vibrant contribution to deterrence. The skepticism exhibited by some commentators hinges on the belief that such a development would be obnoxious, shaping a cure that is definitely worse than the disease.

---

4 In the cartel area, most damages calculations rest on estimating the price increase imposed by colluders on customers; but the range of potentially relevant detriments is much larger, see Friederiszick and Röller (2010).

Accordingly, the basic question reads, more or less, as follows: should private antitrust damages actions be encouraged via a more favorable legal framework than the current one?

3 WHAT THEORY TEACHES

There are two basic approaches to the deterrence of socially harmful behavior: strong enforcement by public agencies, and threat of litigation by private parties. Both approaches are used in most countries, but with varying degrees. The lines between public and private enforcement may blur once the problem is analyzed with a view to designing optimal enforcement institutions, which, as will be seen, are likely to suggest some sort of combination of "public"and "private" features. The crucial challenge becomes that of fine-tuning various parameters of the system, taking into account that, from a "qualitative" point of view, public enforcement is superior in pursuing the objectives of deterrence (more investigative powers, more effective sanctions (jail), better control of their measure, more reliable commitment), and in clarifying the content of the antitrust prohibitions; whereas private enforcement is obviously more geared towards the goal of corrective justice (Wils, 2009).

Under standard neo-classical assumptions, price-fixers behave as rational profit-maximizers. This means that executives conduct an *ex ante* cost–benefit analysis to assess whether the benefit of engaging in illegal conduct is worth taking the risk of being caught and punished. They weigh the expected gains from the cartel against the expected liability (in the form of public fines or damage awards) discounted by the probability of detection and conviction.[5] Accordingly, to achieve optimal deterrence, the antitrust penalty levied against a cartel should, at least, equal the violation's expected profits multiplied by the probability of detection and conviction.[6]

In principle, this would imply that private enforcement can stand as an important second pillar of antitrust policy (Van den Bergh and Camesasca, 2006). But the overall picture, as already stressed by Eger and Weise (2006), is far more complicated. Theory suggests that private enforcement, if effectively designed, would lead to an increase in the probability of detection of an illegal conduct, accuracy of fact-finding, and deterrence; also the overall competitiveness of markets would be beneficially affected. Moreover, the potential for strategic abuse of antitrust laws would be reduced. This would come at some costs, including increased trial costs for private parties; competitiveness of markets overall; and, above all, serious risks of over-deterrence. Let us briefly elaborate on this controversy, confronting pros and cons.

On the one hand, it is often stated that private enforcers, acting as "private attorneys generals," have greater incentive to take enforcement action than public enforcers,[7] and

---

[5] It is worth noting that optimal deterrence, in the economic view, includes also civil damages and criminal penalties, not ever available in different antitrust systems.

[6] The gain-based formulation of the theory (cf. Manzini, 2008) should be, in general, less demanding than the harm-based version. See, however, Aresu (2010).

[7] According to the empirical findings of Lande and Davis (2008), 15 out of the 40 cases canvassed in the study were filed in the absence of government cases or significantly expanded the relief

that by taking action they benefit society through additional deterrence, whereas public enforcers regulate a vast array of industries, and therefore cannot detect anticompetitive practices as easily as private enforcers who experience these practices on a regular basis. In addition, private enforcers are often presumed to be better informed about their particular industry.[8] As Shavell (1984) pointed out, "private parties should generally enjoy an inherent advantage in knowledge over public regulators. For a regulator to obtain comparable information would often require virtually continuous observation of parties' behavior, and thus would be a practical impossibility." Also, Brodley (1995) argues that "competitors and takeover targets are ideal litigants in terms of litigation capability because they are likely to have the skill, knowledge of the industry, and motivation to mount a powerful case with speed and precision." Alluring as they may be, such propositions are not backed by exhaustive empirical support (Segal and Whinston, 2006).[9]

On the other hand, there are reasons to assume that private enforcement might work poorly in antitrust cases. If victims of antitrust law infringements are private consumers, harm and causation are typically not obvious to the victims; the detection of infringements requires investigation by experts, and public authorities are often better informed than the victims. Because the total harm caused by infringements of competition law is often spread across many victims, even well-informed ones have little incentive to bring damages claims. Moreover, facilitating access to civil courts in antitrust cases increases the risk that private damages actions will be abused by competitors. Actually, in the antitrust field plaintiffs are often competitors or takeover targets of defendants: they may have an incentive to deploy private enforcement strategically, that is, to sue even if they know that their competitors did not violate the antitrust laws. Firms may use antitrust laws to prevent large potential competitors from entering their market. Firms can also use antitrust law to prevent their rivals from competing vigorously; extort funds from successful rivals; improve contractual conditions; enforce tacit collusive agreements; respond to existing suits; and prevent hostile takeovers (McAfee et al., 2005; Bebchuk, 1998). The extent to which firms strategically abuse the antitrust laws under private

---

obtained through government enforcement alone. Of the total amount recovered, 43 to 47 percent came from stand-alone suits.

8 A telling example is offered by the *Vitamin* case. Hoffmann-La Roche reported that, out of total costs paid because of its participation in the global vitamins cartel, 2/7 was for fines imposed by public authorities and 5/7 for civil damages (most of them treble damage class actions resolved by settlement). The amount paid in public fines represented 23.7 percent and in civil damages 59.6 percent of the operating profit of the company's vitamins division during the period from 1989 to 1999.

9 Though impressive, the sample examined by Lande and Davis (2008) has been regarded as insufficient (mostly because of ambiguous relationships with precedent government action) to provide a reliable factual basis for the pretence that private suits contribute to autonomous cartel detection. "[N]inguno de ellos es un caso de cártel descubierto y llevado ante los tribunales por particulares. Son todos casos en los que ha habido actividad por parte de los organismos públicos de defensa de la competencia (aunque en algunos no haya habido multas) o casos de abuso de posición dominante, donde el problema de detección no se plantea porque no son prácticas secretas o, casos que pueden calificarse como acuerdos horizontales restrictivos de la competencia – como sucede con los *reverse payments* en litigios sobre patentes entre el titular de una patente farmacéutica y el fabricante de genéricos – pero que no son secretos y no entran en la definición de cártel que contiene, por ejemplo, la Ley de Defensa de la Competencia española" (Águila-Real, 2009).

enforcement also depends crucially on the structure of damage awards in private antitrust cases (Elzinga and Wood, 1988; Easterbrook, 1985). Punitive damages (and the variation on the same theme represented by disgorgement of profits: see the *Mylan* case, a remarkable initiative of the FTC in 1999[10]) reduce firms' incentives to violate antitrust laws, but also increase their incentives to use antitrust laws strategically against their rivals. Firms can use the powerful threat of treble damages to extort funds from successful rivals. The actions that are taken to extort money are often resolved through the payment of a "tax on success" for the firms whose positions are sought after by competitors. But taxes on success discourage investment and innovation, which harms consumers in terms of reduced dynamic efficiency (Gentry and Hubbard, 2000).

In a more parochial way, US-style private enforcement has been deemed almost poisonous. Too often private actions result in remedies that provide lucrative attorney's fees but secure no real benefits for overcharged purchasers; too often they appear parasitic, when not extortionary attempts, which do not add much to public enforcement, and are dramatically "overreaching" (Kovacic, 2008).

In the same vein, with reference to the EU experience, a recurrent criticism hinges upon the risk of overshooting, with a summation of penalties and damages doomed to be definitely over-deterrent. Suppose, in the wake of Prosperetti et al. (2009), that a firm with an annual turnover of €100 million joins a cartel (which is expected to last seven years) and imposes an overcharge of, say, 15 percent. Apply a reasonable discount rate of 8 percent. The total expected profit from the participation to the cartel will be approximately €84 million. Taking note that, in Europe, the average fine for a cartel member climbed in 2007 to €75 million, one should consider that the firm risks paying a €10 million fine (10 percent of the yearly total turnover, which might be referred to a host of products, beside the cartelized one), plus damages of €84 million, plus legal costs of 10 to 20 percent of the awarded damages, plus reputational loss, plus wasted managerial resources in handling litigation: a total bill of over €120 million, which is likely to be grossly excessive.

In more general terms, one might add that damages actions determine over-deterrence also because of the inhibition effects on firms (discouraged from undertaking legal conduct lest it be interpreted as anticompetitive), the prohibitive costs of judicial defense, and the waste of resources involved in the litigation setting. Moreover, in areas where the detection of illegal conduct does not raise serious problems – as happens in contractual contexts of vertical restraints and in the delicate side of abuse of dominance – the risk of over-deterrence deriving from unbalanced favor for the plaintiff's initiative (false positives, leading to the condemnation of pro-competitive acts) would prove to be devastating.

To make things worse, one can consider the dangers of antitrust globalization. Global markets do not have a competition law framework. They are subject to fragmented jurisdictional scrutiny by the individual states, or unions of states, touched upon by the activities of transnational actors. Lack of coordinated efforts is commonly regarded as responsible for the flourishing of unchecked anticompetitive conduct (Gerber, 2010). But it is also possible to conceive of a different by-product. The same violations, spreading

---

10 See *FTC v. Mylan Laboratories, Inc. et al.*, 62 F. Supp. 2d 25 (D.C. Columbia 1999).

all over the world, can be canvassed by several "local" authorities, each of them eager to penalize the multinational infringer, so that condemnations are likely to overlap. The binary pressure of public and private enforcement might exacerbate the problem.

A blatant example is offered by the recent Intel vicissitudes. After being warned, without penalty, to cease its rebates policy by the Japanese antitrust authority in 2005 and condemned to a fine of $26 million by the South Korean equivalent in 2008, the dominator of the CPU market was struck by the highest fine per firm in the history of EU enforcement.[11] While the echo of the European case was still felt, Intel got a comprehensive settlement of its disputes with AMD by, *inter alia*, making a payment of $1.25 billion to AMD in November 2009. A few weeks later the FTC initiated a Section 5 procedure, which has been closed, in August 2010, with a "tough" settlement (but no penalty), which prevents Intel from leveraging its CPU monopoly into other markets. Leaving aside the debate about the different outcomes of the European and US cases and their respective efficacy, it should be noted that, in the wake of the US proceedings, Intel has been left with no choice but to settle also with Nvidia at $1.5 billion (January 2011). It might be argued that stockpiling of sanctions and damages in different jurisdictions for basically the same conduct comes close to a nightmare.

But is the over-deterrence story, in its various declinations, plausible? Or, to reshape the question, can the compound of fines and damages be made, if not optimal, at least workable?

Consider the evils of collusion. Quantifying the direct harm from cartels is difficult. Cartel overcharge may, however, represent the crucial proxy in order to pursue deterrence. Past studies evidenced average overcharge of about 30 percent; data collected through an OECD survey of 2003 pointed to rates between 15 and 20 percent. More recent studies (by Connor, 2009) on a sample of 177 cartels indicate median overcharges of 17 to 21 percent (a previous estimate on a cluster of over 670 cases pointed to average overcharges of 20 percent for domestic cartels and 34 for international ones (Connor and Lande, 2005)).

Also, regarding the average duration of a cartel, estimates vary noticeably. On the one hand, early studies such as Bryant and Eckard (1991) found an average duration of between 5.8 and 7.27 years, with 22 percent of conspiracies lasting more than ten years. Later, Levenstein and Suslow (2002) found the percentage of surveyed cartels that had lasted more than five years to be within 40 percent and 60 percent. Combe and Monnier (2007) analyze the 86 cartels convicted by the European Commission from 1964 to February 2007, and find a median duration of 5.8 years. However, Wils (2006), Schinkel and Rüggeberg (2006) and Bolotova (2006) assume an average duration of five years.[12] A recent analysis (Haucap et al., 2010) of 95 cartels discovered and sanctioned in Germany

---

[11] As remarked by Lande (2009), the spectacular $1.06 billion fine was less than 1 percent of the yearly turnover of the company.

[12] Bolotova (2006) shows that the longer the cartel operates, the larger the overcharges it tends to achieve. If cartel duration is from five to ten years, it tends to achieve overcharges that are 2.88 percentage points higher than overcharges imposed by a cartel that lasted less than five years (reference group). If a cartel operates 10–15 years, its impact on the overcharge level is even greater than in the previous case, and overcharges are between 7.14 and 9.59 percentage points higher than the reference group overcharges.

by the Bundeskartellamt between 1958 and 2005 revealed an average duration of 6.2 years (an estimation which is, however, deemed systematically too short).

When it comes to calculating the detection rate, prospects are even more gloomy, on both sides of the Atlantic Ocean. Although the impossibility of observing how many cartels go undetected makes empirical evidence hardly revealing, opinions are largely converging on the fact that the detection rate falls in the range between 10 and 33 percent (the former figure refers to the estimate of US Sentencing Guidelines (1986), the latter to Landes' study (1983), both regarding the US experience; somewhere in the middle, as will be seen in a while, is the expected rate of detection in Europe); and economists generally agree that the most reliable figure is approximately 15 percent. More recent contributions, such as Wils (2006), assume a 16 percent rate, to be regarded as a conservative (i.e. probably too high) estimate for Europe. Also Craycraft et al. (1997), Schinkel and Rüggeberg (2006) and Motta (2008) assume a 15 percent probability in their papers.

On these bases, it comes as no surprise that Werden and Simon (1987) found, with regard to the US side, that the optimal fine for the average cartel convicted by the Department of Justice from 1975 to 1980 should have been 111 times higher than the fine actually paid. According to Wils (2005), with regard to the European picture, the optimal fine would reach 150 percent of affected sales, and within the range of 5.0 to 7.5 times the overcharge; Motta (2008) estimates that the minimum level of fine (relative to market turnover) necessary to deter cartel formation (if the competitive mark-up is 50 percent and the demand elasticity is 0.6) is around 68 percent per year of the relevant market turnover of the firm; Combe (2006), under rather conservative assumptions, calculates the optimal sanction as being 6.6 times higher than the loss of consumer surplus (thus, for a five-year cartel, 300 percent of annual turnover). And Connor (2010) argues that optimal sanctions ought to be over 300 percent of a cartel's overcharge.

Thus, the available data, tentative as they may be, are largely consistent with cartel formation rates that, despite the growth in fines and the introduction of corporate leniency programs, imply current antitrust sanctions are an insufficient deterrent.

A different (and more optimistic) view has been exposed by the European Commission (2009).[13] Looking at the 18 cartels subject to antitrust decisions during the years 2005 to 2007, and assuming an overcharge of 5 to 15 percent, the Commission has estimated a total harm ranging from around €4 billion to €11 billion. Taking the middle point of this overcharge range – 10 percent – gives a conservative estimate of consumer harm of €7.6 billion due to these cartels. This harm should be confronted with the total amount of fines, which is €5.9: are cartels still convenient? And what about cartels which are not discovered? The harm estimate – the Commission comments – does not take into account "the benefits of deterrence and fostering compliance . . . an additional saving . . ., possibly of the order of some €60 billion, could have accrued."

This shows something which was not doubted at all: that public enforcement is beneficial (but also that it is insufficient, since, if the detection rate is assumed to stay in the range of 15 percent, six cartels out of seven keep faring very well . . .). Completely out of reach remain both the question whether levels of fines capable of achieving optimal deterrence would exceed the offender's ability to pay, triggering serious problems of

[13] Report on Competition Policy 2008, SEC(2009) 10004.

constitutional consistency and likely reluctance of the authorities to impose sanctions that could drive the company out of business, and the subsequent one on public enforcement's capability, under those constraints, to discourage illegal activities. Looking at the existing practice, and given the limits to the viability of high fines, the answer should be negative. In fact, as remarked by Connor (2010), recidivism is widespread and increasing, which implies that violating the antitrust law is still, on the whole, profitable.

4 BEYOND THEORY

Antitrust laws and enforcement agencies have largely followed the conventional wisdom that the primary cure for insufficient deterrence of hard-core cartel activity, such as price-fixing, is to increase corporate fines.

In the US, antitrust laws are supported by criminal fines (up to $100 million for corporations) and convictions (up to a ten-year jail term: Antitrust Criminal Penalty Enhancement and Reform Act of 2004). The criminal enforcement system includes a crown witness system whereby the suspected company representative may get amnesty if sufficient information and cooperation is provided, not only about own involvement in the alleged cartel but also about the other cartel members (leniency program). The evidence provided by the cartel members themselves facilitates the investigation.

Federal antitrust laws are enforced in three main ways:

- *Criminal and civil enforcement actions brought by the Antitrust Division of the Department of Justice*: since May 1999, more than 100 individuals, with at least 20 of them foreign nationals, have been sent to jail; since fiscal 1997, more than $3 billion in criminal fines have been imposed.
- *Civil enforcement actions brought by the Federal Trade Commission*, involving administrative adjudication and state enforcement: state attorneys general can file actions either under state antitrust laws or under federal law, including – since 1976 – as *parens patriae* to seek treble damages on behalf of state residents.
- *Lawsuits brought by private parties asserting damage claims*, whose ratio to public antitrust suits is estimated at between 10 to 1 and 20 to 1. In fact, Section 7 of the Sherman Act and Section 4 of the Clayton Act entitle any firm to bring a lawsuit against a competitor for three times the damages suffered from any violation of the antitrust laws. Private enforcement of the antitrust laws is thus explicitly permitted and indeed encouraged, and supplements public enforcement by the Antitrust Division of the US Department of Justice and the Federal Trade Commission.[14]

[14] Damage claims by private parties against companies involved in competition law infringements are extremely common in the US (in 2008, there were 1,287 private antitrust actions in federal court – state cases are not tabulated – accounting for 96.1 percent of the total number of antitrust cases filed; since 1975, private antitrust actions have accounted for 83.4 to 96.6 percent of all antitrust actions filed). This is, *inter alia*, due to procedural tools such as class actions, contingency fees and treble damages, which have been the focus of a reform of the US leniency program initiated by the US Department of Justice. At any rate, the pivotal role of private enforcement is beyond any doubt. Even though, relative to government fines, about which information is precise,

Some figures will help to frame the overall view. From 1890 to 1997, the DoJ filed 1,134 civil antitrust cases (about 11 per year), with 80 percent concerning merger and cartel cases. From 1915 to 1969, the FTC filed 1,061 cases (about 19 per year). In the period from 1971 to 1999, the number of private antitrust cases varied from 452 to 1528.

Recent trends exhibit a different pattern. Since companies conspire to fix prices through individual employees, and the employer cannot reimburse the penalty imposed on the actual infringer, the DoJ over the past 30 years has sought longer incarcerations, rather than larger individual fines. In 2007, the Antitrust Division secured a record number of jail days (31,391); since then, the trend has been consistent over time: 25,396 in 2009, about 26,000 in 2010. In January 2009, a 61-year-old executive was sentenced to 48 months in jail, the longest incarceration ever imposed for a single antitrust violation. In the following fiscal year 2010, the DoJ filed 60 criminal cases and obtained fines of roughly \$555 million and 63 sentences to imprisonment (the average sentence was 30 months; foreign nationals were sentenced to an average of 10 months in prison).

Yet, given the difficulty in detecting cartels (with a rate that, because of the contribution of leniency programs, has reached an estimated 25 percent (Ginsburg and Wright, 2010)), it is unknown whether the significant increases in criminal fines and jail sentences have significantly reduced the number and duration of illegal cartels. Available evidence would suggest the opposite. Elsewhere, criminal law is seldom resorted to (though as many as 18 national competition laws authorize prison time for price-fixing).

Europe exhibits a different attitude. A few Member States have introduced criminal sanctions for certain antitrust behavior (France, Ireland, Italy, Austria, the UK and Germany). However, probably because of the entrenched tradition of administrative enforcement, there is insufficient support for criminal sanctions in many European Member States, and a top-down introduction of criminal sanctions by the Community remains controversial.

As a consequence, the main impetus has been on levying increasing fines upon companies involved in anticompetitive dealings. Actually, Article 103(1) TFEU instructs the Council to lay down "the appropriate regulations and directives to give effect to the principles set out in Articles 101 and 102." Article 103(2)(a) adds that these regulations or directives shall be designed in particular "to ensure compliance with the prohibitions laid down in Article 101(1) and in Article 102 by making provision for fines." The Council has done so through Regulation 1/2003, Article 23(2) of which empowers the Commission to impose fines on undertakings that, either intentionally or negligently, infringe Article 101 or Article 102 TFEU. The Court of Justice has held that such fines "have as their

antitrust settlement amounts are significantly underreported, it is evident that the \$7.6 billion in international cartel fines collected by the DoJ during 1990–2008 were swamped by the \$26.6 billion in private settlements paid to direct and indirect buyers. The crucial role of private enforcement endangers the most effective tool resorted to in fighting cartels. More and more US companies had found themselves in the dilemma that they successfully obtained a reduction in fine through a leniency application but later had to face millions of dollars of treble damage award payments for the same infringement. This situation seriously put into question a company's incentive to apply for leniency. The new law adopted in the US provides that a company which was the first to file a leniency application may no longer be subject to treble damages payments in any follow-on litigation, but only to the payment of simple damages. However, in order to benefit from this exception, the company has to fully cooperate during the trial.

objective to suppress illegal conduct as well as to prevent it being repeated." Similarly, the Commission has stated that "the purpose of the fines is twofold: to impose a pecuniary sanction on the undertaking for the infringement and prevent a repetition of the offence, and to make the prohibition in the Treaty more effective."

For three decades, from the imposition of the first fines in 1969 (Commission Decision *Quinine* [1969]) to the publication of the 1998 Guidelines, the Commission imposed fines without having published any guidance. In its decisions imposing fines, the Commission always listed a number of factors which it had taken into account in fixing the amount of the fine, but never explained how these factors had brought it to reach the precise figure of the fine. The Court of First Instance nevertheless observed in 1995, in three judgments concerning the Welded steel mesh cartel, that it would be "desirable" for the Commission to make more transparent its method for setting fines. Those judgments led to the publication by the Commission of its 1998 Fining Guidelines.

According to the first paragraph of the 1998 Guidelines, to which the 2006 Guidelines also refer, the principles outlined in these guidelines "should ensure the transparency and impartiality of the Commission's decisions, in the eyes of the undertakings and of the Court of Justice alike, while upholding the discretion which the Commission is granted under the relevant legislation to set fines within the limit of 10 percent of overall turnover." On 1 September 2006, the European Commission published new Guidelines on the method it will use when setting fines on undertakings for violations of the prohibitions on restrictive agreements and abuse of a dominant position laid down in Articles 101 and 102 TFEU and Articles 53 and 54 of the EEA Agreement.

The Guidelines set out a two-step methodology for the setting of fines. First, the Commission will determine a basic amount for each undertaking. Second, it may adjust that basic amount upwards or downwards. The basic amount consists of a percentage of the value (before tax) of the undertaking's sales of goods or services to which the infringement directly or indirectly relates in the relevant geographic area within the EEA. The percentage depends on the gravity of the infringement, gravity which is to be assessed on a case-by-case basis. As a general rule, the percentage applied on account of gravity will be up to 30 percent: for hard-core cartels the percentage will generally be set at the higher end of the scale. To take into account the duration of the infringement, the amount thus determined will be multiplied by the number of years of participation in the infringement. In addition, irrespective of the duration of the undertaking's participation in the infringement, the Commission will, for hard-core cartels, include in the basic amount a sum of between 15 and 25 percent of the value of sales. The Commission may also apply such an additional amount in the case of other infringements.

Once the basic amount of the fine determined, the Commission may make adjustments upwards or downwards for a number of reasons. The basic amount may be increased or decreased on account of aggravating or attenuating circumstances. The Guidelines contain a non-exhaustive list of aggravating circumstances (recidivism, obstruction of investigations, and role of leader or instigator of the infringement) and of attenuating circumstances (including negligence, and authorization or encouragement by public authorities or by legislation). If the increase or decrease on account of other aggravating or mitigating circumstances is not specified, the increase on account of recidivism will be by up to 100 percent of the basic amount for each earlier finding of the same or a similar infringement. The Commission may apply a specific increase for deterrence in the case of undertakings which have a particularly large turnover beyond the sales of goods or services to which the infringement relates and/or to ensure that the fine exceeds the amount of gains improperly made as a result of the infringement where it is possible to estimate that amount. Whenever the amount thus set exceeds the statutory maximum of 10 percent of the total turnover in the preceding business year of the undertaking concerned, as laid down in Article 23(2) of Regulation No 1/2003, it will be capped at that ceiling.

The application of this framework has been impressive. The EU has gone from collecting an average corporate fine of €2 million in 1990–94 to €46 million in 2005–09. In 2010, the provisional amount of fines, relating to five cartel cases, reached the amount of €2.142 million, with the prestressing steel cases scoring €518 million for 17 producers, as many bathroom equipment manufactures fined €622 million, and an impressive €649 million total fine for six LCD panel producers (*Chimney InnoLux*: €300 million).[15]

Article 102 has experienced a much more cautious enforcement. Statistical figures are not provided. But the available data are telling. Leaving aside commitment decisions, there were: six condemnations in 2002; three in 2003; two in 2004 (among them, the *Microsoft* case); one in 2005; none in 2006; one in 2007; none in 2008; one in 2009 (but conspicuous enough: *Intel case*).

Given the number of other possibilities, provided by the Guidelines, to increase the fines (such as aggravating factors, particularly large turnover beyond the affected sales, actual gains from the infringement), it has been suggested that they might approximate a sufficient degree of deterrence (Schinkel, 2007; Motta, 2008), or even "overkill" in some cases (while some serious offenders may still escape with a favorable fine: Van Cayseele and Camesasca, 2007). The more so in view of the improved rate of detection induced by the introduction and implementation of the leniency policy,[16] and of the strong contribution of the NCAs, which, as remarked by Connor (2010), have become – with a total fines amount of $7.4 billion and increased by 39 percent per year from 1994 to

---

[15] This trend does not evoke unanimous enthusiasm: the European Parliament (Resolution of 20 January 2011 on the Report on Competition Policy 2009 (2010/2137(INI)), believes that "the use of ever higher fines as the sole antitrust instrument may be too blunt, not least in view of the job losses that may result from an inability to make payments, and calls for the development of a wider range of more sophisticated instruments covering such issues as individual responsibility, transparency and accountability of firms, shorter procedures, the right of defence and due process, mechanisms to ensure the effective operation of leniency applications (in particular to overcome the interference caused by discovery processes in the US), corporate compliance programmes and the development of European standards; favours a 'carrot-and-stick' approach with penalties that serve as an effective deterrent, in particular for repeat offenders, while encouraging compliance."

[16] A revised Leniency Notice, aiming to aptly reward companies that report cartels, was introduced in 2006. Elaborating the US model, the EU leniency policy offers companies involved in a cartel which self-report and hand over evidence either total immunity from or a reduction of fines which the Commission would have otherwise imposed on them, destabilizing the operation of existing cartels as it seeds distrust and suspicion among cartel members. In order to obtain total immunity under the leniency policy, a company which participated in a cartel must be the first one to inform the Commission of an undetected cartel by providing sufficient information to allow the Commission to launch an inspection at the premises of the companies allegedly involved in the cartel. Companies which do not qualify for immunity may benefit from a reduction of fines if they provide evidence that represents "significant added value" to that already in the Commission's possession and have terminated their participation in the cartel.

2008 – formidable players in the prosecution of international cartels. Relying on this, and on some further elaborations (by Buccirossi and Spagnolo, 2007), it has even been argued that it is not necessary to achieve further deterrence (Aresu, 2010), so that the role for private enforcement in the form of damages actions might be confined to target compensation, possibly via contract law (Castronovo, 2007).

This opinion rings, as a minimum, of overt optimism. The contribution of leniency policy should be considered with some caution: Combe and Monnier (2009) find that the number of detected cartels after 1996 (when leniency programs were introduced in the EU) increased from 1.64 annually (in 1964–96) to 5 annually (between 1997 and 2007). Moreover, jumping from an optimal fine setting (where the impossibility to achieve a reasonably high probability of detection leads to imposing too high fines, which would prove too burdensome for infringers that are actually convicted) to the reassuring idea that a fine smaller than 3 percent would do the job is simply unwarranted and conflicts with the empirical evidence, collected by Connor, that recidivism is widespread and increasing, which implies that violating the antitrust law is still profitable:

> Despite the higher government fines imposed by the EU and the EU's NCAs, because of the near absence of private rights of action, the EU has not been as successful as North America in imposing monetary penalties that might deter international cartels operating in Western Europe.[17]

This view is confirmed by Veljanovski (2011). According to his analysis of 13 published decisions, the fining practice of the Commission under the 2006 Guidelines has been far from compliant. It is certainly true that total fines and fine per prosecuted firm increased significantly; but this was due to less generous reductions of fines under the Commission's leniency program. Available data show that the Commission has not followed the Guidelines; so that, even if the abstract possibility that fines activate proper deterrence keeps being a debatable issue, their actual attitude to discourage illegal behavior is reneged by facts.[18] Veljanovski stresses also that recidivism, one of the main targets of the 2006 Guidelines (with a penalty surcharge up to a maximum of 100 percent for each prior infringement), has been substantially ignored. No firm, irrespective of the number of prior infringements, has been surcharged more than 100 percent. "It appears that the Commission treats the maximum 100 percent as an overall maximum for recidivism rather than for each prior offence."[19]

---

[17] In this regard, it should be noted that the leniency programmes and the judicial review by the European courts contribute to reduce the tangible impact of the penalties (Veljanovsky, 2011).

[18] The basic amount was on average fixed at 18 percent, with a single peak of 25 percent. The entry fee was applied in just one case; and since this additional amount corresponds to gravity percentage for one year, "it penalizes short duration cartels disproportionately more than those of longer duration. Thus, instead of deterring more harmful cartels, it deters those which are short, and presumably less stable, irrespective of the penalty structure." In ten cases where it was possible to rely upon sale figures, a considerable variation emerges with an average of 74.4 percent of the last full year's annual sales before the termination of the cartel. But these figures are misleading as they are based on one year's sales at the end of the cartel and not sales over the whole cartel period, and ignore the fact that only some cartels are detected and punished. Though huge, the European fines do not trigger sufficient deterrence.

[19] "The Commission's practice is perverse. Based on the information in the published decisions, the average percentage surcharge declined from 50 percent for one prior offence, to 25 percent

Summing up. The public interest underlying antitrust prohibitions has often led to emphasizing their public enforcement. In fact, some authors, abiding by the traditional approach, still distinguish between public enforcement, which pursues the public interest in safeguarding effective competition, and private enforcement, aiming at the different – and, in a sense, external – goal of protecting competitors' and consumers' interests. Such a distinction, however, does not do justice to the role of civil courts when they enforce competition law in the context of private litigation: though deciding disputes *inter partes*, they must have regard to the wider impact on the market. In this sense, private interest plays an instrumental role. If, as remarked by most authors, administrative fines will often be insufficient to achieve the optimal level of deterrence, criminal sanctions and/or civil sanctions are a useful complement (with the ensuing caveat that civil sanctions should be coordinated with administrative ones to avoid over-deterrence).

The simple model presented in the Impact Study which accompanied the White Paper[20] explains why private enforcement may effectively act as a complement to public enforcement in a second-best context, where the optimal solution is impossible to achieve:

> It contributes to more effective deterrence by: (i) increasing the probability of detection; and (ii) increasing the infringer's prospective liability by adding expected damage awards to the prospective fines imposed by public enforcers – depending on whether a private suit is stand-alone or follow-on. A cartelist in a jurisdiction with both public and private enforcement would face the following benefit–cost calculation:
>
> $$E(L) = p_g c_g E(F) + p_p c_p E(S) + E(R)$$
>
> Thus, the expected liability faced *ex ante* by a cartelist is the sum of expected public penalties ($E(F)$), expected private damage settlements ($E(S)$) and expected (negative) reputational effects ($E(R)$). This also implies that if the probability of detection with private and public enforcement is greater than under pure public enforcement – and the prospective damage award is significant – then deterrence can be achieved more effectively with both private and public enforcement.[21]

per previous offence where a firm (Akzo in *Calcium Carbide)* had committed four prior offences. The result is that the average penalty declined as the number of prior offences increased – from an average of 50 percent for one prior offence; 30 percent for two to three prior offences; to 25 percent for three or more prior infringements. The incremental surcharge declined more severely to 10 percent from three to four prior offences."

20 Renda, A. et al. (2009),

21 A simple example would help in clarifying this point. "Let 15 percent be the detection/conviction rate under pure public enforcement (*pgcg*), and 10 percent the additional detection/conviction rate with private enforcement (*ppcp*). Further, assume that the prospective settlement value totals 100 million, whereas the expected fine would not be greater than 50 million. This being the case, the deterrence effect contribution under both public and private enforcement would be 1.33 times greater than under pure public enforcement. A widely acknowledged tenet in the literature on optimal fines is that, given the impossibility to raise fines over certain levels, an increase in the probability of detection is more important than the increase in the amount of fines and sanctions in order to achieve more effective deterrence of anticompetitive conduct. Absent this finding, public and private enforcement do not differ noticeably in terms of deterrence potential, and the only advantage of private over public enforcement would lie in the greater potential for corrective justice."

All in all, there seem to be considerable advantages to having a system in place for private actions. First, they help to ensure that the victims of unlawful conduct are compensated. Second, private enforcement of competition laws can be a formidable deterrent to such conduct. Third, allowing private actions takes some of the enforcement burden off public competition agencies, which do not always have sufficient funding to pursue every matter that is worth pursuing. Private claims for damages caused by antitrust violations provide, to say the least, a useful complement for public enforcement. Just a step further, they appear necessary. An additional reason to believe that in the future "a damages litigation culture [will make] itself felt in Europe, and will be beginning to appear in other major jurisdictions" (Riley, 2010).

5 TOWARDS A REALISTIC VIEW

Compared with the US, where about 90 percent of all antitrust cases are private actions (Wils, 2003; Salop and White, 1986), damages claims for infringements of European antitrust law do not fare well. Among many others, an acute problem for private antitrust enforcement is created by the limits of the pan-European court system. The European Union's courts, based in Luxembourg, are only entitled to hear cases arising out of decisions or actions of EU institutions or Member States. Civil actions remain the preserve of the national jurisdictions, each with its own laws and procedures. For plaintiffs that have suffered harm on a pan-European level, bringing individual claims in all these jurisdictions is a daunting prospect. Things are made worse by the many legal hurdles that render problematic any attempt to redress massive but dispersed detriments.

In 2004, the Ashurst study on private enforcement found only 60 cases involving damages claims and 23 damage awards *(plus settlements and arbitral awards)* based on both national and EU competition law, since the adoption of EU and national competition laws. These findings, together with the analysis of the conditions to claim damages in different Member States, supported the statement of "astonishing diversity and total underdevelopment" of antitrust private enforcement in Europe.

A recent and detailed contribution (Peyer, 2010) has challenged the supposed dire state of private enforcement in Germany (and perhaps in Europe) and claims it is just fanciful. From 2005 to 2007, 368 private antitrust cases have been dealt with by German courts (confirming the trend which had been invoked for the past by the Bundeskartellamt: around 900 cases between 2002 and 2005). According to the author, there is room to believe that such a figure is an understatement, just the lowest conceivable bound of a more widespread phenomenon; the opposite credence might depend on the narrow focus on damages litigation, which is admittedly scanty even in Germany. However, even assuming that other remedies (nullity of restrictive agreements; restitution of unjustified enrichment; injunction) are frequently resorted to in contractual settings and the like, the under-deployment of actions for damages as a complement to public enforcement keeps being plausible.

This being the overall scene, the Commission, in the wake of Reg. 1/2003 and with a view to improving the conditions for antitrust damages actions, commissioned an external study to identify the obstacles in the Member States to successful damages action against infringements of EU competition rules. On this basis, it concluded that private enforcement was in a situation of "total underdevelopment." As a next step, the Commission published (in 2005) a Green Paper on damages actions for breach of the EU antitrust rules in order to "to set out different options for further reflections and possible action to improve damages actions." The adoption of the Green Paper was followed by a public consultation. The promotion of antitrust damages actions was seen by the Commission as a means of strengthening the enforcement of EU competition rules. Given the limited resources of competition authorities, the involvement of other players in the market through private enforcement could help the Commission and NCAs to focus on the most severe offenses to EU antitrust laws (and particularly hard-core cartels), while the aggregate effectiveness of these rules would be increased. As suggested by Marcos and Graells (2008), the Commission would be (efficiently) outsourcing some of its enforcement tasks to private individuals through promoting the use of antitrust.

The following move has been, on 2 April 2008, the adoption by the Commission of the White Paper, "Damages actions for breaches of [EU] antitrust rules," presenting a set of proposals – policy choices and specific measures – at both Community and national levels, which would provide better opportunities for full redress for the victims of antitrust violations. The White Paper was supported by a Staff Working Paper and an Impact Assessment, elaborated on the basis of an external report, "Making the antitrust damages actions more effective in the EU: welfare impact and potential scenarios," submitted to the Commission on 21 December 2008.

The White Paper's guiding principles revolve around the idea that compensation for antitrust damages is to be regarded as a fundamental goal. Victims (all victims of all breaches of Articles 101 and 102 in all sectors of the economy) should get full restoration for the prejudice suffered; and law-abiding businesses should not suffer from a competitive disadvantage. An enhanced level of damages actions will also have the effect of increasing deterrence for potential infringers.

Purporting to implement a "genuinely European system," the Commission emphasizes its commitment to preserve an effective public enforcement. However, the crucial role of the public authorities should be complemented by a second pillar, private damages actions, never mind whether relying or not on a prior finding of an infringement by a competition authority (and thus both follow-on and stand-alone suits).

After canvassing the several options identified by the Green Paper, the Commission offers a cautious (and, for many details, still indeterminate) recipe to improve the conditions for antitrust damages claims. The list of relevant issues is long enough. Among them are the following.

Fault requirement The Commission would endorse a presumption of fault, so that, once the victim has shown a breach of Article 101 or 102, the infringer should be liable for damages caused unless he demonstrates that the infringement was the result of an excusable error; note, however, in the resolution adopted on 26 March 2009, the European Parliament stated that

> a culpable act must always be a prerequisite for an action for damages, and that a breach of the EC competition rules must, at the least, be negligent unless national law provides that there is an automatic implication or rebuttable presumption of fault in the case of a breach of the EC competition rules, ensuring the consistent and coherent enforcement of competition law.

Fee shifting The rule sponsored by the Commission would contemplate the possibility, for national courts, of issuing cost orders derogating from the normal cost rules, preferably upfront in the proceedings, and guaranteeing that the claimant, even if unsuccessful, would not have to bear all costs incurred by the other party; whereas the Parliament would leave it to the Member States "to evaluate whether or not to ensure that the asymmetry of resources between the complainant and the defendant in legal proceedings does not deter the bringing of well-founded actions for damages," observing furthermore that "access to justice must also be balanced by strong measures to prevent abuse by, inter alia, frivolous, vexatious or 'blackmailing' actions."

Collective redress According to the Commission, the best choice would be a combination of two complementary mechanisms: representative actions, which are brought by qualified entities (designated in advance or certified on an ad hoc basis), and opt-in collective actions, in which victims expressly decide to combine their individual claims for harm they suffered into one single action. Note, however, that in a subsequent unofficial move (proposed draft Directive, 2009) the Commission itself opted for a representative model where qualified entities would be allowed to bring an action for damages on behalf of a group of injured parties, without any requirement to individually identify all of them, leaving them the right "not to be represented . . . in the representative action" (a rather winding way of evoking mandatory opt-out representative suits).

Binding effect of the NCA decisions According to Article 16(1) of Regulation 1/2003, the findings of the Commission in an antitrust case are to be relied upon as binding proof in civil proceeding for damages: the Commission endorses a rule which would confer analogous effect to NCA final (or finally upheld by a review court) decisions. The European Parliament, however, holds the opposite view that

> a national court should not be bound by a decision of the national competition authority of another Member State without prejudice to rules that provide for the binding effect of decisions that were adopted by a member of the European Competition Network, applying Articles 81 or 82 of the Treaty and in relation to the same subject-matter.

Access to evidence According to the Commission's proposal (in view of the acquis communautaire), national courts should, under specific conditions, have the power to order disclosure inter partes of precise categories of information or evidence relevant to the claim, provided: that the claimant has offered all the facts and means of evidence that are reasonably known and available to him; that they show plausible grounds of action; that he is unable, applying all efforts that can reasonably be expected, to assert the specific facts or to produce the evidence for which disclosure is envisaged; that he has specified sufficiently precise categories of information or evidence to be disclosed; and that the court is satisfied that the envisaged disclosure measure is relevant to the case as well as necessary and proportional in scope.

Quantum of damages As to this delicate calculation, the Commission has announced its intention to provide pragmatic, non-binding assistance (i.e., guidelines) in the difficult task of quantifying damages in antitrust cases, for the benefit of both the national courts and the parties. This commitment produced a study by Oxera et al. (2009), avowedly pursuing two objectives: "finding the most accurate answer possible – the desire to determine the real damage value as closely as possible," and "removing obstacles to private damages actions as a matter of better and more effective access to justice, through approaches that are clear and easy to apply and that fit within the existing EU and national legal frameworks." Several methods and techniques were canvassed, with the specification that, since there is no theoretical reason for preferring one type of method or model over another, the choice of approach will depend on the details of each case (particularly, on the availability and quality of data and information and of the basis on the counterfactual used in a particular model.[22]

Passing-on defense Since damages must be available to anybody proving harm causally linked to the infringement, and unjust enrichment is regrettable, the Commission suggests that defendants should be entitled to invoke the passing-on defense against a claim for compensation of the overcharge (with a standard of proof, for such a defense, not lower than the one imposed on the claimant); on the other hand, indirect purchasers, who can face serious evidentiary difficulties because of their information asymmetry, should be able to rely on a rebuttable presumption that the overcharge was passed on to them. To the contrary, the Parliament would leave courts the option of recourse to established national rules on the link between causality and liability in order to reach just decisions in individual cases.

Interactions between leniency programmes and actions for damages Since "adequate protection" against disclosure in private actions for damages must be ensured for corporate statements submitted by a leniency applicant in order to avoid placing the applicant in a less favorable situation than the co-infringers (otherwise, the threat of disclosure of the confession submitted by a leniency applicant could have a negative influence on the quality of his submissions, or even dissuade an infringer from applying for leniency altogether), the Commission candidly declares its willingness to consider the possibility of limiting the civil liability of the immunity recipient to claims by his direct and indirect contractual partners. But the Parliament, stressing that full exemption of cooperative witnesses from joint and several liability is contrary to the system, rejects such exemption as prejudicial to many victims of breaches of the EU competition rules.

Limitation period The limitation period (whatever it is, according to internal rules) should not start to run before the victim of the infringement can reasonably be expected to have knowledge of the infringement and of the harm it caused him; in order to guarantee that antitrust damages (follow-on) claims are brought more effectively, a new limitation period should start following the final infringement decision of a competition authority or its review court on which the claimant wants to rely in his antitrust damages action.

---

22 In the third quarter of 2011 the Commission is expected to issue a communication devoted to the problems of damages quantification in the antitrust arena.

6 THE WAY AHEAD

It is worth noting that most of the above issues have little (or, at least, a non-exclusive) bearing on antitrust. Rather, they represent by-products of differentiated bodies of procedural and tort law in the Member States, surfacing in several other settings, so that streamlining them with the goal of making antitrust damages actions more effective is, at best, a very partial way of approaching a more general problem – i.e. building a discipline of non-contractual liability with an authentically uniform breath. Whether, for instance, fault is to be presumed while dealing with anticompetitive behavior, as suggested by the Commission (and actually practiced in some jurisdictions, e.g. Italy, in the wake of the specific discipline of unfair competition), or the pre-requisite of culpability is to be demonstrated by the plaintiff as a matter of course, is a question which goes back to the core of the relevant tort system, and is differently solved in the various national contexts; the same holds true for limitation periods (to be applied across the board), which present a dramatic fork, from two to thirty years, as well as for the hotly debated techniques for allowing collective redress and the even more intriguing technicalities of access to evidence. By the same token, the acute difficulties experienced when trying to compute the quantum of antitrust damages is just a variation of widespread judicial resistance to award redress when the proof of prejudice is only virtual and based on counterfactual projections. On this count, one might say that private enforcement of antitrust law has mostly to neutralize a still creeping ideological resistance (the entrenched inclination to recognize the absolute prevalence of public interests as far as market governance is concerned) and to overcome "environmental" hurdles that, as of now, cannot be easily disposed of, simply because they are connected to systemic perspectives.

On the other hand, the aspiration to make the EU right to compensation for antitrust damages more effective could suggest a sectoral strategy, aiming to reshape national rules in so far as they hamper the achievement of the objective of assuring that injured parties be provided the opportunity to effectively exercise that right. This option could be pursued invoking the opportunity to eliminate disparities in the legal regimes and create a level playing field between national jurisdictions as regards both the possibility for private claimants to seek compensation in national proceedings and the reduction of legal uncertainty. Not surprisingly, a trajectory like this has tempted the Commission, as witnessed by the proposed directive that circulated almost clandestinely in 2009, before getting dispersed in the Brussels fog. This strategy, however, would conflate two problems that deserve separate analysis. One concerns the vexing question of harmonization of national disciplines: a process that, as pointed out by a hectic and long-lasting debate, promises evident benefits, while reneging the opportunities stemming from competition of legal systems.[23] Whatever one thinks of harmonization of the European legal panorama as a goal in itself, it goes without saying that the introduction of special rules aiming to incentivize damages actions for antitrust infringements implies an entirely different perspective. Though there exist

[23] A thoughtful reflection about the disparate facets of the drive towards a European civil code in Micklitz (2010).

strong arguments for endorsing such a move – once it is recognized that antitrust damages suits are an indispensable complement in order to fight cartels and the like – a "parochial" solution to problems that plague the whole region of European procedural/tort law appears – given the frictions that have thus far impeded a top-down *reduction ad unum* of European private law – hardly workable.

In light of these considerations, one is driven to conclude that, whilst damages actions should have a greater role than the one currently experienced in Europe, how to get there is – to say the least – problematic. The shortcut of an authoritative intervention, imposing a common frame limited to the antitrust area, lies probably beyond realistic expectations. Accordingly, whether antitrust enforcement will be significantly fueled, in the future, by a more consistent contribution of private suits will depend largely on cultural developments that do not pertain to the antitrust realm.

REFERENCES

Águila-Real, J.A. (2009), "Contra la armonización positiva: la Propuesta de la Comisión para reforzar el *private enforcement* del. Derecho de la Competencia," available at www.indret.com/code/getPdf.php?id=1294&pdf=667_es.pdf.

Aresu, A. (2010), "Optimal contract reformation as a new approach to private antitrust damages in cartel cases," 35 *European Law Review* 349.

Ashurst (2004), "Study on the conditions of claims for damages in case of infringement of EC competition rules – comparative report," available at http://ec.europa.eu/comm/competition/antitrust/others/actions_for_damages/national_reports/spain_en.pdf.

Bebchuk, L.A. (1998), "Negative expected value suits," NBER Working Paper No. W6474.

Bolotova, Y. (2006), "Cartel overcharges: an empirical analysis," available at SSRN: http://ssrn.com/abstract=931211.

Brodley, J.F. (1995) "Antitrust standing in private merger cases: reconciling private incentives and public enforcement goals," 94 *Mich. L. Rev.* 1.

Bryant, P.G. and E.W. Eckard (1991), "Price fixing: the probability of getting caught," 73 *Review of Economics and Statistics* 531.

Buccirossi, P. and G. Spagnolo (2007), "Optimal Fines in the Era of Whistleblowers: Should Price Fixers Still Go To Prison?" in V. Goshal and J. Stennek (eds), *The Political Economy of Antitrust*, Elsevier, North Holland.

Castronovo, C. (2007), "Private law remedies for antitrust violations: a point of view from Italy," in J. Basedow (ed.), *Private Enforcement of EC Competition Law*, Kluwer Law International, Alphen aan den Rijn, 107.

Combe, E. (2006), "Quelle sanctions contre les cartels? Une perspective économique," *Revue international de droit économique*, 11.

Combe, E. and C. Monnier (2007), "Cartel profiles in the European Union," *Concurrences* No. 3-2007, 181.

Combe, E. and C. Monnier (2009), "Fines against hard core cartels in Europe: the myth of over enforcement," Cahiers de recherché PRISM-Sorbonne, available at www.ssrn.com/abstract=1431644.

Connor, J.M. (2009), "Cartels and antitrust portrayed: market effects – private international cartels 1990–2008," available at www.ssrn.com/abstract=1372850.

Connor, J.M. (2010), "Recidivism revealed: private international cartels 1990–2009," available at www.ssrn.com/abstract=1688508.

Connor, J.M. and R.H. Lande (2005), "How high do cartels raise prices: implications for optimal cartel fines," 80 *Tulane L. Rev.* 513.

Craycraft, C., J.L. Craycraft and J.C. Gallo (1997), "Antitrust sanctions and a firm's ability to pay," 12 *Review of Industrial Organization* 171.

Easterbrook, F.H. (1985), "Detrebling antitrust damages," 28 *J. L. & Econ.* 445.

Eger, T. and P. Weise (2006), "Limits to the private enforcement of antitrust law," German Working Papers in Law and Economics, vol. 2007, Article 3.

Elzinga, K.J. and W.C. Wood (1988), "The costs of the legal system in private antitrust enforcement," in L.J. White (ed.), *Private Antitrust Litigation: New Evidence*, MIT Press, Cambridge, MA.

Friederiszich, H.V. and C.-H. Röller (2010), "Quantification of harm in damages actions for antitrust infringements: insights from German cartel cases," ESMT working paper 10–001.
Gentry, W.M. and R.G. Hubbard (2000). "Entrepreneurship and household saving," NBER Working Papers 7894.
Gerber, D.J (2009), "Private enforcement of competition law: US experience and European law," in G.A. Benacchio and M. Carpagnano (ed.), *Il private enforcement del diritto comunitario della concorrenza: ruolo e competenze dei giudici nazionali.* Atti del II Convegno di Studiotenuto presso la Facoltà di Giurisprudenza di Trento 8–9 maggio, CEDAM.
Gerber, D.J. (2010), *Global Competition: Law, Markets, Globalization*, Oxford University Press, Oxford.
Ginsburg, D.H. and J.D. Wright (2010), "Antitrust sanctions," 6 *Competition Policy International*, (2), 3.
Haucap, J., U. Heimeshoff and L.M. Schultz (2010), "Legal and illegal cartels in Germany between 1958 and 2004," DICE discussion papers.
Klöhn, L. (2010), "Private versus public enforcement of laws – a law and economics perspective," paper presented at the Conference: Compensation of private losses – The evolution of torts in the European business law, Münster, November.
Komninos, A. (2008), *EC Private Antitrust Enforcement: Decentralised Application of EC Competition Law by National Courts*, Hart Publishing, Oxford/Portland.
Kovacic, W.E. (2008), "Modern U.S. competition law and the treatment of dominant firms: comments on the Department of Justice and Federal Trade Commission proceedings relating to Section 2 of the Sherman Act," available at http://www.ftc.gov/os/2008/09/080908section2stmtkovacic.pdf, 4, 8.
Lande, R.H. (2009), "Quick – Somebody call Amnesty International! Intel says EU antitrust fine violated human rights" (Federal Trade Commission: Watch, Vol. 746, No. 9, July) available at www.ssrn.com/abstract=1446845.
Lande, R.H. and J.P. Davis (2008), "Benefits from private antitrust enforcement: an analysis of forty cases," 82 *U. San Francisco L. Rev.* 898.
Landes, W.M. (1983), "Optimal sanctions for antitrust violations," 50 *U. Chi. L. Rev.* 652.
Levenstein, M.C. and V.Y. Suslow (2002), "What determines cartel success?" Working paper, University of Michigan Business School, 42.
Manzini, P. (2008), "European antitrust in search of the perfect fine," 31 *World Competition* 3.
Marcos, F. and A.S. Graells (2008), "Towards a European tort law: damages actions for breach of antitrust rules: harmonising tort law through the back door?," *European Review of Private Law* 469.
McAfee, R.P., H.M. Mialon and S.H. Mialon, (2005), "Private v. public antitrust enforcement: a strategic analysis," Working paper, Emory Economics 0523, Emory University (Atlanta) (later published in *92 Journal of Public Economics* (2008) 1863–75).
Micklitz, H.-W. (2010), "The visible hand of European regulatory private law: the transformation of European private law from autonomy to functionalism in competition and regulation," 28 *Yearbook of European law 2009*, 3.
Motta, M. (2008), "On cartel deterrence and fines in the European Union," 29 *E.C.L.R.* 209.
Oxera et al. (2009), *Quantifying Antitrust Damages: Towards Non-binding Guidance for Courts*, Study prepared for the European Commission, available at http://ec.europa.eu/competition/antitrust/actionsdamages/quantification_study.pdf.
Peyer, S. (2010), "Myths and untold stories: private antitrust enforcement in Germany," CCPworking paper 10–12, available at www.ssrn.com/abstract=1672695.
Prosperetti, L., E. Paini and I. Tomasi (2009), *Il danno artitrust*, Il malino, Bologra.
Renda, A. et al. (2009), *Making Antitrust Damages Actions More Effective in the EU: Welfare Impact and Potential Scenarios*, Final report, December 2007.
Riley, A. (2010), "EU competition policy in 2025: a vision of an European internationalist future?" 10 *Competition Policy International*, 1.
Salop, S.C. and L.J. White (1986), "Economic analysis of private antitrust litigation," 74 *Georgetown L. J.* 1001.
Schinkel, M.P. (2007), "Effective cartel enforcement in Europe," 30 *World Competition* 539.
Schinkel, M.P. and J. Rüggeberg (2006), "Consolidating antitrust damages in Europe: a proposal for standing in line with efficient private enforcement," available at www.ssrn.com/ paper= 903282.
Segal, I. and M.D. Whinston (2006), "Private enforcement of antitrust law: a survey," Stanford law and economics Olin working paper No. 335, available at www.ssrn.com/abstract=952067.
Shavell, S. (1984), "Liability for harm versus regulation of safety," 13 *J. Legal Studies* 357.
Van Cayseele, P.J.G. and P.D.N. Camesasca (2007), "The EC Commission's 2006 fine guidelines reviewed from an economic perspective: risking over-deterrence," Amsterdam Center for Law & Economics working paper No. 2007–03, available at www.ssrn.com/abstract=989628.
Van den Bergh, R.J. and P. Camesasca (2006), *European Competition Law and Economics: a Comparative Perspective*, Sweet and Maxwell, London.

Veljanovski, C. (2011), "Deterrence, recidivism and European cartel fines," available at SSRN: http://ssrn.com/abstract=1758639.
Werden, G.J. and M.J. Simon (1987), "Why price fixers should go to prison," 32 *Antitrust Bulletin* (4), 917–37.
Wils, W.P.J. (2003), "Should private enforcement be encouraged in Europe?" 26 *World Competition* 478.
Wils, W.P.J. (2005), "Is criminalization of EU competition law the answer?" 28 *World Competition* 117.
Wils, W.P.J. (2006), "Optimal antitrust fines: theory and practice," 29 *World Competition* 183.
Wils, W.P.J. (2009), "The relationship between public antitrust enforcement and private actions for damages," 32 *Word Competition* 3.

PART 7

DIVERSITY IN UNITY

14 Eastern enlargement of the European Union

Hans-Jürgen Wagener

1 INTRODUCTION

The European Union (EU) is a club with open access, as were its predecessors. Art. 98 of the Treaty establishing the European Community for Coal and Steel of 1951 states: 'Any European State may request to accede to the present Treaty.' All following treaties contain a similar sentence. Since Amsterdam 1997 there is, however, a clause linked to it; in the formulation of the Lisbon Treaty: 'Any European State which respects the values referred to in Article 2 and is committed to promoting them may apply to become a member of the Union' (Art. 49 current TEU). This Article 2 proclaims:

> The Union is founded on the values of respect for human dignity, freedom, democracy, equality, the rule of law and respect for human rights, including the rights of persons belonging to minorities. These values are common to the Member States in a society in which pluralism, non-discrimination, tolerance, justice, solidarity and equality between women and men prevail.

What is a European state has never been specified. But the fact that Cyprus has been accepted as a member and Turkey as a candidate shows that the term may be interpreted rather broadly.

This built-in provision for enlargement by admission of new states respecting basic human rights has one predecessor in the Northwest Ordinance passed by the US Congress in 1787, which envisaged the enlargement of the United States not by extension of the incumbent members but by accession of new states. Enlargement was a strategic option of the Union right from its start. Yet at the end of the formative period of the European Community (EC) at the beginning of the 1960s there were three European integration projects in place: the EC or the Europe of the Six (Benelux, Germany, France, and Italy); the European Free Trade Association (EFTA), the United Kingdom's competitor, or the Europe of the Seven (the UK, Sweden, Norway, Denmark, Austria, Switzerland, and Portugal); and the Council for Mutual Economic Assistance (CMEA), which was not exclusively European and tried to integrate the communist countries east of the Iron Curtain. Only a few countries, namely Finland, Spain, Ireland, Yugoslavia, Albania, and Greece, remained unaligned at that time.

Today, the EU seems to be the only game in town. In several enlargement rounds almost all West European countries joined the Union. EFTA shrank to four members, Switzerland, Liechtenstein, Norway, and Iceland, the last on its way into the EU. The CMEA was disbanded in 1991; ten of its members became members of the EU, the German Democratic Republic by joining the Federal Republic of Germany and nine East-Central and South-East European countries by acceding directly to the EU (Slovenia as part of former Yugoslavia had only an associated status in the CMEA). Enlargement is one of the great success stories of the Union. And the game is not over. At present four countries have their applications pending: Turkey, Croatia, Macedonia, and Iceland (we exclude Switzerland whose application has been put on ice after a negative referendum on the European Economic Area in 1992).

The European Communities were a constitutive element of the political and economic system of post-war Europe, which was characterised by the Cold War and the division into the communist East and the liberal West. When the Soviet empire collapsed in 1989–91, the post-war history of Europe came to an end and Europe was in need of a new ordering. That was the hour of the EC. In Maastricht in 1992 it reconstituted itself as the European Union and widened its scope by the Economic and Monetary Union (EMU). In 1994 it accepted as new members Austria, Finland, and Sweden whose neutrality had lost its import after the fall of the Soviet Union. And it opened the route for Eastern enlargement, the most extensive and ambitious enlargement process so far. The first two rounds of it were completed in 2004 – disregarding the prelude of the German reunification in 1990 – when eight East-Central European countries (Estonia, Latvia, Lithuania, Poland, the Czech Republic, Slovakia, Hungary, and Slovenia) plus Cyprus and Malta joined the Union and in 2007 when two South-East European countries (Bulgaria and Romania) followed.

2 THE COPENHAGEN CRITERIA

Soon after the political turnaround in Eastern Europe and the dissolution of the Soviet Union it became clear that the former communist countries in East-Central and South-East Europe were looking westward politically as well as economically. For these countries it meant leaving behind 40 years or more of Soviet captivity and a return to Europe, where they saw their historical and cultural roots and more or less well-functioning political and economic systems which could serve as models for their process of transformation. The EU was obviously challenged to react immediately to this situation. It did so already in 1989 with the PHARE programme (Poland and Hungary Aid for the Restructuring of Economies), which was later extended to other transition countries. In 1991 followed association agreements with several East-Central European states, as they existed already with other countries. Such agreements mainly create bilateral free trade areas. The first association agreements did not contain a clear membership perspective. The EU was still hesitant whether to open such a perspective or to keep Eastern Europe at arm's length in a kind of special relationship. This changed with the European Council at Copenhagen in June 1993. The association agreements were substituted by so-called Europe Agreements that intensified bilateral cooperation and aid. So trade between the new members and the EU was already almost fully liberalised at the date of accession.

At Copenhagen the incumbent member states finally realised that any arrangement short of full membership would not suffice as a new European order. The task was to structure the process of accession. This was done by specifying conditions for full membership and the procedure whereby their fulfilment would be checked. The Council formulated the criteria rather succinctly:

> Membership requires that the candidate country has achieved stability of institutions guaranteeing democracy, the rule of law, human rights and respect for and protection of minorities,

> the existence of a functioning market economy as well as the capacity to cope with competitive pressure and market forces within the Union. Membership presupposes the candidate's ability to take on the obligations of membership including adherence to the aims of political, economic and monetary union. (Council 1993, p. 13)

Most of the conditions were not new but applied also to previous enlargement rounds. Former planned economies had, of course, first to be transformed into functioning and shock-proof market economies before being able to enter a Union whose governing economic principles are competition and free movement of goods, services, capital, and labour. What makes a functioning market economy was later specified by the Commission. Among other things liberalisation of prices and foreign trade is needed together with a functioning legal system and secure property rights, enforceability of contracts, macro-economic stability, a developed financial sector, and a basic consensus about economic policy. In other words, transformation should be more or less completed when entering the Union. This was a comprehensive programme and an effective stimulus for rapid transformation in the associated countries. When the first eight of them joined the club in 2004, their EBRD transformation score (an index ranging from 1 to 4 reflecting the stage of transition in different legal and economic fields) was, with 3.4, higher than in any other transition country in Eastern Europe (EBRD 2005a, 2005b). The prospect of EU membership was a strong incentive for rapid transformation and has determined the direction of transformation to a large extent.

The 'candidate's ability to take on the obligations of membership' is a rather innocuous formulation for the condition that a candidate has to adopt the full *acquis communautaire*, i.e. the whole body of EU legislation. Already the countries of the first enlargement round had to comply with this condition. However, in 1973 the *acquis* was much smaller than in 2004, when deepening and widening had left hardly any political and economic field untouched by European regulations. It does not suffice, so the 1995 Madrid European Council insisted, to transpose EU legislation into national legislation; it has to be enforced effectively and to this end the national administrative structures have to be adapted. During the accession negotiations the Commission monitored the candidates' progress in this respect. The total *acquis* was segmented into 31 chapters which had to be worked off. It may be seen as an advantage that the former communist countries were transforming their political, economic, and administrative systems anyhow. In particular cases they were helped by specialists from the incumbent member states in so-called twinning programmes.

The Copenhagen Council formulated also a *caveat* for the old member states:

> The Union's capacity to absorb new members, while maintaining the momentum of European integration, is also an important consideration in the general interest of both the Union and the candidate countries. (Council 1993, p. 13)

The transitory regime of free movement of persons is a typical example of old member states claiming a limited capacity to absorb the new members from Eastern Europe. But the real challenge of Eastern enlargement was institutional change. A Union whose governance structure was constructed for a rather narrow scope of policy tasks and a membership of six, in the meantime deepened, widened, and enlarged to 15 members, was in train to accept another 12 and probably more new members. This required some fundamental changes in the administrative structure and above all in the decision making process. In short, enlargement entails reform.

Unlike the candidate transformation countries where for a certain period of time reforms were the order of the day, the old member states had great difficulties to make changes in the constitution of the Union, i.e. the treaties. The applicants did all they could to comply with the Copenhagen criteria, which ultimately led to their accession in 2004. The EU itself did not: neither the Amsterdam nor the Nice Treaty achieved the necessary changes to make a Union of 27 or more members workable. Only after the first round of Eastern enlargement were resolved steps taken with the ultimately failed project of a Constitution for Europe. But its content essentially got saved in the Lisbon Treaty, entering into force after a bumpy ride on 1 December 2009. Instead of fixing the new rules of the game among the old members, the new member states were thus able to co-decide, which may not have been a disadvantage. But it certainly protracted the process of decision making.

3 WHY EASTERN ENLARGEMENT? DIVERSITY AND IDENTITY

Enlargement is always a transition to a Pareto-superior situation. For each party to the agreement has a right to veto it. While it is quite easy to comprehend the interest of Eastern European countries to become members of the EU, this is less clear for some of the incumbent member states. EU membership in conjunction with NATO membership means external security for the newly independent states. The post-World War I idea of a *cordon sanitaire* between Western Europe and the Soviet Union had proven not really healthy. To take part in the single market is a great chance for economic development of countries that during their communist period had fallen back in relation to Western Europe. In addition, the Union's main economic policies, the common agricultural policy and the cohesion policy, would channel financial means into the region and further propel development. As relatively poor countries they would be net receivers of the EU budget for a longer span of time. And finally there was the widespread idea of a return to Europe to which East-Central and South-East Europe felt belonging according to their historical and cultural traditions.

This last idea must have had a considerable weight also within the EU-15. If we distinguish with Schimmelfennig and Sedelmeier (2005a, 2005b) two major motives for enlargement, the rational one of welfare and power maximisation and the constructivist one of values, norms, and identities, it seems rather obvious that old member states that lie at a greater distance from Eastern Europe or that have been chief beneficiaries of agricultural and cohesion policies will hardly improve their situation after enlargement. No wonder that Greece, Spain, Portugal and the Atlantic-oriented countries of the old EU in general were initially less enthusiastic about the prospect of Eastern enlargement. Only the UK was an exception, which may be explained by its notorious aversion to 'creating an ever closer union among the peoples of Europe' (Preamble current TEU): accesion of new member states which are proud of their newly won sovereignty will weaken the federalist camp and strengthen the intergovernmental one. The resistance of Poland and the Czech Republic against the Lisbon Treaty has validated such expectations.

Once there is consensus that accepting the applicants from East-Central and South-East Europe is appropriate, considerations of usefulness move to the back of the stage. This improves the bargaining position of the applicants during the negotiations. Since they do not run the risk of being refused, they may obtain concessions that otherwise would be out of reach. Poland in particular has skilfully negotiated by exploiting in addition the logic of two-level games (Putnam 1988). What at the negotiation table seemed reasonable was shown to be potentially unacceptable in the final national referendum. And a negative Polish referendum would have been a disaster for the new Europe.

Any club that opens its doors to almost double its membership must be afraid of growing diversity. The old identity, the well-established forms of handling club business, the familiar faces will change. Diversity has always been a constitutive trait of the EU. Clearly, any enlargement will increase it. The question is how much diversity the Union can stand without getting bogged down in a dysfunctional stalemate. The answer depends upon two things: the functions the Union is supposed to fulfil and the decision making procedures. Both can adapt to the increasing number of members and national interests. There are four possible paths: to discontinue or even to reverse deepening and widening, which will bring the integration process to a halt; to extend the scope of qualified majority decisions, which will strengthen the federalist mode of governance and reduce national sovereignty; to open the possibility for particular integration projects in which not all member states take part – the so-called Europe of different speeds; or to further develop the culture of compromise seeking, which entails the disadvantage of less transparency of decision making. Post-enlargement experience is too short to tell which of these four non-exclusive alternatives gets priority, but there is a bit of all four to be recognised.

In the context of Eastern enlargement the question of European identity has been widely discussed (see, for example, Fuchs and Klingemann 2002, Buonanno and Deakin 2004, Sjursen 2006). The concept of identity is rather fuzzy. In a multinational political entity it is supposed to substitute for the nation, hardly less fuzzy, as the basis of the nation state. Both should serve to define a demos as a constitutive and legitimating element of the political entity and, hence, also its borders. Historical experience does not confirm the idea. For it is by no means clear whether nation or identity precedes the nation state, or identity is produced by belonging to an integrated political entity. Sure, identity can be based upon a common past, a common culture, common norms. But in order for the past to be recognised and accepted as common, it needs a certain present ideological effort. In other words, European identity may be an endogenous effect of European integration.

Sjursen (2006) distinguishes value based and rights based norms, the latter allowing for a less exclusive identity. Values, however, are exclusive and may yield distinct borders only if they cannot be universalised: were Europe's identity defined as Christian Occident, for instance, Turkey obviously could not have been accepted as a candidate. Identity is generally thought of as an affective attitude that allows identitification with the Union and, hence, stabilises the Union more than mere material advantage. To begin with, the rationale for the Union has been material advantage: peace and the common market, which both are not in need of a distinct identity. A certain identification with the growing community may follow then. For since antiquity we know *patria est, ubicumque est bene* (Cicero). This makes possible higher forms of integration. To be sure, no state, no supranational entity can function without a minimal behavioural consensus.

Fuchs and Klingemann (2002) have shown that the actual Eastern enlargement has a certain logic in that the countries of the EU-27 share a subjectively perceived commonality of democratic values and behaviour even if the sense of a democratic community declines from West to East. Further east of the present EU border they find somewhat different attitudes and behavioural patterns. Within this democratic consensus of member states' societies there is, however, a divide, or rather a slope, concerning attitudes towards the state. Self-reliance and self-responsibility get weaker from West to East; conversely the call for solidarity, which implies a call for the state, increases. Republican virtues like civic engagement and trust in others diminish along the same line. It remains to be seen whether the East's peculiarities are transient Leninist legacies or ingrained attitudes. Anyhow, Eastern enlargement will enhance diversity in many respects.

Does greater diversity make necessary greater flexibility? The Copenhagen criteria said no. New members have to adopt the full *acquis* including Schengen and the EMU, from which incumbent members were allowed to opt out lest they should veto these projects. We may call this a ratchet effect of European integration. Since Nice 2001 the Union has the option of enhanced cooperation. It has been specified in the Lisbon Treaty where it is codified in Art. 20 (current TEU) and Arts 326–34 (TFEU). Member states wishing to establish enhanced cooperation between themselves within the framework of the Union's non-exclusive competences may do so.

A concrete project of enhanced cooperation needs in the Council only the unanimous consent of participating member states – there must be at least nine of them. So there is no need of explicitly opting-out. This also implies that acts adopted in the framework of enhanced cooperation are binding only for the participants. They shall not be regarded as part of the *acquis* which has to be accepted by new candidates (Art. 20(4) current TEU). Had Schengen and the EMU been institutionalised under this rule, new member states would not have been obliged to join them. In fact, the EMU is treated as if it were a project of enhanced cooperation, and neither Sweden nor any of the new member states are summoned to introduce the Euro within a given period of time.

4 CONVERGENCE

Eastern enlargement has been considered a particularly risky project, since the acceding countries were considerably less developed than the EU-15 average. Cohesion, one of the ultimate aims of the Union, depends to a certain extent upon similar welfare levels, otherwise the common budget will be strained too much in order to bring it about. At least such was the apprehension at the beginning of the process. Although the Copenhagen criteria require some convergence, namely institutional convergence or the acceptance of the *acquis* and nominal convergence or macro-economic stability, real convergence is not among the conditions for accession. It should be achieved in due time after becoming a member of the Union.

Of course, it was exactly for real convergence that the new member states were eager to enter the Union. Scale economies and fiercer competition because of the single market, foreign direct investment and net monetary transfers from the Union budget make it a realistic expectation. Indeed, the East European accession countries achieved remarkable results in the roughly three years before and seven years after joining the Union (see Table

Table 14.1 *GDP of East European new member states, 2000–2011*

Country	GDP per capita in PPS (EU-27 = 100)			Average annual growth in per cent		
	2000	2004	2010	2000–2008	2009	2010–11
EU-15	115	113	110	2.05	−4.2	1.7
Slovenia	80	88	85	4.32	−8.0	1.3
Czech Rep.	71	78	80	4.20	−4.7	2.3
Slovakia	50	57	73	5.70	−4.9	3.6
Hungary	54	63	65	3.52	−6.8	1.4
Estonia	45	57	64	7.02	−14.3	5.2
Poland	48	51	63	4.19	1.6	4.0
Lithuania	40	51	57	6.97	−14.8	3.8
Latvia	36	46	51	7.28	−17.7	2.1
Romania	26	34	47	5.84	−6.6	0.1
Bulgaria	28	35	44	5.59	−5.5	1.2

Source: Eurostat.

14.1). The world-wide crisis of 2009 has hit the fastest growers hardest, revealing the vulnerability of these economies. But if the region can resume its pre-crisis development, convergence will happen in the foreseeable future. A rough calculation with growth rates of 2 per cent for the EU-15, 4 per cent for the slower growing East-Central European countries (Poland, the Czech Republic, Slovakia, Hungary, Slovenia), and 6 per cent for the faster growing northern (the Baltic states) and southern (Bulgaria, Romania) new member states yield a time span of about 25 years for Bulgaria, Romania, and Poland to about 10 years for the Czech Republic and Estonia and 5 years for Slovenia to reach the EU-27 average or full β-convergence (Sala-i-Martin 1996). As has previously been the case for Spain, Portugal, Greece, and Ireland, membership of the EU will be beneficial for the economic development of the new members in East-Central and South-East Europe.

The growth performance was export driven. During the communist period the East-European countries were locked into the foreign trade system of the CMEA and the Soviet Union was their largest trading partner. The new member states succeeded within a rather short period to restructure and redirect their foreign trade towards the EU (see Table 14.2). Eastern enlargement has been a major factor in the change. These countries considerably increased their market shares in Western imports. They were attractive as trade partners for the EU-15 because of favourable exchange rates and low labour costs. As the initially notorious current account deficits show, they were also attractive as a market for Western exports. The widespread fear that Eastern enlargement would threaten firms and labour in the old EU turned out to be unfounded, if we look at the economy as a whole. Single sectors of it may have suffered from the competition. Table 14.2 also shows that during the crisis of 2009 the new member states' foreign trade was affected not more, rather less, than the EU-15's. The high foreign trade dependence resulted, however, in a serious fall in output especially in the Baltic states.

Rapid development and convergence have their price. Real exchange rates and labour costs have risen during the first decade of the 2000s as a consequence of rapid growth. Although both are presently still favourable, it is obvious that Eastern Europe

Table 14.2 *Foreign trade of East European new member states, 2000–11*

Country	Export share of EU-27 in per cent	Average annual growth of exports in per cent		Average annual current account deficit in per cent of GDP
	2010	2000–2008	2009	2009–11
EU-27	66.6[a]			1.0
EU-15		4.8	−16.3	1.0
Slovenia	71.6	9.4	−15.6	1.2
Czech Rep.	82.7	12.1	−15.8	3.8
Slovakia	83.9	14.9	−14.0	−0.4
Hungary	76.8	11.6	−16.6	6.5
Estonia	71.9	10.4	−17.4	6.4
Poland	75.5	13.1	−11.6	−0.8
Lithuania	60.6	15.5	−14.5	−1.5
Latvia	64.6	13.5	−11.5	−2.9
Romania	74.3[a]	10.9	−7.7	−5.1
Bulgaria	64.4[a]	9.8	−13.6	−3.3

Note: a 2009.

Source: Eurostat.

cannot compete with cheap labour in East and South Asia and will have to upgrade its production. This, too, is a process of convergence.

One of the more important decisions of the old EU-15 in preparation for enlargement concerned the Union budget. Despite the huge development gap between old and new member states, it was agreed that the financial scope of Brussels should not be extended. Hence, the material basis of EU cohesion policy is rather small: about 0.5 per cent of total GDP of the Union. The sum available for the current budget period (2007–13) is, however, with about €350 billion not negligible. Major receivers of it are the cohesion countries (GDP per capita less than 90 per cent of the Union average in 2001–03) and the convergence regions (NUTS-2 regions with GDP per capita less than 75 per cent of the Union average in 2001–03). All new member states in Eastern Europe with all their regions, except two, qualify as cohesion countries and convergence regions. This implies a fundamental shift in the distribution of EU budgetary means, apart from the fact that accession of 10 + 2 low income countries depresses statistically the Union average, thus excluding hitherto recipient regions. Similar effects influence the budget distribution of the common agricultural policy, since several of the acceding countries still have large agricultural sectors.

Some 50 per cent of the total cohesion budget 2007–13 is earmarked for the new members in Eastern Europe. Although the sum is a small share of total EU GDP, individual recipient countries get between 2 and 3 per cent of their annual GDP. The larger part of these funds is invested in infrastructure projects. A more direct growth effect will be from foreign direct investments which, due to EU membership, flow abundantly into the new member states. These investments are coming in large part from the old member states and they testify to the rapid economic integration of old and new members.

FDI is responsible for about a quarter of gross fixed capital formation in the accession countries (European Commission 2009, p. 84). Its growth impact is due not only to accumulation but also to knowledge and technology transfer, to enhanced competition, and to spillover effects. It is important to see that FDI in Eastern Europe is not restricted to manufacturing but also affects services, above all the financial sector. The rapid development of this sector, almost non-existent under communist rule and indispensable for a functioning market economy, must be ascribed to such foreign engagement. The prospect of EU membership was a major factor influencing this engagement. Investment opportunities were created by transformation of the economic system, in particular by privatisation policy, quite soon after the turnaround of 1989–90. So FDI found its way into Eastern Europe long before the actual accession in 2004 or 2007.

5 MIGRATION

Next to the costs confronting incumbent member states, migration or labour mobility had been the second great concern of Eastern enlargement. The Polish plumber became a *bète noire* in French politics, while he became a relief to many British households. Economic theory predicts that sizeable income differences will be a major pull factor for migration and uncertain employment opportunities a push factor. The economic situation in the individual countries of Eastern Europe is not the same. Unemployment rates vary greatly over the region with a long-term tendency to decline. The same can be said about income differences with the old member states, but their absolute size at the moment of accession was enormous, certainly if calculated at exchange rates.

This situation induced the old member states to require transitory restrictions on free mobility of persons in the accession treaties. In principle there was agreed a 2 + 3 + 2 scheme: incumbent member states were allowed to close their borders for immigrants from the new member states for initially two years, which period could be extended to five years and prolonged for another two years if labour markets would be seriously disturbed by immigration. Three old member states, the UK, Ireland, and Sweden, did not make use of the opportunity with respect to the first eight new member states from Eastern Europe; most of the others opened their borders after two or three years. Only Austria, Belgium, Denmark, and Germany kept up restrictions till April 2011 despite the fact that serious disturbances of the labour market or threat thereof could hardly be perceived. With respect to the new member states of 2007, Bulgaria and Romania, only Sweden and Finland together with the new member states of the first round, except Hungary, allowed for full labour mobility right from the start. Italy and Spain, which before accession had been major targets for emigrants from these two countries, liberalised their immigration policies to a large extent so that these flows continued.

The annual net inflow of citizens of the first accession group into the EU-15 quadrupled in the first three years after 1 May 2004, to a size of about 250 000 persons. While at the end of 2003 there were about 0.9 million foreigners from East-Central Europe in the EU-15, the majority in Austria and Germany, this number had risen to 1.9 million by the end of 2007, and the share of the UK and Ireland in the intake had dramatically increased. In the same period, the number of foreign citizens from Bulgaria and Romania grew from 0.7 million to also 1.9 million, 80 per cent of whom went to Italy and Spain (Brücker et al. 2009). Eastern enlargement has apparently caused the expected migration wave, although not as big as some had feared. But even if the numbers still look impressive, foreign residents from the East European accession states did not exceed 1 per cent of the EU-15 population, while nationals from other EU-15 states made up 1.7 per cent and from non-EU states 4.5 per cent. Of course, these immigrants are very unevenly spread over the total EU-15 area.

A major effect of the selective application of the mobility restrictions was migration diversion from Central Europe, i.e. Austria and Germany, to the British Isles. Between 2003 and 2007 the number of citizens from the first eight East European accession states grew by about 15 per cent in Germany and about 50 per cent in Austria, while it quintupled in the UK and Ireland. The United Kingdom even surpassed Germany as the largest target country for these migration flows. Such are the official estimates. Since illegal immigration into Germany is much easier, and due to the restrictions much more probable, than into the UK, the absolute figures may be somewhat different. The terms emigration and immigration suggest rather misleadingly a permanent dislocation. With most migrants this is not the case. They come with the intention to go back home and stay on average only one year. The main motives are higher consumption, investment in human capital, and savings for material investments at home.

If labour mobility in connection with Eastern enlargement had any impact on national labour markets in the EU-15, it should be perceived first of all in the UK, Ireland, Italy, and Spain, i.e. the countries that received the major share of additional migrants. Any definite analysis is hampered by the very short time series available. Up to 2007, for which period more reliable data are at hand, hardly any negative impact, either increased unemployment or depressed wages, is discernible (Kahanec et al. 2010). Also the fear of extra stress for the national welfare state systems seems to have been unfounded, since the migrants are well integrated into the labour markets of the receiving countries. When in 2009 a major economic crisis set in, the predominant reaction was remigration. At least, such was the preliminary information about experience in the UK and Ireland. The situation in Spain and Italy may have been different. The pattern of migration inflows and outflows varies in general a great deal over the EU-15. The three largest destination countries show quite specific pictures for 2008: Spain had an inflow of 692 000, of which about 10 per cent were Romanians (the largest inflow coming from Morocco and Latin America), and an outflow of 232 000; Germany's inflow was 574 000, of which more than 20 per cent were Poles, and the outflow 563 000, i.e. no net change; and the United Kingdom's inflow was 456 000, of which more than 30 per cent were Poles, and the outflow 243 000 (OECD 2010, pp. 207, 241, 249). Short distance and cheap air fares make quasi-commuting possible (and statistical registration troublesome).

It is remarkable that the general public differs widely as to the labour market effect of Eastern enlargement (Eurobarometer 2009). While in Sweden, Finland, and the Netherlands 58 per cent of a representative sample disagreed with the view that enlargement contributed to job losses in their countries, in Romania, Hungary, Portugal, and Greece 70 per cent or more agreed and even in Germany and France 59 per cent were of that opinion, more than Irish, British or Spanish people, who saw the number of immigrants from Eastern Europe rise most spectacularly. The reasons may be different. In the transition countries people perhaps confound the effects of transformation and of accession to the EU. Greece and Portugal as the poorest old member states perceive perhaps the competition of the new members for cohesion funds and foreign direct investments. In general, the growth and trade enhancing effects of enlargement and integration would disprove such views.

Since after 1 May 2011 labour mobility from the first eight East European accession states has been fully liberalised, a new push and a shift in the direction of the flows can be expected. The size of these flows will depend upon the economic situation in the sending and the recipient countries. On the whole, restructuring unemployment due to transformation in Eastern Europe has come to an end, growth will be resumed after the crisis of 2009, and incomes are rising. This will have a dampening effect on migration. On the other side, labour markets in Austria and Germany will get tighter with a growing excess demand for qualified workers, certainly if the upswing of economic activity after the crisis gains further momentum. This will create ample opportunities for East European emigrants. A purely statistical effect will be the legalisation of illegal workers.

While the effects of migration on the economy of the receiving countries may be expected to be positive in the long run, the sending countries are often seen as losers. Their labour force decreases, they normally send higher qualified persons than the national average (brain drain), and they are left with a larger share of non-occupied persons to be supported by the remaining labour force. The largest numbers are leaving Poland and Romania, since those are the two biggest countries in the region. In relative terms Lithuania, Romania, Bulgaria, Poland, and Slovakia are high mobility countries, whereas the Czech Republic and Hungary exhibit a rather low mobility. The mentioned negative effects are certainly present in the short run together with the rather positive alleviation of unemployment and the financial remittances. In the longer run some more positive effects may appear such as improved human capital of those who return. Even those who do not move may be stimulated by the growing demand at home and abroad to invest in human capital. This is materialising in enhanced tertiary education enrolment in the new member states, which may have a second cause in the restrictive university admission policy of the communist period.

On the whole, there is no indication that opening up borders immediately after Eastern enlargement has had any detrimental effects upon the respective labour markets (see Baas et al. 2010). Did Austria and Germany, then, forgo some positive effects by extending the mobility restrictions to the limit? Arguing theoretically one may be inclined to answer in the affirmative. However, labour mobility is only one flow of productive factors. Austria and Germany were those countries that increased their foreign direct investment engagement in the region considerably together with Eastern enlargement and, consequently, the economic integration with the new member states. In other words, they were using cheap labour and skills on the spot (Marin 2010). Due to short distance and traditional links they had absolute advantages in this respect. The implied gains gave them an edge in international competitiveness manifesting in positive export achievements.

6 EASTERN ENLARGEMENT OF THE EMU

The Economic and Monetary Union (EMU) was included in the treaties at Maastricht 1992 and, hence, has become part of the *acquis communautaire*. It implies that new EU members have to join the EMU and introduce the common currency, the Euro. This important step, however, cannot be taken at the moment of accession, since it is necessarily preceded by a preparatory phase of at least two years, and the accession treaties do not stipulate a time horizon within which the EMU must be joined. The precedent is Sweden, which acceded to the EU in 1995. But although she fulfilled the other Maastricht criteria for EMU membership, she did not enter the Exchange Rate Mechanism II (ERM II), in which a country must prove exchange rate stability for at least two years. So she was able to keep the Swedish crown as wished. The other two voluntary non-Euro states of the EU-15, Denmark and the UK, are opt-out cases, since they were already members at Maastricht and could have vetoed the Euro if opting out would not have been allowed. This alternative is not open for new member states.

There has been a broad discussion about the pros and cons of a common currency in general, and in particular for the new member states which still have not fully completed their post-transformational phase of restructuring and which are, as we saw, considerably less developed than the old EU-15. It is theoretically assumed, and empirically confirmed, that a common currency has a trade enhancing effect and, hence, stimulates growth (Rose 2000; Eicher and Henn 2009). Since a common currency deprives an economy of national exchange rate policy and monetary policy, the theory of optimal currency areas has specified conditions, such as symmetry, flexibility, and integration, under which the loss of sovereignty does no harm (Mundell 1961; McKinnon 1963). Since in a single currency regime there can be only one monetary policy, it seems rather obvious that the economic development of currency union members should be fairly synchronised. Frankel and Rose (1998) have argued, however, that synchronisation or convergence of business cycles need not be an entering condition for monetary union membership, but will be achieved endogeneously once the single currency has been established or a country has joined the union. With respect to the new member states, some have argued that they still need monetary and exchange rate policies as shock absorbers. Others refer to Frankel and Rose or try to show empirically that business cycle asymmetries between old and new members are not larger than within the old EU-15 (Fidrmuc and Korhonen 2006).

The loss of exchange rate policy is even less problematic for open economies. For what they gain by a devaluation on the export side, they lose on the import side. Already McKinnon (1963) has concluded that small open economies are the most suitable candidates for a monetary union. Of the 12 new members of the enlargement rounds 2004 and 2007, five have already joined the EMU (Malta, Cyprus, Slovenia, Slovakia, and Estonia). Another three have either a currency board, i.e. an absolutely fixed exchange with the Euro (Bulgaria and Lithuania), or joined ERM II and fixed the exchange rate with a margin of fluctuation of ± 1 per cent, and not ± 15 per cent as required in that arrangement (Latvia). Those are exactly the smaller accession countries, whereas the four bigger ones, Poland, Romania, Hungary, and the Czech Republic, have floating exchange rates or a crawling band. They think to benefit from monetary sovereignty. This conviction has received a serious blow by the 2009 crisis. Exports fell in the whole region by more or less similar rates, although somewhat less than in the EU-15 (see Table 14.2). But in hard times sovereign currencies of emerging economies are prone to speculative attacks, as the Polish Zloty experienced: it devalued in that year by roughly one quarter.

The chances of the seven not-yet-Euro new members joining the EMU depend on their

Table 14.3 Nominal convergence in EMU candidate countries, 2010

Country	Year	Price stability	Government budgetary position			Exchange rate		Interest rate
		HICP inflation	Excessive deficit	Budget surplus	Gross debt	ERM II	Rate of change	
Bulgaria	2008	12.0	No	+1.8	14.1	No	0.0	5.4
	2009	2.5	No	−3.9	14.8	No	0.0	7.2
	2010	1.7	No	−2.8	17.4	No	0.0	6.9
Czech R.	2008	6.3	Yes	−2.7	30.0	No	10.2	4.6
	2009	0.6	Yes	−5.9	35.4	No	−6.0	4.8
	2010	0.3	Yes	−5.7	39.8	No	2.6	4.7
Latvia	2008	15.3	No	−4.1	19.5	Yes	−0.4	6.4
	2009	3.3	Yes	−9.0	36.1	Yes	−0.4	12.4
	2010	0.1	Yes	−8.6	48.5	Yes	−0.4	12.7
Lithuania	2008	11.1	No	−3.3	15.6	Yes	0.0	5.6
	2009	4.2	Yes	−8.9	29.3	Yes	0.0	14.0
	2010	2.0	Yes	−8.4	38.6	Yes	0.0	12.1
Hungary	2008	6.0	Yes	−3.8	72.9	No	−0.1	8.2
	2009	4.0	Yes	−4.0	78.3	No	−11.5	9.1
	2010	4.8	Yes	−4.1	78.9	No	4.5	8.4
Poland	2008	4.2	Yes	−3.7	47.2	No	7.2	6.1
	2009	4.0	Yes	−7.1	51.0	No	−23.2	6.1
	2010	3.9	Yes	−7.3	53.9	No	8.4	6.1
Romania	2008	7.9	No	−5.4	13.3	No	−10.4	7.7
	2009	5.6	Yes	−8.3	23.7	No	−15.1	9.7
	2010	5.0	Yes	−8.0	30.5	No	2.9	9.4
Sweden	2008	3.3	No	+2.5	38.3	No	−3.9	3.9
	2009	1.9	No	−0.5	42.3	No	−10.4	3.3
	2010	2.1	No	−2.1	42.6	No	6.8	3.3
Reference value		1.0		−3.0	60.0			6.0

Note: Data for 2010 refer either to the period April 2009–March 2010 or to April 2010.

Source: ECB (2010, p. 33).

fulfilling the so-called Maastricht criteria (for a full description see ECB 2010). In May 2010 the situation was as shown in Table 14.3.

Inflation has long been a serious problem in the transformation countries of Eastern Europe, and in many of them it still is too high with respect to the Maastricht criterion, 1.5 per cent above the three 'best performing Member States' (Art. 140(1) TFEU and Protocol). It could be doubted whether an average rate of inflation of –0.5 per cent, i.e. a manifest deflation on which the reference value of the period April 2009–March 2010 in Table 14.3 is based, is a token of best performance. More generally it has been argued that this criterion is unsuitable for catching-up economies. The reason is the so-called 'Maastricht dilemma of real versus nominal convergence' (De Grauwe and Schnabl 2005). The price level of less developed economies is, as a rule, significantly lower than in highly developed countries, since productivity and wages in the tradeables manufacturing sector are lower and, hence, also wages and prices in the non-tradeables service sector. As in the course of catching-up productivity and wages, but not prices, are rising in tradeables, wages and prices, but not productivity, in services go along with the former – there is price convergence and, transitorily, inflation. This is the well-known Balassa–Samuelson theorem. Actually, we should not speak of real *versus* nominal convergence, but of real *cum* nominal convergence. The dilemma is based on the fact that the EU stimulates real convergence and punishes nominal convergence. The favourable price stability record of some of the new member states shows that catching-up inflation need not necessarily take place even if nominal convergence has not yet been completed. The price-dampening competition effect of far-reaching integration is a counteracting force.

Apart from Sweden, only Bulgaria seems to be well prepared to enter the EMU. In this case the qualifying period of two years ERM II participation is rather meaningless, since the successful currency board is a much stronger proof of exchange rate stability. The same would hold for Latvia and Lithuania were it not that their budgets are in high deficit due to the crisis and, hence, the fixed exchange rate had to be defended by high interest rates. Clearly, EMU membership would have reduced this problem. Among the four larger new member states the situation of the Czech Republic looks most promising provided she is successful with implementing budgetary consolidation. However, Czech politicians appear not to be pressing for EMU membership. For the other three the road is apparently even longer. Finally, the Maastricht criteria require not only nominal stability but also institutional convergence, in particular an independent central bank (which is not everywhere in place), carefully monitored by the European Central Bank.

7 NEW BORDERS, NEW NEIGHBOURS

New members to the Union imply new external borders and new neighbours. In consequence of the two rounds of Eastern enlargement the EU now borders with Belarus, the Ukraine, Moldova, Serbia and Croatia. These are European countries and, hence, potential candidates for EU membership. With the accession of Bulgaria and Romania the EU has also reached the Black Sea, across which it borders with Georgia or the three Caucasus republics in general, whose qualification as European countries could be geographically disputed. All these countries are politically or economically difficult neighbours with the exception of Croatia, which most probably will be member as of 1 January 2013.

The prospect of future membership led the EU to differentiate between its neighbours. Turkey has long been sitting in the anteroom of the Union, but now she has candidate status and accession negotiations are under way. The non-members on the Balkan are either candidates already (Croatia and Macedonia) or they are envisaged as such. The other East-European states are included in the European Neighbourhood Policy (ENP), a policy device which is not meant to open the road towards future membership, but merely to closer cooperation. However, since the ENP is addressed also to the Mediterranean neighbours of the Union which clearly are non-European, there is still a difference: the East-European ENP countries may at least hope to become membership candidates. Finally, Russia has a special status. She is not included in the Neighbourhood Policy, but there is a strategic partnership between Russia and the EU.

The basic idea of the ENP is supporting the transition to democracy and a market economy. What has been so successful with the transformation countries in East-Central and South-East Europe and finally has led to Eastern enlargement should be tried also on the wider neighbourhood of the Union. The policy is intended to create a mutual commitment to common values: democracy, human rights, rule of law, good governance, market economy principles, and sustainable development. Typically, the ENP was launched in 2004, the year of the first round of Eastern enlargement (Cremona and Meloni 2007). It has been further developed in its two parts: in 2008 the Euro-Mediterranean partnership was upgraded as Union for the Mediterranean and in 2009 the bilateral ENP cooperation with East-European countries was widened into the more multilateral Eastern Partnership. The ENP and the Strategic Partnership with Russia are financed by the European Neighbourhood and Partnership Instrument, which has only very limited resources.

In the case of the new member states, compliance with the EU expectations, and finally adoption of the complete *acquis communautaire*, was motivated by the realistic perspective of membership. This cannot be expected from the target countries of the ENP. However, some of them are more dependent upon the EU in terms of economic and security policy and even hope to be given in future a membership perspective. Consequently they are more cooperative, as are, for instance, Armenia, Georgia, Moldova, and the Ukraine. Others are less dependent in this respect and show little inclination to adopt European norms; for instance, Algeria, Azerbaijan, Libya, and Syria. The leverage of the ENP is too small to provide effective incentives in these cases (Bendiek 2008).

This does not take away the fact that the EU exerts a strong pull on the population of these countries. They are, on the whole, much less developed than the EU average, even if some are rich in natural resources (oil). The Mediterranean countries, with the exception of Israel, have a lower GDP per capita than the East-European ENP partners, which, in their turn, are below Bulgaria, the poorest EU-27 country (Directorate 2008). The EU is surrounded in the East and South by politically and economically precarious countries with a rather low standard of living, poor goverance, and a notorious record of corruption. There is a strong interest of the Union that these neighbours should catch up and provide sufficient welfare for their citizens.

The new borders have quite naturally an impact upon migration. The increased flows from the new into the old member states have already been dealt with. But the new member states themselves become more and more an attractive destination for people starting further east. This is most clearly visible in the healthcare sector. While qualified, mainly female, personnel from Poland are employed in Austria and Germany (care drain), they are substituted in Poland by less qualified and cheaper workers from the Ukraine, for instance. Population decline, which will take place in the Union in general, has already started in most of the new member states. It remains to be seen how these countries, up to now not accustomed to immigration and foreign-born citizens, will cope with massive migratory pressure.

8 CONCLUSION: FUTURE ENLARGEMENTS

The history of the enlargement process is not at an end. In particular, Eastern enlargement has not been completed yet. The EU has no clear idea about the final stage of

European integration. So it is difficult to predict where the process ultimately will end. For the medium range it is fairly clear that next to the ongoing accession negotiations with Turkey, Macedonia, Croatia, and Iceland, the rest of the Balkans will be the most pressing issue. Among these cases the potential accession of Turkey is comparable to Eastern enlargement; it may even be a larger challenge for the Union. The experience of Eastern enlargement can serve as a guideline for the problems with which the Union will be confronted.

Like any other entrant, Turkey has to fulfil the Copenhagen criteria. For a long period of time this was the stumbling-block for Turkey's membership application. Democracy, rule of law, minority policy, a competitive economic order were considered not sufficiently developed to warrant taking up accession negotiations. These concerns have been overcome and negotiations on 33 chapters of the *acquis* started in 2005. It will be a prolonged process. For there is strong opposition within the EU, and particularly among the population, to the full membership of Turkey. Other than in the case of Eastern enlargement the accession treaty may be put to the popular vote of a referendum. The Austrian and French governments have already signalled their respective intentions, and at present there is a majority against the Turkish membership in Austria, France, Germany, Luxembourg, and Belgium. A single EU member voting against, in parliament or in a referendum, is sufficient to stop the process. One of the Copenhagen criteria is the ability of the Union to accommodate the new member. This was meant in the economic sense. It may turn out that the Union is unable to accommodate Turkey politically.

Geographically Turkey will be by far the largest member state, and given the demographic dynamics its population of about 73 million people in 2010 will very soon overtake that of the presently most populous country, Germany. In other words, by its sheer geographical and population size Turkey has the weight of about three-quarters of all the ten new member states in East-Central and South-East Europe. This weight will make itself felt also in the European Council, where according to the Lisbon Treaty population size determines the vote.

The accession of Turkey will push the Eastern border of the EU more than 1200 km further east with Syria, Iraq, Iran, Azerbaijan, and Armenia as new neighbours. Clearly, Turkey is an Asian country with only 3 per cent of her territory on the European continent. The population is Asian as well. This should not be a principal obstacle to membership. For Finns and Hungarians are Asian immigrants as well and have become good 'Europeans'. However, it is to be expected that in the context of the Turkish accession the question of 'European identity' will be discussed anew. Whatever should be the outcome of that discussion, a European Union with Turkey as a member state will give European integration a new quality and define for the EU a new role in international affairs. What politically is still smacking of European parochialism then has to manifest itself as one of the major players in world politics. It is not clear whether the EU or all of its members have such ambitions, since it enhances the supranational character of the Union.

Economically Turkey is a huge market and a dynamic one, too. The level of development is comparable to the poorest new member states in South-East Europe, Bulgaria and Romania. This implies there will be one additional big claimant for the financial resources of the common agricultural policy and the cohesion policy. Eastern enlargement did not lead to an expansion of the Union budget; the accession of Turkey most probably will not either. The cohesion countries of the Union therefore should not be fans of the Turkish enlargement. Since 1996 Turkey and the EU have been members of a customs union for manufactures and processed agricultural products. So a great deal of potential trade between the two regions will already be realised. However, Eastern enlargement has shown that full membership gives economic integration an additional push from which both sides are benefiting.

If Eastern enlargement has triggered strong concerns about labour market consequences due to migration and competition by a cheap labour force, this will be even more strongly accentuated in the case of Turkey. The strongest opposition to the full membership of Turkey is actually expressed in those countries that have already attracted large groups of immigrants of Turkish origin. Most probably these fears will be as unfounded as in the case of Eastern enlargement, and Southern enlargement for that matter. But they are politically effective. In short, the Turkish enlargement will be the test case for the limits of European integration. If it succeeds, further Eastern enlargement cannot be ruled out.

REFERENCES

Baas, Timo, Herbert Brücker and Andreas Hauptmann (2010), 'Labour Mobility in the Enlarged EU: Who Wins, Who Loses?', in Martin Kahanec and Klaus F. Zimmermann (eds), *EU Labour Markets after Post-Enlargement Migration*, Berlin (Springer), pp. 47–70.

Bendiek, Annegret (2008), 'Wie effektiv ist die Europäische Nachbarschaftspolitik? Sechzehn Länder im Vergleich', SWP-Studie 2008/S 24, Berlin (Stiftung Wissenschaft und Politik).

Brücker, Herbert, et al. (2009), *Labour Mobility within the EU in the Context of Enlargement and the Functioning of the Transitional Arrangements*, Final Report (IAB, CMR, fRDB, GEP, WIFO, wiiw), Nürnberg.

Buonanno, Laurie and Ann Deakin (2004), 'European Identity', in Neill Nugent (ed.), *European Union Enlargement*, Basingstoke (Palgrave), pp. 84–102.

Council of the European Communities (1993), European Council in Copenhagen – Conclusions of the Presidency, 21–22 June, SN 180/93, Brussels.

Cremona, Marise and Gabriella Meloni (eds) (2007), 'The European Neighbourhood Policy: A Framework for Modernisation?', EUI Working Paper Law No. 2007/21, Florence (European University Institute).

De Grauwe, Paul and Gunther Schnabl (2005), 'Nominal versus Real Convergence with Respect to EMU Accession – EMU Entry Scenarios for the New Member States', *Kyklos* 58, pp. 481–99.

Directorate General for Economic and Financial Affairs (2008), 'European Neighbourhood Policy: Economic Review of European Neighbour Countries', European Economy, Occasional Papers 40, August.

EBRD (2005a), *Transition Report 2005: Business Transition*, London (EBRD).

EBRD (2005b), Transition Report update, May, London (EBRD).

Eicher, Theo and Christian Henn (2009), 'One Money, One Market – A Revised Benchmark', IMF Working Paper WP/09/186, Washington (IMF).

Eurobarometer (2009), 'Views on European Union Enlargement', Analytical Report, Flash EB No 257.

European Central Bank (ECB) (2010), Convergence Report, May, Frankfurt a.M.

European Commission (2009), 'Five Years of an Enlarged EU: Economic Achievements and Challenges', European Economy 1/2009.

Fidrmuc Jarko and Iikka Korhonen (2006), 'Meta-analysis of the Business Cycle Correlation between the Euro Area and the CEECs', *Journal of Comparative Economics* 34, pp. 518–37.

Frankel, Jeffrey A. and Andrew K. Rose (1998), 'The Endogeneity of the Optimum Currency Area Criteria', *Economic Journal* 108, pp. 1009–25.

Fuchs, Dieter and Hans-Dieter Klingemann (2002), 'Eastward Enlargement of the European Union and the Identity of Europe', in Jan Zielonka and Peter Mair (eds), *The Enlarged European Union. Diversity and Adaptation*, London (Frank Cass), pp. 19–54.

Kahanec, Martin, Anzelika Zaiceva and Klaus F. Zimmermann (2010), 'Lessons from Migration after EU Enlargement', in Martin Kahanec and Klaus F. Zimmermann (eds), *EU Labour Markets after Post-Enlargement Migration*, Berlin (Springer), pp. 3–46.

Marin, Dalia (2010), 'The Opening-Up of Eastern Europe at 20 – Jobs, Skills and "Reverse Maquiladoras" in Austria and Germany', Bruegel Working Paper 2010–2, Brussels.

McKinnon, Ronald I. (1963), 'Optimum Currency Areas', *American Economic Review* 53, pp. 717–24.
Mundell, Robert A. (1961), 'A Theory of Optimal Currency Area', *American Economic Review* 51, pp. 657–65.
OECD (2010), International Migration Outlook: SOPEMI 2010, Paris (OECD).
Putnam, Robert (1988), 'Diplomacy and Domestic Politics: The Logic of Two Level Games', *International Organization* 42, pp. 427–61.
Rose, Andrew K. (2000), 'One Money, One Market: Estimating the Effect of Common Currencies on Trade', *Economic Policy* 15, pp. 7–46.
Sala-i-Martin, Xavier X. (1996), 'Regional Cohesion: Evidence and Theories of Regional Growth and Convergence', *European Economic Review* 40, pp. 1325–52.
Schimmelfennig, Frank and Ulrich Sedelmeier (eds) (2005a), *The Politics of European Union Enlargement: Theoretical approaches*, London (Routledge).
Schimmelfennig, Frank and Ulrich Sedelmeier (2005b), 'Introduction: Conceptualizing the Europeanization of Central and Eastern Europe', in Frank Schimmelfennig and Ulrich Sedelmeier (eds), *The Europeanization of Central and Eastern Europe*, Ithaca, NY (Cornell University Press), pp. 1–28.
Sjursen, Helene (ed.) (2006), *Questioning EU Enlargement: Europe in Search of Identity*, London (Routledge).

15 The economics of multilingualism in the EU

Jan Fidrmuc

1 INTRODUCTION

In little more than half a century, the EU (including its predecessors) has undergone deep and wide-ranging transformations. It has grown from being a rather loose grouping of six Western European nations to include most European countries, extending from the Baltic to the Black Sea and from the Iberian to the Balkan peninsula. In the process, the European Union has become increasingly heterogeneous. It now counts 27 member countries with diverse historical legacies (from the Roman Empire in the West to the Russian and Ottoman Empires in the East), dramatically different levels of economic development (ranging from rich Luxembourg to poor Bulgaria), various cultural and religious traditions, and a multitude of languages. On the last criterion, the diversity of Europe is perhaps at its most evident: the EU counts 23 official languages at present, compared with just four at the time of its founding.

The list of official EU languages includes some that are spoken by large numbers of people in Europe: German is spoken by approximately 85 million Europeans, while English, French and Italian are each spoken by around 60 million. Some of the official EU languages are also spoken widely outside of Europe: besides English, Spanish and Portuguese are notable examples. On the other hand, several of the official languages are spoken by relatively few: Estonian and Slovene are spoken by approximately 1–2 million while Maltese and Irish are spoken by around half a million each (moreover, the majority of speakers of Maltese and Irish are also fluent in English, another official EU language). This linguistic diversity reflects an overwhelming desire for equality: when joining, each member nation was allowed to put forward its national language as an official language of the EU and all its institutions. The only nation that has not done so is Luxembourg (Luxembourgish is used by the EU as a treaty language only).

Despite this apparent desire for equality, several languages stand out because of their omission. Russian, Turkish and Arabic are spoken by large numbers of Europeans (4.2, 2.2 and 1.6 million EU citizens, respectively), yet they do not enjoy official status. Regional languages are similarly not included, even though some enjoy official or semi-official status in their own country. Catalan, spoken by 4.1 million Europeans, is the most prominent example, followed by Galician and Basque.[1]

[1] All of the above figures refer to the number of native speakers of the various languages as estimated by extrapolating from the 2005 Eurobarometer survey (discussed below) mapping the landscape of languages in Europe. As such, these figures count all native speakers of a given language, not only those in the original country of that language. Only EU citizens are included in the count, thus counting in intra-EU migrants but excluding non-European immigrants. Russian native speakers can be found especially in the Baltic countries as well as in Germany. Turkish is spoken mainly in Germany and Bulgaria. The highest numbers of Arabic speakers are in France,

In the near future, the list of official EU languages can grow further by adding Croatian, Icelandic and Turkish. The last language can get official status either in the wake of Turkey's accession to the EU or because of the reunification of Cyprus. Moreover, Spain's regions are increasingly vocal in their quest for recognition of their languages. It is therefore conceivable that the EU might have as many as 30 official languages in a few years from now.

Multilingualism in the EU stands in sharp contrast with the practice in most nation states. The vast majority of countries in Europe are multilingual, with several regional and/or ethnic-minority languages spoken within their territories. However, most of them espouse strictly monolingual regimes when it comes to official languages, with only a few granting official or semi-official status to regional languages.

The practical and economic implications of multilingualism in the EU are wide-ranging. Official documents must be translated into all official languages. National representatives and members of the European Parliament (MEPs) are free (and often expressly expected) to use their own language when conducting official EU business. EU citizens similarly are entitled to use their language when communicating with European institutions. Implementing such extensive multilingualism is expensive: running translation and interpretation services for the EU of 27 member countries costs over €1 billion annually. It also takes time: translation of official documents into all official languages can take many months. As a result, legal decisions adopted by the EU are often implemented with several months' delay (legal decisions only become valid once they were published in all official languages). The process is prone to errors too, in part because of the growing use of "relay translations" whereby a document or spoken word is translated from one language to another via a "core" language such as English, German or French.

In this chapter, I discuss multilingualism in the EU and its economic implications and analyze some of the alternative arrangements that could be implemented. In the following section, I start by presenting the basic facts about multilingualism and language use in Europe. In that section, I outline the benefits of multilingualism, mainly consisting in avoiding linguistic disenfranchisement, and discuss the prominence of the various European languages in the linguistic landscape of Europe. The analysis documents a clear disconnect between the firm commitment of the EU to maintaining multilingualism in its institutions and the revealed preferences of Europeans: concerning the latter, the people of Europe increasingly coordinate on choosing English as their lingua franca. The following section then complements the discussion of benefits by analyzing the costs of multilingualism. Furthermore, by combining the discussion of benefits and costs of multilingualism, I outline the analytical foundations for identifying an optimal linguistic regime. Finally, the last section summarizes the main findings and argues that extensive multilingualism is neither economically optimal at present nor sustainable in the long term. If political constraints prevent the EU from streamlining its linguistic regime, then the most likely outcome is linguistic reform coming in through the back door: the full range of linguistic services will be maintained for a small subset of official languages

Germany, Italy, the UK and Belgium. The bulk of Catalan and Basque speakers live in Spain, with smaller numbers (much smaller in the case of Catalan) found in France.

while the quality and range of services provided in the remaining languages will gradually deteriorate.

2 LANGUAGES IN THE EU: STYLIZED FACTS AND ECONOMIC BACKGROUND

At the beginning of 2004, the EU had 11 official languages. Since the enlargement in May of that year, which brought in ten new member countries, the number of official languages has almost doubled, to 20 (Cyprus was the only new member country that did not bring with itself a new official language). In 2005, Ireland requested a (somewhat limited) official status for Irish.[2] By 2007, with the EU accession of Bulgaria and Romania, the number of official languages has thus grown to 23.

The right of each member state to nominate its national language as an official language of the EU has been enshrined in the Treaty of Rome and in Regulation 1/1958. The six founding countries shared four official languages: French, German, Italian and Dutch (Luxembourg has never requested the same privilege for Luxembourgish, which is one of its three official languages). Subsequently, following the principle of equality, full recognition of national languages was extended to all new members. This has increased the workload of the EU Directorates-General (DGs) for Translation and Interpretation dramatically. The vast majority (72 percent) of EU documents are currently prepared initially in English.[3] With 23 official languages, each document must therefore be translated 22 times. Moreover, the number of possible combinations requiring translation or interpretation is increasing more than proportionately to the number of languages: with 23 official languages, there are 506 such combinations, compared with 110 when the EU counted 11 official languages and 12 combinations when the EU was founded in 1957.[4] The linguistic services now cost the EU more than €1 billion annually: approximately one-fifth of its administrative budget and one-seventh of the amount spent on average annually on R&D within the FP7 (Seventh Framework Programme).

Linguistic policy is one of the areas where any amendment of the existing practice requires unanimity. Therefore, even if it were in the interest of the majority of EU citizens to demote certain languages, for instance those spoken by relatively few, to a status lower than that of an official EU language, proposing such a change would be futile as at least the country whose language would be affected would be certain to oppose it. It is for this reason that the linguistic regime put in place in 1957 has been maintained until present. Multilingualism was easy to implement – and might have been optimal – when the EU had six members and four languages, none of which had a clear claim to superiority. It is far from obvious that it is optimal – or even sustainable – at present with 27 members and 23 languages.

---

2 The implementation of this decision was postponed until 2007 because of the lack of qualified translators and interpreters.

3 See "EU translation policy here to stay," EurActiv report http://www.euractiv.com/en/culture/eu-translation-policy-stay/article-170516.

4 This calculation treats translation from, say, French to English as being different from that from English to French.

Multilingualism delivers two kinds of benefits to the member countries and their citizens. First, being recognized as an official EU language promotes the international standing and prestige of the language and, indirectly, of its people. This *intangible* benefit is likely to be important especially to small countries. For example, anecdotal evidence suggests that Maltese government institutions make more use of Maltese at the expense of English (both languages have official status in Malta) now that the EU institutions use Maltese for official business with their country. Estonian and Irish may be enjoying similar boosts, following decades of domination by Russian and English, respectively.[5] The EU also helps boost the status of such small languages by hiring translators and interpreters and often actually directly financing their training:[6] this serves to increase the expected return on investing in acquiring proficiency in these languages and thus encourages their teaching and use (especially since not all of those who learn a language because of the prospect of a career in EU institutions will eventually land up in such jobs). These benefits help explain why regions such as Catalonia strive to achieve similar recognition for their languages. Large countries benefit as well, especially if their languages get to be used as working languages by EU bureaucrats: French and German are thus elevated to the status of EU lingua francas, on a par (at least in theory) with English. While such intangible benefits are clearly important, it is very difficult to quantify or measure them, in part because of the missing counterfactual: one cannot evaluate properly the impact of EU multilingualism on the status of languages such as Irish and Maltese because we do not know how those languages would have developed without being official languages of the EU.

Second, multilingualism also bestows important practical, *tangible*, benefits on EU citizens by ensuring that they have access to EU legal documents without requiring translation, that they can communicate with EU institutions in their own language and that their elected representatives can use their language when participating in EU decision making. Ginsburgh and Weber (2005) denote this second effect as preventing *linguistic disenfranchisement*, reflecting the fact that those whose languages are not used by the EU would see their linguistic rights curtailed and would be unable to participate fully in the EU political process and decision making.

While the intangible benefits of multilingualism cannot be quantified, preventing disenfranchisement can be assessed formally by estimating how many people would be disenfranchised under a given linguistic regime. It is important to realize in this context that a person will not be linguistically disenfranchised as long as the EU uses a language that they can speak, whether or not it is their native language. Again, this goes back to the distinction between tangible and intangible benefits of multilingualism discussed above: a Maltese native speaker who also speaks English and Italian is not linguistically disenfranchised as long as the EU uses English or Italian as official languages but fails to enjoy the intangible benefit unless Maltese is adopted as an official language as well. However, the same applies to, for example, an ethnic Turk with German nationality

[5] The fact that Irish MEPs were not able to use Irish in the European Parliament until 2007 was a source of considerable irritation to some Irish representatives in that body.

[6] For example, see "EU still chasing Maltese translators," *Malta Today*, 17 February 2008, http://archive.maltatoday.com.mt/2008/02/17/n4.html.

or a Spaniard who is an ethnic Catalan. Therefore, in my discussion of the costs and benefits of multilingualism, I will consider only the tangible benefits and will disregard the intangible effects.

At the time the EU institutions were being shaped, multilingualism made good sense for two reasons: the EEC started off with only a small number of countries and languages (six and four, respectively), and relatively few people spoke the languages of other countries. At present, neither condition continues to hold: the EU has expanded repeatedly and many Europeans are proficient in foreign languages. A recent survey documented the languages spoken by the nationals of all 27 member countries of the EU. This survey contains extensive information on the use of all official EU languages and some additional languages (Arabic, Chinese, Russian and Turkish as well as some European regional languages and languages spoken by selected ethnic minorities).[7] Two percent of Europeans have two (or more) mother tongues (the share of multilinguals is at its highest in Ireland and Spain, at 8 percent in both countries), while 39 percent speak at least one foreign language (ranging between 17 percent in Hungary and 97 percent in Luxembourg) and 14 percent speak two or more foreign languages (from 4 percent in Ireland to 84 percent in Luxembourg). However, not all languages are equally popular. In fact, with the exception of English, French, German, Spanish and Russian, few European languages are spoken outside of their home country.[8] This is illustrated by Figures 15.1–15.3 (adopted from Fidrmuc and Fidrmuc, 2010), which show the fraction of each country's population speaking the three most popular languages, English, French and German; the figures combine native speakers with those who speak each language as a foreign language but with good or very good (self-assessed) proficiency. Table 15.1 contains the detailed figures, along with similar numbers for additional languages. In the vast majority of European countries, at least 10 percent of the population speak English (Hungary is the only exception with 8 percent English speakers). There are several countries with more than half of the population proficient in English: besides the English-speaking countries, these are Cyprus, Denmark, Malta, the Netherlands and Sweden. The shares of French and German speakers, in contrast, are considerably lower (the Netherlands is the only country where more than half can speak German without the language being an official language there). This pattern is mirrored also in survey responses that reflect attitudes to learning foreign languages (Table 15.2): 67 percent think English is a useful language for one's personal development and career whereas only 22–25 percent think the same about German and French. Attitudes on which languages children should learn are very similar (reassuringly, only 10 percent think no language is useful and only 2 percent believe children should learn no foreign language).

Proficiency in languages can change dynamically over time. In the absence of historical survey data on language skills going back a few decades, we can get useful insight on the dynamics of linguistic skills by considering age cohorts: as people usually learn languages during their school years, proficiency of different age groups approximates the

---

[7] Special Eurobarometer 243: "Europeans and their Languages," November–December 2005. Note that in order to be included in the survey, the respondents had to be EU citizens, though not necessarily nationals of the country in which they were interviewed.

[8] The figures quoted above count all those who speak the language as a foreign language, including foreigners in that language's home country.

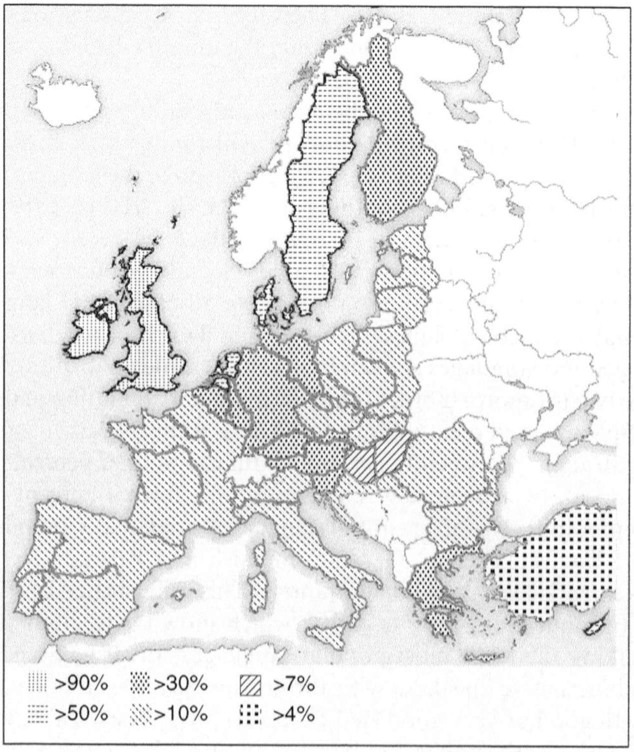

Figure 15.1 Proficiency in English (native, very good or good proficiency)

changes in attitudes to languages. Table 15.3[9] reveals a striking pattern. The proficiency in most languages is remarkably stable over time. The share of young people (aged 15–29) speaking, for example, German and French is nearly the same as the corresponding figure for the oldest group (60+ years of age). The only exception is English: more than half of young Europeans speak it, compared with barely a quarter of the oldest cohort. Moreover, while the share of those speaking English among the oldest differs little from the corresponding figures for German and French, English has taken a big lead among the younger cohorts.

The rising prominence of English should not come as a surprise. It reflects the increasing globalization as well as the accelerating openness of European countries to trade, investment flows and movement of people (whether tourists, labor migrants or students). English has effectively played the role of a modern lingua franca in this process. Language helps facilitate transactions between people in a way similar to the role of money: it serves both as a medium of (communicative) exchange and a store of (informational) value. The role of language in producing *communicative benefits* has been highlighted by, among others, Selten and Pool (1991), Gabszewicz et al. (2005),

---

[9] Again, the figures include both native speakers and those who speak the language with good or very good proficiency.

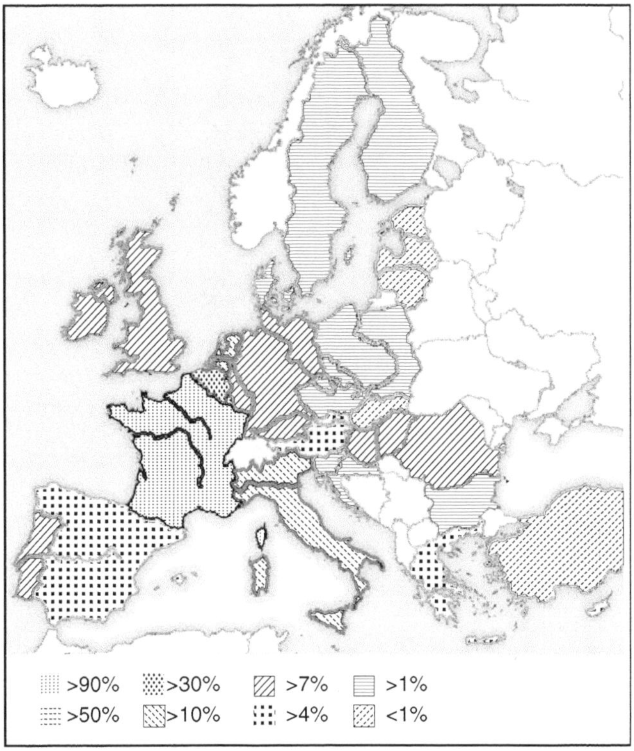

Figure 15.2 Proficiency in French (native, very good or good proficiency)

Ginsburgh et al. (2007), and Ortega and Tangeras (2007). They model the benefits of speaking a particular language as embodied in the opportunities for communicating with other people speaking the same language: the term *communicating* should be understood broadly enough to include also engaging in productive activities and/or trade. The communicative benefits may differ across languages: learning Chinese, for instance, yields greater benefits now than 30 years ago when China was poor and largely closed to the outside world. Similarly, the costs of learning a particular language are not uniformly distributed: some are better at learning languages than others, and some languages are easier to learn while others are more complicated. Importantly, the benefits of learning a language increase with the number of other speakers of that language. Hence, holding everything else constant, people would tend to choose to learn languages of large countries. Moreover, the attractiveness of a language rises further if a large number of other people decide to acquire it as well: given that learning languages is costly, people have a strong motivation to coordinate on a single language that comes to play the role of a lingua franca instead of learning a broad range of different languages.[10]

[10] For the same reason, as Selten and Pool (1991) argue, artificial languages such as Esperanto are destined to fail as few people speak them and they have virtually no native speakers.

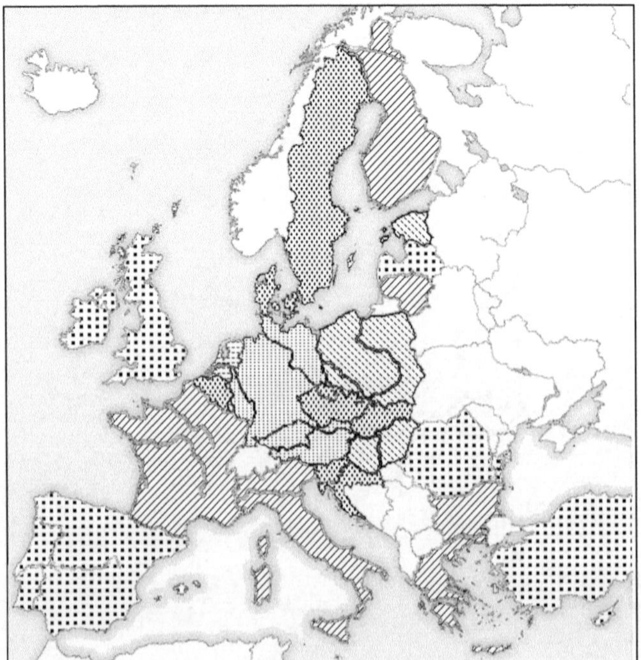

Figure 15.3 Proficiency in German (native, very good or good proficiency)

The individual-level survey discussed above can be used to study the determinants of proficiency in foreign languages as well. The results are summarized in Table 15.4. Given that most languages are spoken almost exclusively by native speakers, the analysis can be carried out only for a few languages. English, French, German, Italian, Spanish, Russian and Dutch are the seven most popular European languages and all have sufficient numbers of non-native speakers to permit the analysis.

The results are illuminating. Younger people are more likely to speak English and German (the effect of age is in fact U-shaped for German, with the minimum attained at the age of 48). The opposite holds for Russian: middle-aged respondents are more likely to speak it (the effect peaks at 55 years of age); this presumably reflects the fact that until the 1990s Russian was widely taught throughout the former Soviet Block.

Having higher education, being self-employed, having a managerial or white-collar occupation and living in an urban area increase the propensity to learn languages. It appears thus that those with higher education and more skills find it more beneficial (and probably also find it easier) to learn foreign languages.

Somewhat less intuitively, being tall has a similar effect on the probability of speaking English and French. This can be explained by the positive relationship between one's height and economic wellbeing during childhood (see Belot and Fidrmuc, 2010, and the references cited therein): growing up in a more affluent household is likely to improve the acquisition of human capital, including foreign-language skills.

Table 15.1 Distribution of main European languages (native speakers and those with good or very good proficiency in percent)

	English	German	French	Italian	Spanish	Polish	Dutch	Russian	Turkish
Austria	45	99	6	5	2	0	0	1	1
Belgium	41	13	71	3	3	1	68	0	1
Bulgaria	16	6	4	1	1	0	0	25	10
Cyprus	51	2	5	1	1	0	0	1	0
Czech Rep.	16	19	2	0	0	2	0	15	0
Denmark	66	27	3	1	2	0	0	0	0
Estonia	25	8	0	0	0	0	0	68	0
Finland	31	5	1	0	0	0	0	1	0
France	20	5	99	5	7	0	0	0	0
Germany	38	99	8	1	2	2	0	8	2
Greece	32	6	5	2	0	0	0	2	1
Hungary	8	9	0	1	0	0	0	1	0
Ireland	99	2	9	0	1	1	0	0	0
Italy	25	4	10	97	3	0	0	0	0
Latvia	15	3	0	0	0	1	0	85	0
Lithuania	14	4	1	0	0	13	0	74	0
Luxembourg	39	88	89	5	1	0	1	0	0
Malta	68	1	5	35	1	0	0	0	0
Netherlands	77	57	19	0	3	0	99	0	0
Poland	18	10	1	1	0	98	0	12	0
Portugal	15	2	9	1	4	0	0	0	0
Romania	14	3	10	2	1	0	0	2	0
Slovak Rep.	17	18	1	0	0	2	0	20	0
Slovenia	41	21	2	9	1	0	0	0	0
Spain	16	2	6	1	98	0	0	0	0
Sweden	67	12	3	1	1	0	0	0	0
UK	99	2	9	1	2	0	0	0	0
EU27	37.4	24.9	19.9	13.3	11.1	8.4	4.9	4.6	0.5

Source: Special Eurobarometer 243: "Europeans and their Languages," November–December 2005.

More surprisingly, political orientation (self-declared) of respondents is also related to the probability of speaking English and French. The respondents were asked to position themselves on a scale between 0 and 10, with 1 representing extreme left and 10 standing for extreme right. Right-wing respondents are more likely to speak English while left-wing individuals are more likely to speak French; political orientation is not significant for any of the other languages (it is especially noteworthy that those who speak Russian are not any more leftist than those who do not). It is not obvious, however, what is the direction of causality here: whether left-wing political orientation makes one more likely to learn French while those with right-wing attitudes choose English, or whether the language that one learns in turn influences one's political opinion, perhaps through exposure to information and news from particular countries (note that the individuals included in this analysis are only those who speak the language in question as a foreign language and therefore this result does not simply reflect the fact that the average Frenchman may be more left-wing than the average Briton).

The analysis accounts for the respondents' country of residence, and the differences

Table 15.2 Attitudes on usefulness of main European languages

	Useful language (percentage)				Children should learn (percentage)			
	English	German	French	Spanish	English	German	French	Spanish
Austria	73	2	15	8	85	2	29	10
Belgium	83	9	54	6	88	7	52	10
Bulgaria	65	34	11	5	87	49	13	6
Cyprus	93	17	34	3	98	18	50	2
Czech Rep.	68	56	5	2	90	68	8	4
Denmark	92	56	7	10	94	64	12	13
Estonia	71	14	2	1	93	23	7	1
Finland	86	18	8	4	84	24	11	3
France	81	19	2	36	90	25	2	45
Germany	81	5	27	13	89	3	44	17
Greece	74	30	21	4	96	50	34	3
Hungary	57	52	3	1	83	73	4	2
Ireland	4	37	58	34	3	42	65	34
Italy	82	15	25	15	85	17	34	18
Latvia	70	17	3	1	94	28	6	1
Lithuania	85	27	4	1	91	34	6	2
Luxembourg	37	60	82	2	61	41	81	3
Malta	88	5	12	2	89	12	23	2
Netherlands	93	48	19	16	90	40	22	22
Poland	70	45	5	2	89	69	7	1
Portugal	51	5	31	6	87	8	58	7
Romania	63	18	33	7	63	18	33	7
Slovak Rep.	70	60	4	1	87	74	7	3
Slovenia	79	61	4	2	97	69	7	3
Spain	72	11	32	5	85	14	44	3
Sweden	96	39	12	21	99	37	17	30
UK	4	29	63	33	4	36	72	38
EU27	67	22	25	15	76	28	33	19

Source: Special Eurobarometer 243: "Europeans and their Languages," November–December 2005.

in the popularity of different languages in different countries are large. They are also not random. Dyen et al. (1992) compiled indicators of linguistic proximity between languages: in essence, these measure the fraction of key words that have the same root. The correlation between the coefficients estimated for country-specific intercepts and linguistic proximity is 0.43 for English, 0.54 for French and 0.33 for German. Hence, more people learn a language if that language is relatively similar to their own.

Besides serving as a medium of communicative exchange and a store of informational value, language also plays a third role: it is a tool of discrimination. A language not only facilitates communication between those who can speak it but also excludes from that communication all those who do not speak it sufficiently well. A good example is the Cockney rhyming slang which was devised by prison inmates in London who wanted to ensure that the prison guards could not understand them. Akerlof and Kranton (2000)

Table 15.3 EU27 proficiency in main European languages by age cohorts (native speakers and those with good or very good proficiency in percent)

	All	15–29	30–44	45–60	> 60
English	37	55	41	32	24
German	25	26	25	24	25
French	20	22	19	20	19
Italian	13	13	13	13	13
Spanish	11	13	11	10	11
Polish	8	8	8	8	8
Dutch	5	5	5	5	5
Turkish	0	1	1	0	0
Russian	5	4	5	5	4

Source: Special Eurobarometer 243: "Europeans and their Languages," November–December 2005.

discuss how a language or accent specific to a particular region or ethnicity becomes a hallmark of one's identity. Deviating or not being able to speak the right language or with the right accent can be met with social sanctions: educated blacks in the US, for example, are disparaged for "speaking white." Those speaking the *wrong* language, similarly, may be subject to discrimination in the labor market (Lang, 1986) and in economic relations generally.

The preceding analysis therefore suggests that individual socio-economic characteristics such as age, education and skill level are associated with the ability to speak foreign languages. Inability to speak a particular language, similarly, may lead to economic discrimination. Is the ability to speak a foreign language, therefore, associated with economic benefits such as higher wages? Most studies that consider this question look at the linguistic skills of immigrants and tend to find that speaking the destination-country language is indeed associated with a wage premium of up to 20 percent (Chiswick and Miller, 2002, 2010). The labor-market position of immigrants, however, is rather specific and therefore the wage premium that accrues to them as a result of speaking another language is not directly comparable with the likely benefits accruing to Europeans speaking foreign languages.

A unique study by Ginsburgh and Prieto-Rodriguez (2011) seeks to address exactly this question. They utilize the European Community Household Panel surveys collected between 1994 and 2001. Crucially, these surveys asked the respondents in nine European countries (Austria, Denmark, Finland, France, Germany, Greece, Italy, Portugal and Spain) about languages that they speak *and* use at their workplace. They argue that the return to speaking a particular language should depend on the relative scarcity of that language. The return to speaking English, for example, ranges from 11 percent in Austria to 39 percent in Spain. Given that French and German are less common, the returns to speaking them are correspondingly higher, as high as 49 percent for French (in Spain) and 46 percent for German (in France).

Toomet (2010), who considers ethnic Russians in Estonia and Latvia, finds comparable results: those speaking English earn a wage premium of 15 percent in Estonia and as much as 40–60 percent (depending on data set used) in Latvia. Speaking the local language, in

Table 15.4 Determinants of proficiency in main European languages

	English		French		German		Italian	
Female	0.236***	(0.059)	0.457***	(0.084)	−0.045	(0.073)	0.368***	(0.162)
Age	−0.065***	(0.009)	0.005	(0.013)	−0.048***	(0.010)	0.007	(0.023)
Age squared	0.0003***	(0.0001)	0.0001	(0.0001)	0.0005***	(0.0001)	−0.0001	(0.0002)
Married	−0.065***	(0.047)	−0.048	(0.072)	−0.039	(0.057)	−0.361***	(0.131)
Left/right	0.031***	(0.010)	−0.033**	(0.015)	0.017	(0.012)	−0.031	(0.025)
Sec. education	1.272***	(0.085)	1.014***	(0.118)	0.874	(0.104)	0.888***	(0.224)
Tert. education	2.321***	(0.088)	1.831***	(0.126)	1.492***	(0.108)	1.377***	(0.248)
Still student	2.758***	(0.123)	2.437***	(0.187)	1.493***	(0.163)	1.394***	(0.343)
Self-employed	0.460***	(0.086)	0.507***	(0.130)	0.300***	(0.119)	0.347	(0.243)
Manager	1.118***	(0.073)	0.578***	(0.115)	0.725***	(0.094)	0.607***	(0.207)
White-collar	0.520***	(0.071)	0.210*	(0.116)	0.402***	(0.096)	0.108	(0.224)
House person	0.059	(0.096)	−0.117	(0.149)	0.259**	(0.130)	−0.512*	(0.294)
Unemployed	0.128	(0.103)	0.089	(0.180)	0.032	(0.144)	0.024	(0.307)
Retired	0.177**	(0.090)	0.190	(0.135)	0.235**	(0.107)	0.184	(0.256)
Height	0.022***	(0.003)	0.013***	(0.005)	0.003	(0.004)	0.008	(0.009)
BMI	−0.091***	(0.026)	0.014	(0.057)	−0.032**	(0.015)	−0.052*	(0.031)
BMI squared	0.001***	(0.000)	−0.001	(0.001)	0.0003	(0.0002)	0.0005	(0.0004)
Small/medium town	0.305***	(0.050)	0.296***	(0.077)	0.101*	(0.062)	0.172	(0.140)
Large town	0.730***	(0.055)	0.376***	(0.084)	0.184***	(0.068)	0.183	(0.141)

	Spanish		Russian		Dutch	
Female	0.202	(0.151)	0.102	(0.095)	−0.365	(0.268)
Age	0.011	(0.022)	0.153***	(0.016)	0.022	(0.037)
Age squared	−0.0002	(0.0002)	−0.0014***	(0.0002)	−0.0003	(0.0004)
Married	−0.293***	(0.122)	0.096	(0.076)	−0.264	(0.216)
Left/right	0.007	(0.028)	0.023	(0.015)	0.067	(0.052)
Sec. education	0.313*	(0.180)	0.788***	(0.137)	0.459	(0.350)
Tert. education	0.692***	(0.196)	1.430***	(0.145)	0.988***	(0.364)
Still student	1.363***	(0.289)	1.205***	(0.240)	1.281**	(0.541)
Self-employed	0.947***	(0.215)	−0.130	(0.144)	0.231	(0.414)
Manager	0.575***	(0.211)	0.355***	(0.121)	0.072	(0.373)
White-collar	0.086	(0.221)	−0.052	(0.117)	0.253	(0.323)
House person	0.386	(0.242)	−0.190	(0.194)	0.608	(0.414)
Unemployed	0.234	(0.301)	−0.042	(0.161)	0.651	(0.401)
Retired	0.581***	(0.233)	−0.246*	(0.130)	0.228	(0.430)
Height	0.003	(0.008)	0.006	(0.005)	−0.023	(0.015)
BMI	−0.071*	(0.040)	−0.044**	(0.018)	0.016	(0.048)
BMI squared	0.0004	(0.0007)	0.0007***	(0.0002)	−0.0003	(0.0005)
Small/medium town	0.104	(0.135)	0.135*	(0.081)	0.148	(0.220)
Large town	0.381***	(0.137)	0.190**	(0.088)	0.515**	(0.248)

Note: Significance levels denoted as ***1%, **5%, *10%.

Source: Special Eurobarometer 243: "Europeans and their Languages," November–December 2005; author's own calculations.

contrast, is not associated with any wage gain, despite the fact that not all ethnic Russians (who account for a considerable share of the populations of these two countries) can speak both Russian and the local language.

In summary, Europeans are at present increasingly proficient in foreign languages and especially in English. The share of those speaking English, furthermore, grows over time, as evidenced by the substantially higher proficiency rate among the young. Most Europeans agree that learning and speaking foreign languages is important; again English takes a privileged place. Those who speak English and other languages, moreover, tend to enjoy higher wages, although these gains may gradually dissipate as more people acquire linguistic skills. Hence, one could argue that the extensive multilingualism espoused by the EU since its inception is now less required than in the past. In the next section, I therefore address this question explicitly, looking at the costs of multilingualism and at the possible scenarios for linguistic reform.

3 MULTILINGUALISM IN THE EU: ASSESSMENT AND ALTERNATIVES

The EU is a leading consumer of linguistic services: translation and interpretation. Every year, it translates 1.8 million pages of written documents and provides interpretation for 11,000 meetings (depending on the linguistic complexity, between 1 and 60 interpreters may be required per meeting). This is costly: providing linguistic services is estimated to cost the EU over €1 billion per year (Fidrmuc and Ginsburgh, 2007). There are also non-monetary costs: the need for translation leads to delays in implementation of decisions and may result in legal ambiguity.[11]

Fidrmuc and Ginsburgh (2007) consider the costs of multilingualism in the EU in the wake of the 2004 enlargement. Providing linguistic services was estimated to cost €1045 million at the time.[12] With 20 official languages, this implies that each document has to be translated 19 times (regardless of the language in which it was originally drafted). The average cost per language thus is €55 million per year (assuming all languages are equally difficult to translate into and from). The average cost per person would appear to be modest at €2.30 per year. This calculation, however, is greatly misleading as translation to each language does not benefit the same number of Europeans. Fidrmuc and Ginsburgh therefore compute the average cost per language and person, considering all speakers of a particular language and then considering only those who would be disenfranchised if their language did not enjoy official status in the EU. The latter calculation is perhaps the best measure of the true cost of multilingualism because it only considers those who actually benefit from having their language included among the official languages of the EU.

---

[11] The EU maintains that each official translation of a legal document has the same legal validity, regardless of whether the document was originally drawn up in that language or not.

[12] Portuese (2010, footnote 8) cites the EU Commissioner for Multilingualism, Leonard Orban, who estimated the cost of linguistic services as being €1.1 billion in 2008. This presumably includes also the effect of the 2007 enlargement, suggesting that the addition of Irish, Romanian and Bulgarian had only a modest economic effect.

Table 15.5 Cost per person by language, EU25

	Pop. (m.)	Cost (€)		Pop. (m.)	Cost (€)
German	90.1	0.6	Hungarian	10.1	5.4
French	64.5	0.9	Swedish	8.9	6.2
English	62.3	0.9	Slovak	5.4	10.2
Italian	57.6	1.0	Danish	5.3	10.4
Spanish	39.4	1.4	Finnish	5.1	10.8
Polish	38.6	1.4	Lithuanian	3.6	15.3
Dutch	21.9	2.5	Latvian	2.4	22.9
Greek	11.3	4.9	Slovene	2.0	27.5
Portuguese	10.8	5.1	Estonian	1.4	39.3
Czech	10.3	5.3	Maltese	0.4	137.5

Source: Fidrmuc and Ginsburgh (2007).

Table 15.5 reproduces the average cost per person per year for each of the 20 languages that had official status in the EU following the 2004 enlargement (Irish, Bulgarian and Romanian were added in 2007 but these languages were not included in the analysis). These calculations consider all persons speaking a particular language (taking account of the fact that some languages are spoken in multiple countries), regardless of what other languages they may be able to speak. The approximate cost per language is thus divided by the population of the country or countries that speak it (note that the calculations only consider the relevant EU countries and thus do not take into account the fact that English, French, Spanish and Portuguese are widely spoken also outside Europe). Not surprisingly, English, French, Italian and especially German, spoken by large numbers of people, are the cheapest. In contrast, Latvian, Slovene and Estonian cost in excess of €20 per person per year and Maltese costs well over €100.

Table 15.6 takes the analysis of costs one step further by considering only those individuals who would be disenfranchised if their language lost official status in the EU. Clearly, for assessing the benefit of accepting a given language as an official language of the EU, it is crucial to consider not only how many people live in the affected country but also how many of them do not speak other official languages. The cost per person, therefore, depends on the number of people speaking the language in question and the fraction of them who do not speak the other languages that would remain official languages of the EU. The choice of languages that would remain official is thus also critical. Four scenarios are considered in this respect: only English, English along with French or German, and all three languages together. The first column lists the population speaking each language and the next four columns report the numbers that would be disenfranchised in each linguistic scenario. In general, allowing for more official languages leads to lower disenfranchisement. Since the cost of providing linguistic services remains the same, the cost per disenfranchised person is therefore generally higher in the scenario with three or two official languages than in the English-only one (except, of course, when one of the official languages is irrelevant, in which case the cost remains the same). With English serving as the sole official language of the EU, large numbers of French, German, Italian, Polish and Spanish speakers would be adversely affected: between 25 and 42 million for

Table 15.6 Cost per disenfranchised person by language, EU25

	Total population	Disenfranchised population (millions)				Cost per person disenfranchised (€)			
		E	EF	EG	EFG	E	EF	EG	EFG
English	62.3	0	0	0	0	0	0	0	0
French	64.5	37.5	0	36.6	0	1.5	0	1.5	0
German	90.1	42.1	40.3	0	0	1.3	1.4	0	0
Italian	57.6	35.1	27.7	34.0	27.1	1.6	2.0	1.6	1.9
Polish	38.6	30.9	30.1	25.9	25.5	1.8	1.8	2.1	2.2
Spanish	39.4	25.2	22.5	24.8	22.1	2.2	2.4	2.2	2.5
Hungarian	10.1	8.6	8.5	7.6	7.5	6.4	6.5	7.3	7.3
Portuguese	10.8	7.0	6.4	6.9	6.3	7.8	8.6	8.0	8.8
Greek	11.3	5.9	5.9	5.8	5.7	9.4	9.4	9.5	9.7
Czech	10.3	7.8	7.8	5.6	5.5	7.0	7.1	9.9	10.0
Slovak	5.4	4.7	4.6	3.9	3.8	11.7	11.8	14.1	14.3
Dutch	21.9	8.4	4.3	5.6	3.3	6.5	12.9	9.8	16.9
Lithuanian	3.6	2.9	2.8	2.6	2.5	19.1	19.3	21.2	21.7
Finnish	5.1	2.0	2.0	1.9	1.8	27.7	27.7	29.1	30.0
Latvian	2.4	1.8	1.8	1.6	1.6	29.8	30.2	33.7	34.2
Swedish	8.9	1.9	1.8	1.7	1.6	29.4	30.9	32.5	34.3
Estonian	1.4	1.0	1.0	0.9	0.9	56.9	56.9	63.4	63.7
Danish	5.3	1.3	1.3	0.9	0.9	41.5	43.2	64.9	64.9
Slovene	2.0	0.9	0.9	0.6	0.5	58.5	59.8	98.2	102.2
Maltese	0.4	0.07	0.07	0.07	0.07	808.8	808.8	808.8	831.3

Source: Fidrmuc and Ginsburgh (2007).

each of these five languages. The costs of providing linguistic services for these languages are then correspondingly low: around or below €2 per disenfranchised person per year. Thereafter, the cost per disenfranchised person starts to increase quite dramatically and can be as high as €800 for Maltese. Adding French or German or both to the list of official languages mainly affects the populations speaking these two languages; the costs for the others do not change too dramatically as a result. The main exceptions to this are Dutch (where adding French and to a lesser extent German makes a substantial difference, presumably because many Flemish Dutch speakers are proficient in French) and Czech, Slovak and Slovene, among whom German appears rather popular.

The differences across languages reflect in part the different sizes of populations speaking them but this is only a part of the story. Another important factor is the number of people who can speak other languages. For example, Dutch is placed between Slovak and Lithuanian, two languages spoken by much smaller numbers of people. This is because the majority of Dutch speakers can also speak English, French or German. Not having Dutch as an official language would therefore result in a similar number of disenfranchised Europeans as in the case of dropping Slovak of Lithuanian from the list of official languages.

The last scenario, with English, French and German as official languages, is probably the most realistic one: these three languages serve as working languages of the EU bureaucracy and therefore it is unlikely that any of them would ever be abandoned. Adopting this scenario would result in costs per disenfranchised person ranging from around €2 (Italian, Spanish and Polish) to 830 (Maltese). One may wonder whether spending €800 or even €100 is optimal and whether the countries in question would be prepared to spend a similar amount if the costs of providing linguistic services were to be borne entirely by them. The present policy of extensive multilingualism financed by the EU implies that the provision of linguistic services for small countries (languages) is cross-subsidized by large countries. Similarly, large countries might in fact prefer to choose a more generous translation/interpretation regime if they were to pay for it by themselves (Fidrmuc and Ginsburgh develop a theoretical model that shows that the extent of linguistic services is increasing in the number of people speaking the language).

The preceding analysis suggests that substantial savings could be made by reducing the extent of linguistic services provided by the EU. This is in fact already happening to some extent. The EU, for instance, increasingly relies on so-called relay translation/interpreting. This practice means that written text or spoken word that is originally in, say, Estonian will not be translated into all of the remaining official languages directly. Instead, it will be translated directly only into English, French and German (and possibly into a few other languages if such direct translations are possible). The remaining languages would then receive a translation from one of these *core* languages. These measures, while cutting the cost of multilingualism, fall well short of a fundamental linguistic-policy reform (and, furthermore, they lower the quality of linguistic services for all non-core languages, not only the marginal ones). The reasons for shying away from a true reform are clear: linguistic policy is one of the areas of EU policy that is subject to unanimity support. Therefore, it is highly likely that at least one country will oppose a move to downgrade a particular language. The degree of implementation of multilingualism, on the other hand, is determined by the European Commission. Therefore, we can expect the EU to introduce further cost-cutting measures without also undertaking a fundamental reform of the linguistic regime in the future.

Let us consider now what would be the optimal approach if the EU were able to garner sufficient support for a linguistic-policy reform aimed at reducing the number of official languages. How many official languages should the EU optimally maintain and which ones? Fidrmuc et al. (2009) address this question and point out that the decision on the optimal number of official languages is ultimately a political one. Instead, they seek to identify the optimal sequence of languages: ordering the 23 languages currently used by the EU according to their contribution to reducing linguistic disenfranchisement. In other words, they identify the optimal sets of official languages for between 1 and 23 languages such that each optimal set of languages results in lower overall disenfranchisement than any other alternative set of languages of the same size.

Table 15.7 presents the result. It reports the optimal ordering in which languages should be given official status, should the EU decide on the choice of official languages anew. Alternatively, for any number m of official languages chosen by the EU decision makers, it reports what should be the mth language and also which languages should be given official status before it. For each step in the sequence, the table also reports the resulting linguistic disenfranchisement.

The first three languages are, not surprisingly, English, German and French. It is interesting to note that German does slightly better than French in reducing linguistic disenfranchisement as the second language in the sequence (see also Fidrmuc et al., 2004). With these three languages only, just over one-third of Europeans would be disenfranchised.

Table 15.7 Sequence of optimal sets of official languages, EU27

1	2	3	4	5	6	7	8	9	10a	10b	10c
EN	1 + GE	2 + FR	3 + IT	4 + SP	5 + PL	6 + RO	7 + HU	8 + PT	9 + CZ	9 + GR	9 + RU
62.6	49.3	37.8	29.5	22.4	16.4	12.9	10.9	9.2	7.7	7.7	7.7
11	12	13	14a	14b	15	16a	16b	17	18a	18b	19
10a+ GR	11 + BG	12 + NL	13 + FI	13 + SW	14a+ SW	15 + LT	15 + SK	15a+ SK	17 + LV	17 + DK	18a+ DK
6.2	5.0	4.0	3.3	3.3	2.7	2.2	2.2	1.7	1.3	1.3	1

Source: Fidrmuc et al. (2009).

Italian, Spanish and Polish are the next three languages. Choosing these six languages would result in a disenfranchisement corresponding to approximately one-sixth of the EU population. Once these six large languages are introduced into the sequence, adding more languages leads only to modest reductions in disenfranchisement (and these gains are typically limited to a single country). The position of each language depends, again, not only on the number of speakers of each language but also on their ability to speak languages that have already been introduced into the sequence. In this way, for example, Hungarian appears in the eighth position, well ahead of languages such as Dutch and Swedish, which are spoken by larger or similar numbers of people. Note that several languages deliver approximately the same reduction in disenfranchisement: this is indicated by listing several alternatives for the same position in the sequence.[13] Finally, the analysis is ended when the remaining disenfranchisement falls to 1 percent; this target is attained with 19 languages. With merely 1 percent of the EU population still linguistically disenfranchised, the gains from adding the other four languages are very limited.

Fidrmuc et al. (2009) also construct a similar sequence considering only young people (thus adopting a forward-looking approach and estimating disenfranchisement that would result in the future, assuming the coming generations will have the same linguistic proficiency as those currently young) and a sequence that considers linguistic proximity between languages (thus in effect assuming that one is not fully disenfranchised if a close enough language is given official status). The resulting sequences are broadly similar to that in Table 15.7 (except Polish and Hungarian are placed at higher positions in the sequence accounting for linguistic proximity as they share little similarity with the languages preceding them).

Of course, the preceding analysis does not say which of these sets should be chosen. It only specifies which languages should be included in a set of official languages of size m, should the EU decision-making bodies choose to restrict the set of official languages to m. However, Fidrmuc et al. point out that the marginal gain from adding more languages falls sharply after the first six languages: English, German, French, Italian, Spanish and Polish. Therefore, choosing these six languages as the official languages of the EU might be a reasonable compromise solution, one that would result in a relatively modest residual disenfranchisement rate.

As I emphasized above, the probability of reaching a consensus in favor of linguistic reform in the EU is rather low, given that the reform would need to be approved with unanimity support. Nevertheless, if such a reform is implemented, then its benefits are likely to go beyond cost savings. Fidrmuc and Fidrmuc (2010) consider the impact of proficiency in foreign languages on international trade. It is well established in the trade literature that countries that share the same official language tend to trade more with each other. Fidrmuc and Fidrmuc, however, go one step further by considering also languages that are widely spoken as foreign ones. Specifically, they compute probabilities that two randomly chosen individuals from two countries will be able to communicate together in English, French or German (regardless of whether the individuals are native speakers of any of these languages or have learned them as foreign languages). They find

[13] Note also that Russian, which is currently not an official language of the EU, would qualify for the ninth place in the sequence, the same position as Czech and Greek.

that linguistic skills, and especially English, exert a significant and positive effect on trade flows in Europe. For example, their results suggest that raising proficiency in English in all EU countries to the level prevailing in the Netherlands would be expected to increase trade in Europe, *ceteris paribus*, by approximately three-quarters.

The gains from improving the linguistic skills of Europeans are thus comparable to those that were envisaged from introducing the common currency in Europe. Crucially, while adopting a common currency is costly because a country must give up its national currency and autonomy over monetary policy, improving linguistic skills in foreign languages does not require abandoning national languages. Reducing the number of official languages in the EU will increase the incentive for Europeans to invest in acquiring and improving proficiency in the core languages (importantly, changes in the linguistic regime at the EU level do not imply that the same linguistic-regime change would have to be implemented at the national level too). Once more Europeans speak English and other languages, trade between their countries is likely to grow and this will have a positive impact on economic growth and overall wellbeing.

Another crucial implication of multilingualism is its effect on innovation. At present, EU countries maintain their separate patent systems: an innovator seeking to protect their invention in all 27 EU countries must apply for patent protection in each country separately. This is costly: not only does it necessitate multiple fees but also the relevant technical documentation needs to be translated into each country's official language. According to Van Pottelsberghe and François (2006), the cost of filing and protecting a patent for 20 years amounts to approximately €130,000 in the EU, compared with €17,000 in both the US and Japan.[14] As a consequence, the number of claims per year (a patent application is composed of on average 7 claims in Japan, 18 in Europe and 23 in the US) is 1 million in Europe, 3 million in Japan and 8 million in the US.

Hence, increasing the use of English and/or formal linguistic reform in the EU has the potential to translate into important economic gains in terms of increased trade and greater innovative activity alike. Again, this does not necessitate that the status of the national languages is diminished in any way, only that English receives greater (formal or informal) recognition in parallel with them. Substantial gains thus may be available at little cost.

4 CONCLUSIONS

The linguistic regime that continues to be in effect in the EU, extensive multilingualism allowing each country to nominate its national language as an official language of the EU, may have been optimal when the process of EU integration began but it is neither optimal nor practical at present. In 1957, when the EEC was founded, it included six countries that had four official languages among them. The scope for European policy making and

[14] It is possible to file the application with the European Patent Office initially only in English, French or German. However, the application needs to be subsequently validated (and the documentation translated) separately for each country for which patent protection is sought. See Van Pottelsberghe and François (2006) for more details.

the impact of EEC policies and decisions on national legal environments were limited. Importantly, the linguistic skills of Europeans were limited as well and there was no clear candidate for a lingua franca among the four EEC languages.

At present, the EU has 27 member countries and 23 official languages. EU rules and decisions have a wide-ranging impact on, and in fact supremacy over, policies and legal frameworks in the member countries. As the scope of EU activities and their legal and practical relevance increase, maintaining the same extent of multilingualism with 23 languages as with four languages in the past is increasingly difficult and costly. It is also less and less needed: present-day Europeans increasingly speak foreign languages and the future generations are likely to continue this trend. English clearly plays the dominant role in Europe at present: it has replaced French as the main language used by the EU bureaucracy and it is the most common foreign language that Europeans choose to learn or that they consider important. While the EU institutions continue to pay lip service to multilingualism, the Europeans themselves increasingly gravitate towards English playing the role of the European lingua franca.

Introducing unilingualism in the EU formally, however, would be premature and politically unacceptable at present. The share of Europeans who speak English well enough, while increasing, is far from being adequate for that. Unilingualism would thus result in excessive linguistic disenfranchisement. Moreover, the cost of maintaining a linguistic regime with multiple languages (while being lower than the costs of 23 official tongues) is modest compared with the benefits that it would entail. A policy of multilingualism with six or perhaps as few as three official languages would serve the EU well: it would ensure that the vast majority of Europeans is not excluded from EU affairs while keeping the costs manageable and helping avoid some of the ills of the current regime such as translation delays and backlogs, errors, and excessive use of relay translations. It would also be similar to the linguistic regime applied by other international organization such as the UN. Importantly, implementing linguistic reform now would preempt the further rise in costs and complexity of linguistic relations in the EU in the wake of future enlargements. Last but not least, adopting a more restrictive linguistic regime would increase the incentive for Europeans to learn foreign languages. This, in turn, would have positive spillover effects for them in terms of higher wages and better opportunities to travel, study or work abroad and for their countries by boosting trade within Europe as well as with the rest of the world.

Garnering political consensus for the reform, however, will be difficult as long as the present practice of applying unanimity to this policy area is maintained. Failure to implement the reform would lead to funds being spent on linguistic services that are increasingly of substandard quality and at the same time less and less required by the Europeans themselves.

REFERENCES

Akerlof, G.A. and Kranton, R.E. (2000), "Economics and Identity," *Quarterly Journal of Economics*, 715–53.

Belot, M. and Fidrmuc, J. (2010), "Anthropometry of Love: Height and Gender Asymmetries in Interethnic Marriages," *Economics and Human Biology*, 8, 361–72.

Chiswick, B.R. and Miller, P.W. (2002), "Immigrant Earnings: Language Skills, Linguistic Concentrations and the Business Cycle," *Journal of Population Economics*, 15, 31–57.

Chiswick, Barry R. and Miller, Paul W. (2010), "Occupational Language Requirements and the Value of English in the US Labor Market," *Journal of Population Economics*, 23(1), 353–72.
Dyen, I., Kruskal, J.B. and Black, P. (1992), "An Indo-European Classification: A Lexicostatistical Experiment," *Transactions of the American Philosophical Society*, 82, Philadelphia: American Philosophical Society.
Fidrmuc, J. and Fidrmuc, J. (2010), "Foreign Languages and Trade," manuscript.
Fidrmuc, J. and Ginsburgh, V. (2007), "Languages in the European Union: The Quest for Equality and its Cost," *European Economic Review*, 51 (6), 1351–69.
Fidrmuc, J., Ginsburgh, V. and Weber, S. (2004), "Le français, deuxième langue de l'Union Européenne?" *Economie Publique*, 15, 43–63.
Fidrmuc, J., Ginsburgh, V. and Weber, S. (2009), "Voting on the Choice of Core Languages in the European Union," *European Journal of Political Economy*, 56–62.
Gabszewicz, J., Ginsburgh, V. and Weber, S. (2005), "Bilingualism and Communicative Benefits," manuscript.
Ginsburgh, V. and Prieto-Rodriguez, J. (2011), "Returns to Foreign Languages of Native Workers in the European Union," *Industrial and Labor Relations Review*, 64(3), 599–618.
Ginsburgh, V. and Weber, S. (2005), "Language Disenfranchisement in the European Union," *Journal of Common Market Studies*, 43, 273–86.
Ginsburgh, V., Ortuno-Ortin, I. and Weber, S. (2007), "Learning Foreign Languages: Theoretical and Empirical Implications of the Selten and Pool Model," *Journal of Economic Behavior and Organization*, 64, 337–47.
Lang, K. (1986), "A Language Theory of Discrimination," *Quarterly Journal of Economics*, 363–82.
Ortega, J. and Tangeras, T.P. (2007), "Unilingual vs Bilingual Education: A Political Economy Analysis," manuscript.
Portuese, A. (2010), "Law and Economics of the European Multilingulism," *European Journal of Law and Economics*, forthcoming and available online.
Selten, R. and Pool, J. (1991), "The Distribution of Foreign Language Skills as a Game Equilibrium," in Reinhard Selten (ed.), *Game Equilibrium Models*, vol. 4, Berlin: Springer-Verlag, 64–84.
Toomet, O. (2010), "Learn English, not the Local Language! Ethnic Russians in Baltic States," manuscript.
Van Pottelsberghe, B. and François, D. (2006), "The Cost Factor in Patent Systems," Working Paper CEB06–002, Centre Emile Bernheim, Université Libre de Bruxelles.

PART 8

MONETARY INSTITUTIONS AND MONETARY POLICY

16 Law and economics of the Monetary Union

Helmut Siekmann

1 HISTORY

From the end of World War II the international monetary system was based on the agreement signed at Bretton Woods on 22 July 1944, which basically encompassed a system of fixed exchange rates with an adjustment procedure and the obligation of the United States of America to redeem dollars into gold. It was combined with the establishment of the International Bank for Reconstruction and Development – the World Bank – and the International Monetary Fund (IMF) and ultimately became the legal basis for the supremacy of the U.S. dollar.

The tensions within the system of fixed exchange rates grew rapidly throughout most of the 1960s partly because of domestic spending programs in the U.S. ("Great Society") and the cost of the Vietnam War. The dollar was considered to be overvalued but the adjustment procedure could not function as the system depended crucially on the fixed convertibility rate between the dollar and gold. As a result the system dissolved between 1968 and 1973. The final turning point was the "temporary" suspension of the dollar's convertibility into gold in August 1971, declared *unilaterally* by U.S. President Richard Nixon. All attempts to re-establish fixed exchange rates in the following months failed, so by March 1973 all major currencies floated against each other.

Although the World Bank and the IMF had been created specifically to make the system of Bretton Woods function smoothly, especially to prevent and to mitigate current account imbalances, both institutions have survived until today. Their growing weight and the assumed new functions, e.g. in the context of the European stabilization facilities and mechanisms,[1] raise serious concerns about the proper legal basis of this practice.

As the system of Bretton Woods provided relatively stable monetary conditions and the European communities had very limited tasks to perform, there was no need for a closer monetary cooperation at the signing of the treaties in 1951 and 1957. Not many years later, the idea of a common currency for the EEC Member States, however, came on the agenda of the European Commission and was first addressed in its Memorandum of 24 October 1962 (the Marjolin Memorandum). Herein the Commission proposed that the customs union should evolve into an economic union by the end of the 1960s with irrevocably fixed exchange rates between the currencies of the Member States.[2] Still, there was no consensus about the economic need of such a common currency.

1 Infra Section 6.4.1.
2 Scheller (2006), p. 17; see also Szász (1999), p. 8.

However, with the increasing strains on the system of Bretton Woods the question became more urgent. The complex system of fixed prices set up under the common agricultural policy was jeopardized by the balance of payment and currency crises inside the European communities. The dragging discussions about a devaluation of the French franc and the revaluation of the German mark[3] contributed to the insecurities.

The incompatibility of frequent exchange rate adjustments or even floating exchange rates within the European Communities (Union) should be kept in mind when deliberating whether Greece should exit the Monetary Union and re-introduce the Greek drachma, which could then be devalued. These ideas, which dominate the advice given by economists on how to solve the current crisis, may seem plausible in a scholarly seminar, but are aloof from the real world and neglect the texture of the European Union.

In February 1969, a report by Raymond Barre, then French member of the Commission and later Prime Minister, proposed greater coordination of economic policies and closer monetary cooperation.[4] In this, he already addressed the two fields which were eventually introduced by the Treaty of Maastricht[5] into the legal framework of the Community and have become the cornerstones of the European Economic and Monetary Union.[6] But until today it has remained an open question whether common economic policies would be an essential prerequisite for the functioning of a monetary union, or whether a monetary union would (automatically) lead to a common economic policy.[7]

1.1 Werner Plan

The Barre report inspired the heads of states and governments to make the economic and monetary union (EMU) an official goal for further integration at their meeting on 1 and 2 December 1969 at The Hague. They agreed that the Council of Ministers should develop a plan to introduce step by step such a union but emphasized that "the development of monetary cooperation should be based on the harmonization of economic policies."[8] Hence, the Council set up a group of experts, chaired by the then Prime Minister of Luxembourg, Pierre Werner, to draw a report on how this goal might be reached by the end of the decade.[9] The group presented its final report in October

---

3 See Siekmann (1985), p. 36 et seq.

4 Commission Memorandum to the Council on the co-ordination of economic policies and monetary co-operation within the Community, submitted on 12 February 1969, Bulletin of the EC no. 1, 1971.

5 Signed 7 February 1992, Official Journal, 29 July 1992, C 191/1.

6 Now Part three, Title VIII of the Treaty on the Functioning of the European Union (TFEU), consolidated version, Official Journal, 30 March 2010, C 83/1 (96).

7 For details see infra, Section 6.1.

8 Final communiqué at no. 8: "a plan by stages should be drawn up by the Council during 1970 with a view to the creation of an economic and monetary union," Compendium of Community Monetary Texts (register no. P 5/88), p. 13 (15); published also in *Krägenau and Wetter* (1993), p. 97; for details about the decision and the following report see Szász (1999), chapter 4.

9 Decision of the Council of 6 March 1970 regarding the procedure in the matter of economic and monetary cooperation, Compendium of Community Monetary Texts (register no. P 5/88), p. 17.

1970.[10] In fulfilment of the expressed expectations a three-stage plan was devised, which was to be realized within a time frame of ten years.[11] Its key elements were:

- total and irreversible convertibility of currencies;
- elimination of margins of fluctuation in rates of exchange;
- irrevocable fixing of parity ratios;
- total liberation of movements of capital;
- Adoption of a single currency, which would guarantee the irreversibility of the undertaking;
- setup of two Community organs: a center of decision making for economic policy and a Community system for the central banks.[12]

In addition to these institutional provisions, it was recommended that "principal decisions of economic policy will be taken at Community level" and that the "budgetary policy of the Member States will be conducted in accordance with Community objectives." In order to achieve this, a "Community survey" was to be effected "before the Governments draw up their budget proposal on a definitive basis."[13] By this, a third element was added to the main goals of the Barre report (first, greater coordination of economic policies, and second, closer monetary cooperation): control of budgetary policy of the Member States, which would ultimately become a major field of dispute and an alleged source of instability.

Thus, the fundamental points which dominate the debate until today were clearly envisaged:

- a *common economic policy* conducted by the Community
- *harmonization of the budgetary policy* of the Member States.

A political union was not considered to be a necessary prerequisite for the monetary union and the single currency. Instead, the economic and monetary union appeared "as a leaven for the development of political union." Only in the long run it appeared "to be unable to do without".[14]

With the collapse of Bretton Woods and the ensuing wave of instability on the foreign exchanges no further measures were taken to implement the plan.

1.2 Delors Plan

After various attempts to bring the free-floating currencies to a closer alignment within the European Community, the drive for a monetary union gained new momentum over

---

10 "Report to the Council and the Commission on the realization by stages of economic and monetary union in the Community," Luxembourg, 8 October 1970. An interim report had been presented to the Council on 20 May 1970.

11 Report, pp. 14, 26.

12 Report, p. 26.

13 Report, p. 27.

14 Report, p. 26.

15 years later. During the summit meeting held in Hanover on 27 and 28 June 1988 it was agreed to form (again) a group of experts and central bank governors to promote the envisaged monetary union. It was chaired by the then president of the Commission, Jacques Delors. The report of the group was presented on 17 April 1989 and proposed the introduction of an economic and monetary union in three stages. During the first step, all obstacles to the free flow of capital within the Community were to be abolished. The beginning of the second step would be marked by the foundation of a European Monetary Institute. With the third step all monetary competences of the Member States were to be transferred to the new European Central Bank.[15] Again, the report emphasized the need for

- a greater coordination of economic policies
- rules on the size and financing of national budget deficits
- the creation of a completely independent institution for the conduct of the monetary policy of the Union, the European Central Bank (ECB).

Even though there was a lot of criticism of the plan, its major elements were accepted in the intense negotiations prior to the Treaty of Maastricht.[16]

1.3 Maastricht Treaty

The Monetary Union and the provisions about the European System of Central Banks (ESCB) were finally introduced by the Treaty of Maastricht in 1992.[17] The EMU's organic law, the Statute of the European System of Central Banks and of the European Central Bank, was not left to ensuing legislation. It was also not left to the new institutions themselves. It was entirely formulated by the signing parties and added to the Treaty as a protocol. A protocol is legally an integral part of the primary law of the EU[18] even though certain very small parts of the statute can be amended in a procedure outside of a revision of the Treaty.[19]

In the course of the negotiations, the United Kingdom obtained a provision which allowed it to refrain from entering the third stage of the EMU even if it fulfilled the convergence criteria.[20] As the Treaty was rejected by means of a referendum in Denmark, the latter was granted an exemption as well.[21]

---

15 Description of the development in depth by Padoa-Schioppa (1994), p. 137 et seq.; Szász (1999), pp. 110–19; Issing (2008a), p. 4 seq.

16 Supra note 5.

17 Supra note 5.

18 Article 51 TEU.

19 This clause has been used in 2008 to change Article 10.2 of the Statute to introduce a rotation system in the Governing Council.

20 "1. Unless the United Kingdom notifies the Council that it intends to adopt the euro, it shall be under no obligation to do so . . . 3. The United Kingdom shall retain its powers in the field of monetary policy according to national law," Protocol (no. 15) on certain provisions relating to the United Kingdom of Great Britain and Northern Ireland, Official Journal C 83, 30 March 2010, p. 284.

21 The exemption had the effect that all Articles and provisions of the Treaty and the Statute of the ECSB referring to a "derogation" should be applicable to Denmark. The admission

1.4 Introduction of the Euro

With the beginning of the year 1999 the last, irrevocable step towards the implementation of the Monetary Union had been taken.[22] The exchange rates of the old currencies towards the euro were irrevocably fixed and the euro was officially introduced in the eleven Member States which had been admitted to the euro. The participating countries were Belgium, Germany, Spain, France, Ireland, Italy, Luxembourg, the Netherlands, Austria, Portugal and Finland.[23] For a period of time it was only used for the inter-bank business parallel to the old currencies. On 1 January 2002, euro notes and coins were introduced, as was also the case in Greece, which had been admitted in the meantime.[24] Cyprus, Malta, Slovenia, and Slovakia followed. Estonia was the last country to join, on 1 January 2011.

The UK and Denmark did not adopt the euro according to the exemptions granted to them.[25] Sweden did not continue in the process of introducing the euro[26] although it fulfilled all the requirements to do so. As a result, Bulgaria, the Czech Republic, Denmark, Latvia, Lithuania, Hungary, Poland, Romania, Sweden and the UK are EU Member States but currently do not use the single European currency.

The term "euro area" describes the Member States in which the euro is legal tender. In addition to these Member States, the euro is used as legal tender in three other European countries on the basis of a formal agreement following Article 219 para. 3 TFEU and these states are allowed to issue euro coins: San Marino,[27] Monaco,[28] and the Vatican.[29] Andorra initially introduced the euro on a unilateral basis. The euro is also used in a number of third countries without a formal agreement and in overseas departments, territories and islands which are either part of or associated with euro area Member States. Non-Member States using the euro as legal tender without an agreement are Montenegro and Kosovo. It is also used in UK Sovereign Base Areas on Cyprus. Furthermore, there are some countries, regions and territories which have

---

procedure of Article 140 TFEU should only be initiated at the request of Denmark, No. 1 and 2 of the Protocol (No. 16) on certain provisions relating to Denmark, Official Journal C83, 30 March 2010, p. 287.

22 Decision of the Council of the European Union meeting in the composition of Heads of State or Government of 3 May 1998, Official Journal L 139, 11 May 1998, p. 30. It was criticized as too early by 155 German professors of economics, Wim Kösters et al. in *Frankfurter Allgemeine* of 9 February1998, p. 15.

23 Regulation (EC) No. 974/98 of the Council, 3/5/1998, Official Journal, 11 May 1998, L 139/1; judged as no infringement of fundamental rights in Germany, Federal Constitutional Court, BVerfGE 97, 350 (370 f.); confirmed BVerfG (K), Neue Juristische Wochenschrift 1998, 3187.

24 The questionable actions of the Greek government preceding it are described by the Commission in its official "Report on Greek Government Deficit and Debt Statistics" of 8 January 2010, COM(2010) 1 final.

25 Supra notes 20 and 21.

26 Automatic consequence of the decision of the EU Council of 3 May 1998 and Article 121 para. 1 phrase 3 TEC.

27 Official Journal, 27 July 2001, C 209, p. 1.

28 Official Journal, 31 May 2002, L 142, p. 59.

29 Official Journal, 25 October 2001, C 299, p. 1; amended by Council decision 2003/738/EC of 7 October 2003.

pegged their currency to the euro: Bulgaria as Member State and Bosnia & Herzegovina as Non-Member State. The euro is, however, not legal tender there.[30]

The agreements with Monaco, San Marino and the Vatican had to be renegotiated mainly to correct some shortcomings in their original implementation and to increase the maximum volume of euro-coins these countries are entitled to issue. The new agreement between the EU and the Vatican came into effect on 1 January 2010, between the EU and Monaco on 1 December 2011; the new agreement with San Marino was concluded 27 March 2012 and is in the process of ratification. Andorra finally concluded a treaty with the EU on 30 June 2011, which allows it to introduce officially the euro and mint euro-coins from 1 July 2013 on.[31]

2 FORMATION

2.1 No Close Political Union

According to the Werner Plan, a common currency for all members of the European Community was to be set up to foster further integration. It was treated as a tool for further integration and not so much a result of the integration, even though in the long run a closer political union appeared to be indispensable.[32] In fact, the Maastricht Treaty introduced the Economic and Monetary Union without a full-fledged political integration. The euro was created as *a currency without a state*.[33] This was done in full awareness of the fact that many critics, namely economists, considered this procedure to be taking the second step before the first.[34] Even if this closer political union was not realized from the beginning, the single currency extends and completes the "single market." To this extent, it worked as "integration via the Economy."[35]

2.2 No Fiscal Federalism or Equalization System

Great care was taken by the framers of the Maastricht Treaty that the Monetary Union did not include any trait of a federal equalization system. All Member States had to remain fully responsible for their finances and absolutely no expectations were

---

30 For more details see: "Monetary and exchange rate arrangements of the euro area with selected third countries and territories," European Central Bank, *Monthly Bulletin*, April 2006, p. 87; European Commission (2008), p. 122. Special rules apply to some overseas territories of Member States which are not part of the territory of the EU, Article 355 TFEU; more in depth treatment by Krauskopf and Steven (1999); Hafke (2000); De Sèze, Marchand and Bardy (2011).

31 Official Journal, 4 February 2010, C 28, p. 1 (Vatican); Official Journal, 28 January 2012, C 23, p. 13 (Monaco); Official Journal, 26 April 2012, C 121, p. 5 (San Marino); Official Journal, 17 December 2011, C 369, p. 1 (Andorra).

32 Supra, Section 1.1.

33 A topic which was treated intensively by one of the leading framers from the German side and later a member of the Executive Board of the ECB, Otmar Issing, see e.g. Issing (2008b).

34 See more infra, Section 6.3.2.

35 Described by Issing (2008c), p. 299 et seq.

to be nourished that outside help would come in case of budgetary problems.[36] The capital markets were to provide the appropriate sanctions for an unsound fiscal policy. Permanent instruments to *prevent* an irresponsible fiscal policy were included in the legal framework besides the screening at the time of admission. Both safeguards[37] allegedly did not fulfill their tasks properly.[38]

In the past, many governments had habitually tried to solve budgetary problems by lowering the internal or external value of the currency or both: inflation and/or devaluation. Both mechanisms usually did not increase the economic strength of the particular country and only helped for a very limited period of time to overcome the inherent structural problems. In the EMU they should – legally – no longer be at the disposition of countries whose currency is the euro.

On the EU level it was envisioned that the problems should be solved at the roots by developing greater economic strength which would eventually result in the necessary convergence. This is also the reason for the existence of the many (coherence) programs of the EU to improve the infrastructure of defined areas or to solve structural economic deficits. They are definitely different from an equalization system as the funds are earmarked and are not at the general disposition of a government. The crucial point is to improve the competitiveness of Member States which are in need.

2.3 The Single Currency as Legal Tender of the Union

The single currency was designed to be the official currency of the European Union; the only official currency in the Union. For this purpose the single currency had to become legal tender in all Member States; the only legal tender.[39] All other currencies or means of payment had to cease in this function. By this, the Member States had to give up a substantial part of their sovereign powers:[40] the power to create and maintain a currency as legal tender and to conduct monetary policy.

The power to create money from a legal point of view was widely considered to be a sovereign right of a ruler but it was not indispensable, as shown by history. There have always been realms without a single currency or a currency of the central state. In any case, the general decision to transfer this sovereign right to the EU had been taken and it was not objected to by the judiciary.[41] Only the scope of this transfer may be debated.

3 THE EUROPEAN SYSTEM OF CENTRAL BANKS AND THE EUROSYSTEM

The Treaty of Maastricht has added monetary policy to the competences of the European Union and provided the necessary institutional setup. This was done by installing the

---

36 Smits (1997), p. 77.
37 More on the safeguards to guarantee permanent stability of the EMU infra in Section 4.
38 Louis (2010), p. 979; for the Stability and Growth Pact see Section 6.3.4.
39 Article 128 para. 1 TFEU.
40 Issing (2008c), p. 301.
41 BVerfGE 89, 155; 97, 350; Siekmann (2011a), Article 88 no. 34 with further references.

entire legal framework for the European System of Central Banks (ESCB). *All* EU Member States, even those that have not adopted the euro because of a special status or because of derogation, are part of the ESCB. It is the system as a whole and not only a subset of it which is charged by the Treaty to "conduct the monetary policy of the Union."[42] This is a consequence of the original idea that the euro was to become the – single – currency of the Union. Despite all disputes and difficulties, monetary policy has become one of the major fields of common power and coherence of the Union.

3.1 Institutional Setup

3.1.1 The general outlay

The ESCB is made up of the European Central Bank (ECB) and the national central banks (NCBs) of all 27 EU Member States.[43] The Governing Council of the ECB decided in November 1998 to adopt the term "Eurosystem" for both the ECB and those national central banks of the Member States whose currency is the euro. This step was taken in order to help the public understand the complex nature of the ESCB and to emphasize that these are the instruments used/implemented by the ESCB in order to carry out its tasks. The Treaty of Lisbon introduced the term into the primary law of the Union.[44]

The ESCB as such has no legal personality and consists of no organs on its own. It is governed by the decision-making bodies of the ECB:[45] the Governing Council and the Executive Board of the ECB and temporarily the General Council, for as long as this body exists.

3.1.2 The European Central Bank

Since the euro was designed to be the official currency of the EU, the ECB is an institution of the EU[46] and not a separate autonomous entity under European law,[47] not a "community" of its own.[48] Whether or not it is an "organ" of the EU is a question of minor importance[49] even if the use of the term "organ" in the German version of the Lisbon Treaty raised some concern at the Bundesbank.[50] However, this is merely a misleading

---

42 Article 127 para. 2 first indent; Article 282 para. 1 phrase 2 TFEU.

43 Article 282 para. 1 TFEU.

44 Article 282 para. 1 phrase 2 TFEU.

45 Article 129 para. 1; Article 282 para. 2 phrase 1 TFEU.

46 ECJ of 10 July 2003 C-11/00, in: Europarecht 2003, p. 847 (870); Dutzler (2003), p. 86: "It [the ECB] is hence, in spite of its separate legal personality and its independence, not a third party to the Community, but an instrument of the Community set up to achieve one of its objectives;" Kempen (2003), Article 107 no. 4; Gaitanides (2005), p. 52; Häde (2011), Article 282 TFEU no. 38; implicitly: Torrent (1999), p. 1230; Amtenbrink and de Haan (2002), p. 73 et seq.

47 Favoring the classification as an independent and separate entity under European law, however: Weber (1998), p. 1465 et seq.; Zilioli and Selmayr (1999), p. 285; (2000), p. 621, 643; (2001), p. 19; critical: Häde (2002), p. 921; (2006), p. 1605 et seq.

48 This is the wording of Selmayr (1999), p. 2433 et seq.

49 See Fang (2006), p. 95 after discussing extensively the question.

50 Deutsche Bundesbank (2003); less skeptical of the ECB: Stellungnahme der Europäischen Zentralbank vom 19 September 2003, Official Journal C 229, 25 September 2003, pp. 7–11.

translation[51] considering that both the English and the French version use the word "institution".[52]

The ECB has a legal personality[53] and enjoys the most extensive legal capacity accorded to legal persons under the respective national laws of each Member State. It has been awarded all the privileges and immunities that are necessary to carry out its tasks. The powers and authorities of the ECB are not delegated. They are directly derived from the Treaty. So the system is not simply one of the many *European agencies* which are derived from secondary law of the Union and which are ultimately responsibly to the Commission.[54]

At its installation, the ECB was not mentioned in the former Article 7 TEC which contained a list of the institutions of the Community. Instead it had a separate legal basis in the Treaty. The Lisbon Treaty changed this and lists the ECB now among other institutions in Article 13 of the Treaty on the European Union (TEU). The ESCB as a whole has retained, however, a separate legal basis.[55]

The ECB was originally endowed with a capital of €5000 million.[56] The sole subscribers and holders of the capital are the national central banks and not the Member States.[57] The capital can be augmented by the bank up to a sum authorized by the EU Council in advance. Already in 2000 the Council granted authority to increase the capital by up to €5000 million.[58] This authorization was used on 15 December 2010. The capital of the bank does not, however, serve the same function as equity in commercial banks as the ECB essentially is a government entity with a special status, and it has the privilege to produce the money needed to pay back its (internal) debt. Capital adequacy rules are not applicable.

The internal structure of the ECB is in principle formed by three bodies: the Governing Council, the Executive Board, and the General Council.

(1) Governing Council The Governing Council of the ECB is made up of the members of the Executive Board of the ECB and the governors of the national central banks of the Eurosystem. It has to meet at least ten times a year. The current frequency is twice a month; usually on the first and third Thursday of each month. The President of the EU Council and a member of the EU Commission are entitled to attend the meetings but without a right to vote.

---

51 Siekmann (2005), p. 50 et seq.

52 Article 13 para. 1 TEU; part 6, title I, chapter 1 TFEU.

53 Article 282 para. 3 phrase 1 TFEU.

54 A comprehensive list is given by Callies (2011), Article 13 TEU, no. 38; see extensively Fischer-Appelt (1999), Görisch (2009). There are in fact growing legal concerns about agencies which shall be granted independence solely on the basis of secondary law like regulatory bodies for the energy market, Article 35 sec. 4 Directive 2009/72/EC of the European Parliament and the Council of 13 July 2009, Official Journal L 211, 14 August 2009, p. 55 – electricity; Article 39 sec. 4 Directive 2009/73/EC of the European Parliament and the Council of 13 July 2009, Official Journal L 211, 14 August 2009, p. 94 – natural gas; Regulation (EC) 714/2009 of the European Parliament and of the Council of 13 July 2009, Official Journal L 211, 14 August 2009, p. 15.

55 Article 282 (1) TFEU.

56 Article 28.1. of the Statute.

57 Article 28.2. of the Statute.

58 Regulation 1009/2000 of 8 May 2000.

The Governing Council's tasks are of utmost importance to the ESCB. The Statute empowers it *inter alia* to formulate the monetary policy, adopt guidelines and take decisions necessary to ensure the performance of the ESCB's responsibilities. The Governing Council takes into account the implications for the euro area as a whole when it makes decisions.

(2) Executive Board The Executive Board is composed of the President and the Vice-President of the ECB and four other members. They are selected "from among persons of recognised standing and professional experience in monetary and banking matters" and are appointed by the European Council, acting by a qualified majority, on a recommendation from the Council, after it has consulted the European Parliament and the Governing Council of the European Central Bank.[59] The board generally meets once a week.

(3) General Council The Treaty on the Functioning of the European Union (TFEU) refers only to two decision-making bodies of the ESCB: the Governing Council and the Executive Board. Nonetheless, the General Council is the third decision-making body of the ECB. It had been constituted only as a temporary body, until all EU Member States have adopted the euro. It consists of the President and the Vice-President of the ECB and the governors of the national central banks of all EU Member States. The other members of the Executive Board, the President of the EU Council and a member of the EU Commission are also allowed to attend the meetings but do not have voting rights.

3.1.3 The national central banks

Within this framework the national central banks are of a double nature. They are created by national law and are subject to national law. Simultaneously they are integral parts of the ESCB.[60] In this capacity they are (partially) a European institution as well. They are instruments in the hands of the ECB to discharge its duties and have to follow its instructions. In this capacity they participate in all immunities and privileges which the law of the Union provides for the ESCB. On the other side, they exert substantial influence on the ECB as the heads or governors of the national central banks are members of the Governing Council of the ECB.

The national central banks of the countries which have not introduced the euro are also members of the ESCB, but, in comparison to the countries that have adopted the euro, they have a special status. These national central banks have retained their monetary sovereignty, which implies that they are still responsible for the national monetary policy whilst they are excluded from taking part in the core activities of the Eurosystem. Even though they do not carry out the primary functions of the Eurosystem, they are committed to the principles of price-stability-oriented monetary policy. Additionally, they are bound to work closely with the Eurosystem in several areas, e.g. statistics. The institutional forum for this cooperation is the General Council.

---

59 Article 11.2. subpara. 1 Statute.

60 Article 14.3. Statute; on their status and integration in the ESCB: Zimmermann (2000), p. 5 et seq.; Dziechciarz (2009).

3.2 Price Stability as Primary Objective

The Monetary Union was designed to be a community rooted in stability. Stability was initially interpreted in terms of price stability alone. Hence, price stability was set as a superior goal for the new monetary system in all legal documents. Financial stability in a wider sense played only a marginal role.[61]

Price stability is laid down as one of the governing principles of the Union in Article 3 para. 3 subpara. 1 of the TEU. With regard to the Monetary Union, it is confirmed at various places in the TFEU, i.e. not only as one among other goals but in fact as its primary objective. To underline the importance and priority of this objective the chapter on monetary policy begins with the phrase: "The primary objective of the European System of Central Banks . . . shall be to maintain price stability."[62]

Only without prejudice to this primary objective, the ESCB shall also support the general economic policies of the Union with regard to contributing to the objectives of the Union as laid down in Article 3 of the TEU.[63] In addition, it shall act in line with the principle of an open market economy with free competition.

The term "price stability" in the legal documents is generally interpreted in the sense of consumer price stability.[64] This is explicitly done by the protocol on the convergence criteria.[65] Consumer price stability is generally measured by the harmonized index of consumer prices (HICP) calculated by the European office of statistics (ESTAT).[66] Asset prices and their tendency to form bubbles were not envisaged by the framers of the Treaty.

3.3 Tasks and Powers

The ECB is entrusted with carrying out the central banking functions for the euro. It commands all the powers necessary to fulfill this task. The banknotes issued by the Eurosystem are the only such notes to have the status of legal tender within the Union.[67] Member States may, however, issue euro coins. They may be regarded as modified "national" means of payment.[68] The right of governments to issue coins has been an old

---

61 It is mentioned in Article 127 para. 5 TFEU as an objective the ESCB shall contribute to: "The ESCB shall contribute to the smooth conduct of policies pursued by the competent authorities relating to the prudential supervision of credit institutions and the stability of the financial system."

62 Article 127 para. 1 phrase 1 TFEU, restated in Article 282 para. 2 phrase 2 TFEU.

63 Article 127 para. 1 phrase 2 TFEU, restated in Article 282 para. 2 phrase 3 TFEU.

64 Endler (1998), p. 65 et seq. with comprehensive discussion of the various alternatives and concepts; Gaitanides (2005), p. 20; Siekmann (2011a), Article 88 no. 29; Blanke (2010), Article 88 no. 67; Häde (2011), Article 127 TFEU no. 3; too vague Herdegen (2010), Article 88 no. 30.

65 Protocol (No. 13) on the convergence criteria, Official Journal C83, 30 March 2010, p. 281.

66 The office has the rank of directorate general of the Commission and is attributed to the Commissioner for administration, audit and fraud prevention. It is not entrenched in the primary law of the Union and has not been awarded a guaranteed independence. Solely in a "practical arrangement" on the "working relations" between the office and the members of the Commission, cabinets and services certain freedoms have been acknowledged (agreement between the competent commissioner, Olli Rehn, and the director general – DG ESTAT – Walter Radermacher of 11 May 2010).

67 Article 128 para. 1 phrase 1 and 2 TFEU; repeated in Article 282 para. 3 phrase 3 TFEU with no additional meaning, see Häde (2011), Article 282 TFEU no. 43.

68 Seiler (2004), p. 67.

tradition even in countries with a central bank which is granted guaranteed independence and a centralized money creating power. There is no material justification to continue with this tradition.[69] The profit for the treasury from minting coins is an insufficient reason. However, prior approval by the ECB is necessary to prevent undue interference with its monetary policy.[70]

Moreover, the ESCB has to carry out four main tasks. These are:

- to define and implement the monetary policy of the Union
- to conduct foreign-exchange operations (which have to be consistent with an international foreign-exchange system in case this has been set up)
- to hold and manage the official foreign reserves of the Member States
- to promote the smooth operation of payment systems.[71]

Although the tasks have been assigned explicitly to the ESCB, at least the monetary policy is performed as a task of the Union. This can be easily derived from the superscription of that part of the Treaty, "union policies and internal actions," as well as the wording in Article 127 para. 2 first indent TFEU.[72] It should, however, be considered that in effect not the entire ESCB is carrying out these tasks but mainly the Eurosystem.[73] The monetary policy is adopted by the Governing Council of the ECB. The Executive Board of the ECB gives instructions to the national central banks in order to implement the monetary policy of the Governing Council. The authority to define and implement the monetary policy of the Union allows the ECB to exert a dominant influence on money market conditions and money market interest rates.

Regarding the powers and competences of the ECB, the primary law of the EU strictly separates monetary policy from economic policy (including fiscal policy).[74] Only under carefully elaborated provisions and to a very limited extent can the ECB act outside the described basic tasks: it shall contribute to the prudential supervision of credit institutions and the stability of the financial system, but only to the conduct of policies pursued by the competent authorities.[75] This is a merely ancillary function. The tasks remain with the "competent authorities." Additional competences or powers are not conferred by these clauses on the ECB. The Council may, however, confer "specific tasks" upon the ECB concerning policies relating to the prudential supervision of credit institutions and other financial institutions with the exception of insurance undertakings.[76] The ECB may also submit opinions to the appropriate Union institutions, bodies, offices or agencies or to national authorities on matters in its fields of competence.[77] All of these carefully

---

69 Siekmann (2011a), Article 88 no. 20.

70 Article 128 para. 1 phrase 2 TFEU.

71 Article 127 para 2. TFEU.

72 Häde (2011), Article 127 no. 11.

73 The Article was designed on the premise that eventually all Member States would introduce the euro and there would be no significant difference between the Eurosystem and the EU.

74 Chapter 1 "Economic Policy" and Chapter 2 "Monetary Policy" of Part three, Title VIII TFEU.

75 Article 127 para. 5 TFEU.

76 Article 127 para. 6 TFEU.

77 Article 127 para. 4 subpara. 2 TFEU.

designed provisions would be superfluous if the ECB could act beyond its basic tasks as laid down in Article 127 para. 2 TFEU.

This shows that the ECB does not have competences to act as "lender of last resort" for credit institutions (banks) or even more so for governments. The support of failing banks or banking systems – aside from providing temporary liquidity to basically solvent banks – is beyond its mandate and powers. As part of economic policy, the primary law has reserved it to the Member States.[78] It also shows that the ECB has no competences of its own in the fields of financial stability and prudential supervision; it may only support measures of the competent authorities. This is also one of the reasons why the tasks of the ECB within the framework of the new European Systemic Risk Board (ESRB) have to be limited and the Board itself does not have sovereign powers.[79]

The ECB does not have to fulfill all its duties by own personnel. It can use the national central banks as its "executive arm."[80] As a result, some of the day-to-day work is performed by the national central banks. This includes also the purchase of "sovereign" bonds and private debt instruments, as in the covered bond program. The legal ownership of these instruments might be essential in case of a default. Also the respective liabilities in this case are an open and not sufficiently scrutinized issue. The primary law explicitly approves that both the ECB and the national central banks may in fact issue euro banknotes[81] but the exclusive responsibility for the material decisions remains with the ECB.

To carry out the tasks entrusted to the ESCB, the ECB has been granted the power to adopt regulations, take decisions, and make recommendations and deliver opinions.[82]

4 SAFEGUARDS FOR PROCURING STABILITY OF THE EURO

Looking at the overall picture, a host of safeguards can be pinpointed which were included in the Maastricht Treaty to ensure that the Monetary Union would be a space of stability not only at its beginning but in fact on a permanent basis. To ensure this lasting stability several carefully designed measures were implemented:

- high admission standards
- far-reaching and absolute independence of the monetary institutions
- no financing of the public sector by the ECB
- no privileged access of the public sector to financing
- strict fiscal discipline
- no liability for the public sector of a Member State.

The design of the Monetary Union as a permanent community of stability (*Stabiltätsgemeinschaft*) was a major aspect for the Federal Constitutional Court

---

78 For the interdiction of support of Members States, see infra 6.4.2.
79 Siekmann (2012), pp. 156, 159–163, 204.
80 Siekmann (2011a), Article 88 no. 44.
81 Article 128 para. 1 phrase 2 TFEU.
82 Article 132 para. 1 TFEU.

of Germany to accept the Maastricht Treaty and the introduction of the euro as constitutional.[83]

4.1 High Admission Standards

Although the single currency was originally designed to become the currency of the European Union it was soon realized that this could not be achieved in one step as the number of members of the Union had rapidly grown. With the growing number, the Union had become increasingly heterogeneous. To achieve the desired minimum homogeneity among the participants of the single currency, restrictive admission standards were set up. A high degree of "sustainable convergence" was required. This convergence is assessed by four criteria:

- the achievement of a high degree of price stability
- the sustainability of the government's financial position
- normal fluctuation of exchange rates within the European Monetary System
- the convergence of long-term interest-rate levels.[84]

These criteria were specified in a protocol pertaining to the Maastricht Treaty,[85] which is part of the Treaty and belongs to the primary law of the Union.[86] They were (later) often referred to as the "Maastricht criteria." To avoid confusion with the criteria for an admissible budget deficit, they should be referred to as "convergence criteria" as in the official wording.[87] However, the convergence criteria are only reference values.[88] The primary law leaves some space for discretion on the part of the deciding bodies. This space was used in the case of Italy, Belgium, and later also Greece.

All Member States were originally expected to adopt the euro at one point in the future once they fulfilled the convergence criteria. Even though the Treaty of Lisbon has diluted this requirement to a certain extent, as it has led to the "official" recognition of two groups of Member States,[89] the initial expectation is still valid.

---

[83] BVerfGE 89, 155 (200, 204): "The Treaty on the Union regulates the Monetary Union as a community lastingly committed to stability and specifically guaranteeing monetary stability." "This concept of the Monetary Union as community of stability ("Stabilitätsgemeinschaft") is foundation and object of the German act of assent" (p. 205); confirmed by BVerfGE 97, 350 (370).

[84] Article 140 para. 1 phrase 3 TFEU.

[85] Protocol (No. 13) on the convergence criteria, Official Journal C83, 30 March 2010, p. 281.

[86] Article 51 TFEU: "The Protocols and Annexes to the Treaties shall form an integral part thereof."

[87] See note 85.

[88] The German Federal Constitutional, however, judges them as binding basis for the consent of Germany to the Treaty, BVerfGE 89, 155 (202 f.); see also Hartmann (1996), p. 135 et seq.

[89] Part three, Title VIII, Chapter 4: Provisions specific to Member States whose currency is the euro; Article 139: "Member States in respect of which the Council has not decided that they fulfil the necessary conditions for the adoption of the euro shall hereinafter be referred to as 'Member States with a derogation.'"

4.2 Independence of Monetary Institutions

An important feature of the ESCB is its independence.[90] The ECB and the national central banks must not seek or take instructions from EU institutions or bodies, from any government of an EU country or from any other body when exercising powers or carrying out tasks conferred upon them by the Treaties and the Statute of the ESCB.[91] This independence is granted not only to the respective bodies but also to their members. This has also been explicitly stated with regard to the members of the decision-making bodies of the national central banks.[92] Especially the latter aspect is crucial for judging the legality of the pressure put on a member of the board of the Bundesbank recently by the president of the Republic and its chancellor. It is an open question, however, whether the guarantee also covers activities by the ECB or the national central banks in banking supervision.

The independence is usually broken down into personal independence and material independence.[93] Personal independence denotes a fixed tenure for governors of the national central banks and members of the Executive Board of the ECB. A minimum term of five years for governors[94] and a non-renewable term of office of eight years for members of the Executive Board[95] are demanded by EU law to strengthen their position.

With regard to the members of the Executive Board, the Treaty allows a removal from office only if a member "no longer fulfills the conditions required for the performance of his duties or if he has been guilty of serious misconduct." However, this cannot be done as a type of "actus contrarius" by the EU Council. Only the European Court of Justice may – on application of the Governing Council or the Executive Board – "retire" such a member compulsorily.[96] A removal from office or any pressure in this direction is illegal, as shown in the present case of the Italian member of the Board, Lorenzo Bini Smaghi. A voluntary resignation may be in compliance with this rule. However, if a resignation at halftime has been agreed upon in advance, as e.g. in the case of the first president of the ECB, Willem Duisenberg, legal doubts remain. Nonetheless it is not binding.[97]

The law of the European Union provides no respective general clause for the members of the governing bodies of the national central banks as they are basically governed by the respective national law. Yet, it provides a minimum standard that a governor may be relieved from office only if he "no longer fulfills the conditions required for the performance of his duties or if he has been guilty of serious misconduct."[98] An action of the national judiciary is not a prerequisite of the EU law. However, "a decision of this effect

---

90 Accepted by the German Federal Constitutional Court as in accordance with the democratic principle, BVerfGE 89, 155 (172, 181, 208); see in depth: Dutzler (2003), pp. 88–109; Gaitanides (2005), pp. 199–279; Siekmann (2005), p. 40 et seq.

91 Article 130 phrase 1 TFEU.

92 Article 130 phrase 1 TFEU: ". . . nor any member of their decision-making bodies . . ."

93 More subdivisions of various kinds are explicated by scholars; see the overview at Siekmann (2005), pp. 8–15; Gaitanides (2005), pp. 45–135; (2007), Article 88 no. 59 et seq.

94 Article 14.2 subpara. 1 Statute.

95 Article 283 para. 2 subpara. 3 TFEU.

96 Article 11.4 Statute.

97 Heun (1998), p. 874; Kempen (2003), Article 108 TEC no. 11; Häde (2011), Article 130 TFEU no. 27.

98 Article 14.2 subpara. 2 phrase 1 Statute.

may be referred to the Court of Justice by the Governor concerned or the Governing Council."[99] No rules were set up for other members of the governing bodies.

This reluctance in regulating the interior composition of the national central banks is plausible but raises serious concerns in view of the independence of the Governing Council of the ECB, which takes the crucial decisions on monetary policy and decides far-reaching questions e.g. the legally and economically highly problematic purchase of sovereign debt, euphemistically named "quantitative easing." At least in some Member States, like Germany, all tenured civil servants can be removed from office by court action and on very limited grounds only; not to mention judges and members of courts of audits, who enjoy a constitutionally guaranteed independence like all parts of the ESCB. This was widely ignored during the recent excitement about a member of the board of the Bundesbank and some years ago about an alleged misconduct of a president of the Bundesbank. Neither the president of the Republic nor the government in Germany have the right to remove an official from office, regardless of what he has committed; also not on the proposal of the Bundesbank. A court action is indispensable.

Material independence indicates that the ECB and the national central banks can freely and uninterruptedly employ all competences and instruments that are necessary for the conduct of their duties. They are to be free to perform the monetary policy in a way they deem suitable. They are authorized to decide how and when to use their instruments without any undue influence from the EU institutions, national government bodies or private institutions. Any kind of pressure is a breach of that guarantee.[100] Even the mere attempt to exert pressure is illegal,[101] regardless of whether from a governmental or private body.[102]

4.3 No Financing of the Public Sector by the ECB

Any type of credit financing of the Union or the Member States by the ECB or by a central bank of a Member State is strictly prohibited. This prohibition is absolutely comprehensive. It holds not only for the Union and central governments but also for all other bodies, offices or agencies, regional, local or other public authorities. It includes all other bodies governed by public law and public enterprises.[103] An exception is only made for those publicly owned credit institutions which can be given the same access as other commercial banks.[104]

In order to secure this interdiction, the ECB and the national central banks may not purchase any debt instruments issued by the public sector. This specifically covers government bonds. However, only the "direct" purchase is forbidden. In this way the

---

[99] Article 14.2 subpara. 2 phrase 2 Statute.

[100] ECJ, C-11/00, margin number 134.

[101] Article 130 phrase 2 TFEU. The English version of the Treaty is in this point, however, not so clear as the German version which explicitly bans the attempt (". . . nicht zu versuchen . . ."); see also Endler (1998), p. 410 et seq.; Kempen (2003), Art. 108 no. 5; Kämmerer (2003), Article 88 no. 27; Siekmann (2011a), Article 88 no. 54.

[102] Louis (1998), p. 43.

[103] Article 123 para. 1 TFEU.

[104] Article 123 para. 2 TFEU.

Eurosystem is enabled to intervene in the markets so as to procure their proper functioning. In no way was it intended to open a back door for an (indirect) financing of governments. The secondary law puts it plainly and unmistakably: "purchases made on the secondary market must not be used to circumvent the objectives of that Article."[105] It is only allowed "in the context of monetary policy operations."[106] As a result, what is euphemistically and misleadingly called "monetizing" of public debt might be allowable for the Federal Reserve System of the U.S. but is clearly illegal for the ECB.

Bearing this in mind, the purchase of government bonds started by the ESCB in early summer 2010 was not without a legal risk from the very beginning. The longer it lasts, the more it becomes legally questionable as the proper functioning of the markets can hardly any longer be used as a justification. So it is *not* a question of the structure of the balance sheet of the ECB when it demands that the support of some of the Member States with debt problems by the ESCB has to be terminated immediately and other instruments, like a (permanent) European Support Mechanism or Monetary Fund[107] is used instead. Nevertheless, despite all legal concerns, the ECB and the national central banks of the Eurosystem resumed the bond buying program in July 2011 and expanded it considerably in size and scope, also now acquiring debt instrument issued by Italy and Spain.

4.4 No Privileged Access of the Public Sector to Financing

In a similar manner any privileged access to financial institutions by Union institutions, bodies, offices or agencies, central governments, regional, local or other public authorities, other bodies governed by public law or public enterprises is strictly prohibited as well.[108] This prohibition is necessary as experience shows that governments prefer to put pressure on the banking system of their country to finance their budgetary deficits, as in the case of Greece. This might be especially true when banks are owned or controlled by government entities. Such a practice increases the danger of contagion and puts additional pressure on the ECB to assist banks as "lender of last resort," thus indirectly financing governments and government entities.

4.5 Strict Fiscal Discipline

4.5.1 Primary law

The primary law requires the "sustainability" of the fiscal policy and thereby offers a rudimentary guideline for the long-term budgetary policy. It declares "the sustainability of the government's financial position" to be the essential criterion for sustainable

---

105 Regulation no. 3603 of 13 December 1993 specifying definitions for the application of the prohibitions referred to in Articles 104 and 104b(1) of the Treaty, Official Journal L 332, 31 December 1993, p. 1, recital p. 1.

106 Hahn (1991), p. 807, from the time of drafting the clause; Heun (1998), p. 875: "unlimited and compulsory interdiction of central bank credits"; Kempen (2003), Article 101 EGV no. 5: only for purposes of open market policy.

107 Infra, Section 6.4.3.

108 Article 124 TFEU.

convergence in the framework of the economic and monetary union.[109] Even if this clause is part of the transitional provisions it can be used as a basis for interpretation of the permanent requirement that "Member States shall avoid excessive government debts."[110] The United Kingdom diluted this clause to some extent in that it promised only to "endeavour to avoid an excessive government deficit."[111]

The compliance with budgetary discipline has to be monitored by the Commission and the Council on the basis of two reference values: the ratio of the planned or actual government deficit to gross domestic product and the ratio of government debt to gross domestic product.[112] The reference values are specified in the protocol (No. 12) on the excessive deficit procedure added to the Maastricht Treaty and pertained in the TFEU.[113] They read as follows:

- 3% for the ratio of the planned or actual government deficit to gross domestic product at market prices;
- 60% for the ratio of government debt to gross domestic product at market prices.[114]

These reference values are part of the primary law of the Union.[115] They are quite frequently referred to as "Maastricht criteria." This might cause confusion as the admission criteria mentioned above are also called "Maastricht criteria." For this reason it should always be made clear which criteria are meant and the latter should be called "convergence criteria."

The monitoring and enforcement of the rules has to be achieved in a complex interaction of the Commission and the Council.[116] They may result in admonition and recommendations.[117] If a Member State persists in failing to put into practice the recommendations, sanctions may be imposed which may eventually entail a non-interest-bearing deposit with the Union or a "fine of an appropriate size."[118] In essence, both the procedural and the substantial rules for enforcing the requirement of permanent budgetary discipline are laid down in the primary law of the Union. However, really effective sanctions have not been embodied. Specifically an *exclusion* of a Member State from the Eurozone is not foreseen and would be illegal.[119] In addition, substantial *discretionary power* remains with the political bodies.

4.5.2 Stability and Growth Pact

At the point of initiation of the Monetary Union, serious concerns were already raised that the procedure provided in the primary law seemed to be too tedious and – above

---

[109] Article 140 para. 1 indent 2 TFEU.
[110] Article 126 para. 1 TFEU.
[111] No 5 of Protocol (No. 15) (supra note 20).
[112] Article 126 para. 2 TFEU.
[113] Protocol (No. 12) on the excessive deficit procedure, Official Journal C83, 30 March 2010, p. 279.
[114] Article 1 of the protocol.
[115] Article 51 TEU.
[116] Article 126 paras 2–13 TFEU.
[117] Article 126 paras 7–9 TFEU.
[118] Article 126 para. 11 subpara. 1.
[119] Kirchhof (1994), p. 72; probably also Herrmann (2010), p. 417.

all – the political determination seemed to lack possibilities to impose appropriate sanctions.[120] Definitions and specifications of the rules on government debt and deficits and the deficit procedure had been provided for by the secondary law of the Union but no reduction of the scope of discretion was imposed for the purpose of imposing sanctions.[121] It was mainly Germany which demanded a "stability pact" preferably with *automatic* sanctions.[122] This would, however, have been barely compatible with the discretionary powers granted to the Commission and the Council through the primary law. A separate treaty – complementing the provisions in the TEC on the Monetary Union – would also have been questionable from a legal point of view.[123] Changing clauses of the primary law of the Union cannot be accomplished this way. Supplementing them in fields which do not yet fall into its competences or which have been left explicitly open to further accords is admissable[124] but of limited effectiveness. That is the reason why the somewhat awkward type of pact at the level of secondary law was finally realized.

Ultimately the so-called Stability and Growth Pact (SGP) was set up by secondary law of the Union. The SGP is not a contract in the common understanding of the word. The term "pact" was retained to emphasize the underlying political consensus[125] even though the term is used in other legal acts of the European Union in the strict sense of the word. It can be taken as a reminiscence of the initially discussed separate treaty. This has been the cause of some confusion among the not so well informed public. Technically the pact consists of one resolution of the European Council,[126] which is not binding, and two – binding – regulations of the Council. One contains mainly substantive provisions[127] and the other mainly procedural rules.[128] The resolution contains a multilateral promise to achieve an almost balanced budget in the medium range.

The regulations are part of the secondary law of the Union. Regulation 1466/97 was

---

120 Zeitler (1995), p. 1611.

121 Council Regulation (EC) No. 3605/93 of 22 November 1993 on the application of the Protocol on the excessive deficit procedure annexed to the Treaty establishing the European Community, Official Journal L 332, 31 December 1993, p. 7; amended several times, codified version: Council Regulation (EC) No. 479/93 of 25 May 2009, on the application of the Protocol on the excessive deficit procedure annexed to the Treaty establishing the European Community, Official Journal L 145, 10 June 2009, p. 1; Council Regulation (EC) No. 3603/93 of 13 December 1993 specifying definitions for the application of the prohibitions referred to in Articles 104 and 104b(1) of the Treaty, Official Journal L 332, 31 December 1993, p. 1.

122 A "Stabilitätspakt für Europa" was presented by the German Minister of Finance on 10 November 1995; see for details Palm (2000), p. 44 et seq., 142; Häde (2006), p. 139; extensively to this and the origins of the Stability and Growth Pact Hentschelmann (2009), p. 205–85.

123 Smits (1997), p. 85; Häde (1996), p. 140.

124 Häde (1996), p. 142.

125 Explicitly expressed in recital no. 2 of both regulations, infra notes 127 and 128.

126 Resolution of the European Council on the Stability and Growth Pact, Amsterdam, of 17 June 1997, Official Journal C 236, 2 August 1997, p. 1.

127 Council Regulation (EC) no. 1466/97 of 7 July 1997 on the strengthening of the surveillance of budgetary positions and the surveillance and coordination of economic policies, Official Journal L 209, 2 August 1997, p. 1; amended by Council Regulation (EC) no. 1055/2005 of 27 June 2005, Official Journal L 174, 7 July 2005, p. 1.

128 Council Regulation (EC) no. 1467/97 of 7 July 1997 on speeding up and clarifying the implementation of the excessive deficit procedure, Official Journal L 209, 2 August 1997, p. 6; amended by Council Regulation (EC) no. 1056/2005 of 27 June 2005, Official Journal L 174, 7 July 2005, p. 5.

based on Article 99 para. 5 TEC and contains an early warning system and the obligation of the Member States to provide a stability program. It is now often named the "preventive part" of the pact. Regulation 1467/97 was based on Article 104 para. 4 TEC and attempts to speed up the procedure and to clarify it in case of an unsustainable deficit. It is called the "dissuasive" or "corrective" part of the pact. It governs the *excessive deficit procedure* (EDP).

Mainly on behalf of France and – ironically – Germany, these regulations were amended in 2005[129] when France and Germany failed to comply with the reference values. Those amendments left the reference criteria untouched, since they are part of the primary law of the Union,[130] but allowed taking more circumstances into account to excuse a failure to meet them. Discretionary powers were extended. Procedural provisions were also changed to make it more difficult to adopt sanctions against non-compliant Member States. In addition to that, the deadlines for imposing sanctions were prolonged.[131] These amendments were preceded by a Council decision not to continue with the deficit procedure against France and Germany, which was later declared not to be in accordance with the European Union law by the Court of Justice.[132]

Whereas the "convergence criteria"[133] were set up to warrant that only Member States which are sufficiently homogeneous in respect to the rest of the euro area could introduce the euro, the rules on economic stability and on budgetary deficits should guarantee the required "community of lasting stability" that the Federal Constitutional Court of Germany had demanded.[134] Beyond the deficit criteria it remained the goal of the EU in the framework of the Monetary Union that the public sector should have an "almost" balanced budget or even a surplus in the medium range to have sufficient leeway for the working of built-in stabilizers.[135]

---

[129] Council Regulation (EC) no. 1055/2005 of 27 June 2005, Official Journal L 174, 7 July 2005, p. 1; Council Regulation (EC) no. 1056/2005 of 27 June 2005, Official Journal L 174, 7 July 2005, p. 5. On 20 March 2005 the ECOFIN Council had adopted a report entitled "Improving the implementation of the Stability and Growth Pact." This report was endorsed by the European Council in its conclusions of 22 March 2005 and is now considered by the ECOFIN Council as an "integral part" of the Pact, see the consolidated version of the "Specifications on the implementation of the Stability and Growth Pact and Guidelines on the format and content of Stability and Convergence Programmes," endorsed by the ECOFIN Council on 7 September 2010, p. 3.

[130] Art. 51 TEU. It might be argued, however, that they could be modified by acts of the secondary law on the basis of Article 126 para. 14 subparagraph 2 TFEU. The protocol could have been replaced on this basis but remained untouched. The legal validity of the regulation was not affected by this, see Hentschelmann (2009), p. 1207.

[131] Severe criticism: Deutsche Bundesbank, *Monatsberichte*, April 2005, p. 15 (20); Stark (2005), p. 64; Zeitler (2006), p. 235; more reserved: Hatje (2006), p. 604.

[132] ECJ, Judgment of 13 July 2004 – C-27/04 (*Commission vs. Council*), *Europäische Zeitschrift für Wirtschaftsrecht*, 2004, p. 465; *Juristen-Zeitung*, 2004, p. 1069 with comment by M. Kotzur; see also Dutzler and Hable (2004); Nicolaysen (2004).

[133] Supra Section 4.1.

[134] Supra section D. BVerfGE 89 155 (200, 202, 204 et seq.); 97, 350 (370, 373, 376)

[135] Council resolution (supra note 126), S. 1; Regulation 1466/97 (supra note 127), recital (2); Regulation 1467/97 (supra note 128), recital (3).

4.6 No Liability for the Public Sector of a Member State

Scholarly debates and the media regularly assume the existence of a so-called "no bail-out" clause. This is premature as a complete interdiction of "bail-outs" is *not* clearly expressed in the Treaties. Specifically, Article 125 para. 1 TFEU only states that the Union and the Member States shall not be liable for the commitments of central governments, regional, local or other bodies governed by public law, or public undertakings of any Member State. Moreover, at least some type of voluntary support is prohibited as neither the Union nor Member States shall "assume" such commitments. The assumption of debt is, however, not identical with financial support of a Member State in need. There is room for interpretation as bilateral payments or credit guarantees must not necessarily be judged as "assuming" a commitment.

These rules do not however, apply to Member States of the European Union whose currency is not the euro. In case a "Member State with a derogation"[136] is in "difficulties or seriously threatened with difficulties as regards its balance of payments" the Council can eventually grant "mutual assistance" and "appropriate methods" in this regard.[137] In case a "sudden crisis" in the balance of payments occurs the Member State may take the necessary protective actions as well.[138]

To complete the argumentation, another clause has to be taken into account. Article 122 para. 2 TFEU allows (voluntary) financial assistance under certain, very restrictive conditions: "Where a Member State is in difficulties or is seriously threatened with severe difficulties caused by natural disasters or exceptional occurrences beyond its control" such an aid may be provided. The clause and the wording are the result of a compromise. By using this phraseology the framers of the Treaty still show that they keenly intended limited support payments for specific, extraordinary situations. Also the term "occurrences beyond its control" might be interpreted in different ways. It was inserted later in the course of the framing process of the Treaty as the original version wanted to restrict the aid only to situations of natural disasters. This way any incentive for circumventing the rules should be excluded. The question is, however, whether this is an exclusive provision banning all other types of aid which do not fulfill its prerequisites.

A complete interdiction of support apart from that could therefore only be the result of careful legal reasoning considering the totality of Articles 122 para. 2, 143 para. 1, and 144 para. 1 TFEU. The purpose of the clauses is clear: the determination of the Member States to comply with the required budgetary discipline was to be strengthened and lenders were to receive a clear signal that there could be a (potential) risk. In effect, the opinion of legal scholars in Germany on the "constitutionality" of financial support by the Union or its Member States is split.[139]

---

136 Terminology introduced by the Treaty of Lisbon, Article 139 para. 1 TFEU.

137 Article 143 para. 1 subpara. 2, para. 2 TFEU.

138 Article 144 para. 1 TFEU.

139 See for references Herrmann (2010), 414 footnote 19; Herrmann is – with some reservations – in favor of constitutionality. Faßbender (2011), p. 800: breach of Article 125 TFEU not justifiable by Article 122 TFEU, p. 802: breach of German constitution law; also critical, Thym (2011), p. 169.

4.7 No Exit from the Monetary Union

The Treaty on European Union and the Treaty on the Functioning of the European Union have been concluded for an unlimited period as Article 53 TEU and Article 356 TFEU. The Monetary Union, as an integral part of the European Union, cannot be dissolved or altered without substantially amending the primary law of the Union.

The movement of the European Community, as a whole, into the third stage of the Monetary Union was construed to be irreversible[140] in order to clarify its institutional stability beyond any doubt. There was no way to leave the Monetary Union, which effectively prevented speculation of market participants against a single Member State.[141] This legal position was reaffirmed by the Treaty, which, by introducing Article 50 TEU, opened a way to completely break away from the Union and not just from the Monetary Union.[142]

A Member State leaving the Monetary Union illegally would run into fundamental legal problems, as monetary sovereignty would still rest with the European Union. The *lex monetae* for all contracts and other transactions would remain with the Union and would have a significant effect on all open claims.[143]

5 MACROECONOMIC SURVEILLANCE AND COMMON FISCAL POLICY

Partially as a consequence of its report on intra-euro-area imbalances[144] the Commission submitted a comprehensive "economic governance package" on 29 September 2010, covering three main subjects:

- reinforcement of Member States' compliance with the Stability and Growth Pact
- broadening of economic surveillance to prevent, detect and correct macroeconomic imbalances and divergences in competitiveness
- strengthening of the enforcement mechanisms.[145]

The measures to prevent and correct macroeconomic imbalances contain

1. an alert mechanism through a scoreboard
2. a preventive surveillance based on discussions with the Member States and in-depth reviews

140 Protocol on the transition to the third stage of Economic and Monetary Union, O.J. C 1992/191/87.

141 Calliess (2011), margin no. 1, with further references to for varying opinions.

142 Kirchhof (1994), p. 72; Athanassiou (2009), p. 21; Hahn and Häde (2010), § 26 margin no. 10; in general see also Herrmann (2010), p. 417; Scott (1998), p. 214, deliberating the application of Article 56 of the Vienna Convention on the Law of Treaties which was highly questionable at that time and is unacceptable following the Treaty of Lisbon.

143 Detailed analysis by Ernst (2012), p. 49; Scott (1998), pp. 207–28, who seems to consider the legality an exit.

144 European Commission (2010).

145 MEMO/10/455, 29 September 2010.

3. an excessive imbalance procedure (EIP) applying to EU Member States
4. an enforcement mechanism for the euro area members.[146]

Altogether six legislative proposals for concrete legal instruments were submitted. Two proposals deal with the amendment of the regulations which constitute in essence the Stability and Growth Pact.[147] The first is based on Article 121 TFEU, the second on Article 126 TFEU. The regulation on the prevention and correction of macroeconomic imbalances is completely new. It was set up to detect imbalances and to establish a corrective procedure ("excessive imbalance procedure" – EIP).[148] The regulation that aims to establish national budgetary frameworks of quality is also new.[149] These requirements for the budgetary frameworks of all Member States are based on Article 126 para. 14 TFEU. In particular, they aim to specify the obligations of national authorities to comply with the provisions of Article 2 of the Protocol (No. 12) on the excessive deficit procedure.

Two regulations deal specifically with the enforcement of rules: one provides an enforcement mechanism for the budgetary surveillance of the euro area Member States[150] and the other deals with the enforcement of actions to correct macroeconomic imbalances in general.[151] The effective enforcement of budgetary surveillance is based on Article 136 in combination with Article 121 para. 6 TFEU. Both regulations allow fines not only for excessive deficits but also for exceeding the debt level of the reference values. The discretionary power of the Council is reduced significantly.[152]

The requested automaticity might be realized indirectly by introducing a "reverse" decisionmaking mechanism ("reverse QMV"). This leads to *semi-automatic sanctions*, as they are derived directly from the normative rule and can only be stopped by a ("reverse")

---

146 MEMO/10/454, 29 September 2010.

147 Proposal for a Council Regulation (EU) amending Regulation (EC) No. 1466/97 on the strengthening of the surveillance of budgetary positions and the surveillance and coordination of economic policies, COM(2010) 526 final, 2010/0280 (COD); adopted as Council Regulation (EU) No. 1175/2011 of the European Parliament and of the Council of 16 November 2011, O.J. L 2011/306/12; proposal for a Council Regulation (EU) amending Regulation (EC) No. 146/97 on speeding up and clarifying the implementation of the excessive deficit procedure, COM(2010) 522 final, 2010/0276 (COD); adopted as Council Regulation (EU) No. 1177/2011 of the European Parliament and of the Council of 8 November 2011, O.J. L 2011/306/33.

148 Proposal for a Regulation of the European Parliament and of the Council on the prevention and correction of macroeconomic imbalances, COM(2010) 527 final, 2010/0281 (COD); adopted as Council Regulation (EU) No. 1176/2011 of the European Parliament and of the Council of 16 November 2011, O.J. L 2011/306/25.

149 Proposal for a Council Directive on requirements for budgetary frameworks of the Member States, COM(2010) 523 final, 2010/0277 (NLE); adopted as Council Directive 2011/85/EU of 8 November 2011, O.J. L 2011/306/41.

150 Proposal for a Regulation of the European Parliament and of the Council on the effective enforcement of budgetary surveillance in the euro area, COM(2010) 524 final, 2010/0278 (COD); adopted as Regulation (EU) No. 1173/2011 of the European Parliament and of the Council of 16 November 2011, O.J. L 2011/306/01.

151 Proposal for a Regulation of the European Parliament and of the Council on enforcement measures to correct excessive macroeconomic imbalances in the euro area, COM(2010) 525 final, 2010/0279 (COD); adopted as Regulation (EU) No. 1174/2011 of the European Proposals 522 and 526 final, p. 3.

152 Proposals 522 and 526 final, p. 3.

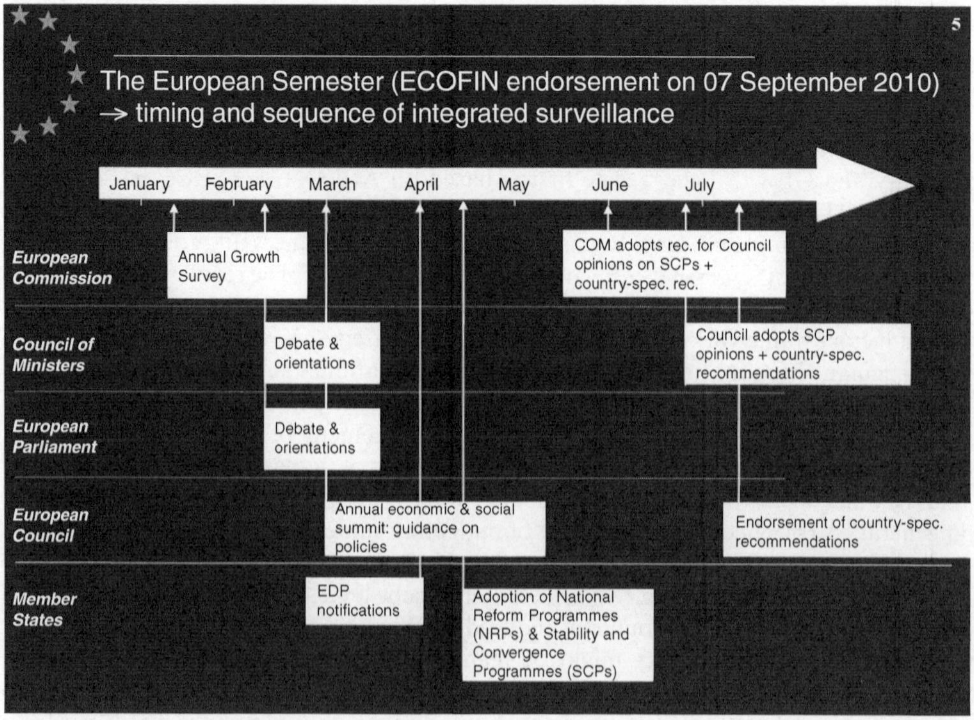

Source: European Commission, MEMO/10/456 of 29 September 2010.

Figure 16.1 The European Semester

decision with a qualified majority. It is assumed that such a majority will be difficult to rally and that sanctions will be the normal case.

The package will in the end also contain a "European Semester" (Figure 16.1) to integrate the multitude of provisions into the national decision-making process.

The package clearly contains elements of a common fiscal policy for the Member States and a first step towards a macroeconomic guidance. In some respects it reminds of the "planification" in France and the "global steering" of the economy (*Globalsteuerung*) which had been attempted in Germany from 1966 onward but had largely failed. On the other hand it will provide the demanded increase of transparency in the budgetary process of the Member States.[153]

To overcome the alleged weaknesses, pressure increased in 2011 to amend the rules on fiscal stability of Member States not only at the level of secondary law but also of primary law. Such an amendment of the primary law requires, however, unanimity, according to Article 48 TEU. As the UK refused to cooperate at the meeting of Heads of State or Government on 30 January 2012, a separate "Treaty on Stability, Coordination and Governance in the Economic and Monetary Union," including a new "fiscal compact,"

[153] Burda and Gerlach (2010), p. 66.

was agreed on by the European leaders at an informal meeting excluding the UK and the Czech Republic. It was concluded that the Treaty is

> aimed at strengthening fiscal discipline and introducing more automatic sanctions and stricter surveillance within the euro area, in particular by introducing a "balanced budget rule". According to the new "fiscal compact" treaty, national budgets are required to be in balance or in surplus, a criterion that would be met if the annual structural government deficit does not exceed 0.5% of nominal GDP. This balanced budget rule must be incorporated within one year into the member states' national legal systems, at constitutional level or equivalent. In the event of deviation from this rule, an automatic correction mechanism would be triggered. It will be defined by each member state on the basis of principles proposed by the European Commission.

The Treaty will be formally signed as an instrument of the Law of Nations at the beginning of March 2012 and has to be ratified by the signatory states.

6 OVERALL ANALYSIS

From the beginning it was an almost relentless mantra of economists that it was not a question of *whether* the single currency would fail but only *when*. To their surprise, the technical introduction procedure went smoothly even though it had been judged as challenging. But this did not discontinue their criticism. Each of the following movements of the dollar–euro exchange rate was accompanied by critical comments and the inevitable prediction of the imminent end of the common currency – regardless of whether it went up or down. It never seemed to reach a level which satisfied economic analysts.

6.1 The "Instrumental" View of the Currency

At the various steps of the introduction of the Monetary Union, economists and politicians had debated extensively, what the "right" path was to be taken.[154] The "economist" view, which included the majority of German economists, considered the removal of all obstacles to a truly integrated single market as essential.[155] The introduction of the common currency would follow almost automatically and was seen as a kind of "coronation" of the economic integration. In contrast, the "monetarist" approach regarded the introduction of the single currency as a tool to enhance (economic) integration. The underlying economic facts and prerequisites for the functioning of a monetary union would play a minor role in this way of thinking.[156] For many economists this was "highly questionable."[157]

Even so, the "monetarist" approach appears to have prevailed, especially as fixed dates were set for the start of the single currency. However, economic facts played a

---

[154] For an early discussion see Mundell (1961), p. 662, who reduces the analysis finally to the question whether Western Europe can be considered to be a "single region," defined by internal factor mobility and external factor immobility, which is to his view essentially "an empirical problem."

[155] It was mainly the Bundesbank seconded by the Dutch central bank which insisted that economic union had to precede monetary union, see for details and references including internal papers Marsh (2009), p. 54 et seq.

[156] For details see: Szász (1999), p. 9; Issing (2008c), p. 302; Marsh (2009), pp. 39–41, 53–7.

[157] Issing (2008c), p. 302; for an early opposite view see Scitkovsky (1958), chapter 2.

strong role in the process. Not a common economic policy was prescribed in the Treaty, but at least strong coordination mechanisms. Not a truly common fiscal policy was installed, but numerical goals for budget deficits were set up, however arbitrary they might be. The vast majority of federal states – with one currency – did not nearly have any similar goals at that time. This is too often ignored in public debates. The admission criteria were almost purely based on economic coherence even if there was room for discretion.

The majority of the framers of the Monetary Union, especially political leaders, assigned the Monetary Union and the single currency the "role of a pacemaker towards political union." Objections were expressed, but mainly from sources which altogether opposed the goal of an evolvement of the European Communities into a federal state.[158] Others thought more in the categories of the Werner plan: development into a political union *parallel* to the introduction of the single currency.[159] However, the question remains whether "integration via the Economy"[160] is a viable approach. Especially using the project of a single currency to foster political objectives raises concerns. From an economist's point of view, it seems hard to perceive how the common currency can promote political unification. Doubts are also expressed that a strong single currency could work as a political prestige project reducing the "might" of the U.S. dollar.[161] On the other hand, the modern "fiat" money is always based on political decisions and is tied closely to legal rules enacted by a sovereign.[162] It is a creation of the legal system, at least the monetary basis of central bank money.[163] As a result, the act of creating a common currency constitutes *in itself* the formation of a closer political union. Another question is the hope or expectation that *additional* political objectives may be achieved by using it and by the working of its institutions.

6.2 The Performance of the Euro

When looking at the overall performance of the euro and the ESCB, it has been a *great success*, both economically and politically. The euro did extremely well during the present financial crisis. The sovereign debt problems of some Member States are predominantly a problem of the Union and of the other Member States if they feel obliged to help but *not* of the monetary system.[164] The U.S. dollar is not endangered because the states of California and Illinois are de facto insolvent and have no legal claim of support by the federal government. An indicator of the success is also the increase in the number of Member States which have been admitted to the euro from 11 to 17 members. Of course, part of this might be the result of strategic behavior, but costs and benefits for the single member have to be analyzed more in depth. Even among skeptical economists there is

158 Mainly the then Prime Minister Margret Thatcher, see Issing (2008c), p. 304.
159 Issing (2008c), p. 303 et seq. with many details.
160 Described by Issing (2008c), p. 299 et seq.
161 Skeptical Issing (2008c), p. 303.
162 Mishkin (2004), p. 48.
163 Groundbreaking despite all criticism, Knapp (1905), pp. 53 et seq., 123, 131, 145.
164 Heun (1998), p. 873 et seq.

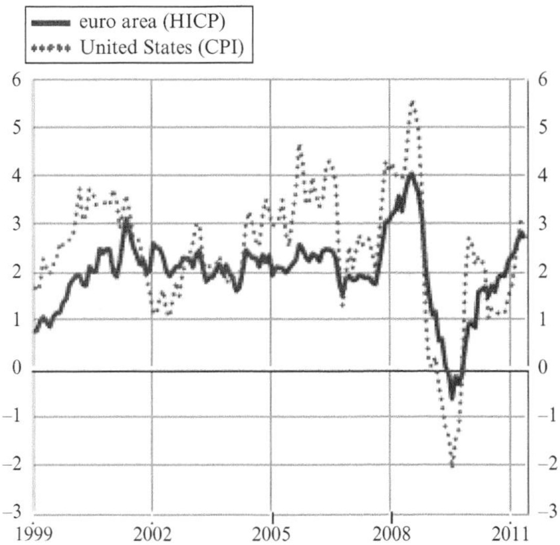

Note: Latest observation refers to April 2011 for the United States and to May 2011 for the euro area.

Source: European Central Bank, *Monthly Bulletin*, June 2011, p. 12.

Figure 16.2 Overall consumer price inflation (year-on-year percentage changes)

little doubt about the performance of the euro as a strong and stable currency, which enjoys worldwide acceptance and is increasingly used as a reserve currency.[165]

The primary objective of *price stability* has been fully achieved. The average annual rate of inflation has been below 2 percent (see Figures 16.2–16.4). By this, the official goal of the ECB has been fulfilled. Overall, the euro has performed better in this respect than the German mark which serves as an unofficial benchmark.

The *external value* of the euro has increased for over ten years. Few currencies have appreciated towards the euro during recent years. The exchange rate to the U.S. dollar remains at an almost all-time high, despite the alleged "euro-crisis." It is of secondary importance whether this outcome (partially) reflects only the weakness of the dollar. The euro has been stable and remained above its fundamental value, which is widely assumed to be between 1.10 and 1.20 USD per euro. (See Figures 16.5 and 16.6)

The above should be kept in mind despite the constant criticism from "experts." Once the exchange rate approaches 1.60, it is allegedly far too high and damages the export sector. As soon as it falls below 1.30, critics assume the end of the euro and a dissolution of the monetary union.

The envisaged *reduction of transaction costs* has also been achieved. Such costs essentially originate from the following sources: transformation of prices into a former currency, procuring and keeping foreign currency, and the risk of exchange rate changes. The latter can, of course, be insured against by means of modern financial instruments

[165] Baldwin and Gros (2010), p. 3; comprehensive coverage by the European Commission (2008); see also the contributions in: Bishop et al. (2008).

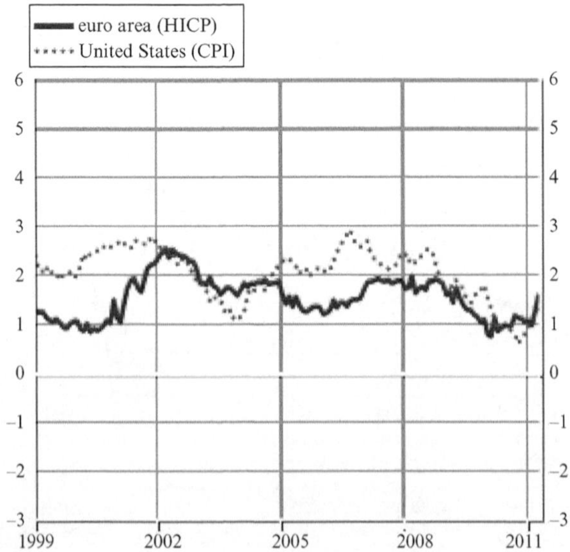

Note: Latest observation refers to April 2011.

Source: European Central Bank, *Monthly Bulletin*, June 2011, p. 12.

Figure 16.3 Consumer price inflation excluding energy and food (year-on-year percentage changes)

but only at a premium. Estimates of the positive effects of the reduced transaction costs run up to 0.5 percent p.a. of additional average growth for the Eurozone as a whole. In addition to that, manifold non-monetary benefits were created for consumers.

Long-term interest rates have been kept low, for some Members of the Eurozone far below the level they had to pay before the introduction of the euro (see Table 16.1). This is not only due to the introduction of the single currency but that is part of it. Low real long-term interest rates in general lead to a reduction in financing costs and may induce (additional) investments. The low interest rates in the Eurozone have, however, proven to be a mixed blessing. They contributed to the rise of a real estate bubble in Ireland and Spain. What was even more detrimental was that they induced several southern European states to increase their consumptive government spending, financed by credits, to a level which was not sustainable. This is, however, not a flaw of the Monetary Union but rather the result of autonomous political and economic decisions, partially in disregard of EU law.

The mere existence of the Monetary Union has been a stabilizing factor in the *present crisis*. An almost certain run for devaluation with severe destabilizing effects could be avoided. A speculative attack on a small currency is also easier than against a big currency which is widely used. Massive intervention by central banks would not have prevented the collapse of the exchange rate system,[166] e.g. in 1969 or 1992 when the dimension of economic and political strains on currencies was far smaller.

[166] Issing (2008c), p. 301.

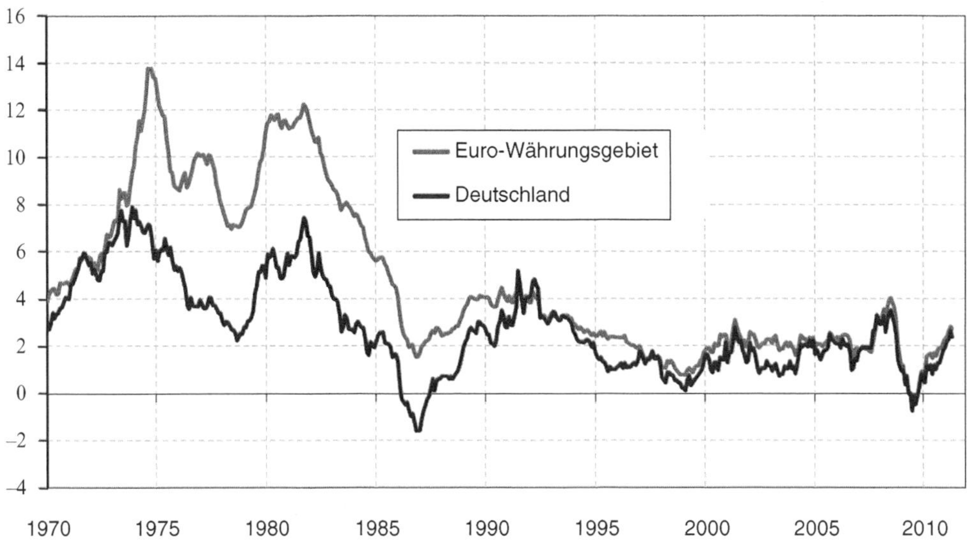

Source: Jürgen Stark, Staatsschuld und Geldpolitik: Lehren aus der globalen Finanzkrise, Rede, Münchner Seminare: CES ifo Group Munich & Süddeutsche Zeitung, Munich, 20 June 2011, slide 2 (European Central Bank).

Figure 16.4 Harmonized index of consumer prices (annual percentage change)

6.3 The Alleged Structural Flaws of the Monetary Union

Economists had been critical of the Monetary Union from the beginning. In their view the European Monetary Union simply could not work, or maybe it should not work.[167] Several fundamental structural flaws are emphasized:

1. unsuitable area for a common currency
2. lack of a state backing the currency
3. insufficient political integration
4. lack of a truly common fiscal policy.

6.3.1 Unsuitable currency area

In the past, governments had quite often tried to solve budgetary problems by lowering the internal or external value of the currency or both: inflation and/or depreciation. Both mechanisms had regularly not improved the internal economic strength of a country in the long run. The often deep-rooted structural problems could only have been solved by a combined effort of the government and the economic agents. It is usually a painful and long-lasting endeavor, which it was lacking. In a monetary union depreciation of

---

[167] Informative is the comprehensive review of the American economic publications on the topic by Jonung/Drea (2009) with the title: “The Euro: It Can’t Happen. It’s a Bad Idea. It Won’t Last.”

Source: European Central Bank, *Monthly Bulletin*, June 2011, S 73.

Figure 16.5 Euro effective exchange rates (EER-20) (monthly averages, 1999 Q1=100)

the currency is not available any more and inflation is substantially limited as long as monetary policy follows the primary goal of price stability, as prescribed by the primary law of the Union.

In view of this reduction of freedom of choice for governments in the area of a single currency, it can be asked whether the EU has been and is a suitable area for a single currency.[168] The theory of optimal currency areas concentrates on

168 American economists were almost only focused on the optimal currency area theory, and that in static way. They mainly did a cost–benefit analysis comparing fully flexible exchange rates with a permanently fixed rate aloof from the real (institutional) setup in Europe. In addition to that, they did not take sufficiently into account the existing factors of political economy in favor of a closer European integration; see Jonung and Drea (2009), pp. 28–30; see also Wilms (1998); Seiter (2002), p. 176–96 who judges the theory as little helpful.

Source: European Central Bank, *Monthly Bulletin*, June 2011, S 73.

Figure 16.6 Bilateral exchange rates (monthly averages, 1999 Q1=100)

regions.[169] An optimal area for a currency is a region, defined by internal factor mobility and external factor immobility.[170] Later the degree of openness of an economy, the product diversity and the stability of real exchange rates were added. The stability of the real exchange rates eventually became the dominant indicator for the convergence of an area necessary for a common currency.[171] Altogether the emphasis was on the cost side. The benefits of a common currency were taken into account later. They are difficult to assess but can – even in theory – turn the evaluation to the positive.

169 Mundell (1961), p. 660.

170 Mundell (1961), p. 661.

171 See the overview at Wilms (1998), pp. 42–6. It is also considered to be the best indicator for both banking crises and currency crises, see Reinhart and Rogoff (2009), p. 381 et seq.

Table 16.1 Macroeconomic performance indicators

		Period averages					
		Euro area		Denmark, Sweden, UK		United States	
		1989–98	1989–2008	1989–98	1999–2008	1989–98	1999–2008
Real GDP	% rate of change	2.2	2.1	2.0	2.7	3.0	2.6
Real GDP per capita	% rate of change	1.9	1.6	1.7	2.2	1.8	1.6
Real GDP per capita	index, US = 100	73	72	74	76	100	100
Employment	% rate of change	0.6	1.3	0.1	0.9	1.5	1.0
Labour productivity	% rate of change	1.6	0.8	1.9	1.8	1.5	1.6
Unemployment	% of labor force	9.3	8.3	7.9	5.2	5.8	5.0
Inflation	%	3.3	2.2	3.4	1.7	3.3	2.8
Fiscal balance	% of GDP	−4.3	−1.7	−3.6	−0.9	−3.3	−2.5
Gross public debt	% of GDP	68.6	68.6	48.7	43.0	67.8	60.7
Long-term interest rate	%	8.1	4.4	8.6	4.9	7.1	4.8
Real long-term interest rate	%	4.7	2.4	4.2	3.3	4.3	2.4

Source: European Commission, *EMU@10*, 2008, p. 19.

Altogether it boils down to an empirical assessment[172] but there is no predefined borderline as it is mainly a dimensional rather than a categorical difference.

When evaluating the different factors, it must not be forgotten that the introduction of the Monetary Union was primarily a political decision and not an economic development.[173] The economic calculation has to be extended by the political benefits derived from such a decision. So a *mere* economic view is too narrow.[174] This does not, however, imply that economic *facts* can or should be neglected in a political project with an economic objective or on "economic rails." Hence, a political project of this kind comes at a cost. The political decision-making bodies have to realize – and some did from the beginning[175] – that such a project might lead to specific expenditures that have to be financed by somebody.

As a result, the introduction of the single currency and the acceptance of new members have to be judged by the marginal net benefit or net cost of the whole project including all political aspects. Although, once a decision has been taken, the cost–benefit structure changes dramatically compared with the ex ante situation.

6.3.2 A currency without a state

A common criticism had been that it would be impossible – or at least not suitable – to form a monetary union without a political union. As a minimum, a well-coordinated economic policy and a common fiscal policy of the members of the Monetary Union

172 Mundell (1961), p. 662.

173 Supra, Section 2.1; acknowledged by Mishkin (2004), p. 49.

174 See Jonung and Drea (2009), p. 30. Wilms (1998), p. 49 considers only an import of credibility and of the efficiency of the monetary policy as a benefit on the macro level.

175 E.g. former German President Richard von Weizsäcker, see Issing (2008c), p. 303.

was considered to be indispensable. In effect, it was also contended that a strong central bank needed a counterpart which would speak with one voice. In addition, it was argued that in times of a crisis, a monetary system needed a clear governmental unit to bear the financial burdens of rescue operations – both for private financial institutions and for governments.

This assessment is partially due to an outdated understanding of a central bank as a commercial unit which has to keep its balance sheet balanced and might need fresh capital when its equity is diminished. However, this does not hold for a public law entity which has the right to produce the money with which it can pay its bills. There is no need – other than for monetary policy reasons – to reduce or even pay out its debt with the consequence of a financial burden to distribute. Partially this view is based on an economic theory of the role of a central bank which might be true in the U.S. but is definitely false in the EU: the ECB is by no means allowed to finance any public sector entity. Even exceptional circumstances do not justify such a serious breach of the law. Otherwise common robbery could be justified too.

Moreover, from a legal point of view it was stipulated that only a state could have a currency and not a supranational organization such as the European Union.[176] For this reason attempts were undertaken to construe the euro as the currency not of the EU but of a group of sovereign states united to form the currency. However, if the appropriate sovereign powers are transferred to a body governing it, no convincing legal reasons exist why a currency cannot exist without a state backing it.[177] Even if the ECB is not considered to be a pillar of the Union but an independent specialized organization of Community law,[178] the ECB within the framework of the ESCB can act as a governing body set up by public law based on a treaty. Historically, even full-fledged states have been established by contract, e.g. the Norddeutsche Bund and its successor, the German Reich of 1870, which is often not mentioned.

6.3.3 Deficits in political integration

As early as 1957 J.E. Meade had stated that a monetary union even of the then only six members of the EEC would require a "single European government." According to his view, "such a government would have to be able to control central-bank monetary policy and governmental budgetary policy throughout Europe."[179] A closer look reveals, however, that a monetary system is not necessarily tied to a (centralized) political system as long as the free flow of goods, labor, and capital is guaranteed, the monetary institutions are granted sufficient powers and independence from politics, and structural discrepancies are being taken care of.[180] This is especially true under the assumption that the monetary system has price stability as its primary objective and no other economic

---

176 See Torrent (1999), p. 1229.

177 Implicitly accepted by Zilioli and Selmayr (2000), p. 643.

178 Zilioli and Selmayr (2000), pp. 621, 643.

179 Meade (1957), p. 388.

180 These are in principle the preconditions Meade (1957) is requiring too and which did not exit in 1957 for the EEC. Only his requirement of one central government is not met but this did not exist with the described powers in federal states. His focus is too much on England, which cannot serve as a role model for federal systems.

policy goals such as growth or employment. It has to be kept in mind that the institutional setup of the Federal Reserve System of the U.S. differs considerably in this respect from the monetary union of the EU.[181]

However, there is a strong call for a political union.[182] The deficit of political integration can be specified as an unfulfilled want of an economic and fiscal government. It is a strongly debated question whether the rules of the primary law (Articles 119–26 TFEU) and of the Stability and Growth Pact have to be expanded to create a body which could be called an *economic government of the EU*. This entity would outline a common economic and fiscal policy and would decide on specific questions of common concern. The proposed economic governance package is a step in this direction.[183]

Yet, such a development could also be judged as a danger for the stability of the currency and the independence of the ECB. Instead of changing the rules, the existing rules ought to be obeyed more strictly.[184]

6.3.4 Lack of a common fiscal policy

A common fiscal policy is *not* indispensable for the functioning of a monetary union. Unsustainable budget deficits and debt levels alone do not destabilize a currency. Contrary to widespread belief, there is no direct link between an irresponsible fiscal policy and the *monetary system* as long as the financing of a fiscal deficit by the central bank is *effectively inhibited* and an obligation for support does not exist. Effective independence is decisive for this.[185] The empirical studies about a contagion between deficit crises and currency crises are usually based on the existence of a national currency, which does not exist in the European Monetary Union.[186] It is an open question whether the EU (not the Monetary Union) could withstand the aggregate pressure of media, politicians, financial institutions and speculators when a Member State would not pay its debt, however small it may be in relation to the whole Union.

Nevertheless, budget deficits and sovereign debt levels are definitely a good predictor for the solvency of a state in the medium range.[187] It is, however, an open question whether the insolvency of a Member State would not be used to put pressure on the institutions of the monetary system, not only through politics but also through the media, which are unwilling or unable to see the difference between a budget problem and a currency problem. In the past many governments tried to solve their budgetary problems by manipulating the monetary system. However, this cannot simply be assumed to happen in the Monetary Union. Even though these manipulations have a long tradition there has been a change: they are legally impossible in the European Monetary Union. It would be

---

181 Mishkin (2004), pp. 350 et seq., 413.

182 See e.g. de Grauwe (2010), p. 31.

183 Supra Section 5.

184 Issing (2008c), p. 306; strongly in favor of a new institutional framework for the euro area including an amendment of the Stability and Growth Pact, new stability rules fort the financial markets, and a European crisis resolution mechanism, Sachverständenrat (2010), p. 89 et seq.

185 See already Heun (1998), p. 873 et seq.

186 See the overview at Karb (2006), p. 168 et seq.

187 Karb (2006), pp. 96, 267.

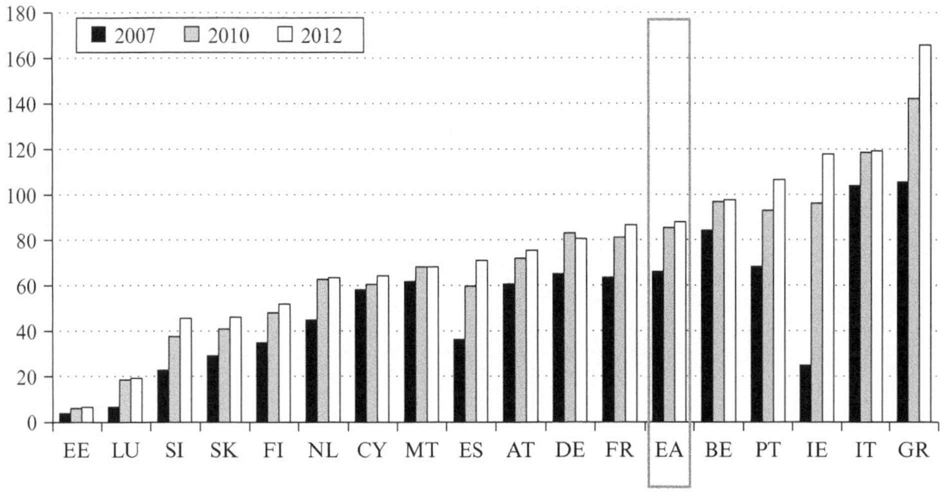

Source: Jürgen Stark, "Staatsschuld und Geldpolitik: Lehren aus der globalen Finanzkrise", Rede, Münchner Seminare: CES ifo Group Munich & Süddeutsche Zeitung, Munich, 20 June 2011, slide 12 (European Central Bank).

Figure 16.7 Debt of general governments (percentage of GDP)

a clear breach of the law, even under extraordinary circumstances. Yet pressure might be increased on the ECB.

So it is prudent to *prevent* budget crises and the insolvency of a Member State. This could be done through sanctions of the markets which are responsible for an unsustainable deficit. However, markets tend to react (too) late and not always in a rational manner.[188] Serious regulatory flaws have also contributed considerably to the malfunction of market forces.[189] The lack of a common fiscal policy might also reduce the ability to even out the upturns and downturns in the course of the cyclical movements of the economy.[190] Hence, effectively enforced legal norms are perhaps the only way to prevent the insolvency of a state.

The norms and the practice, especially the Stability and Growth Pact, allegedly did not fulfill their purpose.[191] Usually the debt criteria are used to demonstrate this without taking into account that they are not strict limits but reference values.[192]

Figure 16.7 and Tables 16.2 and 16.3 demonstrate why it was prudent by the Maastricht Treaty to establish rules about a sustainable fiscal policy of the participating

188 This was known already at the time of framing the monetary union: "Report on economic and monetary union in the European Community," OPOCE, 1989, p. 24; later Beson, in "L'euro dix ans après," Colloque de la CEDECE, 18 June 2010.

189 Infra 6.4.4. Siekmann (2010), pp. 99, 101.

190 Eichengreen (1994), p. 183 et seq.

191 Baldwin and Gros (2010), p. 4; Burda and Gerlach (2010), p. 65; Sachverständigenrat (2010), p. 89 et seq.; earlier similarily Feldmann (2003).

192 Baldwin and Gros (2010), p. 5.

Table 16.2 Net lending/borrowing of general governments (percentage of GDP)

	5-year averages							Spring 2011 forecast			Autumn 2010 forecast	
	1992–96	1997–01	2002–06	2006	2007	2008	2009	2010	2011	2012	2011	2012
Belgium	−5.4	−0.7	−0.6	0.1	−0.3	−1.3	−5.9	−4.1	−3.7	−4.2	−4.6	−4.7
Germany	−3.0	−1.6	−3.3	−1.6	0.3	0.1	−3.0	−3.3	−2.0	−1.2	−2.7	−1.8
Estonia		−0.5	1.5	2.4	2.5	−2.8	−1.7	0.1	−0.6	−2.4	−1.9	−2.7
Ireland	−1.7	2.4	1.2	2.9	0.1	−7.3	−14.3	−32.4	−10.5	−8.8	−10.3	−9.1
Greece	−9.6	−4.2	−5.8	−5.7	−6.4	−9.8	−15.4	−10.5	−9.5	−9.3	−7.4	−7.6
Spain	−5.6	−1.9	0.4	2.0	1.9	−4.2	−11.1	−9.2	−6.3	−5.3	−6.4	−5.5
France	−4.9	−2.1	−3.2	−2.3	−2.7	−3.3	−7.5	−7.0	−5.8	−5.3	−6.3	−5.8
Italy	−6.3	−2.2	−3.5	−3.4	−1.5	−2.7	−5.4	−4.6	−4.0	−3.2	−4.3	−3.5
Cyprus		−3.6	−3.7	−1.2	3.4	0.9	−6.0	−5.3	−5.1	−4.9	−5.7	−5.7
Luxembourg	1.6	4.5	0.6	1.4	3.7	3.0	−0.9	−1.7	−1.0	−1.1	−1.3	−1.2
Malta		−7.6	−5.2	−2.8	−2.4	−4.5	−3.7	−3.6	−3.0	−3.0	−3.0	−3.3
Netherlands	−3.3	0.0	−1.3	0.5	0.2	0.6	−5.5	−5.4	−3.7	−2.3	−3.9	−2.8
Austria	−4.1	−1.6	−2.0	−1.6	−0.9	−0.9	−4.1	−4.6	−3.7	−3.3	−3.6	−3.3
Portugal	−4.6	−3.3	−3.9	−4.1	−3.1	−3.5	−10.1	−9.1	−5.9	−4.5	−4.9	−5.1
Slovenia		−3.1	−2.0	−1.4	−0.1	−1.8	−6.0	−5.6	−5.8	−5.0	−5.3	−4.7
Slovakia		−7.6	−3.9	−3.2	−1.8	−2.1	−8.0	−7.9	−5.1	−4.6	−5.3	−5.0

Finland	−5.8	2.7	3.1	4.0	5.2	4.2	−2.6	−2.5	−1.0	−0.7	−1.6	−1.2
Euro area	−5.0	−1.6	−2.5	−1.4	−0.7	−2.0	−6.3	−6.0	−4.3	−3.5	−4.6	−3.9
Bulgaria		0.5	0.6	1.9	1.1	1.7	−4.7	−3.2	−2.7	−1.6	−2.9	−1.8
Czech Republic		−4.4	−4.5	−2.6	−0.7	−2.7	−5.9	−4.7	−4.4	−4.1	−4.6	−4.2
Denmark	−2.5	0.9	2.6	5.2	4.8	3.2	−2.7	−2.7	−4.1	−3.2	−4.3	−3.5
Latvia		−1.4	−1.2	−0.5	−0.3	−4.2	−9.7	−7.7	−4.5	−3.8	−7.9	−7.3
Lithuania		−4.9	−1.1	−0.4	−1.0	−3.3	−9.5	−7.1	−5.5	−4.8	−7.0	−6.9
Hungary		−5.2	−8.0	−9.3	−5.0	−3.7	−4.5	−4.2	1.6	−3.3	−4.7	−6.2
Poland		−3.9	−4.9	−3.6	−1.9	−3.7	−7.3	−7.9	−5.8	−3.6	−6.6	−6.0
Romania		−4.0	−1.6	−2.2	−2.6	−5.7	−8.5	−6.4	−4.7	−3.6	−4.9	−3.5
Sweden	−7.7	1.0	0.6	2.3	3.6	2.2	−0.7	0.0	0.9	2.0	−0.1	1.0
United Kingdom	−6.1	0.5	−3.0	−2.7	−2.7	−5.0	−11.4	−10.4	−8.6	−7.0	−8.6	−6.4
EU		−1.4	−2.5	−1.5	−0.9	−2.4	−6.8	−6.4	−4.7	−3.8	−5.1	−4.2
USA	−4.2	0.3	−3.7	−2.0	−2.8	−6.2	−11.2	−11.2	−10.0	−8.6	−8.9	−7.9
Japan	−2.5	−7.3	−6.1	−1.6	−2.4	−2.2	−8.7	−9.3	−9.7	−9.8	−6.4	−6.3

Note: ESA 79 up to 1994. ESA 95 from 1995 onwards

Source: *European Commission*, European Economic Forecast, Spring 2011, p. 221.

Table 16.3 Gross debt of general governments (percentage of GDP)

									Spring 2011 forecast		Autumn 2010 forecast	
	2003	2004	2005	2006	2007	2008	2009	2010	2011	2012	2011	2012
Belgium	98.5	94.2	92.1	88.1	84.2	89.6	96.2.	96.8	97.0	97.5	100.5	102.1
Germany	63.9	65.8	68.0	67.6	64.9	66.3	73.5	83.2	82.4	81.1	75.9	75.2
Estonia	5.6	5.0	4.6	4.4	3.7	4.6	7.2	6.6	6.1	6.9	9.5	11.7
Ireland	30.9	29.6	27.4	24.8	25.0	44.4	65.6	96.2	112.0	117.9	107.0	114.3
Greece	97.4	98.9	100.3	106.1	105.4	110.7	127.1	142.8	157.7	166.1	150.2	156.0
Spain	48.7	46.2	43.0	39.6	36.1	39.8	53.3	60.1	68.1	71.0	69.7	73.0
France	62.9	64.9	66.4	63.7	63.9	67.7	78.3	81.7	84.7	86.8	86.8	89.8
Italy	104.4	103.9	105.9	106.6	103.6	106.3	116.1	119.0	120.3	119.8	120.2	119.9
Cyprus	68.9	70.2	69.1	64.6	58.3	48.3	58.0	60.8	62.3	64.3	65.2	68.4
Luxembourg	6.1	6.3	6.1	6.7	6.7	13.6	14.6	18.4	17.2	19.0	19.6	20.9
Malta	69.3	72.4	69.6	64.2	62.0	61.5	67.6	68.0	68.0	67.9	70.8	70.9
Netherlands	52.0	52.4	51.8	47.4	45.3	58.2	60.8	62.7	63.9	64.0	66.6	67.3
Austria	65.5	64.8	63.9	62.1	60.7	63.8	69.6	72.3	73.8	75.4	72.0	73.3
Portugal	55.9	57.6	62.8	63.9	68.3	71.6	83.0	93.0	101.7	107.4	88.8	92.4
Slovenia	27.3	27.4	26.7	26.4	23.1	21.9	35.2	38.0	42.8	46.0	44.8	47.6
Slovakia	42.4	41.5	34.2	30.5	29.6	27.8	35.4	41.0	44.8	46.8	45.1	47.4

Finland	44.5	44.4	41.7	39.7	35.2	34.1	43.8	48.4	50.6	52.2	51.1	53.0
Euro area (a)	69.0	69.4	70.0	68.4	66.2	69.9	79.3	85.4	87.7	88.5	86.5	87.8
Bulgaria	44.4	37.0	27.5	21.6	17.2	13.7	14.6	16.2	18.0	18.6	20.2	20.8
Czech Republic	29.8	30.1	29.7	29.4	29.0	30.0	35.3	38.5	41.3	42.9	43.1	45.2
Denmark	47.2	45.1	37.8	32.1	27.5	34.5	41.8	43.6	45.3	47.1	47.5	49.2
Latvia	14.6	14.9	12.4	10.7	9.0	19.7	36.7	44.7	48.2	49.4	51.9	56.6
Lithuania	21.1	19.4	18.4	18.0	16.9	15.6	29.5	38.2	40.7	43.6	42.8	48.3
Hungary	58.3	59.1	61.8	65.7	66.1	72.3	78.4	80.2	75.2	72.7	80.1	81.6
Poland	47.1	45.7	47.1	47.7	45.0	47.1	50.9	55.0	55.4	55.1	57.2	59.6
Romania	21.5	18.7	15.8	12.4	12.6	13.4	23.6	30.8	33.7	34.8	33.4	34.1
Sweden	51.7	50.3	50.4	45.0	40.2	38.8	42.8	39.8	36.5	33.4	38.9	37.5
United Kingdom	39.0	40.9	42.5	43.4	44.5	54.4	69.6	80.0	84.2	87.9	83.5	86.6
EU (a)	61.8	62.2	62.8	61.5	59.0	62.3	74.4	80.2	82.3	83.3	81.8	83.3

Note: (a) Unconsolidated general government debt. For 2010, this implies a debt ratio, which is 0.3pp. higher for the euro area (0.2pp. higher for the EU) than the consolidated general government debt ratio (i.e. corrected for the intergovernmental loans) published by Eurostat on April 26, 2011.

Source: *European Commission*, European Economic Forecast, Spring 2011, p. 223.

states. This was done to *prevent* a situation where sanctions of the market (high interest rates, denial of loans) would have to be employed in order to remind a member of the Eurozone of its (legal) obligations.[193] The problem is, however, how to force Member States to follow the rules, especially big ones.[194] But this is not a specific European problem of the Monetary Union and Germany has faced similar problems inside the German federation for decades.

The widespread complaint about the lack of a common fiscal policy reveals some ignorance of the design and working of federal systems. The U.S. constitution does not provide for a common fiscal policy of the members of the federation. In contrast to Germany, it also does not interdict grants of the federal government to the states, conditional or unconditional. Often strings are attached to the grants which allow the federal government to exert considerable influence on the policy but this is far from a federal equalization system or even a common taxation.[195] So far there is no clear evidence that the great autonomy of the states in the U.S. has adversely affected the functioning of the dollar. Even the long-run discrepancies inside the U.S. have not threatened the stability of the whole system.

In essence, the EU appears to have more rules to secure a sound fiscal policy of its members than the U.S. has for its states, at least on a constitutional level; and no fundamental criticism exists that the U.S. dollar cannot work in a federation with so little common economic and fiscal policy. Especially rules on (balanced) budgets are definitely state law and requests for financial aid are turned down by the federal government.

Until 2009, the constitution of the Federal Republic of Germany also did *not* contain a clause restricting debt or deficit of the members of the federation. In the German constitution only a weak clause had been introduced in 1969 that both the central state (*Bund*) and its members (*Länder*) should align their fiscal policy to the requirements of the macroeconomic balance and that for *this* reason restrictions on borrowing could be imposed by the federation. In addition to that, it could be decreed that reserves were to be built up during an economic upswing which could be spent during a downturn to stimulate the economy. These rules were strictly reserved to fight business cycles and not to cope with structural deficits, and they played a minor role in practice. An adverse effect on the stability of the currency could not be noticed.

It was not until 2009 that the federal constitution of Germany was amended. For the first time binding rules on deficits for the states (*Länder*) were introduced by the central state (*Schuldenbremse*).[196] Until then the European Union had more legal rules directing the fiscal policy of its Member States than the Federal Republic of Germany, also

---

193 The governments ought to be exposed to the reactions of the markets on their fiscal policy, see Häde (2009), p. 402.

194 Buti (2007), p. 177; doubting the effectiveness of such rules in general, Eichengreen (1994), p. 176; Wyplosz (2010), p. 35: "sanctions cannot be really imposed on democratically elected governments" citing a former work written together with Eichengreen (in *Economic Policy*, vol. 26 (1997), pp. 65–114).

195 See Nicholson and Crotty (2008) investigating the impact of fiscal federalism in the U.S. on state taxation.

196 Article 1 No. 4 Gesetz zur Änderung des Grundgesetzes of 29 September 2009, BGBl I 2248, amending Article 109 of the federal constitution.

in comparison to the central government of Germany. This led to the awkward result – and it was one of the reasons for the fundamental changes to the fiscal federalism in Germany in 2009 – that the federal government could legally not force the Länder to avoid "excessive deficits" in order to fulfill Germany's obligations towards the European Union!

The amendments of the German constitution imposing stiffer rules on the Member States of the federation, abolishing the right of the Länder to run a structural deficit beginning with the fiscal year 2020, raised some constitutional concerns. This was due to the fact that it had been an undisputed right of the members of any form of federation to finance part of their budget by borrowing money. Interdicting any structural deficit except in times of disaster might have taken away too much "sovereignty" from the Länder. They would have lost an essential part of their "statehood" or "sovereignty." This would be a breach of the federal constitution since the amending power is limited in Germany according to Article 79 para. 3 of the federal constitution.[197] A case on this question is pending in the Federal Constitutional Court of Germany.

A similar problem might arise in the event that the EU is transformed into a federation with similar rules on budgets. In a somewhat enigmatic phrase the German Federal Constitutional Court pointed out that the constitution would not empower the representatives of Germany to enter into a federation and thus "give up the right to self-determination of the German people and its sovereignty according to the law of nations."[198] It added that changing the "identity" of the Union and acting *ultra vires* could render those acts of the Union inapplicable in Germany.

6.4 Support of Member States

6.4.1 Preliminary support mechanisms

If the lack of general support mechanisms is considered to be a structural flaw of the Monetary Union, this has been partially mitigated. A support specifically for Greece was organized ad hoc within a few days, followed by an unspecified (general) mechanism a few days later, based on Article 122 para. 2 TFEU. The legality of this procedure is not beyond any doubt, particularly the question of whether or not the prerequisites of that provision are fulfilled. However, the duration of that mechanism has been limited to two years for good reasons. Now a permanent mechanism is being set up including an amendment of the Treaty.

On 25 March 2010, the heads of state and government of the Eurozone Member States initially declared themselves willing to support Greece with bilateral loans in addition to assistance from the International Monetary Fund (IMF). On 23 April 2010, Greece applied for the financial assistance offered. At their meeting on 2 May 2010, Member States of the Eurogroup approved loans up to €110 billion. Individual countries sought to provide a total of €80 billion under strict lending terms which the IMF was to take over a share of €30 billion. The aid was basically granted as credit guarantees on a bilateral

197 New rules imposing rigid limits on the Länder to run a budget deficit are considered to be incompatible with Article 79 para. 3 of the federal constitution, see e.g. Hancke (2009), p. 626.

198 BVerfGE 123, 267 (347 f.) – Lisbon Treaty.

basis. Greece promised to solve its budgetary problems by a rigorous austerity program with spending cuts, tax rises and an overall reduction in social security benefits.

Whether the aid is conform with the principal provisions of the Treaty is questionable. The wording "assume the commitments" in Article 125 para. 1 TFEU would have to be interpreted in a way that new voluntary guarantees by Member States would not be covered. Article 122 para. 2 TFEU could be a basis when considering whether Greece's financial situation was the result of an "exceptional occurrence beyond the control" of Greece.

Only a few days after the rescue operations for Greece, the heads of states and governments of the Member States agreed on 7 May 2010 to set up a support mechanism on a much larger scale for potential financing problems of Member States. The details were further developed by the ministers of finance and economic affairs on 9 May 2010. It was designed to have an accumulated volume of €750 billion, distributed among three pillars:

- European Financial Stability Mechanism (EFSM) (60 billion)
- European Financial Stability Facility (EFSF) (440 billion)
- credits by the International Monetary Fund (IMF) (250 billion).

The lion's share of the aid shall be granted in the form of guarantees and not as direct payments. The good credit ratings of most Member States are to be used to refinance the outstanding debt at much lower costs than the failing countries could have attained. The whole support mechanism is designed to be only of temporary nature and will terminate in 2013.

The *European Financial Stability Mechanism* (EFSM) is an instrument of the European Union. It is financed from general funds of the Union and administered by the Commission.

The Regulation authorizing the Commission to take out loans on behalf of the European Union is expressly based on Article 122 para. 2 TFEU,[199] which allows for EU assistance in the event of natural disasters and other extraordinary emergencies beyond the control of the receiving country. Whether these conditions are actually present is not certain. By virtue of authorizing this borrowing, the highly controversial eurobonds have essentially already been created: not as a direct obligation of the Member States, but as an obligation of the EU. Not only would Member States of the Eurozone have to vouch for payment of these loans, but ultimately also those Member States who have not (yet) introduced the euro.

The *European Financial Stability Facility* (EFSF) has been designed as a special purpose vehicle to borrow money on the capital markets by issuing debt instruments guaranteed by those Member States not in need. The proceeds are passed on to the member in distress. This way there is no direct aid from Member States or the Union to other members. The volume of guarantees was distributed according to the share each member's central bank holds of the capital of the ECB. The liability is limited to that fraction. Technically it was set up on 7 June 2010 as a stock corporation under the law of Luxembourg with seat in Luxembourg City. The state of Luxembourg was the only

---

[199] Regulation (EU) No 407/2010 of 11 May 2010, O.J. L 2011/118/1.

shareholder in order to speed up its creation. The corporation issues bonds which are guaranteed by the various Member States and it was given the desired top rating by the rating agencies.[200] The shares of the corporation were transferred to the Member States of the euro group on a pro-rata basis, corresponding to the capital shares each national central bank holds in the ECB. Further details were outlined in a framework agreement, in which the contractual partners committed to dissolve the company on 30 June 2013, intended to ensure that the EFSF is not an institution of the EU. It was nonetheless still not certain whether its function is compatible with the provisions of European Union law.

While it does serve the requirement of keeping the EU together, the assistance could still be in violation of Article 125 TFEU, the so-called "no bail out" clause. An argument in favor of the latter contention is that the creators of the Maastricht Treaty intended for each state to bear the consequences of its own fiscal policies. If assistance can be expected as soon as the market's own sanctioning mechanisms begin to kick in – higher interest rates, for instance – there would be little incentive to actually adhere to the required sound budgetary policy. The consequences might threaten the coherence of the monetary union, but also that of the EU as a whole. The example of the US, where the federal government does not bail out states with budgetary problems but has one currency for an economic area that is hardly more homogenous than the Eurozone, shows a monetary union's continuation can only be ensured by strict refusal of general budgetary assistance when a Member State of the EU experiences financial distress.[201] A "no bail out" policy is essential and has to be taken seriously, as the creators of the Maastricht Treaty were fully aware.

Legal concerns were taken so seriously that less than a year later the primary laws of the EU were amended. The new Article 136 para. 3 TFEU was created, which now allows for financial support – under very strict conditions – from Member States whose currency is the euro. The important aspect to bear in mind is that this permission was not granted to the EU, but to Member States. Even if this clause can either be interpreted as a mere clarification or as a constitutive regulation, it still limits the freedom of Member States to provide assistance. Otherwise its narrow wording would not make sense.

Bilateral assistance to Greece and the EFSF was judged to be compatible with German constitutional law by the German Federal Constitutional Court in its ruling of 7 September 2011, with certain reservations. The court made no pronouncement on compatibility with EU law, although there would have been reasons for doing so. Above all, the court underscored observance of the budget autonomy of the German Bundestag. In very general terms, the court considers it to be impermissible for the parliament to transfer its "budgetary responsibility" by means of the "undefined budgetary policy authorizations of other agents." In particular, "nor is the law to give rise to mechanisms of a financial nature that [. . .] could lead to unmanageable charges affecting the budget in a significant way in the absence of prior constitutive agreement, whether through

---

200 See for details (2010), p. 973.

201 Henning and Kessler (2012), pp. 6–16, pointing out that this will almost automatically lead to "balanced budget rules" on the Member State level; see, for the convincing reasons for *not* introducing a bankruptcy option as an exit for Member States in financial distress, Spiotto (2011), p. 57 et seq. with telling statistics on the fiscal situation of the US and the Member States of the European monetary union (pp. 83–8); Burns (2011), p. 9 on state defaults in the US.

expenditures or loss of revenues." Budgetary authorities have to make their decisions "free of external decisions on the part of the bodies of the EU and other Member States of the European Union" and had to remain "masters of their own decisions." For this reason, no "permanent mechanisms of international law may be established that might in practice amount to liability for the free decisions of other nations." Yet the court demanded only individual authorization where measures of "great significance in the international or federal context are concerned." Insofar as "supranational agreements are made," which could be of "structural significance" to German budget laws, not only would each individual disposition require approval by the German Parliament, but the existence of adequate parliamentary influence over the manner in which available funds are treated would also have to be ensured.[202] This requirement may only be met by means of a very precise and detailed control of how receiving states manage their budgets on the part of the Federal Republic of Germany as the provider of financial assistance, including the involvement of the German Federal Court of Audit. This explains the ongoing debate over control of the use of assistance funds.

The involvement of the IMF in the support program gives rise to several legal questions. The fund was founded for the purpose of avoiding and rectifying imbalances in balance of payments accounts. However, that the financial support of Member States of the Eurozone is primarily aimed at correcting balance of payments divergences is by no means certain. Far more, it is the preservation of the solvency of public authorities that is the main issue. The designated receivers of this assistance share the same currency and have transferred their monetary sovereignty to the EU and its institutions. Yet the IMF is aimed at balancing out divergences between states with different currencies (articles I (iii) and V section 2(a) of the Agreement adopted at the Conference at Bretton Woods, 22 July 1944.

6.4.2 The support by the ECB

In addition to this three-pronged mechanism, the purchase by the ESCB of debt instruments issued by Member States since early summer 2010 has played a considerable and growing role with the result that a major share of the sovereign debt of the supported members or their banks is already held by the ECB. Only a fraction of it is actually bought and held by the ECB. The rest is carefully distributed among the national central banks. A "restructuring" of sovereign debt would now hit the ESCB to a great extent, although the potential size of that loss is hard to gauge as it is unknown at which discount the instruments were purchased.

The ECB also accepted government bonds of countries with budgetary problems as corollary – partially in conjunction with handing out credits to banks from countries in need. They in turn hold a large fraction of the sovereign debt of their home country. This could also be regarded as an "indirect" financing of sovereign debt by the ECB. The size of the loss in case of a default is hard to assess as well. However, it can be assumed that the corollary includes a sizable safety margin.

Mid-2011, the ECB and the national central banks of the Member States which introduced the euro resumed their securities market program and expanded it to the sover-

[202] Federal Constitutional Court (Bundesverfassungsgericht), Judgement of September 7, 2011 – 2 BvR 987/10, 2 BvR 1485/10, 2 BvR 1099/10 – at no 125–129, 133 et seq.

eign bonds of Italy and Spain. It reached a volume of more than €210 billion. They also substantially lowered the quality of collateral eligible for securing loans to the banking systems of various Member States with the intention to pass on the proceeds to their respective governments. This indirect financing of sovereign was intensified in December 2011 by a three years tender of €489 billion at 1 percent interest (LTRO I). This unusual and questionable operation was resumed at the end of February 2012 with additional €530 billion (LTRO II).[203] A repeat of this is scheduled for the end of February 2012.

The conduct of the ESCB has given rise to considerable concern. The tasks of the ESCB do not include rescuing insolvent banks, banking systems or sovereign public authorities by direct or indirect means, not even in times of extreme need. The primary law of the EU follows a strict separation of economic policy – including budgetary policy – (chapter 1 of part III, title VIII TFEU) and monetary policy (chapter 2 of part III, title VIII TFEU). This may not be compatible with Anglo-Saxon economic thinking and the legal situation in the US, but it is the law in the European monetary union. No independent economic or financial policy responsibilities were transferred to the ECB and the national central banks of the euro area.

It would make little sense to enumerate the "ESCB's fundamental purposes," were it able to assume further tasks in the absence of express authorization. The transfer of further responsibilities to it was rejected when the Maastricht Treaty was drawn up. The only item permitted was a contribution on the part of the "competent authorities" towards the "smooth implementation" of measures taken in the area of "supervision of credit institutions" and "the stability of the financial system." Nor would a sweeping prohibition on financing the loans of sovereign public authorities make any sense if bonds could be purchased on the secondary market virtually at whim. Eventually, this would be a violation of the fundamental principle of limited conferral of competences: "Competences not conferred upon the Union if the Treaties remain with the Member States" (Article 4 and Article 5 para. 2 phrase 2 TEU).

The short-term acquisition of debt instruments on the secondary market may be a further monetary policy measure within the permitted open market policy (Article 18.1 of the ESCB and ECB Statute). The ongoing purchase of government bonds can no longer be justified in terms of the requirements of a "monetary policy transmission mechanism" that is allegedly malfunctioning. This applies particularly to cases where bonds are held long-term. Purchasing programs, which are used to subsidize the interest rates that the market is demanding of solvent Member States down to manageable levels, are no longer monetary policy measures but belong to the realm of fiscal policy, which must be clearly distinguished from monetary policy. The primary laws of the EU unequivocally did not assign the ESCB competence over fiscal and growth policies. Directly or indirectly financing Member States of the EU on the part of the ESCB is, in any event, strictly prohibited. The introduction of a three year tender in December 2011 was an unusual measure, since the average remaining maturity of loans had been around thirty days until then. It has to be judged as a long-term capital injection to banks or sovereigns which is beyond the task of the ESCB.

---

[203] Tender no. 20110149, settled on 22 December 2011, matures 29 January 2015, volume €489.19bn.; tender no. 20120034, settled on 1 March 2012, matures 26 February 2015, volume €529.53bn.

6.4.3 Expanding the competences of the EFSF

On 21 July 2011, the heads of state and governments of the Eurozone announced that they sought to improve the effectiveness of the EFSF and increase its flexibility. While financial support was originally only supposed to be granted in the form of loan and loan facility agreements, support could now be provided in the form of inventory financing loans, lines of credit, loan commitments for recapitalizing financial institutions on behalf of the Member States in question and, in particular, by purchasing bonds on the primary and secondary markets. Interventions in the secondary market were only supposed to be carried out on the basis of ECB analysis, which was previously to confirm the existence of extraordinary market conditions and risks to financial stability. The scope of guarantees was at the same time raised to €780 billion. This was intended to bring the amount actually available to €440 billion. At the same time, interest rates were lowered for receiver countries and the assistances' terms to maturity were extended.

6.4.4 Creation of a permanent support mechanism

The heads of states and government agreed or 17 December 2010 to lay the basis for a permanent support mechanism.[204] As a consequence, at the beginning of July 2011, the Council of economics and finance ministers of the Eurozone signed a framework agreement for a new, permanent stabilizing mechanism meant to succeed both the EFSM and the EFSF. It was intended to enter into effect mid-2013, upon expiry of the temporary assistance mechanisms. At a meeting of the European Council on 9 December 2011, it was decided that the initiative would enter into force earlier, in July 2012. It was recognized that it would be legally prudent to structure it as a (multilateral) support of the members of the Eurozone and not of the EU.[205] That was also one of the reasons why Article 136 para. 3 TFEU was created to provide a sound legal basis for the permanent mechanism.

The German Bundestag has already approved the framework agreement of 11 July 2011, by means of the "Act Concerning the Giving of Guarantees within the Framework of a European Stabilization Mechanism." The most important components of the regulations are:

- A permanent stability mechanism, the European Stabilization Mechanism (ESM), is set up as an international financial institution.
- It is headed by a Board of Governors consisting of the finance ministers of the euro group and/or members of national governments of Member States in charge of the finances.
- Unanimous agreement is required for assistance to be granted.
- The ESM has €700 billion at its disposal. Of the latter amount €80 billion are to be paid in immediately.
- The respective shares of the Member States are once again a function of the capital share of the central banks of those states in the ECB. There is a special provision for Member States with below-average economic capabilities. This means that, unlike the EFSF, the institution will be able to dispose of its own capital.

---

[204] Draft European Council Document EUCO 30/10 of 17 December 2010.
[205] Thym (2011), p. 167.

- The Board of Governors may decide on a capital increase at any time, but only on the condition of mutual agreement. According to IMF procedure, the interest rate is to be one percentage point higher than the funding costs of the ESM; after three years it will be raised to two percentage points. The ESM is to enjoy seniority status over other creditors, subordinate only to the IMF.
- Identically-worded collective action clauses (rules for adapting bonds with a super-majority of bond holders) are to be added to the terms and conditions of all bonds of Eurozone states with terms to maturity of over three years. This is intended to garner the participation of private creditors in the burdens of debt restructuring.
- Assistance is only to be granted under strict conditions.
- The ESM should be able to take on bonds.
- The ESM should be allowed to acquire the bonds of Member States in the primary markets.
- Losses on the part of the ESM are initially to be borne by the institution itself, first from the capital paid in and then later by participating Member States on a pro-rata basis according to their shares.

The German Bundesbank welcomed the establishment of a mechanism as a last resort for warding off existential financial crises. However, three points would have to be observed: (1) the assistance payments must be bound to strict economic and financial policy restrictions; (2) interest rates must be reasonable; and (3) the involvement of credible private creditors in the event of state bankruptcy or default. The decisions of 21 July 2011, however, are in violation of these requirements. They imply another important step towards joint liability and less disciplining on the part of the capital markets, without noticeably enhancing options for control and influence on national financial policy by contrast.

On 9 December 2011, Eurozone heads of state and government agreed to make the following amendments:

- Participation of the private sector, by means of inserting standardized and identical collective action clauses in the terms and conditions of government bonds.
- Amendment of voting rights to include an emergency procedure.

There is also a general consensus to incorporate control on the part of courts of audit, an aspect that was not previously included in the wording of the contract. Unanimity concerning the ESM was attained at the summit meeting of all 27 Member States on 23 January 2012. The "Treaty Establishing the European Stability Mechanism" was signed 2 February 2012 and is in the process of ratification. In an emergency, the ESM may step in and make use of all the principal instruments at its disposal: bond purchases in the primary market, interventions in the secondary market, recapitalizing financial institutions and pension schemes. For the time being, a limit of €500 billion in loan capacity has been set. The heads of state are nonetheless to perform a review at the start of March.

Judging the planned support system, it has to be remembered that budgetary support is not an essential part of a decentralized or even federal system. It might be installed for regions in need as in some, but by no means all, federally organized states. There are federations with great disparities that do not know an equalization system, such as the USA. However, a fiscal equalization system is partially considered to be essential for the functioning of a monetary union but focused on stability and allocation excluding redistribution.[206] To avoid moral hazard and rent seeking when introducing such a mechanism it has to be ensured that

- aid is provided only under strict conditions and controls;
- the necessary structural improvements are not evaded;
- lenders will have to compensate for the benefit of obtaining a debtor who will be supported by the public;
- risk adjusted interest will be charged in the future for sovereign debt.

6.4.5 A new fiscal compact

At the same time, mainly at the request of Germany, an attempt was made towards adopting more effective regulation for imposing permanently sound financial policies among Member States in EU primary laws. This attempt failed since the UK refused to go along with the required amendments to EU treaties. Instead, the heads of state of the Eurozone agreed at the meeting of the European Council on 9 December 2011 to establish regulations along those lines in a separate, international treaty. Currently two treaties on the provision of assistance to Member States of the EU are in the final stages of consultation and implementation in the wake of that meeting:

- a treaty to create an ESM for coping with crises; and
- a fiscal policy treaty (the "new fiscal compact"), primarily for prevention of crises.

According to the agreement reached by the heads of state and government on 9 December 2011, the fiscal agreement is meant to contain the following elements:

- provisions on a balanced budget in national constitutional laws or equivalents;
- limitation of annual structural deficits to a maximum of 0.5 percent of a country's nominal GDP;
- introduction of mechanisms to correct aberrations automatically;
- comprehensive reporting obligations;
- involvement of the European Court of Justice in implementing the above.

The "Treaty on Stability, Coordination and Governance in the Economic and Monetary Union" was signed 2 March 2012. The requirement for a constitutional basis for the obligation to balance public sector budgets was made less stringent, an alternative option for states of emergencies was inserted, the permitted structural deficits were raised to 1 percent of GDP and control on the part of the European Court of Justice was restricted.

The adequacy and usefulness of this kind of agreement is dubious. Even in Germany, regulations on financing public sector deficits on credit have often been violated.

---

206 Francke (1998); *see also* Inman and Rubinfeld (1992), p. 659.

Granting budgetary assistance has only rarely improved the fiscal situation of receiving countries. While instruments for imposing the regulations are necessary, they hit upon serious constitutional difficulties. The same applies to an insolvency act for sovereigns that can only function if receivers in insolvency are equipped with sovereign authority and may intervene in the core responsibilities of a state. In essence, setting up a parallel structure to the primary laws of the EU in key areas of the economic and monetary union is not without its problems.

6.4.6 Beneficiaries

In effect, a large portion of the default risk has been transferred already from private creditors to the public sector without proper compensation. Hence, not only for legal reasons does the purchase of sovereign debt instruments by the ECB have to come to an end but also because of the economically unjustifiable risk transfer. The speculation on an illegal "bail-out" of the debtors would be honored for free.

Moreover, another sizable portion of the sovereign debt of the Member States which need support is held by banks or institutions which are owned, taken over in the course of the crisis or guaranteed by the governments of Germany and France. In this way another part of the default risk has already been taken over tacitly by the taxpayer in those countries.

Since it is unknown at what discount governmental entities including the ECB have acquired sovereign debt instruments or with what safety margin they accepted these instruments as corollary, the size of the transfer is hard to judge. In any case, it is realistic to assume that the profits from lending without an appropriate risk premium to the Member States currently needing support considerably surmount the losses when selling them, so a *substantial subsidy* is being handed out to the crediting financial institutions *by supporting the debtors*. This is the reason why a contribution of the creditors is essential.

6.5 The Coherence Problem

There are signs that internal coherence in the monetary union is eroding (see Figure 16.8). Imbalances in the current accounts are not the result of a weak coherence but a gut indicator. But further details are of significance, such as the appropriation of the financial influx from abroad (see Figure 16.9).

Such developments cannot be mitigated by any form of fiscal federalism, as the examples of the U.S. and the German fiscal federalism demonstrate vividly. To what extent these disparities might have been induced by a common currency is a different question and remains to be analyzed.

Internal coherence of the members of a monetary union may be considered an important factor for its viability. Even in a single currency area three basic adjustment mechanisms remain in case of disparities, mainly with constant and excessive current account imbalances: enhancing competitiveness, movement of labor to a more efficient allocation, and economic growth.

If initial discrepancies are too great or even increasing this might lead to high additional overall costs in the form of support in times of a crisis, as well as programs to foster structural adjustments. This is a political and not primarily an economic decision. Also the EU would have the option to let a region turn into the Mississippi of Europe.

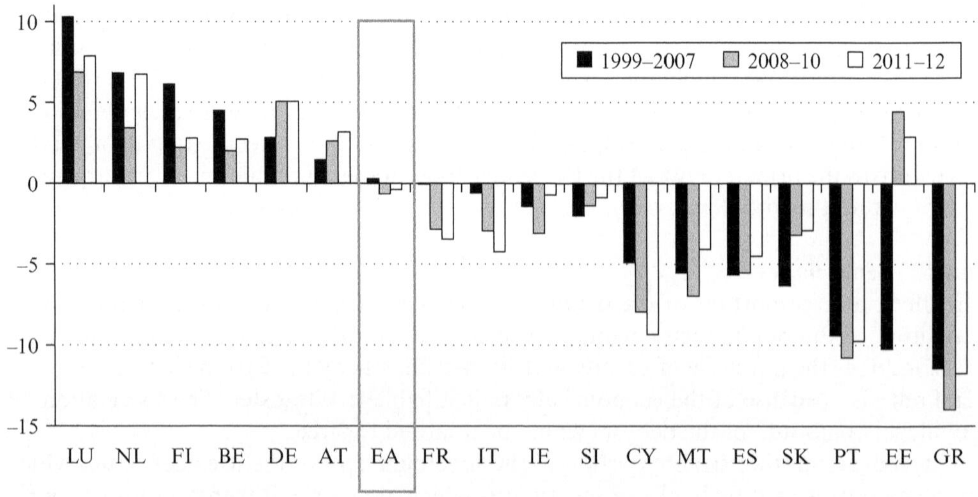

Source: Jürgen Stark, "Staatsschuld und Geldpolitik: Lehren aus der globalen Finanzkrise," Rede, Münchner Seminare: CES ifo Group Munich & Süddeutsche Zeitung, Munich, 20 June 2011, slide 10 (European Central Bank).

Figure 16.8 Current account balance as percentage of nominal GDP

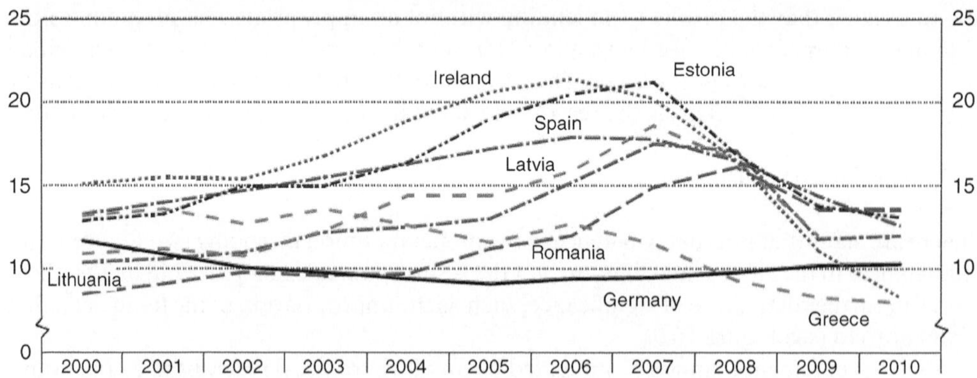

Source: Sachverständigenrat (2010), p. 86.

Figure 16.9 Weight of investments in real estate (percentage of GDP)

In general the EU has decided against that option and attempts to increase coherence by regional development programs. It has collected comprehensive information on the development of coherence in the euro area.[207]

[207] European Commission (2010).

6.6 A "Euro Crisis"?

6.6.1 Foundations

Although many analysts and some politicians have been referring to the crisis as a euro crisis,[208] or even worse an EU crisis, it is essentially not a problem of the currency when a sovereign is not able or not willing to pay its debt. There is no stringent link between the fiscal problems of a state and the currency used in that country as legal tender. Only if a government has the power to print the money it needs in order to pay back its debt might the currency be in danger. This is also why the ECB is not allowed to lend money to the EU or its Member States according to Article 123 TFEU.

In addition to an almost complete failure of financial markets and of economic sciences, the crisis has also demonstrated a total failure of the supervisory system – both of its rules and of their enforcement.

The present turmoil with *sovereign debt* is primarily not a currency problem but the result of discrepancies among Member States. It occurs in any type of interconnected system regardless of whether it uses one or more currencies. There is no link between a government which faces difficulties to finance its budget and the currency used in its country. However, it is a consequence of the financial market crisis and the ensuing depression of the "real" economy. Serious flaws in redesigning financial markets and financial institutions are the major contributing factors. On the lenders' side, ill-conceived capital adequacy rules and laxness towards unsustainable, but individually profitable, leverage ratios are of major significance. The absence of a national currency only forces a government to think about measures to solve its structural problems which are unpopular at home. Not having the questionable exit with inflation and devaluation of the currency might be very healthy in the medium term. It is not a flaw of the Monetary Union that the historically low interest rates in some Member States were not used in a more prudent manner.

6.6.2 A banking crisis

It is still too early to deliver a comprehensive and final analysis of the crisis. Bearing in mind the complexity of what has happened, it is also problematic to devise simple and clear-cut judgments. But, with this "caveat" a few facts appear to be clear:

1. Since the beginning of the crisis and with its current turn into a "sovereign debt crisis," it has been a crisis of financial institutions at its core, i.e. mainly of some big banks, but certainly not all banks.
2. It has now become a crisis of sovereign states and other governmental institutions. They have accumulated debt on a scale which is unsustainable.
3. There always has to be a lender of the underlying money; and to a large extent this money originates from banks and other financial institutions.
4. The risk of sovereign debt write-offs has increasingly been transferred from the market players to the central banks as they bought or accepted sovereign debt as

[208] Paradigmatic: Sachverständigenrat (2010), p. 71 et seq.; Baldwin and Gros (2010), p. 1. *Baldwin* et al. (2010) deliberate even about completing the "Eurozone."

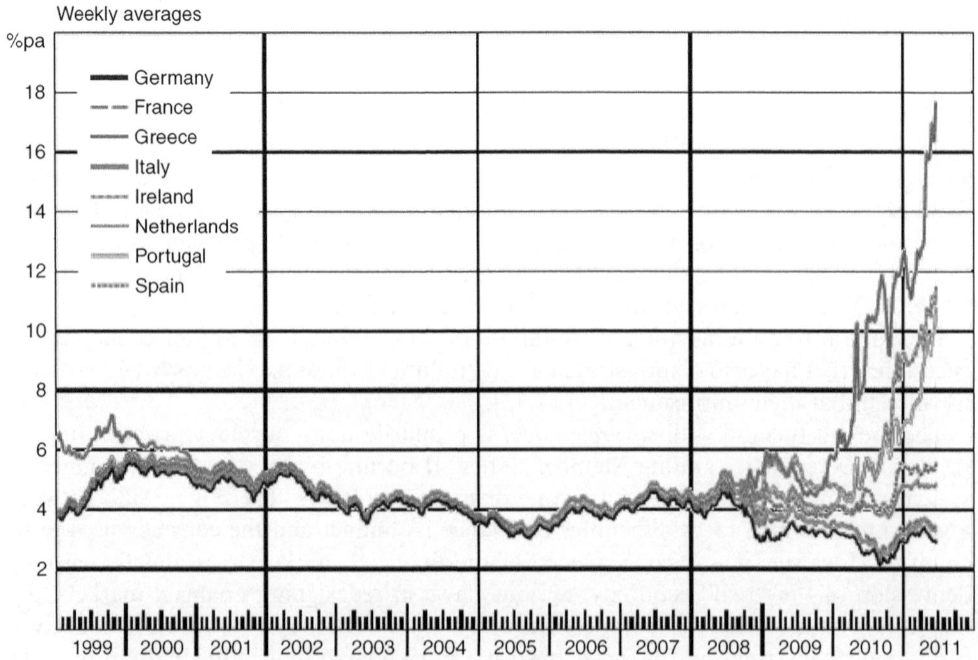

Note: Greece joined the euro area at the beginning of 2001.

Source: *Deutsche Bundesbank,* Monthly Report, June 2011, p. 29.

Figure 16.10 Ten-year government bond yields for selected euro area countries

corollary. This is augmented by the implicit subsidies handed out to creditors of sovereign debt.[209]

Despite all the turns and twists the crisis has taken until today and might take in the future, it was and is in essence a crisis of banks which expand credit and lend too much money and do not charge a risk-adjusted price (interest). This is consistent with the findings of Reinhart and Rogoff who consider the crises in the developed countries predominantly during the last two decades to be caused by banks.[210]

6.6.3 The neglected side of the lenders

So it is worthwhile to focus the analysis more on the side of the lenders. The bank rescue operations that took place directly increased the ratios of government debt to GDP. Private debt was turned into public debt, especially in Ireland but also in Germany. However, things are too complex to simply blame the financial institutions. The legal system substantially contributed to the emergence of the unsustainable sovereign debt

---

[209] Supra, Section 6.4.6.
[210] Reinhart and Rogoff (2009), pp. 141, 173, 348–92.

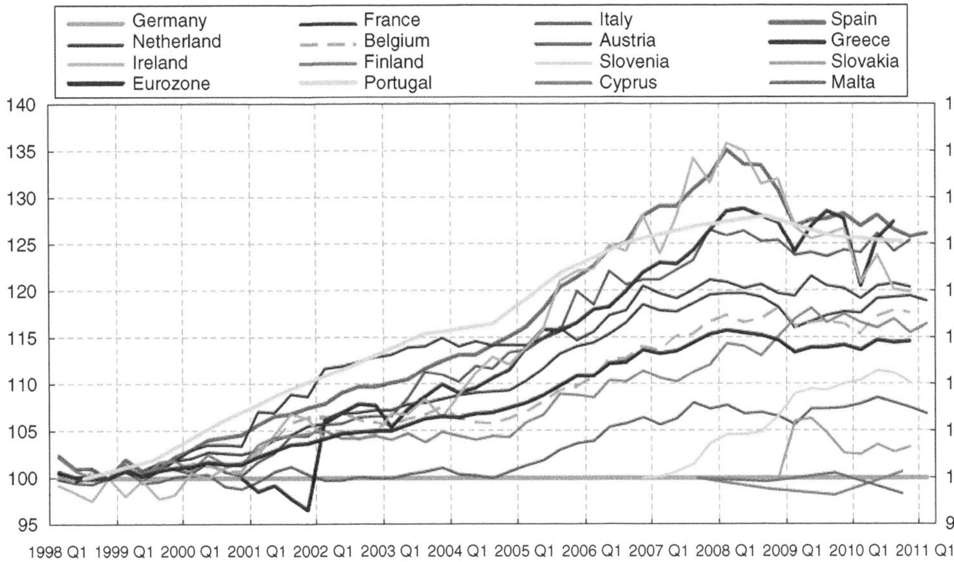

Source: Jürgen Stark, "Staatsschuld und Geldpolitik: Lehren aus der globalen Finanzkrise," Rede, Münchner Seminare: CES ifo Group Munich & Süddeutsche Zeitung, Munich, 20 June 2011, slide 8 (European Central Bank).

Figure 16.11 Development of the unit labor cost in the euro area relative to Germany (1998 Q4 = 100)

situation which has to be resolved now. The *risk weight* was set at *zero* for essentially all sovereign debt in the legal rules on capital adequacy. In other statutes governing financial instruments or institutions, such as insurance laws, it is similar. This made the *irresponsible lending* so attractive alongside the gamble on a "bail-out" in case of need. As a result, market mechanisms were hindered from imposing the necessary sanctions on countries carrying out an unsustainable and irresponsible fiscal policy also from this side. Fatal mistakes were made in the course of deregulation as the *necessary differences* had been made in the previous statutory rules.

Leverage ratios, maturity transformation, and general risk reduction by banks and other financial institutions are the core of the problem, besides the waning competitiveness of some Member States, and both have not yet been sufficiently addressed despite all efforts undertaken so far. Improving competitiveness is often identified when lowering real wages. This certainly helps but the non-economic element might be more important and is often overlooked: superior engineering, good science and reliable workers, and an efficient legal system. These are all hard to achieve.

6.6.4 Solutions

It is an open question whether the EU could tolerate the financial failure of one of its Member States, i.e. one whose currency is the euro. Originally it was clearly intended that there should not be any support. These rules were also intended as a signal to markets that there might be a higher risk with certain "sovereign" debts. Until recently, however, markets completely ignored that signal. Then they overshot in the last months for a while with high fluctuation of spreads. It is hard to blame markets for this even if there might be a strong speculative element. In effect, markets were right since so far a creditor has not suffered any losses with "sovereign" debt from parts of the Eurosystem.

Leaving the Eurosystem or expelling a euro Member State is no viable solution, for two simple reasons: it is economically harmful and it is illegal.[211] Membership in the Monetary Union is irrevocable for good reasons. Monetary systems that provide an exit option are inherently instable. The *structural problems* have to be solved: weak economic growth and weak competitiveness.

The immediate crisis resolution necessities might demand a short-term different approach but that is in essence not a task of the monetary system. Finally an increasing lack of obedience to strict legal norms and contracts has to be observed, and this is – in the medium term – the most frightening aspect of the recent development. That should be kept in mind before keenly designing new rules.

7 CONCLUSION

The European Monetary Union has done very well since its initiation. Price stability has been secured and the external value of the new currency is more than satisfactory. The confidence in it is also demonstrated by an increasing use of the euro as a global reserve currency. It has been a stabilizing factor in the current crisis.

The recent budgetary problems of some Member States are principally not a problem of the Monetary Union. It is therefore unjustifiable to speak of a "euro crisis." However, the Monetary Union restricts the number of possibilities for Member States to solve their financial problems.

The purchase of debt instruments of those Member States by the ECB is questionable from an economic, and more importantly from a legal, point of view. With longer duration, it is legally no longer justifiable.

Financial support for Member States in severe financial distress might be acceptable as a temporary crisis resolution mechanism. A permanent support mechanism needs a basis in the primary law of the EU.

The treatment of the risk of "sovereign" debt in the legal framework for financial institutions needs urgent improvement. Especially the capital requirements for credit institutions have to be adjusted.

REFERENCES

Amtenbrink, Fabian and de Haan, Jakob (2002), "The European Central Bank: An Independent Specialised Organization of Community Law – a Comment," *Common Market Law Review*, 39: 65.

Athanassiou, Phoebus (2009), "Withdrawal and Expulsion from the EU and EMU," ECB Legal Working Paper Series No. 10.

---

211 Despite the fact that the Treaty of Lisbon opened the door for a *voluntary exit*: Article 50 TFEU; for references see note 119.

Baldwin, Richard and Daniel Gros (2010), "Introduction: The Euro in Crisis – What to Do?" in Richard Baldwin, Daniel Gros and Luc Laeven (eds), *Completing the Eurozone Rescue: What More Needs to Be Done*, Centre for Economic Policy Research (CEPR), June.

Baldwin, Richard, Daniel Gros and Luc Laeven (eds) (2010), *Completing the Eurozone Rescue: What More Needs to Be Done*, Centre for Economic Policy Research (CEPR), June.

Bishop, Graham et al. (eds) (2008), *10 Years of the Euro: New Perspectives for Britain*.

Blanke, Hermann-Josef Blanke (2010), in Hermann von Mangoldt, Friedrich Klein and Christian Starck (eds), *Kommentar zum Grundgesetz*, 6th edn.

Burda, Michael C. and Stefan Gerlach (2010), "A Credible Stability and Growth Pact: Raising the Bar for Budgetary Transparency," in Richard Baldwin, Daniel Gros and Luc Laeven (eds), *Completing the Eurozone Rescue: What More Needs to Be Done*, Centre for Economic Policy Research (CEPR), June, p. 65.

Burns, Debra Brubaker (2011), "Too Big to Fair and Too Big to Pay: States, Their Public-pension Bills, and the Constitution," *Hastings Constitutional Law Quarterly*, (Fall): 1–35.

Buti, Marco (2007), "Will the New Stability and Growth Pact Succeed? An Economic and Political Perspective," in Fritz Breuss (ed.), *The Stability and Growth Pact*, New York: Springer, p. 153.

Callies, Christian (2011), in Christian Callies and Matthias Ruffert (eds), *EUV/AEUV*, 4th edn.

De Grauwe, Paul (2010), "How to Embed the Eurozone in a Political Union," in Richard Baldwin, Daniel Gros and Luc Laeven (eds), *Completing the Eurozone Rescue: What More Needs to Be Done*, Centre for Economic Policy Research (CEPR), June, p. 29.

De Sèze, Nicolas, Aurélie Marchand and Romain Bardy (2011), "L'outre-mer français et l'euro," *Bulletin de la Banque de France*, 186(4): 89.

Deutsche Bundesbank (2003), "Zur Währungsverfassung nach dem Entwurf einer Verfassung für die Europäische Union," in *Monatsbericht*, November, p. 67.

Dutzler, Barbara (2003), *The European System of Central Banks: An Autonomous Actor?* New York: Springer.

Dutzler, Barbara and Angelika Hable (2004), "Das Urteil des Europäischen Gerichtshofs zum Stabilitäts- und Wachstumspakt – eine Klarstellung?" *Integration – Vierteljahreszeitschrift des Instituts für Europäische Politik* 27: 301.

Dziechciarz, Beata (2009), *Rechtliche Integration der nationalen Zentralbanken in das Europäische System der Zentralbanken und in das Eurosystem*, Baden-Baden: Nomos.

Eichengreen, Barry (1994), "Fiscal Policy and EMU," in Barry Eichengreen and Jeffrey Frieden (ed.), *The Political Economy of the European Monetary Unification*, Boulder, CO: Westview Press, p. 167.

Endler, Jan (1998), *Europäische Zentralbank und Preisstabilität*.

Ernst, Wolfgang (2012), "Privatrechtliche Folgen eines Ausscheidens einzelner Staaten aus der Euro-Währung – Ein Problemaufriss," *ZIP*, p. 49.

European Commission (2008), *EMU@10: Successes and Challenges after Ten Years of Economic and Monetary Union*.

European Commission (2010), *Surveillance of Intra-Euro-Area Competitiveness and Imbalances*, European Economy I-2010.

Fang, Paul (2006), "Die Europäische Zenteralbank," Diss. jur. St. Gallen.

Faßbender, Kurt (2010), "Der europäische 'Stabilisierungsmechanismus' im Lichte von Unionsrecht und deutschem Vergassungsrecht," *NVwZ*, p. 799.

Feldmann, Horst (2003), "Der Stabilitäts- und Wachstumspakt in der Praxis: Eine Bilanz der ersten vier Jahre," *List Forum für Wirtschafts- und Finanzpolitik*, 29: 114.

Fischer-Appelt, Dorothee (1999), *Agenturen der Europäischen Gemeinschaft*.

Francke, Hans-Hermann (1998), "Europäische Währungsunion mit europäischem Finanzausgleichssystem und europäischer Sozialpolitik," in Hans-Hermann Francke, Eberhart Ketzel and Hans-Helmut Kotz (eds), "Europäische Währungsunion," Beiheft zu *Kredit und Kapital*, Heft 14, p. 181.

Gaitanides, Charlotte (2005), *Das Recht der Europäischen Zentralbank*.

Gaitanides, Charlotte (2007), in Karl Heinrich Friauf and Wolfram Höfling (eds), *Berliner Kommentar zum Grundgesetz* (loose-leaf).

Görisch, Christoph (2009), *Demokratische Verwaltung durch Unionsagenturen*.

Häde, Ulrich (1996), "Ein Stabilitätspakt für Europa? Zur Zulässigkeit völkerrechtlicher Verträge zwischen den Mitgliedstaaten der EU," *Europäische Zeitschrift für Wirtschaftsrecht*, p. 138.

Häde, Ulrich (2002), Book report on Zilioli and Selmayr, *The Law of the European Central Bank* (2001), *Europarecht*, p. 920.

Häde, Ulrich (2006), "Zur rechtlichen Stellung der Europäischen Zentralbank," in *Wertpapier-Mitteilungen*, p. 1605.

Häde, Ulrich (2009), "Haushaltsdisziplin und Solidarität im Zeichen der Finanzkrise," *Europäische Zeitschrift für Wirtschaftsrecht*, p. 399.

Häde, Ulrich (2011), in Christian Callies and Matthias Ruffert (eds), *EUV/AEUV*, 4th edn, Vienna: Manz.

Hafke, Heinz Christian (2000), "Rechtliche Aspekte der Währungsbeziehungen zwischen Mitgliedstaaten der

Europäischen Währungsunion und Territorien außerhalb des Geltungsbereichs des EGV, Zeitschrift für Europarechtliche Studien," p. 25.

Hahn, Hugo J. (1991), "The European Central Bank: Key to European Monetary Union or Target?" *Common Market Law Review*, 28: 783.

Hahn, Hugo J. and Ulrich Häde (2010), *Währungsrecht*, 2nd edition, Munich: Beck.

Hancke, Johannes (2009), "Defizitbegrenzung im Bundesstaat – Verfassungsmäßigkeit einer verbindlichen Verschuldungsregel für die Bundsländer," *Deutsches Verwaltungsblatt*, p. 621.

Hartmann, Uwe (1996), "Öffentliche Finanzpolitik in der EU – Rechtlicher Rahmen und dessen Diskussion im Vorfeld der Regierungskommission," *Europäische Zeitschrift für Wirtschaftsrecht*, p. 133.

Hatje, Hatje (2006), "Die Reform des Stabilitäts- und Wachstumspaktes," *Die öffentliche Verwaltung*, p. 597.

Henning, C. Randall and Martin Kessler (2012), "Fiscal Federalism: US History for Architects of Europe's Fiscal Union," Bruegel Essay and Lecture Series.

Hentschelmann, Kai (2009), *Der Stabilitäts- und Wachstumspakt*.

Herdegen, Matthias (2010), in Theodor Maunz et al. (founders and editors), *Grundgesetz* (loose-leaf).

Herrmann, Matthias (2010), "Griechische Tragöde – der währungsverfassunghsrechtliche Rahmen für die Rettung, den Austritt oder den Ausschluss von überschuldeten Staaten aus der Eurozone," *Europäische Zeitschrift für Wirtschaftsrecht*, p. 413.

Heun, Werner (1998), "Die Europäische Zentralbank in der Währungsunion," *Juristen-Zeitung*, p. 866.

Inman, Robert P. and Daniel L. Rubinfeld (1992), "Fiscal Federalism in Europe," *European Economic Review*, 36: 654.

Issing, Otmar (2008a), *Der Euro: Geburt, Erfolg, Zukunft*, Munich: Franz Vahlen.

Issing, Otmar (2008b), "The Euro – A Currency Without a State," Center for Financial Studies, Working Paper No. 2008/51.

Issing, Otmar (2008c), "The Euro: Does a Currency Need a State?" *International Finance*, 11: 297.

Jonung, Lars and Eoin Drea (2009), "The Euro: It Can't Happen. It's a Bad Idea. It Won't Last: US Economists on the EMU, 1989–2002," European Commission, Economic Papers 395, December.

Kämmerer, Eoin (2003), in Ingo von Münch and Philip Kunig (eds), *Grundgesetz-Kommentar*, 4/5th edn, Munich: Beck.

Karb, Volker (2006), *Währungskrisen und staatliche Schuldenkrisen*.

Kempen, Bernhard (2003), in Rudolf Streinz (ed.), *EUV/EGV*.

Kirchhof, Paul (1994), "Die Mitwirkung Deutschlands an der Wirtschafts- und Währungsunion," in *Festschrift Franz Klein*, p. 61.

Knapp, Georg Friedrich (1905), *Staatliche Theorie des Geldes*, Leipzig: Duncker & Humblot.

Krägenau, Henry and Wolfgang Wetter (1993), *Europäische Wirtschaftsunion*.

Krauskopf, Bernd and Christine Steven (1999), "Die Einführung des Euro in außereuropäischen Territorien und währungsrechtliche Regelungen im Verhältnis zu Drittstaaten," *EuZW*, 10: 650–54.

Louis, Jean-Victor (1998), "A Legal and Institutional Approach for Building a Monetary Union," *Common Market Law Review*, 35: 33.

Louis, Jean-Victor (2010), Guest Editorial: "The no-bailout clause and rescue packages," *Common Market Law Review*, 47: 971.

Marsh, David (2009), *The Euro: The Politics of the New Global Currency*, New Haven, CT and London: Yale University Press.

Meade, James E. (1957), "The Balance-of-Payments Problems of a European Free-Trade Area," *The Economic Journal*, 67: 379.

Mishkin, Frederic S. (2004), *The Economics of Money, Banking, and Financial Markets*, 7th edn, Boston, MA: Pearson.

Mundell, Robert (1961), "A Theory of Optimum Currency Areas," *American Economic Review*, 39: 657.

Nicholson-Crotty, Sean (2008), "Fiscal Federalism and Tax Effort in the U.S. States," *State Politics and Policy Quarterly*, 8: 109.

Nicolaysen, Gert (2004), Der EuGH zum Defizitverfahren nach Art. 104 EGV, Urteil vom 13. Juli, *Deutsches Verwaltungsblatt*, p. 1321.

Padoa-Schioppa, Tommaso (1994), *The Road to Monetary Union in Europe: The Emperor, the Kings, and the Genies*, Oxford: Clarendon Press.

Palm, Sean (2000), *Preisstabilität in der Europäischen Wirtschafts- und Währungsunion*.

Reinhart, Carmen M. and Kenneth S. Rogoff (2009), *This Time is Different: Eight Centuries of Financial Folly*, Princeton: Princeton University Press.

Sachverständigenrat zur Begutachtung der gesamtwirtschaftlichen Entwicklung (2010), "Chancen für einen stabilen Aufschwung," Jahresgutachten 2010/11.

Scheller, Hanspeter K. (2006), *The European Central Bank*, 2nd edn, Frankfurt a.M.: European Central Bank.

Scitkovsky, Tibor (1958), *Economic Theory and Western European Integration*, Stanford, CA: Stanford University Press.

Scott, Hal S. (1998), "When the Euro Falls Apart," *International Finance*, 1(2): 207–28.

Seiler, Christian (2004), "Das Europäische System der Zentralbanken (ESZB) als Verantwortungsverbund: Systemgebundene Aufgabenerfüllung durch einen eigenständigen Kompetenzträger," *Europarecht*, p. 52.

Seiter, Corina (2002), "Vergleich historischer Währungsunionen und Zentralbanksysteme als Lehrstück für die Europäische Wirtschafts- und Währungsunion," Diss. Bremen 2003.

Selmayr, Martin (1999), "Wie unabhängig ist die Europäische Zentralbank?" *Wertpapier-Mitteilungen*, p. 2429.

Siekmann, Helmut (1985), *Institutionalisierte Einkommenspolitik in der Bundesrepublik Deutschland: gesetzliche Regelung und bisherige Praxis*, Munich: F. Vahlen.

Siekmann, Helmut (2005), "Die Unabhängigkeit von EZB und Bundesbank nach geltendem Recht und dem Vertrag über eine Verfassung für Europa," Institute for Law and Finance, Working paper series no. 35.

Siekmann, Helmut (2010), "Die Neuordnung der Finanzmarktaufsicht," *Die Verwaltung*, 43, 95–115.

Siekmann, Helmut (2011a), in Michael Sachs (ed.), *Grundgesetz*, 6th edn, Munich: C.H. Beck.

Siekmann, Helmut (2011b), "Europäisierung der Finanzmarktaufsicht," Institute for Monetary and Financial Stability, Working Paper Series No. 47.

Siekmann, Helmut (2012), "Neuorganisation der Fenanzaufsicht," in Stefan Kaedlbach (ed.), *Nach der Finanzkrise*, pp. 131–220.

Smits, René (1997), *The European Central Bank: Institutional Aspects*, The Hague and Boston: Kluwer Law International.

Spiotto, James E. (2011), "Role of Public Employee Pensions in Contributing to State Insolvency and the Possibility of a State Bankruptcy Chapter," prepared statement for the Hearing before the Subcommittee on Courts, Commercial and Administrative Law of the Committee on the Judiciary, House of Representatives 112th Congress, 1st session, 14 February 2011, Serial No. 112-25, pp. 54–95.

Stark, Jürgen (2005), "Zur 'Reform' des Stabilitäts- und Wachstumspakts," in *Orientierungen zur Wirtschafts- und Gesellschaftspolitik*, p. 64.

Szász, André (1999), *The Road to European Monetary Union*, New York: St. Martin's Press.

Thym, Daniel (2011), "Euro-Rettungsschirm: zwischenstaatliche Rechtskonstruktion und verfassungsgerichtliche Kontrolle," *Europäische Zeitschrift für Wirtschaftsrecht*, p. 167.

Torrent, Ramon (1999), "Whom is the European Central Bank the Central Bank of?" *Common Market Law Review*, 36: 1229.

Weber, Martin (1998), "Das Europäische System der Zentralbanken," *Wertpapier-Mitteilungen*, p. 1465.

Willms, Manfred (1998), "Die Europäische Währungsunion im Lichte der Theorie optimaler Währungsräume," in Hans-Hermann Francke, Eberhart Ketzel and Hans-Helmut Kotz (eds), "Europäische Währungsunion," Beiheft zu *Kredit und Kapital*, Heft 14, p. 41.

Wyplosz, Charles (2010), "The Eurozone's Levitation," in Richard Baldwin, Daniel Gros and Luc Laeven (eds), *Completing the Eurozone Rescue: What More Needs to Be Done*, Centre for Economic Policy Research (CEPR), June, p. 33.

Zeitler, Franz-Christoph (1995), "Die Europäische Währungsunion als Stabilitätsgemeinschaft," *Wertpapier-Mitteilungen*, p. 1609.

Zeitler, Franz-Christoph (2006), "Was bleibt vom Stabilitäts- und Wachstumspakt?" in *Festschrift für Reiner Schmidt*, p. 223.

Zilioli, Chiara and Martin Selmayr (1999), "The External Relations of the Euro Area: Legal Aspects," *Common Market Law Review*, 36: 273.

Zilioli, Chiara and Martin Selmayr (2000), "The European Central Bank: An Independent Specialized Organization of Community Law," *Common Market Law Review*, 37: 591.

Zilioli, Chiara and Martin Selmayr (2001), *The Law of the European Central Bank*, Oxford and Portland, OR: Hart.

Zimmermann, Beate (2000), "Die nationalen Zentralbanken als Bestandteile des Europäischen Systems der Zentralbank," Diss.jur. Würzburg.

Index